Economic Cooperation
in Latin America, Africa, and Asia

Economic Cooperation
in Latin America, Africa, and Asia

A Handbook of Documents

Edited by
Miguel S. Wionczek

The M.I.T. Press
Massachusetts Institute of Technology
Cambridge, Massachusetts, and London, England

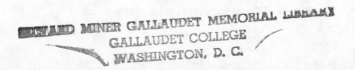

Library of Congress catalog card number: 68–22829

dweet 13.50

Preface

According to the Final Act of the first United Nations Conference on Trade and Development (UNCTAD), held in Geneva in the spring of 1964,

> regional economic groupings, integration or other forms of economic cooperation should be promoted among developing countries as a means of expanding their intra-regional and extra-regional trade and encouraging their economic growth and their industrial and agricultural diversification with due regard to the special features of development of the various countries concerned as well as their economic and social systems.[1]

Over the past ten years more than a dozen customs and monetary unions, common markets, free trade zones, and other regional cooperative arrangements have been proposed or established in Latin America, Africa, and Asia. It is estimated that at one point or another some fifty underdeveloped states joined or expressed willingness to join such multinational arrangements. Some of these cooperative schemes, especially those in West Africa, have never gotten off the ground. Others were torn apart at a very early stage by deep political conflicts (the Federation of Rhodesia and Nyasaland, the common market of the Federation of Malaya and Singapore, and the Rwanda-Burundi customs and monetary union, for example). Nine regional economic cooperation arrangements with a total membership of forty-six states — something like one half of the underdeveloped countries — survived initial difficulties and function today with varying effectiveness. The trials and tribulations of most of these economic cooperation attempts are largely unknown outside the countries directly involved. Knowledge of even the Latin American Free Trade Association

[1] United Nations Conference on Trade and Development, *Proceedings,* Vol. I: *Final Act and Report* (New York, 1964), p. 11.

(LAFTA) and the Central American Common Market (CACM), two schemes that received considerable publicity, is largely limited to a small group of people directly involved in the problems of the economic development of that part of the world.

The purpose of this collection of annotated documents related to economic integration movements in the southern hemisphere is twofold: to provide a guide to those in the economically advanced countries who study current developments in the economic "peripheries" of the world or participate in policy-making processes affecting these areas; and to offer some help to those experts and policy makers in Latin America, Africa, and Asia who consider regional economic integration a potentially important weapon in the search for accelerated development and industrialization in their respective countries.

Most multinational cooperation experiments in the southern hemisphere have been created autonomously, with very little knowledge of similar ventures elsewhere. Although much is heard about the similarity of the problems arising in the underdeveloped south, few actual contacts exist — on the intellectual, professional, or institutional levels — among the three economically backward continents. Even among the United Nations regional economic commissions in Latin America, Africa, and Asia, working contacts are both highly sporadic and limited to the expert level. Although the establishment of UNCTAD is helping to increase exchanges of development experience throughout the southern hemisphere, the transmission of actual experience in the field of regional economic cooperation from one continent to another is still largely accidental. It is hoped that this volume will contribute to filling one of the existing gaps in the dissemination of the important and considerable store of knowledge accumulated over the past ten years in Latin America, Africa, and Asia.

This volume of documents is not directed to a broad public. Legal texts generally make rather dull reading, and international treaties and agreements, despite their great importance, are mostly consulted by a limited number of experts and policy makers. It may well be, however, that if one accepts the proposition set forth here — that in most cases traditional approaches to the issue of underdevelopment are leading both the developed and the backward countries into a blind alley of self-deception — the potential importance of this particular collection of documents will be apparent.

The preparation of this volume hardly would have been possible without the cooperation of many people scattered around the world and involved either directly or indirectly in the elaboration and implementation of distinct regional economic cooperation schemes. Warm thanks and appreciation must be extended to those international civil servants, official delegates to international meetings, and university professors in the developing countries who clearly went beyond the line of duty in helping this writer collect the basic and ancillary documentation and who offered additional relevant information and comments based on their own experiences. The following persons must be specially mentioned here, although they are in no way responsible for the content of the introductory essay and the notes accompanying the legal texts: Carlos M. Castillo, Secretary-General of the Central American Common Market; Sidney Dell, Director of the UNCTAD office at United Nations headquarters; Jorge Gonzalez del Valle, Executive Director of the International Monetary Fund; Reginald H. Green, Adviser to the Treasury of the United Republic of Tanzania; Felipe Herrera, President of the Inter-American Development Bank; Kazam Kazerouni of the Plan Organization of Iran; Karl E. Lachman, Chief, Fiscal and Financial Branch of the United Nations Secretariat; Marcel Landy, Chief, Trade Section of the United Nations Economic Commission for Africa; Giovanni Mancini, African Development Bank; Michel Norro, Université Louvain in Kinshasa, Congo; and Fuad Rouhani, Secretary-General of Regional Cooperation for Development (RCD). Javier Marquez, Director of the Center for Latin American Monetary Studies in Mexico City, deserves special thanks for his sympathetic and understanding attitude toward the editor's frequent absences from the Center during his travels throughout Latin America and Africa.

The editor also would like to express his deep appreciation to the Carnegie Endowment for International Peace, which supported this venture financially, to the Endowment's Editor-in-Chief, Anne Winslow, for considering the project worthwhile and helping to bring it to fruition, and to Valeriana Kaleb, also from the Endowment, for editorial assistance in the early stages of the volume.

MIGUEL S. WIONCZEK

April 1968
Cambridge, Massachusetts

Contents

ix

Present Status and Prospects of Economic Integration
Movements in the Developing Countries

Political Atomization and Economic Backwardness
of the Southern Hemisphere

The number of countries that have achieved political independence in the past twenty years exceeds that of the original signatories of the United Nations Charter at the San Francisco Conference in 1945. To a roster of some eighty independent states that presently form an informal bloc of the developing countries within the United Nations Conference on Trade and Development (UNCTAD), twenty will probably be added before 1975, when it is expected that the process of political decolonization of Latin America, Africa, and Asia finally will have run its course. Thus within the foreseeable future we will be living in a world in which some thirty-five economically advanced and socially coherent states of the Northern Hemisphere — whether capitalist or socialist — will be facing over one hundred political units of all possible sizes and levels of underdevelopment dispersed throughout the world's South and burdened with population explosions.

These "new" states escape classification in other than geographical and development terms. They comprise some countries whose statehood started in ancient times: in Latin America a considerable number of states with 150 years of political independence, and some entities, including most African states, that have had no unitary political tradition since the Middle Ages. The group includes feudal monarchies, regressive dictatorships, one-party states managed by dynamic, modernizing elites, and several parliamentary democracies of the Western type. The populations of a few of these units exceed or equal those of the largest industrialized countries. At the other end of the spectrum, however, are scores of states

1

with populations of less than several million. Of the countries that will achieve independence within the near future, about twenty (many of them islands) have populations under one million.

The resource endowments in the new states also present no orderly pattern. Some are known to be potentially extremely rich — Brazil, the Congo (Kinshasa), Zambia, and Indonesia — but many others seem to possess little beyond the superficial symbols of political independence. The great majority of these states have a per capita income of less than $200 a year. All of their governments are strongly bent upon rapid achievement of economic independence — equated by their elites with industrialization — and face increasing popular pressure for the rapid implementation of some kind of welfare state. The underdeveloped South learned the concepts of economic independence, industrialization, and social welfare from the developed North. To a large degree the responsibility for the transfer of these ideas southward falls not only upon well-meaning political and economic reformers and innovators from the world's North but also upon the former foreign political overlords and economic exploiters of the South during the colonial period. The transfer started around the turn of the century and accelerated greatly after the Second World War. As a consequence the second half of the twentieth century has on its hands the seemingly impossible task of bringing, with considerable speed, some measure of economic independence, industrial development, and social welfare to a rapidly multiplying number of independent or quasi-independent political units that together account for two thirds of the global population.

The achievement of these goals implies concurrently the modernization of the relatively backward societies, the diversification of their productive structures, and a substantial transfer of the modern technology that largely accounts for the accelerated progress of the North. Even if it were assumed, unrealistically, that the flow of economic and technical assistance to the underdeveloped regions could be greatly expanded from present levels, only a small minority of the developing countries could fulfill the conditions necessary to utilize such assistance effectively and become viable and relatively prosperous economic entities within the reasonable future. Until recently these countries were mostly passive participants in the historical process in which educational methods, production processes, and technology were gradually built up and perfected over a long period within the framework of economically large and socially cohesive units. It took only one generation, however, for political and economic nationalism to extend all over the globe.

It is precisely because the key ingredients responsible for economic growth and social welfare originated in the North under specific and difficult to duplicate conditions that the transfer and adaptation of the means to achieve these goals to the present situation in the new countries are yielding such meager results to all parties concerned. A feeling of frustration with the process is spreading throughout both the North and the South. While the rich societies, including the socialist countries, show a rapidly diminishing willingness to participate in economic aid programs, the social and political tensions in the South are visibly growing. They are translating themselves not only into the deterioration of political relations with the advanced sector of the world economy but also into the strengthening of a parochial type of political and economic nationalism in the underdeveloped regions themselves.

If the politically atomized underdeveloped regions, taking their cue from the industrialized world, are struggling for economic growth and increased social welfare, the question that arises is: How many of the close to one hundred politically independent but economically small units are in a position to advance toward these goals at a pace their societies are willing to accept? This is a crucial question, since a low growth rate coupled with too great expectations of welfare creates politically and socially disruptive situations that affect both growth and welfare. Considering the serious constraints arising from the present working of the world economy and from the general internal backwardness of the states of the South as well as the size of their domestic markets, probably only a small minority of these countries are about to cross the line dividing the world into its poor and its relatively affluent halves or can see on the horizon the moment when they will do so. There are three such states in Latin America (Mexico, Brazil, and long-stagnant, semiaffluent Argentina); probably only two in nonwhite Africa (the United Arab Republic and Nigeria); and four in Asia (Pakistan, India, Malaysia, and the Philippines). Although some of these countries are still extremely poor on the whole, all are rather large political and economic units, have domestic markets that warrant the industrial effort, and rely on modernizing elites. This short list can be expanded somewhat by the addition of a few countries that either represent clearly special cases (Israel and Taiwan) or happen to have at their disposal rich oil resources guaranteeing a continuous flow of foreign exchange for economic development (Venezuela, Algeria, Libya, and Iran). Thus a total of some fifteen independent developing states can expect, with a reasonable degree of assurance, that their inward-directed economic development will bring them in the reasonable future some measure of economic independence, industrial power, and general welfare to satisfy the expectations of their societies.

Among the remaining underdeveloped independent states, a few, for example, the Congo (Kinshasa) and Indonesia, are relatively large and potentially very rich in resources, but their absolute degree of backwardness seems to offer an impenetrable barrier to rapid development. In practically all of the sixty remaining countries, the difficulties arising from backwardness are compounded by very limited resource bases and small populations. It is in this last group — comprising, among others, Jamaica, Haiti, Honduras, Panama, Ecuador, Guyana, Mali, Chad, Rwanda, Tanzania, Botswana, Somalia, Jordan, Iraq, Nepal, and Laos — that pressure for economic development and social welfare cannot be relieved by the traditional means of building separate national economies. Such an approach will fail to bring them not only to the welfare level of the poorest of the advanced countries (Greece, Turkey, or Portugal) but even to the present level of such semideveloped states as Mexico and the United Arab Republic. It would be too much, however, to expect that all of these small entities, having achieved the status of independent political units, could simply give up their socioeconomic goals because of apparent economic unviability. Neither is it possible to envisage their forced incorporation into larger political units or their reincorporation into colonial empires that they chose to leave regardless of possible economic disadvantages. A "hands-off" policy toward festering centers of hunger and potential internal violence is also very unattractive; violence is contagious and creates complicated and dangerous situations in a world still divided into the spheres of influence of major industrial powers with distinct, and often hostile, ideologies.

Even the hopeful assumption that in many of the smaller backward countries there are still considerable unexploited possibilities for economic development on a national scale through agricultural improvement and utilization of national resources for export does not really brighten the long-term development prospect. In practically every country, even if a well-planned development strategy is applied, there is a clear time limit within which such possibilities will be exhausted. After a first stage of development, import substitution may be practiced for some time with limited industrialization schemes. A two-stage development strategy would offer these countries some relief, for about one decade, and probably would bring them within reach of a per capita income level of $200 a year. Such an achievement might be looked upon from the outside as a considerable improvement compared with the present situation, but it would be a far cry from the kind of sustained growth and general welfare that is expected all over the world. Thus the question of what can be done in the majority of the developing countries after 1975 remains unsolved.

In most of the underdeveloped areas — for rather obvious reasons — the Hong Kong model of industrial development, aimed at expanding manufactured exports to advanced countries, has little future. On the other hand, although traditional forms of international trade stopped being the engine of growth some time ago, at the present levels of $100–$150 per capita income, domestic savings can be increased rapidly only at the price of holding down consumption for a considerable time. Substantial relief to the fifty or more small and backward economies through the international flow of capital is also unlikely. Unless they are of strategic value for some world power, these countries receive little public foreign aid. Moreover, the disruption of institutional links inherited from colonial times and the sociopolitical tensions arising in the Southern Hemisphere from the postindependence frustration are bringing about the decline of private capital flows. This situation can hardly be remedied by multinational agreements intended to provide safety and a proper climate for international financial and industrial capital. Other complex mechanisms and motivations are at work in this respect. In the nineteenth century, either private capital followed the flag or the flag followed capital. Today it is difficult to envisage large private foreign investments going where neither foreign flags nor foreign capital are particularly welcome and where uncertainty reigns concerning the future behavior of highly nationalistic societies.

In a period of declining economic aid from public sources and growing frustration in the underdeveloped South, it is doubtful that the resources gap obvious in practically every development plan will be filled by foreign private capital. From the viewpoint of the owners of capital, most such ventures simply do not look sound, while alternatives for relatively safe investment are more than plentiful in the North. What is worse yet is that southward flows are not absolutely necessary from the viewpoint of the economic needs of the developed societies considered as a whole.

Theoreticians of economic imperialism at the turn of the century may have been right in insisting that the advanced countries badly needed the underdeveloped regions as sources of raw materials and markets for manufactures. However, the radical intellectuals of previous generations were unable to foresee the nature and speed of the technological change presently taking place in the Northern Hemisphere. It is apparent from world trade statistics that the dependence of the developed countries upon the primary producing Southern Hemisphere is diminishing rapidly. If it were possible to put aside military considerations, great-power politics, and the past interests of foreign investors, it might almost be concluded that, except for the dozen or so viable economic units mentioned before, the Southern Hemisphere is becoming a burden rather than an asset to the developed and affluent societies that controlled the destinies of Latin America, Africa, and Asia over the last three centuries. Today the market opportunities for the Western countries are greater in Eastern Europe than in Africa, Southeast Asia, and large parts of Latin America taken together. There is more oil in the Northern Hemisphere than was thought even ten years ago. In the long run, no insurmountable obstacles seem to preclude substituting synthetic products for real coffee or plastics for most metals. Neither should one assume that the dependence of the advanced countries on the supply of foodstuffs produced in the temperate, less developed areas of the South will increase in the foreseeable future. Even Eastern Europe is rapidly solving its agricultural difficulties, and few operations similar to the large long-term sales of Cuban sugar to the Soviet Union can be envisaged. In brief, the North needs the South less and less. As someone remarked recently, the South is becoming largely irrelevant to the economies of the advanced countries.

The great impact of modern technology upon both the economically advanced and the backward nations has not been grasped sufficiently by either group to have elicited a comprehensive, mutually acceptable approach to the problem of development. Although we live under radically new technological conditions, the *economic* approach of the North to worldwide development continues to be traditional. Meanwhile the *political* approach to the same problem in the underdeveloped regions tends to model itself upon the nineteenth-century experiences of the industrial countries. Both sides are applying methods that are inappropriate for the solution of an urgent new problem. Consequently, very little development is achieved, scarce real and financial resources are squandered, and much time and good will are lost. The situation is far more critical today than when economic development as a paramount issue was first brought to the attention of intellectual elites and policy makers in the advanced countries shortly after the end of the Second World War. The moment is rapidly approaching when we will have to elaborate and apply nontraditional policies for the solution of nontraditional problems in the world peripheries.

Search for a Multinational Approach to Economic Development

The idea of this volume was born someplace between the Pacific coast of South America and East Africa during various trips undertaken by this writer in recent years. The writer's travels in the Southern Hemisphere led to his discovery that many people in many parts in the underdeveloped world are arriving simultaneously, despite little contact with each other, at similarly pessimistic conclusions about the prospects for an inward-directed economic development effort within relatively weak national states as well as about the efficiency of the outside aid distributed on a state-by-state basis. The disappointing results of such policies led to discussions — first among development experts and later among a few statesmen and policy makers in the economically backward regions — of the possibility of extending economic development beyond the limits of national states (that is, of establishing some kind of complementary multi-national economic groupings).

In Latin America this search for multinational approaches toward development dates from the early 1950s. It began under the creative influence of Raúl Prebisch, then Executive Secretary of the United Nations Economic Commission for Latin America (ECLA). Independently, but at about the same time, Asian economists associated with the United Nations Economic Commission for Asia and the Far East (ECAFE) initiated studies of the prospects for regional economic cooperation in South and Southeast Asia. Later, in the early 1960s, the youngest United Nations regional commission — the Economic Commission for Africa (ECA) — became a center for African intellectuals and their non-African colleagues searching for some more rational approach to the continent's urgent economic growth problems.

In each continent the urgency of accelerating development was due to a different set of circumstances. By 1955 it was evident that Latin America would be unable to continue, within individual national borders, the industrialization process that intensified under the abnormal conditions prevalent during the Second World War and the following decade. In Asia, where except for India and Pakistan very few possibilities for inward-directed development were ever present, individual economies moved very slowly, and intraregional trade started to decline because of autarkic agricultural policies and the rapid saturation of small markets by new but largely primitive consumer goods industries. The acceleration of development seemed especially urgent in Africa, which represents the extreme and most recent example of a sudden division of a continent into many politically independent but economically backward units. It is difficult to visualize how tiny Africa is in terms of markets or what great efforts are necessary to create a functioning modern economy under such conditions. Africa covers a fifth of the land surface of the earth, yet, according to ECA estimates, the output of goods and services of the continent (excluding the Republic of South Africa) is less than that of Benelux. Inhabited by 270 million people, 90 per cent of whom live at subsistence level, the continent is presently divided into more than forty political entities.

In Latin America and Africa, steps were taken toward the establishment of broad continental common markets. Future historians will have the fascinating task of discerning between the political and economic motivations underlying these early intellectual experiments. A similar approach has never been tried in Asia, probably because of various overriding political factors. The heart of Asia is occupied by two major world powers, the Soviet Union and China; on the continent's southern perimeter are two warring but large and economically self-contained units, India and Pakistan; and military conflicts have been ravaging Southeast Asia for the past quarter of a century. But in both Latin America and Africa (if Latin America can be considered a continent) the continental approach seemed to be especially attractive on political grounds. Since the disappearance of the Spanish and Portuguese empires from that part of the world in the early nineteenth century, Latin America has always proclaimed the existence of some kind of Latin American unity: first vis-à-vis European powers and later the United States. Bolívar's dream of political unity never disappeared from Latin American political folklore. In Africa, latter-day Bolívars were even more plentiful immediately after the continent's decolonization. The pan-African common market idea launched in the early 1960s was closely linked to the African political unity movement directed against European domination of that part of the world since the sixteenth century. Those who shortly after the political decolonization of Africa had a chance to discuss with the new elites its future and its prospects for economic cooperation remember the largely emotional arguments in favor of the continental economic unit. Any less ambitious proposals for organizing subregional groupings of neighboring newly independent states amounted in African eyes to an attempt to divide Africa once again, allegedly for the purpose of furthering neocolonialist interests.

Neither of these maximalist approaches was very successful. In Africa the vision of an African common market had disappeared by 1965. By the same date the pan–Latin American economic integration movement embodied in the Latin American Free Trade Association (LAFTA) had run into heavy and growing difficulties. The results of the present rescue operations undertaken belatedly with assistance from the United States appear somewhat doubtful. It seems that the continental approaches in Latin America and Africa overestimated the strength of political unity feelings and underestimated the difficulties of welding together largely nationalistic societies differing in size and level of development. In both continents the concept of regional unity of interests is tenuous despite common cultural, linguistic, and religious traditions in Latin America or the common heritage of colonialism in Africa. If Simón Bolívar in his later years compared the task of uniting Latin America with that of plowing the sea, the task in Africa would have been still more difficult.

In the past, pan–Latin Americanism has amounted to little more than the ability of twenty relatively weak countries sharing the common destiny of underdevelopment to organize circumstantial coalitions for the purpose of increasing their bargaining power in the face of the United States. Each member of this informal club concurrently tries to cultivate a special relationship with the superpower of the Western Hemisphere. When the immediate needs of this special relationship collide with the interests of the region, short-run considerations prevail as a rule. An even more complex maze of regional political links and special relationships with former colonial powers exists in Africa, where the picture is further complicated by the presence of the Republic of South Africa. Some disinterested and perhaps cynical observers of international politics go as far as to suggest that if the United States were to disappear from the Western Hemisphere and the Republic of South Africa from the African continent, the concepts of Latin American and African unity would rapidly wither away.

There is some truth in this harsh observation. It might be supported by voluminous evidence: endless political and territorial conflicts and open and intractable disagreements on many basic intraregional economic issues in Latin America for which the United States can hardly be blamed, and the frequency and violence of the serious political and economic conflicts that have plagued independent Africa since its decolonization and cannot be traced back to neocolonialist machinations from outside. Whatever Latin Americans and Africans as two separate groups may have in common vis-à-vis the industrial North, intraregional power politics are the daily diet of the two underdeveloped continents.

Weak and small countries play this game as subtly or brutally — according to the occasion — as the advanced and affluent nationalist societies. The persistence of intraregional politics represents one obstacle to the maximalist type of regional economic cooperation involving a continent. The presence of ambivalent bilateral relationships with the extraregional powers makes for another obstacle, and a third arises from the extension of the power politics raging in the North to the backward peripheries.

Another basic reason why pan–Latin American economic cooperation attempts have run into great difficulties at an early stage and why the idea of an African common market had to be abandoned completely can be found in the fact that it was originally expected that the application to economic integration of traditional approaches suitable for advanced countries would bring rapid political and economic benefits to all participants in these ambitious ventures. In the minds of the political elites that embraced these broad schemes in both continents, the Latin American common market and the African common market were to represent an answer to the challenge of the large economic blocs that had emerged in the Northern Hemisphere over a long period of time. According to textbooks and conventional wisdom, the success of these large units within the Western capitalist world was due to the opening of markets to free trade while allegedly Adam Smith's invisible hand obligingly took care of the rest. This highly simplistic approach, which cannot be supported by the history of economic development in Western Europe and the United States, was bound to be especially unsuitable for the conditions prevailing today in the underdeveloped world. In each of the backward continents, no infrastructure links between different parts existed, trade flows were directed mainly to the outside world, differences in underdevelopment levels within each region were staggering, and the relationship of real economic power among the prospective participants was extremely uneven. Thus the odds were overwhelming against the success of economic cooperation experiments centering on the liberalization of trade among highly unequal partners in both Latin America and Africa.

The Latin American Free Trade Association, which replaced the original idea of a Latin American common market, brought under the same roof the region's few industrial giants and a number of small and much more backward countries. If a continental common market had ever been implemented in Africa, it would have brought together an array of even more unequal partners: on the one hand, several relatively dynamic and rapidly developing countries like the United Arab Republic, Kenya, Ivory Coast, and Ghana, and, on the other, a score of states with economic assets amounting to only a few hundred miles of poor roads, a few antiquated consumer goods plants, and a weak and primitive agriculture.

Since the African common market has never been established, it is useless to speculate about what might have happened to it. Within LAFTA, however, frictions arising from the strength of economic nationalism and the inequality of economic power among its members were felt from the very beginning. They became only more acute when the absence of early support from the advanced countries made it impossible to establish special regional cooperation mechanisms to help improve the relative position within the area of the smaller partners in the venture. Consequently, LAFTA became for all practical purposes a weak preferential trade zone, a largely ineffective umbrella over the heads of several groups with conflicting immediate interests: three large countries — Argentina, Brazil, and Mexico — which in theory can "go it alone"; the so-called middle group — Colombia, Chile, Peru, Uruguay, and Venezuela — which probably need regional economic cooperation more than the others; and the most backward states — Ecuador and Paraguay, joined later by Bolivia. The middle and small LAFTA members claim, with different degrees of vehemence, that the freeing of regional trade brought them no tangible benefits. Some of them even insist that their position vis-à-vis the larger members has actually deteriorated when measured by trade flows. While there are reasons to believe that the larger republics reaped some benefits from LAFTA trade liberalization, these gains do not seem important enough to force the beneficiaries to offer any meaningful nontrade compensation to the remaining LAFTA members. Thus, with each country following its own development policies, no tangible progress was achieved in industrial integration, harmonization of trade policies toward the outside world, or monetary and transport cooperation. At the same time, from the viewpoint of the continent's development needs, the net gains from a free trade zone proved negligible.

Some neoclassical economists who never saw the reason for cooperation among a group of largely noncomplementary and underdeveloped economies might use this disappointing experience as a proof that any form of economic cooperation among developing countries is a futile exercise. But it is also possible that the LAFTA failure is due not to the general inapplicability of the idea of regional economic cooperation to the developing world but to the choice of a wrong strategy. In the Latin American experiment, emphasis on trade liberalization as the principal ingredient of regional integration brought about neither meaningful trade expansion nor acceleration of development. It is in a way ironical that when the United States finally decided in 1965 to lend its support to the LAFTA experiment it still assigned major emphasis to integration techniques and approaches borrowed from Western European experience that do not seem to work in the general context of underdevelopment.

Preconditions for Regional Economic Cooperation in the Context of Underdevelopment

As the legal texts included in this volume demonstrate, in addition to languishing LAFTA, seven different economic cooperation schemes, with a total participation of thirty-three countries, presently exist in Latin America, Africa, and Asia: the Central American Common Market, the East African Common Market, the Central African Economic and Customs Union, the West African Customs Union, the Arab common market, the economic cooperation scheme for the Maghrib countries, and Regional Cooperation for Development in Western Asia. Although the origin of one of them, the East African Common Market, goes back as far as the end of the First World War, its structure was completely revamped in 1966–1967. All of the remaining schemes have begun to operate only during the past few years, even though the preparatory work for some preceded the beginning of the present decade.

The only common characteristic of these arrangements is that each is limited to a relatively small group of countries that, in addition to covering a compact geographic area, are united to some degree by common political or sociocultural traditions. Thus the Central American Common Market comprises the area that, after the dissolution of the Spanish empire in the early nineteenth century, formed for a short period the Federal Republic of Central America. Three customs union arrangements in the sub-Sahara follow closely the political or administrative divisions of the colonial era by covering what until a few years ago were known as French West Africa, French Equatorial Africa, and British East Africa. Two cooperative schemes in the Arab world comprise the United Arab Republic and adjoining parts of the Middle East, and the Maghrib countries, respectively. Finally, some historical and cultural affinities can also be found in the only Asian regional arrangement, Regional Cooperation for Development, which includes Turkey, Iraq, and Pakistan. It is worth noting that in each of these small cooperative groupings the differences in development levels among the participating countries are reasonably small. It would be difficult to deny, however, that in at least two, the Arab common market and the East African Common Market, the presence of one dominant state can be detected — the United Arab Republic in the first and Kenya in the second.

Dissimilarities in the operating aspects of the seven subregional economic groupings are so great that no comparative analysis of their legal structures or of the scope of the commitments of participating countries seems possible. All of them involve some measure of regional liberalization of trade, but liberalization mechanisms vary considerably from one group to another. In some instances full customs unions or common markets have already been established or are gradually being built up; there is one very limited free trade zone, the Arab common market; and two envisage trade liberalization as a distant future goal, presumably to be achieved by the gradual expansion and strengthening of bilateral trade agreements concurrent with extension of the most-favored-nation clause to the remaining members of the grouping. Interestingly enough, in most of these cooperation schemes the trade liberalization program is not considered the decisive element of the regional economic integration and cooperation process, although it represents a general framework. In this respect these schemes differ basically from the approaches adopted by the developed countries in the past. In the most unorthodox arrangement — Regional Cooperation for Development — the kernel of cooperation is an industrial integration program involving the establishment of a large group of mutually complementary industries distributed among member countries in accordance with their resource endowments.

The rationale for this departure from traditional approaches to economic integration — perceived as necessary almost a decade ago by the intellectual fathers of LAFTA but not implemented by its actual builders — is rather obvious. The purpose of all these schemes is to achieve economic diversification and to accelerate industrialization directly without waiting until the liberalization of largely nonexistent trade induces economic development in a round-about way. In most of the regional agreements industrial complementarity or cooperative industrialization is given as high a priority as trade liberalization itself. Thus, for example, the General Treaty on Central American Economic Integration addresses itself directly to the issue of industrial integration by endorsing the agreement on regional integration industries concluded prior to the treaty itself. The Central African Economic and Customs Union treaty commits the contracting parties "to harmonize their industrialization policies, development plans and transport policies with a view to promoting balanced development and diversification of the economies of the member States."

Coordination of economic development and industrialization policies is also provided for in the Agreement for Economic Unity among Arab League States, signed in 1962, which offered a basis for subsequent agreement on the Arab common market. A cooperation scheme involving the Maghrib countries puts industrial harmonization and coordination ahead of trade expansion; and, finally, Regional Cooperation for Development, involving three West Asian countries, centers not on trade liberalization but on coordination of new industrial projects.

It must be admitted that the translation of regional industrialization plans into reality has until now presented serious difficulties. Many factors are responsible for this disappointing state of affairs. Probably the most important obstacle arises from the fact that, for any developing country, industrialization is much more than a preferred road to development offering an important source of badly needed employment and a way to save some foreign exchange at an early stage; it is a status symbol. In multilateral trade negotiations related to the implementation of a regional economic cooperation scheme, a broad consensus can be reached by interested parties because certain difficult situations — due to pressures exerted by vested interests in each country — can be taken care of by resorting to rules of exception or escape clauses. But agreement on the distribution of new industrial activities is more difficult to reach. Unless a well-thought-out program providing a series of possible *quid pro quos* through the submission of a wide range of feasible concrete projects is at hand, each member country will press for maximum *immediate* gains in the industrial field, that is, will try to put its hands on as many industries as possible. In the absence of an early group agreement each member will opt for the implementation of its own industrialization program with very little regard either for consumer welfare or for the interests of the region as a whole. In a world composed of nationalist political units bent upon industrialization, limitations on sovereignty in trade matters are more easily accepted than the renunciation of industrial sovereignty. Throughout the developing world, Lord Keynes's exhortation directed to British economic policy makers in the midst of the Great Depression is followed unreservedly: "We wish . . . to be our own masters and to be as free as we can make ourselves from the interferences of the outside world." It does not help much to insist that the industrial sovereignty of a small developing country is very spurious indeed. Moreover, this apparent sovereignty is often encouraged by interferences of the outside world. The experience of the Central American Common Market with the regime for integration industries and the tribulations of the East

African Common Market when its members, immediately after their independence, unsuccessfully tried to arrive at an agreement concerning the distribution of new industrial activities point toward the existence of these disruptive external elements.

Whatever form future industrial cooperation takes within the framework of a small regional grouping — the harmonization of industrial development plans, a common investment policy, or joint elaboration of individual industrial projects — the grouping's success will depend upon solution of the thorny problem of distributing new industries in a way considered equitable by all participants. As demonstrated by the disappointing experiences of LAFTA and the difficulties of smaller cooperation schemes, the liberalization of trade among countries with different development levels and divergent resource endowments puts into motion a process that gives benefits to those who need them relatively less at the expense of those who probably need them most. Nurkse, Myrdal, Prebisch, and Singer did not invent this process. The way it functions is well known to students of the economic history of nineteenth-century Italy, Germany, and the United States. But for unclear reasons, those who advocate the integration of developing countries through trade liberalization mechanisms alone conveniently forget not only historical evidence but even the present experiences of many advanced countries. Within individual states, some nontrade mechanisms have always existed for arresting or cutting down the growing regional disparities caused by freeing the movement of production factors. Such nontrade equilibrating mechanisms also must be built into multinational economic cooperation schemes; if the regional development process is left to trade liberalization and to market forces alone, these schemes are bound to fail. This fact of life is gaining recognition in the developing countries, as demonstrated by the continuous and growing appearance in regional groupings of nontrade mechanisms meant to assure what some of the international treaties contained in this volume call balanced, or equilibrated, development.

Initially the concept of reciprocal and equitable distribution of benefits was limited to the equilibrium of trade flows. Since such an equilibrium is easier to achieve by trade restriction than by trade expansion, the concept of equal participation in integration gains has been gradually broadened to comprise four essential aspects of economic integration for development: balance-of-payments effects, over-all growth rates, industrialization, and relative levels of development. As the texts presented in this collection show, more and more developing countries accept the following proposition:

. . . in order to operate efficiently, an integration program should be based on an aggregate of regional and national policies that prevent the emergence of severe disequilibrium in intraregional trade; guarantee comparable long-term rates of development; and, at the same time, shorten the economic distance within the zone and assure that all members in the union will participate in the industrialization process.[1]

The need to fulfill these conditions clearly makes extremely doubtful all of the ambitious plans for continental integration in the developing world. Ecuador and Argentina, Afghanistan and Malaya, and the United Arab Republic and Mali have nothing in common except geographical position within their respective continents. This is obviously not enough for meaningful economic cooperation. If by way of *reductio ad absurdum* it occurred to someone to establish a cooperation scheme encompassing, among others, Portugal, West Germany, and Albania and built it upon the trade liberalization concept, it is clear that such a scheme would not be able to work. Fortunately, basic preconditions for viable economic cooperation can be created — and gradually are being established — in smaller regional groupings. A growing number of these geographically modest arrangements comprise, in addition to an agreement providing for gradual trade liberalization, some of the following elements: a regional development bank; a regional mechanism for financial settlements and for monetary policy coordination; a regime harmonizing incentives for regional and external private investment; an instrument for the promotion of industrial specialization by agreement; and a formula for the equitable distribution of customs revenues and other taxes, with due account being taken of the development needs of the most backward participants.

The Central American Common Market contains almost all these instruments of economic cooperation: a development bank with substantial resources, a payments clearing house, a regional technological institute, and a system harmonizing tax incentives. This explains to a large degree why the Central American experiment is the most successful of all. The East African Common Market relies upon the support of a common services organization in the field of infrastructure, and its new draft treaty provides for the establishment of a regional development bank. The Central African Economic and Customs Union has a solidarity fund, an investment code, and an arrangement for the distribution of

[1] Miguel S. Wionczek, "Requisites for Viable Integration," in Miguel S. Wionczek, ed., *Latin American Economic Integration: Experiences and Prospects* (New York: Frederick A. Praeger, 1966), p. 13.

fiscal revenues through the ingenious system of the *taxe unique* (single tax). The Arab common market envisages the establishment of a development bank, a multilateral payments arrangement, and a number of joint service organizations. The West Asian scheme provides for cooperation in industry, commerce, transport, communications, and other fields. An extremely interesting arrangement for a common market in the Federation of Malaysia, which broke down at a very early stage, probably because of acute political conflicts between Malaya and Singapore, contained measures that were expected to assure for all participants some equitable gains from industrialization, fair distribution of customs revenues, and development aid to the most backward parts of the Federation.

The experiences of the relatively successful regional cooperation agreements, as well as of those that failed or are languishing, strongly suggest that, in addition to a series of regional mechanisms needed to provide some measure of equitable distribution of gains among the participating countries, a common policy of the aid-providing developed countries vis-à-vis an integrating area is absolutely necessary. If the cooperation mechanism is limited to trade liberalization and if aid policies to the area are not coordinated or are left to the free working of international finance, the results are bound to be disruptive even in the short run. When the direction of capital flows, in addition to the benefits of trade liberalization, favors the leading economies of the region, the already existing differences in development levels and potentialities rapidly increase. Since this openly contradicts the objectives of regional cooperation and the expectations of the more backward members, disruptive political tensions brought about by a deficient integration mechanism may bring greater estrangement among the participating countries than existed before the beginning of the cooperation experiment. This is clearly true of the Latin American Free Trade Association after six years of unsuccessful attempts to extend cooperation to nontrade fields. Similar negative effects of the intraregional scramble for equal participation in gains can be detected in the Arab common market and in the East African Common Market.

Most of these strains obviously could be avoided if the more advanced participants were willing or able to forgo some benefits accruing to them through the regional grouping for the sake of the poorer partners. However, if one recalls the climate of economic nationalism now prevalent in the developing world and the staggering problems facing each underdeveloped country, it is completely futile to advocate such a solution. A country willing to abdicate some immediate gains for future

common benefits in effect slows down its own painful and far from satisfactory progress and for some time subsidizes the "underdeveloped"
neighboring countries. The "richer" members of a grouping do not,
however, feel responsible for the "poorer" ones; the greater underdevelopment of the latter may be a result of historical conditions, the random
distribution of natural resources, or past policies of extraregional developed powers. Unfortunately, a more underdeveloped member of a regional grouping does not see the situation in the same terms. From its
viewpoint, the misfortunes of the present are added to the misfortunes of
the past. Those of the present are obviously related to the unjust functioning of the cooperation scheme — and someone has to be blamed for
that. Thus Malaya was afraid of economic and industrial domination by
Singapore, Paraguay and Ecuador feel exploited by the advanced members of LAFTA, and Tanzania believes that it is being abused by Kenya.
The conflict surges at all possible levels of underdevelopment. The
Rwanda-Burundi customs and monetary union, renegotiated after the
withdrawal of Belgium from that part of Central Africa, broke down in
1962 not only because of deep tribal conflicts but because Bujumbura — in
Burundi — was the only development pole in the two countries. Consequently, the Rwandese were afraid, not without reason, that all benefits
of the union would accrue to the neighboring state.

It is unreasonable to expect that any regional economic grouping will
be able to solve the basic problem of achieving relatively balanced multinational development with its own means. Thus the case for the coordination of external aid to regional cooperation arrangements rests upon
three major considerations. First, the economic development of most of the
economies of the new states — because of their minuscule size and backwardness — will be impossible unless they join in their efforts to organize
a regional division of labor, especially in the field of industrialization.
Second, the regionalization of aid would increase the over-all performance
of economic aid where the total flow of external aid is not expanding *pari
passu* with the needs of the underdeveloped world. Third, only the coordination and regionalization of external aid can assure the abandonment of
the futile inward-directed development policies of many economically
unviable political units, or prevent them from adopting beggar-
your-neighbor policies when the expectations of traditionally oriented cooperation schemes are not fulfilled.

Awareness of this situation led the UNCTAD group of experts on
economic integration to recommend in the spring of 1966 that developed
countries urgently consider joint action in support of numerous cooperation arrangements in the Southern Hemisphere through (a) the provision

of additional funds for regional and multinational projects, since willingness to provide these funds might be an effective means of overcoming resistance to trade liberalization and economic cooperation among developing countries; (b) special attention to the need for financing regional preinvestment and feasibility studies to ensure that an adequate number of such projects would be forthcoming in support of regional cooperation schemes; and (c) special consideration of the need to cushion balance-of-payments risks resulting from trade liberalization or integration measures — either through existing international financial bodies or through regional payment facilities assisted by donor countries.[2]

A report by the UNCTAD Secretariat on trade expansion and economic integration among developing countries, released in the summer of 1966, again raised the question of how the advanced countries and international institutions might help the developing states find suitable solutions of the crucial problem arising in most regional cooperation schemes — that of assuring the more underdeveloped partners an equitable share in the benefits expected from integration. According to the UNCTAD report,

> a firm expression of the readiness of the developed countries and of the [international] institutions . . . to support such solutions, if that support is requested by particular groups of developing countries, might ease the developing countries' negotiating problems and might also help to prevent future difficulties that might be due to insufficient consideration of the less advanced partner's needs. It would underscore the developed countries' awareness of the real nature of the problem of integration in the developing part of the world, and it would show that the international community attaches great importance to a type of integration which would not widen the differences between the relatively rich and the poor among developing countries and which would not limit such efforts to the richer countries of a region, with the less advanced ones being left out and lagging ever more behind.[3]

External Assistance to Regional Cooperation Schemes

The recent establishment of three continental development banks — the Inter-American Development Bank (IDB), the African Development Bank, and the Asian Development Bank — points to a gradual worldwide

[2] United Nations Conference on Trade and Development, *Trade Expansion and Economic Co-operation among Developing Countries: Report of the Committee of Experts* (Sales No. 67.II.D.2; Geneva, 1966), p. 29.

[3] United Nations Conference on Trade and Development, *Trade Expansion and Economic Integration among Developing Countries: Report by the Secretariat* (Sales No. 67.II.D.20; New York, 1967), p. 30.

acceptance of the importance of the regional approach toward the problem of underdevelopment. Only a decade ago Latin American initiatives calling for the establishment of an inter-American financial agency were considered untimely and unnecessary by the economically advanced countries. In the mid-fifties it still was claimed that the financing of development needs was satisfactorily managed through either bilateral channels or worldwide agencies such as the International Bank for Reconstruction and Development. When the Inter-American Development Bank was finally established in 1960, its charter was not at all explicit with respect to its important potential function as a source of financing and technical assistance for regional economic cooperation schemes. The only indirect reference to this function is a sentence in the article of the charter dealing with the purposes of the institution. According to this statement, the IDB was "to cooperate with the member countries to orient their development policies toward a better utilization of their resources, in a manner consistent with the objectives of making their economies *more complementary* [italics added]. . . ." From the very beginning, however, the IDB has actively participated in the formulation of practical solutions to problems arising in the implementation of Latin American economic cooperation schemes. In the words of IDB's president,

> . . . the bank's interest [in this type of activity] . . . stems from the conviction that, in the absence of economic integration, it will be impossible to remove some of the fundamental obstructions to the economic and social development of Latin American countries.[4]

This supporting action has taken many forms, such as the establishment of a program for financing intraregional exports of capital goods, the setting up of a preinvestment fund for Latin American integration, the extension of loans to the Central American Bank for Economic Integration (CABEI), and IDB participation in regional studies and research projects undertaken in cooperation with the United Nations Economic Commission for Latin America and other regional agencies. Presently, the Inter-American Development Bank is putting special emphasis on multinational projects — mainly in the field of infrastructure — that, if well-designed and implemented, may in the long run improve prospects for the more efficient functioning of the Latin American Free Trade Association and even open the way for the establishment of a Latin American common market. Behind the idea of multinational infra-

---

[4] Felipe Herrera, "The Inter-American Development Bank and Latin American Integration," in Wionczek, *Latin American Economic Integration*, p. 216.

structure projects lies the belief that they may create in the region strong vested interests favoring broader cooperation as well as offer immediate benefits to the less developed Latin American republics.

The charter of the African Development Bank is somewhat more explicit about the institution's role in supporting regional cooperation schemes. It declares that the Bank will give special priority to projects or programs that in nature or scope concern several members, and to projects or programs intended to make the economies of its members increasingly complementary. In December 1965 the Bank's Board of Governors agreed that the agency would finance particularly those projects that are included within regional development programs, and that special preference would be accorded to all projects that may benefit two or more member countries and thus stimulate inter-African cooperation.

The charter of the Asian Development Bank goes still further. First, it commits the institution to "giving priority to those regional, subregional as well as national projects and programmes which will contribute most effectively to the harmonious economic growth of the region as a whole, and having special regard to the needs of the smaller or less developed member countries in the region," and, second, to meeting "requests from members in the region to assist them in the co-ordination of their development policies and plans with a view to achieving better utilization of their resources, making their economies more complementary."

A comparison of the three charters reveals the evolution of the concept of the role of a continental development bank. Increasing emphasis is being placed on the financial support of regional and subregional cooperation arrangements. The charter of the Asian Development Bank goes beyond this, clearly noting the urgent need for fostering more balanced growth in the region as a whole, keeping in mind the special difficulties of the least developed Asian countries. Thus the problem of the growing lag between the richer and the poorer underdeveloped countries, which has been largely responsible for serious frictions arising in regional cooperation arrangements, finally has been brought into sharp focus. Multilateral aid, provided only partially by the advanced countries, is expected to help to eliminate these particularly explosive political frictions.

Thus a new approach to aid seems to be emerging. In contrast to traditional country-to-country aid disbursement or worldwide distribution of economic assistance by global international agencies, the channeling of some part of external aid through continental development banks offers considerable advantages from the viewpoint of regional economic groupings. Moreover, international financial agencies are also beginning to take note, albeit slowly, of the existence of regional economic arrangements. Some recent credit operations of the World Bank in East Africa seem, for example, to be designed in such a way as to offer badly needed support to the East African Common Market.

Extending external aid to regional cooperation schemes by financing a multinational infrastructure or industrial projects of regional interest is not, however, an easy enterprise — whether such aid originates in global financial agencies or in continental development banks. Two limiting factors enter the picture. First, because of the limited magnitude of the total aid potentially available, national governments continue to show a clear preference for securing external resources for exclusively national projects; and, second, precisely because of this preference, there is an acute scarcity of multinational projects suitable for external financing. The Inter-American Development Bank was the first regional agency to recognize that in such a situation some special mechanisms and procedures would have to be created for the purpose of launching this type of project without creating the politically unacceptable impression that they were being imposed from outside upon independent political units. This was why IDB established a preinvestment fund for Latin American integration.

It is quite possible, however, that in small cooperation arrangements subregional development banks or corporations might offer a more efficient and speedier solution. One such agency, the Central American Bank for Economic Integration, has proved quite successful. The access of this bank to sizable financial resources from outside — the United States and IDB — is largely responsible for the Central American Common Market's rapid progress with a minimum of intra-area frictions. In Africa an East African Development Bank has been established. In the Middle East the Arab common market agreement provided for a pan-Arab development institution. It was expected, largely on extraregional political grounds, that financial support for this grouping would come from Kuwait, a state whose foreign exchange resources are considerably larger than those needed for its own economic development. Because of intra-Arab political strife an Arab development bank has never started functioning, but it would have accelerated and made easier economic cooperation in the Middle East. It is only to be hoped that other subregional development agencies will be established, particularly in various parts of Africa and Asia, for the purpose of (1) mobilizing and channeling some extraregional resources to integrating areas and (2) undertaking the difficult task of promoting industrial cooperation and the preparation of infrastructure projects of multinational scope. If such development agencies were assured of external financial support on a more or less continuous basis, the objective of balanced or equitable regional development might be much easier to achieve than under the present circumstances.

There are signs that support for the idea of economic aid regionalization is growing stronger in the advanced countries. In the United States, the 1967 Presidential message to Congress on foreign aid for the first time took note of the movement toward regional cooperation in the Southern Hemisphere, stating that "the resources available for development are too scarce to scatter among many countries when greater promise lies in joint action" and that "the United States will encourage regional economic development to the maximum extent consistent with the economic and political realities in each region." Some additional resources are to be provided by the United States for special loan operations on concessional terms envisaged by both the Asian and the African Development Banks. To avoid external political interference in the activities of the African Bank, its charter explicitly bars non-African countries from ordinary membership. The readiness of the United States to help the African Development Bank, without enjoying the political benefits of membership, is an encouraging sign. Similar arrangements aimed at the establishment of a Latin American integration fund under the aegis of IDB are being worked out. Such a fund has been advocated for a long time by all regional agencies working on Latin American economic cooperation.

A number of factors make economic cooperation more difficult in Latin America than in other regions. First, the differences in development levels and in the degree of industrialization within the area presently covered by LAFTA are wider than in other smaller regional cooperation arrangements. Second, the unsatisfactory performance of LAFTA during its first five years of existence only increased frictions in the area and exacerbated fears in the smaller countries of possible economic domination by the larger republics. Moreover, in the three leading countries, strong industrial groups show great fear that trade liberalization will affect their privileged positions within highly protected domestic markets. Under such conditions much more is expected now from a Latin American regional development fund than would have been expected at the beginning of the decade, when difficulties arising from the integration process were not yet clearly perceived.

To satisfy all the parties concerned, a regional integration fund in

Latin America will have to be in a position to take care of many problems at the same time. It will have to count upon enough resources to (a)
finance a number of multinational infrastructure projects to provide evidence that closer economic cooperation can bring immediate benefits to
all parties concerned; (b) provide special assistance to those poorer members who, rightly or wrongly, feel not only that they are not participating
in the benefits of the cooperation program but also that they are its victims; and (c) dispel the fear of the backward sectors of national industries
in the larger countries that they may be wiped out by regional free trade.
Thus a Latin American integration fund will have to be, simultaneously,
a promoter of relatively large and expensive multinational projects, a pro-
vider of considerable resources for the acceleration of growth in the poorer
countries, and a source of funds for the modernization and reconversion
of antiquated industries in the relatively advanced republics.

Shortly before the Meeting of American Chiefs of State in Punta del
Este in April 1967, the United States informally offered financial support
of $100 million a year for Latin American economic integration. This
offer clearly is not proportionate to the resources needed to accelerate
trade liberalization in Latin America and to transform LAFTA into a regional common market. Under present circumstances it is difficult to envisage that the large resources needed to cope with all of the problems
arising from the acceleration of Latin American integration can be
mobilized unless the United States radically reorients its aid policies in
Latin America or unless the Inter-American Development Bank dedi-
cates most of its funds to the support of the Latin American integration
experiment. The first proposition seems politically unrealistic. The second
would hardly be acceptable to the great majority of IDB members, who
consider that agency an important source of financing for national
development programs that are very tenuously related to regional economic needs.

In Africa and Asia, relatively small resources, if judiciously applied,
may provide considerable help for the existing or planned small subregional economic cooperation groupings. But in Latin America the acceleration of the integration process on a continental scale would imply
a much larger external economic assistance and a far greater degree of
intraregional willingness to cooperate than exists at present.

Prospects for the Next Decade

What direction will regional economic cooperation experiments in Latin
America, Africa, and Asia take within the next decade? Despite the su-

perficially impressive declaration of intent issued at the Punta del Este Meeting of Chiefs of State of the American continent in April 1967, the odds of organizing a Latin American common market are less than even. The Punta del Este declaration overstresses the trade liberalization content of this future market and gives too little emphasis to other much more important ingredients of a geographically wide cooperation scheme undertaken by countries at different development levels. The declaration contains few ideas that were not agreed upon in principle within the LAFTA context but found impossible to implement. It is one thing to agree in broad terms to harmonize economic policies and foster sectoral industrial cooperation agreements and another to work out and set in motion mutually agreed upon operative mechanisms that by their very nature restrict the sovereignty of individual countries in such highly sensitive fields as economic development planning and industrialization.

In this respect, the presidential declaration is extremely vague:

> The Latin American common market will be based on the improvement of the two existing integration systems: the Latin American Free Trade Association (LAFTA) and the Central American Common Market (CACM). The two systems will initiate simultaneously a process of convergence by stages of cooperation, closer ties and integration, taking into account the interest of Latin American countries not yet associated with these systems, in order to provide their access to one of them.[5]

The implementation of this agreement will be supervised by a committee composed of the executive organs of LAFTA and the Central American Common Market. Such a committee, in turn, "will encourage meetings at the ministerial level, in order to insure that Latin American integration will proceed as rapidly as possible, and, in due course, initiate negotiation of a general treaty or the protocols required to create the Latin American common market." The expressions "the improvement of the existing integration systems," "a process of convergence by the stages of cooperation," "as rapidly as possible," and "in due course," considered together with the fact that the major LAFTA members rejected at Punta del Este a proposal to establish a ministerial executive committee to draft by a specific date a Latin American common market treaty, strongly suggest that the road to agreement on such a treaty will be an extremely long one.

Moreover, the presidential declaration provides no clear indication of how the problem of the grievances of the middle-sized and smaller Latin

[5] Organization of American States, *Declaration of the American Presidents*, Meeting of American Chiefs of State, Punta del Este, Uruguay, April 12–14, 1967 (OAS/Ser.K/XIV/1.1; Washington, D.C.).

American republics is to be solved except that the solution will be based "on the provisions of the Montevideo Treaty and its complementary resolutions." Unless a special effort is made to give additional aid to these states and to assign to them new industrial projects of regional interest, it is difficult to see how the present frictions within LAFTA can disappear. The declaration's only new approach to Latin American integration is the provision for the acceleration of the construction of a multinational infrastructure and for the mobilization of financial and technical resources "to contribute to the solution of problems in connection with the balance of payments, industrial readjustments and retraining of the labor force that may arise from a rapid reduction of trade barriers during the period of transition toward a common market." But the extremely important question of the magnitude of these resources is left unanswered.

It is expected that high priority will be given to multinational projects, but many such projects may cement relations among small groups of neighboring countries rather than expand the scope of continental cooperation. It will take a long time to create a network of such multinational projects linking together all of the future common market's participants. Moreover, one should not exclude altogether the possibility of a scramble for economic aid for such projects in which the larger countries will be at a considerable advantage precisely because they are larger and more developed and thus can be the first to elaborate and submit for financial aid projects that are multinational in scope but heavily biased in their own favor. For the orderly and equitable functioning of a Latin American common market some kind of regional planning in the area would be needed, but such planning is hardly in the cards, given the meager results of national planning in Latin America under the aegis of the Alliance for Progress.

The April 1967 Punta del Este meeting probably offered the last chance to put some content into the idea of Latin American integration along maximalist lines. If this opportunity is not taken, however, Latin America will not necessarily revert to the pre-1960 situation. The Central American Common Market has achieved a momentum that should permit its continuous move forward independently of the future of LAFTA. Some kind of economic cooperation is also emerging among the newly independent small countries in the Caribbean. Within LAFTA itself one can envisage a distinct potential for a growing rapprochement among some smaller neighboring countries, for example, Venezuela, Colombia, and Ecuador or Peru, Chile, and Bolivia. They might be willing to advance economic cooperation faster than the rest of the present LAFTA membership, and in the recent past they have given some indication of considering such an alternative approach if their grievances against the big three (Argentina, Brazil, and Mexico) are not redressed. The presidential declaration in fact opens a door to such schemes by accepting the idea of transitional arrangements providing for accelerated trade liberalization within subregions and for concurrent industrial cooperation agreements whose benefits would not be extended to other members of a future Latin American common market. Within a decade, therefore, we may see in Latin America several limited economic cooperation groupings instead of one large common market. It is impossible to predict whether they will one day converge into a regional common market.

In Africa, from the moment the continental market idea was definitely abandoned, the United Nations Economic Commission for Africa has slowly been elaborating a scheme for economic development cooperation in four subregions: North Africa (from Morocco to Sudan), West Africa (from Mauritania to Nigeria), Central Africa (including the Congo [Kinshasa]), and "greater" East Africa (from Ethiopia to Zambia). Very little has been achieved as yet in respect to these subregional economic communities, as ECA calls them, except in greater East Africa and West Africa, where initial agreements have been reached to accelerate economic cooperation in the industrial and infrastructure fields. The absence of any tangible progress is explained by the fact, among others, that practically each of the four regions includes countries that have close economic links with different former metropolitan powers. The agreement on the association of eighteen African states with the European Common Market and the proliferation of monetary areas in the continent, which also involve strong links with various ex-colonial powers, are considered immediate obstacles to ECA plans. The origin of the difficulties no doubt goes much deeper. One might assume that the division of Africa into four future subregional economic communities aims not only to facilitate economic cooperation in that part of the world but also to weaken the postcolonial relations of the majority of the newly independent states with the former metropolitan areas, but in fact these ECA-promoted subregions were established very arbitrarily. They are quite large subregions — each larger in physical terms than Western Europe. Many of the countries thrown into these ECA-sponsored subregions not only have little common political tradition (except possibly in North Africa) but have never in the past engaged in any economic relations, nor do they now have even the crudest infrastructure links. It is quite difficult, for example, to envisage any kind of meaningful economic cooperation between Sudan and Morocco, Senegal and Nigeria, or Ethiopia and Zambia. At present they have nothing to trade with each other. Moreover, the distances and the economic and institutional obstacles involved are so great that the prospects for industrial cooperation in these large areas seem extremely remote even in the distant future. Economic cooperation might be made more feasible if, since the African countries are unable to undertake this task on their own, someone were willing to underwrite the forbidding cost of building up the basic infrastructure of each of the four subregions, especially transport and communication networks, thus bringing closer together the most important prospective members of the proposed communities. Even then it defies human imagination to foresee the emergence of conditions that would permit the degree of complementarity defensible on economic grounds. It seems that ECA's strategy still contains a large degree of political wishful thinking and disregards many important economic factors. Since the smaller groupings involving a limited number of neighboring countries as yet do not show willingness to merge into larger and more unwieldy communities, it is within the realm of possibility that by the end of the next decade Africa will witness the presence of some ten smaller groupings built on the grounds of political expediency and immediate economic interests. Some countries, for example, the Congo (Kinshasa), Ethiopia, or Sudan, may opt for staying out of such small and relatively compact groupings but may attempt to expand their trade relations with neighbors for whatever the trade expansion may be worth. Even such very pragmatic and, to many Africans, politically objectionable solutions would represent some progress in comparison with the immediate postindependence situation. One might also assume, and not only hope, that the former colonial powers will also revise their present policies in Africa once it becomes clear to everyone concerned that the present economic atomization of the continent does not pay political dividends to any outside power. Such an adjustment of the policies of the Northern Hemisphere would represent a considerable contribution to the achievement of African economic unity, which is still very distant, but to making Africa less unviable than it is at present from the viewpoint of long-term economic development.

In Asia the problem continues to be extremely acute in the southeastern part of the continent. Over the past decade more plans for limited economic cooperation were probably advanced in Southeast Asia than anywhere else. In addition to the stillborn common market of Malaya and Singapore, the Association of South Asia (ASA) — a cooperative effort involving Malaya, the Philippines, and Indonesia (Maphilindo) — and similar schemes were propounded; but none has ever passed the stage of preliminary political negotiations and declarations of intent. Southeast Asia is not only internally divided; it is also the field of the most violent power politics clash between the Western powers and China. The last period of peace in that part of the world — a colonial peace — ended in 1940. A quarter century of wars and intense intraregional and internal conflicts does not provide the preconditions for any kind of regional economic cooperation. The prospects are very bleak indeed, unless some kind of peace is brought to the countries that used to belong to the former French colonial empire, unless some *modus vivendi* is established between extraregional powers, and unless the conflicts between local societies and large Chinese minorities are resolved. Only then might some regional cooperation schemes be implemented in the Mekong River basin and among the island countries off the Asian coast. The political problems confronted are so great, however, that it is impossible at this stage to visualize any permanent forms of economic cooperation beyond the expansion of trade by traditional means. Multilateralization of aid through the Asian Development Bank might be very helpful in that respect and might possibly give some substance to the long-ready plans for multinational cooperation in the Mekong area under the most adverse conditions.

Even if it is assumed that the prospects for regional economic cooperation in Southeast Asia are extremely doubtful, the progress of limited integration schemes in western Asia and in the Middle East might make the problems of Asian economic development somewhat more tractable. It is quite possible that by the mid-1970s two relatively viable and large economic units — the Arab common market and the West Asian regional cooperation scheme — will emerge on the western perimeter of the continent in place of the present dozen inward-directed and independent but economically backward units.

It is hoped that this brief survey of the present state and prospects for economic cooperation experiments in the three underdeveloped continents strongly supports this writer's main proposition: that such schemes offer one of the very few ways available to the Southern Hemisphere to break the present vicious circle of social backwardness, economic stagnation, and parochial nationalism. Whether this difficult road of regional economic cooperation will be followed at a speed commensurate with the magnitude of unresolved problems depends as much on the countries directly involved as on the advanced Northern Hemisphere.

PART I

COMMON MARKETS, FREE TRADE ZONES,
AND REGIONAL INDUSTRIAL COOPERATION SCHEMES

CHAPTER ONE

Latin American Free Trade Association

The concept of Latin American economic cooperation for the purpose of accelerating the region's development and industrialization emerged within the United Nations Economic Commission for Latin America (ECLA) at the beginning of the 1950s. The major Latin American republics had by that time completed the first stage of industrialization, which concentrated on consumer goods industries, but the area was severely hit by the decline of world demand for its traditional primary exports. Although ECLA had been working on adapting economic development theory to particular Latin American conditions since its establishment in 1948, until the mid-1950s no one in the region had any clear notion of the institutional form that such cooperation might imply. The concept of regional cooperation based on trade preferences appeared for the first time in studies elaborated in the mid-1950s by the ECLA Trade Committee, created — primarily by the countries already participating actively in intraregional trade — expressly to analyze and help resolve problems related to commercial policy, payments, maritime transport, and other aspects of trade. At that time practically all intra–Latin American trade, except for Venezuela's intraregional exports of oil, was concentrated in the south of the subcontinent, that is, in Argentina, Brazil, Chile, Paraguay, and Uruguay.

It was at the Inter-American Economic Conference in Buenos Aires in the fall of 1957 that the idea of regional economic cooperation was fully discussed for the first time. A few months later, in January 1958, the first meeting of the ECLA Working Group on the Latin American Common Market was held in Santiago, Chile. By the spring of 1959 the Working Group, composed of leading economists, many of whom occupied important positions in their respective governments, had elaborated a series of fundamental principles and basic recommendations calling for

33

the early establishment of a common market covering the whole of the subcontinent. They recommended that a Latin American common market be established in two stages. During the first ten-year stage, a substantial reduction of restrictions on trade among the participants would be carried out, with the scope of the reduction depending upon the commodity category. During the second stage, the reduction of tariffs and other trade restrictions within the area would be completed and a single customs tariff vis-à-vis the rest of the world established. The Working Group proposed special treatment for the least developed republics and also stressed the importance of organizing a regional payments agreement and of fostering specific subregional complementarity and specialization agreements primarily in the industrial field.

This proposal, submitted to the ECLA Trade Committee at the ECLA conference in Panama City in May 1959, did not prosper because of the unwillingness of the Latin American countries to accept such far-reaching commitments and because of the parallel initiative of the southernmost republics to establish a subregional free trade zone. Shortly before the ECLA conference, Argentina, Brazil, Chile, and Uruguay — the countries accounting for some three fourths of inter–Latin American trade — had finished drawing up a detailed draft of a treaty envisaging the establishment within a ten-year period of a free trade zone with the possible participation of other republics.

In spite of the basic clash between the two schemes, the fact that the four-country project left adherence to the proposed free trade zone open to other Latin American republics offered a way out. Bolivia, Paraguay, and Peru were invited to participate in the negotiation of a free trade arrangement; Mexico and Venezuela were asked to send observers to a high-level conference convoked in Montevideo in September 1959 to prepare a final draft of a free trade zone treaty. By that time the initial draft had been expanded to include various important features of the ECLA Working Group plan and embodied detailed provisions on the treatment to be granted to the less advanced member countries; its reciprocity and escape clauses had been redefined; and the chapter on the expansion of trade and economic complementarity had been considerably strengthened.

Subsequent negotiations ended with the signing in February 1960 of the Montevideo Treaty, which established the Latin American Free Trade Association (LAFTA). The seven original members (Argentina, Brazil, Chile, Mexico, Paraguay, Peru, and Uruguay) were joined by Colombia and Ecuador in 1961 and by Venezuela in 1966. In early 1967 Bolivia, the only country that participated in the 1960 negotiations but abstained from signing the Treaty, also ratified the LAFTA Treaty.

Reflecting the project elaborated in 1958 and 1959 by the southernmost republics, the Montevideo Treaty concentrated on gradual trade liberalization. It provided for the freeing of regional trade flows through the negotiated establishment of (a) national schedules specifying annual concessions to be granted by each member country to other members, and (b) a common schedule listing the products on which the contracting parties collectively agreed to eliminate all tariff duties and other restrictions affecting commerce within the free trade area over a period not to exceed twelve years.

Each member country committed itself to granting to other LAFTA contracting parties annual tariff reductions equivalent to 8 per cent of the weighted average applicable to third countries. The common schedule was to constitute, in terms of the aggregate value of intra-LAFTA trade, 25 per cent of such trade after the first three years; 50 per cent after six years; 75 per cent after nine years; and "substantially all of such trade" by mid-1973, the end of the twelve-year period.

The Treaty established escape clauses to be applied (a) if imports of products from the area under the liberalization program "have, or are liable to have, serious repercussions on specific activities of vital importance to the national economy"; and (b) if a seriously unfavorable over-all balance-of-payments situation arises. These escape clauses may be resorted to only for short emergency periods and are not applicable to the goods included in the common schedule. The Treaty also elaborated a special regime for trade in agricultural products.

In addition to liberalizing trade and pursuing the more ambitious objectives originally formulated by the ECLA Working Group, the LAFTA signatories agreed, in principle, to expand cooperation beyond the field of trade. Their agreements on these goals were expressed in both the Preamble (a general statement of intentions) and Chapter III of the Montevideo Treaty, and they have been expanded and spelled out in more detail in various resolutions adopted by the LAFTA Conference at its annual meetings. Chapter III of the Treaty committed signatories to facilitate "the increasing integration and complementarity of their economies" by making "every effort . . . to reconcile their import and export régimes, as well as the treatment they accord to capital, goods and services from outside the Area." Furthermore, Article 16 of Chapter III of the Treaty envisaged "progressively closer co-ordination of the corresponding industrialization policies" through agreements "among representatives of the economic sectors concerned." It also recommended negotiation of "mutual agreements on complementarity by industrial sectors."

The Montevideo Treaty established two LAFTA organs: a Conference of the Contracting Parties and a Standing Executive Committee assisted by a Secretariat. The United Nations Economic Commission for Latin America and the Inter-American Economic and Social Council of the Organization of American States were requested to act as technical advisers to the Association. In 1965 it was decided that the foreign ministers of LAFTA countries would hold annual meetings and that, at an early date, a LAFTA Council of Ministers of Foreign Relations would be established as the highest organ of the Association. Because of Chile's refusal to sign a necessary protocol to the Treaty at the second ministerial meeting held in Montevideo in late 1966, the Council of Ministers did not come into being until the spring of 1967.

The first few years of LAFTA's life marked considerable progress in trade negotiations, which were translated into a relatively rapid expansion of trade within Latin America. Following the extension of close to 10,000 tariff concessions on individual products negotiated in six successive annual rounds before the end of 1966, intra-LAFTA trade expanded, in terms of exports f.o.b., from $299 million (6 per cent of global export trade of the nine member countries) in 1961 to $675 million (slightly over 10 per cent of their total export trade) in 1966. Although by the mid-sixties the trade of some newcomers — Mexico, Peru, and Ecuador — had grown very considerably from the low levels registered at the end of the 1950s, the bulk of the commercial exchange continued to be concentrated in the three southern republics — Argentina, Brazil, and Chile — which have a long tradition of reciprocal trade. In 1961 these three countries accounted for 77 per cent of intra-LAFTA exports and 73 per cent of its imports. In 1966 their joint participation in intra-LAFTA exports and imports was still 71 and 68 per cent, respectively. Leaving aside the special case of land-locked Paraguay, only in Argentina and Uruguay did exports to LAFTA in 1966 represent more than one eighth of their global export trade. If the list of countries whose imports from the zone exceeded that percentage in 1966 is longer — it includes Argentina, Brazil, Chile, and Uruguay — this is partly because of the decline in Chilean and Uruguayan global imports in that year as a result of balance-of-payments difficulties. Detailed data on trade diversification by products are still unavailable beyond 1964, but it seems that not too much progress was achieved in this area. In 1964 foodstuffs and other primary products still represented close to 75 per cent of intra-LAFTA trade compared to some 80 per cent at the time of the signing of the Montevideo Treaty.

Besides trade liberalization, which was partly responsible for the expansion of commercial flows within the area, LAFTA's only other achievements during the first years of its existence were the mapping out of the region's resource complementarity and the identification of the nature of the obstacles to broader economic cooperation. The detailed diagnosis of these problems in voluminous studies carried out by ECLA, the LAFTA Secretariat, and the Inter-American Development Bank, among others, has not been translated into any concerted regional action. Some minor cooperative steps, such as the signing of a regional maritime transport convention, the setting up of a rudimentary payments clearing system, or the establishment by the Inter-American Development Bank of two small funds for the support of Latin American integration, are obviously welcome, but they can hardly be considered substitutes for the absence of progress in three key fields: acceleration of the trade liberalization process, regional industrial cooperation, and coordination of economic policies toward the rest of the world.

The deadlock on these three basic fronts has been accompanied by growing frictions among LAFTA members concerning unequal shares in the benefits arising from the scheme as measured by trade flows. At the time of the signing of the LAFTA Treaty, it was recognized that Paraguay and Ecuador, the poorest LAFTA countries, would need unilateral trade and nontrade concessions to compensate for their inability to participate on an equal footing in a trade liberalization scheme involving much more industrially advanced countries. Several years later, however, there emerged another group, composed of middle-sized countries — Chile, Colombia, Peru, and Uruguay. This group also claimed that the three industrial giants of Latin America — Argentina, Brazil, and Mexico — were reaping all of the advantages of the scheme through exports of highly priced manufactured goods to the rest of the region. Although the case for the "middle group" (especially with respect to Colombia and Uruguay) cannot be easily defended, the fact remains that trade deficits of Chile, Colombia, and Uruguay with the LAFTA region continued to grow while Peru's considerable surplus within the area largely disappeared.

The need to adopt joint measures in favor of the members of the "middle group" to "stimulate the establishment or expansion of certain productive activities for which the size of the respective national markets is inadequate or the development of which is of region-wide interest" was officially recognized at the third Conference of the Contracting Parties in late 1963. Since no practical action followed this recognition of the new problem, the heads of state of the LAFTA members from the Pacific coast of South America (small and middle countries) met in Bogotá, Colombia, in August 1966 for the purpose of accelerating cooperation and establishing an informal common front vis-à-vis the three largest LAFTA members. By accentuating intra-LAFTA differences, the Bogotá meeting brought to the surface latent tendencies toward the establishment of small subregional blocs, tendencies that had been avoided in 1960, at least apparently, by a compromise between the southernmost republics and the sponsors of an all-inclusive Latin American common market scheme.

Growing general dissatisfaction with LAFTA progress was officially expressed for the first time in the spring of 1963 in a joint declaration issued by the presidents of Brazil and Chile. Their statement, supported immediately by Argentina, called for a special conference of LAFTA foreign ministers to establish a high-level permanent consultative body for all integration matters. The initiative of Brazil and Chile coincided with the publication of a study by Raúl Prebisch just before his retirement from the post of ECLA Executive Secretary. To avoid LAFTA stagnation this study, *Towards a Dynamic Development Policy for Latin America*, suggested a number of joint regional measures, including a commitment of all parties concerned to bring down, within the period covered by the 1960 Treaty, the tariff average on all products to 15 per cent and to eliminate all quantitative trade restrictions; to negotiate simultaneously a number of industrial complementarity agreements; to redefine the principle of reciprocity; and to establish a regional investment fund.

Similar and even more far-reaching proposals subsequently originated in a Special Committee set up in 1964 by the LAFTA Conference to analyze the growing deadlock in the implementation of the Montevideo Treaty, and in a document submitted in the spring of 1965 to all Latin American heads of state by Raúl Prebisch, Secretary-General of UNCTAD; Felipe Herrera, President of the Inter-American Development Bank; José Antonio Mayobre, Executive Secretary of ECLA; and Carlos Sanz de Santamaría, Chairman of the Inter-American Committee of the Alliance for Progress. The four wise men — as they are called in Latin America — recommended the establishment of a regional common market by 1975 by means of annual across-the-board tariff cuts involving a series of closely related commitments by all participating countries to be fulfilled within a period of ten years, the definition of quantitative targets for the permissible maximum level of intrazonal customs duties to be attained in the subsequent stages of trade liberalization, the gradual elimination of quantitative and other nontariff restrictions, the coordination of commercial policies vis-à-vis the rest of the world, and the establishment of definite preferences in the common external tariff. According to this proposal the gradual establishment of a common external tariff would start with the bringing into line of customs duties for raw materials and intermediate products and with the establishment of sectoral common external tariffs with respect to commodities covered by future zonal complementarity or industrial integration agreements. At first these agreements were to involve a limited number of industries, whose economies of scale, external economies, advantages of suitable location, and high operational efficiency were of paramount importance from the viewpoint of the Latin American industrialization process — for example, iron and steel, some nonferrous metals, certain groups of heavy chemicals and petrochemicals, and the manufacture of motor vehicles, ships, and heavy industrial equipment.

The proposed common market would not only absorb the Central American Common Market (CACM) but would also include the small Caribbean countries presently left out of the two economic cooperation schemes in Latin America. This new expanded arrangement would require agreement on a regional investment policy (including the formulation of a statute providing a clear and uniform definition of the terms offered by Latin American countries and their common market to foreign capital); the setting up of a payments union with temporary credit facilities; and the supplementing of the Inter-American Development Bank's fund for medium-term financing of intrazonal trade in capital goods by the establishment of regional machinery for trade insurance and reinsurance.

The institutional framework of the proposed common market would include a council of ministers to act as the regional economic community's highest political authority. The common market would be administered by an executive board composed of a president and four to six members chosen by the ministerial council. Serving as an advisory group would be a Latin American parliament made up of delegates of Latin American national legislatures. Finally, the Inter-American Development Bank would become the "bank of integration" and would be charged with the preparation of surveys and regional investment projects.

The foreign ministers of the LAFTA countries met in Montevideo at the end of 1965 and again at the end of 1966. The few positive contributions resulting from the first meeting were a proposal to set up a permanent LAFTA Council of Ministers of Foreign Relations; a recommendation that the Inter-American Development Bank create a fund for financing feasibility studies for investment projects of regional interest; and a recommendation that LAFTA's Standing Executive Committee prepare a regional shipping convention draft and an agreement on the transit of nationals of LAFTA countries throughout the region. The results of the second ministerial meeting were even less tangible. In addition to several insignificant resolutions, the foreign ministers signed two protocols on the solution of controversies arising from the implementation of the 1960 Treaty and on the free movement of nationals of LAFTA countries within the area. A third protocol that was to create the permanent council of LAFTA foreign ministers was left pending because of Chile's unwillingness to sign it. The foreign minister of Chile took the position that there was no need for such a council as long as the LAFTA foreign ministers were unable to agree on any specific measure aimed at accelerating the regional cooperation program. The content of the resolutions adopted at the two ministerial meetings unfortunately demonstrates the absence of any substantial agreement on proposals submitted to the Latin American heads of state in early 1965 by Prebisch, Herrera, Mayobre, and Sanz de Santamaría. Consequently, the conviction that LAFTA is facing a deep crisis and is running the danger of becoming an inconsequential preferential trade zone started rapidly spreading in Latin America in late 1966.

In April 1967, in response to a United States initiative dating back to the spring of the previous year, a meeting of the presidents of American states was held in Punta del Este. Latin American economic integration was at the head of the agenda of that meeting. The Action Program signed at the Punta del Este conference by all participants except the President of Ecuador calls for the progressive establishment, beginning in 1970, of the Latin American common market, "which should be substantially in operation within a period of no more than 15 years." This common market is to be based on the improvement of the two existing integration schemes: LAFTA and the Central American Common Market. According to the Action Program, "the two systems will initiate simultaneously a process of convergence by stages of cooperation, closer ties and integration, taking into account the interests of Latin American countries not yet associated with these systems, in order to provide their access to one of them." For the purpose of coordinating various measures that may eventually lead to a Latin American common market, a committee composed of representatives of the executive organs of LAFTA and the CACM will be established. The committee is to encourage meetings at the ministerial level and to initiate, in due course, the negotiation of a general treaty or of protocols required to create the Latin American common market.

At the Punta del Este conference the chiefs of state of the member countries of LAFTA agreed to instruct their respective ministers of foreign affairs to adopt at the forthcoming meeting of the Council of Ministers of Foreign Relations of LAFTA the measures necessary to implement the following decisions: (a) the acceleration of the process of converting LAFTA into a common market through a programed elimination of duties and tariff restrictions, tariff harmonization in order to establish progressively a common external tariff, and the progressive coordination of economic policies; and (b) the conclusion of temporary subregional agreements, with provisions for reducing tariffs within the subregions and harmonizing the treatment of third nations more rapidly than under the general agreement on a Latin American common market.

It was agreed that the participation of the least developed LAFTA members in the formation of a regional common market would be based on the provisions of the Montevideo Treaty and its complementary resolutions, and that action would be taken "to facilitate free access of products of the LAFTA member countries of relatively less economic development to the market of the other LAFTA countries and to promote the installation and financing in the former countries of industries intended for the enlarged market." The "middle group" of states — Chile, Colombia, Peru, Uruguay, and Venezuela — was promised that its situation would be taken into account in temporary subregional agreements on accelerated trade liberalization.

The extreme vagueness of the commitments made at the Punta del Este conference makes it extremely difficult to evaluate the chances for their early implementation. The future both of LAFTA and of the proposed regional common market had not been decided as had been expected by the end of 1967 at the level of the Council of Ministers of LAFTA. Any attempts to postpone decisions of substance to later meetings of the Council will suggest strongly that no compromise between the divergent interests of the three groups of LAFTA members — the big three, the "middle group," and the most underdeveloped countries — can be arrived at at this stage.

Bibliographic References

Baerrensen, Donald W., Martin Carnoy, and Joseph Grunwald. *Latin American Trade Patterns.* Washington, D.C.: The Brookings Institution, 1965.

Balassa, Bela. *Economic Development and Integration.* Mexico City: Centro de Estudios Monetarios Latinoamericanos, 1965.

Dell, Sidney. *A Latin American Common Market?* New York: Oxford University Press, 1966.

Economic Commission for Latin America. *The Economic Development of Latin America and Its Principal Problems,* by Raúl Prebisch. New York: United Nations, 1950.

———. *The Latin American Common Market.* New York: United Nations, 1959.

———. *Multilateral Economic Co-operation in Latin America.* Vol. I: *Texts and Documents.* (United Nations Publication, Sales No. 62.II.G.3.) New York: United Nations, Department of Economic and Social Affairs, 1962.

———. *Towards a Dynamic Development Policy in Latin America.* New York: United Nations, 1963.

Haas, Ernst B. *"The Uniting of Europe* and the Uniting of Latin America," *Journal of Common Market Studies,* Vol. V, No. 4 (June 1967).

Haas, Ernst B., and Philippe C. Schmitter. *The Politics of Economics in Latin American Regionalism.* Denver, Colo.: University of Denver Press, 1965.

Herrera, Felipe. "The Inter-American Development Bank and the Latin American Integration Movement," *Journal of Common Market Studies* (Oxford), Vol. V, No. 2 (December 1966).

Inter-American Development Bank. *Multinational Investment Programs and Latin American Integration.* A report prepared by Development and Resources Corporation. New York, September 1966. Mimeographed.

Mikesell, Raymond F. "Towards Regional Trading Groups in Latin America." In Albert O. Hirschman, ed., *Latin American Issues: Essays and Comments.* New York: Twentieth Century Fund, 1961.

Navarrete, Jorge. "Latin American Economic Integration: A Survey of Recent Literature," *Journal of Common Market Studies,* Vol. IV, No. 2 (December 1965).

Perloff, Harvey S., and Rómulo Almeida. "Regional Economic Integration in the Development of Latin America," *Economía Latinoamericana* (Washington, D.C.), Vol. I, No. 2 (November 1963).

Prebisch, Raúl, Felipe Herrera, José Antonio Mayobre, and Carlos Sanz de Santamaría. "Proposals for the Creation of the Latin American Common Market," *Journal of Common Market Studies,* Vol. V, No. 1 (September 1966).

Urquidi, Víctor L. *Free Trade and Economic Integration in Latin America.* Berkeley, Calif.: University of California Press, 1962.

Wionczek, Miguel S., ed. *Latin American Economic Integration: Experiences and Prospects.* New York: Frederick A. Praeger, 1966.

———. "Latin American Integration and United States Economic Policies." In Robert W. Gregg, ed., *International Organization in the Western Hemisphere.* Syracuse, N.Y.: Syracuse University Press, 1967.

TREATY ESTABLISHING A FREE TRADE AREA AND INSTITUTING THE LATIN AMERICAN FREE TRADE ASSOCIATION*

The Governments represented at the Inter-Governmental Conference for the Establishment of a Free Trade Area among Latin American Countries,

Persuaded that the expansion of present national markets, through the gradual elimination of barriers to intra-regional trade, is a prerequisite if the Latin American countries are to accelerate their economic development process in such a way as to ensure a higher level of living for their peoples,

Aware that economic development should be attained through the maximum utilization of available production factors and the more effective co-ordination of the development programmes of the different production sectors in accordance with norms which take due account of the interests of each and all and which make proper compensation, by means of appropriate measures, for the special situation of countries which are at a relatively less advanced stage of economic development,

Convinced that the strengthening of national economies will contribute to the expansion of trade within Latin America and with the rest of the world,

Sure that, by the adoption of suitable formulae, conditions can be created that will be conducive to the gradual and smooth adaptation of existing productive activities to new patterns of reciprocal trade, and that further incentives will thereby be provided for the improvement and expansion of such trade,

* The Montevideo Treaty was originally concluded and signed by Argentina, Brazil, Chile, Mexico, Paraguay, Peru, and Uruguay in Montevideo, Uruguay, February 18, 1960. The signatory governments deposited their respective instruments of ratification on May 2, 1960. The instruments of accession by Colombia, Ecuador, Venezuela, and Bolivia were deposited on September 30, 1961, November 3, 1961, August 31, 1966, and February 14, 1967, respectively. The text of the Treaty is an unofficial translation from the Spanish prepared by the United Nations Economic Commission for Latin America (ECLA) and published in United Nations, Department of Economic and Social Affairs, *Multilateral Economic Co-operation in Latin America*, Vol. I: *Text and Documents* (Sales No. 62.II.G.3; New York, 1962). The unofficial translations of Protocols No. 1, 2, 3, 4, and 5 and of Resolutions I and II, adopted by the Montevideo conference as annexes to the Treaty, appeared in the same ECLA publication.

Certain that any action to achieve such ends must take into account the commitments arising out of the international instruments which govern their trade,

Determined to persevere in their efforts to establish, gradually and progressively, a Latin American common market and, hence, to continue collaborating with the Latin American Governments as a whole in the work already initiated for this purpose, and

Motivated by the desire to pool their efforts to achieve the progressive complementarity and integration of their national economies on the basis of an effective reciprocity of benefits, decide to establish a Free Trade Area and, to that end, to conclude a Treaty instituting the Latin American Free Trade Association; and have, for this purpose, appointed their plenipotentiaries who have agreed as follows:

CHAPTER I: NAME AND PURPOSE

ARTICLE 1

By this Treaty the Contracting Parties establish a Free Trade Area and institute the Latin American Free Trade Association (hereinafter referred to as "the Association"), with headquarters in the city of Montevideo (Eastern Republic of Uruguay).

The term "Area," when used in this Treaty, means the combined territories of the Contracting Parties.

CHAPTER II: PROGRAMME FOR TRADE LIBERALIZATION

ARTICLE 2

The Free Trade Area, established under the terms of the present Treaty, shall be brought into full operation within not more than twelve (12) years from the date of the Treaty's entry into force.

ARTICLE 3

During the period indicated in article 2, the Contracting Parties shall gradually eliminate, in respect of substantially all their reciprocal trade, such duties, charges and restrictions as may be applied to imports of goods originating in the territory of any Contracting Party.

For the purposes of the present Treaty the term "duties and charges" means customs duties and any other charges of equivalent effect — whether fiscal, monetary or exchange — that are levied on imports.

The provisions of the present article do not apply to fees and similar charges in respect of services rendered.

ARTICLE 4

The purpose set forth in article 3 shall be achieved through negotiations to be held from time to time among the Contracting Parties with a view to drawing up:

a. National Schedules specifying the annual reductions in duties, charges and other restrictions which each Contracting Party grants to the other Contracting Parties in accordance with the provisions of article 5; and

b. a Common Schedule listing the products on which the Contracting Parties collectively agree to eliminate duties, charges and other restrictions completely, so far as intra-Area trade is concerned, within the period mentioned in article 2, by complying with the minimum percentages set out in article 7 and through the gradual reduction provided for in article 5.

ARTICLE 5

With a view to the preparation of the National Schedules referred to in article 4, sub-paragraph (*a*), each Contracting Party shall annually grant to the other Contracting Parties reductions in duties and charges equivalent to not less than eight (8) per cent of the weighted average applicable to third countries, until they are eliminated in respect of substantially all of its imports from the Area, in accordance with the definitions, methods of calculation, rules and procedures laid down in the Protocol.

For this purpose, duties and charges for third parties shall be deemed to be those in force on 31 December prior to each negotiation.

When the import régime of a Contracting Party contains restrictions of such a kind that the requisite equivalence with the reductions in duties and charges granted by another Contracting Party or other Contracting Parties is unobtainable, the counterpart of these reductions shall be complemented by means of the elimination or relaxation of those restrictions.

ARTICLE 6

The National Schedules shall enter into force on 1 January of each year, except that those deriving from the initial negotiations shall enter into force on the date fixed by the Contracting Parties.

ARTICLE 7

The Common Schedule shall consist of products which, in terms of the aggregate value of the trade among the Contracting Parties, shall constitute not less than the following percentages, calculated in accordance with the provisions of the Protocol:

Twenty-five (25) per cent during the first three-year period;
Fifty (50) per cent during the second three-year period;

Seventy-five (75) per cent during the third three-year period;
Substantially all of such trade during the fourth three-year period.

ARTICLE 8

The inclusion of products in the Common Schedule shall be final and the concessions granted in respect thereof irrevocable.

Concessions granted in respect of products which appear only in the National Schedules may be withdrawn by negotiation among the Contracting Parties and on a basis of adequate compensation.

ARTICLE 9

The percentages referred to in articles 5 and 7 shall be calculated on the basis of the average annual value of trade during the three years preceding the year in which each negotiation is effected.

ARTICLE 10

The purpose of the negotiations — based on reciprocity of concessions — referred to in article 4 shall be to expand and diversify trade and to promote the progressive complementarity of the economies of the countries in the Area.

In these negotiations the situation of those Contracting Parties whose levels of duties, charges and restrictions differ substantially from those of the other Contracting Parties shall be considered with due fairness.

ARTICLE 11

If, as a result of the concessions granted, significant and persistent disadvantages are created in respect of trade between one Contracting Party and the others as a whole in the products included in the liberalization programme, the Contracting Parties shall, at the request of the Contracting Party affected, consider steps to remedy these disadvantages with a view to the adoption of suitable, non-restrictive measures designed to promote trade at the highest possible levels.

ARTICLE 12

If, as a result of circumstances other than those referred to in article 11, significant and persistent disadvantages are created in respect of trade in the products included in the liberalization programme, the Contracting Parties shall, at the request of the Contracting Party concerned, make every effort within their power to remedy these disadvantages.

ARTICLE 13

The reciprocity mentioned in article 10 refers to the expected growth in the flow of trade between each Contracting Party and the others as a whole, in the products included in the liberalization programme and those which may subsequently be added.

CHAPTER III: EXPANSION OF TRADE AND ECONOMIC COMPLEMENTARITY

ARTICLE 14

In order to ensure the continued expansion and diversification of reciprocal trade, the Contracting Parties shall take steps:

a. To grant one another, while observing the principle of reciprocity, concessions which will ensure that, in the first negotiation, treatment not less favourable than that which existed before the date of entry into force of the present Treaty is accorded to imports from within the Area;

b. To include in the National Schedules the largest possible number of products in which trade is carried on among the Contracting Parties; and

c. To add to these Schedules an increasing number of products which are not yet included in reciprocal trade.

ARTICLE 15

In order to ensure fair competitive conditions among the Contracting Parties and to facilitate the increasing integration and complementarity of their economies, particularly with regard to industrial production, the Contracting Parties shall make every effort — in keeping with the liberalization objectives of the present Treaty — to reconcile their import and export régimes, as well as the treatment they accord to capital, goods and services from outside the Area.

ARTICLE 16

With a view to expediting the process of integration and complementarity referred to in article 15, the Contracting Parties:

a. Shall endeavour to promote progressively closer co-ordination of the corresponding industrialization policies, and shall sponsor for this purpose agreements among representatives of the economic sectors concerned; and

b. May negotiate mutual agreements on complementarity by industrial sectors.

ARTICLE 17

The complementarity agreements referred to in article 16, sub-paragraph (b), shall set forth the liberalization programme to be applied to products of the sector concerned and may contain, *inter alia,* clauses designed to reconcile the treatment accorded to raw materials and other components used in the manufacture of these products.

Any Contracting Party concerned with the complementarity programmes shall be free to participate in the negotiation of these agreements.

The results of these negotiations shall, in every case, be embodied in protocols which shall enter into force after the Contracting Parties have decided that they are consistent with the general principles and purposes of the present Treaty.

CHAPTER IV: MOST-FAVOURED-NATION TREATMENT

ARTICLE 18

Any advantage, benefit, franchise, immunity or privilege applied by a Contracting Party in respect of a product originating in or intended for consignment to any other country shall be immediately and unconditionally extended to the similar product originating in or intended for consignment to the territory of the other Contracting Parties.

ARTICLE 19

The most-favoured-nation treatment referred to in article 18 shall not be applicable to the advantages, benefits, franchises, immunities and privileges already granted or which may be granted by virtue of agreements among Contracting Parties or between Contracting Parties and third countries with a view to facilitating border trade.

ARTICLE 20

Capital originating in the Area shall enjoy, in the territory of each Contracting Party, treatment not less favourable than that granted to capital originating in any other country.

CHAPTER V: TREATMENT IN RESPECT OF INTERNAL
TAXATION

ARTICLE 21

With respect to taxes, rates and other internal duties and charges, products originating in the territory of a Contracting Party shall enjoy, in the territory of another Contracting Party, treatment no less favourable than that accorded to similar national products.

ARTICLE 22

Each Contracting Party shall endeavour to ensure that the charges or other domestic measures applied to products included in the liberalization programme which are not produced, or are produced only in small quantities, in its territory, do not nullify or reduce any concession or advantage obtained by any Contracting Party during the negotiations.

If a Contracting Party considers itself injured by virtue of the measures mentioned in the previous paragraph, it may appeal to the competent organs of the Association with a view to having the matter examined and appropriate recommendations made.

CHAPTER VI: SAFEGUARD CLAUSES

ARTICLE 23

The Contracting Parties may, as a provisional measure and providing that the customary level of consumption in the importer country is not thereby lowered, authorize a Contracting Party to impose non-discriminatory restrictions upon imports of products included in the liberalization programme which originate in the Area, if these products are imported in such quantities or under such conditions that they have, or are liable to have, serious repercussions on specific productive activities of vital importance to the national economy.

ARTICLE 24

The Contracting Parties may likewise authorize a Contracting Party which has adopted measures to correct its unfavourable over-all balance of payments to extend these measures, provisionally and without discrimination, to intra-Area trade in the products included in the liberalization programme.

The Contracting Parties shall endeavour to ensure that the imposition of restrictions deriving from the balance-of-payments situation does not affect trade, within the Area, in the products included in the liberalization programme.

ARTICLE 25

If the situations referred to in articles 23 and 24 call for immediate action, the Contracting Party concerned may, as an emergency arrangement to be referred to the Contracting Parties, apply the measures provided for in the said articles. The measures adopted must immediately be communicated to the Committee mentioned in article 33, which, if it deems necessary, shall convene a special session of the Conference.

ARTICLE 26

Should the measures envisaged in this chapter be prolonged for more than one year, the Committee shall propose to the Conference, referred to in article 33, either *ex officio* or at the request of any of the Contracting Parties, the immediate initiation of negotiations with a view to eliminating the restrictions adopted.

The present article does not affect the provisions of article 8.

CHAPTER VII: SPECIAL PROVISIONS CONCERNING AGRICULTURE

ARTICLE 27

The Contracting Parties shall seek to co-ordinate their agricultural development and agricultural commodity trade policies, with a view to securing the most efficient utilization of their natural resources, raising the standard of living of the rural population, and guaranteeing normal supplies to consumers, without disorganizing the regular productive activities of each Contracting Party.

ARTICLE 28

Providing that no lowering of its customary consumption or increase in anti-economic production is involved, a Contracting Party may apply, within the period mentioned in article 2, and in respect of trade in agricultural commodities of substantial importance to its economy that are included in the liberalization programme, appropriate nondiscriminatory measures designed to:

a. Limit imports to the amount required to meet the deficit in internal production; and

b. Equalize the prices of the imported and domestic product.

The Contracting Party which decides to apply these measures shall inform the other Contracting Parties before it puts them into effect.

ARTICLE 29

During the period prescribed in article 2 an attempt shall be made to expand intra-Area trade in agricultural commodities by such means as agreements among the Contracting Parties designed to cover deficits in domestic production.

For this purpose, the Contracting Parties shall give priority, under normal competitive conditions, to products originating in the territories of the other Contracting Parties, due consideration being given to the traditional flows of intra-Area trade.

Should such agreements be concluded among two or more Contracting Parties, the other Contracting Parties shall be notified before the agreements enter into force.

ARTICLE 30

The measures provided for in this chapter shall not be applied for the purpose of incorporating, in the production of agricultural commodities, resources which imply a reduction in the average level of productivity existing on the date on which the present Treaty enters into force.

ARTICLE 31

If a Contracting Party considers itself injured by a reduction of its exports attributable to the lowering of the usual consumption level of the importer country as a result of the measures referred to in article 28 and/or an anti-economic increase in the production referred to in the previous article, it may appeal to the competent organs of the Association to study the situation and, if necessary, to make recommendations for the adoption of appropriate measures to be applied in accordance with article 12.

CHAPTER VIII: MEASURES IN FAVOUR OF COUNTRIES AT A RELATIVELY LESS ADVANCED STAGE OF ECONOMIC DEVELOPMENT

ARTICLE 32

The Contracting Parties, recognizing that fulfilment of the purpose of the present Treaty will be facilitated by the economic growth of the countries in the Area that are at a relatively less advanced stage of economic development, shall take steps to create conditions conducive to such growth.

To this end, the Contracting Parties may:

a. Authorize a Contracting Party to grant to another Contracting Party which is at a relatively less advanced stage of economic development within the Area, as long as necessary and as a temporary measure, for the purposes set out in the present article, advantages not extended to the other Contracting Parties, in order to encourage the introduction or expansion of specific productive activities;

b. Authorize a Contracting Party at a relatively less advanced stage of economic development within the Area to implement the programme for the reduction of duties, charges and other restrictions under more favourable conditions, specially agreed upon;

c. Authorize a Contracting Party at a relatively less advanced stage of economic development within the Area to adopt appropriate measures to correct an unfavourable balance of payments, if the case arises;

d. Authorize a Contracting Party at a relatively less advanced stage of economic development within the Area to apply, if necessary and as a temporary measure, and providing that this does not entail a decrease in its customary consumption, appropriate non-discriminatory measures designed to protect the domestic output of products included in the liberalization programme which are of vital importance to its economic development;

e. Make collective arrangements in favour of a Contracting Party at a relatively less advanced stage of economic development within the Area with respect to the support and promotion, both inside and outside the Area, of financial or technical measures designed to bring about the expansion of existing productive activities or to encourage new activities, particularly those intended for the industrialization of its raw materials; and

f. Promote or support, as the case may be, special technical assistance programmes for one or more Contracting Parties, intended to raise, in countries at a relatively less advanced stage of economic development within the Area, productivity levels in specific production sectors.

CHAPTER IX: ORGANS OF THE ASSOCIATION

ARTICLE 33

The organs of the Association are the Conference of the Contracting Parties (referred to in this Treaty as "the Conference") and the Standing Executive Committee (referred to in this Treaty as "the Committee").

ARTICLE 34

The Conference is the supreme organ of the Association. It shall adopt all decisions in matters requiring joint action on the part of the Contracting Parties, and it shall be empowered, *inter alia*:

   a. To take the necessary steps to carry out the present Treaty and to study the results of its implementation;

   b. To promote the negotiations provided for in article 4 and to assess the results thereof;

   c. To approve the Committee's annual budget and to fix the contributions of each Contracting Party;

   d. To lay down its own rules of procedure and to approve the Committee's rules of procedure;

   e. To elect a Chairman and two Vice-Chairmen for each session;

   f. To appoint the Executive Secretary of the Committee; and

   g. To deal with other business of common interest.

ARTICLE 35

The Conference shall be composed of duly accredited representatives of the Contracting Parties. Each delegation shall have one vote.

ARTICLE 36

The Conference shall hold: (*a*) a regular session once a year; and (*b*) special sessions when convened by the Committee.

At each session the Conference shall decide the place and date of the following regular session.

ARTICLE 37

The Conference may not take decisions unless at least two-thirds ($\frac{2}{3}$) of the Contracting Parties are present.

ARTICLE 38

During the first two years in which the present Treaty is in force, decisions of the Conference shall be adopted when affirmative votes are cast by at least two-thirds (⅔) of the Contracting Parties and providing that no negative vote is cast.

The Contracting Parties shall likewise determine the voting system to be adopted after this two-year period.

The affirmative vote of two-thirds (⅔) of the Contracting Parties shall be required:

a. To approve the Committee's annual budget;

b. To elect the Chairman and Vice-Chairmen of the Conference, as well as the Executive Secretary; and

c. To fix the time and place of the sessions of the Conference.

ARTICLE 39

The Committee is the permanent organ of the Association responsible for supervising the implementation of the provisions of the present Treaty. Its duties and responsibilities shall be, *inter alia*:

a. To convene the Conference;

b. To submit for the approval of the Conference an annual work programme and the Committee's annual budget estimates;

c. To represent the Association in dealings with third countries and international organs and entities for the purpose of considering matters of common interest. It shall also represent the Association in contracts and other instruments of public and private law;

d. To undertake studies, to suggest measures and to submit to the Conference such recommendations as it deems appropriate for the effective implementation of the Treaty;

e. To submit to the Conference at its regular sessions an annual report on its activities and on the results of the implementation of the present Treaty;

f. To request the technical advice and the co-operation of individuals and of national and international organizations;

g. To take such decisions as may be delegated to it by the Conference; and

h. To undertake the work assigned to it by the Conference.

ARTICLE 40

The Committee shall consist of a Permanent Representative of each Contracting Party, who shall have a single vote.

Each Representative shall have an Alternate.

ARTICLE 41

The Committee shall have a Secretariat headed by an Executive Secretary and comprising technical and administrative personnel.

The Executive Secretary, elected by the Conference for a three-year term and re-eligible for similar periods, shall attend the plenary meetings of the Committee without the right to vote.

The Executive Secretary shall be the General Secretary of the Conference. His duties shall be, *inter alia*:

    a. To organize the work of the Conference and of the Committee;

    b. To prepare the Committee's annual budget estimates; and

    c. To recruit and engage the technical and administrative staff in accordance with the Committee's rules of procedure.

ARTICLE 42

In the performance of their duties, the Executive Secretary and the Secretariat staff shall not seek or receive instructions from any Government or from any other national or international entity. They shall refrain from any action which might reflect on their position as international civil servants.

The Contracting Parties undertake to respect the international character of the responsibilities of the Executive Secretary and of the Secretariat staff and shall refrain from influencing them in any way in the discharge of their responsibilities.

ARTICLE 43

In order to facilitate the study of specific problems, the Committee may set up Advisory Commissions composed of representatives of the various sectors of economic activity of each of the Contracting Parties.

ARTICLE 44

The Committee shall request, for the organs of the Association, the technical advice of the secretariat of the United Nations Economic Commission for Latin America (ECLA) and of the Inter-American Economic and Social Council (IA-ECOSOC) of the Organization of American States.

ARTICLE 45

The Committee shall be constituted sixty days from the entry into force of the present Treaty and shall have its headquarters in the city of Montevideo.

CHAPTER X: JURIDICAL PERSONALITY — IMMUNITIES AND PRIVILEGES

ARTICLE 46

The Latin American Free Trade Association shall possess complete juridical personality and shall, in particular, have the power:

    a. To contract;

b. To acquire and dispose of the movable and immovable property it needs for the achievement of its objectives;

c. To institute legal proceedings; and

d. To hold funds in any currency and to transfer them as necessary.

ARTICLE 47

The representatives of the Contracting Parties and the international staff and advisers of the Association shall enjoy in the Area such diplomatic and other immunities and privileges as are necessary for the exercise of their functions.

The Contracting Parties undertake to conclude, as soon as possible, an Agreement regulating the provisions of the previous paragraph in which the aforesaid privileges and immunities shall be defined.

The Association shall conclude with the Government of the Eastern Republic of Uruguay an Agreement for the purpose of specifying the privileges and immunities which the Association, its organs and its international staff and advisers shall enjoy.

CHAPTER XI: MISCELLANEOUS PROVISIONS

ARTICLE 48

No change introduced by a Contracting Party in its régime of import duties and charges shall imply a level of duties and charges less favourable than that in force before the change for any commodity in respect of which concessions are granted to the other Contracting Parties.

The requirement set out in the previous paragraph shall not apply to the conversion to present worth of the official base value (*aforo*) in respect of customs duties and charges, providing that such conversion corresponds exclusively to the real value of the goods. In such cases, the value shall not include the customs duties and charges levied on the goods.

ARTICLE 49

In order to facilitate the implementation of the provisions of the present Treaty, the Contracting Parties shall, as soon as possible:

a. Determine the criteria to be adopted for the purpose of establishing the origin of goods and for classifying them as raw materials, semi-manufactured goods or finished products;

b. Simplify and standardize procedures and formalities relating to reciprocal trade;

c. Prepare a tariff nomenclature to serve as a common basis for the presentation of statistics and for carrying out the negotiations provided for in the present Treaty;

d. Determine what shall be deemed to constitute border trade within the meaning of article 19;

e. Determine the criteria for the purpose of defining "dumping" and other unfair trade practices and the procedures relating thereto.

ARTICLE 50

The products imported from the Area by a Contracting Party may not be re-exported save by agreement between the Contracting Parties concerned.

A product shall not be deemed to be a re-export if it has been subjected in the importer country to industrial processing or manufacture, the degree of which shall be determined by the Committee.

ARTICLE 51

Products imported or exported by a Contracting Party shall enjoy freedom of transit within the Area and shall only be subject to the payment of the normal rates for services rendered.

ARTICLE 52

No Contracting Party shall promote its exports by means of subsidies or other measures likely to disrupt normal competitive conditions in the Area.

An export shall not be deemed to have been subsidized if it is exempted from duties and charges levied on the product or its components when destined for internal consumption, or if it is subject to drawback.

ARTICLE 53

No provision of the present Treaty shall be so construed as to constitute an impediment to the adoption and execution of measures relating to:

a. The protection of public morality;

b. The application of security laws and regulations;

c. The control of imports or exports of arms, ammunition and other war equipment and, in exceptional circumstances, of all other military items, in so far as this is compatible with the terms of article 51 and of the treaties on the unrestricted freedom of transit in force among the Contracting Parties;

d. The protection of human, animal and plant life and health;

e. Imports and exports of gold and silver bullion;

f. The protection of the nation's heritage of artistic, historical and archaeological value; and

g. The export, use and consumption of nuclear materials, radioactive products or any other material that may be used in the development or exploitation of nuclear energy.

ARTICLE 54

The Contracting Parties shall make every effort to direct their policies with a view to creating conditions favourable to the establishment of a Latin

American common market. To that end, the Committee shall undertake studies and consider projects and plans designed to achieve this purpose, and shall endeavour to co-ordinate its work with that of other international organizations.

CHAPTER XII: FINAL PROVISIONS

ARTICLE 55

The present Treaty may not be signed with reservations nor shall reservations be admitted at the time of ratification or accession.

ARTICLE 56

The present Treaty shall be ratified by the signatory States at the earliest opportunity.

The instruments of ratification shall be deposited with the Government of the Eastern Republic of Uruguay, which shall communicate the date of deposit to the Governments of the signatory and successively acceding States.

ARTICLE 57

The present Treaty shall enter into force for the first three ratifying States thirty days after the third instrument of ratification has been deposited; and, for the other signatories, thirty days after the respective instrument of ratification has been deposited, and in the order in which the ratifications are deposited.

The Government of the Eastern Republic of Uruguay shall communicate the date of the entry into force of the present Treaty to the Government of each of the signatory States.

ARTICLE 58

Following its entry into force, the present Treaty shall remain open to accession by the other Latin American States, which for this purpose shall deposit the relevant instrument of accession with the Government of the Eastern Republic of Uruguay. The Treaty shall enter into force for the acceding State thirty days after the deposit of the corresponding instrument.

Acceding States shall enter into the negotiations referred to in article 4 at the session of the Conference immediately following the date of deposit of the instrument of accession.

ARTICLE 59

Each Contracting Party shall begin to benefit from the concessions already granted to one another by the other Contracting Parties as from the date of entry into force of the reductions in duties and charges and other restrictions negotiated by them on a basis of reciprocity, and after the minimum obligations referred to in article 5, accumulated during the period which has elapsed since the entry into force of the present Treaty, have been carried out.

ARTICLE 60

The Contracting Parties may present amendments to the present Treaty, which shall be set out in protocols that shall enter into force upon their ratification by all the Contracting Parties and after the corresponding instruments have been deposited.

ARTICLE 61

On the expiry of the twelve-year term starting on the date of entry into force of the present Treaty, the Contracting Parties shall proceed to study the results of the Treaty's implementation and shall initiate the necessary collective negotiations with a view to fulfilling more effectively the purposes of the Treaty and, if desirable, to adapting it to a new stage of economic integration.

ARTICLE 62

The provisions of the present Treaty shall not affect the rights and obligations deriving from agreements signed by any of the Contracting Parties prior to the entry into force of the present Treaty.

However, each Contracting Party shall take the necessary steps to reconcile the provisions of existing agreements with the purposes of the present Treaty.

ARTICLE 63

The present Treaty shall be of unlimited duration.

ARTICLE 64

A Contracting Party wishing to withdraw from the present Treaty shall inform the other Contracting Parties of its intention at a regular session of the Conference, and shall formally submit the instrument of denunciation at the following regular session.

When the formalities of denunciation have been completed, those rights and obligations of the denouncing Government which derive from its status as a Contracting Party shall cease automatically, with the exception of those relating to reductions in duties and charges and other restrictions, received or granted under the liberalization programme, which shall remain in force for a period of five years from the date on which the denunciation becomes formally effective.

The period specified in the preceding paragraph may be shortened if there is sufficient justification, with the consent of the Conference and at the request of the Contracting Party concerned.

ARTICLE 65

The present Treaty shall be called the Montevideo Treaty.

In witness whereof the undersigned Plenipotentiaries, having deposited their full powers, found in good and due form, have signed the present Treaty on behalf of their respective Governments.

Done in the city of Montevideo, on the eighteenth day of the month of February in the year one thousand nine hundred and sixty, in one original in the Spanish and one in the Portuguese language, both texts being equally authentic. The Government of the Eastern Republic of Uruguay shall be the depositary of the present Treaty and shall transmit duly certified copies thereof to the Governments of the other signatory and acceding States.

PROTOCOL NO. 1: ON NORMS AND PROCEDURES FOR NEGOTIATIONS

On the occasion of the signing of the Treaty establishing a free trade area and instituting the Latin American Free Trade Association (Montevideo Treaty), the signatories, thereunto duly authorized by their Governments, hereby agree upon the following Protocol:

TITLE I

CALCULATION OF WEIGHTED AVERAGES

1. For the purposes of article 5 of the Montevideo Treaty, it shall be understood that, as a result of the negotiations for the establishment of the National Schedules, the difference between the weighted average of duties and charges in force for third countries and that which shall be applicable to imports from within the area shall be not less than the product of eight per cent (8%) of the weighted average of duties and charges in force for third countries multiplied by the number of years that have elapsed since the Treaty became effective.

2. The reduction mechanism shall therefore be based on two weighted averages: one corresponding to the average of the duties and charges in force for third countries; and the other to the average of the duties and charges which shall be applicable to imports from within the Area.

3. In order to calculate each of these weighted averages, the total amount that would be represented by the duties and charges on aggregate imports of the goods under consideration shall be divided by the total value of these imports.

4. This calculation will give a percentage (or *ad valorem* figure) for each weighted average. It is the difference between the two averages that shall be

not less than the product of the factor 0.08 (or eight per cent) multiplied by the number of years elapsed.

5. The foregoing formula is expressed as follows:

$$t \leqq T\,(1 - 0.08n)\ \text{in which}$$

t = weighted average of the duties and charges that shall be applicable to imports from within the area;

T = weighted average of duties and charges in force for third countries;

n = number of years since the Treaty entered into force.

6. In calculating the weighted averages for each of the Contracting Parties, the following shall be taken into account:

(a) Products originating in the territory of the other Contracting Parties and imported from the Area during the preceding three-year period and further products included in the National Schedule concerned as a result of negotiations;

(b) The total value of imports, irrespective of origin, of each of the products referred to in sub-paragraph (a), during the three-year period preceding each negotiation; and

(c) The duties and charges on imports from third countries in force as on 31 December prior to the negotiations, and the duties and charges applicable to imports from within the Area entering into force on 1 January following the negotiations.

7. The Contracting Parties shall be entitled to exclude products of little value from the group referred to in sub-paragraph (a), provided that their aggregate value does not exceed five per cent (5%) of the value of imports from within the Area.

TITLE II

EXCHANGE OF INFORMATION

8. The Contracting Parties shall provide one another, through the Standing Executive Committee, with information as complete as possible on:

(a) National statistics in respect of total imports and exports (value in dollars and volume, by countries both of origin and of destination), production and consumption;

(b) Customs legislation and regulations;

(c) Exchange, monetary, fiscal and administrative legislation, regulations and practices bearing on exports and imports;

(d) International trade treaties and agreements whose provisions relate to the Treaty;

(e) Systems of direct or indirect subsidies on production or exports, including minimum price systems; and

(f) State trading systems.

9. So far as possible, these data shall be permanently available to the Contracting Parties. They shall be specially brought up to date sufficiently in advance of the opening of the annual negotiations.

TITLE III

NEGOTIATION OF NATIONAL SCHEDULES

10. Before 30 June of each year, the Contracting Parties shall make available to one another, through the Standing Executive Committee, the list of products in respect of which they are applying for concessions and, before 15 August of each year (with the exception of the first year, when the corresponding final date shall be 1 October), the preliminary list of items in favour of which they are prepared to grant concessions.

11. On 1 September of each year (with the exception of the first year, when the corresponding date shall be 1 November), the Contracting Parties shall initiate the negotiation of the concessions to be accorded by each to the others as a whole. The concessions shall be assessed multilaterally, although this shall not preclude the conduct of negotiations by pairs or groups of countries, in accordance with the interest attaching to specific products.

12. Upon the conclusion of this phase of the negotiations, the Standing Executive Committee shall make the calculations referred to in title I of this Protocol and shall inform each Contracting Party, at the earliest possible opportunity, of the percentage whereby its individual concessions reduce the weighted average of the duties and charges in force for imports from within the Area, in relation to the weighted average of duties and charges applicable in the case of third countries.

13. When the concessions negotiated fall short of the corresponding minimum commitment, the negotiations among the Contracting Parties shall be continued, so that the list of reductions of duties and charges and other restrictions to enter into force as from the following 1 January may be simultaneously published by each of the Contracting Parties not later than 1 November of each year.

TITLE IV

NEGOTIATION OF THE COMMON SCHEDULE

14. During each three-year period and not later than on 31 May of the third, sixth, ninth and twelfth years from the time of the Treaty's entry into force, the Standing Executive Committee shall supply the Contracting Parties with statistical data on the value and volume of the products traded in the Area during the preceding three-year period, indicating the proportion of aggregate trade which each individually represented.

15. Before 30 June of the third, sixth and ninth years from the time of the Treaty's entry into force, the Contracting Parties shall exchange the lists of products whose inclusion in the Common Schedule they wish to negotiate.

16. The Contracting Parties shall conduct multilateral negotiations to establish, before 30 November in the third, sixth, ninth and twelfth years, a Common Schedule comprising goods whose value meets the minimum commitments referred to in article 7 of the Treaty.

TITLE V

SPECIAL AND TEMPORARY PROVISIONS

17. In the negotiations to which this Protocol refers, consideration shall be given to those cases in which varying levels of duties and charges on certain products create conditions such that producers in the Area are not competing on equitable terms.

18. To this end, steps shall be taken to ensure prior equalization of tariffs or to secure by any other suitable procedure the highest possible degree of effective reciprocity.

In witness whereof the respective representatives have signed the Protocol.

Done at the City of Montevideo, on the eighteenth day of the month of February in the year one thousand nine hundred and sixty, in one original in the Spanish and one in the Portuguese language, both texts being equally authentic.

The Government of the Eastern Republic of Uruguay shall act as depositary of the present Protocol and shall send certified true copies thereof to the Governments of the other signatory and acceding countries.

PROTOCOL NO. 2: ON THE ESTABLISHMENT OF A PROVISIONAL COMMITTEE

On the occasion of the signing of the Treaty establishing a free trade area and instituting the Latin American Free Trade Association (Montevideo Treaty), the signatories, thereunto duly authorized by their Governments, taking into consideration the need to adopt and co-ordinate measures to facilitate the entry into force of the Treaty, hereby agree as follows:

1. A Provisional Committee shall be set up, composed of one representative of each signatory State. Each representative shall have an alternate.

At its first meeting the Provisional Committee shall elect from among its members one Chairman and two Vice-Chairmen.

2. The terms of reference of the Provisional Committee shall be as follows:

(*a*) To draw up its rules of procedure;

(*b*) To prepare, within sixty days from the date of its inauguration, its work programme, and to establish its budget of expenditure and the contributions to be made by each country;

(*c*) To adopt the measures and prepare the documents necessary for the presentation of the Treaty to the Contracting Parties of the General Agreement on Tariffs and Trade (GATT);

(*d*) To convene and prepare for the first Conference of Contracting Parties;

(*e*) To assemble and prepare the data and statistics required for the first series of negotiations connected with the implementation of the liberalization programme provided for in the Treaty;

(*f*) To carry out or promote studies and research, and to adopt whatsoever measures may be necessary in the common interest during its period of office; and

(g) To prepare a preliminary draft agreement on the privileges and immunities referred to in article 47 of the Treaty.

3. In technical matters, the Provisional Committee shall be assisted in an advisory capacity by the United Nations Economic Commission for Latin America (ECLA) and the Inter-American Economic and Social Council (IA-ECOSOC), of the Organization of American States, in accordance with the relevant Protocol.

4. The Provisional Committee shall appoint an Administrative Secretary and other requisite staff.

5. The Provisional Committee shall be inaugurated on 1 April 1960, and its quorum shall be constituted by not less than four members. Up to that date, the Officers of the Inter-Governmental Conference for the Establishment of a Free Trade Area among Latin American Countries shall continue to discharge their functions, for the sole purpose of establishing the Provisional Committee.

6. The Provisional Committee shall remain in office until the Standing Executive Committee, provided for in article 33 of the Treaty, has been set up.

7. The Provisional Committee shall have its headquarters in the City of Montevideo.

8. The Officers of the above-mentioned Conference are recommended to request the Government of the Eastern Republic of Uruguay to advance the necessary sums to cover the payment of staff salaries and the installation and operational expenses of the Provisional Committee during the first ninety days. These sums shall be subsequently reimbursed by the States signatories of the present Treaty.

9. The Provisional Committee shall approach the signatory Governments with a view to obtaining for the members of its constituent delegations, as well as for its international staff and advisers, such immunities and privileges as may be needful for the performance of their duties.

In witness whereof the respective representatives have signed the present Protocol.

Done at the City of Montevideo, on the eighteenth day of the month of February in the year one thousand nine hundred and sixty, in one original in the Spanish and one in the Portuguese language, both texts being equally authentic. The Government of the Eastern Republic of Uruguay shall act as the depositary of the present Protocol and shall send certified true copies thereof to the Governments of the other signatory and acceding countries.

PROTOCOL NO. 3: ON THE COLLABORATION OF THE UNITED NATIONS ECONOMIC COMMISSION FOR LATIN AMERICA (ECLA) AND OF THE INTER-AMERICAN ECONOMIC AND SOCIAL COUNCIL (IA-ECOSOC) OF THE ORGANIZATION OF AMERICAN STATES

On the occasion of the signing of the Treaty establishing a free trade area and instituting the Latin American Free Trade Association (Montevideo Treaty), the signatories, thereunto duly authorized by their Governments, hereby agree as follows:

1. With reference to the provisions of article 44 of the Treaty and in view of the fact that the secretaries of ECLA and of IA-ECOSOC have agreed to assist the organs of the Latin American Free Trade Association with advice on technical matters, a representative of each of the secretariats in question shall attend the meetings of the Standing Executive Committee of the above-mentioned Association when the business to be discussed is, in the Committee's opinion, of a technical nature.

2. The appointment of the representatives referred to shall be subject to the prior approval of the members of the said Committee.

In witness whereof the respective representatives have signed the present Protocol.

Done at the City of Montevideo, on the eighteenth day of the month of February in the year one thousand nine hundred and sixty, in one original in the Spanish and one in the Portuguese language, both texts being equally authentic. The Government of the Eastern Republic of Uruguay shall act as the depositary of the present Protocol and shall send certified true copies thereof to the Governments of the other signatory and acceding countries.

PROTOCOL NO. 4: ON COMMITMENTS TO PURCHASE OR SELL PETROLEUM AND PETROLEUM DERIVATIVES

On the occasion of the signing of the Treaty establishing a free trade area and instituting the Latin American Free Trade Association (Montevideo Treaty), the signatories, thereunto duly authorized by their Governments, hereby agree:

To declare that the provisions of the Montevideo Treaty, signed on 18 February 1960, are not applicable to commitments to purchase or sell petroleum and petroleum derivatives resulting from agreements concluded by the signatories of the present Protocol prior to the date of signature of the above-mentioned Treaty.

In witness whereof the respective representatives have signed the present Protocol.

Done at the City of Montevideo, on the eighteenth day of the month of February in the year one thousand nine hundred and sixty, in one original in the Spanish and one in the Portuguese language, both texts being equally authentic.

The Government of the Eastern Republic of Uruguay shall act as depositary of the present Protocol and shall send certified true copies thereof to the Governments of the other signatory and acceding countries.

PROTOCOL NO. 5: ON SPECIAL TREATMENT IN FAVOUR OF BOLIVIA AND PARAGUAY

On the occasion of the signing of the Treaty establishing a free trade area and instituting the Latin American Free Trade Association (Montevideo

Treaty), the signatories, thereunto duly authorized by their Governments, hereby agree:

To declare that Bolivia and Paraguay are at present in a position to invoke in their favour the provisions in the Treaty concerning special treatment for countries at a relatively less advanced stage of economic development within the Free Trade Area.

In witness whereof the respective representatives have signed the present Protocol.

Done at the City of Montevideo, on the eighteenth day of the month of February in the year one thousand nine hundred and sixty, in one original in the Spanish and one in the Portuguese language, both texts being equally authentic.

The Government of the Eastern Republic of Uruguay shall act as depositary of the present Protocol and shall send certified true copies thereof to the Governments of other signatory and acceding countries.

RESOLUTION I: MEETINGS OF GOVERNMENTAL REPRESENTATIVES OF CENTRAL BANKS

The Inter-Governmental Conference for the Establishment of a Free Trade Area among Latin American Countries,

In view of the report submitted to the Conference by the Meeting of Governmental Representatives of Central Banks, held at Montevideo in January 1960,

Considering the desirability of continuing the studies on payments and credits to facilitate the financing of intra-Area transactions and therefore the fulfilment of the purposes of the Treaty establishing a Free Trade Area and instituting the Latin American Free Trade Association,

Decides:

1. To take note of the above-mentioned report;

2. To request the Provisional Committee to convene informal meetings of governmental experts from the central banks of Argentina, Bolivia, Brazil, Chile, Mexico, Paraguay, Peru and Uruguay, which shall be organized by the secretariat of the United Nations Economic Commission for Latin America (ECLA);

3. To establish that the object of these meetings shall be the continuance of the studies on credits and payments to facilitate the financing of intra-Area transactions and therefore the fulfilment of the purposes of the aforesaid Treaty;

4. To request the United Nations Economic Commission for Latin America (ECLA), the Inter-American Economic and Central Council (IA-ECOSOC) of the Organization of American States and the International Monetary Fund for their advice and technical assistance;

5. To extend the invitation to experts from the central banks of such countries as may have acceded to the said Treaty.

RESOLUTION II: MORATORIUM GRANTED TO BOLIVIA
FOR SIGNATURE OF THE TREATY

The Inter-Governmental Conference for the Establishment of a Free Trade Area among Latin American Countries,

Considering the generous spirit of co-operation displayed by Bolivia in its participation in the negotiations for the conclusion of the Treaty establishing a Free Trade Area and instituting the Latin American Free Trade Association.

Mindful of the motives adduced by the delegation of Bolivia to explain why, for reasons of *force majeure*, it is unable to sign the above-mentioned Treaty on the present occasion.

Decides to grant the Government of Bolivia a moratorium of four (4) months during which it will be free to accede to the aforesaid Treaty as a signatory State.

PROTOCOL INSTITUTING THE COUNCIL OF MINISTERS OF FOREIGN RELATIONS OF THE LATIN AMERICAN FREE TRADE ASSOCIATION*

The Representatives of the Governments of Contracting Parties to the Treaty of Montevideo, assembled in the Council of Ministers of the Latin American Free Trade Association, in accordance with the provisions of Article 60 of the Treaty, agree to the following:

ARTICLE 1

Articles 33, 34, 35, 36, 37, 38, and 39 of the Treaty of Montevideo are hereby modified and will read as follows:

ARTICLE 33

The Council of Ministers of Foreign Relations of the Contracting Parties (herein termed "the Council"), the Conference of the Contracting Parties (herein termed "the Conference"), and the Standing Executive Committee (herein termed "the Committee") are bodies of the Association.

ARTICLE 34

The Council is the highest body of the Association and will adopt decisions pertaining to the conduct of its policy at the highest level. As such, it will be empowered:

a. To dictate general rules permitting the better fulfillment of the objectives of this Treaty, especially those directed towards the harmonious acceleration of the economic and social development and integration of the Contracting Parties;

* This protocol was signed by Argentina, Brazil, Colombia, Ecuador, Mexico, Paraguay, Peru, Uruguay, and Venezuela in Montevideo, Uruguay, December 12, 1966 and adhered to by Chile on April 12, 1967. The text reproduced here is an unofficial translation from *Acta Final de la Primera Reunión del Consejo de Ministros de la Asociación Latinoamericana de Libre Comercio* (Montevideo, December 7–12, 1966), published in *Comercio Exterior* (Mexico City), Supplement to Vol. XVII, No. 1 (January 1967). [Editor's note.]

b. To review the results of tasks accomplished within the Association, and establish fundamental guidelines to serve as a basis for the working programs of the other bodies of the Association;

c. To be cognizant of and resolve matters that it considers appropriate among those referred to it by the Conference or the Committee;

d. To establish basic rules regulating the Association's relations with third countries, regional associations, and international agencies or bodies;

e. To delegate to the Conference or Committee the authority to make decisions on specific subjects, directed towards the better fulfillment of the objectives of the Treaty;

f. To agree to amendments to the Treaty within the terms of Article 60;

g. To modify its own voting system and that of the Conference, in accordance with the provisions of Article 38; and

h. To establish its own bylaws.

The Council will be constituted by the Ministers of Foreign Affairs of the Contracting Parties. However, should any of the latter have assigned responsibility for Association matters to a Minister or Secretary of State other than the Minister of Foreign Affairs, it may be represented on the Council by the respective Minister or Secretary.

ARTICLE 35

The terms of reference of the Conference will be:

a. To promote the conduct of the negotiations envisaged in Article 4 and evaluate their results;

b. To fulfill the tasks entrusted to it by the Council;

c. To consider and resolve, within the limits of its competence, matters submitted to it by the Committee;

d. To adopt, within the limits of its competence, measures needed for the implementation of the Treaty and the respective protocols;

e. To approve the Committee's annual work program and the Association's budget of expenditures, and determine the amounts to be contributed by each Contracting Party;

f. To approve its own bylaws and those of the Committee;

g. To appoint the Executive Secretary of the Committee; and

h. To attend to any other matters of common interest not included in the policy conducted by the Association at the highest level.

The Conference will be constituted by duly accredited Delegations of the Contracting Parties. Each Delegation will be entitled to one vote.

ARTICLE 36

Both the Council and the Conference will meet in regular sessions once a year. At each Period of Sessions they will determine the site and date of the next annual period of regular sessions, without prejudice to the Committee's authority to decide upon a new site and date should supervening reasons make this necessary. Each of the two bodies will meet in special sessions when convened by the Committee.

ARTICLE 37

Neither the Council nor the Conference shall meet or make decisions without the attendance of at least two thirds (⅔) of the Contracting Parties.

ARTICLE 38

Until the Council establishes a different voting system, its decisions and those of the Conference will be adopted with affirmative votes by at least two thirds (⅔) of the Contracting Parties, provided that none of the votes are negative.

Abstention will not represent a negative vote. Absence during voting will be considered abstention.

However the Council may, with affirmative votes on the part of two thirds (⅔) of its members:

a. Elect a Chairman and two Vice-Chairmen; and

b. Determine the site and date of the next regular session.

With the affirmative votes of two thirds (⅔) of the Contracting Parties, the Conference may:

a. Approve the Association's annual budget of expenditures;

b. Elect a Chairman, two Vice-Chairmen, and an Executive Secretary; and

c. Determine the site and date of the next regular session.

ARTICLE 39

The Committee is the Association's permanent executive body, charged with ensuring the application of the provisions of this Treaty. Among others, its terms of reference and obligations will be:

a. To convene the Council and the Conference and provide an appropriate provisional agenda in each case;

b. To submit to the Conference for its approval an annual work plan and a draft annual budget of the Association's expenditures;

c. To represent the Association in contacts with third countries and international agencies or bodies, with a view to dealing with matters of common interest. It will also represent the Association in contracts and other acts under public and private law;

d. To perform any studies, suggest any measures, and propose to the Council and the Conference any recommendations it considers appropriate for the better fulfillment of the Treaty;

e. To submit to the regular sessions of the Council and the Conference an annual report on its activities, and on the results of the application of this Treaty;

f. To request technical advice when it considers it appropriate, as well as the collaboration of individuals and national and international agencies;

g. To make the decisions delegated to it by the Council or the Conference; and

h. To perform the tasks entrusted to it by the Council or the Conference, and those specifically incumbent upon it by virtue of the provisions of this Treaty and the protocols thereof.

ARTICLE 2

This Protocol may not be signed with reservations, nor will reservations be accepted at the time of its ratification. The instruments of ratification will be deposited with the Secretariat of the Standing Executive Committee of the Latin American Free Trade Association, who will inform the Governments of the States signing this Protocol of the date for depositing the instruments.

ARTICLE 3

This Protocol will become effective thirty days after all the instruments of ratification of the Contracting Parties have been deposited.

In witness whereof the respective duly accredited Plenipotentiaries affix their signatures to an original of this Protocol in the Spanish and Portuguese languages, both texts being equally valid, in the city of Montevideo on the twelfth day of December nineteen hundred and sixty-six.

SELECTED RESOLUTIONS OF LAFTA
CONTRACTING PARTIES*

RESOLUTION 17 (I): APPLICATION OF THE PROVISIONS OF CHAPTER VIII OF THE TREATY OF MONTEVIDEO

The Conference of Contracting Parties, at its first session,

In view of the provisions of Chapter VIII and Article 34 of the Treaty of Montevideo; and

Considering the need to establish uniform standards for a more effective application of the provisions of Chapter VIII of the Treaty

Resolves that

1. Entitlement to benefit from the provisions of Chapter VIII of the Treaty shall be limited to those member countries of the Latin American Free Trade Association whose situation as relatively less developed countries within the Area is recognized by the Contracting Parties.

2. A request for the application of one or other of the advantages envisaged in Article 32 shall contain:

(a) a specification of the advantage or advantages requested;

(b) an account of the factors that would permit a judgement to be made whether the benefits requested are necessary for the Party concerned, and adequate for the achievement of the desired objectives;

(c) an indication of the period for which authorization is requested — in

* Unofficial translations from the Spanish texts made public by the LAFTA Secretariat in Montevideo after each annual meeting of the Conference of LAFTA Contracting Parties. The Spanish texts, except for Resolutions 202 and 203, were published in Asociación Latinoamericana de Libre Comercio, Comité Ejecutivo Permanente, *Serie Instrumentos*, Tomo I: *Tratado de Montevideo y Resoluciones de las Conferencias I, I–E y II* (Montevideo, 1963), and Tomo II: *Resoluciones: Conferencias III, II–E, IV y V* (Montevideo, 1966). Resolutions 202 and 203 were published in Asociación Latinoamericana de Libre Comercio, "Acta Final de la Segunda Reunión del Consejo de Ministros de Relaciones Exteriores de la ALALC," *Sintesis Mensual* (Montevideo), No. 28 (October 1967). The translations of Resolutions 17 (I), 68 (III), 70 (III), 71 (III), 74 (III), 75 (III), 77 (III) and 99 (IV), made by Sidney Dell and published in his book, *A Latin American Common Market?* (New York: Oxford University Press, 1966), pp. 311–329, are reproduced here with the kind permission of the translator and the Oxford University Press. [Editor's note.]

the case of benefits under paragraph (*a*) of Article 32 — as well as of the products in respect of which advantages not extended to other Contracting Parties are sought, the extent of such advantages, and the nature of the productive activities the installation or expansion of which it is desired to stimulate;

(d) the manner and rate at which the relatively less developed Contracting Party concerned proposes to comply with the programme for reduction of duties, if the benefits requested are those of paragraph (*b*) of Article 32.

(e) a demonstration of the existence or prospect of balance of payments disequilibrium and a specific indication of the measure or measures for which authorization is requested, if the benefits are those of paragraph (*c*) of Article 32.

(f) in the case of the benefits envisaged in paragraph (*d*) of Article 32, an indication of the productive activities of basic importance which it is considered necessary to protect, immediately or in future, an enumeration of the measures for which authorization is sought and the period for which they would be applied. In addition, data should be supplied concerning the consumption, production, and imports of the products concerned.

3. The Contracting Parties may authorize a relatively less developed Contracting Party to be granted simultaneously all or some of the benefits envisaged under Article 32 of the Treaty. The fact that a Contracting Party may have previously been granted one or more of these benefits shall not prevent the authorization of a new benefit.

4. The Contracting Parties, in authorizing the granting to a relatively less developed Contracting Party of advantages not extended to other Contracting Parties, shall fix the period during which such authorization shall be effective.

5. During the period in which the authorization is effective, any Contracting Party which has granted the benefits indicated in paragraph (*a*) of Article 32 may include in its programme of liberalization the products to which such benefits relate, and may negotiate the whole or part of the benefits affecting each product with the remaining Contracting Parties, except in so far as it may have been agreed with the relatively less developed country concerned that such negotiations should not take place for a certain time.

In the latter event, the Contracting Party concerned, in requesting the authorization provided for in the paragraph under reference, shall indicate the benefits that are not subject to negotiation and the period during which this situation will be maintained.

6. The Contracting Parties may extend the period of authorization laid down under paragraph (*a*) of Article 32 with respect to all or some of the benefits provided if, at the end of the period, the Contracting Party receiving the benefits is still in the position of a relatively less developed country within the Area and if the objectives for which the benefits had been granted have still not been realized.

A request for extension shall be presented at the session of the Conference immediately preceding the expiration of the period initially provided.

7. If the authorization granted in conformity with paragraph (*a*) of Article

32 is not extended at the end of the period provided, the benefits shall be automatically extended to the remaining Contracting Parties, in accordance with the provisions of Article 18 of the Treaty, except in those cases in which a Contracting Party which had given such concessions withdraws them at the end of the period concerned — providing that such withdrawal is in accordance with what has been agreed or resolved by the Contracting Parties — or incorporates the products concerned in its programme of liberalization, negotiating for similar concessions itself.

8. The Contracting Parties, in granting the authorization referred to in paragraph (*b*) of Article 32, shall indicate specifically the particular rate at which the relatively less developed Contracting Party may comply with the minimum requirements of the programme for reducing duties, laid down in Article 5 of the Treaty, noting the stages and percentages by which that programme shall be carried out.

The period for such reductions may not extend beyond that laid down in Article 2 of the Treaty, except as agreed under Article 61 of the Treaty.

9. The authorization indicated in paragraph (*c*) of Article 32 may be granted by the Contracting Parties if the provisions of Chapter VI of the Treaty would not be sufficient for the correction of a disequilibrium in the balance of payments of a relatively less developed Contracting Party.

10. In granting the authorization referred to in paragraph (*d*) of Article 32, the Contractting Parties shall fix the period during which the relatively less developed country shall be allowed to impose the measures indicated in that paragraph and the period for which such measures, once applied, may be maintained.

The measures referred to may include, among others, quantitative restrictions on imports, the modification of tariffs, and price fixing arrangements.

11. The collective steps and the promotion of special programmes indicated in paragraphs (*e*) and (*f*) of Article 32 shall be undertaken at the request of the relatively less developed country concerned. Without prejudice to the above, the organs of the Association may make whatever recommendations they consider appropriate.

The Contracting Parties shall facilitate the practical application of these provisions of the Treaty.

12. The Contracting Parties may, at the request of one or more of the Parties, suspend any of the authorizations granted for the application of the measures envisaged in Article 32 of the Treaty, when

(a) it is agreed to withdraw recognition as a relatively less developed country owing to the cessation of the circumstances in which such recognition was granted; or

(b) it is proved that the special circumstances justifying the provision of the benefits in question have ended.

The suspension envisaged in the present Article, where necessary, shall be applied taking into account the provisions of Article 7 of the present resolution.

13. The Committee shall propose to the Conference whatever modifications in the present provisions may appear to be necessary in practice for the more effective application of the provisions of Chapter VIII of the Treaty.

EXPLANATORY NOTES

During the elaboration of the preceding provisions, certain clarifications have been achieved which it is convenient to set forth in explicit form, so as to ensure the fullest realization of the objectives of Chapter VIII of the Treaty, and avoid as far as possible difficulties of interpretation.

For this reason, and in view of the fact that the clarifications referred to cannot be included within the text of the resolution itself, it has been considered appropriate to add the present Explanatory Notes, which should stand annexed to the resolution.

1. Article 32 of the Treaty does not constitute an exception to the general provisions of the Treaty. Nevertheless, paragraphs (*a*) and (*b*) of that Article are exceptions to the provisions of Articles 5 and 18 of the Treaty, just as paragraphs (*c*) and (*d*) constitute exceptions to the provisions of Chapter VI.

Consequently, the relatively less developed countries, without prejudice to the benefits accorded to them by Article 32, shall, in common with the other Contracting Parties, enjoy all the rights and be subject to all the obligations emanating from the Treaty.

2. Paragraph (*a*) of Article 32 enables the Contracting Parties to authorize any Contracting Party to concede certain benefits, in addition to those contained in its liberalization programme, to another Contracting Party at a relatively less developed stage of economic development within the Area, which benefits shall not be affected by the provisions of Article 18 of the Treaty. Consequently, the Contracting Party granting any benefit may, within the limits of the authorization concerned, provide and maintain such benefit in a manner and for a period which it considers appropriate, and may even reach agreement with the relatively less developed country concerned not to withdraw nor negotiate nor modify in any other way the exclusive character of such benefit.

3. In order to avoid the application of measures restricting trade in products included in the liberalization programme, it is considered necessary to reserve the provisions of paragraph (*c*) of Article 32 for those cases in which the correction of a disequilibrium cannot be achieved through the application of Chapter VI of the Treaty.

4. The provisions of paragraph (*b*) of Article 32 are independent of those of Chapter VI, and the Contracting Parties may therefore authorize the joint application of the measures indicated in both places.

October 11, 1961

RESOLUTION 68 (III): SYSTEM OF VOTING
OF THE CONFERENCE

The Conference of the Contracting Parties, at its third session,
In view of Article 38 of the Treaty of Montevideo,

Considering that since the first two years of the operation of the Treaty have elapsed, it is necessary to establish the system of voting in the Conference of the Contracting Parties that will apply henceforth; and

That experience in the application of the Treaty suggests the need for gradual elimination of the provision whereby the adoption of decisions by the Conference is subject to there being no negative vote.

Resolves that

1. Except in the case of explicit provision to the contrary, decisions of the Conference shall continue to be adopted when affirmative votes are cast by at least two-thirds ($\frac{2}{3}$) of the Contracting Parties provided that no negative vote is cast.

2. The Contracting Parties shall determine, as they consider necessary, the cases to be added to those envisaged in paragraphs (a), (b), and (c) of Article 38 of the Treaty, which provide for decisions to be adopted by the affirmative votes of at least two-thirds ($\frac{2}{3}$) of the Contracting Parties.

October 4, 1963

RESOLUTION 70 (III) CRITERIA FOR DRAWING UP THE COMMON SCHEDULE

The Conference of Contracting Parties, at its third session,

In view of Articles 4, 7 and 8 of the Treaty of Montevideo and the Protocol on Norms and Procedures for Negotiations,

Considering the need to define certain concepts so as to facilitate the negotiation of the Common Schedule,

Resolves that

1. The inclusion of a product in the Common Schedule binds each of the Contracting Parties to eliminate completely, before 2 June 1973, duties and restrictions of any kind affecting the import of that product if it originates in the territory of any other Contracting Party. Consequently, the inclusion of a product in the Common Schedule does not in itself imply an obligation to reduce or eliminate restrictions on the import of that product before the above-mentioned date.

2. The products which may be included in the Common Schedule at each stage of its drawing up do not necessarily have to appear in the National Schedules and their inclusion shall be effected without indication of the import régime to be applied.

3. The irrevocability referred to in Article 8 of the Treaty shall begin to apply from the date of signature of the Act of Negotiations in which the first Common Schedule is drawn up, in relation to the products included in that Common Schedule and the import régime agreed for these products in so far as they appear in the National Schedules.

November 21, 1963

RESOLUTION 71 (III): SITUATION OF COUNTRIES WITH INADEQUATE MARKETS

The Conference of Contracting Parties, at its third session,

Considering that the Contracting Parties, in the Preamble to the Treaty, have recognized that the economic development of the Area should be attained through the maximum utilization of available factors of production and the more effective co-ordination of the development programmes of the different production sectors in accordance with norms which take due account of equitable conditions of competition and of the interests of each and every one of the Contracting Parties;

That the principle established in that Preamble whereby the expansion of present national markets is a fundamental prerequisite for the acceleration of the economic development of the Contracting Parties has particular relevance for certain sectors of production in those countries whose internal demand is insufficient for the expansion of these activities;

That in consequence, in order to facilitate the achievement of the objectives of the Treaty it is necessary to make special provision for the situation of those countries having sectors of production that are insufficiently developed or that are confronted with national markets insufficiently large for the expansion or establishment of the productive activities concerned;

That at the same time in the above-mentioned Preamble it is stated that, by the adoption of suitable formulae, conditions can be created that will be conducive to stimulating the expansion of existing productive activities, formulae that may be extended to apply also to new industries of region-wide importance;

That in addition to the case of countries already designated as relatively less advanced, the narrowness of the national market for the development of certain industrial activities is common to Chile, Colombia, Peru and Uruguay, and

That it is indispensable to adopt joint measures enabling the countries mentioned in the previous paragraph to develop their economies in harmony and in parallel with the remaining Contracting Parties,

Resolves:

1. To recognize that in order to achieve a balanced and harmonious economic development of the Area it is necessary to adopt joint measures in favour of Chile, Colombia, Peru and Uruguay which would stimulate the establishment or expansion of certain productive activities for which the size of the respective national markets is inadequate or the development of which is of region-wide interest.

The countries already designated as relatively less advanced shall benefit from the provisions of the preceding paragraph.

2. To declare the firm intention of the Contracting Parties to assure the effective participation, through a fair distribution of benefits, of the countries mentioned in the preceding Article, as well as those already designated as rela-

tively less advanced, in the Complementarity Agreements and any other type of multi-national arrangements providing for the initiation or expansion of regional productive activities. To this end, the Contracting Parties shall take into account the possibility of applying, where relevant, the principles established in Article 3, paragraph (*b*) of Resolution 48 (II) and in Article 8, paragraph (*c*) of Resolution 49 (II).

3. The Contracting Parties consider that within the framework of the Treaty it is possible to adopt joint measures adequate for the execution of a specific programme for the establishment or expansion of productive activities for the countries referred to in Article 1, the soundness of that programme being recognized by the Committee[1] in accordance with the information and advance plans presented. At the same time, the Contracting Parties undertake to do everything necessary to facilitate the execution of such a programme.

4. The Committee, in its programme of sectoral meetings and of activities. of the Advisory Committee on Industrial Development, shall give priority to the examination of any initiatives presented by the Contracting Parties mentioned in Article 1 and those already designated as relatively less advanced, in accordance with the objectives of this Resolution, and shall determine the respective solutions or, where the situation so requires, shall propose to the Conference the adoption of any measures that it may consider appropriate for implementing these solutions.

November 21, 1963

RESOLUTION 74 (III): APPLICATION OF CHAPTER VIII
OF THE TREATY. PLAN OF OPERATIONS AND
SPECIAL MEASURES IN FAVOUR OF COUNTRIES
AT A RELATIVELY LESS ADVANCED STAGE OF
ECONOMIC DEVELOPMENT

The Conference of Contracting Parties, at its third session,

In view of Chapter VIII of the Treaty of Montevideo and Resolution 62 (II) of the Conference

Considering that the Committee,[2] in fulfilment of the recommendations of Resolution 62 (II), has proposed certain practical and effective rules for fostering, through special operations and concrete measures, the growth of the economies of countries at a relatively less advanced stage of economic development within the Area, and

That the Contracting Parties have repeatedly affirmed their readiness to consider the application of measures favouring the relatively less developed countries to the fullest extent possible, so as to permit these countries to over-

[1] References to 'the Committee' in this and other resolutions are to the Standing Executive Committee established under ch. ix of the Treaty of Montevideo.

[2] See footnote to Resolution 71 (III).

come the inequalities in which they find themselves in relation to other Contracting Parties,

Resolves:

I. To approve the following Plan of Operations and Special Measures which the Contracting Parties may apply in favour of relatively less developed countries within the Area:

(a) SPECIAL OPERATIONS

When a relatively less developed country wishes to take advantage of the Plan, it shall submit for the study and approval of the Committee, a Programme of Special Operations which would permit it to accelerate its rate of economic development by means of:

1. Financial Assistance

Through loans or special operations, the Contracting Parties, may give aid, in accordance with their capacity to do so, to each one of the relatively less developed countries within the Area, principally by:

(i) Supplying machinery, equipment, installations, tools and instruments required for infrastructural projects (roads, bridges, airfield runways, transport and communications media, power facilities and others);

(ii) Supplying equipment and installations for industrial and agricultural schools for the training of skilled labour;

(iii) Supplying basic texts, installations and equipment for technical courses in the universities and other specialized centres;

(iv) Establishing lines of development credit for financing imports from within the Area, of seed, insecticides, fertilizer, raw materials or other goods required in the basic productive activities of the relatively less developed countries; and

(v) Facilitating financial agreements aimed at the creation of a fund, composed of cash contributions, with the objective of supplementing the resources of the development banks of the relatively less developed countries so as to supply working capital for productive activities of region-wide interest.

2. Technical Assistance

The Contracting Parties shall provide technical assistance, in accordance with their capacities, corresponding to the needs of each of the relatively less developed countries in the Area, principally by:

(i) Supplying experts, technicians and instructors to work within the countries concerned;

(ii) Providing fellowships for the training of technicians, skilled workers and business administrators from the relatively less developed countries, at the centres for professional and technical training of the other Contracting Parties.

(iii) Preparing and executing specific projects, such as: highly specialized engineering works; programmes of plant and animal health; works of irrigation, drainage, canal building and dam building; rural urbanization; agricultural colonization; reafforestation; the care and conservation of the navigable courses of rivers, and

(iv) Studying market possibilities and identifying industries, of region-wide interest, with a view to locating them on the territory of the relatively less developed countries within the Area.

(b) SPECIAL MEASURES

1. The Standing Executive Committee is authorized to study and approve collective negotiations with international financial institutions such as the Inter-American Development Bank, the International Bank for Reconstruction and Development and the Alliance for Progress, in support of requests for financial and technical assistance that have been or may be presented to these bodies by relatively less developed countries, with a view to obtaining finance for the expansion of existing productive activities or the development of new ones, including initiatives for the development of infrastructural projects.

2. The Standing Executive Committee is authorized to study and present for the consideration of the Contracting Parties any requests which relatively less developed countries may present for maintaining margins of preference for a certain time in respect of one or more products mentioned in such requests and which had been the subject of negotiations in accordance with Resolutions 12 (I) and 38 (II).

3. The Committee is authorized to carry out studies and, on the basis of such studies, to adopt measures or prepare draft resolutions, as the case may be, which relatively less developed countries may request in the application of other provisions envisaged in Article 32 of the Treaty dealing, in particular, with the following:

(i) The identification of industries which would produce exportable products, principally intended to supply the regional market, which could be located in countries declared as being at a relatively less advanced stage of economic development under Resolutions 12 (I) and 38 (II), and

(ii) The programme of expected liberalization which would permit the installation and ensure the effective operation of the industries referred to in the preceding paragraph.

II. The operations contemplated in paragraph (a) of Article I are intended to supplement and not to replace the normal sources of financial or technical assistance which each relatively less developed country may obtain directly from the appropriate international agencies.

III. The Committee shall include a chapter dealing with the implementation of the present Resolution in its annual report to the Conference of the Contracting Parties.

November 21, 1963

RESOLUTION 75 (III): PROGRAMME FOR CO-ORDINATING ECONOMIC AND COMMERCIAL POLICIES AND FOR HARMONIZING SYSTEMS OF FOREIGN TRADE CONTROL

The Conference of Contracting Parties, at its third session,

In view of the provisions of Articles 15, 16, 27 and 54 of the Treaty of Montevideo, Agreement No. 2 of the first meeting of Central Banks on commercial policy and Agreements Nos. 1 and 2 of the first meeting on the planning, development and orientation of industrial development.

Considering that the diversity in the economic policies of LAFTA countries imposes grave limitations on economic integration and on the process of liberalizing the intra-regional trade of the Contracting Parties;

That, in particular, diversity in the treatment of imports from third countries gives rise to the following problems among others:

(a) Growing complexity of the process of negotiation because of the multiplicity and heterogeneity of duties and restrictions applied to the same product in different countries;

(b) Differences in the margin of preference and, consequently, in the commercial stimulus provided in the various countries by the liberalization of the same category of products;

(c) Difficulty in the application of the principle of reciprocity, laid down in the Treaty of Montevideo, to give fundamental orientation to the negotiations;

(d) Distortion of normal conditions of competition between producers in the region;

(e) Difficulties arising from differences in the cost of inputs imported from outside the region, affecting the location of new investments, and

(f) Extreme complexity of the problem of defining and controlling the regional origin of products subject to liberalization;

That in order to achieve the balanced economic and social development of the Area and to comply with the objectives laid down in the Treaty Articles and Agreements mentioned above it is necessary to correct the anomalies in question, by harmonizing the economic and commercial policies of the Contracting Parties;

That these objectives should be achieved gradually by means of adequate norms taking into account the interests of each and every Contracting Party.

Resolves:

1. The Contracting Parties, in accordance with the provisions of Articles 15 and 54 of the Treaty, agree to undertake the studies required for the elaboration of a programme of co-ordination of their economic and commercial policies and for harmonizing their systems of foreign trade control.

2. This programme, which shall be carried out in stages, shall take into account all aspects of economic policy relevant for the process of integration. To

assist in formulating the programme, the Committee[3] shall request the Advisory Committees on Industrial Development, on Agricultural Questions and on Monetary Questions to carry out during the first five months of 1964 an examination of the policies of the Contracting Parties in the areas of their respective competence and the identification of the problems which, in each case, have a bearing on the process of integration.

The results of the work of the Advisory Committees mentioned above shall be analysed by the Special Committee envisaged in the present Resolution, which shall produce a report for consideration by the Conference at its fourth regular session.

3. The first phase of the programme shall aim at harmonizing commercial policies, beginning by an analysis of the customs arrangements of the Contracting Parties. To this end the Committee shall entrust the Advisory Committee on Customs Questions, which shall be convened in the month of February 1964, with the following studies:

(a) Revision of NABALALC so as to make it suitable for adoption as the Common Customs Nomenclature;

(b) Identification of the customs duties and charges of equivalent effect and of restrictions applied to the importation of each product in the various countries;

(c) Conversion of these customs duties and charges with equivalent effect into ad valorem terms, based on the c.i.f. value of the products;

(d) Classification under NABALALC of the charges and restrictions emerging from the work envisaged under paragraphs (b) and (c) above;

(e) Comparison of the charges and restrictions in force in each of the Contracting Parties in respect of each product, and

(f) Other studies considered necessary for examining the possibility of establishing a Common External Tariff.

4. The Committee is requested to create a Special Committee, composed of high level experts from each of the Contracting Parties to undertake the examination of the results of the work of the Advisory Committees referred to in Articles 2 and 3 of the present Resolution and to prepare a report proposing the basic measures considered necessary for achieving the objectives of the present Resolution, for consideration at the fourth regular session of the Conference.

5. The Contracting Parties shall designate the representatives of the Advisory Committee on Customs Questions and shall complete the establishment of the Advisory Committees mentioned in Article 2 before 31 December 1963.

6. The Contracting Parties shall furnish the Committee with the information necessary for the carrying out of the present Resolution and shall ensure the participation of the national technicians required for undertaking the work in question.

November 21, 1963

[3] See footnote to Resolution 71 (III).

RESOLUTION 77 (III): COORDINATION OF
AGRICULTURAL POLICIES

The Conference of Contracting Parties, at its third session,

In view of Articles 27 and 29 of the Treaty and Resolution 41 (II) of the Conference

Considering that under Resolution 11 (I) the Conference recommended the Committee[4] to convene meetings of experts to study regional problems in the field of agriculture;

That the Committee, under Resolution 36, created the Advisory Committee on Agricultural Questions, to carry out technical studies for the agricultural sector and to accelerate effective compliance with the provisions of the Treaty regarding agricultural complementarity;

That a harmonization of the agricultural development policies of the Contracting Parties would tend particularly to bring about overall utilization of the possibilities for trade in agricultural products within the Area;

That the co-ordination of these development policies can only be achieved in the light of a full understanding of the present situation of agriculture in each country in the Area, and

That although the work of the Advisory Committee will have to include the examination of all questions relevant to the above-mentioned objectives, it is convenient to establish an agreed tentative programme of prior studies, as a basis for an immediate plan of action,

Resolves:

1. To request the Standing Executive Committee to carry out the following tasks, with the assistance of the Advisory Committee on Agricultural Questions:

   (a) The study and evaluation of programmes of agricultural expansion and investigation in member countries, related to the existing agricultural situation, as a basis for regional co-ordination;

   (b) The study and analysis of requirements and availabilities of basic production equipment, with a view to increasing regional trade in these products;

   (c) The examination of seasonal characteristics of regional production, with a view to an orderly increase in commercial transactions to supplement local supplies;

   (d) The establishment of priorities for sectoral meetings on agricultural products, and

   (e) The study of measures for expanding regional trade in agricultural products and stimulating the exports of these products to extra-regional markets.

2. Without prejudice to the carrying out of the work indicated in the preceding Article, which has high priority, the Advisory Committee on Agricultural Questions is requested to analyse the present structure of agriculture and cattle-raising in each of the member countries of the Area, with spe-

[4] See footnote to Resolution 71 (III).

cial reference to the conditions of production, distribution and marketing.

3. The Committee[5] shall prepare a minimum plan of action embodying measures designed to achieve the co-ordination of the agricultural development policies of the member countries of LAFTA.

November 21, 1963

RESOLUTION 99 (IV): NORMS AND PROCEDURES FOR COMPLEMENTARITY AGREEMENTS

The Conference of Contracting Parties, at its fourth regular session,
In view of Articles 15, 16, and 17 of the Treaty
Decides to approve the following norms and procedures for Complementarity Agreements.

I. NATURE AND OBJECTIVES

1. Complementarity Agreements, which constitute a means of promoting economic integration, should lead to the harmonious economic development of the Area and have the following objectives, among others:

(a) To accelerate the fulfilment of the programme of liberalization of duties and restrictions on industrial products;

(b) To facilitate the inclusion in the liberalization programme of products which do not yet form part of intra-regional trade;

(c) To create conditions favourable for the promotion of investments which would tend to accelerate economic and social development, raise the level of employment and improve the utilization of the resources of the Area;

(d) To make possible the maximum utilization of the available factors of production in the sector concerned and an adequate co-ordination of the relevant development plans;

(e) To facilitate programmes of sectoral integration that may be established by the Contracting Parties;

(f) To contribute, through the adoption of specific norms, to the narrowing of differences between the levels of economic development of the countries of Area;

(g) To give special attention, in planning and drawing up Complementarity Agreements, to the situation of the relatively less developed countries and to the need, in compliance with the provisions of Article 32 of the Treaty, to create opportunities for them to participate adequately in such Agreements;

(h) To stimulate complementarity between industrial activities designed to supply the needs of the Area; and

(i) To ensure equitable conditions of competition so as to increase industrial productivity, promote an improvement in quality and a reduction

[5] See footnote to Resolution 71 (III).

in prices and to enhance the competitiveness of the products of the Area in world markets.

II. CONTENTS OF THE AGREEMENTS

2. Complementarity Agreements drawn up under the provisions of Articles 15, 16 and 17 of the Treaty, shall without fail contain norms to govern the programme of liberalization to be established for the products included in such Agreements.

3. The programme of liberalization of each Complementarity Agreement shall:

   (a) Specify the products included in the Agreement, in conformity with the specifications and corresponding code-numbers of NABALALC;[6]

   (b) Indicate the manner in which duties and restrictions applying to the products specified shall be eliminated, it being understood that the rate of liberalization may differ as between countries and products included in the Agreement;

   (c) Provide for the maintenance of the margins of preference agreed upon for the products included in the liberalization programme; and

   (d) Define the requirements as to origin to which the products concerned shall be subject, in accordance with the general norms approved by the Conference.

4. Complementarity Agreements shall contain clauses providing for accession to the Agreements which shall be such as to facilitate the participation of other Contracting Parties.

5. Contracting Parties participating in a Complementarity Agreement shall endeavour to include in such Agreement provisions relating to:

   (a) Harmonization of treatment accorded to imports from third countries related to products included in the sector concerned, as also of raw materials and components employed in the manufacturing process in question;

   (b) Co-ordination of governmental programmes and incentives, with a view to facilitating sectoral complementarity and harmonizing the treatment accorded to capital and services originating either within or outside the Area and involving the sector in question; and

   (c) Regulations to prevent unfair trade practices, in line with the general norms adopted by the Conference.

6. Complementarity Agreements may include, among others, clauses relating to:

   (a) Irrevocability of concessions or conditions regulating the withdrawal of concessions relating to one or more products of the sector;

   (b) Special treatment in application of Chapter VIII of the Treaty;

   (c) Treatment to be applied in implementation of Article 2 of Resolution 71 (III);

   (d) Denunciation of the Agreement;

   (e) Special procedures for settling disputes; and

---

[6] NABALALC is the common customs nomenclature adopted by LAFTA.

(f) Administration of the Agreement.

7. A Contracting Party at a relatively less advanced stage of economic development participating in an Agreement may, in accordance with Article 32, paragraph (a) of the Treaty, be granted benefits through concessions not extended to other Contracting Parties, under conditions laid down in the relevant Resolution of the Conference.

8. Clauses providing for denunciation shall deal with the following points *inter alia*:

(a) Formalities of denunciation;

(b) The period at the end of which the denunciation shall begin to take effect; and

(c) Effects of the denunciation in respect of the liberalization programme contained in the Agreement and of the rights and obligations of participating Contracting Parties deriving therefrom.

III. CONCLUSION OF AGREEMENTS

9. Negotiations for the conclusion of Complementarity Agreements shall be open to the participation of all Contracting Parties.

10. The Contracting Parties proposing to conclude a Complementarity Agreement shall communicate its text to the Standing Executive Committee through their representatives, and shall provide the most complete information possible on the nature of the Draft Agreement. The Committee shall in turn inform the other Contracting Parties of the intention to conclude the Agreement.

11. The negotiations shall not begin before forty-five days have elapsed from the date that the Committee receives the communication referred to in the preceding Article.

12. At the request of any Contracting Party, the beginning of the negotiations shall be deferred for a supplementary period of up to sixty days.

13. The periods referred to in Articles 11 and 12 above may be reduced or eliminated by decision of the Committee, in accordance with the system of voting laid down in Article 38 of the Treaty.

14. Between the date of the communication and the commencement of negotiations, the Committee shall analyse the material presented, and supplement it with the necessary technical studies for the information of the Contracting Parties; it shall examine the possibilities for other Contracting Parties to participate in the Agreement; it shall formulate, where appropriate, any recommendations which it may consider advisable; and to this end it may request of the sponsoring Parties any additional information that it may consider necessary.

15. In the negotiations for drawing up Complementarity Agreements and for accession to such Agreements, the Contracting Parties shall take full account of the situation of the relatively less developed countries, as well as of conditions of production in the countries of the Area, especially in the cases envisaged in Resolution 71 (III).

16. Agreements shall consist of Protocols signed by plenipotentiaries duly accredited by the Contracting Parties.

17. The Secretariat of the Committee shall be the depositary of the Protocols, of which it shall supply authentic copies to all Contracting Parties.

18. Immediately after the respective Protocol has been signed, the Complementarity Agreements shall be submitted for the examination of the Committee, which shall pronounce on their compatibility with the general principles and objectives of the Treaty within a period of thirty days from the date on which the Standing Executive Committee received the Protocol in question.

19. Complementarity Agreements may enter into force only after they have been declared compatible with the general principles and objectives of the Treaty, in the manner provided in Article 17 of the Treaty, and in accordance with the terms of Article 18 of the present Resolution.

20. Complementarity Agreements shall remain open to the accession of the remaining Contracting Parties. Such accession shall take effect definitively as soon as the requisite negotiations have been completed and the necessary Protocols have been signed by the countries participating in the Agreement and by the acceding Party, which Protocols shall be deposited with the Secretariat of the Association.

21. The Contracting Parties expressly agree that those Contracting Parties not participating in a Complementarity Agreement shall enjoy the benefits granted reciprocally between the Parties participating in the Agreement only if they provide adequate compensation.

22. Contracting Parties proposing to accede to a Complementarity Agreement shall initiate the negotiations referred to in Article 20 not earlier than thirty days nor later than 120 days from the date on which they communicate their intention to the Standing Executive Committee.

23. The obligations required of an acceding Contracting Party shall, as a maximum, not exceed the cumulative obligations undertaken since the entry into force of the Agreement by the Contracting Party that has assumed the greatest such obligations, taking into account the provisions of Article 15 of the present Resolution.

24. In case of any dispute regarding the interpretation of the conditions required for the entry into force of the Agreement in respect of an acceding Contracting Party, the latter may submit the case to the Committee, which shall undertake the necessary negotiations for conciliation.

25. In all cases, benefits negotiated under Complementarity Agreements shall be automatically extended, without the provision of compensation, to the relatively less developed countries, independently of any negotiation or accession to the Agreements.

IV. RELATION TO THE LIBERALIZATION PROGRAMME OF THE TREATY

26. Liberalization programmes established by Complementarity Agreements shall be formulated taking into account their auxiliary character in relation to the liberalization programme instituted under Chapter 2 of the Treaty of

Montevideo. They shall therefore be limited to the period indicated in Article 2 of the Treaty.

V. EXECUTION OF THE AGREEMENTS

27. Contracting Parties participating in a Complementarity Agreement shall supply information periodically on the progress of the Agreement to the Committee, which shall render an annual report on this matter to the Conference at its regular sessions, including in such report an account of experience gained in the application of this Resolution.

28. A Contracting Party not participating in an Agreement may at any time request additional information on the progress of such Agreement, through the Committee.

29. At the request of any Contracting Party participating in a Complementarity Agreement, the organs of the Association shall endeavour to take such measures as would be necessary to correct any anomalies arising in the course of its execution, particularly in the event that one or more Contracting Parties, whether or not they are participants in the Agreement, adopt measures which cause or threaten to cause disturbances in the normal functioning of the Agreement.

30. If as a consequence of the application of the norms laid down in the present Resolution serious and persistent imbalance occurs in the industrial development of the Contracting Parties affecting the harmonious economic development of the Area, the means of correcting such imbalance shall be examined by the Standing Executive Committee, at the request of any Party that considers it has suffered damage, with a view to adopting measures that it regards as adequate for this purpose.

VI. SPECIAL CLAUSE

31. The present Resolution supersedes Resolution 48 (II) of the Conference.

December 8, 1964

RESOLUTION 117 (V): CREATION OF THE COUNCIL OF MINISTERS

The Conference of Contracting Parties, at its fifth session,

Bearing in mind the resolutions contained in the final Act of the Meeting of Ministers of Foreign Relations of the Contracting Parties to the Treaty of Montevideo, held pursuant to the provisions of Resolution 112 (IV);

Whereas the development of the integration process will be facilitated if the Ministers or Secretaries of State in charge of implementing the foreign policies of the LAFTA countries meet periodically to adopt decisions pertaining to the conduct of the Association's policy at the highest level; and

For this reason a Council of Ministers of Foreign Relations of LAFTA should be created immediately, and an instrument prepared to establish it fully as an institution;

Resolves:

First. To create the Council of Ministers of Foreign Relations of the Latin American Free Trade Association, for whose organization as an institution an appropriate instrument will be signed.

Second. To entrust the Standing Executive Committee with preparing and submitting to the governments of the Contracting Parties a draft of the instrument referred to in the first article, as soon as possible so that it may be considered by the Ministers of Foreign Relations at their first meeting.

Third. Until such time as the Council of Ministers has been fully created as an organ of the Association, it will meet at least once a year at the Conference of Contracting Parties to the Treaty of Montevideo. The latter will be convened to this end for special sessions, on the date and site determined by the Ministers of Foreign Relations at their previous meeting, or at the initiative of the Standing Executive Committee when deemed necessary by the Parties.

Fourth. To charge the Standing Executive Committee with proceeding, as envisaged in the foregoing article, to convene the first meeting of the Council of Ministers at the headquarters of the Association as soon as the draft referred to in the second article has been prepared.

Fifth. Contracting Parties who have assigned the responsibility for LAFTA matters to a Minister or Secretary of State other than the Minister of Foreign Relations may be represented on the Council by the respective Minister.

December 30, 1965

RESOLUTION 202 (CM–II/VI–E): NORMS FOR SUBREGIONAL AGREEMENTS

The Council of Ministers, gathered at the sixth extraordinary session of the Conference of Contracting Parties to the Treaty of Montevideo,

In view of the Declaration of the Presidents of America,

Resolves:

First. To charge the Conference with establishing, at its seventh ordinary session, the norms on which subregional agreements shall be based.

Second. The norms established shall comply with — among others — the following principles:

1. Subregional agreements may be concluded between two or more Contracting Parties in terms that comply with the text of the Declaration of the Presidents of America, contained in Chapter I, Section 2.

2. Each subregional agreement shall establish terms for accelerating trade policy in relation to programed elimination of duties and the establishment of a common external tariff. It shall also determine measures for intensifying industrialization and achieving greater harmonization of the respective national legislations.

3. The program of elimination of duties shall be general and not restricted to specific sectors.

4. Subregional agreement stipulations shall take into account the commitments of undersigning countries in relation to their national schedules, special schedules, the common schedule, and applicable decisions adopted in the Declaration of the Presidents of America.

5. Industrial complementarity agreements concluded by participants in subregional agreements shall comply with the pertinent guidelines of the Treaty of Montevideo and Conference resolutions and shall be open to all other Contracting Parties on the same terms.

6. Subregional agreements shall be transitory and as such shall fix the date of entry into effect and duration.

7. Contracting Parties participating in a subregional agreement shall designate the executive agency that shall undertake administration of the agreement.

8. All subregional agreements shall be subject to prior approval by the Contracting Parties that delegate this faculty to the Standing Executive Committee. The Conference shall annually examine the progress of the agreements during its ordinary sessions.

9. Subregional agreement dispositions shall not affect the rights and obligations derived from the Treaty of Montevideo and LAFTA resolutions, which shall be applied in those areas not covered by the agreement.

10. Subregional agreements shall contain adherence norms compatible with the objectives of the Treaty of Montevideo.

September 2, 1967

RESOLUTION 203 (CM–II/VI–E): BASES FOR A SUBREGIONAL AGREEMENT AMONG COLOMBIA, CHILE, ECUADOR, PERU, AND VENEZUELA

The Council of Ministers, gathered at the sixth extraordinary session of the Conference of Contracting Parties to the Treaty of Montevideo,

In view of the Declaration of the Presidents of America,

Resolves:

First. To approve the bases for a subregional agreement presented by Colombia, Chile, Ecuador, Peru, and Venezuela contained in the document annexed to this Resolution.

Second. To delegate to the Standing Executive Committee the faculty of establishing the compatibility of the undersigned subregional agreement with the bases approved in the first article of this Resolution and the principles enumerated from 1 to 10 in the second article of Resolution 202 (CM–II/VI–E) of the Council of Ministers' second meeting.

Third. The Conference of Contracting Parties, in its ordinary sessions, shall analyze the progress of the subregional agreement and its compatibility with the major objectives of the Treaty of Montevideo.

September 2, 1967

ANNEX
BASES FOR A SUBREGIONAL AGREEMENT
ELABORATED BY COLOMBIA, CHILE, ECUADOR,
PERU, AND VENEZUELA

Chapter I: Preamble

The Bogotá Declaration signatory countries are convinced that in order to facilitate more adequate participation in the integration process provided for in the Treaty of Montevideo, it is urgently necessary to foster the substantial expansion of their respective internal markets by means of a transitory subregional agreement set up to accelerate the conversion of LAFTA into a common market. This would permit the signatory countries to fulfill, together with other Contracting Parties, under conditions of greater equilibrium, the commitments derived from the Treaty of Montevideo.

The Presidents of America, assembled in Punta del Este in April of this year, agreed to facilitate the conclusion of subregional agreements among the countries of Latin America.

In compliance with the Bogotá Declaration, representatives of Colombia, Chile, Ecuador, Peru, and Venezuela held successive meetings in the course of the year in Viña del Mar, Quito, and Caracas. Representatives of Bolivia participated in the last of these meetings as observers.

The bases established for the subregional agreement take into very special account the strict fulfillment of commitments created by the Treaty of Montevideo and the compatibility of these commitments with those assumed in the subregional agreement. Moreover, the transitory nature of the preferential systems proposed in the agreement is underscored, with the understanding that these special systems will cease to be applied to the extent that they become absorbed into more general commitments undertaken within the LAFTA framework in the process of achieving a common market.

In consideration of these guidelines and of the preamble and dispositions of the Treaty of Montevideo, the representatives of the Governments of Colombia, Chile, Ecuador, Peru, and Venezuela have elaborated the following bases for a subregional agreement:

Chapter II: Program of Internal Elimination of Duties

The program of elimination of duties and nontariff restrictions, including restraints of an administrative, financial, and foreign exchange nature, shall be regulated according to the following norms:

A. PRODUCTS INCLUDED, OR WHICH SHALL BE INCLUDED, IN THE LAFTA COMMON SCHEDULE

Products included in the common schedule as of the date of the agreement shall be totally freed from duties or restrictions 180 days after that date. Products later added to the common schedule shall be totally freed from duties and restrictions 90 days after the date of their incorporation into the said list.

B. MANUFACTURED GOODS AND AGRICULTURAL AND MINING PRODUCTS NOT CURRENTLY PRODUCED IN ANY OF THE COUNTRIES OF THE SUBREGION

These products shall be totally freed from duties and restrictions 180 days after the corresponding lists have been drawn up. To this effect, within a maximum period of 60 days from the date the agreement is undersigned, all participating countries shall designate sectorial groups of experts to prepare these lists, which shall be completed within 180 days.

C. OTHER PRODUCTS

Without affecting the exceptions specified in Sections D and F, products not encompassed in Sections A and B shall be totally freed from duties and restrictions at a date to be established by the subregional agreement, substantially prior to that indicated in the Declaration of the Presidents of America for converting LAFTA into a common market.

The terms and time limits in which elimination of duties and restrictions shall become effective shall be determined by agreement among the participating countries.

Elimination or reduction of duties and restrictions shall go into effect on January first of the year following the date of the respective agreement, unless another date is fixed. Elimination or reduction of duties and restrictions shall be put into effect by all participating countries in the terms and time limits established, except in the case of Ecuador, which shall be governed by the conditions established in Section E.

D. PRODUCTS INCORPORATED INTO COMPLEMENTARITY AGREEMENTS

The following industrial sectors shall be excepted from the norms specified in the preceding sections:

1. Basic metallurgy;
2. Nonmetallic minerals;
3. Chemicals and petrochemicals, with special emphasis on fertilizers;
4. Wood, cellulose, and paper;
5. Metallic machine products, particularly automotive parts and capital goods;
6. Electrical and electronic products; and
7. Processed foodstuffs, and those other sectors that lend themselves to industrial complementarity agreements.

In these instances the process of elimination of duties shall be guided by the norms of the respective agreement.

E. SPECIAL SYSTEM FOR ECUADOR

1. With regard to Ecuador, the subregional agreement shall fully apply the principles and dispositions of the Treaty of Montevideo, as well as those contained in LAFTA Conference resolutions on behalf of relatively less developed countries.

2. In order to obtain the subregion's harmonious development, the other participating countries shall commit themselves to free Ecuadorian products from duties and restrictions, promptly and substantially, in order to assure

it a stable market. For this purpose, and no more than ninety (90) days after the date on which the agreement goes into effect, Ecuador shall present to the other participating countries a schedule of goods it produces from which it and the other countries shall choose, within a period of sixty (60) days, the products to be totally freed, in terms not extended to the other countries, in order to maintain a sufficient preferential margin during the periods to be established. The elimination of duties and restrictions thus agreed upon shall go into effect no later than thirty (30) days after termination of the afore-mentioned 60-day period. The schedule submitted by Ecuador may be based on a report to be prepared upon that country's request by a group of international organization experts and annexed to the said schedule.

3. Ecuadorian products not included in the schedule to which the preceding point refers shall be incorporated into successive schedules for elimination of duties and restrictions, also not extended to other countries. Such schedules shall be acted upon every six months so that the process may be completed five years before the date established for total tariff elimination within the subregion. The new schedules shall be subject to the dispositions contained in Chapter III relative to the minimum common external tariff. Under certain circumstances that might be particularly detrimental to Ecuador's economic situation, or when it becomes necessary to stimulate certain production lines for subregional consumption, Ecuador shall be granted special facilities to adjust itself to the said tariff. These special facilities shall be transitory and shall not exceed the conditions considered necessary to promote production in sectors agreed upon, or to prevent dislocations that might otherwise occur.

4. Ecuador shall gradually free common schedule products as agreed upon within the time limit specified in Article 2 of the Treaty of Montevideo. Products included in the common schedule on which the countries of the subregion have granted Ecuador special concessions shall be excluded from these reductions of duties. The exclusion shall be restricted to the country or countries granting the respective concession.

5. Ecuador shall effect the reductions of duties to which Section C of Chapter II (Other Products) refers, gradually, more slowly, and within a time limit not more than five years beyond the date on which respective elimination of duties among the other countries takes place. This time limit may be revised according to the results that Ecuador obtains in its trade with the other countries of the subregion. Ecuador shall be granted during a period not exceeding five years beyond that applicable to the other countries conditions more favorable and more compatible with its possibilities for harmonizing tariff concessions to third countries. These conditions shall consist of a reduction, the size of which shall be determined on undersigning the agreement, in the minimum common external tariff. The rate shall be gradually reduced in each case, in terms previously established by the Contracting Parties.

6. The Contracting Parties shall make the utmost effort to assure that, benefiting from the opportunities that the development of the subregional market may afford, Ecuador obtain adequate specialization and equitable distribution of investments within the subregion through proper programing. To this effect, the Contracting Parties shall take into account the guidelines and

spirit of Articles 4 and 5 of Resolution 100 (IV) and item (e) of numbers 1 and 5 of Resolution 157 (VI), of the LAFTA Conference.

7. The countries of the subregion recognize the convenience of Ecuador's participation in industrial complementarity agreements.

F. SCHEDULE OF EXCEPTIONS

The schedule of products incorporated into the agreement with a given total of NABALALC (LAFTA-Brussels tariff nomenclature) subpositions proposed by the participating countries, in the proportion corresponding to the indicated total, shall be excepted from the preceding dispositions. Should the proposals of one or more countries coincide, they shall be entitled to propose new subpositions in substitution of those repeated.

Reductions of duties on products incorporated into the schedules thus formed shall be adjusted to general commitments adopted in the course of LAFTA's general process.

G. REDUCTIONS OF DUTIES VIS-À-VIS LAFTA

Reductions of duties effected within the framework of the subregional agreement shall not be extended to the other LAFTA countries. Nevertheless, agreements adopted in compliance with the Treaty of Montevideo, the LAFTA program for elimination of duties and for the establishment of a common external tariff shall take precedence over agreements concluded within the subregion, whenever LAFTA agreements represent an advance over those of the subregion.

Chapter III: Minimum Common External Tariff

Whenever a given product is incorporated into the process of elimination of duties and restrictions, in compliance with the norms established in the preceding chapter, a minimum common external tariff on imports of these products from outside the subregion shall be fixed, according to the following dispositions:

(a) In the case of products covered in Sections A and B of the previous chapter, the countries shall adjust the treatment they apply to countries outside the subregion simultaneously with the total elimination of duties agreed upon. The paramount factor to be considered in this area is the effect that the minimum common external tariff will have on the economy and living costs of each of the participating countries;

(b) The same treatment shall be applied to all other totally freed products, subsequently incorporated;

(c) In the case of products not totally freed from duties and restrictions at the time of their incorporation into the program, a minimum common external tariff shall be determined, together with the respective treatment, as well as terms and time limits of application;

(d) When fixing a minimum common external tariff on a given product, the treatment that shall be applied to imports of substitute products shall also be determined. At the same time, an effort shall be made to establish the minimum common external tariff that shall be placed on imports of semifinished goods and raw materials used in the manufacture of products incorporated into the program of elimination of duties and restrictions;

(e) In every instance, the minimum common external tariff may be modified at any time by common consent;

(f) In the case of products that appear on LAFTA National Schedules of one or more countries, the treatment agreed upon with regard to imports from LAFTA countries not forming part of this agreement shall be maintained, without affecting the preceding norms;

(g) In the case of products incorporated into industrial complementarity agreements, only norms regarding the common external tariff contained in the respective agreement shall be applied; and

(h) Once the levels of a common external tariff have been established by LAFTA, they shall take precedence over the treatment applied in compliance with subregional agreement norms.

Chapter IV: Requirements of Origin

The dispositions and requirements agreed upon by LAFTA regarding origin shall be applied to products incorporated into the process of elimination of duties and restrictions. Nevertheless, at the time of incorporation, or at a later date, special norms of origin may be established.

Chapter V: Safeguard Clauses

The dispositions on safeguard clauses contained in Chapters VI and VII of the Treaty of Montevideo shall be fully applicable.

Authorization already granted by LAFTA to a member of the subregion for application of safeguard clauses shall continue in effect. However, on signing the subregional agreement, the country shall endeavor to reduce the authorized time limit or to eliminate it gradually by groups of products in favor of the countries of the subregion.

Chapter VI: Trade Competition

In order to prevent unfair competition within the subregion, as well as that produced by imports from countries outside the subregion, the countries shall adopt the necessary measures to avoid the damage caused by dumping or other unfair trade practices.

Participating countries shall commit themselves not to favor their exports by subsidies or other measures that may dislocate normal competitive conditions within the subregion.

Chapter VII: Coordination of Economic Policies

Participating countries shall coordinate their development, monetary, exchange, fiscal, foreign trade, and investment policies.

To this end, they shall foster the conclusion of agreements among the responsible organizations in each of these areas, among others: planning agencies, central banks, foreign trade organizations, and those devoted to industrial, agricultural, and mining promotion.

Chapter VIII: Administration of the Subregional Agreement

The administration of the subregional agreement shall be the domain of the Joint Commission created in Viña del Mar on June 23, 1967, which shall function as an Executive Commission and top policy-making agency. Its functions and attributions shall be determined by a set of special regulations that shall be submitted to the participating countries for approval.

Chapter IX: Final Dispositions

The subregional agreement shall contain dispositions regarding entry into effect, incorporation of new members, and liquidation and shall establish the fact that its rulings shall not affect the rights and obligations derived from the Treaty of Montevideo, which shall be applied in supplementary form, nor the principles and resolutions adopted by LAFTA.

Special treatment established in the case of Ecuador in Section E of Chapter II shall be extended to all relatively less developed countries that sign the agreement.

Caracas   *August 16, 1967*

EXCERPTS FROM ACTION PROGRAM AGREED UPON BY THE AMERICAN PRESIDENTS*

CHAPTER I: LATIN AMERICAN ECONOMIC INTEGRATION AND INDUSTRIAL DEVELOPMENT

1. PRINCIPLES, OBJECTIVES, AND GOALS

Economic integration is a collective instrument for accelerating Latin American development and should constitute one of the policy goals of each of the countries of the region. The greatest possible efforts should be made to bring it about, as a necessary complement to national development plans.

At the same time, the different levels of development and economic and market conditions of the various Latin American countries must be borne in mind, in order that the integration process may promote their harmonious and balanced growth. In this respect, the countries of relatively less economic development, and, to the extent required, those of insufficient market, will have preferential treatment in matters of trade and of technical and financial cooperation.

Integration must be fully at the service of Latin America. This requires the strengthening of Latin American enterprise through vigorous financial and technical support that will permit it to develop and supply the regional market efficiently. Foreign private enterprise will be able to fill an important function in assuring achievement of the objectives of integration within the pertinent policies of each of the countries of Latin America.

Adequate financing is required to facilitate the economic restructuring and adjustments called for by the urgent need to accelerate integration.

It is necessary to adopt all measures that will lead to the completion of Latin American integration, above all those that will bring about, in the shortest time possible, monetary stability and the elimination of all restrictions, including administrative, financial, and exchange restrictions, that obstruct the trade of the products of the area.

* Excerpts from the official text published in Organization of American States, *Declaration of the American Presidents*, Meeting of American Chiefs of State, Punta del Este, Uruguay, April 12–14, 1967 (OAS/Ser.K/XIV/1.1; Washington, D.C.). Chapters III–VI are not reproduced here since they are not directly relevant to the subject matter of this volume. [Editor's note.]

To these ends, the Latin American Presidents, agree to take action on the following points:

a. Beginning in 1970, to establish progressively the Latin American Common Market, which should be substantially in operation within a period of no more than fifteen years.

b. The Latin American Common Market will be based on the improvement of the two existing integration systems: the Latin American Free Trade Association (LAFTA) and the Central American Common Market (CACM). The two systems will initiate simultaneously a process of convergence by stages of cooperation, closer ties, and integration, taking into account the interest of the Latin American countries not yet associated with these systems, in order to provide their access to one of them.

c. To encourage the incorporation of other countries of the Latin American region into the existing integration systems.

2. MEASURES WITH REGARD TO THE LATIN AMERICAN FREE TRADE ASSOCIATION (LAFTA)

The Presidents of the member states of LAFTA instruct their respective Ministers of Foreign Affairs, who will participate in the next meeting of the Council of Ministers of LAFTA, to be held in 1967, to adopt the measures necessary to implement the following decisions:

a. To accelerate the process of converting LAFTA into a common market. To this end, starting in 1970, and to be completed in a period of not more than fifteen years, LAFTA will put into effect a system of programmed elimination of duties and all other nontariff restrictions, and also a system of tariff harmonization, in order to establish progressively a common external tariff at levels that will promote efficiency and productivity, as well as the expansion of trade.

b. To coordinate progressively economic policies and instruments and to harmonize national laws to the extent required for integration. These measures will be adopted simultaneously with the improvement of the integration process.

c. To promote the conclusion of sectoral agreements for industrial complementation, endeavoring to obtain the participation of the countries of relatively less economic development.

d. To promote the conclusion of temporary subregional agreements, with provision for reducing tariffs within the subregions and harmonizing treatments toward third nations more rapidly than in the general agreements, in keeping with the objectives of regional integration. Subregional tariff reductions will not be extended to countries that are not parties to the subregional agreement, nor will they create special obligations for them.

Participation of the countries of relatively less economic development in all stages of the integration process and in the formation of the Latin American Common Market will be based on the provisions of the Treaty of Montevideo and its complementary resolutions, and these countries will be given the greatest possible advantages, so that balanced development of the region may be achieved.

To this same end, they have decided to promote immediate action to facilitate free access of products of the LAFTA member countries of relatively less economic development to the market of the other LAFTA countries, and to promote the installation and financing in the former countries of industries intended for the enlarged market.

The countries of relatively less economic development will have the right to participate and to obtain preferential conditions in the subregional agreements in which they have an interest.

The situation of countries characterized as being of insufficient market shall be taken into account in temporary preferential treatments established, to the extent necessary to achieve a harmonious development in the integration process.

It is understood that all the provisions set forth in this section fall within or are based upon the Treaty of Montevideo.

3. MEASURES WITH REGARD TO THE CENTRAL AMERICAN ECONOMIC INTEGRATION PROGRAM

The Presidents of the member states of the Central American Common Market, commit themselves:

a. To carry out an action program that will include the following measures, among others:

(1) Improvement of the customs union and establishment of a Central American monetary union;

(2) Completion of the regional network of infrastructure;

(3) Promotion of a common foreign-trade policy;

(4) Improvement of the common market in agricultural products and implementation of a joint, coordinated industrial policy;

(5) Acceleration of the process of free movement of manpower and capital within the area;

(6) Harmonization of the basic legislation required for economic integration.

b. To apply, in the implementation of the foregoing measures, and when pertinent, the temporary preferential treatment already established or that may be established, in accordance with the principle of balanced development among countries.

c. To foster closer ties between Panama and the Central American Common Market, as well as rapid expansion of trade and investment relations with neighboring countries of the Central American and Caribbean region, taking advantage, to this end, of their geographic proximity and of the possibilities for economic complementation; also, to seek conclusion of subregional agreements and agreements of industrial complementation between Central America and other Latin American countries.

4. MEASURES COMMON TO LATIN AMERICAN COUNTRIES

The Latin American Presidents commit themselves:

a. Not to establish new restrictions on trade among Latin American countries, except in special cases, such as those arising from equalization of tariffs and other instruments of trade policy, as well as from the need to assure the initiation or expansion of certain productive activities in countries of relatively less economic development.

b. To establish, by a tariff cut or other equivalent measures, a margin of preference within the region for all products originating in Latin American countries, taking into account the different degrees of development of the countries.

c. To have the measures in the two preceding paragraphs applied immediately among the member countries of LAFTA, in harmony with the other measures referring to this organization contained in the present chapter and, insofar as possible, to extend them to nonmember countries in a manner compatible with existing international commitments, inviting the latter countries to extend similar preference to the members of LAFTA, with the same qualification.

d. To ensure that application of the foregoing measures shall not hinder internal readjustments designed to rationalize the instruments of trade policy made necessary in order to carry out national development plans and to achieve the goals of integration.

e. To promote acceleration of the studies already initiated regarding preferences that LAFTA countries might grant to imports from the Latin American countries that are not members of the Association.

f. To have studies made of the possibility of concluding agreements of industrial complementation in which all Latin American countries may participate, as well as temporary subregional economic integration agreements between the CACM and member countries of LAFTA.

g. To have a committee established composed of the executive organs of LAFTA and the CACM to coordinate implementation of the foregoing points. To this end, the committee will encourage meetings at the ministerial level, in order to ensure that Latin American integration will proceed as rapidly as possible, and, in due course, initiate negotiation of a general treaty or the protocols required to create the Latin American Common Market. Latin American countries that are not members shall be invited to send representatives to these meetings and to those of the committee of the executive organs of LAFTA and the CACM.

h. To give special attention to industrial development within integration, and particularly to the strengthening of Latin American industrial firms. In this regard, we reiterate that development must be balanced between investments for economic ends and investments for social ends.

5. MEASURES COMMON TO MEMBER COUNTRIES OF THE ORGANIZATION OF AMERICAN STATES (OAS)

The Presidents of the member states of the OAS, agree:

a. To mobilize financial and technical resources within and without the hemisphere to contribute to the solution of problems in connection with the balance of payments, industrial readjustments, and retraining of the labor force that may arise from a rapid reduction of trade barriers during the period of transition toward the common market, as well as to increase the sums available for export credits in intra–Latin American trade. The Inter-American Development Bank and the organs of both existing integration systems should participate in the mobilization of such resources.

b. To mobilize public and private resources within and without the hemisphere to encourage industrial development as part of the integration process and of national development plans.

c. To mobilize financial and technical resources to undertake specific feasibility studies on multinational projects for Latin American industrial firms, as well as to aid in carrying out these projects.

d. To accelerate the studies being conducted by various inter-American agencies to promote strengthening of capital markets and the possible establishment of a Latin American stock market.

e. To make available to Central America, within the Alliance for Progress, adequate technical and financial resources, including those required for strengthening and expanding the existing Central American Economic Integration Fund, for the purpose of accelerating the Central American economic integration program.

f. To make available, within the Alliance for Progress and pursuant to the provisions of the Charter of Punta del Este, the technical and financial resources needed to accelerate the preparatory studies and work involved in converting LAFTA into a common market.

CHAPTER II: MULTINATIONAL ACTION FOR INFRASTRUCTURE PROJECTS

The economic integration of Latin America demands a vigorous and sustained effort to complete and modernize the physical infrastructure of the region. It is necessary to build a land transport network and improve all types of transport systems to facilitate the movement of persons and goods throughout the hemisphere; to establish an adequate and efficient telecommunications system and interconnected power systems; and jointly to develop international watersheds, frontier regions and economic areas that include the territory of two or more countries. In Latin America there are in existence projects in all these fields, at different stages of preparation or implementation, but in many cases the completion of prior studies, financial resources, or merely the coordination of efforts and the decision to bring them to fruition are lacking.

The Presidents of the member states of the OAS agree to engage in determined action to undertake or accelerate the construction of the infrastructure required for the development and integration of Latin America and to make better use thereof. In so doing, it is essential that the groups of interested countries or multinational institutions determine criteria for assigning priorities, in view of the amount of human and material resources needed for the task.

As one basis for the criteria, which will be determined with precision upon consideration of the specific cases submitted for study, they stress the fundamental need to give preferential attention to those projects that benefit the countries of the region that are at a relatively lower level of economic development.

Priority should also be given to the mobilization of financial and technical resources for the preparation and implementation of infrastructure projects that will facilitate the participation of landlocked countries in regional and international trade.

In consequence, they adopt the following decisions for immediate implementation:

1. To complete the studies and conclude the agreements necessary to accelerate the construction of an inter-American telecommunications network.

2. To expedite the agreements necessary to complete the Pan American Highway, to accelerate the construction of the Bolivarian Highway (Carretera Marginal de la Selva) and its junction with the Trans-Chaco Highway and to support the studies and agreements designed to bring into being the new highway systems that will join groups of countries of continental and insular Latin America, as well as the basic works required to develop water and airborne transport of a multinational nature and the corresponding systems of operation. As a complement to these agreements, negotiations should be undertaken for the purpose of eliminating or reducing to a minimum the restrictions on international traffic and of promoting technical and administrative cooperation among land, water, and air transport enterprises and the establishment of multinational transport services.

3. To sponsor studies for preparing joint projects in connection with watersheds, such as the studies commenced on the development of the River Plate basin and that relating to the Gulf of Fonseca.

4. To allocate sufficient resources to the Preinvestment Fund for Latin American Integration of the IDB for conducting studies that will make it possible to identify and prepare multinational projects in all fields that may be of importance in promoting regional integration. In order that the aforesaid Fund may carry out an effective promotion effort, it is necessary that an adequate part of the resources allocated may be used without reimbursement, or with reimbursement conditioned on the execution of the corresponding projects.

5. To mobilize, within and outside the hemisphere, resources in addition to those that will continue to be placed at the disposal of the countries to support national economic development programs, such resources to be devoted especially to the implementation of multinational infrastructure projects that can represent important advances in the Latin American economic integration process. In this regard, the IDB should have additional resources in order to participate actively in the attainment of this objective.

Central American Common Market

The Central American economies are characterized by heavy dependence on a few commodity exports. In 1961 coffee, bananas, and cotton accounted for 75 per cent of the exports of the five countries presently participating in the Central American Common Market (CACM) — Costa Rica, El Salvador, Guatemala, Honduras, and Nicaragua. In the same year, 46 per cent of the region's national income originated in agriculture, while manufacturing, the next largest contributor, represented only 16 per cent. The area's underdevelopment, dependence on primary export-oriented activities, and the absence of complementarity among the five minuscule economies were for a long time considered extremely serious obstacles to regional economic cooperation. Nevertheless, the Central American Common Market represents the most successful example of regional integration in the entire underdeveloped sector of the world.

The first attempts to bring about some degree of economic cooperation among the five Central American republics go back to the beginning of the 1950s. The authorship of the idea of Central American economic integration belongs to the United Nations Economic Commission for Latin America (ECLA), upon whose initiative a Central American Economic Cooperation Committee was formed in 1952. With a membership comprising the ministers of economy of the five countries, and assisted by several specialized subcommittees and various regional agencies, this committee has been in charge of the program ever since. It took almost ten years, however, to create the basic preconditions for the economic cooperation mechanism embodied in the General Treaty on Central American Economic Integration, signed in Managua, Nicaragua, in December 1960. It is generally agreed, within as well as outside the region, that the key factors responsible for the relative success of the Central American integration experiment during its preparatory stages and its first five years of existence were the concurrent and rapidly growing availability of a cohesive group of government officials, a continuous flow of technical assistance from ECLA, a series of systematic surveys and studies of Central America's resources and growth potential, and increasing experience with the problems involved in trade liberalization.

The first formal multilateral cooperation mechanism in the region was the Multilateral Treaty on Free Trade and Central American Economic Integration signed by El Salvador, Guatemala, and Honduras in 1958. The treaty provided for the establishment of a common market through the gradual addition of products to the free trade list by interested parties over a period of ten years. Concurrently with the 1958 treaty, two other important regional agreements were reached: one on the establishment of a regional development bank (Central American Bank for Economic Integration) and another on the distribution of new industrial activities throughout the area under the Régime for Central American Integration Industries. Prior to these agreements, several regional institutes, such as the Central American Institute for Industrial Research and the Central American College for Public Administration, were established.

A new and broader treaty, signed in December 1960 in Managua, Nicaragua, by four of the Central American republics (with Costa Rica delaying its formal entry until July 1962) for the purpose of superseding the 1958 treaty, committed the contracting parties, in principle, to free all regional trade and establish a common market by mid-1966. A relatively brief list of exceptions was annexed to the Managua Treaty. It comprised those products whose immediate liberation from trade restraints, whether customs duties or quantitative restrictions, might seriously affect already existing productive activities or occasion substantial losses in fiscal revenue. Four different kinds of special treatment were reserved for goods appearing on the list of exceptions. The first involved the application, over a maximum period of five years, of a preferential tariff based on a fixed or progressively descending rate. This treatment was to be applied generally to those consumer goods manufactured in individual member countries that would require time to adjust to new regional competitive conditions. The second type of special treatment, amounting to import or export controls or import quotas, was to be applied to certain basic foodstuffs. The third type of treatment was to cover a limited number of nondurable consumer goods, which were to be permitted to enter free trade only after customs duties equalization had been achieved in respect to both finished products and raw materials.

Finally, special treatment was also reserved for certain items to be produced by industrial plants established on a regional basis.

By mid-1966 about 98 per cent of the tariffs on items in intra–Central American trade had been eliminated. Uniform customs duties against the rest of the world had been introduced for over 80 per cent of the national import tariff items; the remaining customs duties are to be equalized gradually over an additional five-year period. Attempts to cut progressively the list of exceptions — which still contains a number of important commodities, including transportation equipment, electric appliances, crude and refined oil, and some agricultural products — also are proceeding successfully. These goods, which in 1966 accounted for about one fourth of the Central American exports, are expected to enter free intrazonal trade and have uniform external tariffs by 1970. It is also anticipated that by 1970 the area will have a common customs administration.

The Managua Treaty's immediate freeing of a large proportion of actual and potential trade, made possible by the relatively low level of industrialization and by the absence of large disparities in over-all development, spared the Central American countries the complicated and bitter trade negotiations that represent a major stumbling block of the Latin American Free Trade Association. Consequently, intrazonal trade expanded very rapidly. Intra–Central American exports f.o.b. rose from $36.9 million in 1961 to about $175 million — according to preliminary figures — in 1966. Their share in the region's total export trade increased during the same period from 8 to over 20 per cent. A considerable diversification of trade composition by products was registered concurrently. Trade in manufactures, including chemicals, represented 64 per cent of intrazonal commercial transactions in 1965. Although Guatemala and El Salvador, the two relatively more industrialized Central American republics, continue to account for some 60 per cent of the total intraregional trade, the rate of increase in trade flows to and from Costa Rica, Honduras, and Nicaragua exceeds that of the two more advanced countries. Except for Nicaragua, which has a traditional trade deficit with the Common Market, no major commercial imbalances seem to be emerging, contrary to fears expressed in Costa Rica and Honduras in the early stages of regional cooperation. In view of its backwardness relative to the rest of the area, Honduras received some unilateral trade and nontrade concessions from the other member countries.

The establishment of the Central American Common Market brought about a considerable increase in foreign capital inflow. The clear preference shown by foreign direct investors in recent years for buying out of already existing and locally owned industrial firms tends to make foreign capital participation in the Common Market a political issue of growing importance. The future distribution of new region-oriented industrial activities is potentially another difficult issue. The impressive intrazonal expansion of trade registered since the end of the 1950s has resulted mainly from the modernization and fuller use of the capacity of existing productive facilities, especially in consumer manufactures. However, relatively little investment has gone into new industrial activities, and the Régime for Central American Integration Industries cannot yet be considered a success. Extensive suspicion of foreign investment is compounded in some member countries of the Common Market by the fear that any acceleration of industrial growth may lead to the concentration of new industries in the two more advanced countries (Guatemala and El Salvador). Conversely, the conviction is growing both among public officials directly involved in the Central American integration program and among private entrepreneurs that the absence of substantial new investment in the industrial sector may lead to the progressive stagnation of intrazonal trade at its present level.

After more than half a decade of Central American success with the free trade experiment, attention is thus being shifted to issues such as regional investment policy and the distribution of new industrial activities. The existence of the Central American Bank for Economic Integration and of various regional cooperation mechanisms in the monetary, industrial research, and public administration training fields is extremely helpful to the Central American Common Market. Considerable assistance is also expected from the Fund for Economic Integration, established in 1965 at the Central American Bank with United States financial aid. It is generally agreed within the area that the basis for close economic integration has already been established in Central America and that with additional external aid the Common Market may be able to contribute in a decisive way to the modernization and the diversification of the economies of the five participating countries.

The issue of the link between the Central American Common Market and the Latin American Free Trade Association was raised at the Meeting of American Chiefs of State held in Punta del Este, Uruguay, in April 1967. It was agreed on that occasion that LAFTA and CACM "will initiate simultaneously a process of convergence" into a Latin American common market to be established progressively by 1985. The heads of state of the five Central American republics committed themselves, among other things, to acceleration of their subregional economic integration through the improvement of the customs union and the establishment of a monetary union, the completion of a regional network of infrastructure, the development of a common foreign trade policy, the implementation of a joint coordinated industrial policy, and the harmonization of basic economic legislation. The Punta del Este agreement also calls for closer ties between the CACM and Panama and for the expansion of trade and investment relations between Central America and the Caribbean area. No deadlines were set for the implementation of this CACM program, which presumably will be set in motion gradually starting in 1970.

Bibliographic References

Castillo, Carlos. *Growth and Integration in Central America.* New York: Frederick A. Praeger, 1967.

Cochrane, J. D. "United States Attitudes Towards Central American Integration," *Inter-American Economic Affairs* (Washington, D.C.), Autumn 1964.

Economic Commission for Latin America. *Multilateral Economic Co-operation in Latin America,* Vol. I: *Texts and Documents.* (United Nations Publication, Sales No. 62.II.G.3.) New York: United Nations, Department of Economic and Social Affairs, 1962.

———. *Possibilities for Integrated Industrial Development in Central America.* New York: United Nations, 1964.

Hansen, Roger D. *Central America: Regional Integration and Economic Development.* Washington, D.C.: National Planning Association, 1967.

Herrarte, Alberto. *La unión de Centroamérica.* Segunda Edición. Guatemala City: Centro Editorial del Ministerio de Educación Pública, 1964.

Mills, Joseph C. "Problems of Central American Industrialization." In Miguel S. Wionczek, ed., *Latin American Intergration: Experiences and Prospects.* New York: Frederick A. Praeger, 1966.

Moscarella, Joseph. "Economic Integration in Central America." In Wionczek, *Latin American Integration.*

Nye, Joseph S., Jr. *Central American Regional Integration.* Carnegie Endowment for International Peace, *International Conciliation* (New York), No. 562 (March 1967).

Pincus, Joseph. *The Central American Common Market.* Mexico City: U.S. Department of State, Agency for International Development, September 1962.

Wionczek, Miguel S. "Experiences of the Central American Economic Integration as Applied to East Africa," *Industrialization and Productivity* (United Nations, New York), Bulletin 11 (1968).

GENERAL TREATY ON CENTRAL AMERICAN ECONOMIC INTEGRATION*

The Governments of the Republics of Guatemala, El Salvador, Honduras and Nicaragua,

For the purpose of reaffirming their intention to unify the economies of the four countries and jointly to promote the development of Central America in order to improve the living conditions of their peoples,

Mindful of the need to expedite the integration of their economies, consolidate the results so far achieved and lay down the principles on which it should be based in the future,

Having regard to the commitments entered into in the following instruments of economic integration:

Multilateral Treaty on Free Trade and Central American Economic Integration;

Central American Agreement on the Equalization of Import Duties and Charges and its Protocol on the Central American Preferential Tariff;

Bilateral treaties on free trade and economic integration signed between Central American Governments;

Treaty on Economic Association signed between Guatemala, El Salvador and Honduras,

Have agreed to conclude the present Treaty and for that purpose have appointed as their respective plenipotentiaries:

H.E. The President of the Republic of Guatemala: Mr. *Julio Prado García Salas*, Minister for Co-ordinating Central American Integration, and Mr. *Alberto Fuentes Mohr*, Head of the Economic Integration Bureau

* Signed by Guatemala, El Salvador, Honduras, and Nicaragua in Managua, Nicaragua, December 13, 1960, and adhered to by Costa Rica on July 23, 1962. The text reproduced here is an unofficial translation from the Spanish prepared by the United Nations Economic Commission for Latin America (ECLA) and published in United Nations, Department of Economic and Social Affairs, *Multilateral Economic Co-operation in Latin America*, Vol. I: *Text and Documents* (Sales No. 62.II.G.3; New York, 1962). [Editor's note.]

The H. Junta de Gobierno of the Republic of El Salvador: Mr. *Gabriel Piloña Araujo,* Minister for Economic Affairs, and Mr. *Abelardo Torres,* Under-Secretary for Economic Affairs

H.E. The President of the Republic of Honduras: Mr. *Jorge Bueso Arias,* Minister for Economic and Financial Affairs

H.E. The President of the Republic of Nicaragua: Mr. *Juan José Lugo Marenco,* Minister for Economic Affairs

who, having exchanged their respective full powers, found to be in good and due form, have agreed as follows:

CHAPTER I: CENTRAL AMERICAN COMMON MARKET

ARTICLE I

The Contracting States agree to establish among themselves a common market which shall be brought into full operation within a period of not more than five years from the date on which the present Treaty enters into force. They further agree to create a customs union in respect of their territories.

ARTICLE II

For the purposes of the previous article the Contracting Parties undertake to bring a Central American free-trade area into full operation within a period of five years and to adopt a standard Central American tariff as provided for in the Central American Agreement on the Equalization of Import Duties and Charges.

CHAPTER II: TRADE REGIME

ARTICLE III

The Signatory States shall grant each other free-trade treatment in respect of all products originating in their respective territories, save only for the limitations contained in the special régimes referred to in Annex A of the present Treaty.

Consequently, the natural products of the Contracting States and the products manufactured therein shall be exempt from import and export duties including consular fees, and all other taxes, dues and charges levied on imports and exports or charged in respect thereof, whether they be of a national, municipal or any other nature.

The exemptions provided for in this article shall not include charges or fees for lighterage, wharfage, warehousing or handling of goods, or any other charges which may legally be incurred for port, storage or transport services;

nor shall they include exchange differentials resulting from the existence of two or more rates of exchange or from other exchange arrangements in any of the Contracting States.

Goods originating in the territory of any of the Signatory States shall be accorded national treatment in all of them and shall be exempt from all quantitative or other restrictions or measures, except for such measures as may be legally applicable in the territories of the Contracting States for reasons of health, security or police control.

ARTICLE IV

The Contracting Parties establish special interim régimes in respect of specific products exempting them from the immediate free-trade treatment referred to in article III hereof. These products shall be automatically incorporated into the free-trade régime not later than the end of the fifth year in which the present Treaty is in force, except as specifically provided in Annex A.

The products to which special régimes apply are listed in Annex A and trade in them shall be carried on in conformity with the measures and conditions therein specified. These measures and conditions shall not be amended except by multilateral negotiation in the Executive Council. Annex A is an integral part of this Treaty.

The Signatory States agree that the Protocol on the Central American Preferential Tariff, appended to the Central American Agreement on the Equalization of Import Duties and Charges, shall not apply to trade in the products referred to in the present article for which special régimes are provided.

ARTICLE V

Goods enjoying the advantages stipulated in this Treaty shall be designated as such on a customs form, signed by the exporter and containing a declaration of origin. This form shall be produced for checking by the customs officers of the countries of origin and destination, in conformity with Annex B of this Treaty.

If there is doubt as to the origin of an article and the matter has not been settled by bilateral negotiation, any of the Parties affected may request the intervention of the Executive Council to verify the origin of the article concerned. The Council shall not consider goods as originating in one of the Contracting States if they originate or are manufactured in a third country and are only simply assembled, wrapped, packed, cut or diluted in the exporting country.

In the cases mentioned in the previous paragraph, importation of the goods concerned shall not be prohibited provided that a guaranty is given to the importing country in respect of payment of the import duties and other charges to which the goods may be liable. The guaranty shall be either forfeited or refunded, as the case may be, when the matter is finally settled.

The Executive Council shall lay down regulations governing the procedure to be followed in determining the origin of goods.

ARTICLE VI

If the goods traded are liable to internal taxes, charges or duties of any kind levied on production, sale, distribution or consumption in any of the signatory countries, the country concerned may levy an equivalent amount on similar goods imported from the other Contracting State, in which case it must also levy at least an equivalent amount for the same respective purposes on similar imports from third countries.

The Contracting Parties agree that the following conditions shall apply to the establishment of internal taxes on consumption:

a. Such taxes may be established in the amount deemed necessary when there is domestic production of the article in question, or when the article is not produced in any of the Signatory States;

b. When the article is not produced in one Signatory State but is produced in any of the others, the former State may not establish taxes on consumption of the article concerned unless the Executive Council so authorizes;

c. If a Contracting Party has established a domestic tax on consumption, and production of the article so taxed is subsequently begun in any of the other Signatory States, but the article is not produced in the State that established the tax, the Executive Council shall, if the State concerned so requests, deal with the case and decide whether the tax is compatible with free trade. The States undertake to abolish these taxes on consumption, in accordance with their legal procedures, on receipt of notification to this effect from the Executive Council.

ARTICLE VII

No Signatory State shall establish or maintain regulations on the distribution or retailing of goods originating in another Signatory State when such regulations place, or tend to place, the said goods in an unfavourable position in relation to similar goods of domestic origin or imported from any other country.

ARTICLE VIII

Items which, by virtue of the domestic legislation of the Contracting Parties, constitute State monopolies on the date of entry into force of the present Treaty, shall remain subject to the relevant legislation of each country and, if applicable, to the provisions of Annex A of the present Treaty.

Should new monopolies be created or the régime of existing monopolies be changed, the Parties shall enter into consultations for the purpose of placing Central American trade in the items concerned under a special régime.

CHAPTER III: EXPORT SUBSIDIES AND
UNFAIR TRADE PRACTICES

ARTICLE IX

The Governments of the Signatory States shall not grant customs exemptions or reductions in respect of imports from outside Central America of articles adequately produced in the Contracting States.

If a Signatory State deems itself to be affected by the granting of customs import franchises or by governmental imports not intended for the use of the Government itself or of its agencies, it may submit the matter to the Executive Council for its consideration and ruling.

ARTICLE X

The Central Banks of the Signatory States shall co-operate closely in order to prevent any currency speculation that might affect the rates of exchange and to maintain the convertibility of the currencies of the respective countries on a basis which, in normal conditions, shall guarantee the freedom, uniformity and stability of exchange.

Any Signatory State which establishes quantitative restrictions on international monetary transfers shall adopt whatever measures are necessary to ensure that such restrictions do not discriminate against the other States.

Should serious balance-of-payments difficulties arise which affect, or are apt to affect, monetary relations in respect of payments between the Signatory States, the Executive Council, acting of its own accord or at the request of one of the Parties, shall immediately study the problem in co-operation with the Central Banks for the purpose of recommending to the Signatory States a satisfactory solution compatible with the maintenance of the multilateral free-trade régime.

ARTICLE XI

No Signatory State shall grant any direct or indirect subsidy favouring the export of goods intended for the territory of the other States, or establish or maintain any system resulting in the sale of such goods for export to any other Contracting State at a price lower than that established for the sale of similar goods on the domestic market, due allowance being made for differences in the conditions and terms of sale and taxation and for any other factors affecting price comparability.

Any measure involving the fixing of, or discrimination in, prices in a Signatory State which is reflected in the establishment of sales prices for specific goods in the other Contracting States at levels lower than those that would result from the normal operation of the market in the exporting country shall be deemed to constitute an indirect export subsidy.

If the importation of goods processed in a Contracting State with raw materials purchased under conditions of monopoly at artificially low prices should threaten existing production in another Signatory State, the Party which considers itself affected shall submit the matter to the consideration of the Executive Council for a ruling as to whether an unfair business practice is in fact involved. The Executive Council shall, within five days of the receipt of the request, either give its ruling or authorize a temporary suspension of free trade, while permitting trade to be carried on subject to the award of a guaranty in the amount of the customs duties. This suspension shall be effective for thirty days, within which period the Executive Council shall announce its final decision. If no ruling is forthcoming within the five days stipulated, the Party concerned may demand a guaranty pending the Executive Council's final decision.

However, tax exemptions of a general nature granted by a Signatory State with a view to encouraging production shall not be deemed to constitute export subsidies.

Similarly, any exemption from internal taxes levied in the exporting State on the production, sale or consumption of goods exported to the territory of another State shall not be deemed to constitute an export subsidy. The differentials resulting from the sale of foreign currency on the free market at a rate of exchange higher than the official rate shall not normally be deemed to be an export subsidy; if one of the Contracting States is in doubt, however, the matter shall be submitted to the Executive Council for its consideration and opinion.

ARTICLE XII

As a means of precluding a practice which would be inconsistent with the purposes of this Treaty, each Signatory State shall employ all the legal means at its disposal to prevent the export of goods from its territory to the territories of the other States at a price lower than their normal value, if such export would prejudice or be liable to prejudice the production of the other States or retard the establishment of a national or Central American industry.

Goods shall be deemed to be exported at a price lower than their normal value if their export price is less than:

a. The comparable price in normal trade conditions of similar goods destined for domestic consumption in the exporting country; or

b. The highest comparable price of similar goods for export to a third country in normal trade conditions; or

c. The cost of production of the goods in the country of origin, plus a reasonable amount for sales expenses and profit.

Due allowance shall be made in every case for existing differences in conditions and terms of sale and taxation and for any other factors affecting price comparability.

ARTICLE XIII

If a Contracting Party deems that unfair trade practices not covered in article XI exist, it cannot impede trade by a unilateral decision but must bring the matter before the Executive Council so that the latter can decide whether in fact such practices are being resorted to. The Council shall announce its decision within not more than 60 days from the date on which it received the relevant communication.

If any Party deems that there is evidence of unfair trade, it shall request the Executive Council to authorize it to demand a guaranty in the amount of the import duties.

Should the Executive Council fail to give a ruling within eight days, the Party concerned may demand such guaranty pending the Executive Council's final decision.

ARTICLE XIV

Once the Executive Council has given its ruling on unfair trade practices, it shall inform the Contracting Parties whether, in conformity with this Treaty, protective measures against such practices should be taken.

CHAPTER IV: TRANSIT AND TRANSPORT

ARTICLE XV

Each of the Contracting States shall ensure full freedom of transit through its territory for goods proceeding to or from the other Signatory States as well as for the vehicles transporting these goods.

Such transit shall not be subject to any deduction, discrimination or quantitative restriction. In the event of traffic congestion or other instances of *force majeure*, each Signatory State shall treat the mobilization of consignments intended for its own population and those in transit to the other States on an equitable basis.

Transit operations shall be carried out by the routes prescribed by law for that purpose and shall be subject to the customs and transit laws and regulations applicable in the territory of transit.

Goods in transit shall be exempt from all duties, taxes and other charges of a fiscal, municipal or any other character levied on transit, irrespective of their destination, but may be liable to the charges usually applied for services rendered which shall in no case exceed the cost thereof and thus constitute *de facto* import duties or taxes.

CHAPTER V: CONSTRUCTION ENTERPRISES

ARTICLE XVI

The Contracting States shall grant national treatment to enterprises of other Signatory States engaged in the construction of roads, bridges, dams, irrigation systems, electrification, housing and other works intended to further the development of the Central American economic infrastructure.

CHAPTER VI: INDUSTRIAL INTEGRATION

ARTICLE XVII

The Contracting Parties hereby endorse all the provisions of the Agreement on the Régime for Central American Integration Industries, and, in order to ensure implementation among themselves as soon as possible, undertake to sign, within a period of not more than six months from the date of entry into force of the present Treaty, additional protocols specifying the industrial plants initially to be covered by the Agreement, the free trade régime applicable to their products and the other conditions provided for in article III of the Agreement.

CHAPTER VII: CENTRAL AMERICAN BANK FOR ECONOMIC INTEGRATION

ARTICLE XVIII

The Signatory States agree to establish the Central American Bank for Economic Integration which shall be a juridical person. The Bank shall act as an instrument for the financing and promotion of a regionally balanced, integrated economic growth. To that end they shall sign the agreement constituting the Bank, which shall remain open for the signature or accession of any other Central American State which may wish to become a member of the Bank.

It is, however, established that members of the Bank may not obtain guaranties or loans from the Bank unless they have previously deposited their instruments of ratification of the following international agreements:

The present Treaty;

Multilateral Treaty on Free Trade and Central American Economic Integration, signed on 10 June 1958;

Agreement on the Régime for Central American Integration Industries, signed on 10 June 1958; and

Central American Agreement on the Equalization of Import Duties and Charges, signed on 1 September 1959, and its *Protocol* signed on the same day as the present Treaty.

CHAPTER VIII: TAX INCENTIVES TO INDUSTRIAL DEVELOPMENT

ARTICLE XIX

The Contracting States, with a view to establishing uniform tax incentives to industrial development, agree to ensure as soon as possible a reasonable equalization of the relevant laws and regulations in force. To that end they shall, within a period of six months from the date of entry into force of the present Treaty, sign a special protocol specifying the amount and type of exemptions, the time limits thereof, the conditions under which they shall be granted, the systems of industrial classification and the principles and procedures governing their application. The Executive Council shall be responsible for co-ordinating the application of the tax incentives to industrial development.

CHAPTER IX: ORGANS

ARTICLE XX

The Central American Economic Council, composed of the Ministers of Economic Affairs of the several Contracting Parties, is hereby established for the purpose of integrating the Central American economies and co-ordinating the economic policy of the Contracting States.

The Central American Economic Council shall meet as often as required or at the request of any of the Contracting Parties. It shall examine the work of the Executive Council and adopt such resolutions as it may deem appropriate. The Central American Economic Council shall be the organ responsible for facilitating implementation of the resolutions on economic integration adopted by the Central American Economic Co-operation Committee. It may seek the advice of Central American and international technical organs.

ARTICLE XXI

For the purpose of applying and administering the present Treaty and of undertaking all the negotiations and work designed to give practical effect to the Central American economic union, an Executive Council, consisting of one titular official and one alternate appointed by each Contracting Party, is hereby established.

The Executive Council shall meet as often as required, at the request of one of the Contracting Parties or when convened by the Permanent Secretariat, and its resolutions shall be adopted by majority vote. In the event of disagreement, recourse will be had to the Central American Economic Council in order that the latter may give a final ruling.

Before ruling on a matter, the Executive Council shall determine unanimously whether the matter is to be decided by a concurrent vote of all its members or by a simple majority.

ARTICLE XXII

The Executive Council shall take such measures as it may deem necessary to ensure fulfilment of the commitments entered into under this Treaty and to settle problems arising from the implementation of its provisions. It may likewise propose to the Governments the signing of such additional multilateral agreements as may be required in order to achieve the purpose of Central American economic integration, including a customs union in respect of their territories.

The Executive Council shall assume, on behalf of the Contracting Parties, the functions assigned to the Central American Trade Commission in the Multilateral Treaty on Free Trade and Central American Economic Integration and the Central American Agreement on the Equalization of Import Duties and Charges, as well as those assigned to the Central American Industrial Integration Commission in the Agreement on the Régime for Central American Integration Industries, as well as the powers and duties of the joint commissions set up under bilateral treaties in force between the Contracting Parties.

ARTICLE XXIII

A Permanent Secretariat is hereby instituted, as a juridical person, and shall act as such both for the Central American Economic Council and the Executive Council established under this Treaty.

The Secretariat shall have its seat and headquarters in Guatemala City, capital of the Republic of Guatemala, and shall be headed by a Secretary-General appointed for a period of three years by the Central American Economic Council. The Secretariat shall establish such departments and sections as may be necessary for the performance of its functions. Its expenses shall be governed by a general budget adopted annually by the Central American Economic Council and each Contracting Party shall contribute annually to its support an amount equivalent to not less than fifty thousand United States dollars (US$50,000), payable in the respective currencies of the Signatory States.

Members of the Secretariat shall enjoy diplomatic immunity. Other diplomatic privileges shall be granted only to the Secretariat and to the Secretary-General.

ARTICLE XXIV

The Secretariat shall ensure that this Treaty, the Multilateral Treaty on Free Trade and Central American Economic Integration, the Agreement on the Régime for Central American Integration Industries, the Central American Agreement on the Equalization of Import Duties and Charges, bilateral or multilateral treaties on free trade and economic integration in force between any of the Contracting Parties, and all other agreements relating to Central American economic integration already signed or that may be signed hereafter, the interpretation of which has not been specifically entrusted to another organ, are properly executed among the Contracting Parties.

The Secretariat shall ensure implementation of the resolutions adopted by the Central American Economic Council and the Executive Council established under this Treaty and shall also perform such functions as are assigned to it by the Executive Council. Its regulations shall be approved by the Economic Council.

The Secretariat shall also undertake such work and studies as may be assigned to it by the Executive Council and the Central American Economic Council. In performing these duties, it shall avail itself of the studies and work carried out by other Central American and international organs and shall, where appropriate, enlist their co-operation.

CHAPTER X: GENERAL PROVISIONS

ARTICLE XXV

The Signatory States agree not to sign unilaterally with non-Central American countries any new treaties that may affect the principles of Central American economic integration. They further agree to maintain the "Central American exception clause" in any trade agreements they may conclude on the basis of most-favoured-nation treatment with any countries other than the Contracting States.

ARTICLE XXVI

The Signatory States agree to settle amicably, in the spirit of this Treaty, and through the Executive Council or the Central American Economic Council, as the case may be, any differences which may arise regarding the interpretation or application of any of its provisions. If agreement cannot be reached, they shall submit the matter to arbitration. For the purpose of constituting the arbitration tribunal, each Contracting Party shall propose to the General Secretariat of the Organization of Central American States the names of three magistrates from its Supreme Court of Justice. From the complete list of candidates, the Secretary-General of the Organization of Central American States and the Government representatives in the Organization shall select, by drawing lots, one arbitrator for each Contracting Party, no two of whom may be nationals of the same State. The award of the arbitration tribunal shall require the concurring votes of not less than three members, and shall have the effect of res judicata for all the Contracting Parties so far as it contains any ruling concerning the interpretation or application of the provisions of this Treaty.

ARTICLE XXVII

The present Treaty shall, with respect to the Contracting Parties, take precedence over the Multilateral Treaty on Free Trade and Central American Economic Integration and any other bilateral or multilateral free trade instruments signed between the Contracting Parties; it shall not, however, affect the validity of those agreements.

The provisions of the trade and economic integration agreements referred to in the previous paragraph shall be applied between the respective Contracting Parties in so far as they are not covered in the present Treaty.

Pending ratification of the present Treaty by any of the Contracting Parties, or in the event of its denunciation by any of them, the trade relations of the Party concerned with the other Signatory States shall be governed by the commitments entered into previously under the existing instruments referred to in the preamble of the present Treaty.

ARTICLE XXVIII

The Contracting Parties agree to hold consultations in the Executive Council prior to signing any new treaties among themselves which may affect free trade.

The Executive Council shall examine each case and determine the effects that the conclusion of such agreements might produce on the free trade régime established in the present Treaty. On the basis of the Executive Council's examination, the Party which considers itself affected by the conclusion of these new treaties may adopt whatever measures the Council may recommend in order to protect its interests.

ARTICLE XXIX

For the purposes of customs regulations relating to free trade, the transit of goods and the application of the Central American Standard Import Tariff, the Contracting Parties shall, within a period of one year from the date of entry into force of the present Treaty, sign special protocols providing for the adoption of a Central American Standard Customs Code and the necessary transport regulations.

CHAPTER XI: FINAL PROVISIONS

ARTICLE XXX

This Treaty shall be submitted for ratification in each State in conformity with its respective constitutional or legislative procedures.

The instruments of ratification shall be deposited with the General Secretariat of the Organization of Central American States.

The Treaty shall enter into force, in the case of the first three States to ratify it, eight days following the date of deposit of the third instrument of ratification and, in the case of the States which ratify it subsequently, on the date of deposit of the relevant instrument.

ARTICLE XXXI

This Treaty shall remain effective for a period of twenty years from the date of its entry into force and shall be renewable indefinitely.

Upon expiry of the twenty-year period mentioned in the previous paragraph, the Treaty may be denounced by any of the Contracting Parties. Denunciation shall take effect, for the denouncing State, five years after notification, and the Treaty shall remain in force among the other Contracting States so long as at least two of them remain parties thereto.

ARTICLE XXXII

The General Secretariat of the Organization of Central American States shall act as depositary of this Treaty and shall send a certified copy thereof to the Ministry of Foreign Affairs of each of the Contracting States and shall also notify them immediately of the deposit of each instrument of ratification as well as of any denunciation which may be made. When the Treaty enters into force, it shall also transmit a certified copy thereof to the Secretary-General of the United Nations for the purposes of registration as set forth in Article 102 of the United Nations Charter.

ARTICLE XXXIII

The present Treaty shall remain open for the accession of any Central American State not originally a party thereto.

PROVISIONAL ARTICLE

As soon as the Government of the Republic of Costa Rica formally accedes to the provisions of this Treaty, the organs hereby established shall form part of the Organization of Central American States (OCAS) by an incorporation agreement; and the OCAS shall be reorganized in such a way that the organs established by this Treaty retain all their structural and functional attributes.

In witness whereof the respective plenipotentiaries have signed the present Treaty in the City of Managua, capital of the Republic of Nicaragua, this thirteenth day of the month of December nineteen hundred and sixty.

DOCUMENT 6

AGREEMENT ON THE RÉGIME FOR CENTRAL AMERICAN INTEGRATION INDUSTRIES*

The Governments of the Republic of Guatemala, El Salvador, Honduras, Nicaragua and Costa Rica,

Having regard to the objectives of the Central American Economic Integration Programme which was undertaken through the Central American Economic Co-operation Committee and, in particular, to article XXI of the Central American Multilateral Free Trade and Economic Integration Treaty,

Desirous of strengthening the natural and traditional bonds of brotherhood which unite their countries, and of co-operating towards the solution of their common economic problems,

Having as their basic aim the improvement of the living standards of the Central American peoples and the rational use, for that purpose, of their natural resources, and being convinced that, within the economic development programmes of the Central American Isthmus, the integration of their economies offers favourable prospects for the expansion of trade between their countries and for a more rapid industrialization process on the basis of mutual interest,

Have decided to conclude the present Agreement, which prescribes a Régime for Central American Integration Industries, and for that purpose have appointed as their respective plenipotentiaries:

H.E. the President of the Republic of Guatemala: *José Guirola Leal,* Minister of Economic Affairs;

H.E. the President of the Republic of El Salvador: *Alfonso Rochac,* Minister of Economic Affairs;

H.E. the President of the Council of Ministers exercising the powers of the Executive of the Republic of Honduras: *Fernando Villar,* Minister of Economic Affairs and Finance;

---

* Signed by Guatemala, El Salvador, Honduras, Nicaragua, and Costa Rica in Tegucigalpa, Honduras, June 10, 1958. Guatemala signed "with a reservation regarding Article XI of this Treaty, in accordance with the provisions of paragraph 3, subparagraph (b) of Article 149 of the Constitution of the Republic." The text reproduced here is an unofficial ECLA translation published in United Nations, Department of Economic and Social Affairs, *Multilateral Economic Co-operation in Latin America,* Vol. I: *Text and Documents* (Sales No. 62.II.G.3; New York, 1962). [Editor's note].

H.E. the President of the Republic of Nicaragua: *Enrique Delgado,* Minister of Economic Affairs; and

H.E. the President of the Republic of Costa Rica: *Wilburg Jiménez Castro,* Vice-Minister of Economic Affairs and Finance

who, having exchanged their full powers, found in good and due form, have agreed as follows:

ARTICLE I

The Contracting States undertake to encourage and promote the establishment of new industries and the specialization and expansion of existing industries within the framework of Central American economic integration, and agree that the development of the various activities which are or may be included in such a programme shall be effected on a reciprocal and equitable basis in order that each and every Central American State may progressively derive economic advantages.

ARTICLE II

The Contracting States declare their interest in the development of industries with access to a common Central American market. These shall be designated Central American integration industries and shall be so declared jointly by the Contracting States, through the agency of the Central American Industrial Integration Commission established in conformity with article VIII of this Agreement.

The Contracting States shall regard as Central American integration industries those industries which, in the judgement of the Central American Industrial Integration Commission, comprise one or more plants which require access to the Central American market in order to operate under reasonably economic and competitive conditions even at minimum capacity.

ARTICLE III

The application of the present Régime to the Central American integration industries is subject to signature by the Contracting States, in respect of each of the said industries, of an additional protocol stipulating:

a. The country or countries in which the industrial plants covered by this Régime are to be initially situated, the minimum capacity of the said plants and the conditions under which additional plants are to be subsequently admitted into the same or other countries;

b. The quality standards for the products of the said industries and any other requirements that may be deemed convenient for the protection of the consumer;

c. The regulations that may be advisable as regards the participation of Central American capital in the enterprises owning the plants;

d. The common Central American tariffs which shall be applied to the products of Central American integration industries; and

e. Any other provisions designed to ensure the attainment of the objectives of this Agreement.

ARTICLE IV

The products of plants which form part of a Central American integration industry and which are covered by the present Régime, shall enjoy the benefits of free trade between the territories of the Contracting States.

The products of plants which form part of the same industry but which are not covered by the Régime, shall enjoy in the Contracting States successive annual reductions of ten per cent in the applicable uniform Central American tariff, from the date specified in the relevant additional protocol. As from the tenth year, such products shall enjoy the full benefits of free trade.

Except as provided in the preceding paragraph and in any other provisions of this Agreement or of the additional protocols, all trade in commodities produced by the Central American integration industries shall be governed by the provisions of the Central American Multilateral Free Trade and Economic Integration Treaty.

ARTICLE V

In conformity with the provisions of article IV of the Central American Multilateral Free Trade and Economic Integration Treaty, the Central American Trade Commission shall give priority consideration to the equalization of the customs duties and other charges levied upon imports of commodities that are similar to or substitutes for the commodities produced by the Central American integration industries covered by the additional protocols to this Agreement, as well as upon imports of raw materials and of the containers necessary for their production and distribution.

ARTICLE VI

Since the Contracting States intend to grant to the Central American integration industries ample fiscal incentives, the enterprises owning industrial plants covered by the present Régime shall enjoy, in the territory of the countries where such plants are or may be established, the benefits and exemptions prescribed by the national legislation of the country concerned.

ARTICLE VII

Except in cases of emergency, the Governments of the Contracting States shall not grant customs duty exemptions or reductions below the Central

American common tariff on any imports from countries outside Central America of goods which are equal or similar to or substitutes for goods manufactured in any of the Central American countries by plants of industrial integration industries, nor shall they apply to such imports preferential exchange rates equivalent to such exemptions or reductions.

The Governments and other State bodies shall also give preference in their official imports to the products of the Central American integration industries.

ARTICLE VIII

In order to ensure due application of this Agreement and of the additional protocols, the Contracting States agree to establish a Central American Industrial Integration Commission, to which each of the Contracting States shall appoint a special representative; the Commission shall meet as frequently as its work may require or at the request of any of the Contracting States.

The Commission or any of its members may travel freely in the Contracting States in order to study matters within the Commission's competence in the field, and the authorities of the Contracting States shall provided them with whatever information and facilities may be necessary for the proper discharge of their functions.

The Commission shall have a permanent secretariat which shall be under the responsibility of the General Secretariat of the Organization of Central American States.

The Commission shall adopt its rules of procedure unanimously and shall prescribe the regulations relating to the conduct of matters within its competence, in particular the regulations relating to the conditions and form in which, in each specific case, the views of private enterprise shall be heard.

ARTICLE IX

Individuals or bodies corporate desiring the incorporation of a given plant into the present Régime shall present an application to that effect to the Secretariat of the Central American Industrial Integration Commission and accompany it with the required information.

When the Secretariat has sufficient information available, it shall advise the Commission of the application. If the Commission finds that the project meets the aims of this Agreement, the application shall be referred for an opinion to the Central American Research Institute for Industry or to any other person or body that the Commission considers competent. Such opinion shall take into account the technological and economic aspects of the project and, in particular, the market prospects, and the costs incurred shall be borne by the interested parties.

The Commission shall decide on the project on the basis of the said opinion, and if it finds the project capable of being realized, shall make whatever recommendations it considers pertinent to the Governments of the Contracting

States on the conclusion of the protocol covering the industry concerned and on the conditions to be stipulated.

When the projecct refers to a plant which forms part of an industry already covered by a protocol, the Commission may, in conformity with the terms of the relevant protocol and of this article, declare that the plant shall be admitted to the benefits of the present Régime and advise to that effect the Governments of the Contracting States.

ARTICLE X

The Central American Industrial Integration Commission shall submit an annual report on its activities to the Contracting States.

The Commission shall periodically carry out studies with a view to enabling the Governments to evaluate the results of the application of the present Régime.

The Commission may propose to the Contracting States measures favourable to the development of the Central American integration industries and to the efficient functioning of their plants. The Commission may also propose to the Governments any measures necessary to resolve any problems arising from the application of this Agreement.

ARTICLE XI

The Contracting States agree to settle amicably, in the spirit of this Agreement, any differences which may arise in the interpretation or application of any of its provisions or of the additional protocols. If agreement cannot be reached, they shall submit the matter to arbitration. For the purpose of constituting the arbitral tribunal, each Contracting State shall propose to the General Secretariat of the Organization of Central American States the names of three judges from its Supreme Court of Justice. From the complete list of candidates, the Secretary-General of the Organization of Central American States and the Government representatives in the Organization shall select, by drawing lots, a tribunal composed of five arbitrators, no two of whom may be nationals of the same State. The award of the arbitral tribunal shall require the concurring votes of not less than three members and shall be binding on all the Contracting States so far as it contains any ruling concerning the interpretation or application of the provisions of this Agreement and of the additional protocols.

ARTICLE XII

This Agreement shall be submitted for ratification in each Contracting State in conformity with its respective constitutional or legislative procedures.

This Agreement shall come into force on the date of deposit of the last instrument of ratification. It shall remain in force for twenty years and shall be tacitly renewable for successive periods of ten years.

Any Contracting State may withdraw from this Agreement provided that notice of withdrawal is given not later than two years before the date on which the initial or any other subsequent period of validity expires.

If a Contracting State gives notice of withdrawal after the prescribed time limit but before a new period of validity has commenced, such notification shall be valid, but the Agreement shall remain in force for two further years after the beginning of the new period.

In the event of denunciation of this Agreement, the same shall remain in force as regards its additional protocols until the expiry of the latter.

Should a Contracting State denounce this Agreement, the other Contracting States shall determine whether the Agreement shall cease to have effect between all the Contracting States or whether it shall be maintained between such Contracting States as have not denounced it.

The additional protocols to this Agreement shall be approved in conformity with the constitutional or legislative procedures of each country.

ARTICLE XIII

The General Secretariat of the Organization of Central American States shall act as depositary of this Agreement and shall send a certified copy thereof to the Ministry of Foreign Affairs of each of the Contracting States. It shall also notify the Contracting States of the deposit of the relevant instruments of ratification as well as of any denunciation which may occur within the prescribed time-limit. When the Agreement comes into force, it shall also transmit a certified copy thereof to the Secretary-General of the United Nations, for registration in conformity with Article 102 of the United Nations Charter.

TRANSITIONAL ARTICLE

In order to promote an equitable distribution of the Central American industrial integration plants, the Contracting States shall not award a second plant to any one country until all of the five Central American countries have each been assigned a plant in conformity with the protocols specified in article III.

In witness whereof the respective plenipotentiaries have signed this Agreement.

Done in the city of Tegucigalpa, D.C., capital of the Republic of Honduras, on June 10, 1958.

CHAPTER THREE

Caribbean Free Trade Association

The idea of political and economic cooperation among British colonial territories in the Caribbean was discussed for the first time in the final decades of the nineteenth century. It originated in that period with local white elites bent upon increasing their negotiating power in commercial matters vis-à-vis the metropolis. Nothing came from these plans, and the issue of regional cooperation was revived more than a half century later in a completely different political context — the final stage of British direct rule in the West Indies.

The Federation of the West Indies, comprising eleven islands with a total population of slightly over three million, was established in 1958, but it disintegrated three years later when the largest participant, Jamaica, decided to secede. The reasons for the Federation's demise were both political and economic. The Federation of the West Indies was considered by the local populations as a British stratagem aimed at shifting the major part of the burden of the financial support of the lesser Caribbean islands from the British Treasury to the area itself. The participating territories were offered a large measure of self-government and dominion status in exchange for the commitment on the part of the larger islands (Jamaica and Trinidad) to put a part of their own fiscal resources at the disposal of the small and very backward members of the Federation and to free the movement of labor throughout the area. This last issue and the relative power of the federal government became especially intractable during both the pre-1958 negotiations and the short life of the scheme. The lesser Caribbean islands (Antigua, Barbados, and Grenada, among others) insisted on the free movement of people in the region and a strong federal government. Jamaica and Trinidad were neither willing to open their doors to immigration from the poorer islands nor to give them political power in the Federation. Although all the participants in the short-lived Federation are clearly very underdeveloped, the differences in their relative level of development and the political consequences of this situation doomed the Federation from its start. In the years following the end of the Federation, all the major islands (Jamaica, Trinidad and Tobago, and Barbados) became independent, while the lesser islands achieved a status of self-rule within the Commonwealth. Of the two British possessions on the mainland bordering the Caribbean Sea (British Guiana and British Honduras), British Guiana achieved full independence in 1966.

While no economic rapprochement took place in the region during the period of its progressive decolonization, a limited agreement on trade liberalization was negotiated between the then British Guiana, Barbados, and Antigua in the fall of 1965. It led to the signing by the three interested parties on December 15, 1965 of an Agreement establishing the Caribbean Free Trade Association (CARIFTA). The Principal Agreement, amplified by a Supplementary Agreement signed in December 1966, was to be ratified by the respective governments before the end of 1967. The CARIFTA arrangement of 1965 was modeled upon the European Free Trade Association treaty, and its purpose was "to promote the expansion and diversification of trade in the area of the Association." All basic commodities, listed in one of the annexes to the agreement, were to enjoy free trade under the condition that they contain no imported inputs. Import duties on manufactures were to be eliminated gradually over a five-year period ending on January 1, 1971. Only manufactures with a minimum 50 per cent value added through processing in the member countries were to qualify for free trade treatment. Quantitative restrictions on imports from the area were to be lifted, but they could be reintroduced in the case of balance-of-payments difficulties. CARIFTA was to be managed by a Council in which each country would have one vote, and all decisions would be taken unanimously. The Agreement was open for the accession of other countries in the region, and its preamble suggested a possibility of "the ultimate creation of a viable economic community of Caribbean Territories."

In October 1967 a Conference of Heads of Government of the Commonwealth Caribbean countries (four independent states — Barbados, Guyana, Jamaica, and Trinidad — and seven self-governing British territories — Antigua, Dominica, Grenada, Montserrat, St. Kitts, St. Lucia, and St. Vincent), held in Barbados, proposed the establishment of a widened free trade area based on the original CARIFTA agreement with necessary modifications. Officials of the eleven Caribbean countries met in Jamaica in December 1967 and agreed that the government of Guyana would prepare a draft of a supplementary agreement to the 1965 CARIFTA convention for discussion and final approval at a regional meeting of Ministers of Trade set for February 1968. The ministerial meeting was held in Georgetown, Guyana, with participation of all Commonwealth Caribbean countries but Jamaica. However, after the Ministers of Trade meeting had approved with certain amendments the supplementary agreement and had submitted it for the signature of all the eleven countries, Jamaica made public at the end of March 1968 its decision to join the enlarged CARIFTA. The major issue that gave rise to Jamaica's absence from the Georgetown negotiations was that while other participating countries enjoy duty-free imports of raw materials, after independence the Jamaican government introduced import taxes on these commodities. It is understood that before announcing its decision to adhere to the new CARIFTA agreement, Jamaica's authorities promised local producers to lift import duties on raw materials to be used in processing goods for export to the area.

Antigua, Barbados, and Guyana became members of the enlarged CARIFTA automatically. Six remaining smaller territories joined it in April 1968, and Jamaica signed the agreement in late June 1968.

The Georgetown agreement basically follows the 1965 CARIFTA agreement in that it provides for the establishment of a limited-in-scope free trade zone by May 1, 1968. Immediate elimination of import duties and quantitative restrictions will affect the commodities traded within the area — as long as they fulfill certain area origin requirements — with the exception of two major groups: (a) goods subject to specific agreements entered into by any member with a third country before February 22, 1968, and (b) goods expressly enumerated in annexes to the agreement. Duties and other restrictions on the commodities belonging to the second group will be eliminated gradually over a five-year period in the more advanced CARIFTA member countries (Jamaica, Trinidad and Tobago, Barbados, and Guyana) and over a ten-year period in the smaller self-governing territories.

Intra-area trade in agricultural commodities is subject to special marketing arrangements. The 1968 CARIFTA agreement provides for rudimentary regional cooperation in respect to the approximation of investment incentives legislation and for periodic consultations on economic and financial policies. The operation of the agreement will be supervised by a Council in which each member country will have one vote. On all matters of substance, decisions are to be taken unanimously, and in remaining cases by a two thirds majority. A Regional Secretariat was established to administer the implementation of the free trade zone provision, with financial contributions for the upkeep of that regional agency ranging from 39 per cent for Jamaica to 0.7 per cent for Montserrat.

In 1964 the value of trade among the eleven Commonwealth Caribbean countries, half of them re-exports, amounted to $31.2 million, less than 4 per cent of the total imports of the area. Petroleum and rice (both subject to special arrangements under CARIFTA) constituted 50 per cent of the Commonwealth Caribbean trade, and Guyana and Trinidad were responsible for three quarters of the regional trade. Smaller territories represent important and growing outlets for manufactures produced in Jamaica, Barbados, and Trinidad. Fifteen per cent of the Jamaican exports of manufactured goods were sold in the area in 1964. The Leeward and Windward islands accounted for 15 per cent of Trinidad's total export trade.

Independently from the CARIFTA arrangement, a project for a Caribbean Development Bank with external financial backing was submitted for the consideration of the Commonwealth Caribbean countries (including the Bahamas and British Honduras, which do not participate in the CARIFTA arrangement) by the U.N. Development Program in mid-1967. A meeting of technical experts, held in Georgetown, Guyana, in August 1967 approved the project, but Jamaica's unwillingness to join the Bank postponed its establishment. The project set the Caribbean Development Bank's initial capital at $50 million, 60 per cent of which was to be subscribed within the area and the rest by the United States, Canada, and Great Britain.

Bibliographic References

Beckford, G. L., and M. H. Guscott. *Intra-Caribbean Agricultural Trade.* University of the West Indies, Institute of Social and Economic Research, *Studies in Regional Economic Integration*, Vol. 2, No. 2. Jamaica, 1967.

Brewster, Havelock, and Clive Y. Thomas. *The Dynamics of West Indian Economic Integration.* University of the West Indies, Institute of Social and Economic Research, *Studies in Regional Economic Integration*, Vol. 1. Jamaica, 1967.

Demas, William G. *The Economics of Development in Small Countries, with Special Reference to the Caribbean.* Montreal: McGill University Press, 1965.

Segal, Aaron. *The Politics of Caribbean Economic Integration.* University of Puerto Rico, Institute of Caribbean Studies, Special Study No. 6. Río Piedras, Puerto Rico, 1968.

CARIBBEAN FREE TRADE ASSOCIATION: TEXT CONSOLIDATING THE PROVISIONS OF THE PRINCIPAL AGREEMENT AND THE SUPPLEMENTARY AGREEMENT*

The Governments of the Signatory Territories:

Sharing a common determination to fulfill within the shortest possible time the hopes and aspirations of the peoples of the Caribbean Territories for full employment and improved living standards;

Conscious that these goals can most rapidly be attained by the optimum use of available human and other resources and by accelerated, co-ordinated, and sustained economic development;

Aware that the broadening of domestic markets through the elimination of barriers to trade between the Territories is a prerequisite to such development;

Convinced that such elimination of barriers to trade can best be achieved by the immediate establishment of a free trade area which will contribute to the ultimate creation of a viable economic community of Caribbean Territories;

Mindful of the different levels of development attained by the Territories of the Caribbean;

Have agreed as follows:

---

* Signed by Antigua, Barbados, and British Guiana at Dickenson Bay, Antigua, December 15, 1965. The Supplementary Agreement was signed, after British Guiana achieved independence under the new name of Guyana, by Antigua in Georgetown, Guyana, December 10, 1966; Barbados in Bridgetown, Barbados, December 13, 1966; and Guyana in Georgetown, Guyana, December 10, 1966. This consolidated text of the provisions in the Principal Agreement establishing the Caribbean Free Trade Association (CARIFTA) and the Supplementary Agreement negotiated by the Commonwealth Caribbean governments was prepared in March 1968 for the use of the member countries by the United Nations Economic Commission for Latin America, Office for the Caribbean, in Port of Spain, Trinidad. Annexes C, D, E, and F, covering rules regarding area origin for tariff purposes and basic materials list, a list related to protective revenue duties, a list of products covered by export duties, and a list of governmental measures assisting foreign trade, respectively, have been omitted from this text. [Editor's note.]

ARTICLE 1: ASSOCIATION

1. An Association to be called the Caribbean Free Trade Association (hereinafter referred to as "The Association") is hereby established.

2. The Members of the Association, hereinafter referred to as "Member Territories" shall be the Territories on behalf of the Governments of which this Agreement is ratified in accordance with Article 31 and such other Territories as participate therein by virtue of paragraph 1 of Article 32, and for the purposes hereof, "Territories" includes sovereign states internationally recognised.

3. The institutions of the Association shall be a Council and such organs as are mentioned in paragraph 3 of Article 28.

4. The Caribbean Free Trade Association shall operate over the areas of the Member Territories collectively called the Caribbean Free Trade Area (hereinafter referred to as "The Area").

ARTICLE 2: OBJECTIVES

The objectives of the Association shall be:
(a) to promote the expansion and diversification of trade in the area of the Association;
(b) to secure that trade between Member Territories takes place in conditions of fair competition;
(c) to encourage the balanced and progressive development of the economies of the Area in keeping with paragraphs 3 to 10 of the Resolution adopted at the Fourth Conference of the Heads of Government of Commonwealth Caribbean Countries and set out in Annex A;
(d) to foster the harmonious development of Caribbean trade and its liberalisation by the removal of barriers to it;
(e) to ensure that the benefits of free trade are equitably distributed among the Member Territories.

ARTICLE 3: EXCLUSION FROM THIS AGREEMENT

1. The provisions of this Agreement shall not affect the rights and obligations under any agreements entered into by any of the Parties to this Agreement before the effective date hereof and notified to the Council:

Provided, however, that each Party shall take any steps at its disposal which are necessary to reconcile the provisions of any of such agreements with the purposes of this Agreement.

Provided further that, in case of any nonobservance of any provisions of this Agreement on the part of a Member Territory pursuant to its exemption in that behalf by virtue of the foregoing provisions of this Article, any other Member Territory which considers that it would enjoy any benefit under this Agreement but for such exemption may, if no satisfactory settlement is reached between the Member Territories concerned, refer the matter to the Council, which may, by majority decision, authorise any Member Territory to suspend to the first-mentioned Member Territory the application of such obligations under this Agreement as the Council considers meet, due regard being had to the report of such committee (if any) as may have been constituted in accordance with Article 27 to examine the matter, and paragraphs 2 and 5 of Article 26 shall apply *mutatis mutandis* in the case of any reference under this proviso as they apply in the case of a reference under paragraph 1 of Article 26.

2. All such agreements shall be registered in such form as the Council shall decide and by way of such service in that behalf as shall be arranged pursuant to subparagraph (b) of paragraph 1 of Article 29.

3. The Council shall annually review the observance by Parties to this Agreement of the first proviso to paragraph 1 of this Article and may from time to time, by majority vote, recommend to any of them the taking of any steps for the purposes of that proviso.

4. For the purposes of this Article, "agreements" means any agreements concluded by instruments, or any arrangements made in writing which the Council decides, by majority vote, constitute agreements for those purposes, but does not include any agreement or arrangements entered into by a Party hereto, not being the Government of Grenada, in respect of which negotiations commenced after the 22nd February, 1968.

ARTICLE 4: IMPORT DUTIES

1. Subject to the provisions of Annex B, Member Territories shall not apply any import duties on goods which are eligible for Area tariff treatment in accordance with Article 5.

2. For the purposes of this Article and Annex B, the term "import duties" means any tax or surtax of customs and any other charges of equivalent effect — whether fiscal, monetary, or exchange — which are levied on imports, except duties notified under Article 7 and other charges which fall within that Article.

3. The provisions of this Article do not apply to fees and similar charges in respect of services rendered, and nothing in paragraph 2 of this Article shall be construed to exclude from the application of paragraph 1 of this Article any tax or surtax of customs on any product neither the like of which, nor a competitive substitute for which, is produced in the importing Member Territory, or to extend such application to nondiscriminatory internal charges on any such product.

4. For the purposes of paragraph 3 of this Article:

(a) "nondiscriminatory" means nondiscriminatory as between goods eligible for Area tariff treatment as aforesaid and goods not so eligible;

(b) a charge shall not be deemed other than internal by reason only that it is collected at the time and place of importation.

ARTICLE 5: AREA ORIGIN FOR TARIFF PURPOSES

1. For the purposes of Articles 4 to 8, goods shall, subject to Annex C, be accepted as eligible for Area tariff treatment if they are consigned from a Member Territory to a consignee in the importing Member Territory and if they are of Area origin under any one of the following conditions:

(a) that they have been wholly produced within the Area;

(b) that they fall within a description of goods listed in a Process List to be established by decision of the Council and have been produced within the Area by the appropriate qualifying process described in that List;

(c) that they have been produced within the Area and that the value of any materials imported from outside the Area or of undetermined origin which have been used at any stage of the production of the goods does not exceed 50 per cent of the export price of the goods.

2. For the purposes of subparagraphs (a), (b), and (c) of paragraph 1 of this Article, materials listed in the Basic Materials List which forms the Schedule to Annex C, which have been used in the state described in that List in a process of production within the Area, shall be deemed to contain no element imported from outside the Area.

3. Nothing in this Agreement shall prevent a Member Territory from accepting as eligible for Area tariff treatment any imports consigned from another Member Territory, provided that the like imports consigned from any Member Territory are accorded the same treatment.

4. Provisions necessary for the administration and effective application of this Article are contained in Annex C.

5. The Council may decide to amend the provisions of this Article, Annex C, and the Process List established under subparagraph (b) of paragraph 1 of this Article.

6. The Council shall from time to time examine in what respect this Agreement can be amended in order to ensure the smooth operation of the origin rules.

7. Nothing in this Agreement shall require a Member Territory to accept as eligible for Area tariff treatment any imports consigned from another Member Territory and consisting of, or manufactured from, oils and fats as defined by clause 2 of the Oils and Fats Agreement, or any of such oils or fats, where the Government of one of such Territories is a party to the Oils and Fats Agreement, and the Government of the other of such Territories is not a party to that Agreement, being the Agreement made on January 26, 1967 between the Governments of Barbados, Dominica, Grenada, Guyana, St. Lucia, St. Vincent, and Trinidad and Tobago or any Agreement amending or replacing the same.

ARTICLE 6: DEFLECTION OF TRADE

1. For the purposes of this Article, trade is said to be deflected when
(a) imports into a Member Territory of consignments of a particular product from another Member Territory are increasing —
    (i) as a result of the reduction or elimination in the importing Member Territory of duties and charges on that product in accordance with Articles 4 or 7, and
    (ii) because the duties or charges levied by the exporting Member Territory on imports of raw materials or intermediate products, used in the production of the product in question, are significantly lower than the corresponding duties or charges levied by the importing Member Territory, and
(b) this increase in imports causes or would cause serious injury to production which is carried on in the importing Member Territory.

2. The Council shall keep under review the question of deflections of trade and their causes. It shall take such decisions as are necessary in order to deal with the causes of deflection of trade by amending the rules of origin in accordance with paragraph 5 of Article 5 or by such other means as it may consider appropriate.

3. If a deflection of trade of a particularly urgent nature occurs, any Member Territory may refer the matter to the Council. The Council shall take its decision as quickly as possible and, in general, within one month. The Council may, by majority decision, authorise interim measures to safeguard the position of the Member Territory in question. Such measures shall not continue for longer than is necessary for the procedure under paragraph 2 above to take place, and for not more than two months unless, in exceptional cases, the Council, by majority decision, authorises an extension of this period by not more than two months.

4. A Member Territory which is considering the reduction of the effective level of its duties or charges on any product not eligible for Area tariff treatment shall, as far as may be practicable, notify the Council not less than thirty days before such reduction comes into effect, and shall consider any representations by other Member Territories that the reduction is likely to lead to a deflection of trade. Information received under this paragraph shall not be disclosed to any person outside the service of the Association or the Governments of Member Territories.

5. When considering changes in their duties or charges on any product not eligible for Area tariff treatment, Member Territories shall have due regard to the desirability of avoiding consequential deflections of trade. In case of any such change, any Member Territory which considers that trade is being deflected may refer the matter to the Council in accordance with Article 26.

6. If, in the consideration of any complaint in accordance with Article 26, reference is made to a difference in the level of duties or charges on any product not eligible for Area tariff treatment, that difference shall be taken

into account only if the Council finds by majority vote that there is a deflection of trade.

7. The Council shall review from time to time the provisions of this Article and may decide to amend those provisions.

ARTICLE 7: REVENUE DUTIES AND INTERNAL TAXATION

1. Subject to the provisions of Annex D, Member Territories shall not:
(a) apply directly or indirectly to imported goods any fiscal charges in excess of those applied directly or indirectly to like domestic goods, nor otherwise apply such charges so as to afford effective protection to like domestic goods; or
(b) apply fiscal charges to imported goods of a kind which they do not produce, or which they do not produce in substantial quantities, in such a way as to afford effective protection to the domestic production of goods of a different kind which are substitutable for the imported goods, which enter into direct competition with them and which do not bear, directly or indirectly, in the country of importation, fiscal charges of equivalent incidence.

2. A Member Territory shall notify the Council of all fiscal charges applied by it where, although the rates of charge, or the conditions governing the imposition or collection of the charge, are not identical in relation to the imported goods and to the like domestic goods, the Member Territory applying the charge considers that the charge is, or has been made, consistent with subparagraph (a) of paragraph 1 of this Article. Each Member Territory shall, at the request of any other Member Territory, supply information about the application of paragraph 1 of this Article.

3. For the purposes of this Article and Annex D:
(a) "fiscal charges" means revenue duties, internal taxes and other internal charges on goods;
(b) "revenue duties" means customs duties and other similar charges applied primarily for the purpose of raising revenue; and
(c) "imported goods" means goods which are accepted as being eligible for Area tariff treatment in accordance with Article 5.

ARTICLE 8: EXPORT DRAWBACK

Each Member Territory may refuse to accept as eligible for Area tariff treatment goods which benefit from export drawback allowed by Member Territories in which the goods have undergone the processes of production which form the basis of the claim to Area origin. In applying this paragraph, each Member Territory shall accord the same treatment to imports consigned from all other Member Territories.

For the purposes of this Article:

(a) "export drawback" means any arrangement for the refund or remission, wholly or in part, of import duties applicable to imported materials, provided that the arrangement, expressly or in effect, allows refund or remission if certain goods or materials are exported, but not if they are retained for home use;

(b) "remission" includes exemption for materials brought into free ports and other places which have similar customs privileges;

(c) "duties" means (i) all charges on or in connection with importation, except fiscal charges to which Article 7 applies and (ii) any protective element in such fiscal charges;

(d) "materials" and "process of production" have the meanings assigned to them in Rule 1 of Annex C.

ARTICLE 9: PROHIBITION OF EXPORT DUTIES

1. Member Territories shall not apply any export duties.

2. The provisions of this Article shall not prevent any Member Territory from taking such measures as are necessary to prevent evasion, by means of re-export, of duties which it applied to exports to territories outside the Area.

3. For the purposes of this Article, "export duties" means any duties or charges with equivalent effect imposed on or in connection with the exportation of goods from any Member Territory to a consignee in any other Member Territory.

4. Nothing in this Article shall preclude a Member Territory from applying to any commodity listed in Annex E, within ten years from the effective date of this Agreement, export duty not exceeding that applicable by the Member Territory to such commodity immediately before the effective date of this Agreement.

5. Any Member Territory which, pursuant to paragraph 4 of this Article, applies or continues to apply export duty to any commodity listed in Annex E shall notify the Council of every commodity on which export duty is applied and the rate of such duty. The Council shall keep under review the question of such export duties and may at any time by majority vote make recommendations designed to moderate any damaging effect of those duties.

ARTICLE 10: COOPERATION IN CUSTOMS ADMINISTRATION

Member Territories shall take appropriate measures, including arrangements regarding administrative cooperation, to ensure that the provisions of Articles 4 to 8 and of Annexes B, C, and D are effectively and harmoniously applied, taking account of the need to reduce as far as is possible the formalities imposed on trade and of the need to achieve mutually satisfactory solutions of any difficulties arising out of the operation of those provisions.

ARTICLE 11: FREEDOM OF TRANSIT

Products imported into, or exported from, a Member Territory shall enjoy freedom of transit within the Area and shall only be subject to the payment of the normal rates for services rendered.

ARTICLE 12: DUMPED AND SUBSIDISED IMPORTS

1. Nothing in this Agreement shall prevent any Member Territory from taking action against dumped or subsidised imports consistently with any international obligations to which it is subject.

2. Any products which have been exported from one Member Territory to a consignee in another Member Territory and have not undergone any manufacturing process since exportation shall, when reimported into the first Member Territory, be admitted free of quantitative restrictions and measures with equivalent effect. They shall also be admitted free of customs duties and charges with equivalent effect, except that any allowance by way of drawback, relief from duty or otherwise, given by reason of the exportation from the first Member Territory, may be recovered.

3. If any industry in any Member Territory is suffering or is threatened with material injury as the result of the import of dumped or subsidised products into another Member Territory, the latter Member Territory shall, at the request of the former Member Territory, examine the possibility of taking, consistently with any international obligations to which it is subject, action to remedy the injury or prevent the threatened injury.

ARTICLE 13: QUANTITATIVE IMPORT RESTRICTIONS

1. Subject to anything to the contrary in any agricultural marketing arrangements made pursuant to paragraph 6 of Annex A and laid down in a Protocol between the Parties to this Agreement, a Member Territory shall not apply any quantitative restrictions on imports of goods from any other part of the Area.

2. For the purposes of the preceding paragraph, "Quantitative restrictions" means prohibitions or restrictions on imports into any Member Territory from any other part of the Area whether made effective through quotas, import licenses, or other measures with equivalent effect, including administrative measures and requirements restricting import.

3. The provisions of this Article shall not prevent any Member Territory from taking such measures as are necessary to prevent evasion, of any prohibitions or restrictions which it applies to imports from territories outside the Area.

ARTICLE 14: QUANTITATIVE EXPORT RESTRICTIONS

1. Subject as mentioned in paragraph 1 of Article 13, a Member Territory shall not apply any prohibitions or restrictions on exports to any other part of the Area, whether made effective through quotas or export licences or other measures with equivalent effect.

2. The provisions of this Article shall not prevent any Member Territory from taking such measures as are necessary to prevent evasion, of any prohibitions or restrictions which it applies to exports to territories outside the Area.

ARTICLE 15: GENERAL EXCEPTIONS

Provided that such measures are not used as a means of arbitrary or unjustifiable discrimination between Member Territories, or as a disguised restriction on the interterritorial trade of the Area, nothing in Articles 13 and 14 shall prevent the adoption or enforcement by any Member Territory of measures

(a) necessary to protect public morals;

(b) necessary for the prevention of disorder or crime;

(c) necessary to protect human, animal, or plant life or health;

(d) necessary to secure compliance with laws or regulations relating to customs enforcement, or to the classification, grading, or marketing of goods, or to the operation of monopolies by means of state enterprises or enterprises given exclusive or special privileges;

(e) necessary to protect industrial property or copyrights or to prevent deceptive practices;

(f) relating to gold or silver;

(g) relating to the products of prison labour;

(h) imposed for the protection of national treasures of artistic, historic, or archeological value; or

(i) necessary to prevent or relieve critical shortages of foodstuffs in any exporting Member Territory.

ARTICLE 16: SECURITY EXCEPTIONS

1. Nothing in this Agreement shall prevent any Member Territory from taking action which it considers necessary for the protection of its essential security interests, where such action:

(a) is taken to prevent the disclosure of information;

(b) relates to trade in arms, ammunition, or war materials or to research, development, or production indispensable for defence purposes, provided that such action does not include the application of import duties or the quantitative restriction of imports except in so far as such restriction is permitted in accordance with Article 15 or is authorised by decision of the Council;

(c) is taken to ensure that nuclear materials and equipment made available for peaceful purposes do not further military purposes; or

(d) is taken in time of war or other emergency in international relations.

2. Nothing in this Agreement shall prevent any Member Territory from taking action to perform any obligations to which it is subject for the purpose of maintaining international peace and security.

ARTICLE 17: GOVERNMENT AIDS

1. A Member Territory shall not maintain or introduce:

(a) the forms of aid to export of goods to any other part of the Area of the kinds which are described in Annex F; or

(b) any other form of aid, the main purpose or effect of which is to frustrate the benefits expected from such removal or absence of duties and quantitative restrictions as is required by this Agreement.

2. If the application of any form of aid by a Member Territory, although not contrary to paragraph 1 of this Article, frustrates the benefits expected from such removal or absence of duties and quantitative restrictions as is required by this Agreement and provided that the procedure set out in paragraphs 1 to 3 of Article 26 has been followed, the Council may, by majority decision, authorise any Member Territory to suspend to the Member Territory which is applying the aid the application of such obligations under this Agreement as the Council considers appropriate.

3. The Council may decide to amend the provision of this Article and of Annex F.

4. The provisions of this Article:

(a) shall not apply in respect of interterritorial trade within the Area in any agricultural products until such time as Member Territories shall agree upon the regional policy with respect to the production and marketing, including the subsidization, of agricultural products;

(b) exclusive of subparagraph (a) of paragraph 1 and paragraph 3, shall not apply in respect of interterritorial trade within the Area in any manufactured goods until Member Territories have agreed upon a regional policy with respect to incentives to industry.

ARTICLE 18: PUBLIC UNDERTAKINGS

1. Member Territories shall ensure the elimination in the practices of public undertakings, of:

(a) measures the effect of which is to afford protection to domestic production which would be inconsistent with this Agreement if achieved by means of a duty or charge with equivalent effect or quantitative restriction or Government aid; or

(b) trade discrimination on grounds of Territorial origin in so far as it frustrates the benefits expected from such removal or absence of duties and quantitative restrictions as is required by this Agreement.

2. In so far as the provisions of Article 19 are relevant to the activities of public undertakings, that Article shall apply to them in the same way as it applies to other enterprises.

3. Member Territories shall ensure that new practices of the kind described in paragraph 1 of this Article are not introduced.

4. Where Member Territories do not have the necessary legal powers to control the activities of regional or local government authorities or enterprises under their control in these matters, they shall nevertheless endeavour to ensure that those authorities or enterprises comply with the provisions of this Article.

5. The Council shall keep the provisions of this Article under review and may decide to amend them.

6. For the purpose of this Article, "public undertakings" means central, regional, or local government authorities, public enterprises, and any other organisation by means of which a Member Territory by law or in practice controls or appreciably influences imports from, or exports to, any other part of the Area.

7. The provisions of this Article shall not apply in respect of interterritorial trade within the Area:

(a) in agricultural products until such time as Member Territories shall agree upon a regional policy with respect to the production and marketing, including the subsidization, of agricultural products;

(b) in manufactured goods until Member Territories have agreed upon a regional policy with respect to incentives to industry.

ARTICLE 19: RESTRICTIVE BUSINESS PRACTICES

1. Member Territories recognise that the following practices are incompatible with this Agreement in so far as they frustrate the benefits expected from such removal or absence of duties and quantitative restrictions as is required by this Agreement:

(a) agreements between enterprises, decisions by associations of enterprises, and concerted practices between enterprises which have as their object or result the prevention, restriction, or distortion of competition within the Area;

(b) actions by which one or more enterprises take unfair advantage of a dominant position within the Area or a substantial part of it.

2. If any practice of the kind described in paragraph 1 of this Article is referred to the Council in accordance with Article 26, the Council may, in any recommendation in accordance with paragraph 3 or in any decision in accordance with paragraph 4 of that Article, make provision for publication of a report on the circumstances of the matter.

3. (a) In the light of experience gained, the Council shall consider before April 30, 1970, and may consider at any time thereafter, whether further or different provisions are necessary to deal with the effect of restrictive business practices or dominant enterprises on the interterritorial trade of the Area.

(b) Such review shall include consideration of the following matters:
  (1) specification of the restrictive business practices or dominant enterprises with which the Council should be concerned;
  (2) methods of securing information about restrictive business practices or dominant enterprises;
  (3) procedures for investigations;
  (4) whether the right to initiate inquiries should be conferred on the Council.
(c) The Council may decide to make the provisions found necessary as a result of the review envisaged in subparagraphs (a) and (b) of this paragraph.

ARTICLE 20: ESTABLISHMENT

1. Each Member Territory recognises that restrictions on the establishment and operation of economic enterprises therein by persons belonging to other Member Territories should not be applied, through accord to such persons of treatment which is less favourable than that accorded in such matters to persons belonging to that Member Territory, in such a way as to frustrate the benefits expected from such removal or absence of duties and quantitative restrictions as is required by this Agreement.

2. Member Territories shall not apply new restrictions in such a way that they conflict with the principle set out in paragraph 1 of this Article.

3. A Member Territory shall notify the Council within such period as the Council may decide of particulars of any restrictions which it applies in such a way that persons belonging to another Member Territory are accorded in the first-mentioned Territory less favourable treatment in respect of the matters set out in paragraph 1 of this Article than is accorded to persons belonging thereto.

4. The Council shall consider before April 30, 1970, and may consider at any time thereafter, whether further or different provisions are necessary to give effect to the principles set out in paragraph 1 of this Article and may decide to make the necessary provisions.

5. Nothing in this Article shall prevent the adoption and enforcement by a Member Territory of measures for the control of entry, residence, activity, and departure of persons where such measures are justified by reasons of public order, public health or morality, or national security of that Member Territory.

6. For the purposes of this Article:
(a) a person shall be regarded as belonging to a Member Territory if such person —
  (i) is a citizen of that Territory;
  (ii) has a connection with that Territory of a kind which entitles him to be regarded as belonging to, or, if it be so expressed, as being a native of, the Territory for the purposes of such laws thereof relating to immigration as are for the time being in force; or

(iii) is a company or other legal person constituted in the Member Territory in conformity with the law thereof and which that Territory regards as belonging to it, provided that such company or other legal person has been formed for gainful purposes and has its registered office and central administration, and carries on substantial activity, within the Area;

(b) "economic enterprises" means any type of economic enterprises for production of or commerce in goods which are of Area origin, whether conducted by individuals or through agencies, branches, or companies or other legal persons.

ARTICLE 21: BALANCE-OF-PAYMENTS DIFFICULTIES

1. Notwithstanding the provisions of Article 13 any Member Territory may, consistently with any international obligations to which it is subject, introduce quantitative restrictions on imports for the purpose of safeguarding its balance of payments.

2. Any Member Territory taking measures in accordance with paragraph 1 of this Article shall notify them to the Council, if possible before they come into force. The Council shall examine the situation and keep it under review and may at any time by majority vote make recommendations designed to moderate any damaging effect of these restrictions or to assist the Member Territory concerned to overcome its difficulties. If the balance-of-payments difficulties persist for more than 18 months and the measures applied seriously disturb the operation of the Association, the Council shall examine the situation and may, taking into account the interests of all Member Territories, by majority decision devise special procedures to attenuate or compensate for the effect of such measures.

3. A Member Territory which has taken measures in accordance with paragraph 1 of this Article shall have regard to its obligation to resume the full application of Article 13 and shall, as soon as its balance-of-payments situation improves, make proposals to the Council on the way in which this should be done. The Council, if it is not satisfied that these proposals are adequate, may recommend to the Member Territories alternative arrangements to the same end. Decisions of the Council pursuant to this paragraph shall be made by majority vote.

ARTICLE 22: DIFFICULTIES IN PARTICULAR SECTORS

1. If, in a Member Territory:

(a) an appreciable rise in unemployment in a particular sector of industry or region is caused by a substantial decrease in internal demand for a domestic product, and

(b) this decrease in demand is due to an increase in imports consigned from other Member Territories as a result of the progressive reduction or the elimination of duties, charges, and quantitative restrictions in accordance with Articles 4, 7, and 13, that Member Territory may, notwithstanding any other provisions of this Agreement,

(i) limit those imports by means of quantitative restrictions to a rate not less than the rate of such imports during any period of twelve months which ended within twelve months of the date on which the restrictions come into force; the restrictions shall not be continued for a period longer than eighteen months, unless the Council, by majority decision, authorises their continuance for such further period and on such conditions as the Council considers appropriate; and

(ii) take such measures, either instead of or in addition to restriction of imports in accordance with subparagraph (i) of this paragraph, as the Council may, by majority decision, authorise.

2. In applying measures in accordance with paragraph 1 of this Article, a Member Territory shall give like treatment to imports consigned from all Member Territories.

3. A Member Territory applying restrictions in accordance with subparagraph (i) of paragraph 1 of this Article shall notify them to the Council, if possible before they come into force. The Council may at any time consider those restrictions and may, by majority vote, make recommendations designed to moderate any damaging effect of those restrictions or to assist the Member State concerned to overcome its difficulties.

4. This Article shall have effect until April 30, 1973.

5. Before May 1, 1973, if the Council considers that some provision similar to those in paragraphs 1 to 3 of this Article will be required thereafter, it may decide that such provisions shall have effect for any period after that date.

ARTICLE 23: APPROXIMATION OF INCENTIVE LEGISLATION

1. A tax of any kind in a Member Territory shall not, by the introduction or extension of incentive provisions at any time after this Agreement takes effect, be rendered liable to mitigation to any extent to which no tax of that kind elsewhere in the Area (if any) is rendered, by incentive provisions previously introduced or extended, liable to mitigation:

Provided that, in resolving any question whether any breach by a Member Territory of its obligations for the purposes of this Article is to be apprehended or has resulted from the introduction or extension of any incentive provisions, the Council shall take into account the over-all level and structure of taxation and the general economic circumstances in that Member Territory as compared with other Member Territories.

2. The Council may, by majority decision, authorise any Member Territory to withhold, from imports of any products in relation to the manufacture of which it has been established to the satisfaction of a majority of the Council

that any such breach by another Member Territory has resulted as aforesaid, treatment the benefit whereof is applicable in conformity with any provisions of this Agreement to such imports.

3. A Member Territory which is considering the introduction or alteration of any incentive provisions shall, as far as may be practicable, notify the Council not less than thirty days before such introduction or alteration comes into effect, and shall consider any representations with respect thereto by other Member Territories, any of which may refer the matter to the Council under Article 26 if a breach of this Article is apprehended. Information received under this paragraph shall not be disclosed to any person outside the service of the Association or the Governments of Member Territories.

4. The Council may on its own initiative recommend to Member Territories proposals for the approximation of incentive provisions within the Area. Such proposals may include schemes for the increase or reduction of concessions within the Area consistently with the provisions of the foregoing Articles of this Agreement, and may be implemented notwithstanding anything provided in paragraph 1 of this Article. The Council may take any appropriate measure provided for in this Agreement in furtherance of the objectives of this Article.

5. The Council may from time to time review the provisions of this Article and may decide to amend those provisions.

6. For the purposes of this Article:

"incentive provisions" means any legislation or practice providing for the granting of concessions for the purpose of encouraging the establishment or development of manufacturing industry;

"concessions" means any tax exemptions or remissions or refunds of tax;

"tax" includes any impost, duty, or due.

ARTICLE 24: ECONOMIC AND FINANCIAL POLICIES

Member Territories recognise that the economic and financial policies of each of them affect the economies of other Member Territories and intend to pursue those policies in a manner which serves to promote the objectives of the Association. They shall periodically exchange views on all aspects of those policies. The Council may make recommendations to Member Territories on matters relating to these policies to the extent necessary to ensure the attainment of the objectives of the smooth operation of the Association.

ARTICLE 25: INVISIBLES

The Council shall as soon as practicable, having due regard to international obligations, decide the treatment to be given to invisible transactions and transfer amongst Member Territories with a view to promoting the objectives of this Agreement.

ARTICLE 26: GENERAL CONSULTATIONS AND COMPLAINTS PROCEDURE

1. If any Member Territory considers that any benefit conferred upon it by this Agreement or any objective of the Association is being or may be frustrated and if no satisfactory settlement is reached between the Member Territories concerned, any of those Member Territories may refer the matter to the Council.

2. The Council shall promptly, by majority vote, make arrangements for examining the matter. Such arrangements may include a reference to an examining committee constituted in accordance with Article 27. Before taking action under paragraph 3 of this Article, the Council shall so refer the matter at the request of an Member Territory concerned. Member Territories shall furnish all information which they can make available and shall lend their assistance to establish the facts.

3. When considering the matter, the Council shall have regard to whether it has been established that an obligation under this Agreement has not been fulfilled and whether and to what extent any benefit conferred by this Agreement or any objective of the Association is being or may be frustrated. In the light of this consideration and of the report of any examining committee which may have been appointed, the Council may, by majority vote, make to any Member Territory such recommendations as it considers appropriate.

4. If a Member Territory does not or is unable to comply with a recommendation made in accordance with paragraph 3 of this Article and the Council finds, by majority vote, that an obligation under this Agreement has not been fulfilled, the Council may, by majority decision, authorise any Member Territory to suspend to the Member Territory which has not complied with the recommendation the application of such obligations under this Agreement as the Council considers appropriate.

5. Any Member Territory may, at any time while the matter is under consideration, request the Council to authorise, as a matter of urgency, interim measures to safeguard its position. If it is found by majority vote of the Council that the circumstances are sufficiently serious to justify interim action, and without prejudice to any action which it may subsequently take in accordance with the preceding paragraphs of this Article, the Council may, by majority decision, authorise a Member Territory to suspend its obligations under this Agreement to such an extent and for such a period as the Council considers appropriate.

ARTICLE 27: EXAMINING COMMITTEES

The examining committees referred to in Article 26 shall consist of persons selected for their competence and integrity, who, in the performance of their duties, shall neither seek nor receive instructions from any Territory or from any authority or organisation other than the Association. They shall be appointed, on such terms and conditions as may be decided, by majority vote of the Council.

ARTICLE 28: THE COUNCIL

1. It shall be the responsibility of the Council:
   (a) to exercise such powers and functions as are conferred upon it by this Agreement;
   (b) to supervise the application of this Agreement and keep its operation under review;
   (c) to consider whether further action should be taken by Member Territories in order to promote the attainment of the objectives of the Association and to facilitate the establishment of closer links with other countries, unions of countries, or international organisations.

2. Each Member Territory shall be represented in the Council and shall have one vote.

3. The Commonwealth Caribbean Regional Secretariat shall be the principal administrative organ of the Association and the Council may entrust it, and may set up other organs, committees, and bodies and entrust them, with such functions as the Council considers necessary to assist it in accomplishing its tasks. Decisions of the Council pursuant to this paragraph shall be made by majority vote.

4. In exercising its responsibility under paragraph 1 of this Article, the Council may take decisions which shall be binding on all Member Territories and may make recommendations to Member Territories.

5. Decisions and recommendations of the Council shall be made by unanimous vote, except in so far as this Agreement provides otherwise. Decisions or recommendations shall be regarded as unanimous unless any Member Territory casts a negative vote. A decision or recommendation of the Council pursuant to any such provision as aforesaid requires the affirmative votes of not less than two thirds of all Member Territories, and reference in any such provision to a majority shall, in relation to the Council, be construed accordingly.

6. The Council may, by its decision to confer any authority under this Agreement, impose conditions to which such authority shall be subject.

ARTICLE 29: ADMINISTRATIVE ARRANGEMENTS OF THE ASSOCIATION

1. The Council shall take decision for the following purposes:
   (a) to lay down the Rules of Procedure of the Council and of any bodies of the Association, which may include provision that procedural questions may be decided by majority vote;
   (b) to make arrangements for the Secretariat services required by the Association;

(c) to establish the financial arrangements necessary for the administrative expenses of the Association, and the procedure for establishing an annual budget.

2. The expenses of the Association shall be shared between Member Territories in conformity with the appropriate basis of Territorial contributions to the annual budget of the Commonwealth Caribbean Regional Secretariat, approved at the Conference of Ministers of Trade held in Guyana on February 21 and 22, 1968, or in such other manner as the Council may decide.

ARTICLE 30: RELATIONS WITH INTERNATIONAL ORGANISATIONS

The Council, acting on behalf of the Association, shall seek to procure the establishment of such relationships with other international organisations as may facilitate the attainment of the objectives of the Association.

ARTICLE 31: RATIFICATIONS REQUIRED FOR EFFECTIVENESS

1. This Agreement shall be subject to ratification by the Legislatures of all the Signatory Territories.

2. Instruments signifying such ratification shall be deposited with the Government of Antigua, which shall notify the other Signatory Territories, and, subject to the next following paragraph, this Agreement shall take effect as soon as the number of Signatory Territories has been ascertained consistently with paragraphs 4 and 5 of this Article and all such instruments have been so deposited.

3. If prior to the ratification of this Agreement by any Signatory Territory that Territory indicates by notice to the Government of Antigua that difficulties have arisen in relation to carrying any provision of this Agreement into effect, the Agreement shall not take effect with respect to that Territory except in accordance with the terms of a supplementary agreement between all the Signatory Territories providing for the resolution of such difficulties.

4. Any Commonwealth Caribbean Country by whose Government an instrument signifying its endorsement of the Resolution set out in Annex A has been deposited with the Government of Antigua shall be deemed for the purposes of this Agreement to be a Signatory Territory as from the date of such deposit, which shall be notified to the other Signatory Territories by the Government of Antigua.

5. Notwithstanding anything to the contrary in this Agreement, the preceding paragraph shall not apply on or after May 1, 1968 to a Commonwealth Caribbean Country unless, before that date, there has been deposited an instrument signifying ratification by its Legislature of this Agreement, pursuant to the deposit by its Government of an instrument of endorsement, in accordance with this Article.

ARTICLE 32: JOINING ASSOCIATION

1. Any Territory, though it be not a signatory hereto, may participate in this Agreement, subject to prior approval of the Council of the Territory's participation in this Agreement on terms and conditions decided by the Council. The instrument duly signifying the agreement of the Government of the Territory to its participation in this Agreement on the terms and conditions decided as aforesaid shall be deposited with the Government of Antigua which shall notify all other Member Territories. This Agreement shall have effect in relation to the participating Territory as, and from the time, indicated in the Council's decision.

2. The Council may pursuant to any decision thereof in that behalf seek to procure the creation of an association consisting of Member Territories and any other Territory, union of Territories, or international organisation, and embodying such reciprocal rights and obligations, common actions, and special procedures as may be appropriate.

ARTICLE 33: WITHDRAWAL

Any Member Territory may withdraw from participation in this Agreement provided that the Government thereof gives twelve months' notice in writing to the Government of Antigua, which shall notify the other Member Territories.

ARTICLE 34: AMENDMENT

1. Except where provision for modification is made elsewhere in this Agreement, including the Annexes to it, an amendment to the provisions of this Agreement shall be submitted to the Governments of Member Territories for acceptance if it is approved by decision of the Council, and it shall have effect provided it is accepted by all such Governments. Instruments of acceptance shall be deposited with the Government of Antigua, which shall notify the other Member Territories.

ARTICLE 35: ACQUISITION OF SOVEREIGN STATUS

1. If a Member Territory, upon becoming a sovereign state recognised internationally, intimates its willingness to continue to participate in this Agreement, then, notwithstanding its having become such a state, this Agreement shall continue to have effect in relation to it.

2. For the purposes of paragraph 1 of this Article, any intimation thereunder shall be given by notice to the Government of Antigua, which shall notify all other Member Territories.

ARTICLE 36: ANNEXES

The annexes to this Agreement are an integral part of this Agreement.

ARTICLE 37: LEGAL CAPACITY, PRIVILEGES, AND IMMUNITIES

1. The legal capacity, privileges, and immunities to be recognised and granted by the Member Territories in connection with the Association shall be laid down in a Protocol to this Agreement.

2. The Council, acting on behalf of the Association, may conclude with the Government of the Territory in which the headquarters will be situated an agreement relating to the legal capacity and the privileges and immunities to be recognised and granted in connection with the Association.

ARTICLE 38: PROTECTION OF GUYANESE PETROLEUM PRODUCTS

1. Notwithstanding anything in this Agreement, any quantitative restriction within the meaning of Article 13 may, during any period for which the Government of Guyana is a party to any protective agreement in that behalf relating to a petroleum product produced in Guyana, be applied on imports into Guyana of that petroleum product from any other part of the Area:

Provided that no such restriction shall be so applied on imports of any petroleum product, other than Bunker C, asphalt, or road oil, during any year except with a view to preventing the importation of that petroleum product into Guyana to any extent in excess of:

(a) one third of such amount of that petroleum product as is reasonably considered by the Government of Guyana to be marketable in Guyana during such year; or

(b) the difference between such amount of that petroleum product as is reasonably considered by the Government of Guyana to be marketable in Guyana during such year and any lesser amount of that petroleum product which is reasonably considered by the said Government to be producible in Guyana during such year,

whichever is more.

2. During any period first hereinbefore in this Article referred to in connection with a petroleum product produced in Guyana, customs duties shall, at rates not lower than those in force when this Agreement takes effect, be applicable to any permitted imports into Guyana of that petroleum product from outside the Area.

3. Not later than:

(a) the commencement, during any year, of any period mentioned in paragraph 2 of this Article;

(b) the commencement, during any such period, of any year,

Guyana shall notify to the Council the amounts mentioned in paragraph (b) of the proviso to paragraph 1 of this Article in relation to that year and shall, at the request of any Member Territory, inform the Council in strictest confidence of the reasons of the Government of Guyana for arriving at such amounts.

4. In this Article, "that petroleum product" includes any like or substitutable petroleum product.

5. This Article shall not have effect for longer than 15 years from the commencement of a period mentioned in paragraph 2 of this Article.

ARTICLE 39: PROMOTION OF INDUSTRIAL DEVELOPMENT IN LESS-DEVELOPED TERRITORIES

Upon any application made in that behalf by the less-developed Territories as defined in Annex B, the Council may, if necessary as a temporary measure in order to promote the development of an industry in any of those Territories, authorise by majority decision such Territories to suspend Area tariff treatment of any description of imports eligible therefor on grounds of production in the other Member Territories, any of whom may, during the period for which such authorisation is in force, suspend Area tariff treatment of the like description of imports eligible therefor on grounds of production in the less-developed Territories.

ANNEX A

RESOLUTION ADOPTED BY FOURTH HEADS OF GOVERNMENT CONFERENCE ON REGIONAL INTEGRATION

Free Trade should be introduced with respect to all intra-Commonwealth Caribbean trade by May 1, 1968, subject to a list of reserved commodities which would be freed within a five-year period for the more-developed countries and within a ten-year period for the less-developed countries; subject to special provisions for appeal by a less-developed Territory to the governing body of the Free Trade Area for further extension in any case where serious injury may be done to a territorial industry.

2. The Governments should approach the task of freeing of trade, by using the CARIFTA Agreement as a basis with suitable modifications.

3. The Commonwealth Caribbean countries shall immediately take steps to initiate studies to determine whether the objective of achieving trade expansion to the mutual benefit of the member states can be facilitated by the establishment of a common external tariff in whole or in part.

4. The principle should be accepted that certain industries may require for their economic operation the whole or a large part of the entire regional market protected by a common external tariff or other suitable instrument. The location of such industries and the criteria to be applied in respect thereof, as well as the implementation of the principle accepted above, should be the

subject of immediate study — such study to have special regard to the situation of the relatively less-developed countries.

5. Subject to existing commitments a regional policy of incentives to industry should be adopted as early as possible on the basis of studies mentioned in Resolution 7 below, bearing in mind the special needs of the less-developed countries for preferential treatment, such as soft loans.

6. Marketing agreements for an agreed list of agricultural commodities should be sought to come into effect at the same time as the commencement of free trade, and the territories in the region should examine the possibility of restricting imports from extraregional sources of agricultural products that are produced within the region and are available for satisfying regional demand.

7. The principle of seeking to establish more industries in the less-developed countries should be accepted, and the ECLA Secretariat should be asked to undertake feasibility studies immediately with a view to identifying industries which should be located in the less-developed countries and to devising special measures for securing the establishment of such industries in these countries. These studies should be submitted to governments no later than one year after the commencement of free trade.

8. The Commonwealth Caribbean countries should endeavour to maintain and improve regional carriers to facilitate the movement of goods and services within the region.

9. The Commonwealth Caribbean countries should agree to negotiate with the Shipping Conference the rationalisation of freight rates on extraregional traffic.

10. The ECLA Secretariat for the Caribbean should be asked to undertake a number of studies, for example, studies on the harmonising of incentives and the feasibility of establishing certain regional industries.

11. A Committee of Ministers should be set up immediately, functioning as a subcommittee of the Heads of Government Conference, with general responsibility for the establishment of Free Trade Area.

ANNEX B

1. Special arrangements are provided in this Annex for the progressive elimination by less-developed Territories, within ten years from the effective date of this Agreement in conformity with paragraph 4, of import duties on such products as are itemised according to the Standard International Trade Classification (original) as follows:

SITC Item No.	Description of Product
Ex 048–04	Biscuits, sweetened or unsweetened.
Ex 657–03	Coir products, mats and matting.
Ex 899–13	Brushes made with plastic bristles, except paint brushes and artists' brushes.

2. Special arrangements are provided in this Annex for the progressive elimination by less-developed Territories within ten years from the effective date of this Agreement in conformity with paragraph 4, and by other Member

Territories within five years from that date in conformity with paragraph 3, of import duties on such products as are itemised according to the Standard International Trade Classification (original) as follows:

SITC Item No.	Description of Product
053	Fruits preserved and fruit preparations, except frozen citrus concentrates and citrus segments.
121–01	Tobacco unmanufactured (including scrap tobacco and tobacco stems).
122	Manufactured tobacco except cigars.
Ex 533	Prepared paints, enamels, lacquer and varnishes. Ships' bottom compositions, putty and all other (including driers).
Ex 552–02	Cleansing preparations with soap (detergents).
Ex 632	Crates and wooden containers.
Ex 721–04	Radio and television sets.
Ex 721–19	Accumulators.
Ex 821	Wood furniture, metal furniture.
Ex 821–09	Mattresses.
Ex 841	Underwear and shirts of knitted fabrics. Underwear, shirts and nightwear of fabrics other than knitted. Outerwear of non-knitted textile fabrics.
Ex 851–01	Slippers and house footwear, wholly or mainly of leather.
Ex 851–02	Footwear wholly or mainly of leather.

3. On and after each of the following dates, a Member Territory may apply an import duty on any product eligible for Area tariff treatment, being a product the duty on which is to be eliminated by the Member Territory within five years as mentioned in the foregoing provisions of this Annex, at a level not exceeding the percentage of the basic duty specified against that date:

Effective date hereof	100 per cent
May 1, 1969	80 per cent
May 1, 1970	60 per cent
May 1, 1971	40 per cent
May 1, 1972	20 per cent
May 1, 1973	9 per cent

4. On and after each of the following dates, a less-developed Territory may apply import duty on any product eligible for Area tariff treatment, being a product the duty on which is to be eliminated by the Territory within ten years as mentioned in the foregoing provisions of this Annex, at a level not exceeding the percentage of the basic duty specified against that date:

Effective date hereof	100 per cent
May 1, 1973	50 per cent
May 1, 1978	0 per cent

5. Notwithstanding anything hereinbefore provided, special arrangements for the progressive elimination by Member Territories of import duty on any product listed in this Annex shall, in case of its being produced in any such Member Territory at the effective date hereof, come into operation on that date and, in any other case, shall come into operation, in so far as applicable, if and when such production commences in any of the Member Territories to which any of such arrangements have for the time being reference and the percentages of basic duty which are thenceforth applicable as prescribed by this Annex in relation to that product may be applied thereto accordingly.

6. Any less-developed Territory which considers that serious injury may be done to an industry in such Territory by the total elimination of import duty on any product as required by paragraph 4 may refer the matter to the Council, which may, by majority decision, authorise the continued application by any less-developed Territory of import duty on such product after April 30, 1978, due regard being had to the report of such committee (if any) as may have been constituted in accordance with Article 27 to examine the matter, and paragraphs 2 and 5 of Article 26 shall apply *mutatis mutandis* in the case of any reference under this paragraph as they apply in the case of a reference by a Member Territory to the Council under that Article.

7. For the purpose of this Annex:
   (a) "basic duty" means, in respect of any product imported into a Member Territory, the import duty applicable in that Territory, immediately before the effective date hereof, to imports of such a product from the other Territories becoming Members of the Association;
   (b) "paragraph" means a paragraph of this Annex;
   (c) "less-developed Territories" means Member Territories including neither Barbados, Guyana, Jamaica, nor Trinidad and Tobago.

8. Nothing in this Agreement shall preclude any agreement made between the less-developed Territories, and notified by them to the Council, whereby their import duties on any of the products listed in this Annex and imported from the less-developed Territories shall at any time be eliminated by all the less-developed Territories or reduced by not less than such percentage of their respective basic duties as may be so agreed between them, notwithstanding that no corresponding elimination or reduction be made by them in respect of such products imported from the other Member Territories except in so far as it may be necessary so to do for the purposes of compliance with this Annex.

PROTOCOL LAYING DOWN AGRICULTURAL MARKETING ARRANGEMENTS MENTIONED IN ARTICLE 13 OF THE AGREEMENT FOR ESTABLISHMENT OF THE CARIBBEAN FREE TRADE ASSOCIATION

The Signatory Governments:
Being the Governments of the Signatory Territories within the meaning of Article 31 of the Agreement for establishment of the Caribbean Free Trade Association;

Desirous of encouraging the agricultural development of the Caribbean Free Trade Area as a whole by ensuring that commodities capable of being produced in the Area are in fact produced and distributed at prices remunerative to growers and reasonable to consumers;

Conscious of the importance of agriculture in the economies of the region, particularly to those of the less-developed Territories;

Have agreed as follows:

1. In this Protocol, unless the context otherwise requires:

"the Agreement" means the Agreement for establishment of the Association, as modified by a Supplementary Agreement for the purpose of widening the area of the Association;

"the Area" means the area widened as aforesaid;

"the Association" means the Caribbean Free Trade Association;

"commodity" means any commodity listed in the Annex to this Protocol;

"Member Territory" shall have the meaning assigned thereto by paragraph 2 of Article 1 of the Agreement;

"participating Government" means any Signatory Government belonging to a Member Territory;

"Secretariat" means the Secretariat providing services for which arrangements are made under subparagraph (b) of paragraph 1 of Article 29 of the Agreement.

2. (1) No participating Government shall import or permit the importation of any commodity, except in conformity with the terms of this Protocol.

    (2) Except in conformity with the terms of any binding recommendations pursuant to subparagraph (1)(c) of paragraph 7 and subparagraph (2) of paragraph 8, no participating Government shall export any commodity mentioned in such list as may be established by virtue of any such recommendation in the light of negotiations between participating Governments with respect to the supply of specified amounts of the commodities so mentioned, account being taken in such negotiations of the objective of satisfying the demands of the Area and the desirability of maintaining and encouraging earnings from markets outside the Area.

    (3) Pursuant to information supplied by participating Governments as required by paragraph 6 (in conformity with subparagraph [6] whereof "import" in the following provisions of this subparagraph shall be construed), the Secretariat will allocate markets for each commodity among Member Territories proportionately —

        (a) as regards importing Member Territories, to their respective import requirements; and

        (b) as regards exporting Member Territories, to the availability for export to the Area from them, respectively,

    of the commodity in question.

3. Subject to paragraphs 4 and 5, imports of any commodity into a Member Territory shall be from within the Area:

Provided that, during a period of three years commencing with the date of the coming into operation of this Protocol, imports of any commodity into a Member Territory from outside the Area may, in the aggregate for each of those years, amount to not more than thirty per centum of the imports of such commodity into that Member Territory from outside the Area during the year 1966.

4. (1) Imports of any commodity into a Member Territory from outside the Area, not being allowed under the proviso to paragraph 3, are permissible by prior sanction of the Secretariat at the Member Territory's request made through notification thereof by its Government to the Secretariat.

(2) The Secretariat shall give such sanction only when a deficit in reference to the commodity in question has been declared to exist in the said Member Territory under subparagraph (4) of paragraph 6.

5. Any participating Government may import as mentioned in subparagraph (1) of paragraph 4, but without the sanction of the Secretariat, or may permit to be so imported, planting material for any crop, or breeding stock for livestock, for which any commodity is a product.

6. (1) Not later than September 30 in every year, and before the commencement of each of such other periods as the Secretariat may from time to time appoint for the purpose, every participating Government shall notify estimates of its Territory's import requirements and production, and of the availability for export therefrom, of each commodity during the next following year or during that period, as the case may be, to the Secretariat.

(2) The Secretariat shall, in reference to each commodity produced in the Area, inform participating Governments regularly whether, and to what extent (if any),
   (a) such production is likely to be available; and
   (b) there is likely to be a shortage of that commodity,
   for export.

(3) The participating Government of every Member Territory shall from time to time inform the Secretariat of
   (a) such imports of any commodity into that Territory as it requires to obtain by purchase; and
   (b) such exports from that Territory of any commodity produced in the Area as are suppliable on sale.

(4) A deficit of any commodity shall be deemed for the purposes of subparagraph (2) of paragraph 4 to exist when
   (a) any purchase requirements of the commodity have, after being notified by the Government of any Member Territory to the Secretariat in conformity with subparagraph (3)(a) of this paragraph, remained unsatisfied; or

    (b) there has been any such shortage of the commodity as is mentioned in subparagraph (2) of this paragraph,

for such period not exceeding four weeks as the Secretariat shall consider appropriate for the purpose, and the Secretariat shall, upon the expiration of that period, declare the existence of such deficit in the said Member Territory or in the Member Territories affected by the said shortage, as the case may be.

(5) Participating Governments shall furnish the Secretariat at its request with such statistics and other information as may be required for the proper functioning of this Protocol.

(6) Every reference in the foregoing provisions of this paragraph to exportation shall be construed as a reference to exportation to Member Territories and no reference in those provisions to importation shall be construed to include a reference to importation under the proviso to paragraph 3 or paragraph 5.

7. (1) The Secretariat shall convene a Conference in every year for the following purposes:

    (a) to consider the f.o.b. price to be fixed under subparagraph (2) of paragraph 8 for exports during the next following year of each commodity from one Member Territory to another;

    (b) to review the list in the Annex to this Protocol, the working of this Protocol, and the list, if any, established in pursuance of subparagraph (2) of paragraph 2;

    (c) to consider any matter connected with this Protocol and referred to the Conference by any participating Government,

and to make recommendations thereon.

(2) The Secretariat may convene a special Conference whenever the circumstances so require.

(3) Every Conference shall consist of the delegates of the participating Governments, one delegate (with such advisers as may be considered necessary) to be nominated by each Government.

(4) Every Conference shall elect its chairman from among the delegates nominated thereto.

(5) Every Conference shall be serviced by the Secretariat.

8. (1) Every such Conference as aforesaid shall be advisory to participating Governments, and its decisions shall be framed in that sense.

(2) A recommendation of any such Conference when accepted by two thirds of the participating Governments shall become binding on all the participating Governments, except with respect to matters in the case of which it has been prescribed, by agreement between the participating Governments, that unanimity among them is required for the purpose.

9. (1) It shall be the responsibility of the Secretariat:

    (a) to ensure that information with respect to export availability and import requirements is furnished, and imports are authorised, in conformity with the provisions of this Agreement;

  (b) to inform all participating Governments of requests and arrangements for the purchase and sale within the Area, and the importation into the Area, of any commodity;

  (c) otherwise, subject to the provisions of subparagraph (3) of this paragraph, to administer this Agreement.

 (2) The Secretariat shall compile and circulate to participating Governments periodically and regularly statistics relating to production and trade in agricultural products in the Area.

 (3) Every participating Government shall be responsible for the administration within its Territory of this Agreement and shall notify to the Secretariat all importations of any commodity into the Territory from outside the Area.

10. This Protocol shall come into operation when the Agreement takes effect.

In witness whereof the undersigned, duly authorised, have signed the present Protocol for the Governments herein below mentioned, respectively.

Done in a single copy which shall be deposited with the Government of Antigua by which certified copies shall be transmitted to all other Signatory Governments.[1]

PROTOCOL LAYING DOWN MARKETING ARRANGEMENTS FOR SUGAR PURSUANT TO ARTICLE 13 OF AND PARAGRAPH 6 OF ANNEX "A" TO THE AGREEMENT FOR ESTABLISHMENT OF THE CARIBBEAN FREE TRADE ASSOCIATION

The Signatory Governments:

Being the Governments of the Signatory Territories within the meaning of Article 31 of the Agreement for establishment of the Caribbean Free Trade Association;

Conscious of the vital role which the production of sugar plays in the economies of some territories in the Caribbean Free Trade Area;

Recognising that the different arrangements which exist for determining the prices at which sugar is sold for consumption in the territories of the Area could, under the terms of the Agreement, lead to the movement of sugar from one sugar producing territory in the Area to another;

Desirous of avoiding the adverse economic effects which such movement of sugar from one sugar producing territory in the Area to another is likely to produce,

Have agreed as follows:

1. For the purposes of this Protocol, unless the context otherwise requires:

---

[1] This Protocol on Agricultural Marketing Arrangements is followed by an annex listing twenty-two agricultural, livestock, and poultry products subject to such arrangements. [Editor's note.]

"the Agreement" means the Agreement for establishment of the Association as modified by a Supplementary Agreement for the purpose of widening the area of the Association;

"the Area" means the Area widened as aforesaid;

"the Association" means the Caribbean Free Trade Association;

"Member Territory" has the meaning assigned thereto by paragraph 2 of Article 1 of the Agreement;

"participating Government" means any Signatory Government of a Member Territory;

"sugar" means unrefined cane sugar.

2. Notwithstanding the provisions of Article 13 of the Agreement, any Member Territory in which sugar is produced may, subject to paragraph 3, and consistently with any international obligations to which it is subject, apply any quantitative restriction within the meaning of Article 13 on imports into that Territory of sugar from any other part of the Area.

3. Any Member Territory taking measures in accordance with paragraph 2 shall notify them to the Council, if possible before they come into force.

4. This Protocol shall come into operation when the Agreement takes effect.

In witness whereof the undersigned, duly authorised, have signed the present Protocol for the Governments herein below mentioned, respectively.

Done in a single copy which shall be deposited with the Government of Antigua by which certified copies shall be transmitted to all other Signatory Governments.

CHAPTER FOUR

East African Economic Community

Regional economic cooperation in what in colonial times was known as British East Africa, comprising the territories of Kenya, Uganda, and Tanganyika, started during the First World War. Over the following thirty years it led gradually to the establishment of a de facto common market supported by a common currency area and a score of common services in the fields of infrastructure, transport and communications, fiscal matters, and higher education, among others. During the political decolonization of the region (1961–1963) the scope of economic cooperation in East Africa was probably broader than anywhere else in the developing world. In the immediate postcolonial period attempts were made to transform the economic cooperation scheme into a full-fledged political federation of the three newly independent states. Not only did these attempts fail but extremely serious frictions developed between Kenya, Uganda, and Tanzania (which emerged in 1964 as a federation between Tanganyika and Zanzibar) over the unequal distribution of benefits ensuing from the common market and the common services arrangements. At various points in 1964 and 1965 the breakdown of this regional economic cooperation scheme looked almost inevitable, and in fact cooperation in certain specific fields was suspended or curtailed.

Facing the possibility of a total disintegration of the scheme, the heads of the participating countries in August 1965 set up a tripartite ministerial commission headed by Kjeld Philip, a United Nations expert of Danish nationality. After almost two years of work the Philip Commission elaborated a draft Treaty for East African Co-operation, which provided for the establishment of an East African Community and overhauled and formalized an agreement concerning the East African Common Market. The Treaty was signed by the Presidents of Kenya, Uganda, and

Tanzania in Kampala, Uganda, on June 6, 1967 and entered into force on December 1, 1967.

The magnitude of the task faced by the Philip Commission and the spirit of mutual accommodation needed to overcome numerous serious difficulties arising from the dissatisfaction of Uganda and Tanzania with the working of the scheme inherited from colonial times cannot be properly evaluated without a review of the history of the East African Common Market and the East African Common Services Organization (EACSO), two basic parts of the cooperation program.

A common market was achieved in the region in a number of stages long before the independence of three East African states. Its legal basis consisted of a series of ordinances issued by British colonial authorities between 1918 and 1947 and amplified during the 1950s by Acts of the East African Central Legislative Assembly. An agreement between Kenya and Uganda, dating from 1918, on the free transfer of domestically produced goods and the amalgamation of their customs authorities marked the beginning of the regional common market. In 1919/20 a common currency area under the East African Currency Board and a Common Court of Appeal for East Africa were established. In 1923 Tanganyika, although still retaining a separate customs department, was brought into a common market arrangement (Tanganyika's customs department was merged with that of Kenya and Uganda only in 1949). The interwar period also witnessed the gradual emergence of the regional common services, which at first took the form of railway systems coordination and amalgamation of the postal and telegraph services. Common services were further strengthened and expanded during the Second World War within the framework of coordination of the Allied war effort, under the guidance of the Conference of Governors of British East Africa that functioned in the area between 1926 and 1948.

In 1948, upon the initiative of the British government and in view of the growing scope of regional economic cooperation, a single regional authority, the East Africa High Commission, was established. The creation of the High Commission did not involve a closer political union or a merger of the three territorial governments. They continued to have direct relations with the Secretary of State for the Colonies in London, and they retained their own constitutions and exclusive responsibility for basic administration and police services, health and education, agriculture, animal health, labor, housing, and public works. Together with its secretariat and a legislative arm, the Central Legislative Assembly, the High

Commission took charge of multiple aspects of regional cooperation. The East African Currency Board, however, was directly dependent upon the British Treasury and continued to function independently.

After the establishment of the High Commission, the area's railway systems were finally merged; a common rail transport tariff was introduced; postal and telecommunication services were put on a self-sustaining basis; the Income Tax and Customs and Excise Departments were reorganized into efficient agencies for the collection of taxes and duties for the whole region; and a regional scheme was introduced for the licensing of new industries. By the end of the 1950s the High Commission administered about thirty interterritorial services and departments. The legal structure of regional cooperation was substantially strengthened by a number of Acts passed by the Central Legislative Assembly and having effect in all three territories. Important as the activities of the two regional bodies were, their centralizing power was circumscribed by the dependence of the High Commission on grants from the territorial governments and by the restrictions imposed upon the Legislative Assembly, which was enjoined from passing regional legislation in such important matters as customs and excise tariff rates, commercial legislation, and economic development policies. At the same time, despite the considerable contribution of existing cooperation arrangements to the economic growth and welfare of the region, the growing participation of the African population in territorial self-government brought about serious frictions about the distribution of the benefits of economic integration among the three colonial territories.

These frictions increased after independence, with large sectors of African public opinion in Uganda — and even more in Tanganyika — insisting that an undue share of the benefits from free trade, new industrial activities, and common services was accruing to Kenya, the most developed member of the scheme. Criticisms ranged from assertions that the benefits received by Uganda and Tanganyika (later Tanzania) represented only a fraction of those accruing to Kenya to accusations that Kenya's economic and specifically industrial development was taking place at a loss to the two other economies. Shortly before independence an Economic and Fiscal Commission, sent from London and known in the area as the Raisman Commission, investigated the matter and concluded that the common market and the common services had benefited the whole of East Africa and that, although participation in the benefits had not been equal, none of the territories would have been better off on its own. To placate Uganda and Tanganyika, at the Raisman Commission's recommendation, a Distributable Pool Fund was established under the administration of the High Commission to provide for the financing of common services and for the redistribution of revenue among the territories. The redistribution formula called for some transfer of net fiscal resources from Kenya to Uganda and Tanganyika. The Fund received annually 40 per cent of the income tax from companies and 6 per cent of the customs and excise duty receipts collected in East Africa. After applying half of the proceeds to the financing of common services, it distributed the rest equally among the three territories. However, the establishment of the Distributable Pool Fund failed to end the dissatisfaction of Uganda and Tanganyika. After independence — followed by the complete failure of attempts, fostered principally by Tanganyika, to achieve a political federation — conflicts between the three countries increased in intensity, primarily because of the lack of balance in interterritorial trade flows and the subsequent losses of customs revenue by the two less developed members of the scheme and because of the concentration of new industrial activities in Kenya and the benefits accruing to that country from the location of the East African Common Services Organization in its capital, Nairobi.

The uneven distribution of the benefits of a regional economic integration scheme became an issue in East Africa at an early stage of the common market arrangements. It was Kenya, a relatively advanced country well endowed in natural resources and non-African entrepreneurial talent, that led the movement toward integration. While Uganda and Tanganyika continued as traditional peasant-based, export-oriented economies, Kenya, in the early twenties, became a development pole of the area, with a fairly diversified and highly productive agriculture and a rapidly growing light industry sector. Already in the interwar period some experts on the economics of East African integration maintained that the East African Common Market was established to provide additional outlets for Kenya's agriculture and industry.

The different economic and financial policies of Great Britain toward the three territories during the 1900–1950 period and the especially high priority given to building up infrastructure in Kenya, together with the concentration of common administrative and other services in that country, strongly suggest that in colonial times Great Britain followed a conscious policy of building up Kenya as a development center not only for East Africa but also for what is known as the Greater East African region, which extends from southern Sudan to the northern parts of the Rhodesias. Since the mid-1920s, large subsidies from the metropolitan power — a protective tariff around the East African common market and differential transport rates taxing imports and favoring interregional trade and exports to the rest of the world — were used to foster Kenya's development. Devoid of any industrial base, both Uganda and Tanganyika protested against the high external common market tariff and the railway rate policies in the area, and complained about the loss of fiscal revenues caused by the substitution of Kenya products for dutiable foreign imports. Some adjustments in colonial policies were made in 1930–1932 to placate Uganda and Tanganyika. The controversy became forgotten, however, during the following two decades, first because of major over-all difficulties brought to the area by the Great Depression, and later because of the traditional commodity export boom that in East Africa lasted from the beginning of the Second World War to the end of the Korean conflict.

Only with the general deterioration of world commodity trade in the mid-1950s did the issue of the alleged economic exploitation of Uganda and Tanganyika by Kenya through common market and common services devices again appear on the East African scene. The two less developed participants claimed this time that the unification of fiscal policies within the common market worked in favor of Kenya, that they were losing substantial revenue through the substitution of Kenya's goods for foreign imports and suffering additional losses through terms of trade deterioration, and that they were forgoing a chance to industrialize while not sharing the benefits that Kenya received from the rapid growth of its manufacturing sector, which by 1960 represented 70 per cent of the manufacturing output of East Africa. The Raisman Commission attempted in 1961 to alleviate political tensions in the area by recommending the establishment of a Distributable Pool Fund. Because of the growing trade imbalances arising from the advanced production structure of the Kenya economy and a rapid, albeit largely unilateral, expansion of interterritorial trade, the establishment of the Fund brought very limited relief.

In the period 1954–1963 intraregional exports increased from $16.2 million to $55.4 million, and their participation in the area's global exports increased from 13 to 17 per cent. In the mid-1960s almost half of the interterritorial trade consisted of manufactures, demonstrating that the postwar industrialization of East Africa, largely concentrated in Kenya, depended heavily on the existence of a protected regional market. As in the past, Kenya continued to be the main supplier of goods entering interterritorial trade. Between 1959 and 1963 its share in regional exports averaged 63 per cent compared with 27 per cent for Uganda and 10 per cent for Tanganyika. The last-mentioned country was in turn the largest importer from the area (with an average share of 41 per cent), followed by Uganda (30 per cent) and Kenya (29 per cent).

Shortly after independence, Tanganyika's — and to a lesser extent Uganda's — persistent trade deficit was taken up by the heads of the new states in the context of future industrial policies for the region. Under the Kampala Agreement (April 1964) and the existing industrial licensing scheme, Tanganyika was given the exclusive right to establish three new region-oriented industries, Uganda two, and Kenya only one. It was agreed, furthermore, that a country having a large interterritorial trade deficit and intending to expand or start an industry that could be operated efficiently and economically in one country might apply quotas against similar imports from the rest of East Africa. Although the agreement on the distribution of new industrial activities on a regional scale was never implemented and regional trade imbalances continued, in 1965 Tanzania began to restrict imports from the region despite violent protests from Kenya. The emergence of interterritorial trade restrictions, together with the decision of the three countries to dissolve the common currency area formed in 1920 and to establish separate national central banks, intensified the widespread fear that the common market and common services arrangements might eventually break down completely.

It was in this atmosphere of crisis in political and economic relations that the Philip Commission was established in August 1965 to salvage the regional cooperation scheme. Its terms of reference were defined as follows: to examine existing arrangements in East Africa for cooperation between Kenya, Tanzania, and Uganda and to present recommendations acceptable to all parties concerned on the future functioning of the common market (taking due regard of the establishment of separate national currencies); the extent to which the existing common services should continue; the financing of the common services arrangements; the distribution of the management of common services throughout the area; and the new constitutional, legal, and administrative arrangements needed to promote economic cooperation in East Africa.

At the very beginning of the new treaty negotiations it became clear that despite the growing differences concerning internal economic policies between Kenya and Uganda on the one hand and Tanzania on the other, there was common agreement on the highest political level in the area that the breakdown of the economic cooperation arrangement must be avoided and that the common market would be able to function in the future only if it provided for a more balanced economic growth of the area. Although broad political consensus existed, a number of thorny problems remained to be solved. These related to the equitable distribution of benefits from free trade and regional industrialization and to the fact that, after the breakdown of the common currency area in 1965, each country had started implementing its own autonomous monetary and development policies. The early stages of the work of the Philip Commission confirmed that among the central issues to be resolved through tripartite negotiations the following were outstanding: the secular trend toward interregional trade imbalances in favor of Kenya; the concentration of new industrial activities in the same country; and the preponderant role of Nairobi, the capital of Kenya, as the administrative center for common services. It took the Philip Commission over a year to work out solutions in principle for these contentious issues. The drafting of the new treaty was finished in December 1966, and in early 1967 the text was submitted to the three heads of state for final revision and approval. At that time only one major problem remained to be solved: the size of Kenya's indirect financial assistance to Uganda and Tanzania through a proposed East African Development Bank. All three countries were expected to make equal contributions to the Bank, but the two less developed members asked to receive larger drawing rights than Kenya. The final formula, agreed to in late May 1967, assured Uganda and Tanzania of $38\frac{3}{4}$ per cent each and Kenya of the remaining $22\frac{1}{2}$ per cent of the total credits, loans, and investments to be made by the regional bank over the first ten years of its existence.

The Treaty for East African Co-operation, which entered into force on December 1, 1967, expands the scope of regional cooperation and at the same time represents an ingenious effort to eliminate the sources of past frictions among member countries. It provides for the strengthening of the common market, the decentralization of the East African Common Services Organization, the establishment of an East African Development Bank, and a large measure of monetary cooperation within the framework of the newly established East African Community. The aim of the Community, as defined in the Treaty, is "to strengthen and regulate the industrial, commercial and other relations of the Partner States to the end that there shall be accelerated, harmonious and balanced development and sustained expansion of economic activities the benefits whereof shall be equally shared." The parts of the treaty dealing with the Common Market are expected to remain in force for fifteen years; at the end of this period they will be reviewed. A common customs tariff on all goods imported into the region from foreign states will be perfected and maintained, and customs duties will be paid to a consuming state. All internal tariffs and quantitative restrictions on intra–East African trade will be rescinded. East African goods are defined as those produced in the area with value added during the processing of imported inputs being no less than 30 per cent. Certain agricultural products are excepted from free trade. In addition to a common external tariff, a common excise tax on excisable goods manufactured, processed, or produced in the member states will be introduced. Proceeds from this tax, which is to be collected by a regional fiscal agency, will be paid to consuming states.

To promote balanced industrial development, the member countries agreed to negotiate a common scheme of fiscal incentives. Moreover, the balancing of trade and the fostering of industrialization in the two less developed states, Uganda and Tanzania, will be supported by the device of a transfer tax. The Treaty provides that a member state experiencing a deficit in its total trade in specified manufactured goods with the other two states may impose transfer taxes on such goods originating in those countries. The transfer tax can be applied only if similar goods are being manufactured, or are expected to be manufactured shortly, in the deficit state. The value of goods imported from the area and affected by a transfer tax cannot exceed the value of the current deficit in the trade of manufactured goods with the other members of the common market, and no transfer tax can be imposed for more than eight years. The present system of industrial licensing for certain new activities will continue for twenty years from the date of the original agreement reached in 1964. The schedule of manufactures subject to regional industrial licensing will remain unchanged.

With respect to financial and monetary cooperation, in addition to the establishment of a regional development bank, the treaty provides that, subject to exchange control laws and regulations not in conflict with the Treaty, remittances among the member countries will be made at official par value without exchange commission. It also provides for freedom of current account payments between countries, but allows control of capital payments and transfers under specified conditions. The member countries commit themselves to harmonize their monetary policies to the extent required for the functioning of the common market through quarterly consultations among the governors of the three central banks. Finally, provision is made for the extension of reciprocal credits, up to defined limits and for a period of not more than three years, by one member state to another that is in need of balance-of-payments assistance.

To govern the Community and to settle disputes, the Treaty authorizes the establishment of an executive institution, the East African Authority, consisting of the three heads of state and three assisting East African ministers (one from each country). Five councils are to be established — for the Common Market, Communications, Economic Consultative and Planning, Finance, and Research and Social. An East African Legislative Assembly, consisting of nine members appointed from each country, the East African Ministers, the Secretary General, the Counsel to the Community, and the Chairman, is also to be formed. Disputes are to be settled by a Common Market Tribunal whose decisions must be reached by a majority. The four corporations within the Community — the East African Railways Corporation, the East African Harbours Corporation, the East African Posts and Telecommunications Corporation, and the East African Airways Corporation — are expected to continue to operate as self-sustained business enterprises. The headquarters of the Community, the development bank, and the four corporations will be distributed among the member countries, and the headquarters of the Community will be located in Arusha, Tanzania.

Bibliographic References

Clark, Paul G. *Development Planning in East Africa.* Nairobi: East African Publishing House, 1965.

Great Britain. Colonial Office. *East Africa: Report of the Economic and Fiscal Commission.* London: H.M. Stationery Office, 1961. Cmnd. 1279.

Hazelwood, Arthur. "The East African Common Market: Importance and Effects," Oxford University Institute of Economics and Statistics, *Bulletin,* Vol. 28, No. 1 (February 1966).

———. *Rail and Road in East Africa: Transport Coordination in Under-developed Countries.* Oxford: Basil Blackwell, 1964.

Ilett, J. "Designated Product Common Market," *The East African Economics Review* (Nairobi), Vol. 9, No. 2 (December 1962).

Leys, C., and P. Robson, eds. *Federation in East Africa: Opportunities and Problems.* Nairobi: Oxford University Press, 1965.

Massell, Benton F. *East African Economic Union: An Evaluation and Some Implications for Policy.* Santa Monica, Calif.: The RAND Corporation, December 1963.

Ndegwa, Philip. *The Common Market and Development in East Africa.* Nairobi: East African Publishing House, 1965.

Newlyn, W. T. "Monetary Systems and Integration," *The East African Economics Review,* Vol. 11, No. 1 (June 1964).

Nye, Joseph S., Jr. *Pan-Africanism and East African Federation.* Cambridge, Mass.: Harvard University Press, 1965.

Rosberg, Carl G., with Aaron Segal. *An East African Federation.* Carnegie Endowment for International Peace, *International Conciliation* (New York), No. 543 (May 1963).

Segal, Aaron. *East Africa: Strategy for Economic Co-operation.* Nairobi: The East African Institute of Social and Cultural Affairs, 1965.

Wionczek, Miguel S. "Experiences of the Central American Economic Integration as Applied to East Africa," *Industrialization and Productivity* (United Nations, New York), Bulletin 11 (1968).

TREATY FOR EAST AFRICAN CO-OPERATION*

Whereas the United Republic of Tanzania, the Sovereign State of Uganda and the Republic of Kenya have enjoyed close commercial, industrial and other ties for many years:

And whereas provision was made by the East Africa (High Commission) Orders in Council 1947 to 1961 for the control and administration of certain matters and services of common interest to the said countries and for that purpose the East Africa High Commission and the East Africa Central Legislative Assembly were thereby established:

And whereas provision was made by the East African Common Services Organization Agreements 1961 to 1966 (upon the revocation of the East Africa [High Commission] Orders in Council 1947 to 1961) for the establishment of the East African Common Services Organization with the East African Common Services Authority as its principal executive authority and the Central Legislative Assembly as its legislative body:

And whereas the East African Common Services Organization has, since its establishment, performed on behalf of the said countries common services in accordance with the wishes of the said countries and its Constitution:

And whereas the said countries, while being aware that they have reached different stages of industrial development and resolved to reduce existing industrial imbalances, are resolved and determined to foster and encourage the accelerated and sustained industrial development of all of the said countries:

And whereas the said countries, with a view to strengthening the unity of East Africa, are resolved to abolish certain quantitative restrictions which at present affect trade between them and are desirous of pursuing a policy towards the most favourable development of the freest possible international trade:

---

* Signed by Tanzania, Uganda, and Kenya at Kampala, Uganda, June 6, 1967. The Charter of the East African Development Bank, figuring as Annex VI to the Treaty, is reproduced separately as Document 28 in Part III of this volume. Some of the fifteen annexes (II, III, IV, VII, XI, XII, and XIII) have been omitted here for reasons of brevity. The text of the Treaty reproduced here is that published in a pamphlet of the same title, printed on behalf of the East African Common Services Organization by the Government Printer, Nairobi, Kenya, June 1967 (GPK 5673 — 3m — 5/67). [Editor's note.]

And whereas the said countries having regard to the interests of and their desire for the wider unity of Africa are resolved to co-operate with one another and with other African countries in the economic, political and cultural fields:

And whereas the said countries are resolved to act in concert for the establishment of a common market with no restrictions in the long term on trade between such countries:

Now therefore the Government of the United Republic of Tanzania, the Government of the Sovereign State of Uganda and the Government of the Republic of Kenya

Determined to strengthen their industrial, commercial and other ties and their common services by the establishment of an East African Community and of a Common Market as an integral part thereof

Agree as follows:

PART I: PRINCIPLES

CHAPTER I
THE EAST AFRICAN COMMUNITY

Article 1: Establishment and Membership of the Community

1. By this Treaty the Contracting Parties establish among themselves an East African Community and, as an integral part of such Community, an East African Common Market.

2. The East African Community is in this Treaty referred to as "the Community" and the East African Common Market is referred to as "the Common Market."

3. The members of the Community, in this Treaty referred to as "the Partner States," shall be the United Republic of Tanzania, the Sovereign State of Uganda and the Republic of Kenya.

Article 2: Aims of the Community

1. It shall be the aim of the Community to strengthen and regulate the industrial, commercial and other relations of the Partner States to the end that there shall be accelerated, harmonious and balanced development and sustained expansion of economic activities the benefits whereof shall be equitably shared.

2. For the purposes set out in paragraph 1 of this Article and as hereinafter provided in the particular provisions of this Treaty, the Community shall use its best endeavours to ensure:

    (a) the establishment and maintenance, subject to certain exceptions, of a common customs tariff and a common excise tariff;

    (b) the abolition generally of restrictions on trade between Partner States;

    (c) the inauguration, in the long term, of a common agricultural policy;

    (d) the establishment of an East African Development Bank in accordance with the Chapter contained in Annex VI to this Treaty;

(e) the retention of freedom of current account payments between the Partner States, and freedom of capital account payments necessary to further the aims of the Community;

(f) the harmonization, required for the proper functioning of the Common Market, of the monetary policies of the Partner States and in particular consultation in case of any disequilibrium in the balances of payments of the Partner States;

(g) the operation of services common to the Partner States;

(h) the co-ordination of economic planning;

(i) the co-ordination of transport policy;

(j) the approximation of the commercial laws of the Partner States; and

(k) such other activities, calculated to further the aims of the Community, as the Partner States may from time to time decide to undertake in common.

Article 3: Institutions of the Community

1. The institutions of the Community (established and regulated by Parts III and IV of this Treaty) shall be:

the East African Authority
the East African Legislative Assembly
the East African Ministers
the Common Market Council
the Common Market Tribunal
the Communications Council
the Finance Council
the Economic Consultative and Planning Council
the Research and Social Council,

and such other corporations, bodies, departments and services as are established or provided for by this Treaty.

2. The institutions of the Community shall perform the functions and act within the limits of the powers conferred upon them by this Treaty or by any law.

3. The institutions of the Community shall be assisted in the exercise of their functions by a central secretariat of officers in the service of the Community.

4. Persons employed in the service of the Community, the Corporations or the Bank, and directors and alternate directors of the Bank:

(a) shall be immune from civil process with respect to acts performed by them in their official capacity; and

(b) shall be accorded immunities from immigration restrictions or alien registration, and where they are not citizens of a Partner State, such facilities in relation to exchange regulations, as the Authority may determine.

5. Experts or consultants rendering services to the Community, the Corporations or the Bank shall be accorded such immunities and privileges in the Partner States as the Authority may determine.

Article 4: General Undertaking as to Implementation

The Partner States shall make every effort to plan and direct their policies with a view to creating conditions favourable for the development of the Common Market and the achievement of the aims of the Community and shall co-ordinate, through the institutions of the Community, their economic policies to the extent necessary to achieve such aims and shall abstain from any measure likely to jeopardize the achievement thereof.

PART II: THE EAST AFRICAN COMMON MARKET

CHAPTER II
EXTERNAL TRADE

Article 5: Common Customs Tariff

1. The Partner States, recognizing that a common external customs tariff is a basic requirement of the Common Market and subject to paragraphs 2 and 3 of this Article, agree to establish and maintain a common customs tariff in respect of all goods imported into the Partner States from foreign countries.

2. A Partner State may, with the agreement of the Ministers of the Partner States responsible for public finance, depart from the common external customs tariff in respect of the importation of a particular item into that State.

3. The Partner States agree to undertake early consultations in the Common Market Council with a view to the abolition generally of existing differences in the external customs tariff.

Article 6: Remission of Customs Duty

1. The Partner States agree not to exempt, remit or otherwise relieve from payment of customs duty any goods originating in a foreign country and imported by the Government of a Partner State if:

(a) such goods are imported for the purpose of resale or for any purpose other than consumption or use by that Government; and

(b) in the case of goods provided by way of aid, by any government or organization, either *gratis* or on terms less stringent than those appropriate to ordinary commercial transactions, such goods are intended for the purpose of resale or consumption in, or are transferred to, any country other than the Partner State which is the recipient of such goods.

2. The Partner States agree that the Community and the Corporations shall be enabled to import free of customs duty any goods required for the purpose of their operations except such goods as are intended for sale, or are sold, to the public.

Article 7: External Trade Arrangements

No Partner State shall enter into arrangements with any foreign country whereunder tariff concessions are available to that Partner State which are not available to the other Partner States.

Article 8: Deviation of Trade Resulting from Barter Agreements

1. If as a result of any barter agreement involving a particular kind of manufactured goods, entered into between a Partner State or any body or person therein, and a foreign country, or any body or person therein, there is, in respect of that kind of manufactured goods, a significant deviation of trade away from goods coming from and manufactured in another Partner State to goods imported in pursuance of that agreement, then the Partner State into which such goods are so imported shall take effective measures to counteract such deviation.

2. In paragraph 1 of this Article "barter agreement" means any agreement or arrangement by which manufactured goods are imported into a Partner State, being goods for which settlement may be effected, in whole or in part, by the direct exchange of goods.

3. In order to determine whether a deviation of trade in a particular kind of manufactured goods has occurred for the purposes of this Article, regard shall be had to all relevant trade statistics and other records concerning that kind of manufactured goods of the East African Customs and Excise Department for the six months immediately preceding a complaint that a deviation has occurred and to the average of the two comparable periods of six months in the twenty-four months which preceded the first importation of goods under the barter agreement.

CHAPTER III
INTRA–EAST AFRICAN TRADE

Article 9: External Goods — General Principles

1. The Partner States agree that where customs duty has been charged and collected on any goods imported into a Partner State (hereinafter in this paragraph referred to as "the importing State") from a foreign country then such goods shall not be liable to further customs duty on transfer to any other Partner State (hereinafter referred to as "the receiving State"):

Provided that where the rate of customs duty applicable to such goods in the receiving State exceeds that charged and collected in the importing State any excess of duty so arising may be charged and collected.

2. Each of the Partner States shall grant full and unrestricted freedom of transit through its territory for goods proceeding to or from a foreign country indirectly through that territory to or from another Partner State; and such transit shall not be subject to any discrimination, quantitative restrictions, duties or other charges levied on transit.

3. Notwithstanding paragraph 2 of this Article:

(a) goods in transit shall be subject to the customs laws; and

(b) goods in transit shall be liable to the charges usually made for carriage and for any services which may be rendered, provided such charges are not discriminatory.

4. The Partner States agree that each Partner State shall be entitled to prohibit or restrict the import from a foreign country into it of goods of any particular description or derived from any particular source.

5. Where goods are imported from a foreign country into one Partner State, it shall be open to each of the other Partner States to restrict the transfer to it of such goods whether by a system of licensing and controlling importers or by other means:

Provided that, in the application of any restriction referred to in this paragraph, regard shall be had to the practicability of such restriction where goods have been repacked, blended, or otherwise processed.

6. The provisions of paragraphs 4 and 5 of this Article shall not apply to any goods which, under the provisions of Article 11 of this Treaty, fall to be accepted as goods originating in a Partner State.

Article 10: Customs Duty Collected to Be Paid to Consuming State

1. Where any goods, which are imported into a Partner State from a foreign country and in respect of which customs duty has been charged and collected in that State (in this paragraph referred to as "the collecting State") are transferred to one of the other Partner States (in this paragraph referred to as "the consuming State"), the following provisions shall apply:

(a) if the duty collected in the collecting State was a specific duty or if the goods are transferred to the consuming State in their original packages, the collecting State shall pay the full amount of the duty collected to the consuming State;

(b) if the duty collected in the collecting State was an *ad valorem* duty and the goods are transferred to the consuming State other than in their original packages, the collecting State shall pay to the consuming State an amount equal to 70 per cent of the duty which would have been payable if the value of the goods for duty had been taken to be the ordinary retail price; and for this purpose "ordinary retail price" means the price at which the goods could be expected to sell at the time and place of their transfer to the consuming State:

Provided that the Authority may by order from time to time alter the amount to be paid by the collecting State to the consuming State under this sub-paragraph and the method of calculation thereof;

(c) if the duty collected was an *ad valorem* duty and the goods are transferred other than in their original packages and an alteration of the relevant tariff has been made in the collecting State within a material time, then, for the purpose of calculating the sum to be paid under sub-paragraph (b) of this paragraph, duty shall be deemed to have been collected in accordance with the tariff actually in force six weeks before the transfer of the goods.

2. Where any goods, which are imported from a foreign country into a Partner State (in this paragraph referred to as "the importing State") are

chargeable to customs duty in that State, but the duty has been remitted either in whole or in part, and are subsequently transferred to one of the other Partner States (in this paragraph referred to as "the consuming State") the importing State shall, notwithstanding the said remission, pay to the consuming State the amount which would have been paid to the consuming State in accordance with paragraph 1 of this Article had the duty been collected but to the extent only that such duty would have been chargeable and collected if the goods had been imported directly into the consuming State.

Article 11: No Internal Tariff on East African Goods

1. Except as is provided in paragraph 2 of this Article no Partner State shall impose a duty in the nature of a customs duty or import duty in respect of goods which are transferred to that Partner State from one of the other Partner States and originate in the Partner States.

2. Paragraph 1 of this Article is subject to the rights and powers of Partner States to impose transfer taxes in accordance with and subject to the conditions contained in this Treaty.

3. For the purpose of this Treaty, goods shall be accepted as originating in the Partner States where:

(a) they have been wholly produced in the Partner States; or
(b) they have been produced in the Partner States and the value of materials imported from a foreign country or of undetermined origin which have been used at any stage of the production of the goods does not exceed 70 per cent of the ex-factory value of the goods.

4. Rules for the administration and application of this Article are contained in Annex I to this Treaty.

5. The Common Market Council shall from time to time examine whether the rules contained in Annex I to this Treaty can be amended to make them simpler and more liberal and to ensure their smooth and equitable operation, and the Authority may by order from time to time amend or add to Annex I.

Article 12: No Quantitative Restrictions on East African Goods

1. Except as is provided in this Article, each of the Partner States undertakes that, at a time not later than the coming into force of this Treaty, it will remove all the then existing quota, quantitative or the like restrictions or prohibitions which apply to the transfer to that State of goods originating in the other Partner States (including agricultural products) and, except as may be provided for or permitted by this Treaty, will thereafter refrain from imposing any further restrictions or prohibitions:

Provided that this paragraph shall not preclude a Partner State introducing or continuing or executing restrictions or prohibitions affecting:

(a) the application of security laws and regulations;
(b) the control of arms, ammunition and other war equipment and military items;
(c) the protection of human, animal or plant health or life, or the protection of public morality;

(d) transfers of gold, silver and precious and semi-precious stones;

(e) the control of nuclear materials, radio-active products or any other material used in the development or exploitation of nuclear energy; or

(f) the protection of its revenue where another Partner State has, in accordance with paragraph 2 of Article 17 of this Treaty, departed from a common excise tariff.

2. It is agreed that each of the Partner States shall have the right to impose restrictions and prohibitions against the transfer of goods from the other Partner States which originate in the other Partner States, insofar as may be necessary from time to time to give effect to the contractual and other obligations entered into by each of the States and listed in Annex II to this Treaty.

3. It is agreed that each of the Partner States shall have the right to impose quantitative restrictions or prohibitions in respect of certain agricultural products in the circumstances provided for by Article 13 of this Treaty.

4. If a Partner State encounters balance of payment difficulties, taking into account its overall position, that Partner State may, for the purpose only of overcoming such difficulties, impose quantitative restrictions on the goods of the other Partner States, subject to the following conditions being satisfied, namely that:

(a) the proposed quantitative restrictions do not contravene its obligations under the General Agreement on Tariffs and Trade or its obligations under the rules of the International Monetary Fund; and

(b) restrictions have been imposed on the import of goods from foreign countries and are inadequate to solve the difficulties; and

(c) the restrictions imposed under this paragraph shall in no case operate against the goods of Partner States more unfavourably than the restrictions imposed on the goods of foreign countries; and

(d) consultation concerning the proposed quantitative restrictions has first taken place within the Common Market Council and thereafter, while such restrictions remain in force, the Common Market Council shall keep the operation thereof under review.

Article 13: Exception for Certain Agricultural Products

1. Notwithstanding the obligation of the Partner States in respect of agricultural products referred to in paragraph 1 of Article 12 of this Treaty, it is declared that each of the Partner States shall, to the extent set out in Annex III to this Treaty, have the right to impose quantitative restrictions against the transfer of the agricultural products of the other Partner States which are basic staple foods or major export crops, subject to special marketing arrangements and listed in that Annex.

2. The Authority may from time to time amend or add to Annex III to this Treaty.

Article 14: Long-Term Aim as to Agriculture

Notwithstanding Articles 12 and 13 of this Treaty, it is declared that, in the long term, it is the aim and intention of the Partner States that the provisions of this Treaty relating to the establishment and maintenance of the Common Market should extend to agriculture and trade in agricultural products and that the development of the Common Market in respect of agricultural products should be accompanied by co-operation and consultation in the field of agricultural policy among the Partner States so that in particular, within the framework of the Community, trade arrangements between the national agencies or marketing boards of the Partner States may be entered into directly within a single system of prices and a network within the Partner States as a whole of marketing services and facilities.

Article 15: Customs Duty on Goods Used in Manufacture

1. Where goods which are imported into a Partner State from a foreign country and in respect of which customs duty is charged and collected in that State (in this Article referred to as "the collecting State") are wholly or in part used in the collecting State in the manufacture of other goods (in this Article referred to as "the manufactured goods"), and the manufactured goods are subsequently transferred to another Partner State (in this Article referred to as "the consuming State"), the collecting State shall pay to the consuming State the full amount of the duty collected in the collecting State in respect of the goods imported into the collecting State and used in the manufacture of the manufactured goods subsequently transferred to the consuming State.

2. Where goods which are imported into a Partner State (in this paragraph referred to as "the importing State") from a foreign country are chargeable to customs duty in that State but the duty has been remitted either in whole or in part and the goods are wholly or in part used in the importing State in the manufacture of other goods (in this paragraph referred to as "the manufactured goods"), and the manufactured goods are subsequently transferred to another Partner State (in this paragraph referred to as "the consuming State"), the importing State shall, notwithstanding the said remission, pay to the consuming State the amount of the duty chargeable in respect of goods imported into the importing State and used in the manufacture of the manufactured goods subsequently transferred to the consuming State to the extent that such duty would have been chargeable and collected if the goods had been imported into the consuming State.

3. Notwithstanding paragraphs 1 and 2 of this Article, if the value of the imported goods which are used in the manufacture of any manufactured goods transferred as a separate consignment is less than one hundred shillings in the currency of the State of manufacture, then in that case only no payment of duty shall be made to the consuming State under this Article.

Article 16: Discriminatory Practices

1. The Partner States recognize that the following practices are incompatible with this Treaty to the extent that they frustrate the benefits expected from the removal or absence of duties and quantitative restrictions on trade between the Partner States:

(a) one channel marketing;

(b) discriminatory rates of taxes, duties or other charges levied in a Partner State on any goods originating in another Partner State;

(c) dumping; and

(d) discriminatory purchasing.

2. In paragraph 1 of this Article:

(a) "one channel marketing" means any arrangement for the marketing of goods, whether regulated by law or otherwise, which, by limiting the channels by which such goods may be marketed, has effect to exclude competition in the marketing of such goods;

(b) "discriminatory rates of taxes, duties or other charges" means rates of taxes, duties or other charges imposed upon goods by a Partner State which place such goods in an unfavourable position with regard to sale by comparison with similar goods originating in that Partner State or imported from any other country;

(c) "dumping" means the transfer of goods originating in a Partner State to another Partner State for sale:

(i) at a price less than the comparable price charged for similar goods in the Partner State where such goods originate (due allowance being made for the differences in the conditions of sale or in taxation or for any other factors affecting the comparability of prices); and

(ii) under circumstances likely to prejudice the production of similar goods in that Partner State; and

(d) "discriminatory purchasing" means any arrangement or practice whereby a Partner State or any body or person therein gives preference to the purchase of goods originating from a foreign country when suitable goods originating within the Partner States are available on comparable terms including price.

CHAPTER IV
EXCISABLE GOODS

Article 17: Common Excise Tariff

1. Subject to paragraphs 2 and 3 of this Article, the Partner States agree to establish and maintain a common excise tariff in respect of excisable goods manufactured, processed or produced in the Partner States.

2. For revenue purposes, a Partner State may, in special circumstances and after consultation between the Ministers of the Partner States responsible for public finance, depart from the common excise tariff in respect of the manufacture, processing or production of particular excisable goods in that State:

Provided that a Partner State before acting under this paragraph shall have due regard to the administrative practicability of enforcing the departure contemplated and to whether the proposed departure would be likely to affect detrimentally the proper functioning of the Common Market.

3. The Partner States acknowledge their intention to remove presently existing differences in the excise tariff which the Common Market Council

may determine to be undesirable in the interests of the proper functioning of the Common Market.

Article 18: Excise Duty to Be Paid to Consuming State

1. Where goods which are liable to excise duty in one of the Partner States (in this Article referred to as "the collecting State") are transferred to another Partner State (in this Article referred to as "the consuming State") the East African Customs and Excise Department shall collect excise duty either at the rate in force in respect of the collecting State or, where the rate in force in respect of the consuming State is higher than that in force in respect of the collecting State, at that rate.

2. Where the rate of excise duty in force in respect of the consuming State is lower than that in force in respect of the collecting State, the owner or other transferor of goods referred to in paragraph 1 of this Article shall receive from the East African Customs and Excise Department, on proof of transfer to the consuming State, a refund of the difference between those rates of duty.

3. The East African Customs and Excise Department shall, in respect of goods liable to excise duty transferred from the collecting State to the consuming State, pay to the consuming State the amount of the excise duty collected at the rate in force in that State.

CHAPTER V
MEASURES TO PROMOTE BALANCED INDUSTRIAL DEVELOPMENT

Article 19: Fiscal Incentives

The Partner States declare that they shall use their best endeavours to agree upon a common scheme of fiscal incentives towards industrial development which shall apply within the Partner States.

Article 20: Transfer Tax

1. As a measure to promote new industrial development in those Partner States which are less developed industrially transfer taxes may, with the aim of promoting industrial balance between the Partner States, be imposed, notwithstanding paragraph 1 of Article 11 of this Treaty, in accordance with and subject to the conditions and limitations imposed by this Treaty.

2. In this Article, "manufactured goods" means the goods defined, or otherwise listed, in Annex IV to this Treaty. The Authority may by order from time to time amend or add to Annex IV.

3. Subject to this Article, a Partner State which is in deficit in its total trade in manufactured goods with the other two Partner States may impose transfer taxes upon manufactured goods which are transferred to that State and originate from either of the other Partner States.

4. Subject to this Article, a Partner State may impose transfer taxes upon

the manufactured goods of a Partner State being goods of a value not exceeding the amount of the deficit in trade in manufactured goods between the State which is imposing the transfer tax and the State of origin of the goods upon which the tax is to be imposed.

5. For the purposes of paragraphs 3 and 4 of this Article the deficit in trade in manufactured goods between Partner States shall at any time be taken to be that indicated in the most recently published annual trade statistics produced by the East African Customs and Excise Department and where, in any particular case, the manufactured goods of a Partner State upon which a transfer tax may under this Article be imposed are not readily identifiable within the trade statistics referred to in this paragraph, the Common Market Council may determine the extent to which any goods comprised in such statistics contribute to the amount of any deficit in any trade.

6. A Partner State may impose a transfer tax upon manufactured goods only if at the time the tax is imposed goods of a similar description are being manufactured in that State or are reasonably expected to be manufactured in that State within three months of the imposition of the tax, and for the purposes of this paragraph goods shall be deemed to be of a similar description to other goods if, in addition to similar function, constituent parts or content, they are of such a nature as will enable them actively to compete in the same market as those other goods:

Provided that this paragraph shall not preclude the imposition, but not the bringing into operation, of a suspended transfer tax at any time:

Provided further that, if a transfer tax is imposed in the reasonable expectation that the manufacture of particular goods will commence within three months of the imposition of the tax and such manufacture does not commence within that period:

(a) the Partner State imposing the transfer tax shall, within twenty-one days, revoke it unless, before the expiration of that period, that Partner State has obtained the directive of the Common Market Council that, conditional upon the commencement of manufacture within a further period of three months, the revocation of such tax may be deferred for such further period;

(b) notwithstanding that a transfer tax has been revoked, for the reason that the Common Market Council has not within three months of the imposition of such tax given the directive referred to in sub-paragraph (a) of this proviso, it shall be competent to that Council, where application in that behalf has been made by a Partner State within three months of the imposition of such tax, to direct that, conditional upon the commencement of manufacture within a further period of three months, such tax may be reimposed.

7. A Partner State may impose a transfer tax upon a particular kind of manufactured goods only if at the time the tax is imposed, or within three months thereafter if the tax is imposed in the reasonable expectation that the manufacture of such goods will commence within three months, the industry

within the tax imposing State has the capacity to produce in the ensuing year:

(a) a quantity of goods equivalent to not less than 15 per cent of the domestic consumption within that Partner State of goods of that particular kind in the period of twelve months immediately preceding the imposition of the tax; or

(b) goods of that particular kind having an ex-factory value of not less than 2,000,000 shillings.

8. The rate of transfer tax shall be determined by the Partner State which imposes it, but the rate for a particular item shall not exceed:

(a) where the duty is chargeable *ad valorem* or *ad valorem* as an alternative to the specific duty, 50 per cent of the rate of duty prescribed by the customs tariff of the tax imposing State in respect of the import of the same kind of item; or

(b) where the duty is a specific duty with no alternative *ad valorem*, 50 per cent of the *ad valorem* equivalent of the specific duty;

but if the same kind of item is not chargeable with any duty on import no transfer tax may be imposed.

9. For the purposes of paragraph 8 of this Article, the *ad valorem* equivalent of the specific duty on a particular item shall be the percentage which is equivalent to that proportion which the aggregate of the duties collected on all items of that kind imported into the tax imposing State in a period of one year bears to the total value of those items, calculated from the date used in compiling the most recently published annual trade statistics produced by the East African Customs and Excise Department:

Provided that, if in the course of the period covered by such annual trade statistics the relevant rate of specific duty was altered, the *ad valorem* equivalent of the specific duty shall be calculated with reference only to imports entered after the alteration of the rate of duty:

Provided further that, in the calculation of the *ad valorem* equivalent of the specific duty, no account shall be taken of manufactured goods which have been either exempted from the payment of customs duty or in respect of which the customs duty has been remitted:

Provided further that, in relation to goods subject to specific duty with no alternative *ad valorem*, where there has been no importation of such goods into the tax imposing State and consequently no *ad valorem* equivalent can be determined, the rate of transfer tax shall not exceed 50 per cent of the specific duty thereon.

10. Where, in accordance with this Article, a Partner State has imposed a transfer tax upon manufactured goods and subsequently the rate of customs duty chargeable in that State on goods of the same kind is reduced, so that by virtue of paragraph 8 of this Article the tax falls to be reduced, that State shall, within twenty-one days of such reduction, reduce the tax accordingly:

Provided that, where the relevant item in the customs tariff is expressed only as a specific duty, the obligation to reduce the tax shall be performed as soon as the *ad valorem* equivalent of the specific duty as defined in paragraph 9 of this Article can be recalculated, on the basis of statistics produced by the East African Customs and Excise Department, in respect of imports into the tax imposing State for a period of three months following the reduction in the customs tariff.

11. Transfer tax shall be assessed on the value of the manufactured goods upon which it is imposed, which shall be taken to be the value set out in Annex V to this Treaty:

Provided that, in the case of manufactured goods transferred under a contract of sale and entered for the payment of transfer tax, tax shall be deemed to have been paid on that value if, before the goods are released after transfer, tax is tendered and accepted on a declared value based on the contract price and for the purposes of this proviso:

(a) the declared value of any goods shall be their value as declared by or on behalf of the buyer in the country to which the goods are being transferred in making entry of the goods for transfer tax;

(b) that value shall be deemed to be based on the contract price if, but only if, it represents that price properly adjusted to take account of circumstances differentiating the contract from such contract of sale as is contemplated by Annex V to this Treaty; and

(c) the rate of exchange to be used for determining the equivalent in the currency of the country to which the goods are transferred of any foreign currency shall be the current selling rate for sight drafts in the country to which the goods are transferred as last notified before the time when the goods are entered for transfer:

Provided further that, where under Article 15 of this Treaty the Partner State in which the goods are manufactured is liable to pay to the Partner State which has imposed the transfer tax the full amount of customs duty collected in respect of goods imported and used in the manufacture of the manufactured goods, the amount of such duty paid over shall be deducted from the value provided for by this Article:

Provided further that, where under Article 18 of this Treaty the Partner State in which the goods are manufactured is liable to pay to the Partner State which has imposed the transfer tax the full amount of excise duty collected in respect of goods manufactured or processed or used in the manufacture of the manufactured goods, the amount of such duty paid shall be deducted from the value provided for by this Article.

12. The Authority may from time to time make rules for the administration and operation of paragraph 11 of this Article and of Annex V to this Treaty and may from time to time amend or add to such rules.

13. Subject to this Treaty, the assessment, collection, administration and management generally of all transfer taxes imposed under this Treaty shall be performed by the East African Customs and Excise Department, but the costs and expenses thereof, including any costs and expenses incurred in establishing the system of such assessment and collection, shall be borne by the Partner States which impose such transfer taxes in such manner as the Finance Council may from time to time determine.

14. Every transfer tax shall expire, unless sooner revoked, eight years after the date of its first imposition; and for the purposes of this paragraph no regard shall be had, in the case of a suspended transfer tax, to the date when, if at all, such tax is brought into operation.

15. Every transfer tax imposed under this Treaty shall be revoked fifteen years after the coming into force of this Treaty unless such tax has sooner expired.

16. Notwithstanding paragraphs 14 and 15 of this Article, the Partner States agree that, for the purpose of evaluating the effectiveness of the transfer tax system as an instrument for attaining the aims of the Community, and in particular its effectiveness as a measure to promote a more balanced industrial development, they will undertake joint consultations to review and reappraise the system five years after the first imposition of a transfer tax under this Treaty.

17. If, as a result of a Partner State imposing a transfer tax upon a particular kind of manufactured goods, there is, in respect of manufactured goods of that kind coming into the Partner State which has imposed the transfer tax, a significant deviation of trade away from goods coming from and manufactured in the Partner State whose goods are subject to the transfer tax, to goods imported from a foreign country, then the Partner State which has imposed the transfer tax shall take measures to counteract such deviation and the other Partner States shall, where appropriate, take steps, in co-operation with that Partner State, to make such measures effective.

18. In order to determine whether a deviation of trade in a particular kind of manufactured goods has occurred for the purpose of paragraph 17 of this Article, regard shall be had to the information concerning that kind of manufactured goods in the trade statistics of the East African Customs and Excise Department (or otherwise recorded by that Department) for the six months immediately preceding a complaint that a deviation has occurred and to the average of the two comparable periods of six months in the twenty-four months which preceded the imposition of the transfer tax.

19. If a transfer tax is imposed by a Partner State upon a particular kind of manufactured goods originating in one of the other Partner States, and subsequently not less than 30 per cent of the total ex-factory value of sales, in any period of twelve months, of manufactured goods of that kind originating in the tax imposing State is sold for transfer to the other Partner States, the transfer tax shall be revoked.

20. If a transfer tax is imposed by a Partner State upon a particular kind of manufactured goods originating in the other Partner States, or one of them, and subsequently not less than 30 per cent of the total ex-factory value of sales, in any period of twelve months, of manufactured goods of that kind originating in the tax imposing State is sold for transfer to the other Partner States or to a foreign country, a Partner State may, if it considers that in the circumstances the tax ought not to continue in force, having regard to all relevant matters and to this Treaty, raise the matter within the Common Market Council and the Council may direct that the Partner State which imposed the tax shall revoke it.

21. If a Partner State which is entitled to impose transfer taxes transfers to the other Partner States in any year beginning on the 1st January manufactured goods originating in that Partner State and amounting in total value to not less than 80 per cent of the total value (measured on a fair and comparable basis in accordance with the annual trade statistics produced by the East African Customs and Excise Department) of manufactured goods transferred into that Partner State from the other Partner States during that year (and originating in those Partner States), that Partner State shall not thereafter be entitled to impose any new transfer tax or bring any suspended transfer tax into operation; but this paragraph shall not affect any subsisting transfer tax.

22. If a transfer tax is imposed by a Partner State upon a particular kind of manufactured goods, the manufacture of which is regulated under the East African industrial licensing laws in operation in the Partner States (or any laws which may be enacted in replacement of those laws in pursuance of Article 23 of this Treaty), the Partner State whose goods are subject to the transfer tax may, if it considers that there are such exceptional circumstances that the tax ought not to continue in force, having regard to all relevant matters and to this Treaty, raise the matter within the Common Market Council and if the Council after due consideration finds that such circumstances exist the Partner State which imposed the tax shall revoke it.

23. Each Partner State shall take effective action to prevent manufactured goods originating in a Partner State being transferred to another Partner State at a price lower than their true value if such transfer is likely to prejudice the production of similar goods by that other Partner State or retard or prevent the establishment of an industry to produce such goods in that State.

24. For the purpose of paragraph 23 of this Article:

(a) manufactured goods shall be considered to be transferred at a price lower than their true value if, due allowance having been made in each case for differences in conditions of sale, taxation or for any other factors affecting the comparability of prices, their price on transfer is less than —

   (i) the comparable price, in ordinary trading conditions, of similar goods destined for domestic consumption in the State in which they were produced; or

   (ii) the comparable price of similar goods on their export to a foreign country in ordinary trading conditions; or

   (iii) the cost of production of the goods in the Partner State where they are produced, together with a reasonable addition in respect of distribution and sales costs and profit; and

(b) "effective action" shall include the making available of facilities for enquiry relating to any allegation, by a Partner State, of transfer of goods to that Partner State at a price lower than the true value of such goods and where, on reference to the Common Market Council, the fact of such transfer at such lower value has been established, the taking of such measures as, in relation to any industry, shall be calculated to prevent its recurrence.

25. No Partner State shall directly or indirectly subsidize the transfer of any manufactured goods from that Partner State, or establish, maintain or support any system whereby such goods are sold for transfer to another Partner State at a price lower than the comparable price charged for similar goods on the domestic market, due allowance being made for differences in the conditions of sale or in taxation and for any other factors affecting the comparability of prices.

26. For the purpose of paragraph 25 of this Article, tax incentives or refunds of a general and non-discriminatory nature granted by a Partner State with a view to encouraging production within that State of goods shall not constitute a transfer subsidy, provided they do not frustrate the purpose of the transfer tax system and are not inconsistent with this Treaty.

27. The Partner States agree that no transfer tax may be imposed upon manufactured goods which are required by the Community or by any of the Corporations for the purpose of their operations, otherwise than upon such goods as are intended for sale, or are sold, to the public.

Article 21: Establishment of the East African Development Bank

1. There is hereby established a Development Bank, to be known as the East African Development Bank.

2. The East African Development Bank is in this Treaty referred to as "the Bank."

Article 22: Charter of the Bank

The Charter of the Bank shall be that set out in Annex VI to this Treaty.

CHAPTER VI
INDUSTRIAL LICENSING

Article 23: Present System to Continue

1. Subject to this Article, the Partner States agree to continue the industrial licensing system formulated in the three East African Industrial Licensing laws now in operation in the Partner States, whereby the manufacture of certain articles scheduled under the said laws is regulated and the East African Industrial Council is empowered to grant industrial licences in respect of the manufacture of such articles.

2. It is agreed that the industrial licensing system shall continue until the expiration of twenty years from the commencement of the said East African Industrial Licensing laws.

3. It is agreed that no additions shall be made to the schedules of articles, the manufacture of which is subject to industrial licensing under the said East African Industrial Licensing laws.

4. Subject to paragraph 5 of this Article, the Partner States agree to support the early replacement of the said East African Industrial Licensing laws by one law to be introduced into the East African Legislative Assembly for enactment as an Act of the Community.

5. It is agreed that the law proposed in paragraph 4 of this Article shall

generally be in similar terms to the said East African Industrial Licensing laws, except that an appeal shall lie to the Industrial Licensing Appeal Tribunal on a matter of law only.

CHAPTER VII
CURRENCY AND BANKING

Article 24: No Exchange Commission

The Partner States undertake to make arrangements through their central banks, subject only to exchange control laws and regulations which do not conflict with this Treaty, whereby:

(a) their respective currency notes shall be exchanged without undue delay within the territories of the Partner States at official par value without exchange commission:

Provided that the Finance Council may at its discretion authorize the central banks to make such charge, upon the exchange of currency, as will be sufficient only to meet the cost of transfer of such currency to the Partner State of its origin; and

(b) remittances may be effected without undue delay between the Partner States at official par value of the respective currencies, that is to say without exchange commission.

Article 25: Payments and Capital Transfers

1. Each Partner State undertakes to permit, in the currency of the Partner State in which the creditor or beneficiary resides, all *bona fide* payments on current account falling within the definition of current account payments set out in Annex VII to this Treaty, and undertakes to ensure that all necessary permissions and authorities are given without undue delay.

2. Each Partner State undertakes to permit payments and transfers on capital account except to the extent that a Partner State may consider that control of certain categories of such payments and transfers is necessary for furthering its economic development and an increase in trade consistent with the aims of the Community:

Provided that no such control shall be imposed by a Partner State in such a manner as to prejudice the ability of the Community, the Bank or the Corporations to perform the functions conferred upon any of them by this Treaty or under any law.

3. The Authority may from time to time by order amend or add to Annex VII to this Treaty.

Article 26: Inter-State Settlements

The central banks of the Partner States shall open accounts with each other over which settlements shall be effected between them in a currency acceptable to the creditor.

Article 27: Economic and Monetary Policy

1. Each of the Partner States agrees to pursue an economic policy aimed at ensuring the equilibrium of its overall balance of payments and confidence in its currency.

2. The Partner States will endeavour to harmonize their monetary policies to the extent required for the proper functioning of the Common Market and the fulfilment of the aims of the Community, and for this purpose agree that the Governors of the three central banks shall meet at least four times in every year to consult, and to co-ordinate and review their monetary and balance of payments policies.

Article 28: Reciprocal Credits

1. If a Partner State is in difficulties as regards its balance of payments and has already exercised its drawing rights under the first credit tranche beyond the gold tranche with the International Monetary Fund, such State may, from time to time, request assistance in the way of credits for balance of payments support from any other Partner State with which it had a payments deficit in the last period of twelve months for which information is available and, subject to this Article, such a request shall be granted. Credits granted under this Article shall be in the currency of the Partner State granting the credits.

2. A Partner State shall not be obliged by this Article to allow credits at any one time to be outstanding in excess of an amount equivalent to the value of one-sixth of the goods transferred from the Partner State granting the credits to the recipient Partner State in the last period of twelve months for which information is available.

3. Except by agreement, a Partner State shall not be obliged by this Article to grant credits which in any year beginning on the 1st January exceed in total one-twelfth of the value of the goods transferred from the Partner State granting the credits to the recipient Partner State in the preceding year.

4. Credits granted in pursuance of this Article shall be for a period not exceeding three years and interest shall be paid half-yearly on the amounts outstanding at the rate of 4 per cent per annum for the first year, 5 per cent per annum for the second year and 6 per cent per annum for the third year.

CHAPTER VIII:
CO-OPERATION IN OTHER RESPECTS

Article 29: Co-operation in Particular Fields

The Partner States declare their intention to consult with one another through the appropriate institutions of the Community for the purpose of co-ordinating their respective policies in such fields of governmental activity as they may, from time to time, consider necessary or desirable for the efficient and harmonious functioning and development of the Common Market, and in particular, but without prejudice to the generality of the foregoing declaration, the Partner States agree:

(a) that the Tax Board established by Article 88 of this Treaty shall, if requested by any Partner State, render assistance in the study of and correlation between taxes managed and collected by the Community and taxes managed and collected directly by authorities in that Partner State, and shall render such further assistance in matters appertaining to fiscal planning as may be desired by any Partner State;

(b) that the Counsel to the Community shall advise the Partner States on, and endeavour to promote, the harmonization of the commercial laws in operation in the Partner States;

(c) that it is their intention to co-operate in the co-ordination of their surface transport policies and to consult thereon within the Communications Council as may from time to time be desirable; and

(d) in order to assist their respective national planning, to engage in consultations within the Economic Consultative and Planning Council and between the planning authorities of each of the Partner States and those of the Community.

PART III: PRINCIPAL COMMON MARKET MACHINERY

CHAPTER IX
THE COMMON MARKET COUNCIL

Article 30: Responsibilities of the Common Market Council

It shall be the responsibility of the Common Market Council established by Article 53 of this Treaty:

(a) to exercise such powers and perform such duties as are conferred or imposed upon it by this Treaty;

(b) to ensure the functioning and development of the Common Market in accordance with this Treaty and to keep its operation under review;

(c) to settle problems arising from the implementation of this Treaty concerning the Common Market;

(d) to receive and consider references making, refuting or concerning allegations as to the breach of any obligation under this Treaty in relation to the Common Market or as to any action or omission affecting the Common Market alleged to be in contravention of this Treaty and determine every such reference as follows:

    (i) by issuing a binding directive to a Partner State or States; or

    (ii) by making recommendations to a Partner State or States; or

    (iii) by recording that the reference shall be deemed to be abandoned, settled or otherwise disposed of; or

    (iv) by recording an inability to agree in relation to the reference;

(e) to consider what further action should be taken by Partner States and the Community in order to promote the attainment of the aims of the Community and to facilitate the establishment of closer economic and commercial links with other States, associations of States or international organizations;

(f) to request advisory opinions from the Common Market Tribunal in accordance with this Treaty.

Article 31: Common Market Functions of the Central Secretariat

1. The central secretariat shall keep the functioning of the Common Market under continuous examination and may act in relation to any particular matter which appears to merit examination either on its own initiative or upon the request of a Partner State made through the Common Market Council and the central secretariat shall, where appropriate, report the results of its examination to the Common Market Council.

2. The central secretariat shall undertake such work and studies and perform such services relating to the Common Market as may be assigned to it by the Common Market Council, and shall also make such proposals thereto as it considers may assist in the efficient and harmonious functioning and development of the Common Market.

3. For the performance of the functions imposed upon it by this Article, the central secretariat may collect information and verify matters of fact relating to the functioning of the Common Market and for that purpose may request a Partner State to provide information relating thereto.

4. The Partner States agree to co-operate with and assist the central secretariat in the performance of the functions imposed upon it by this Article and agree in particular to provide any information which may be requested under paragraph 3 of this Article.

CHAPTER X
THE COMMON MARKET TRIBUNAL

Article 32: Establishment of the Common Market Tribunal

1. There is hereby established a judicial body, to be known as the Common Market Tribunal, which shall ensure the observance of law and of the terms of this Treaty in the interpretation and application of so much of this Treaty as appertains to the Common Market.

2. The Common Market Tribunal is in this Treaty referred to as "the Tribunal."

Article 33: Composition of the Tribunal

1. Subject to this Article, the Tribunal shall be composed of a Chairman and four other members, all of whom shall be appointed by the Authority.

2. The Chairman of the Tribunal shall be chosen from among persons of impartiality and independence who fulfil the conditions required for the holding of the highest judicial office in their respective countries of domicile or who are jurists of a recognized competence.

3. Of the members of the Tribunal other than the Chairman, each of the

Partner States shall choose one, and the fourth shall be chosen by the Chairman and the other three members acting in common agreement.

4. The members chosen under paragraph 3 of this Article shall be chosen from among persons of impartiality and independence who are qualified for appointment by reason of their knowledge or experience in industry, commerce or public affairs.

Article 34: Term of Office and Temporary Membership of the Tribunal

1. The Chairman and the other members of the Tribunal shall hold office for such period, being not less than three years, as may be determined in their respective instruments of appointment, and in fixing such periods of office regard shall be had to the desirability of securing a measure of continuity in the membership of the Tribunal.

2. All members of the Tribunal shall be eligible for re-appointment.

3. If a member of the Tribunal is temporarily absent or otherwise unable to carry out his functions, the Authority shall, if such absence or inability to act appears to the Authority to be likely to be of such duration as to cause a significant delay in the work of the Tribunal, appoint a temporary member chosen in the same manner as was the absent or disabled member in accordance with Article 33 of this Treaty, to act in place of the said member.

4. If a member of the Tribunal, other than the Chairman, is directly or indirectly interested in a case before the Tribunal, he shall immediately report the nature of his interest to the Chairman, who, if he considers that the member's interest is such that it would be undesirable for him to take part in that case, shall make a report to the Authority; and the Authority shall appoint a temporary member, chosen in the same manner as was the interested member, to act for that case only in place of the interested member.

5. If the Chairman is directly or indirectly interested in a case before the Tribunal he shall, if he considers that the nature of his interest is such that it would be undesirable for him to take part in that case, make a report to the Authority; and the Authority shall appoint a temporary Chairman, chosen in the same manner as was the substantive Chairman, to act as Chairman for that case only in place of the substantive Chairman.

6. A temporary Chairman or temporary member appointed under this Article shall have, during the period he is acting, all the functions of the Chairman or member, as the case may be.

Article 35: Competence of the Tribunal

The Tribunal shall be competent to accept and adjudicate upon all matters which pursuant to this Treaty may be referred to it, and shall also possess the jurisdiction specifically conferred on it by this Chapter.

Article 36: References to the Tribunal by a Partner State

1. Where a Partner State has made a reference to the Common Market Council in pursuance of paragraph (d) of Article 30 of this Treaty, and the reference has not been determined by the Common Market Council in accord-

ance with that paragraph within one month of the reference being made, that Partner State may refer the matter in dispute to the Tribunal.

2. Where a reference has been made to the Common Market Council in pursuance of paragraph (d) of Article 30 of this Treaty and the reference has been determined by the Council by recording an inability to agree in relation to the reference, a Partner State which is aggrieved by such determination may within two months thereof refer the matter in dispute to the Tribunal.

3. Where a reference has been made to the Common Market Council in pursuance of paragraph (d) of Article 30 of this Treaty, and a binding directive has been issued by the Common Market Council to a Partner State, and in the opinion of one of the other Partner States that directive is not complied with by the Partner State to which it is directed within the period fixed therein, that other Partner State may refer the question of such non-compliance to the Tribunal.

Article 37: Decisions of the Tribunal

1. The Tribunal shall consider and determine every reference made to it by a Partner State pursuant to this Treaty in accordance with the Statute of the Common Market Tribunal and its rules of procedure, and shall deliver in public session a reasoned decision which, subject to the provisions of the said Statute as to rectification and review, shall be final and conclusive and not open to appeal:

Provided that, if the Tribunal considers that in the special circumstances of the case it is undesirable that its decision be delivered in public, the Tribunal may make an order to that effect and deliver its decision before the parties privately.

2. The Tribunal shall deliver one decision only in respect of every reference to it, which shall be the decision of the Tribunal reached in private by majority verdict. In the event of the members of the Tribunal being equally divided, the Chairman shall have a casting vote.

3. If a member of the Tribunal does not agree with the majority verdict reached in respect of any reference, he shall not be permitted to deliver a dissenting opinion nor record his dissent in public.

Article 38: Advisory Opinions of the Tribunal

The Common Market Council may request the Tribunal to give an advisory opinion regarding questions of law arising from the provisions of this Treaty affecting the Common Market, and the Partner States shall in the case of every such request have the right to be represented and take part in the proceedings.

Article 39: Interim Orders and Directions of the Tribunal

The Tribunal may, in any case referred to it, make any interim order or issue any directions which it considers necessary or desirable.

Article 40: Intervention

A Partner State which is not a party to a case before the Tribunal may intervene in that case, but its submissions shall be limited to supporting or opposing the arguments of a party to the case.

Article 41: Acceptance of the Tribunal's Decisions

1. The Partner States undertake not to submit a dispute concerning the interpretation or application of this Treaty, so far as it relates to or affects the Common Market, to any method of settlement other than those provided for in this Treaty.

2. Where a dispute has been referred to the Common Market Council or to the Tribunal, the Partner States shall refrain from any action which might endanger the solution of the dispute or might aggravate the dispute.

3. A Partner State shall take, without delay, the measures required to implement a decision of the Tribunal.

Article 42: Statute and Rules of the Tribunal

1. The Statute of the Tribunal shall be that set out in Annex VIII to this Treaty.

2. The Tribunal shall, after consultation with the Common Market Council, make its rules of procedure and may in like manner from time to time amend or add to any such rules.

PART IV: THE FUNCTIONS OF THE EAST AFRICAN COMMUNITY AND ITS INSTITUTIONS

CHAPTER XI
FUNCTIONS AND PROCEDURE

Article 43: Functions of the Community

1. The Community shall, on behalf of the Partner States, through its appropriate institutions, perform the functions given to it, and discharge the responsibilities imposed upon it, by this Treaty in relation to the establishment, functioning and development of the Common Market.

2. (a) The Community shall, on behalf of the Partner States, administer the services specified in Part A of Annex IX to this Treaty, and for that purpose shall, subject to this Treaty, take over from the Common Services Organization such of those services as are in existence at the date of the coming into force of this Treaty.

   (b) The Authority may by order from time to time amend or add to Part A of Annex IX to this Treaty.

3. The Corporations shall, on behalf of the Partner States and in accordance with this Treaty and the laws of the Community, administer the services specified in Part B of Annex IX to this Treaty, and for that purpose shall

take over from the Common Services Organization the corresponding services administered by the Common Services Organization at the date of the coming into force of this Treaty.

4. The Community shall provide machinery to facilitate the co-ordination of the activities of the Partner States on any matter of common interest.

5. Subject to this Treaty, the Community shall so regulate the distribution of its non-physical investments as to ensure an equitable contribution to the foreign exchange resources of each of the Partner States.

6. The Community shall so arrange its purchases within the Partner States as to ensure an equitable distribution of the benefits thereof to each of the Partner States.

7. Subject to this Treaty, the Community may enact measures with respect to the matters set out in Annex X to this Treaty.

8. The Community shall, in accordance with this Treaty, provide a Court of Appeal, a Common Market Tribunal and an East African Industrial Court.

Article 44: Provision of Services on an Agency Basis

1. The Community and the Corporations may, with the approval of the Authority, enter into arrangements with any Government or international organization for providing services, and may provide and administer such services accordingly.

2. The Community may enter into arrangements with any of the Corporations for providing services, and may provide and administer such services accordingly.

3. Arrangements made under this Article shall normally provide for the Community or the Corporation concerned to be reimbursed for any expenditure incurred.

Article 45: Procedure within the Community

1. The procedural provisions set out in Annex XI to this Treaty shall be followed within the Community.

2. If there is a doubt as to the procedure to be followed in any particular case, or if no procedure is prescribed by or under this Treaty, the procedure to be followed may be determined by the Authority.

CHAPTER XII
THE EAST AFRICAN AUTHORITY

Article 46: Establishment of the East African Authority

There is hereby established an Authority to be known as the East African Authority, which shall, subject to this Treaty, be the principal executive authority of the Community.

Article 47: Composition of the Authority

1. The Authority shall consist of the President of the United Republic of Tanzania, the President of the Sovereign State of Uganda and the President of the Republic of Kenya.

2. If a member of the Authority is unable to attend a meeting of the Authority and it is not convenient to postpone the meeting, he shall, after consultation with the other members of the Authority, appoint a person holding office as a Minister of his Government to represent him at such meeting only, and a person so appointed shall for the purpose of that meeting have all the powers, duties and responsibilities of the member of the Authority for whom he is acting.

Article 48: Functions of the Authority

1. The Authority shall be responsible for, and have the general direction and control of, the performance of the executive functions of the Community.

2. The Authority shall be assisted in the performance of its functions under this Article by the Councils and the East African Ministers.

3. The Authority may give directions to the Councils and to the East African Ministers as to the performance of any functions conferred upon them, and such directions shall be complied with.

CHAPTER XIII
EAST AFRICAN MINISTERS

Article 49: Appointment of East African Ministers

1. There shall be three East African Ministers.

2. The Partner States shall each nominate one person, qualified under paragraph 3 of this Article, for appointment as an East African Minister, and the Authority shall appoint the persons so nominated to be East African Ministers.

3. A person shall be qualified to be appointed an East African Minister if he is qualified to vote under the national electoral laws of the Partner State nominating him:

Provided that if at the time of his appointment as an East African Minister a person holds office as a Minister, a Deputy, Junior or Assistant Minister or a Parliamentary Secretary in the Government of a Partner State, he shall immediately resign from that office and may not thereafter hold such an office while he remains an East African Minister.

4. If an East African Minister is temporarily absent from the territories of the Partner States, or for some other reason is temporarily unable to perform his duties, the Partner State which nominated him for appointment may, and at the request of the other East African Ministers shall, nominate some other person, qualified to vote under its national electoral laws, for temporary appointment as an East African Minister; and the Authority shall appoint the person so nominated to be an Acting East African Minister in the place of the Minister who is absent or unable to act.

5. An Acting East African Minister shall hold office until the person in whose place he is acting returns to the territories of the Partner States or is able to resume his duties, as the case may be, and delivers notification thereof in writing to the Secretary General for transmission to the Authority.

6. An Acting East African Minister shall while he is holding office have all the functions, responsibilities, powers, duties and privileges of the substantive East African Minister.

Article 50: Tenure of Office of East African Ministers

An East African Minister shall not be appointed for a fixed term but shall vacate his office upon the happening of any of the following events:
  (a) if he transmits his resignation in writing to the Authority and the Authority accepts his resignation;
  (b) if he ceases to be qualified for appointment as an East African Minister;
  (c) if the Authority terminates his appointment, which it shall do upon the request in writing of the Partner State which nominated him.

Article 51: Functions of East African Ministers

1. It shall be the responsibility of the East African Ministers to assist the Authority in the exercise of its executive functions to the extent required by and subject to the directions of the Authority, and to advise the Authority generally in respect of the affairs of the Community.

2. In addition to the responsibilities conferred on them by paragraph 1 of this Article, the East African Ministers shall perform the functions conferred on them by this Treaty in respect of the Councils, the Assembly and other matters.

3. The Authority may allocate particular responsibilities to each of the East African Ministers.

4. The Authority may, in respect of any responsibilities which it confers upon the East African Ministers, specify which matters shall be performed by them acting in common agreement and which may be performed by a single East African Minister.

5. It shall be the responsibility of the East African Ministers, with the assistance of representatives of the East African Airways Corporation and such other persons as may be appropriate, to negotiate bi-lateral air services agreements on behalf of the Partner States and to conduct such negotiations in accordance with the criteria laid down by the Communications Ministerial Committee of the Common Services Organization and any amendment of such criteria which may be made by the Communications Council.

6. Each of the Partner States undertakes that it will grant to the East African Minister nominated by it a status within its territory commensurate with that of a Minister of its Government, and shall permit that East African Minister to attend and speak at meetings of its Cabinet.

CHAPTER XIV
DEPUTY EAST AFRICAN MINISTERS

Article 52: Deputy East African Ministers

1. The Authority may, if at any time it considers it desirable, appoint three Deputy East African Ministers.

2. If the Authority decides to appoint three Deputy East African Ministers, the Partner States shall each nominate one person, qualified under paragraph 3 of this Article, for appointment as a Deputy East African Minister; and the Authority shall appoint the persons so nominated to be Deputy East African Ministers.

3. A person shall be qualified to be appointed a Deputy East African Minister if he is qualified to vote under the national electoral laws of the Partner State nominating him:

Provided that if, at the time of his appointment as a Deputy East African Minister, a person holds office as a Minister, a Deputy, Junior or Assistant Minister or a Parliamentary Secretary in the Government of a Partner State, he shall immediately resign from that office and may not thereafter hold such an office while he remains a Deputy East African Minister.

4. A Deputy East African Minister shall not be appointed for a fixed term but shall vacate his office upon the happening of any of the following events:
   (a) if he transmits his resignation in writing to the Authority and the Authority accepts his resignation;
   (b) if he ceases to be qualified for appointment as a Deputy East African Minister;
   (c) if the Authority terminates his appointment, which it shall do upon the request in writing of the Partner State which nominated him.

5. Where Deputy East African Ministers have been appointed and thereafter the number of Deputy East African Ministers falls below three, a person or persons shall be nominated and appointed in the manner provided by this Article to fill the vacancy or vacancies.

6. Subject to any directions given or instructions issued by the Authority, it shall be the responsibility of the Deputy East African Ministers to assist the East African Ministers in the performance of their functions and to perform such duties as may be imposed on them by the Authority or by this Treaty.

CHAPTER XV
THE COUNCILS

Article 53: Establishment of the Councils

There shall be established as institutions of the Community the following Councils:
   (a) the Common Market Council;
   (b) the Communciations Council;
   (c) the Economic Consultative and Planning Council;
   (d) the Finance Council; and
   (e) the Research and Social Council.

Article 54: Composition of the Councils

1. The composition of the Councils shall be as follows:
   (a) the Common Market Council shall consist of the three East African Ministers, together with nine other members, of whom three shall be

designated by each Partner State from among the persons holding office as Minister of its Government;

(b) the Communications Council shall consist of the three East African Ministers, together with three other members, being the persons holding office as Ministers responsible for matters relating to communications in the respective Governments of the Partner States;

(c) the Economic Consultative and Planning Council shall consist of the three East African Ministers, together with nine other members, of whom three shall be designated by each Partner State from among the persons holding office as Minister of its Government;

(d) the Finance Council shall consist of the three East African Ministers, together with three other members, being the persons holding office as the Ministers responsible for matters relating to public finance in the respective Governments of the Partner States; and

(e) the Research and Social Council shall consist of the three East African Ministers, together with nine other members, of whom three shall be designated by each Partner State from among the persons holding office as Minister of its Government.

2. If an East African Minister is unable to attend a meeting of a Council, he may, if at the time there are persons holding office as Deputy East African Ministers, appoint one of them, by notice in writing delivered to the Secretary General, to act as a member of that Council for that meeting and a person so appointed shall, in respect of the meeting for which he is appointed to act, have all the rights and duties of a member of the Council.

3. If a Minister of the Government of a Partner State is unable to attend a meeting of a Council of which he is a member, that Partner State may, by notice in writing delivered to the Secretary General, appoint some other person who is a Minister, a Deputy, Junior or Assistant Minister or a Parliamentary Secretary of its Government to act as a member of that Council for that meeting, and a person so appointed shall, in respect of the meeting for which he is appointed to act, have all the rights and duties of a member of the Council.

4. If under paragraph 1 of this Article a Partner State designates one of its Ministers to be a member of a Council or terminates such a designation, it shall give notice thereof in writing to the Secretary General.

Article 55: Functions of the Councils

The Common Market Council. 1. The function of the Common Market Council shall be the discharge of the responsibilities imposed upon it by Article 30 of this Treaty.

The Communications Council. 2. Subject to any directions given by the Authority, and subject to this Treaty and to any law of the Community, the Communications Council shall perform the duties and have the powers which are set out in Annex XIII to this Treaty, and shall provide a forum for consultation generally on communications matters.

The Economic Consultative and Planning Council. 3. The functions of the Economic Consultative and Planning Council shall be:

(a) to assist the national planning of the Partner States by consultative means; and

(b) to advise the Authority upon the long-term planning of the common services.

The Finance Council. 4. Subject to this Treaty, the functions of the Finance Council shall be to consult in common on the major financial affairs of the Community, and to consider and approve major financial decisions relating to the services administered by the Community, including their estimates of expenditure and related loan and investment programmes. In this paragraph "the Community" shall not include the Bank.

The Research and Social Council. 5. The functions of the Research and Social Council shall be to assist, by consultative means, in the co-ordination of the policies of each of the Partner States and the Community regarding research and social matters.

CHAPTER XVI
THE EAST AFRICAN LEGISLATIVE ASSEMBLY

Article 56: Establishment and Composition of the East African Legislative Assembly

1. There is hereby established for the Community a legislative body, to be known as the East African Legislative Assembly, which shall exercise the powers conferred upon it by this Treaty.

2. The members of the Assembly shall be:

(a) the three East African Ministers;

(b) the three Deputy East African Ministers (if any);

(c) twenty-seven appointed members; and

(d) the Chairman of the Assembly, the Secretary General and the Counsel to the Community.

3. The Chairman of the Assembly shall preside over and take part in its proceedings in accordance with the rules of procedure of the Assembly made by the Authority in accordance with paragraph 17 of Annex XI to this Treaty.

4. The Assembly shall have a Public Accounts Committee, which shall be constituted in the manner provided in the rules of procedure of the Assembly and shall perform the functions provided in respect thereof in the said rules of procedure; and the Assembly may have such other committees as may be provided for or permitted under the said rules of procedure.

Article 57: Appointment of Members of the Assembly

1. Of the twenty-seven appointed members of the Assembly each Partner State shall appoint nine in accordance with such procedure as each Partner State decides.

2. A person shall be qualified to be appointed a member by a Partner State if he is a citizen of that Partner State and is qualified to be elected a member of its legislature under its electoral laws, and is not an officer in the service of the Community or a servant of a Corporation or the Bank.

3. If an appointed member of the Assembly is temporarily absent from the territories of the Partner States, or for some other reason is temporarily unable to perform his duties, the Partner State which appointed him may appoint some other person, qualified under paragraph 2 of this Article, to be a temporary appointed member in his place; and a temporary appointed member shall, unless his period of office is terminated by the Partner State which appointed him, hold office until the person in whose place he is acting returns to the territories of the Partner States or is able to resume his duties, as the case may be, and so notifies the Chairman of the Assembly in writing.

4. A temporary appointed member of the Assembly shall, while holding office, have all the responsibilities, powers and privileges of the substantive appointed member.

Article 58: Tenure of Office of Appointed Members

1. Subject to this Article, an appointed member of the Assembly shall hold office until the legislature of the Partner State which appointed him first meets after it is next dissolved.

2. An appointed member of the Assembly shall vacate his seat in the Assembly upon the happening of any of the following events:
   (a) upon the delivery of his resignation in writing to the Chairman of the Assembly;
   (b) upon his ceasing to be qualified for appointment as an appointed member;
   (c) upon his appointment as a Minister, a Deputy, Junior or Assistant Minister or a Parliamentary Secretary in the Government of a Partner State;
   (d) upon his appointment as an East African Minister or as a Deputy East African Minister;
   (e) upon his having been absent from the Assembly for such period and in such circumstances as are prescribed by the rules of procedure of the Assembly.

Article 59: Acts of the Community

1. The enactment of measures of the Community shall be effected by means of Bills passed by the Assembly and assented to on behalf of the Community by the Heads of State of the Partner States and every measure that has been duly passed and assented to shall be styled an Act.

2. When a Bill has been duly passed by the Assembly the Chairman of the Assembly shall submit the Bill to the Heads of State of the Partner States.

3. Every Bill that is submitted to the Heads of Sate under paragraph 2 of this Article shall contain the following words of enactment:

"Enacted by the President of the United Republic of Tanzania, the President of the Sovereign State of Uganda and the President of the Republic of Kenya on behalf of the East African Community, with the advice and consent of the East African Legislative Assembly."

Article 60: Assent to Bills

1. The President of the United Republic of Tanzania, the President of the Sovereign State of Uganda and the President of the Republic of Kenya may assent or withhold assent to a Bill.

2. A Bill that has not received the assent provided for in paragraph 1 of this Article within nine months of the date upon which it was passed by the Assembly shall lapse.

CHAPTER XVII
STAFF OF THE COMMUNITY

Article 61: Offices in the Community

1. There shall be the following offices in the service of the Community:
   (a) a Secretary General, who shall be the principal executive officer of the Community;
   (b) a Counsel to the Community; and
   (c) an Auditor-General.

2. There shall be such other offices in the service of the Community as, subject to any Act of the Community, the Authority may determine.

3. In this Treaty, "officers in the service of the Community" does not include an office in the service of a Corporation or of the Bank.

Article 62: Establishment of the East African Community Service Commission

1. There is hereby established a service commission to be known as the East African Community Service Commission for all offices in the service of the Community.

2. The Service Commission shall consist of such number of members as the Authority shall from time to time determine.

3. The Authority shall appoint the members of the Service Commission by instrument in writing, which shall specify the period of office of the member concerned.

4. A person shall not be qualified to be appointed a member of the Service Commission if he holds office as a Minister, a Deputy, Junior or Assistant Minister or a Parliamentary Secretary in the Government of a Partner State, or is a member of the Legislative Assembly or a member of the legislature of a Partner State.

5. A member of the Service Commission shall vacate his office:
   (a) upon the expiry of the period of office specified in his instrument of appointment;
   (b) if he delivers his resignation in writing to the Secretary General for transmission to the Authority; or
   (c) if he ceases to be qualified for appointment as a member.

6. A member of the Service Commission may be removed from office by the Authority for inability to perform the functions of his office, whether

arising from infirmity of mind or body or for any other sufficient cause, or for misbehaviour, but shall not otherwise be removed from office.

Article 63: Appointment and Disciplinary Control of the Secretary General and Certain Other Officers

1. The Secretary General of the Community shall be appointed by the Authority.

2. The Counsel to the Community and the holders of such other offices in the service of the Community as the Authority may, by notice in the Gazette, determine shall be appointed by the Authority afer consultation with the Service Commission and with the Secretary General.

3. If the Secretary General or any person appointed under paragraph 2 of this Article is absent from the territories of the Partner States, or is unable through illness or for any other reason to perform the functions of his office, the Authority may appoint a person to act in the place of the Secretary General or of such person, as the case may be, during the period of the absence or inability to act and the person so appointed shall have, while he is so acting, the same powers and responsibilities as the substantive holder of the office.

4. For the purposes of the exercise of the power of disciplinary control and dismissal, the persons appointed under paragraph 2 of this Article shall be subject to the jurisdiction of the Service Commission.

Article 64: Functions of the Service Commission

1. Subject to this Treaty and to any Act of the Community, the Service Commission shall, on behalf of the Community, make appointments to offices in the service of the Community, and shall exercise the powers of disciplinary control and dismissal over persons holding or acting in such offices.

2. For the purposes of paragraph 1 of this Article, references to appointments shall be construed as including references to appointments on promotion and on transfer, and appointments of persons in an acting capacity.

3. The Service Commission may, by order published in the Gazette, and with the approval of the Authority, delegate, subject to such conditions as it may think fit, any of its functions under this Article to any of its members or to any officer of the Community either generally or in respect of any particular class of cases.

4. This Article shall not apply to the Judges of the Court of Appeal for East Africa or to the members of the Common Market Tribunal.

CHAPTER XVIII
FINANCES OF THE COMMUNITY

Article 65: The General Fund and Special Funds

1. There shall be a General Fund of the Community, and such special funds as may from time to time be established by an Act of the Community.

2. Subject to this Treaty, all moneys received by the Community from whatever source shall be paid into the General Fund, except:

(a) the divisible income tax, the remaining divisible income tax and the divisible customs and excise duties;

(b) sums which fall to be paid into the Distributable Pool Fund under Article 67 of this Treaty; and

(c) sums which are required by an Act of the Community to be paid into one of the special funds referred to in paragraph 1 of this Article.

Article 66: Expenditure from the General Fund

1. All expenditure of the Community, other than expenditure which is required by an Act of the Community to be met from one of the special funds referred to in Article 65 of this Treaty, shall be met from the General Fund.

2. There may be met from the General Fund:

(a) the estimated net annual recurrent expenditure of the University of East Africa;

(b) one-half of the estimated net annual recurrent expenditure of Makerere University College, the University College, Dar es Salaam, and University College, Nairobi; and

(c) expenditure towards the cost of any service provided by the Community under Article 44 of this Treaty, or of any activity which the Authority declares to be in furtherance of the aims of the Community:

Provided that the expenditure under sub-paragraphs (a) and (b) of this paragraph shall cease on the 30th June 1970 or upon the cessation of the arrangements under which the University Colleges mentioned in sub-paragraph (b) of this paragraph are constituent colleges of the University of East Africa, whichever is the sooner.

3. No money shall be paid out of the General Fund unless:

(a) the payment has been authorized by an Appropriation Act of the Community; or

(b) the money is required to meet expenditure charged on the General Fund under this Treaty or by an Act of the Community:

Provided that, if an Appropriation Act for a particular financial year has not come into operation by the first day of that financial year, the Authority may from time to time authorize the payment of money out of the General Fund to meet any expenditure which may properly be met thereout, but so that:

(i) the amount paid out in any particular month for any particular head of expenditure shall not exceed one-twelfth of the total appropriation for the previous financial year for that head;

(ii) the authorization shall not extend beyond the 30th day of September in the same financial year or such earlier date as that on which the Appropriation Act may come into operation; and

(iii) any money paid out under this proviso shall be brought into account when payments are being made under the Appropriation Act.

4. No money shall be paid out of the General Fund except in the manner prescribed by an Act of the Community.

5. The Authority shall cause detailed estimates of the receipts into and the payments out of the General Fund to be prepared for each financial year and shall cause them to be laid before a meeting of the Assembly in the financial year preceding that to which they relate.

6. A Bill for an Appropriation Act providing for the sums necessary to meet the estimated expenditure (other than expenditure charged on the General Fund under this Treaty or by an Act of the Community) to be paid out of the General Fund shall be introduced into the Assembly as soon as practicable after the estimates have been laid before a meeting of the Assembly under paragraph 5 of this Article.

7. If in any financial year it is found:

(a) that the amount appropriated by the Appropriation Act is insufficient to meet any particular head of expenditure or that a need has arisen for expenditure from the General Fund for which no amount has been appropriated by that Act; or

(b) that any expenditure has been incurred for any purpose in excess of the amount appropriated to that purpose by the Appropriation Act, or for a purpose to which no amount has been appropriated by that Act,

the Authority shall cause a supplementary estimate of expenditure in respect thereof to be prepared and laid before the Assembly, and a Bill for a Supplementary Appropriation Act, providing for the sums necessary to meet the estimated expenditure (other than expenditure charged on the General Fund under this Treaty or by an Act of the Community) to be paid out of the General Fund, shall be introduced into the Assembly as soon as practicable after the supplementary estimate has been so laid before the Assembly.

8. Notwithstanding paragraph 3 of this Article, if at any time it appears to the East African Ministers to be necessary for money to be paid out of the General Fund to meet unforeseen expenditure which either:

(a) is of a special character, and may properly be provided for in an Appropriation Act but has not been so provided for; or

(b) will result in an excess on a vote contained in an Appropriation Act, and which in either case cannot without serious injury to the public interest be postponed until a Supplementary Appropriation Act can be enacted, the East African Ministers may, in anticipation of such enactment, authorize payment from the General Fund of the sums required to meet such expenditure:

Provided that:

(i) the total sum so authorized shall not at any time exceed 500,000 Tanzania shillings; and

(ii) a Bill for a Supplementary Appropriation Act in respect of the payments shall be introduced into the Assembly as soon as practicable thereafter.

Article 67: The Distributable Pool Fund

1. There shall be a Distributable Pool Fund of the Community.
2. There shall be paid into the Distributable Pool Fund:
(a) a sum equal to 20 per cent of the income tax collected by the East African Income Tax Department on gains or profits of companies engaged in manufacturing or finance business (less 20 per cent of the proportion of the cost of collection referred to in paragraph 1 (b) of Article 68 of this Treaty):

> Provided that, where the tax is collected on or after the effective date and before the final date, the percentages shall be 10 per cent; and

(b) a sum equal to 3 per cent of the amount of customs duty and excise duty collected by the East African Customs and Excise Department (less a rateable proportion of the cost of collection referred to in paragraph 3 of Article 68 of this Treaty):

> Provided that, where the customs duty or excise duty is collected on or after the effective date and before the final date, the percentage shall be one and one half per cent.

3. Notwithstanding paragraph 2 of this Article, no payment shall be made into the Distributable Pool Fund in respect of income tax collected on or after the final date or in respect of customs duty or excise duty collected on or after the final date.
4. The Distributable Pool Fund shall be distributed among the Partner States in equal shares.

Article 68: Distribution of the Principal Revenue

1. From the amount of income tax collected by the East African Income Tax Department, there shall be deducted:
(a) the cost of collection, which shall be paid into the General Fund; and
(b) so much of the amount as represents income tax on gains or profits of companies engaged in manufacturing or finance business (less a rateable proportion of the cost of collection), which shall be dealt with in accordance with paragraph 4 of this Article,
and the balance (in this Treaty referred to as "the divisible income tax") shall be divided among the Partner States in accordance with paragraph 7 of this Article.

2. In this Article and in Article 67 of this Treaty, the "gains or profits of companies engaged in manufacturing or finance business" means the income defined in the provisions of Annex XII to this Treaty.
3. From the amount of customs duty and excise duty collected by the East African Customs and Excise Department, there shall be deducted the cost of collection, which shall be paid into the General Fund, and the balance shall be dealt with in accordance with paragraph 4 of this Article.
4. From the amounts which, under paragraph 1 (b) and paragraph 3 of

this Article, are to be dealt with in accordance with this paragraph, there shall be deducted:

- (a) the sums which, under Article 67 of this Treaty, fall to be paid into the Distributable Pool Fund; and
- (b) such sums as are required to make up (with the moneys in the General Fund) the amount of expenditure to be met from the General Fund; and
  - (i) for the period from the coming into force of this Treaty until the final date as defined in Article 70 of this Treaty, such sums shall be charged against the moneys referred to in paragraph 1 (b) and paragraph 3 of this Article in the ratio which 20 per cent of the moneys referred to in paragraph 1 (b) bears to 3 per cent of the moneys referred to in paragraph 3 respectively; and
  - (ii) after the said final date, the proportions in which those sums shall be charged against the moneys referred to in paragraph 1 (b) and paragraph 3 of this Article respectively shall correspond to the relative sizes of those two amounts of money,

and the residue of the money referred to in paragraph 1 (b) of this Article (in this Treaty referred to as "the remaining divisible income tax") and the residue of the money referred to in paragraph 3 of this Article (in this Treaty referred to as "the divisible customs and excise duties") shall each be divided among the Partner States in accordance respectively with paragraphs 7 and 8 of this Article.

5. The money divided between the Partner States under paragraph 4 of this Article shall be paid direct by the East African Income Tax Department or the East African Customs and Excise Department, as the case may be, to the Partner States.

6. Revenue from transfer taxes payable to a Partner State under Article 20 of this Treaty, less the costs and expenses to be borne by that Partner State under paragraph 13 of that Article, shall be paid direct by the East African Customs and Excise Department to that Partner State, and the said costs and expenses shall be paid into the General Fund.

7. There shall be paid by the East African Income Tax Department to each of the Partner States that portion of the remaining divisible income tax as, according to law, may be ascertained as relating to income accruing in, or derived from, that Partner State.

8. There shall be paid by the East African Customs and Excise Department to each of the Partner States that portion of the divisible customs and excise duties which arises from customs and excise duties collected in respect of goods imported into, or manufactured in, that Partner State and consumed in that Partner State, together with such portion of the divisible customs and excise duties as falls to be paid to that State in accordance with Articles 10, 15 and 18 of this Treaty.

Article 69: Remuneration of the Holders of Certain Offices

1. There shall be paid to the holders of the offices of:
   (a) Judge of the Court of Appeal for East Africa;

(b) Chairman or other member of the Tribunal;
(c) Chairman of the Assembly;
(d) Chairman or other member of the Service Commission; and
(e) Auditor-General,

such salaries as may be prescribed by an Act of the Community.

2. The salaries payable to the holders of the offices specified in paragraph 1 of this Article shall be paid from and are hereby charged on the General Fund.

3. A holder of any of the offices specified in paragraph 1 of this Article shall not have his salary or any of his other terms and conditions of service altered to his disadvantage after his appointment.

Article 70: Interpretation of This Chapter

In this Chapter of this Treaty:

"cost of collection" means the expenditure of the East African Income Tax Department or the East African Customs and Excise Department, as the case may be, less appropriations in aid and less the costs and expenses referred to in paragraph 6 of Article 68 of this Treaty;

"divisible customs and excise duties" has the meaning given to it in paragraph 4 of Article 68 of this Treaty;

"divisible income tax" has the meaning given to it in paragraph 1 of Article 68 of this Treaty;

"effective date" means the first day of the month following the date on which a transfer tax is first imposed under this Treaty;

"final date" means the first day of the month following the first anniversary of the date on which the Republic of Kenya has paid in full the second instalment to the paid-in capital stock of the Bank pursuant to Article 5 of the Charter of the Bank;

"financial year" means the period from the 1st day of July to the succeeding 30th day of June;

"remaining divisible income tax" has the meaning given to it in paragraph 4 of Article 68 of this Treaty.

CHAPTER XIX
THE CORPORATIONS WITHIN THE COMMUNITY

Article 71: Establishment of the Corporations

1. There shall be within the Community, as institutions of the Community, the Corporations specified in paragraph 2 of this Article and the Corporations shall, subject to this Treaty, be constituted in such manner as shall be provided by law.

2. The Corporations shall be:

The East African Railways Corporation;
The East African Harbours Corporation;

The East African Posts and Telecommunications Corporation; and
The East African Airways Corporation.

Article 72: Principles of Operation

1. It shall be the duty of each of the Corporations to conduct its business according to commercial principles and to perform its functions in such a manner as to secure that, taking one year with another, its revenue is not less than sufficient to meet its outgoings which are properly chargeable to revenue account, including proper allocations to the general reserve and provision in respect of depreciation of capital assets, pension liabilities and interest and other provision for the repayment of loans and further to ensure that, taking one year with another, its net operating income is not less than sufficient to secure an annual return on the value of the net fixed assets in operation by the Corporation of such a percentage as the Authority may from time to time direct:

Provided that the Authority may at any time, if it thinks fit, relieve the East African Airways Corporation from any obligation to secure an annual return on the value of net fixed assets in operation by the Corporation.

2. For the purpose of paragraph 1 of this Article:
   (a) "net operating income" shall be determined by subtracting from gross operating revenues all operating and administrative expenses, including taxes (if any) and adequate provision for maintenance and depreciation; and
   (b) "value of the net fixed assets in operation" shall be the value of such assets less accumulated depreciation as shown in the statement of accounts of the Corporation:

   Provided that, if the amounts shown in such statements of accounts do not reflect a true measure of value of the assets concerned because of currency revaluations, changes in prices or similar factors, the value of the fixed assets shall be adjusted adequately to reflect such currency revaluations, changes in prices or similar factors.

3. It shall be the duty of each Corporation, in performing its obligations under paragraph 1 of this Article, to have regard to its revenues in the territories of the Partner States as a whole and not to its revenues in any particular Partner State or area within the territories of the Partner States.

4. Subject to this Treaty, the Corporations shall so regulate the distribution of their non-physical investments as to ensure an equitable contribution to the foreign exchange resources of each of the Partner States, taking into account *inter alia* the scale of their operations in each Partner State.

5. The Corporations shall so arrange their purchases within the Partner States as to ensure an equitable distribution of the benefits thereof to each of the Partner States, taking into account *inter alia* the scale of their operations in each Partner State.

6. The Corporations shall be exempted from income tax and from stamp duty.

Article 73: Control of the Corporations

1. There shall be a Board of Directors for each of the Corporations which shall be, subject to this Treaty, responsible for its policy, control and management through the Director-General.

2. The Authority, the Communications Council and the Board of Directors and the Director-General of each Corporation shall, in respect of that Corporation, and in addition to any other powers and duties conferred or imposed on them by this Treaty or by any Act of the Community, have the powers and perform the duties specified in Annex XIII to this Treaty.

Article 74: Composition of Boards of Directors of the Corporations

1. Subject to this Article, the Boards of Directors of the Corporations, other than the East African Airways Corporation, shall each be composed of a Chairman, who shall be appointed by the Authority, the Director-General, who shall be a director *ex officio*, and six other members who shall be appointed in the manner provided by paragraph 2 of this Article.

2. Of the six members of the Boards of Directors to be appointed under paragraph 1 of this Article, three shall be appointed one each by the Partner States, and three shall be appointed by the Authority which shall have regard to the desirability of appointing persons with experience in commerce, industry, finance or administration or with technical experience or qualifications.

3. The Board of Directors of the East African Airways Corporation shall be composed of a Chairman, who shall be appointed by the Authority, the Director-General, who shall be a director *ex officio*, and eight other members of whom two each shall be appointed by the Authority and the Partner States, and the appointing authorities shall have regard to the desirability of appointing persons with experience in commerce, industry, finance or administration or with technical experience or qualifications.

4. A member of the legislature of a Partner State or a member of the Assembly shall not, while he remains such a member, be appointed to a Board of Directors.

Article 75: Resident Directors

1. The three directors appointed by the Partner States to the Board of Directors of the East African Railways Corporation shall be styled Resident Directors.

2. The Board of Directors of the East African Posts and Telecommunications Corporation may resolve (and may if it so desires rescind such a resolution) that the three directors appointed to the Board of Directors of that Corporation by the Partner States shall be styled Resident Directors and in that event paragraph 3 of this Article shall apply.

3. Each Resident Director shall have the duty of being the main link between the Partner State which appointed him and the Corporation of which he is a director, and for that purpose he shall reside and have his office in the capital of that Partner State and shall also be a member of the General Purposes Committee of the Board of Directors; but a Resident

Director shall have no executive functions in relation to the Corporation other than his function as one of the directors of the Corporation.

Article 76: Directors-General of the Corporations

1. There shall be a principal executive officer, who shall be styled the Director-General, for each of the Corporations and, subject to this Treaty, a Director-General shall be responsible for the execution of the policy of the Board of Directors.

2. The Authority shall be responsible for the appointment, disciplinary control and termination of appointment of the Director-General of each of the Corporations:

Provided that, except in the case of the appointment of the first Director-General of a Corporation, the Authority shall exercise its powers under this paragraph after consultation with the Board of Directors.

Article 77: Appointment and Disciplinary Control of Staff of the Corporations

1. The Corporations shall employ such staff as may be necessary for the efficient conduct of their operations.

2. The Board of Directors of each Corporation shall be responsible for the appointment, disciplinary control and dismissal of all staff of that Corporation other than the Director-General.

3. A Board of Directors may, subject to such conditions as it shall think fit, delegate any of its functions under paragraph 2 of this Article to the Director-General or to any other member of the staff of the Corporation or to any committee or board established by the Board of Directors.

4. The Board of Directors of each of the Corporations shall introduce and maintain procedures whereby staff aggrieved by the exercise of powers delegated under paragraph 3 of this Article may appeal to a higher authority.

5. For the purpose of Article 76 of this Treaty, and this Article, references to appointments shall be construed so as to include references to appointments on promotion and on transfer or secondment and appointments of persons in an acting capacity.

Article 78: Annual Accounts of the Corporations

1. A Board of Directors shall ensure that proper accounts and proper records are kept in relation to the revenue and expenditure of the Corporation, and shall ensure that within six months of the end of each financial year of the Corporation, or such longer period as the Communications Council may allow in any particular case, a statement of accounts of the Corporation is prepared, in accordance with the best commercial standards and any directions which may be issued by the Authority, and transmitted to the Auditor-General.

2. Upon the return of the statement of accounts, certified by the Auditor-General, and the receipt of his report thereon, the Board of Directors shall immediately transmit that statement of accounts and report of the Auditor-General to the Communications Council which shall cause the same to be

presented to the Assembly without delay and, in any event, before the expiry of nine months from the end of the financial year to which they relate or such longer period as the Communications Council may allow in any particular case.

Article 79: Annual Reports of the Corporations

A Board of Directors shall, within nine months after the end of each financial year, prepare a report upon the operations of the Corporation during that year and shall transmit such report to the Communications Council which shall cause the same to be presented to the Assembly with the statement of accounts and report of the Auditor-General referred to in Article 78 of this Treaty.

CHAPTER XX
THE COURT OF APPEAL FOR EAST AFRICA

Article 80: The Court of Appeal for East Africa

There shall be a Court of Appeal for East Africa which shall be constituted in such manner as may be provided by Act of the Community, and the Court of Appeal for Eastern Africa established by the East African Common Services Organization Agreements 1961 to 1966 shall continue in being under the name of the Court of Appeal for East Africa and shall be deemed to have been established by this Treaty, notwithstanding the abrogation of those Agreements by this Treaty.

Article 81: Jurisdiction of the Court of Appeal

The Court of Appeal for East Africa shall have jurisdiction to hear and determine such appeals from the courts of each Partner State as may be provided for by any law in force in that Partner State and shall have such powers in connection with appeals as may be so provided.

CHAPTER XXI
PENSIONS AND TRADE DISPUTES

Article 82: Pension Rights

1. This Article applies to any benefit payable under any law providing for the grant of pensions, compensation, gratuities or like allowances to persons who are, or have been, officers or servants of the Community, the Corporations, the Common Services Organization or of the East Africa High Commission in respect of their services as such officers or servants, or to the widows, children or personal representatives of such persons in respect of such services.

2. The law applicable to any benefits to which this Article applies shall, in relation to any person who has been granted or is eligible for such benefits, be that in force on the relevant date or any later law that is no less favourable to the person.

3. In this Article, "the relevant date" means:

(a) in relation to any benefits granted before the coming into force of this Treaty, the date upon which those benefits were granted;

(b) in relation to any benefits granted after the date upon which this Treaty comes into force, to or in respect of any person who was an officer or servant of the Common Services Organization before that date or any benefits for which any such person may be eligible, the date immediately preceding the date on which this Treaty comes into force; and

(c) in relation to any benefits granted to or in respect of any person who first becomes an officer or servant of the Community or of a Corporation after the date upon which this Treaty comes into force, the date upon which he first becomes such an officer or servant.

4. Where a person is entitled to exercise an option as to which of two or more laws might apply in his case, the law specified by him in exercising the option shall, for the purpose of this Article, be deemed to be more favourable to him than any other law.

5. Any benefits to which this Article applies shall:

(a) in the case of benefits that are payable in respect of the service of any person who at the time he ceased to be an officer or servant of the East Africa High Commission or the Common Services Organization was in the service of the East African Posts and Telecommunications Administration, be a charge upon the funds of the East African Posts and Telecommunications Corporation;

(b) in the case of benefits that are payable in respect of the service of any person who at the time he ceased to be an officer or servant of the East Africa High Commission or the Common Services Organization was in the service of the East African Railways and Harbours Administration, be a charge upon the funds of either the East African Railways Corporation or the East African Harbours Corporation as the Authority may, in respect of such person, by notice in the Gazette determine;

(c) in the case of benefits that are payable in respect of the service of any person who, immediately preceding his retirement, was an officer or servant of the East African Posts and Telecommunications Corporation, the East African Railways Corporation or the East African Harbours Corporation, be a charge upon the funds of that Corporation;

(d) in the case of any other benefits, be a charge upon the General Fund of the Community or such special fund as may be established for that purpose by an Act of the Community.

6. Where under any law any person or authority has a discretion:

(a) to decide whether or not any benefits to which this Article applies shall be granted; or

(b) to withhold, reduce in amount or suspend any amounts which have been granted,

those benefits shall be granted and may not be withheld, reduced in amount or suspended unless the appropriate body concurs in the refusal to grant the benefits or, as the case may be, the decision to withhold them, reduce them in amount or suspend them.

7. Where the amount of any benefit to which this Article applies that may be granted to any person is not fixed by law, the amount of the benefits to be granted to him shall be the greatest amount for which he is eligible unless the appropriate body concurs in his being granted benefits of a smaller amount.

8. For the purpose of this Article "the appropriate body" means:

(a) in the case of benefits that have been granted or may be granted in respect of the services of any person who, at the time that he ceased to be an officer or servant of the Community, was subject to the jurisdiction of the Service Commission established by this Treaty, that Commission; and

(b) in the case of an officer or servant of any of the Corporations, the body appointed by that Corporation for the purpose of paragraphs 6 and 7 of this Article.

9. Reference in this Article to officers or servants of the Community shall include reference to the Judges, officers and servants of the Court of Appeal for East Africa.

Article 83: Investment of Money Accruing for the Payment of Pensions

Upon the coming into force of this Treaty, and until such time as the Authority may determine, the net accruals to money held by the Community or the Corporations for the payment of pensions shall be invested in such stock of the former East Africa High Commission as the Authority may specify; and thereafter such net accruals shall be invested in such stock of the Partner States as the Authority may specify, having regard to the relative proportions of the financial provisions made each year by the Community or the Corporations in respect of pensions for the citizens of each Partner State employed in their service.

Article 84: Settlement of Trade Disputes

The law relating to the settlement of trade disputes in force in any Partner State shall apply to employment or service under the Community and the Corporations, and to persons in such employment or service, within that State; so however that any such law shall provide that:

(a) any power therein conferred upon any tribunal, court or other authority to make binding awards or orders in respect of the salaries or other conditions of service of persons in employment or service under the Community or the Corporations, and any power incidental thereto, shall be conferred upon, and be exercised by, the East African Industrial Court provided for in Article 85 of this Treaty; and

(b) any award or order made by the East African Industrial Court which accords with paragraph 2 of Article 85 of this Treaty shall be binding.

Article 85: The East African Industrial Court

1. There shall be established a tribunal to be styled the East African Industrial Court, in this Article referred to as "the Industrial Court," which shall be constituted by:

(a) the Chairman, or other member nominated by the Chairman, of the Permanent Labour Tribunal established under the Permanent Labour Tribunal Act 1967 of Tanzania;

(b) the president, or the deputy president if so nominated by the president, of the Industrial Court established under the Trade Disputes (Arbitration and Settlement) Act 1964 of Uganda; and

(c) the President, or other member nominated by the President, of the Industrial Court established under the Trades Disputes Act 1965 of Kenya.

2. The Industrial Court shall exercise the powers referred to in Article 84 of this Treaty in accordance with the principles laid down from time to time by the Authority.

3. The persons referred to in paragraph 1 of this Article shall, in the order set out therein, preside over the sittings of the Industrial Court.

4. The Industrial Court shall regulate its own procedure.

5. The Authority may determine the fees, emoluments or allowances to be paid to members of the Industrial Court.

CHAPTER XXII
DECENTRALIZATION, THE LOCATION OF HEADQUARTERS AND THE EAST AFRICAN TAX BOARD

Article 86: Decentralization and Related Measures

The Partner States agree that the measures in Annex XIV to this Treaty, which relate to decentralization of the operations of the Corporations and of certain of the services administered by the Community, shall be put into effect by the authorities concerned in accordance with the said Annex.

Article 87: Location of Headquarters

1. It is agreed that:

(a) the headquarters of the Community, including the Tribunal and the central secretariat, shall be at Arusha in Tanzania;

(b) the headquarters of the Bank shall be at Kampala in Uganda;

(c) the headquarters of the East African Railways Corporation shall be at Nairobi in Kenya;

(d) the headquarters of the East African Harbours Corporation shall be at Dar es Salaam in Tanzania;

(e) the headquarters of the East African Posts and Telecommunications Corporation shall be at Kampala in Uganda; and

(f) the headquarters of the East African Airways Corporation shall be at Nairobi in Kenya.

2. The authorities concerned shall implement paragraph 1 of this Article as soon as possible.

Article 88: The East African Tax Board

1. There is hereby established an advisory body, to be known as the East African Tax Board.

2. The Tax Board shall consist of:
(a) three members appointed one each by the Minister responsible for public finance in each of the Partner States;
(b) the Commissioner-General of the East African Income Tax Department;
(c) the Commissioner-General of the East African Customs and Excise Department;
(d) the three Commissioners of Income Tax in the Partner States;
(e) the three Commissioners of Customs and Excise in the Partner States; and
(f) a senior officer of the central secretariat of the Community designated by the Secretary General.

3. The members appointed under sub-paragraph (a) of paragraph 2 of this Article shall hold the office of Chairman of the Tax Board in rotation.

4. The functions of the Tax Board shall be:
(a) to render assistance as provided for in paragraph (a) of Article 29 of this Treaty;
(b) to keep under review the administration of the East African Income Tax Department and the East African Customs and Excise Department including the allocation and distribution or revenue collected by those Departments;
(c) to ensure the best possible co-operation between the East African Income Tax Department and the East African Customs and Excise Department;
(d) to study the correlation between the taxes managed and collected by the Community and taxes managed and collected directly by authorities in the Partner States, to make proposals to improve this correlation and to report annually thereon to the Finance Council;
(e) if requested by any Partner State, to render assistance in relation to taxation planning; and
(f) to make an annual report to the Finance Council concerning the operation of the East African Income Tax Department and of the East African Customs and Excise Department, and the organization and the personnel situation in those Departments.

CHAPTER XXIII
AUDIT

Article 89: Audit of Accounts

1. The public accounts of the Community and of all officers and authorities of the Community shall be audited and reported on by the Auditor-General and for that purpose the Auditor-General and any person authorized by him in that behalf shall have access to all books, records, returns and other documents relating to those accounts.

2. It shall be the duty of the Auditor-General to verify that the revenue collected by the East African Income Tax Department and the East African Customs and Excise Department has been allocated and distributed in ac-

cordance with this Treaty and to include a certificate to that effect in his report.

3. The Auditor-General shall submit his reports under paragraph 1 of this Article to the East African Ministers who shall cause the same to be laid before the Assembly.

4. The accounts of the Corporations and of all officers and authorities of the Corporations shall be audited by the Auditor-General, and for that purpose the Auditor-General and any person authorized by him in that behalf shall have access to all books, records, returns and other documents relating to those accounts and upon receipt of a statement of accounts transmitted to him under paragraph 1 of Article 78 of this Treaty the Auditor-General shall examine it, certify it and report on it and shall return the statement with his certificate and report to the Board of Directors of the Corporation concerned in sufficient time to enable compliance with paragraph 2 of Article 78 of this Treaty.

5. In the performance of his functions under this Article, the Auditor-General shall not be subject to the direction or control of any person or authority.

PART V: TRANSITIONAL AND GENERAL

CHAPTER XXIV
TRANSITIONAL

Article 90: Transitional Provisions

The transitional provisions contained in Annex XV to this Treaty shall apply.

CHAPTER XXV
GENERAL

Article 91: Commencement of the Treaty

This Treaty shall come into force on the first day of December 1967.

Article 92: Duration of the Treaty

1. Parts II and III of this Treaty, together with so much of the other Parts of the Treaty as appertains to the Common Market or the Common Market Council, shall remain in force for 15 years after coming into force and shall be reviewed by the Partner States before the expiry of that period.

2. Subject to paragraph 1 of this Article, this Treaty shall have indefinite duration.

Article 93: Association of Other Countries with the Community

The Partner States may together negotiate with any foreign country with a view to the association of that country with the Community or its participation in any of the activities of the Community or the Corporations.

Article 94: Modification of the Treaty

1. This Treaty may be modified at any time by agreement of all the Partner States.

2. Notwithstanding paragraph 1 of this Article, Annex VI to this Treaty shall only be amended in accordance with Article 52 of that Annex.

Article 95: Implementation Measures of the Partner States

1. Each of the Partner States undertakes to take all steps within its power to secure the enactment and the continuation of such legislation as is necessary to give effect to this Treaty, and in particular:

(a) to confer upon the Community the legal capacity and personality required for the performance of its functions; and

(b) to confer upon Acts of the Community the force of law within its territory.

2. A Partner State shall not, by or under any law of that Partner State, confer any power nor impose any duty upon an officer or authority of the Community, or of a Corporation as such, except with the prior consent of the Authority.

Article 96: Effect of Annexes, Rules and Orders

1. The Annexes to this Treaty shall form an integral part of this Treaty.

2. Rules and orders made by the Authority pursuant to this Treaty shall be binding on the institutions of the Community and the Partner States.

Article 97: Abrogation of Existing Agreements

1. Subject to this Treaty, the East African Common Services Organization Agreements 1961 to 1966 are hereby abrogated.

2. Subject to this Treaty, all the existing agreements between the Partner States or any of them concerning the imposition of customs and excise duties and the allocation and distribution of customs and excise revenue collected by the East African Customs and Excise Department are hereby abrogated.

3. Subject to this Treaty, all the existing agreements between the Partner States or any of them concerning the allocation and distribution of revenue collected by the East African Income Tax Department are hereby abrogated.

4. Subject to this Treaty, the Agreement dated the 22nd November 1961 made between the Governments of the Trust Territory of Tanganyika, the Protectorate of Uganda and the Colony and Protectorate of Kenya in pursuance of section 42A of the East Africa (High Commission) Order in Council 1947 with respect to payments into and out of the Distributable Pool Fund of the East Africa High Commission is hereby abrogated.

Article 98: Interpretation

1. In this Treaty, except where the context otherwise requires:

"Act of the Community" means an Act of the Community enacted in accordance with this Treaty or an Act of the Common Services Organization or an Act of the East Africa High Commission;

"appointed member" means an appointed member of the Assembly appointed under Article 57 of this Treaty;

"Assembly" means the East African Legislative Assembly established by Article 56 of this Treaty;

"Auditor-General" means the Auditor-General of the Community provided for by Article 61 of this Treaty;

"Authority" means the East African Authority established by Article 46 of this Treaty;

"Bank" means the East African Development Bank established by Article 21 of this Treaty;

"Board of Directors," except in Annex VI to this Treaty, means the Board of Directors of a Corporation;

"central banks" means the Bank of Tanzania, the Bank of Uganda and the Central Bank of Kenya;

"Chairman of the Assembly" means the Chairman of the East African Legislative Assembly provided for by paragraph 2 of Article 56 of this Treaty;

"Chairman of the Tribunal" means the Chairman of the Common Market Tribunal provided for by Article 33 of this Treaty;

"common customs tariff" and "common excise tariff" imply an identical rate of tariff imposed in the same manner;

"Common Market" means the East African Common Market established by Article 1 of this Treaty;

"common services" means the services specified in Annex IX to this Treaty;

"Common Services Organization" means the East African Common Services Organization established by the East African Common Services Organization Agreements 1961 to 1966;

"Community" means the East African Community established by Article 1 of this Treaty;

"Corporation" means a corporation specified in paragraph 2 of Article 71 of this Treaty;

"Council" means a council established by Article 53 of this Treaty;

"Counsel to the Community" means the Counsel to the Community provided for by Article 61 of this Treaty;

"current account payments" means the payments so defined in Annex VII to this Treaty;

"customs duty" includes suspended duty;

"customs laws" means the East African Customs Management Act 1952;

"Deputy East African Ministers" means the Deputy East African Ministers appointed under Article 52 of this Treaty;

"Director-General," except in Annex VI to this Treaty, means the Director-General of a Corporation provided for by Article 76 of this Treaty;

"East African Ministers" means the East African Ministers appointed under Article 49 of this Treaty;

"foreign country" means any country other than a Partner State;

"Gazette" means the Official Gazette of the Community;

"General Fund" means the General Fund provided for by Article 65 of this Treaty;

"goods in transit" means goods being conveyed between a Partner State and a foreign country and passing through another Partner State or States, and "transit" shall be construed accordingly;

"Heads of State" means the President of the United Republic of Tanzania, the President of the Sovereign State of Uganda and the President of the Republic of Kenya;

"import" with its grammatical variations and cognate expressions means to bring or cause to be brought into the territories of the Partner States from a foreign country;

"Industrial Licensing laws" means the East African Industrial Licensing Ordinance (Tanzania Cap. 324), the East African Industrial Licensing Act (Uganda Cap. 102) and the East African Industrial Licensing Act (Kenya Cap. 496);

"Industrial Licensing Tribunal" means the Tribunal established by the law referred to in paragraph 4 of Article 23 of this Treaty;

"manufactured goods" means the goods defined or otherwise listed in Annex IV to this Treaty;

"Minister" in relation to a Partner State includes the Vice-President of that Partner State;

"Partner States" means the United Republic of Tanzania, the Sovereign State of Uganda and the Republic of Kenya;

"Resident Director" means a director of a Corporation who is styled a Resident Director under Article 75 of this Treaty;

"salaries and other conditions of service" includes wages, overtime pay, salary and wage structures, leave, passages, transport for leave purposes, pensions and other retirement benefits, redundancy and severance payments, hours of duty, grading of posts, medical arrangements, housing, arrangements for transport and travelling on duty, and allowances;

"Secretary General" means the Secretary General of the Community provided for by Article 61 of this Treaty;

"Service Commission" means the East African Community Service Commission established by Article 62 of this Treaty;

"suspended transfer tax" means a transfer tax the operation of which is suspended at the time of its introduction;

"Tax Board" means the East African Tax Board established by Article 88 of this Treaty;

"transfer tax" includes suspended transfer tax;

"Tribunal" means the Common Market Tribunal established by Article 32 of this Treaty;

"University of East Africa" means the University of East Africa constituted by the University of East Africa Act 1962.

2. In this Treaty, a reference to a law shall be construed as a reference to that law as from time to time amended, added to or replaced.

ANNEX I: RULES FOR THE ADMINISTRATION AND APPLICATION OF ARTICLE 11

Interpretation

1. (1) In these Rules:
"materials" includes products, parts and components used in the production of goods;

"produced" and "a process of production" include the application of any operation or process with the exception of any operation or process which consist only of one or more of the following:

> (a) packing, wherever the packing materials may have been produced;
> (b) splitting up into lots;
> (c) sorting or grading;
> (d) marking;
> (e) putting up into sets.

> (2) Energy, fuel, plant, machinery and tools used in the production of goods within the Partner States and materials used in the maintenance of such plant, machinery and tools shall be regarded as wholly produced within the Partner States when determining the origin of goods.

> (3) In determining the place of production of marine products and goods in relation to a Partner State, a vessel of a Partner State shall be regarded as part of the territory of that State and in determining the place from which such goods originated, marine products taken from the sea, or goods produced therefrom at sea, shall be regarded as having their origin in the territory of a Partner State if they were taken by, or produced in, a vessel of that State and have been brought directly to the territories of the Partner States.

> (4) For the purposes of paragraph (3) of this rule, a vessel which is registered or licensed under any law in force within the Partner States shall be regarded as a vessel of the State in which it is so registered or licensed.

Goods Wholly Produced in the Partner States

2. For the purposes of paragraph 3 of Article 11 of this Treaty, the following are among the products which shall be regarded as wholly produced in the Partner States:

(a) mineral products extracted from the ground within the Partner States;

(b) vegetable products harvested within the Partner States;

(c) live animals born and raised within the Partner States;

(d) products obtained within the Partner States from live animals;

(e) products obtained by hunting or fishing conducted within the Partner States;

(f) marine products taken from the sea by a vessel of a Partner State;

(g) used articles fit only for the recovery of materials provided that they have been collected from users within the Partner States;

(h) scrap and waste resulting from manufacturing operations within the Partner States;

(i) goods produced within the Partner States exclusively from one or both of the following:

(i) products within sub-paragraphs (a) to (h);

(ii) materials containing no element imported from outside the Partner States or of undetermined origin.

Application of Percentage Criterion

3. For the purposes of sub-paragraph (b) of paragraph 3 of Article 11 of this Treaty, the following rules shall apply:

(a) any materials which meet the condition specified in sub-paragraph (a) of paragraph 3 of that Article shall be regarded as containing no element imported from outside the Partner States;

(b) the value of any materials which can be identified as having been imported from a foreign country shall be their c.i.f. value accepted by the East African Customs and Excise Department on clearance for home consumption less the amount of any transport costs incurred in transit through the territory of other Partner States;

(c) if the value of any materials imported from a foreign country cannot be determined in accordance with paragraph (b) of this rule, their value shall be the earliest ascertainable price paid for them in the territory of the Partner State where they were used in a process of production;

(d) if the origin of any materials cannot be determined, such materials shall be deemed to have been imported from a foreign country and their value shall be the earliest ascertainable price paid for them in the territory of the Partner State where they were used in a process of production;

(e) the ex-factory value of the goods shall be the price paid or payable for them to the exporter in the territory of the Partner State where the goods were produced, that price being adjusted where necessary to a f.o.b. or free at frontier basis in that territory;

(f) the value under paragraphs (b), (c) or (d) of this rule or the ex-factory value under paragraph (e) of this rule may be adjusted to correspond with the amount which would have been obtained on a sale in the open market between buyer and seller independent of each other; this amount shall also be taken to be the ex-factory value when the goods are not the subject of a sale.

Unit of Qualification

4. (a) Each article in a consignment shall be considered separately.
   (b) For the purposes of paragraph (a) of this rule:
      (i) tools, parts and accessories which are transferred with an article, the price of which is included in that of the article or for which no separate charge is made, shall be considered as forming a whole with the article so long as they constitute the standard equipment customarily included on the sale of articles of that kind;
      (ii) in cases not within sub-paragraph (i) of this paragraph, goods shall be treated as a single article if they are so treated for the purpose of assessing customs duty on like articles.
   (c) An unassembled or disassembled article which is imported in more than one consignment because it is not feasible for transport or production reasons to transfer it in a single consignment may, at the option of the transferee, be treated as one article.

Segregation of Materials

5. (a) For those products or industries where it would be impracticable to segregate physically materials of similar character but different origin used in the production of goods, such segregation may be replaced by an appropriate accounting system which ensures that no more goods are deemed to originate in the Partner States than would have been the case if it had been possible physically to segregate the materials.
   (b) Any such accounting system shall conform to such conditions as may be agreed upon by the Common Market Council in order to ensure that adequate control measures will be applied.

Treatment of Mixtures

6. (a) In the case of mixtures, not being groups, sets or assemblies of separable articles dealt with under rule 4, a Partner State may refuse to accept as originating in the Partner States any product resulting from the mixing together of goods which would qualify as originating in the Partner States with goods which would not so qualify, if the characteristics of the product as a whole are not essentially different from the characteristics of the goods which have been mixed.

(b) In the case of particular products where it is recognized by the Common Market Council to be desirable to permit mixing of the kind described in paragraph (a) of this rule, such products shall be accepted as originating in the Partner States in respect of such part thereof as may be shown to correspond to the quantity of goods originating in the Partner States used in the mixing subject to such conditions as may be agreed by the Common Market Council.

Certificates of Origin

7. The transferor of any goods from one Partner State to another Partner State shall, if required by law or by the appropriate authority, provide a certificate of the origin of such goods, determined in accordance with the provisions of paragraph 3 of Article 11 of this Treaty and of these rules, signed or otherwise authenticated by the manufacturer of such goods.

ANNEX V: VALUE OF GOODS LIABLE TO TRANSFER TAX

1. (1) The value of any goods liable to transfer tax shall be taken to be the normal price, that is to say the price which they would fetch when they are entered for the payment of transfer tax (or, if they are not so entered, at the time of transfer) on a sale in the open market between a buyer in the country to which the goods are transferred and a seller in the country from which the goods are transferred independent of each other.

(2) The normal price of any goods liable to transfer tax shall be determined on the following assumptions:

(a) that the goods are treated as having been delivered to the buyer at the point of entry into the country to which the goods are being transferred; and

(b) that the seller will bear freight, insurance, commission and all other costs, charges and expenses incidental to the sale and the delivery of the goods at that point of entry; but

(c) that the buyer will bear any tax chargeable in the country to which the goods are being transferred.

2. A sale in the open market between buyer and seller independent of each other presupposes:

(a) that the price is the sole consideration; and

(b) that the price paid is not influenced by any commercial, financial or other relationship, whether by contract or otherwise, between the seller or any person associated in business with him and the buyer or any person associated in business with him (other than the relationship created by the sale of the goods in question); and

(c) that no part of the proceeds of the subsequent resale, use or disposal of the goods will accrue directly or indirectly to the seller or any person associated with him.

3. Where the goods to be valued:

(a) are manufactured in accordance with any patented invention or are goods to which any registered design has been applied; or

(b) are transferred under a foreign trade mark or are transferred for sale (whether or not after further manufacture) under a foreign trade mark,

the normal price shall be determined on the assumption that the price covers the right to use the patent, design or trade mark in respect of the goods.

4. For the purposes of paragraph 3 of this Annex, the expression "trade mark" includes a trade name and a get up, and a foreign trade mark is a trade mark used for the purpose of indicating that goods in relation to which it is used are those of:

(a) a person by whom the goods to be valued have been grown, produced, manufactured, selected, offered for sale or otherwise dealt with outside the country to which the goods are transferred; or

(b) a person associated in business with any such person as is referred to in sub-paragraph (a) of this paragraph; or

(c) a person to whom any such person as is mentioned in sub-paragraph (a) or (b) of this paragraph has assigned the goodwill of the business in connection with which the trade mark is used.

5. Two persons shall be deemed to be associated in business with one another if, whether directly or indirectly, either one of them has any interest in the business or property of the other, or both have a common interest in any business or property, or some third person has an interest in the business or property of both of them.

ANNEX VIII: STATUTE OF THE COMMON MARKET TRIBUNAL

ARTICLE 1
PRELIMINARY

The Tribunal shall be constituted and shall perform its duties in accordance with this Treaty and this Statute.

ARTICLE 2
OATH AND DECLARATION

1. Before entering upon their duties, the members of the Tribunal shall in public session individually undertake, by oath or affirmation, to perform their duties impartially and conscientiously and to preserve the secrecy of the Tribunal's deliberations.

2. When entering upon their duties, the members of the Tribunal shall make a declaration to the effect that they will, both during and after the

termination of their office, respect the obligations resulting therefrom and in particular the duty of exercising honesty and discretion as regards the acceptance, after their term of office, of certain positions or benefits, and will abide by the direction of the Tribunal in cases of doubt.

ARTICLE 3
HOLDING OF OTHER OFFICES

Except with the consent of the Authority, a member of the Tribunal shall neither hold any political office or any office in the service of a Partner State, the Community or a Corporation, nor engage in any trade, vocation or profession.

ARTICLE 4
RESIGNATION

1. The Chairman of the Tribunal may at any time resign his office by letter delivered to the Secretary General for transmission to the Authority, but his resignation shall not take effect until his successor enters upon his duties.

2. A member of the Tribunal other than the Chairman may at any time resign his office by letter delivered to the Chairman of the Tribunal for transmission to the Authority, but his resignation shall not take effect until his successor enters upon his duties.

ARTICLE 5
REPLACEMENT OF MEMBER

A member of the Tribunal appointed to replace a member whose term of office has not expired shall be appointed in the same manner as was that member and for the remainder of that member's term of office.

ARTICLE 6
REGISTRAR AND STAFF

1. There shall be a Registrar of the Tribunal who shall hold office in the service of the Community and whose functions shall, subject to this Statute and to the rules of procedure of the Tribunal, be determined by the Tribunal.

2. Before entering upon his duties, the Registrar of the Tribunal shall undertake, by oath or affirmation sworn or made before the Tribunal in public session, to perform his duties impartially and conscientiously and to preserve the secrecy of the Tribunal's deliberations.

3. The Tribunal shall have such officials and staff, who shall hold office in the service of the Community, as may be necessary to enable it to perform its functions.

ARTICLE 7
SEAT OF THE TRIBUNAL

The seat of the Tribunal shall be at Arusha in Tanzania, but the Tribunal may in any particular case sit and exercise its functions elsewhere within the Partner States if it considers it desirable.

ARTICLE 8
SESSIONS OF THE TRIBUNAL

1. The Tribunal shall remain permanently in session, except for judicial vacations, and the dates and length of such vacations shall be determined by the Chairman with due regard for its obligations.

2. Subject to this Statute and to the rules of procedure, the Tribunal shall sit in plenary session only with all its members present:

Provided that, in any case where the Tribunal has commenced the hearing of a case before it and not more than one member of the Tribunal is unable to continue such hearing and is temporarily absent therefrom, it shall be competent to the Tribunal, notwithstanding the temporary absence of such member and with the agreement of the parties to the case before it, to continue and determine the hearing of such case.

ARTICLE 9
FUNCTIONS OF THE CHAIRMAN

Notwithstanding paragraph 2 of Article 8 of this Statute, the rules of procedure may impose functions upon the Chairman of the Tribunal sitting alone in relation to administrative, procedural and other preliminary matters not being matters falling to be dealt with by the Tribunal by interim order under Article 39 of this Treaty.

ARTICLE 10
DUTY TO ATTEND

Members of the Tribunal shall be bound, unless they are prevented from attending by illness or other serious reasons duly explained to the Chairman, to hold themselves permanently at the disposal of the Tribunal.

ARTICLE 11

1. Matters in dispute shall be referred to the Tribunal by a reference addressed to the Registrar specifying the subject matter of the dispute and the parties to it.

2. The Registrar shall immediately send a copy of the reference to all concerned.

ARTICLE 12
REPRESENTATION BEFORE THE TRIBUNAL

Every party to a case before the Tribunal shall be represented by a person appointed by that party for the case; a representative need not be an advocate but he may be assisted by an advocate entitled to appear before a superior court of any of the Partner States.

ARTICLE 13
PROCEEDINGS

1. The proceedings of the Tribunal shall consist of a written part and an oral part.
2. The written part of the proceedings shall include the reference, the application, the response to the application, the reply, the rejoinder and the submissions, together with all papers and documents in support.
3. The written part of the proceedings shall be presented to the Registrar, in the order and within the time fixed by the rules of procedure or by the Tribunal in any particular case, and a copy of every paper or document presented by one party shall be communicated to the other party.
4. The oral part of the proceedings shall consist of the hearing by the Tribunal of witnesses, experts, representatives and advocates.

ARTICLE 14
HEARINGS

The hearing before the Tribunal shall be under the control of the Chairman and shall be in public, unless the Tribunal decides otherwise or a party requests that the public be not admitted.

ARTICLE 15
PRODUCTION OF DOCUMENTS

1. The Tribunal may at any time request the parties to produce all documents and supply all information or explanations which the Tribunal considers desirable. Formal note shall be taken of any refusal.
2. The Tribunal may also request a Partner State, which is not a party to the case, or an institution of the Community to supply all information which the Tribunal considers necessary for the proceedings.

ARTICLE 16
INQUIRIES AND EXPERT OPINIONS

The Tribunal may, in relation to any proceedings and at any time, charge any person, body or institution with the task of carring out an inquiry or giving an expert opinion.

ARTICLE 17
WITNESSES

1. During the hearing relevant questions may be put to the witnesses and experts under the conditions laid down by the rules of procedure.

2. During the hearing the Tribunal may examine the experts and witnesses and ask questions of the representatives and advocates.

3. The Tribunal shall have, with respect to defaulting witnesses, the powers granted to the superior court in the Partner State where it is at the relevant time sitting, and may impose sanctions accordingly.

4. Minutes shall be kept of each hearing and shall be signed by the Chairman and the Registrar.

ARTICLE 18
LIST OF CASES

The list of cases shall be fixed by the Chairman.

ARTICLE 19
COSTS

Unless otherwise decided by the Tribunal, each party shall bear its own costs.

ARTICLE 20
ADVISORY OPINIONS

1. A request for an advisory opinion under Article 38 of the Treaty shall be made by means of a written request containing an exact statement of the question upon which an opinion is required and shall be accompanied by all documents likely to be of assistance.

2. Upon receipt of a request under paragraph 1 of this Article, the Registrar shall forthwith give notice thereof to the Partner States and notify them that the Tribunal will be prepared to accept, within a time to be fixed by the Chairman, written submissions, or to hear, at a hearing held for the purpose, oral submissions relating to the question.

3. The Tribunal shall, unless for special reasons it makes an order to the contrary, deliver an advisory opinion in public session.

4. In the exercise of its advisory function the Tribunal shall be guided by the provisions of this Statute relating to references to the extent which it considers them applicable.

ARTICLE 21
INTERPRETATION OF DECISIONS

In the case of difficulty as to the meaning or scope of a decision or an advisory opinion, the Tribunal shall interpret it upon the request of any party or any institution of the Community establishing an interest therein.

ARTICLE 22
REVISION

1. An application for revision of a decision may be made to the Tribunal only if it is based upon the discovery of some fact of such nature as to be a decisive factor, which fact was, when the decision was delivered, unknown to the Tribunal and to the party claiming revision.

2. On an application for revision, the procedure shall commence, where the application is admissible, with a decision of the Tribunal explicitly finding that the new fact alleged does exist and is of such a character as to lay the case open to revision, and declaring the application admissible on that ground.

3. Before declaring an application for revision of a decision to be admissible, the Tribunal may require prior compliance with the terms of the decision.

4. No application for revision of a decision may be made after the expiry of five years from the date of the decision.

ARTICLE 23
AMENDMENT OF THE STATUTE

The Authority may, after consultation with the Tribunal, by order from time to time amend or add to this Statute, and the Tribunal may propose amendments or additions to this Statute.

ANNEX IX: SERVICES TO BE ADMINISTERED BY THE COMMUNITY OR BY THE CORPORATIONS

PART A
SERVICES TO BE ADMINISTERED BY THE COMMUNITY

1. The secretariat of the Community, including services relating to the Common Market and the Chambers of the Counsel to the Community.
2. The East African Directorate of Civil Aviation.
3. The East African Meteorological Department.
4. The East African Customs and Excise Department.
5. The East African Income Tax Department.
6. The East African Industrial Council.
7. The East African Literature Bureau.
8. The Auditor-General's Department.
9. The East African Community Service Commission.
10. The East African Legislative Assembly.
11. The East African Agriculture and Forestry Research Organization.
12. The East African Freshwater Fisheries Research Organization.
13. The East African Marine Fisheries Research Organization.
14. The East African Trypanosomiasis Research Organization.
15. The East African Veterinary Research Organization.
16. The East African Leprosy Research Centre.

17. The East African Institute of Malaria and Vector-Borne Diseases.
18. The East African Institute for Medical Research.
19. The East African Virus Research Organization.
20. The East African Industrial Research Organization.
21. The East African Tropical Pesticides Research Institute.
22. The East African Tuberculosis Investigation Centre.
23. Services arising from the operations of the East African Currency Board.
24. Services for the administration of grants or loans made by the government of any country, any organization or any authority, for the purposes of projects or services agreed between the Authority and the Partner States.
25. Services, including statistical services, for the purposes of co-ordinating the economic activities of the Partner States.
26. Services for the purposes of any body or authority established in pursuance of paragraph 4 of Article 43 of this Treaty.
27. Services for the purposes of the East African Industrial Court established by Article 85 of this Treaty.

PART B
SERVICES TO BE ADMINISTERED BY THE CORPORATIONS

1. The East African Railways Corporation — services and facilities relating to rail, road and inland waterways transport and inland waterways ports.
2. The East African Harbours Corporation — harbour services and facilities (other than inland waterways ports).
3. The East African Posts and Telecommunications Corporation — posts, telecommunications and other associated services.
4. The East African Airways Corporation — services and facilities relating to East African and international air transport.

ANNEX X: MATTERS WITH RESPECT TO WHICH ACTS OF THE COMMUNITY MAY BE ENACTED

1. Finances of the Community.
2. Appropriations from the General Fund.
3. Audit of the accounts of the Community and the accounts of the Corporations.
4. Civil aviation.
5. Customs, excise and transfer tax — administrative and general provisions (but not including tariff, rates of tax and allowances).
6. Income tax — administrative and general provisions (but not including rates of tax and allowances).
7. Powers, privileges and immunities of the East African Legislative Assembly and the Chairman and members thereof.
8. Research within the Partner States.
9. Control of pesticides.
10. The University of East Africa; Makerere University College; the University College, Dar es Salaam; and University College, Nairobi.

11. The East African Staff College.
12. The East African Examinations Council.
13. Meteorology.
14. The East African Land Survey Certificate.
15. Pensions, gratuities and other retirement benefits payable out of the funds of the Community or the Corporations.
16. Staff of the Community, the East African Community Service Commission, and staff of the Corporations.
17. Posts and telegraphs, telephones, radio communications and other associated matters.
18. Services and facilities relating to rail, road and inland waterways transport and inland waterways ports.
19. Harbour services and facilities (other than inland waterways ports).
20. Borrowing for the purposes of the Community and the Corporations.
21. The Common Market Tribunal.
22. The Court of Appeal for East Africa (but not including the jurisdiction or powers of the Court).
23. Legal proceedings by or against the Community and the Corporations, or any officers or authorities thereof.
24. Statistics.
25. Industrial licensing in East Africa.
26. The establishment of advisory or consultative bodies in respect of any service or Corporation or in respect of any matter of common interest to the Partner States.
27. Any matter, not mentioned elsewhere in this Annex, which is incidental to the execution, performance or enforcement of any function conferred by this Treaty or by an Act of the Community upon any institution or authority, or officer in the service, of the Community, or upon any authority or servant of a Corporation.

ANNEX XIV: DECENTRALIZATION AND RELATED MEASURES

PART A
SERVICES ADMINISTERED BY THE COMMUNITY

The East African Customs and Excise Department

1. (a) There shall be appointed for each Partner State a Commissioner of Customs and Excise who shall be an officer in the service of the Community.

(b) There shall be a Commissioner-General of the East African Customs and Excise Department who shall, subject to this Treaty and to any law, have the general control of the Department.

(c) Subject to the general control of the Commissioner-General, a Commissioner of Customs and Excise shall control the operations of the Department, including revenue collection, within the Partner State for which he is Commissioner, and shall have the duty to supply the Minister responsible for finance of that Partner State with such information, including statistical information, as may be required from time to time by that Minister.

(d) Notwithstanding sub-paragraph (c) of this paragraph, the Commissioner-General shall retain control over functions which are necessary to ensure effective co-ordination in the three Partner States.

The East African Income Tax Department

2. (a) There shall be appointed for each Partner State a Commissioner of Income Tax who shall be an officer in the service of the Community.

(b) There shall be a Commissioner-General of the East African Income Tax Department who shall, subject to this Treaty and to any law, have the general control of the Department.

(c) Subject to the general control of the Commissioner-General, a Commissioner of Income Tax shall control the operations of the Department, including revenue collection, within the Partner State for which he is Commissioner, and shall have the duty to supply the Minister responsible for finance of that Partner State with such information, including statistical information, as may be required from time to time by that Minister.

(d) Notwithstanding sub-paragraph (c) of this paragraph, the Commissioner-General shall retain control over functions which are necessary to ensure effective co-ordination in the three Partner States.

Directorate of Civil Aviation

3. (a) There shall be appointed for each Partner State a Director of Civil Aviation who shall be an officer in the service of the Community.

(b) There shall be a Director-General of Civil Aviation who shall, subject to this Treaty and to any law, have the general control of the Directorate.

(c) The Director of Civil Aviation for a Partner State shall be responsible to the Director-General but shall have as much control of the operations of the Directorate as is practical within the territory of the Partner State for which he is Director.

(d) The area of control of each Director shall be determined by the Director-General and need not correspond exactly with the territorial boundaries of the Partner States.

(e) In accordance with a programme to be agreed by the East African Ministers, Sub-Flight Information Centres shall be established at Dar es Salaam and Entebbe to handle air movements, in Tanzania and Uganda respectively, below flight level 145 as from time to time determined in accordance with the rules for international air navigation of the International Civil Aviation Organization.

(f) The programme referred to in sub-paragraph (e) of this paragraph shall give priority to the establishment of the Sub-Flight Information Centre at Dar es Salaam.

East African Meteorological Department

4. (a) The operations of the Department shall in each Partner State be placed under the control of a senior officer in the service of the Community.

   (b) Each of the senior officers responsible for the operations of the Department in a Partner State shall have comparable status and responsibilities and their functions and the services which they control shall be gradually developed in accordance with the availability of staff and finance.

PART B
THE CORPORATIONS

The East African Railways Corporation

1. (a) Strong and functionally comparable regional railway headquarters, including revenue and accounting services, shall be established in Dar es Salaam, Kampala and Nairobi.

   (b) The Board of Directors and the Communications Council shall, when considering the capital development programme of the Corporation, give a high priority to sanctioning expenditure to enable:

   (i) Mwanza to become the operating headquarters of the inland marine services (but the workshops and dockyard shall remain at Kisumu);

   (ii) diesel locomotive facilities and carriage and wagon depots to be established in Uganda.

   (c) The Board of Directors and the Communications Council shall, within sensible operating and financial parameters and for an initial period to be agreed, give preference to Tanzania and to Uganda in establishing new services and facilities.

   (d) The Board of Directors and the Communications Council shall give consideration to the initiation of a preliminary economic and engineering survey of a possible new line of communication between Musoma, Arusha and Tanga.

The East African Harbours Corporation

2. The Board of Directors and the Communications Council shall, when considering the capital development programme of the Corporation, give special consideration to the development of harbours in Tanzania.

The East African Posts and Telecommunications Corporation

3. (a) Strong and functionally comparable regional headquarters, including revenue and accounting services, shall be established in Dar es Salaam, Kampala and Nairobi.

   (b) The implementation of sub-paragraph (a) of this paragraph shall involve a measure of devolution of functions from the headquarters of the Corporation to the regional headquarters in each Partner

State and there shall be a corresponding adjustment of establishments.

The East African Airways Corporation

4. The Board of Directors and the Communications Council shall ensure that future development should, so far as possible, be sited in Uganda and Tanzania, the first priority being given to development in Uganda, and in particular that:

(i) a workshop be established in Uganda for the overhaul of all Pratt and Whitney piston engines; and

(ii) the maintenance and overhaul base for Friendship, Dakota and other piston-engined aircraft be transferred to Entebbe.

ANNEX XV: TRANSITIONAL PROVISIONS

1. The amounts collected by the East African Income Tax Department and the East African Customs and Excise Department which immediately before the coming into force of this Treaty fall to be paid to the Distributable Pool Fund of the Common Services Organization but have not been so paid, shall, upon the coming into force of this Treaty, be paid to the Distributable Pool Fund of the Community.

2. Until rules governing the procedure of the Assembly are made under paragraph 17 of Annex XI to this Treaty, the Standing Orders of the Central Legislative Assembly, established by Article 16 of the Constitution of the Common Services Organization, shall apply for regulating the procedure of the Assembly with such modifications as the Authority may prescribe by order published in the Gazette of the Community.

3. The Service Commission established by Article 62 of this Treaty shall assume its functions under this Treaty on such date as may be appointed by the Authority by notice published in the Gazette of the Community and until that date those functions shall be performed by the Secretary General.

4. Upon the coming into force of this Treaty, the Secretary General and the Legal Secretary of the Common Services Organization shall assume the offices of Secretary General of the Community and Counsel to the Community respectively and shall be deemed to have been appointed thereto under Article 63 of this Treaty.

5. Until provision is made by Act of the Community for the salary of an office to which Article 69 of this Treaty applies there shall be paid to the holder of that office such salary as shall be determined by the Authority.

6. Until the Assembly first meets after the coming into force of this Treaty, the Authority may, in anticipation of the enactment of an Appropriation Act in accordance with Article 66 of this Treaty and notwithstanding the provisions of that Article, authorize money to be paid from the General Fund for any purpose for which the Assembly might lawfully appropriate money in accordance with this Treaty in any case where the payment of such money is not already provided for in any law.

7. References:

(a) in sub-paragraph (a) of paragraph 5 of Article 82 of this Treaty, to a charge upon the funds of the East African Posts and Telecommunications Corporation shall, in respect of any period commencing on the day of the coming into force of this Treaty and ending on the day of the establishment of that Corporation, be construed as references to a charge upon the Posts and Telecommunications Fund; and

(b) in sub-paragraph (b) of paragraph 5 of Article 82 of this Treaty, to a charge upon the funds of the East African Railways Corporation or of the East African Harbours Corporation shall, in respect of any period commencing on the day of the coming into force of this Treaty and ending on the day of the establishment of those Corporations, be construed as references to a charge upon the Railways and Harbours Fund.

Done at Kampala, Uganda, on the sixth day of June, in the year one thousand nine hundred and sixty-seven.

In faith whereof the undersigned have placed their signatures at the end of this Treaty and the Annexes thereto.

CHAPTER FIVE

Central African Economic and Customs Union

With the rest of former French Africa, the four territories comprising the Central African region — Congo (Brazzaville), Gabon, Central African Republic, and Chad — achieved political independence in the summer of 1960. The establishment of the Equatorial Customs Union (Union Douanière Equatoriale, or UDE) preceded their independence by about one year. Delegations from the local semiautonomous governments of the four territories met in Paris in January 1959, where they decided to create a regional customs arrangement. At a conference held in Brazzaville in June of the same year, the Prime Ministers of the four provisional governments formally approved a series of treaties creating, in addition to the customs union, a Council of Prime Ministers of the Central African states and several joint service organizations in the fields of communications, postal services, and geological surveys. Although these service organizations disappeared after independence, the customs union not only survived but became progressively strengthened under the aegis of the Council of Prime Ministers, which in 1961 was transformed into the Council of Heads of State.

The original UDE treaty, amplified in 1960, provided for the free movement of goods and capital throughout the territories of the four states, a common external tariff, a solidarity fund composed of 20 per cent of the proceeds from import taxes, and harmonization of the fiscal treatment of industrial investments.

This last aspect of UDE represents a unique feature of the Central African arrangement, one that is absent from all other common market or customs union schemes in the developing countries. The harmonization of the fiscal treatment of industrial investment was achieved in UDE by two measures: the *taxe unique* (single tax) and the investment code. The *taxe unique,* which is tantamount to an excise duty, is collected on finished products at the source of production in return for the exemption of manufacturers from import duties on raw materials and equipment coming from third countries. The rates of the *taxe unique* are considerably lower than the import duties and taxes on equivalent imports, and the proceeds from this excise tax are transferred to the treasuries of member countries consuming products of regional origin that are covered by this fiscal arrangement. The purpose of the *taxe unique* is threefold: (a) to encourage the local manufacture of consumer goods; (b) to compensate for a fall in fiscal revenue resulting from a fall in import duties on equivalent goods and to distribute the revenue fairly; and (c) to ensure sufficient control over exemptions granted on imports of raw materials or equipment used in local manufacture while encouraging the infant industries concerned. The *taxe unique* scheme was amplified by a common investment regime, which provided for the incorporation of enterprises needing access to markets of two or more member countries into the *taxe unique* scheme and for the reduction of duties on imported equipment and installations. The investment code also provided for the harmonization of fiscal charges pertaining to enterprises working for a single domestic market or to enterprises of particular importance for the development of a member country of UDE. Decisions concerning these two types of enterprises were to be made at the national level, while those concerning "regional" industries were to be handled by the UDE authorities.

The Equatorial Customs Union was joined by Cameroon in June 1961 — after the merger of the former French and British Cameroons into one independent state. By mid-1962 an external common tariff for the five countries had been established. Two years later, in 1964, the contracting parties to the UDE-Cameroon treaty decided to enter a more comprehensive stage of economic cooperation, including (in addition to the free movement of goods and capital) the coordination of development policies, especially in the field of infrastructure and industrialization. The treaty creating the Central African Economic and Customs Union (UDEAC) was signed in Brazzaville in early December 1964 and entered into force on January 1, 1966.

The new regional arrangement is directed by the Council of Heads of State and by a Management Committee, composed of the ministers of the treasury and the ministers of economic development (or their representatives) from each member country. The Council, which meets at least once a year, coordinates the general customs and economic policies of the participating countries, while the Management Committee, authorized by the Council, takes care of matters pertaining to common external customs tariffs; customs legislation and regulations; harmonization of internal taxes; the investment code; and the harmonization of industrialization projects, development plans, and transport policy. The signatories of the UDEAC treaty have made clear on various occasions that they envisage the establishment of multinational industrial projects and the distribution of new industrial firms throughout the region in the future. Even before the negotiation of the new, broader treaty in January 1964, an agreement had been reached by the five heads of state to establish a single petroleum refinery for the entire region at Port Gentil, Gabon. An industrial complementarity scheme in cotton textiles also is reported to be under consideration.

Intraregional trade in the UDEAC area is still relatively small. It amounted to 3,713 million CFA francs (close to $15 million) in 1964 and 4,545 million CFA francs ($18 million) in 1965 — 5 and 6 per cent of the total export trade of the five member countries. Two land-locked republics, Chad and the Central African Republic are, respectively, the largest exporter to and the largest importer from the region.

The percentage of intra-UDEAC trade is larger than that of any other African subregional economic cooperation arrangement except for the East African Common Market. The fact that UDEAC proved able to solve successfully two of the most difficult problems of regional cooperation — the distribution of customs proceeds and transit trade — offers reason to believe that its plans for industrial cooperation have a fair chance of success. A link between the republics participating in UDEAC and Congo (Kinshasa) envisaged by the United Nations Economic Commission for Africa would probably enhance further the viability of economic cooperation in that part of the world.

Bibliographic References

Anguilé, André G., and Jacques E. David. *L'Afrique sans frontières.* Monaco: Société des Editions Paul Bory, 1965.

Economic Commission for Africa. *Report of the Sub-Regional Meeting on Economic Co-operation in Central Africa, Brazzaville, 18–23 April 1966* (E/CN.14/CA/-ECOP/5.) Addis Ababa, May 14, 1966. Mimeographed.

————. *Treaty Establishing a Central African Economic and Customs Union.* (E/CN.14/WP.1/6.) Addis Ababa, January 5, 1966. Mimeographed.

Gillet, Jean-François. *Les organismes communs aux Etats de l'Afrique Centrale.* Brazzaville: n.p., 1965.

République du Congo. Commissariat au Plan. *Code des investissements et textes annexes.* Brazzaville, 1963.

CONVENTION ESTABLISHING A
CENTRAL AFRICAN ECONOMIC AND CUSTOMS UNION*

The President of the Federal Republic of Cameroon,
The President of the Central African Republic,
The President of the Republic of the Congo (Brazzaville),
The President of the Gabon Republic,
The President of the Republic of Chad,

Having regard to the Convention regulating economic and customs relations between the States of the Equatorial Customs Union and the Federal Republic of Cameroon, signed at Bangui on June 23, 1961;

Having regard to the Protocol of Agreement signed on February 11, 1964 at Fort-Lamy,

Determined to promote the gradual and progressive establishment of a Central African Common Market,

Convinced that the extension of present national markets, through the removal of barriers to interregional trade, the adoption of a procedure of equitable distribution of industrialization projects and the co-ordination of development programmes for the various production sectors will greatly contribute to the improvement of the living standard of their peoples,

Desirous of strengthening the unity of their economies and of ensuring their harmonious development through the adoption of measures which take into account the interests of each and all while adequately compensating through appropriate measures the special situation of the economically less-developed countries,

Determined to participate through the establishment of such a subregional economic group in the creation of a true African Common Market.

Have decided to establish a Central African Economic and Customs Union
Have agreed as follows:

---

* Signed by Cameroon, Central African Republic, Congo (Brazzaville), Gabon, and Chad in Brazzaville, December 1964. The text reproduced here is an unofficial translation from the French prepared by the United Nations Economic Commission for Africa and distributed as a mimeographed ECA document (E/CN.14/WP.1/6—OAU/Trad/5) on the occasion of the Joint Meeting of the ECA Working Party on Intra-African Trade and the OAU Ad Hoc Committee of Fourteen on Trade and Development, Addis Ababa, March 28–April 2, 1966. [Editor's note.]

PART ONE: INSTITUTIONS

ARTICLE I

By the present Treaty, the High Contracting Parties establish among themselves a Central African Economic and Customs Union (CAECU) hereinafter referred to as the "Union."

The Union shall be open to any independent and sovereign African State requesting admission; the admission of a new State shall require the unanimous consent of the members which make up the Union.

ARTICLE 2

The achievement of the tasks incumbent upon the Union shall be ensured by:

> the Council of Heads of State,
> the Management Committee,
> the General Secretariat.

TITLE I
THE COUNCIL OF HEADS OF STATE

Chapter I: Organization

ARTICLE 3

The Council shall be constituted by the meeting of the Heads of State or of their representatives invested with the power of decision. The Heads of State may be accompanied by Ministers and Experts.

ARTICLE 4

The Council shall meet as often as necessary and at least once a year.

ARTICLE 5

The office of President shall be exercised each year by each of the Heads of States, in rotation, according to the alphabetical order of the States, unless otherwise unanimously decided by the Heads of State. The Presidency shall change at the opening of the first meeting of each calendar year.

Should any new States adhere to the Union, their Heads of State would assume the Presidency of the Council after the State signatory to this Treaty which is last in alphabetical order.

ARTICLE 6

In the event that a national vacancy in government deprives the Council of its President, the Presidency shall be assumed by the Head of State next in alphabetical order of the States.

ARTICLE 7

The President shall set the date and place of meetings and shall convene the members of the Council.

ARTICLE 8

In case of emergency, members of the Council, upon decision of its President, may be consulted in their own country.

Chapter II: Competence

ARTICLE 9

The Council shall be the supreme organ of the Union for the achievement of the objectives laid down in this Treaty and under the conditions herein set forth:

1. it shall determine and co-ordinate the Customs and economic policy of the Member States;

2. it shall have a power of decision and shall supervise the Management Committee;

it shall establish its own rules of procedure and approve the rules of procedure of the Management Committee;

it shall decide upon the headquarters of the Union;

it shall appoint the Secretary-General of the Union;

it shall draw up the budget of the Union and set the annual contribution of each Member State, on the proposal of the Management Committee;

it shall decide upon tariff negotiations with third countries and the application of the general tariff;

it shall decide in the last resort on all questions concerning which the Management Committee has not been able to reach a unanimous decision;

3. it shall arbitrate in disputes arising between member States concerning the application of this Treaty.

Decisions of the Council concerning economic, customs and fiscal legislation shall be taken by the delegation of the powers of the National Legislative Assemblies in accordance with the institutional rules of each State.

Chapter III: Decisions, Notification, Enforcement

ARTICLE 10

The decisions of the Council shall be taken unanimously. They shall be legally enforceable in the member States one full day after the arrival of the Official Gazette of the Union in the capital of each member State.

These decisions shall also be published in the Official Gazettes of the five States.

The Council may decide that its decisions are to be published according to the emergency procedure.

TITLE II
MANAGEMENT COMMITTEE

Chapter I: Organization

ARTICLE 11

The Management Committee shall be composed of two members per State:

the Minister of Finance or his representative;

the Minister responsible for problems of economic development or his representative.

The delegation of each State, which shall be entitled to speak and to vote, must include at least one Minister.

The members of the Management Committee may be accompanied by not more than four Experts per delegation.

ARTICLE 12

The Committee may invite any qualified person to a meeting on a consultative basis but not for deliberative purposes.

The Committee shall meet as often as necessary and at least twice a year.

ARTICLE 13

The Office of Chairman shall be exercised each year by one of the two Ministers of each State, in rotation according to the alphabetical order of the States. The Chairmanship shall change at the opening of the first meeting of each calendar year.

Should any new States adhere to the Union, their Ministers would assume the Chairmanship of the Committee after the State signatory to this Treaty which is last in alphabetical order.

ARTICLE 14

In the event that a national vacancy in government deprives the Management Committee of its Chairman, the Chairmanship shall be assumed by one of the Ministers of the State next in alphabetical order of the States.

ARTICLE 15

The Chairman shall set the date and place of meetings and shall convene the members of the Committee.

ARTICLE 16

In case of emergency, members of the Committee may be consulted in their own country.

Meetings of the Committee are valid only if all the member States are represented by at least one Minister.

Chapter II: Competence

ARTICLE 17

The Committee shall act under the authority conferred on it by the Council. Its competence shall include the following subjects:

> tariff and statistical nomenclature,
> common external customs tariff,
> tariff or duties and fiscal charges on importation,
> single tax,
> Customs Code,
> customs legislation and regulations,
> harmonization of internal taxes,
> Investment Code,
> harmonization of industrialization projects, development plans and transport policy,
> consultation regarding exit duties, export information on products of common interest as well as on wage and social systems.

The conditions under which the Committee shall exercise its competence are stipulated in the following titles.

Chapter III: Decisions of the Committee, Notification, Enforcement

ARTICLE 18

The decisions of the Committee shall be taken unanimously. They shall become legally enforceable in the member States one full day after the arrival of the Official Gazette of the Union in the capital of each member State.

Such decisions shall also be published in the Official Gazettes of the five States.

The Committee may decide that its decisions are to be published according to the emergency procedure.

It may also make recommendations and express wishes.

TITLE III
GENERAL SECRETARIAT

ARTICLE 19

The Secretariat of the Council and that of the Committee shall be assured by the Secretary-General of the Union, assisted by administrative staff.

The Secretary-General shall be appointed by a decision of the Council of Heads of State. He shall be placed under the direct authority of the President of the Council.

ARTICLE 20

The General Secretariat shall be made up of the following divisions:

a division for foreign trade, fiscal matters, statistics, and typewriting;
a development and industrialization division.

Other divisions may be established as required by decision of the Council.

ARTICLE 21

In the performance of their duties the Secretary-General and the staff of the Secretariat shall not seek or receive instructions from any government or from any national or international entity. They shall refrain from any action which might reflect on their position as international officials.

The staff rules and regulations of the General Secretariat shall be determined by a decision of the Council.

ARTICLE 22

The Contracting States shall forward to the Secretary-General of the Union, for information, the text of all laws and regulations, decisions of a fiscal, customs or economic character and all decisions concerning the granting of privileged treatment within the internal competence of the States. The Secretary-General shall distribute those texts to the member States.

TITLE IV
LEGAL PERSONALITY

ARTICLE 23

The Union shall have legal personality and in particular the necessary authority to:
  (a) contract;
  (b) acquire or transfer movable and immovable property as required for the achievement of its objectives;
  (c) take out loans;
  (d) engage in legal proceedings;
  (e) accept donations, legacies and liberalities of any kind.
For this purpose it shall be represented by the President of the Council of Heads of State, who may delegate his powers.

The legal capacity to enter into contracts, to acquire or transfer movable and immovable property and to take out loans shall be exercised by the President, with the prior consent of the Heads of all the Contracting States.

ARTICLE 24

The Council of the Union shall determine the immunities to be granted to the Union, to the representatives of the contracting parties and to the staff of the General Secretariat in the territory of the member States.

TITLE V
FINANCIAL PROVISIONS

ARTICLE 25

The budget of the institutions of the Union shall be drawn up annually by the Council of Heads of State. It shall be made applicable by the President of the Council.

ARTICLE 26

The expenditures of the institutions of the Union shall be covered by equal contributions from each member State.

PART TWO: THE CUSTOMS UNION, HARMONIZATION OF INTERNAL FISCAL SYSTEMS, INVESTMENT CODES

ARTICLE 27

The Union shall constitute a single customs territory within which there shall be free movement of persons, goods, merchandise, services and capital.

TITLE I
CUSTOMS LEGISLATION AND REGULATIONS

ARTICLE 28

The Customs Union established between the five States shall cover the exchange of all goods; subject to the reservations and the conditions fixed in this Title, it shall comprise:

the adoption of a common customs and fiscal import tariff in their relations with third countries;

the prohibition, as between the member States, of all duties and charges on importation and exportation.

ARTICLE 29

The member States shall adopt, apply and maintain common customs legislation and regulations with respect to duties and charges on importation.

Such common legislation and regulations shall essentially consist of the customs code and its implementing texts, the tariff, the customs and statistical nomenclature and the other texts and regulations regarding customs which are required for the proper application of import duties and charges.

At its first meeting the Management Committee shall indicate the particular points of customs legislation and regulations on which unification should be sought first; for this purpose, it shall establish a programme of work and a timetable.

The unification of the systems applied in the member States with respect to exceptional and conditional exemptions from import duties and charges must, in any event, be completed not later than three months after the date of entry into force of this Treaty.

ARTICLE 30

The common customs and fiscal import tariff shall be drawn up by the Management Committee and adopted by the Council before the end of the first six months of 1965, so that it can be put into force simultaneously in the five States not later than 1 January 1966.

It shall include:

(a) the customs duty of the common external tariff instituted by Act. No. 16/62 in the States of Equatorial Africa and Decree No. 62 DF 223 in the Federal Republic of Cameroon;

the common fiscal charge on imports;

the common turnover tax on imports;

(b) the additional import charge, the rate of which may differ from one State to another.

Where the rules governing the computation, levy collection, or dispute of other duties and charges existing in the States are the same as with respect to import duties, they shall be eliminated if need be by incorporation in one or more of the duties and charges listed above, other than the customs duty.

ARTICLE 31

The States shall inform the Management Committee of the rates of the additional import charge provided for in Article 30 (b) and of any variations therein. At the request of a member State, consultations may be held on the matter in the Management Committee.

ARTICLE 32

Products and merchandise originating in member States shall, when transferred from one member State to another member State for consumption therein, be exempt from all import and export duties and charges, except in the event of application of the safeguard clauses provided for in Articles 40 and 41 below.

However, products and merchandise manufactured in the member States shall, when transferred from one member State to another member State for consumption therein, be subject to the single tax system in accordance with the terms of Part IV of this Treaty.

The Management Committee shall establish the list of such products and merchandise.

As from the date of entry into force of this Treaty, the import quotas applicable to the products and merchandise in question shall, in trade between the States of Equatorial Africa on the one hand and the Federal Republic of Cameroon on the other, be eliminated.

Imported merchandise acquired on the consumer market in a member State and transferred to another member State shall be exempt from all duties and charges upon exit from the consigning country and upon admission into the receiving country.

However, in the case of commercial transactions, a statistical check as to the quantity and value of such merchandise shall be made when it crosses the frontiers.

During a transitional period, the duration of which shall not exceed three years as from the date of entry into force of this Treaty, the importing State shall reimburse to the State of actual consumption the amount of the duties and charges corresponding to the transactions recorded.

The procedures for such reimbursements shall be determined by the Management Committee not later than three months following the entry into force of this Treaty.

Export duties and charges shall remain within the competence of each member State.

However, the member States undertake to hold bilateral or multilateral consultations to determine the tariffs and, if necessary, the market values applicable to similar productions or production of common interest.

TITLE II
APPORTIONMENT OF IMPORT AND EXPORT DUTIES

The product of duties and charges paid to the customs upon importation into a member State shall accrue to the budget of the member State in which the merchandise is declared as having entered into consumption.

To this end, declaration forms for delivery of goods to the consumer market shall be made uniform between the five member States and shall provide for a declaration by the country of destination of the merchandise.

The product of export duties and charges collected by the customs when merchandise leaves the member States shall accrue to the budget of the State of origin of the goods.

Certificates of origin shall be produced in support of export declarations; the Management Committee shall draw up a model certificate of origin and determine conditions for its use.

The Management Committee shall draw up a list of the common customs offices in the member States authorized to collect duties and charges for the account of States other than that in which they are situated.

In these offices separate accounts shall be kept for each member State. A duplicate of the accounts shall be forwarded at the end of each month to the customs administration of the States for whose account collections have been made.

The corresponding revenue shall be transferred by Treasury transaction.

The Management Committee shall establish procedures for keeping the accounts of the customs offices common to the five States and likewise procedures for verifying those accounts and transferring customs revenue from one State to another.

ARTICLE 37

In order to facilitate as much as possible customs declarations in the State of destination of imported goods, the States undertake to make general use of transit régimes for transport by sea, air, land and inland waterways.

ARTICLE 38

In a spirit of solidarity, and to take account of any errors in indicating the State of consumption and of advantages deriving from transit activities, in particular for coastal States, a percentage of the import duties and charges levied by the common customs office of the five States, shall be paid into a Common Solidarity Fund.

The rate of this deduction shall be determined by the Council on a proposal by the Management Committee.

The proceeds of the Solidarity Fund shall be refunded to the member States according to the apportionment percentages to be set annually by the Council on a proposal of the Management Committee.

ARTICLE 39

The Council shall determine the date on which the apportionment procedure for import duties and charges as referred to in Articles 35 to 38 above shall become effective.

TITLE III
SAFEGUARD CLAUSES

ARTICLE 40

In the event that in order to meet its development needs or industrialization requirements, a member State envisages the introduction of quantitative restrictions with respect to products and merchandise imported from third countries, it shall so immediately inform the Management Committee.

If need be, the Management Committee shall decide on any measures necessary to prevent trade diversions.

ARTICLE 41

Should there be disturbances in an economic sector of one or more member States or should difficulties arise which might cause substantial deterioration

in a regional economic situation, the Management Committee may, in deroga-
tion from the provisions of this Title, take or authorize the member State or
States concerned to take the necessary measures to restore a sound situation.

TITLE IV
HARMONIZATION OF INTERNAL FISCAL SYSTEMS

ARTICLE 42

The Management Committee shall examine the conditions in which the
legislation of the five member States in respect of direct taxes and, if necessary, indirect taxes not levied by customs administration, can be harmonized
in the common interest.

The Management Committee shall submit proposals to the Council not
later than three months following the entry into force of this Treaty.

The Council shall draw up directives for the approximation of laws and
regulations.

ARTICLE 43

In its work, the Management Committee shall aim at encouraging the installation and functioning of undertakings, in the same fiscal conditions, in
the five States.

In particular, it shall try to achieve the harmonization of the rules determining the basis for computation and, so far as possible, the rates of the
following taxes:

tax on industrial and commercial profits;

internal turnover tax;

tax on income from securities.

ARTICLE 44

To this end, the member States undertake to communicate to each other
regularly within the Management Committee, all relevant information on
their fiscal policy and to consult each other so far as possible before introducing or modifying the basis for computation of taxes or the rate thereof.

TITLE V
INVESTMENT CODES

ARTICLE 45

The Management Committee shall prepare and submit to the Council, not
later than 1 July 1965, a draft outline Code to govern the fiscal and financial
conditions prevailing on the Union market. With a view to harmonization,
the member States shall eliminate or correct, within one year following the
entry into force of this Treaty, any provisions in their national Code which
are contrary to the provisions of the common outline Code.

ARTICLE 46

The provisions of the national Codes, as submitted to the Management Committee and, where applicable, harmonized according to its directives may not be further modified unilaterally.

PART THREE: APPORTIONMENT OF INDUSTRIALIZATION PROJECTS, HARMONIZATION OF DEVELOPMENT PLANS AND TRANSPORT POLICY

TITLE I
PRINCIPLES

ARTICLE 47

The High Contracting Parties agree to harmonize their industrialization policies, development plans and transport policies with a view to promoting the balanced development and diversification of the economies of the member States of the Union, within a framework which would permit the multiplication of exchanges between the States and an improvement in the living standards of their peoples.

TITLE II
HARMONIZATION OF DEVELOPMENT PLANS AND TRANSPORT POLICIES

The member States decide that, as from the date of entry into force of this Treaty, they will communicate to each other documents indicating on their respective economic situations and, for future years, their development plans or programmes and annual reports on the execution of such plans and programmes.

They shall also keep each other informed of their plans for improving and developing communication routes which may be of interest to one or more other States, as well as of their national regulations on transport and movement.

ARTICLE 49

The above-mentioned documents shall be addressed by each State to the General Secretariat of the Union.

The General Secretariat shall make a comprehensive study thereof with a view to presenting to the Management Committee and to the Council a review of the economic situation of the Union during the period considered.

Such review shall report any distortions which may have been observed, in particular as regards the harmonization objectives defined in Article 47, and shall make proposals for correcting such distortions.

The documents and reviews shall be forwarded to the States by the Secretary-General.

In these tasks he obtains assistance from Experts or study institutes approved by the Committee.

ARTICLE 50

The study of these documents shall be included in the agenda for the ensuing meeting of the Management Committee, which shall give an opinion regarding them. That opinion shall be communicated to the Council which shall decide as to any measures to be taken.

TITLE III
INDUSTRIAL CO-OPERATION

ARTICLE 51

In this field, a distinction shall be made as between the following:
(a) industries mainly devoted to exports outside the Union;
(b) industries affecting the market of a single State for which no economic, fiscal or customs advantages are requested from the other States of the Union;
(c) industrial projects affecting the market of a single State which concern a production existing already in another State of the Union or the creation of which is also envisaged in the development plans or programmes of another State of the Union;
(d) industrial projects, the market for which is and will remain limited to two States, for which harmonization can be sought as between those two States;
(e) industrial projects affecting the market of more than two States and for which harmonization is directly sought within the Union.

The provisions of this Article shall apply to all industrial undertakings including those having the status of joint venture corporations or State agencies.

ARTICLE 52

Industries within categories (a) and (b) may be created in each of the member States concerned without intervention by the Union institutions.

However, and in the absence of prior consent from the Management Committee, the market of industries in category (b) shall remain limited to the State in which they are situated and may not be extended to that of the other member States.

The State concerned shall regularly forward to the General Secretariat a list of the industries thus created, together with all relative economic data, and an exchange of views may take place in the Management Committee on that information.

ARTICLE 53

Industrial projects within category (d) shall be the subject of a joint report and shall be notified jointly by the two States concerned to the other States of the Union, through the intermediary of the General Secretariat.

Investment projects regarding industries in categories (c) and (e) must be communicated to the States of the Union by the State in whose territory the industry is to be situated.

To this end, before any decision is taken to proceed with the plan, and before any definitive undertakings are given to interested third parties, each project shall be notified to the General Secretariat, together with supporting documentation, for forwarding to each member State.

Any member State may request the Secretary-General to make a study of projects in categories (c), (d) and (e), in relation to the harmonization objectives defined in Article 47 of the Treaty.

Such study shall be carried out by experts or study institutes approved by the Committee.

The General Secretariat shall transmit the report to all the States.

ARTICLE 54

The project shall comprise full relevant information of an economic, financial, legal, technical, fiscal, and customs nature.

The Committee shall decide what the file shall include.

ARTICLE 55

The States shall be consulted in their own territory according to the procedure referred to in Article 53 of the Treaty, and must reply within two months as from the date of the communication from the General Secretariat. Failure to reply within the two-month period shall be construed as signifying approval of the project. In case of express disagreement, the project shall be submitted to the Management Committee which may, if appropriate, decide what rate or rates of single tax should be applied to the project, and as regards industries in category (e), what system should be granted under the Investment Code.

ARTICLE 56

As regards category (e) projects, in taking its decision the Management Committee shall base itself on the following criteria:

raw materials situation,

volume of investments already made in the various States of the Union, and comparison of advantages thus granted by each State to its partners,

desirability of compensating the relatively lower degree of economic development of certain States of the Union.

ARTICLE 57

After consulting the Ministries of Planning in the member States, the Secretary-General shall have a general industrialization plan prepared for the Union, covering projects within category (e) of Article 51 above, such plan being drawn up for all industrial sectors in relation to the harmonization objectives defined in Article 47. In this task, he may obtain assistance from study institutes approved by the Committee.

The industrial development plan for the Union shall be submitted for approval to the Council, after the Management Committee has given its opinion, not later than one year following the entry into force of the Treaty.

ARTICLE 58

In the event that, in a member State an industrial production which has not been the subject of a harmonization measure and has not been brought under the single tax system, reaches the market of one or more other member States, the State or States which considers its interests impaired may either prohibit access to its territory for the products in question or may, as a temporary measure, introduce a countervailing charge, the rate of which shall not exceed the overall fiscal charge on similar products when imported from third countries, with the exception, however, of the duties of the common external customs tariff.

The State or States concerned shall, not later than one month following such decisions, notify them to the Management Committee which shall decide on appropriate measures to be taken, subject to consultation of the Council.

The safeguard measures taken by the requesting member State or States shall remain applicable pending the decision of the Committee and the Council which shall be legally enforceable forthwith.

PART FOUR: SINGLE TAX

ARTICLE 59

The "single tax" (*taxe unique*) system shall apply to all domestic industrial production whose market extends or is likely to extend to the territory of several member States.

ARTICLE 60

The single tax shall be exclusive of the following:

duties and charges applicable upon importation on raw materials and essential products used in industry for the preparation of manufactured products in the form in which they enter into trade;

all internal charges on raw materials and essential products used in industry as well as on manufactured products.

The single tax shall be levied and settled in the State in which the manufacturing industry is situated for the account of the State in which the products are consumed, in accordance with the applicable rules regarding customs duties and with the provisions of Article 36 of this Treaty.

The rules for customs disputes shall be applied in establishing infractions and taking proceedings against them.

The Management Committee shall determine the regulations and the rates for the single tax; they shall be subject to review.

During the transitional period, which shall end on January 1, 1972, the rates of the single tax may be different in respect of a like product, according to the place of production.

Thereafter, the Management Committee may, on an exceptional basis and at the request of a member State, authorize the maintenance of different rates according to States, for a given production.

However, subject to any recourse to the provisions of Article 41, the differences existing between the rates of the single tax shall not be increased and shall be progressively reduced following an annual review.

The rates of the single tax shall in particular be calculated on the basis of the following elements:

exemption from duties and charges of all kinds granted on imported or domestic products,

other privileges and protective measures of a customs or fiscal nature granted in the past or still accorded to undertakings in particular by virtue of their admission to priority treatment under Investment Codes,

any disparities in production conditions for similar articles.

Within three months following the entry into force of this Treaty, the Management Committee shall determine the contents of the file to be submitted by undertakings requesting admission to the single tax system.

PART FIVE: FREE MOVEMENT OF PERSONS, SERVICES, AND CAPITAL, RIGHT OF ESTABLISHMENT

The situation of persons and the right of establishment are governed by the Convention signed on September 8, 1961 by the member States of the African and Malagasy Union.

Movements of capital within the Union shall not be subject to any restrictions other than those provided for under the exchange regulations currently in force.

PART SIX: GENERAL AND FINAL PROVISIONS

ARTICLE 65

The rights and obligations resulting from Conventions concluded prior to the entry into force of this Treaty between one or more member States, on the one hand, and one or more third countries, on the other hand, shall not be affected by the provisions of this Treaty.

In so far as such Conventions are not compatible with this Treaty, the member State or States concerned shall take all appropriate steps to eliminate any incompatibility found to exist. Member States shall, if necessary, assist each other in order to achieve this purpose and shall, where appropriate, adopt a common attitude.

Member States shall, in the application of the Conventions referred to in the first paragraph, take due account of the fact that the advantages granted under this Treaty by each member State form an integral part of the establishment of the Union and are therefore inseparably linked with the creation of common institutions, the conferring of competences upon such institutions and the granting of the same advantages by all other member States.

This Treaty shall enter into force following its ratification in accordance with constitutional practice by each of the Contracting States.

The instruments of ratification shall be deposited with the Government of the Congo, hereby designated as the depositary Government.

Once the depositary Government has received instruments of ratification, it shall forthwith notify them to all the contracting parties and to the Secretary-General of the Union.

ARTICLE 66

Any modifications to this Treaty must be ratified by each State in the forms required by its internal legislation.

ARTICLE 67

This Treaty may be modified in the forms provided for its adoption.

It may be denounced by any member State. Such denunciation shall take effect in respect of the denouncing State only as from 1 January following its notification to the President of the Council and not earlier than six months following such notification.

Denunciation by one or more Contracting States shall not cause the dissolution of the Union.

Such dissolution may be decided upon only by the Council of Heads of State which shall determine the modalities for apportioning the assets and liabilities.

However, the Council shall determine the principle and modalities for indemnification in the event that a Contracting State withdraws from the Union.

CONVENTION ON THE TREATMENT OF INVESTMENTS
IN THE EQUATORIAL CUSTOMS UNION*

The treatment of investments in the States which are members of the Equatorial Customs Union shall be in harmony with the following conditions and policies:

The economic development which results from the activity of existing enterprises and their expansion and from the establishment of new enterprises makes it imperative to confirm and, as circumstances may require, to specify more clearly the guarantees of security, freedom and stability indispensable for the persons and property already established and for new resources which may be brought in.

The member States of the Customs Union have already taken a clear stand in this regard by the democratic character of their institutions, by the agreements which they have concluded within the Community, by their association with the European Common Market and, in a more general way, by their adherence to the Charter of the United Nations and to the international treaties in force relating thereto.

Because of their attachment to human freedoms, they have in particular solemnly confirmed the principle of freedom of establishment and freedom of movement for all persons and the free exercise of gainful activity with due respect for the precepts of law and order. The right of private property is guaranteed on all their territories. The free movement of capital and goods is guaranteed within the Customs Union and in its relations with the States that belong to the franc area. As regards the other currency areas, the only restrictions are those which result from the requirements of the exchange policy of the franc area.

The present Convention has been drawn up in conformity with these principles in order both to guarantee the security of existing enterprises and to encourage the establishment of new activities in the States.

With a view to encouraging the establishment of large productive enterprises financed by foreign capital in the States of the Customs Union, arrangements

* Signed by Chad, Gabon, Congo (Brazzaville), and the Central African Republic in Brazzaville, November 12, 1960. The text given here is an unofficial translation from the official French-language text published in République du Congo, Commissariat au Plan, *Code des investissements et textes annexes* (Brazzaville, 1963). [Editor's note.]

have already been made and agreements concluded within the framework of the legislation in force to guarantee to investors the stability indispensable for the establishment and operation of their enterprises as regards the conditions of establishment and fiscal treatment.

The evolution of the institutions in the Republics necessitates an adaptation of these former arrangements in order to bring their procedures into conformity with the new order of things without thereby impairing in any way the reciprocal rights and obligations of the parties.

Economic and social advancement cannot, however, be achieved solely through the establishment and activity of large entities which have the effect primarily of creating localized centers of prosperity, increasing budgetary resources and enabling a country to participate in the world economy.

At the same time it is important to encourage the development of new activities of varying scope that will be conducive to greater economic diversification and an increase in purchasing power.

The present Convention therefore embodies measures conducive to the emergence of enterprises offering all the desirable guarantees. It shall apply to all investments regardless of origin. Its provisions may be applied to nationals as well as to aliens.

It also encourages the modernization or expansion of existing enterprises. It enables potential investors to obtain a comprehensive view of the conditions favorable to the establishment and expansion of their activities.

Such are the guiding principles underlying this Convention. It fully reserves to the Governments, through the procedure of prior approval, the choice of the enterprises to be given the benefit of these provisions by reason of the relevance of their projects to the economic and social development of the countries. It also establishes a graduated scale of benefits varying according to the importance of the projects. Its purpose is to create between the States and private enterprises, by regulatory and contractual means, an atmosphere of trust and partnership beneficial to the legitimate interests of investors and the higher interests of the States.

Between:
The *Governments* of:

    the Central African Republic,
    the Gabonese Republic,
    the Republic of the Congo,
    the Republic of Chad,

members of the Equatorial Customs Union, agreement has been reached on the following provisions:

TITLE I: GENERAL PROVISIONS

Article 1

The provisions of this Convention have been adopted by common agreement of the four signatory States.

Any grant of benefits which are superior or similar to those provided for in this Convention but are granted according to rules different from those laid down herein shall be subject to the prior consent of the Conference of Prime Ministers after consultation with the Management Committee of the Equatorial Customs Union.

Article 2

With the exception of activities in the commercial sector, the benefits provided for in this Convention shall be available to any enterprise or establishment if it is to be set up in one of the States of the Equatorial Customs Union for the purpose of engaging there in a new activity or of expanding an existing activity.

TITLE II: APPROVAL

Article 3

The admission of an enterprise to the benefits of one of the investment systems provided for in Title III shall be subject to the prior approval of the Government of the State concerned in the case of Systems A and C, and of the Management Committee of the Equatorial Customs Union in the case of System B.

Article 4

Approval for inclusion in Systems A and C shall be granted according to the procedure followed in the particular State.

The decision granting approval shall specify the purpose and the capital investment program of the enterprise and shall enumerate the activities for which the approval was granted and any obligations that may be incumbent on the enterprise. It shall indicate to which of the systems provided for in Title III the approved enterprise is admitted.

Any operations carried on by an approved enterprise which are not expressly related to the activities enumerated in the decision granting approval shall remain subject to the fiscal and other provisions of the ordinary law.

Article 5

Approval for inclusion in System B, together with the conditions for the application thereof, shall be granted by decision of the Management Committee of the Equatorial Customs Union on the proposal of the State in which the activity of the enterprise is carried on.

Article 6

The conditions and procedure for withdrawal of approval are specified for each of the investment systems provided for in Title III.

TITLE III: INVESTMENT SYSTEMS

Article 7

In consideration of the imperative need for social progress in Africa, the conditions of approval may be relaxed by the signatory States in favor of certain enterprises, especially as regards the amount of capital to be invested, and arrangements may be made to facilitate access to credit facilities.

Any relaxation of the conditions of approval and any arrangements made as aforesaid shall be established in each particular case by the decree granting approval and, where necessary, by a contract between the approved enterprise and the State or the public agencies designated by the State.

SECTION I: SYSTEM A

Article 8

An enterprise or establishment referred to in Article 2 shall qualify for inclusion in System A if its activity is confined to the territory of only one of the contracting States.

Article 9

Approval for inclusion in System A grants entitlement to the following fiscal benefits:

The admission of installation material and equipment at the reduced rates of import duty and turnover tax on imports provided for in the customs legislation in force.

Exemption for a specified period determined in the light of the nature and importance of the approved activity:

a. from import duties and charges on raw materials and products which enter entirely or on some of their components found in manufactured or processed products;

b. from duties and taxes on raw materials and products that are destroyed or basically altered in the course of the operations directly related to manufacturing, on raw materials and products intended for conditioning and on the nonreusable packaging of the products manufactured or processed.

Specification in the decision granting approval:

a. of the rate of the export duties applicable to the products prepared, manufactured or processed by the enterprise for export, such duties being possibly reduced or nil;

b. of the amount of the land, mining or forestry royalty, such royalty being possibly reduced or nil;

c. of a temporary exemption from or a reduction in the profits tax, property taxes and the merchandizing and business tax as provided for in the tax codes of the States.

Article 10

Products manufactured by enterprises entitled to System A benefits which are sold in the State in which they are produced shall be exempt from the internal turnover tax. Such products may be made subject to an internal tax on consumption; the rate of the latter tax, which may be variable, and the dates on which it is to become applicable shall be specified in the decision granting approval.

The application of the stabilized fiscal arrangements provided for in System A with the addition of the internal tax on consumption may not in any case impose on the enterprise a fiscal burden greater than that which would result from the application of the ordinary law.

Article 11

With a view to encouraging production reinvestment, an enterprise approved for inclusion in System A shall be allowed, for a specified period, to deduct from the amount on which the tax on industrial and commercial profits is based a fraction of the part of the profit actually reinvested during the specified period in the territory concerned, either directly or through other companies in which the enterprise has become a shareholder for the purpose of carrying out the approved programs.

The conditions for applying the provisions of this article shall be specified separately by each country.

Article 12

During the time that the aforementioned fiscal arrangements are in effect, no import duty or charge, no new charge or tax and no duty or surcharge of a fiscal character may be levied, save as otherwise provided in the decision granting approval, in addition to the taxes and charges existing on the date of the granting of approval.

Article 13

Enterprises approved for inclusion in System A shall be liable to the withdrawal of such approval according to the procedure followed for the granting thereof; the party to whom the approval was granted must first be given a hearing and shall be entitled to exercise the rights of defense.

A decision to withdraw approval may not be made until formal notice has been given without any action being taken thereon within a period of at least sixty days and may be made only in consequence of serious deficiencies that have been duly noted.

An appeal against the decision may be lodged with the competent administrative tribunal.

Where, however, the major portion of the contributions to the initial capital of an enterprise was of foreign origin, the decision granting approval may provide for an international arbitrator in lieu of the aforementioned procedure.

SECTION II: SYSTEM B

Article 14

An enterprise or establishment referred to in Article 2 shall qualify for inclusion in System B if its market extends to the territory of two or more of the member States of the Equatorial Customs Union.

Article 15

Approval for inclusion in System B grants entitlement to the benefits of the "single tax" [*taxe unique*] system as provided for and codified in Act No. 12/60–75 of the Conference of Prime Ministers, dated May 17, 1960.

The fiscal benefits of System B are as follows:

The admission of installation material and equipment at the reduced rates of import duty and turnover tax on imports provided for in the customs legislation in force.

Exemption from import duties and charges on raw materials and essential products used for the manufacture of products in the form in which they are delivered for sale.

Exemption, under the conditions specified in the decision granting approval, from all internal taxes on the products or goods manufactured and on the raw materials or essential products of local origin used for the manufacture thereof.

Exemption from the single tax on the products manufactured under this system and intended for export outside the member States of the Equatorial Customs Union. The benefit of this exemption shall, however, be subject to the prior consent of the Management Committee of the Equatorial Customs Union.

Specification in the decision granting approval:

a. of the rate of the export duties applicable to the products prepared, manufactured or processed by the enterprise for export, such duties being possibly reduced or nil;

b. of the amount of the land, mining or forestry royalty, such royalty being possibly reduced or nil;

c. of a temporary exemption from or reductions in the profits tax, the merchandizing and business tax and other taxes as provided for in the tax codes of the States.

Article 16

The provisions of Article 11 applicable to System A may be extended to the enterprises approved for inclusion in System B.

Article 17

The rate of the single tax applicable to a particular product manufactured by an enterprise or establishment approved for inclusion in System B shall be determined in the Act by which that product and the manufacturers thereof are made subject to the single tax system. This rate may be nil or variable. In any case the application of the single tax system may not impose on the enterprise a fiscal burden greater than that which would result from the application of the ordinary law.

Article 18

No legislative or regulatory decision made by a State or between States, which takes effect on a date subsequent to that of the approval of an enterprise for benefits under Systems A and B, may have the effect of restricting the foregoing provisions in regard to the said enterprise.

The enterprises approved for inclusion in Systems A and B may, moreover, apply for the benefit of any more favorable provision that may be included in the tax and customs legislation of a State or in legislation in force between the States.

The said enterprises may be granted such benefit by a decision of the Government of the State concerned in the case of System A and by consent of the Management Committee of the Equatorial Customs Union in the case of System B.

Article 19

Withdrawal of approval from enterprises admitted to System B benefits shall be effected according to the procedure provided in Article 5 for the granting of approval.

SECTION III: SYSTEM C

Article 20

Enterprises having capital importance for the economic development of a State, requiring a large investment and not classifiable in any of the cases provided for in Article 15, may obtain stabilization of their fiscal treatment in accordance with the terms and conditions set out in this section.

Article 21

The duration of the fiscal arrangements provided for in this section may not exceed twenty-five years in addition, where applicable, to the period normally required for installation, which may not exceed five years except in the case of projects requiring an unusually long time to carry out.

The starting date and duration of the arrangements shall be specified in the decision granting approval.

Article 22

During the period specified in Article 21 for the application of the stabilized fiscal arrangements, the said arrangements shall guarantee to the enterprise to which they are extended stability as regards the assessment base, the rates and the collection procedures of the taxes, fiscal charges and fiscal duties of any kind which are applicable to the enterprise on the starting date of the arrangements.

Article 23

During the period specified in Article 21 for the application of the arrangements provided for in this section, any legislative or regulatory provision which might be inconsistent with the provisions of Article 22 shall not apply to the enterprises benefiting from the system defined in this section.

Article 24

If the ordinary fiscal system is modified, the enterprise benefiting from stabilized fiscal arrangements may request the benefit of such modification.

The enterprise may also request to be put back under the ordinary fiscal system.

Article 25

Where an enterprise becomes seriously deficient in complying with the provision laid down in pursuance of the decree granting approval under Article 4, the advantage of long-term fiscal treatment may be withdrawn, subject to the following conditions:

The Prime Minister shall give the enterprise official notice that it must take the necessary action to eliminate the situation brought about by its deficiency. If no action is taken on such notice within a reasonable period, the Prime Minister shall instruct an advisory commission, the membership of which shall be as specified below, to ascertain, in a written decision stating the reasons on which it is based, the failure of the enterprise to comply with its obligations in pursuance of the decision granting approval.

The advisory commission shall consist of one expert appointed by the Prime Minister, a second expert appointed by the enterprise and a third expert who shall be appointed by agreement between the first two or, if they are unable to reach agreement, he shall be designated, at the request of the Prime Minister or the enterprise, by an outstanding person of international renown and recognized competence in the field of public law or by an international arbitral tribunal. Such person or tribunal shall be designated in the decision granting approval referred to in Article 4.

If the enterprise has not designated its expert within two months after being requested to do so in an extrajudicial writ delivered to its registered office, the decision of the first expert shall be deemed to be the decision of the commission.

The advantage of long-term fiscal treatment may be withdrawn according to the procedure followed for the granting thereof.

TITLE IV: CONTRACTS OF ESTABLISHMENT

Article 26

Approved enterprises, meeting the conditions set out in Article 27, may enter into a contract of establishment with the Government imposing on them certain obligations and granting them certain guarantees in accordance with the terms and conditions specified in this title.

Article 27

The project submitted by the enterprise must be of special importance; more specifically, it must contribute to the execution of the plans for the economic and social development of the country or correspond to a productive activity which has a priority status.

Article 28

Companies founding or holding shares in the enterprises referred to above may likewise benefit from the provisions of the contract insofar as concerns their participation in the activities of such enterprises in the State concerned.

Article 29

The text of the contract shall be subject to approval according to the procedure followed in each State. The same shall apply to any endorsements to the contract.

Article 30

The contract of establishment may not include any undertaking on the part of the State concerned which would have the effect of relieving the enterprise of losses, expenses or lack of earnings due to technological progress or economic conditions or to factors peculiar to the enterprise.

Article 31

The contract of establishment shall specify:
a. its duration;
b. the general operating conditions, the minimum capital equipment and production programs, the obligations assumed by the enterprise with regard to training or to the socially beneficial activities provided for in the said programs, and the particular obligations of the enterprise regarding the portion of its output to be used to meet the demands of the internal market;
c. the various guarantees provided by the State concerned, and in particular:

Guarantees of the stability of certain legal, economic and financial conditions, especially as regards the transfer of funds, and guarantees of nondiscrimination insofar as the laws and regulations applicable to companies are concerned;

Guarantees of stability as regards the marketing of products and the sale of the output of the enterprise;

Priority treatment as regards the supply of raw materials or of any products or goods necessary for the operation of the enterprise;

Guarantees regarding the access and mobility of labor, freedom of employment and the free choice of persons supply or performing services;

The benefits, as applicable, of all or part of the fiscal arrangements provided for in the systems set out in Title III;

The terms and conditions, where applicable, for the use of such water, electric power and other resources as may be necessary for the operation of the enterprise, and the terms and conditions for the transport of the products to the place of shipment and for the use of the existing facilities or of those provided by or for the enterprise at such place of shipment.

d. the terms and conditions for extending the contract, the grounds for voidance of the contract or for the forfeiture of any noncontractual rights, and the procedure for the application of penalties for nonfulfillment of their obligations by the parties concerned.

Article 32

The provisions of the contract of establishment may be modified only by mutual consent of the parties and only by way of endorsements under the conditions specified in Article 29.

Article 33

The settlement of disputes arising from the application of the provisions of a contract of establishment and the determination of any compensation due to one party by reason of nonfulfillment by the other party of the obligations assumed may be made the subject of an arbitration procedure which shall be further specified in each contract.

Such arbitration procedure shall specifically provide for:

a. the designation of an arbitrator by each of the parties;

b. the designation, in the event of the arbitrators being unable to reach agreement, of a third arbitrator by agreement between the parties or, if they are unable to reach agreement, by a highly qualified authority who shall be designated in the contract;

c. the definitive character of the arbitral award, which shall be made by a majority of the arbitrators, being masters of their own procedure and deliberating according to the principles of equity.

TITLE V: MISCELLANEOUS PROVISIONS

Article 34

The special system of treatment accorded, before the promulgation of the present Convention, to enterprises carrying on their activity in the State concerned shall remain in full force.

If the special system of treatment provides for the stabilization of fiscal arrangements, the enterprise benefiting therefrom may be allowed to negotiate a contract of establishment as provided in Title IV with the Government of the State concerned.

The provisions of such stabilized fiscal arrangements shall be incorporated in and form an integral part of the said contract.

Article 35

Enterprises which were approved for the benefits of long-term fiscal treatment and for benefits under a contract of establishment before the promulgation of the present Convention shall be authorized, as the need arises, to conclude with the Government of the State concerned any contract necessary for adapting the earlier provisions and agreements to the new provisions, provided that such action shall not result in any diminution of the reciprocal advantages and obligations of the parties.

The contracts referred to in this article shall be negotiated on the initiative of the Government or enterprise concerned.

Article 36

The present Convention shall come into force according to the procedure followed in each State and shall be published in the Official Gazettes of the four member States of the Equatorial Customs Union.

ACT CODIFYING AND REGULATING THE SINGLE TAX [TAXE UNIQUE] IN THE STATES OF EQUATORIAL AFRICA*

The Conference of Prime Ministers of the States of Equatorial Africa

Considering Protocol No. 1 signed in Paris on January 17, 1959 by the delegations of the States of the former Federation of French Equatorial Africa;

Considering the Protocol of Agreement of June 23, 1959, relating to the transitional provisions for the application of Protocol No. I of January 17, 1959, as from July 1, 1959;

Considering the Convention of June 23, 1959, establishing the Fiscal, Economic and Customs Union, in particular Articles 18 and 22 thereof, and the Convention of December 7, 1959, in particular Article 13 thereof;

Considering the Customs Code, in particular Article 122 *quater* thereof;

Considering Decision No. 66/49 of September 7, 1949, of the Great Council of French Equatorial Africa specifying the duties and taxes applicable to imports and exports, together with the subsequent amendments thereto;

Considering Decision No. 48/58 of May 19, 1958, of the Great Council instituting a "single tax" [*taxe unique*] on sugar, and the subsequent amendments thereto, in particular Act No. 24/59 of December 7, 1959, of the Conference of Prime Ministers;

Considering Acts Nos. 25 and 26/59 of December 7, 1959, of the Conference of Prime Ministers instituting a "single tax" on aluminum household goods and plastic footwear;

At its meeting of May 17, 1960,

Has adopted the following Act:

---

* Act No. 12/60–75. Signed by the Central African Republic, Gabon, Chad, and the Congo (Brazzaville) in Fort-Lamy, Chad, May 17, 1960. The text given here is an unofficial translation from the official French-language text published in République du Congo, Commissariat au Plan, *Code des investissements et textes annexes* (Brazzaville, 1963). [Editor's note.]

I: PRINCIPLES OF THE SINGLE TAX

Article 1

There shall be brought under the single tax system certain types of local industrial production, the market for which extends or is capable of being extended to the territory of two or more of the States of the Equatorial Customs Union.

The enterprises engaging in such production must, in addition, furnish proof of its clearly industrial character and particulars of the size and nature of their investment and the volume of their output.

An enterprise shall be placed under the single tax system by decision of the Management Committee of the Equatorial Customs Union on the proposal of the State in which the activity of the enterprise is carried on.

Discontuance of the single tax system shall be decided upon according to the same procedure.

Article 2

Collection of the single tax shall exclude collection of import duties and charges on raw materials and *essential* products used for the manufacture of products in the form in which they are delivered for sale.

Article 3

It shall likewise exclude the collection of any internal tax either on the raw materials and *essential* products used in the manufacturing process or on the products manufactured.

The terms and conditions for the application of these provisions shall be specified for each particular case in the order instituting the system.

Article 4

The receipts from the single tax shall be apportioned each quarter among the member States of the Equatorial Customs Union in proportion to their consumption of locally manufactured products subject to the said tax and in accordance with the rates of the tax applicable in each State.

Article 5

The Customs and Indirect Taxes Service shall be responsible for the settlement of the single tax and for furnishing the data needed for the apportionment of the receipts among the States; it shall, as necessary, be assisted by the Direct Taxes Service and the Registration Service.

II: RAW MATERIALS AND PRODUCTS ENTERING INTO THE MANUFACTURE OF THE PRODUCTS SUBJECT TO THE SINGLE TAX

Article 6

In order to obtain exemption from import duties and charges, the manufacturers admitted to the single tax system must submit to the competent department of Customs and Indirect Taxes:

1. An annual import plan enumerating by type, quantity and value the raw materials and products qualifying for the exemption that the manufacturer proposes to import in the course of the next annual period to meet his production requirements;

2. Either annually or as the need arises but in any case not less than fifteen days before the arrival of the goods, an application for free admission in the form of the annexed model (Annex I) for each of the products or raw materials which are to be imported. The said application shall be prepared in four copies, one green, one pink and two white; after the authorization for free admission has been affixed, these various copies shall be distributed as follows:

one white copy to the importer, who shall present it to the customs clearance office on each occasion that the product to which the application refers is imported;

one pink copy to the customs clearance office, which shall use it as a control copy;

one green copy to the agency responsible for the inspection or surveillance of the plant;

one white copy to the department files.

Where the manufacturers referred to above have occasion to obtain their supplies from local raw materials and products which are themselves subject to the single tax system, the procedure to be followed shall be the same as for raw materials and products that are imported.

Article 7

The manufacturers benefiting from the single tax system must, in addition, keep records of the materials and products admitted free of duty so as to be able at any time to furnish evidence of the use of such materials and products or of the supplies thereof on hand. The registers, cards and various documents used for the purposes of such records must have been numbered and initialed beforehand by the head of the customs office responsible for the supervision and inspection of the plant in question.

III: PRODUCTION: REGULATION OF MANUFACTURING PLANTS

Article 8

The manufacture of products meeting the conditions for being placed under the single tax system may not begin until a statement has been submitted to the Customs Service.

The statement shall specify the name or firm name and the address of the manufacturer and the working arrangements in the plant. It shall be accompanied by a plan of the various buildings comprising the establishment. The plan shall clearly indicate all the exits.

Article 9

The single tax system may not begin to apply until a qualified representative of the Customs Service has ascertained:

1. that the plant and its appurtenances have only one exit that is customarily open, the others being equipped with a closing device so arranged that communication with the outside is impossible without the authorization of the Service;

2. that the enclosing walls have a minimum height of 2.5 meters;

3. that exterior windows and openings are equipped with a device (iron grating or the like) making it impossible for them to be used for the removal of products;

4. that there is no interior communication between the plant or its appurtenances and adjacent buildings from which the plant is not entirely separated.

The foregoing conditions may, however, be moderated at the request of the parties concerned, due regard being made to the site of the plant and the type of production in which it is engaged.

Article 10

If there is any stoppage of production, a further statement must be submitted as soon as possible before the stoppage occurs but in no case more than fifteen days after the stoppage.

The same shall apply in the event of any change in the working arrangements in the plant.

Article 11

The manufacturing plants shall be subject to intermittent inspection.

They may, however, as an exceptional measure be subjected to regular surveillance by decision of the head of the competent department of Customs and Indirect Taxes if the interests of public health or of the Treasury so require or in consequence of duly noted fraudulent practices.

The costs of inspection or surveillance shall be borne by the manufacturers.

Article 12

The manufacturers shall be required to allow inspections by agents of the Customs Service, to admit such agents to factory, workshop, warehouse and other premises within the confines of the establishment and to show them the raw materials and the products already manufactured which the manufacturers have on hand.

They shall also be required to supply to the said agents without charge and at the place where they are requested to do so such furnishings as may be necessary for carrying out such inspections.

Article 13

Every manufacturer shall, in a special register, keep an account of the products manufactured and delivered, in correlation with the records of the raw materials and products entering into the manufacturing process.

The said register must have been numbered and initialed beforehand by the head of the customs office responsible for the supervision and inspection of the plant.

The relevant entries shall be made in the register on a daily basis without blank spaces or erasures.

The register shall be presented, on request, to the agents of the Customs Service, who shall initial the same.

The balance of the items in the account must agree with the quantities supplied or in stock. There must also be agreement between the entries in the account and the information on the production vouchers, circulation passes and ten-day returns, and between the entries in the account and the commercial accounts of the plant.

The manufacturer shall also be required to present to the customs agents responsible for exercising supervision such registers, copies of invoices and other vouchers as relate to the sales made by the establishment.

Article 14

Manufactured products which are not immediately shipped shall be placed in a warehouse or depot under the conditions prescribed by the customs regulations in respect of private bonded warehouses.

IV: RATE OF THE SINGLE TAX, COLLECTION OF THE TAX

Article 15

The rate of the single tax as it applies to a particular product shall be specified in the instrument by which the said product and the manufacturer thereof are brought under the single tax system. It shall be determined in relation to the duties and taxes of every kind from which the essential products have been exempted.

Article 16

Where the single tax is established on an *ad valorem* basis, the selling price ex-factory shall represent the value to be declared as the basis of assessment. The manufacturer shall then be required to submit the corresponding invoices in support of his ten-day return.

Article 17

Products manufactured under the single tax system and intended for export outside the States of the Equatorial Customs Union may be exempted from the single tax. The said products shall be so exempted when they are delivered, as raw materials or, broadly speaking, as products incorporated into the manufacturing process, to a plant coming under the single tax system.

Article 18

Settlement of the tax shall be effected by the Customs Service, and payment of the tax shall be made by those from whom it is due, in conformity with the customs regulations in force.

Article 19

The tax shall be due from the manufacturers as soon as the products leave the plant either to be stored or to be marketed. In the case, however, of prolonged storage, the manufacturers may be granted the benefits provided for in respect of private bonded warehouses.

An exemption from the tax may, on production of the relevant vouchers, be granted in respect of manufacturing deficits arising from natural causes.

Manufacturing waste that has commercial value shall be subject to import duties and charges.

Manufactured products shall be declared by the manufacturers to the customs office responsible for supervision and inspection as soon as they are produced. The manufacturers shall for this purpose prepare daily production vouchers in the form of the annexed model (Annex II), which shall be printed on white paper. The said vouchers shall be filed according to a system of continuous numbering.

On the first, eleventh and twenty-first of each month, the manufacturers shall, for the purposes of payment of the tax, submit, in duplicate, a return in the form of the annexed model (Annex III), which shall be printed on yellow paper and in which the quantities leaving the manufacturing plant during the preceding ten-day period shall be stated.

V: CIRCULATION OF PRODUCTS SUBJECT TO THE SINGLE TAX

Article 20

Products manufactured under the single tax system shall bear, on the product itself if that is technically feasible or, if not, on the inner and outer packaging, a trade mark or some kind of notation enabling the products to be identified as locally manufactured and as issuing from the establishment where they were produced.

The manufacturers shall make known to the competent department of Customs and Indirect Taxes the design of such trade marks and the character of any notations which may be placed on the said packaging.

Article 21

Products manufactured under the single tax system and intended for domestic consumption may circulate freely within the States of the Equatorial Customs Union, subject to compliance with the regulations hereinafter laid down with regard to inter-State trade.

Article 22

Products manufactured under the single tax system and intended for export outside the States of the Equatorial Customs Union shall, if benefiting from the exemption provided for in Article 17, be conveyed within the shortest possible time to the customs office closest to the manufacturing plant for the purpose of being declared to such office for export. While being so conveyed, they shall be accompanied by a Model I circulation pass printed on white paper and detached from a counterfoil book, the said pass to be in the form of the annexed model (Annex IV). The manufacturer shall complete, in duplicate, a "notice of exempt shipment," which shall be in the form of the annexed model (Annex V) and shall be printed on pink paper; he shall address one copy to the customs office responsible for the supervision of his plant and shall attach the second copy to the export declaration.

The customs office through which export is effected shall attach a certificate of release to the pass and shall deliver the pass to the manufacturer, who shall retain it in support of the special records which he is obliged to keep. The said office shall attach the certificate of export to the notice of duty-free export and shall transmit the said notice to the customs office responsible for the supervision of the plant.

Article 23

Products manufactured under the single tax system and intended to be delivered, as raw materials or as products to be incorporated into the manufacturing process, to an establishment subject to the same system shall be subject, as regards transport and delivery to the plant of destination, to the same formalities as products intended for duty-free export. The plant of destination shall note on the pass and on the copy of the notice of exempt shipment the date on which the products were entered in its special records and the date of such entry and shall return the said pass and copy to its supplier, who shall transmit the copy of the notice of exempt shipment on which the aforementioned particulars have been noted to the customs office responsible for the supervision of the supplier's plant.

Article 24

For the purposes of the single tax the term "wholesale dealer" means any dealer who, within the limits of the Equatorial Customs Union, carries out in the course of a month inter-State transactions for the sale of such quantities of products subject to the tax as exceed a figure specified in the instrument instituting the system.

Article 25

Dealers carrying out wholesale transactions as referred to in Article 24 shall submit a declaration to the customs office closest to the place where they reside stating that they are assuming the status of "wholesale dealer" for the purposes of the single tax. In support of such declaration they shall state the address of the commercial establishment or establishments for which they assume responsibility in any capacity whatsoever and which carry out inter-State transactions for the sale of the products subject to the single tax.

The declarations shall be centralized in the central customs office of the district in which the said establishments are situated, and they shall be entered in a register especially opened for the purpose. The registration number shall be communicated to the dealer concerned so as to be used as a permanent reference.

Article 26

The "wholesale dealers" may not receive or ship products subject to the single tax in a State of the Equatorial Customs Union other than that in which they carry on their activity except under cover of a Model II circulation pass printed on green paper and detached from a counterfoil book, the said pass to be in the form of the annexed model (Annex VI).

The sales and shipments aforesaid shall, as soon as they take place, be entered in a special register that has been duly numbered and initialed by the Customs Service.

Within eight days after the end of each quarter, the wholesale dealers shall declare to the Customs Service the quantities of products which they have sold or shipped as aforesaid. The declarations shall be made on forms of the annexed type (Annex VII) printed on green paper, and a separate declaration shall be made for each product subject to the single tax.

VI: LEGAL PROCEDURES IN RESPECT OF THE SINGLE TAX

Article 27

Any action or attempted action whereby raw materials or products admitted free of duties and charges by virtue of the provisions of this Act are made available for consumption outside the manufacturing plant or are diverted from their destination shall, unless such action has been previously authorized by the Customs Service and unless the duties and charges normally required have been previously paid, be deemed to constitute an act of contraband importation and shall be subject to the provisions of the Customs Code applicable to such cases.

Article 28

If the records prescribed by Article 7 are not properly kept, or if they are inaccurate, incorrect or incomplete, the manufacturer shall, without prejudice to any penalties incurred under the preceding articles, be liable to a fine equal to the value of the undeclared raw materials and products on which he has been granted an exemption from import duties and charges.

Article 29

Failure to submit the statements prescribed by Articles 8 and 10 shall be punishable by confiscation of the manufacturing equipment.

Article 30

Any infraction of the provisions of this Act which, in any manner whatsoever, has the direct or indirect effect of jeopardizing the collection of the single tax shall be punishable by a fine equal to five times the amount of the tax so jeopardized but in no case less than 50,000 francs, without prejudice to the actual recovery of the tax; such infractions shall specifically include:

failure to comply with the provisions of Article 9;

the fact that the account prescribed by Article 13 is not properly kept or is inaccurate, incorrect or incomplete;

a false statement of the value referred to in Article 6;

making available in an improper or fraudulent manner for consumption any of the products exempted from the tax by virtue of the provisions of Article 17 and failure to comply with the legal formalities relating to such exemptions as provided in Articles 22 and 23;

the submission of false returns under Article 19.

Where the aforementioned infractions do not jeopardize the collection of the tax, either because the rate of the tax is nil or for any other reason, only the fine of 50,000 francs shall be imposed.

Article 31

Manufacturers and whoelsale dealers as defined in this Act who fail to keep the special register, to submit the declaration or to use the pass prescribed by Articles 25 and 26, or who are responsible for such inaccuracies discovered in those documents as are apt to jeopardize the correct distribution of the proceeds of the single tax among the States, shall be liable to a fine of 50,000 francs for each infraction that is substantiated.

Article 32

Any infraction of the provisions of this Act shall be substantiated and punished in the same way as an infraction of the customs regulations and shall be tried by the courts having jurisdiction in customs matters.

The provisions of the Customs Code relating to the privileges of officials of the Customs and Indirect Taxes Service shall also apply.

VII: TRANSITIONAL PROVISIONS

Article 33, Article 34. Omitted.[1]

Article 35

The present Act, which shall come into force on July 1, 1960, shall be registered, published in the official gazettes of the four States of Equatorial Africa and shall be communicated wherever there shall be need to do so.

---

[1] The French text reads: "Art. 33, art. 34, pour mémoire." [Editor's note.]

CHAPTER SIX

West African Customs Union

In June 1959, concurrently with the political decolonization of Africa at the end of the fifties, seven of the eight independent states that emerged in the area previously known as French West Africa — Senegal, Mauritania, Mali, Upper Volta, Niger, Ivory Coast, and Dahomey — signed a convention establishing a West African Customs Union (Union Douanière d'Afrique Occidentale — UDAO). The territory of the customs union comprised the six members of the West African monetary union (endowed with a common central bank) and Mali, which decided to adhere to the customs union although it had broken away from the franc zone.[1] The purpose of the 1959 convention was to preserve the free flow of domestically produced and imported goods throughout the area that had existed under the colonial regime. The customs union convention provided that products of regional origin would be exempt from tariffs and that customs revenue collected on imports from third countries would be equitably distributed among the members of the customs union.

In light of the crucial importance of customs proceeds in the national budgets of the participating countries, the fact that the members of UDAO were unable to agree on a formula for the distribution of those proceeds made the West African customs union inoperative at an early stage. One country after another introduced revenue tariffs on goods in transit from the outside world. The unilateral application of excise taxes on imported goods only compounded the difficulties of cooperation. The situation deteriorated further when the three land-locked countries (Mali, Upper Volta, and Niger) considered themselves the victims of certain policies followed by those member countries with access to the sea and thus a

---

[1] In February 1967 the government of Mali made public its decision to rejoin the franc zone.

direct commercial link with the outside world. In fact, the 1959 UDAO convention was never fully implemented except between Senegal and Mauritania.

A new Convention, elaborated with French technical assistance by experts from the seven member countries of UDAO, was approved at a meeting of the West African Customs Union Committee in Paris in March 1966. It was formally subscribed to by the ministers of the seven countries at a meeting of the authorities of the new customs union (Union Douanière des Etats de l'Afrique Occidentale — UDEAO) in Abidjan, Ivory Coast, in early June 1966.

Under the 1966 Convention, products originating in a member country of UDEAO will not be subject to any quantitative restrictions when sold to other member countries, but they will be subject to an internal tax by an importing member of the customs union. Such an internal tax will amount, in principle, to 50 per cent of the customs tariff on similar imported goods, and to 70 per cent of the external tariff in the case of goods competing with domestic production. Goods assembled in a member country from parts imported from the rest of the world will receive preferential access to the markets of the remaining members of UDEAO only according to quotas previously negotiated bilaterally. While an external common tariff is being established, customs proceeds on goods in transit are to be transferred by the countries of entry to the country of final destination.

The 1966 West African Customs Union Convention is considerably less ambitious than the 1964 Central African Economic and Customs Union Convention, which, in addition to establishing a common external tariff and the *taxe unique* (single tax) on industrial goods produced and traded in the area, provides for the harmonization of domestic fiscal systems, investment policies, development plans, and industrialization measures. However, the UDEAO Convention represents some improvement over the 1959 convention in that it establishes two executive organs and a permanent secretariat. The highest authority of the UDEAO, the Council of Ministers, is to meet annually. A Committee of Experts is to meet twice a year and prepare studies and recommendations on the implementation of the Convention.

Recent studies on the prospects of intra–West African trade, prepared either independently within the area or under the auspices of the United Nations Economic Commission for Africa (ECA), strongly suggest that there is considerable room for the expansion of regional trade. Between 1960 and 1963 trade within West Africa (including the present members of UDEAO and former British colonial territories) represented between 2 and 4 per cent of the global foreign trade of the region. Most of this trade consisted of raw materials, foodstuffs, and especially livestock exported from the land-locked sub-Sahara countries to the rest of the region. According to ECA, assuming the future improvement of transport facilities and the harmonization of fiscal treatment for products originating in the area, possibilities exist for the commercial exchange of cereals, cotton goods, footwear and other consumer nondurables, cement, and plastics, among others.

One major point that will have to be clarified in the not too distant future, and one that may have a direct bearing on the functioning of the West African Customs Union, is the relationship between UDEAO and the proposed West African Economic Community. Formal proposals for a community comprising both former French and former British territories in West Africa as well as Liberia were first made at the United Nations Economic Commission for Africa's meeting for the West African subregion in Niamey, Niger, in October 1966. These proposals for a West African Economic Community envisage a loose form of association as a first step toward eventual integrated economic planning and development. They closely follow the philosophy of ECA, which aims to foster economic cooperation based not upon the limits of groupings inherited from the colonial past but upon the four major subregions of Africa: North Africa, from Morocco to Sudan; East Africa, from Zambia to Ethiopia; Central Africa, including Congo (Kinshasa); and West Africa, from Senegal to Nigeria.

The ECA proposals place special emphasis on the subregional approach to industrialization and on the solution of transport problems. At the Niamey meeting, attended by all seven members of UDEAO as well as Ghana, Liberia, Nigeria, and Togo, the representatives of the participating countries recommended the signing of draft articles of association for a West African Economic Community. If the respective governments follow this recommendation, they will commit themselves to negotiate a treaty for the formal creation of the Community. However, the draft articles of association endorsed at the Niamey meeting merely express the general intentions of economic cooperation, trade expansion, and mutual consultation. Their only concrete outcome might be the establishment of an interim Council of Ministers with working subcommittees on transport, energy, industry, and other matters.

The problem of regional economic cooperation in West Africa is highly complicated by the side-by-side existence of French-speaking and English-speaking countries, great differences in political and administrative traditions, the presence of at least two monetary areas (franc and pound sterling), and many other factors. The first West African Customs Union established by French-speaking states in 1959 never functioned, and many other — often conflicting — proposals have never reached the implementation stage. Two examples of these unfruitful initiatives are the Liberian proposal in mid-1960 for the establishment of an Organization of West African Economic Cooperation and the joint initiative made four years later by Guinea, Ivory Coast, Liberia, and Sierra Leone for the creation of a free trade zone among those countries. Although the latter group set up a Ministerial Committee in Monrovia in February 1965 and established an Interim Organization for West African Cooperation a few months later in Freetown, Sierra Leone, thus far nothing concrete has resulted from the initiative.

Bibliographic References

Economic Commission for Africa. "A Note on the Projected Free Trade Area in West Africa," *Foreign Trade Newsletter* (Addis Ababa), No. 11 (March 1965).
———. *Prospects for Increasing Intra-West African Trade.* (E/CN.14/WA/ECOP/-3.) Addis Ababa, September 14, 1966. Mimeographed.
———. *Report of the West African Industrial Coordination Mission.* (E/CN./14/-246.) Addis Ababa, January 7, 1964.
Hodgkin, Thomas, and Ruth Schachter. *French-Speaking West Africa in Transition.* Carnegie Endowment for International Peace, *International Conciliation* (New York), No. 528 (May 1960).
Liberia, Government of. *Proposals for the Organization of West African Economic Cooperation.* Monrovia, June 15, 1960. Mimeographed.
"U.D.E.A.O. — Signature de la nouvelle convention douanière," *Marchés Tropicaux* (Paris), June 11, 1966.
"Vie des organismes régionaux," *Bulletin d'Afrique Noire* (Paris), No. 424 (June 29, 1966).

CONVENTION ESTABLISHING THE CUSTOMS UNION OF THE STATES OF WEST AFRICA*

Article 1

The signatory States have decided to establish among themselves a Customs Union of West African States, hereinafter referred to as the Union.

TITLE I

SCOPE

Article 2

The member states shall apply a common external tariff and uniform customs laws and regulations.

COMMON EXTERNAL TARIFF

Article 3

The common external tariff shall be constituted by the customs duty. It shall be within the exclusive competence of the Union.

The common external tariff shall comprise a minimum tariff and a general tariff which shall be three times the minimum tariff.

No tariff concession may be granted which is lower than the minimum tariff.

Article 4

The Union may be authorized to enter into tariff negotiations with a country or an international organization on behalf of the member States.

The Council of Ministers may, moreover, authorize a member State to

* Signed by Dahomey, Ivory Coast, Mali, Mauretania, Nigeria, and Upper Volta at the thirteenth session of the Committee of the Customs Union of West African States in Abidjan, Ivory Coast, June 3, 1966. The text given here is an unofficial translation from the original French, made available to the editor by the Secretariat of the United Nations Conference on Trade and Development (UNCTAD). [Editor's note.]

negotiate intermediate tariffs between the general tariff and the minimum tariff with third States, but such tariffs shall apply only in the signatory State.

PRODUCTS ORIGINATING IN THE UNION

Article 5

Products grown, mined or manufactured in a member State shall be regarded as products originating in the Union.

Operations consisting merely of conditioning or intended to ensure the preservation of goods imported from third countries shall not be regarded as manufacturing operations.

Article 6

Products originating in the Union and introduced into a member State shall be subject to taxes and duties, of whatever form, which, in the aggregate, shall be equal to 50 per cent of the total rate of the most favorable taxes and duties applicable to a similar imported product.

Finished articles obtained in a member State that are merely assembled from detached parts imported from third countries shall be entitled to the benefits of the fiscal treatment provided for in the first paragraph of this article only within the limit of a quota established by common agreement between the two member States concerned.

Wherever an industry in one member State is apt to compete with a similar industry in another member State, the latter shall be authorized by the Council of Ministers of the Union to raise the taxes and duties defined above to 70 per cent of the total rate referred to in the first paragraph.

The foregoing provisions shall be without prejudice to the arrangements affecting the particular trade relations established between certain member States that are in effect on the date on which this Convention comes into force.

Article 7

Products originating in the Union may move without restriction within the Union.

In order, however, to remedy any economic disequilibrium which might result in a member State, quantitative restrictions may be imposed by that State, on condition that it notifies the Council of Ministers of the Union forthwith.

PRODUCTS ORIGINATING IN THIRD COUNTRIES

Article 8

Where products originating in third countries are received for purposes of consumption in one member State and are transferred to another member State, the said products shall be subject to the import duties and charges which apply to them according to their origin.

The aforementioned products shall be admitted to the State of destination only on the presentation of a customs certificate from which it is evident that the duties and charges paid in the State of first arrival will be reimbursed to the shipper.

Unless otherwise decided by the State of destination, the said certificate shall be accompanied by an invoice from which it is clearly apparent what amounts of taxes and charges were previously paid in the member State from which the reshipment is effected.

Any other system of reimbursement shall be left to the discretion of the member States concerned.

TITLE II

INSTITUTIONS

Article 9

The institutions of the Union shall be as follows:

the Council of Ministers
the Committee of Experts
the General Secretariat.

THE COUNCIL OF MINISTERS

Article 10

The Council of Ministers shall be the supreme organ of the Union.

Each State shall be represented on the Council by its Minister of Finance or by a member of its Government.

The Council shall meet once a year in regular session and may hold special sessions at the request of its President.

The Council shall meet successively in each State, each session being held in a different State according to the alphabetical order of the States.

The office of President shall be held in rotation by the representative of the State in which the Council is meeting. In the interval between sessions, the representative of the State in which the next session is to be held shall act as President.

The Council of Ministers alone shall have the power of decision.

Its decisions shall be taken by such majority as it shall itself determine. The decisions shall be binding on each member State and shall become enforceable, according to the constitutional procedures of each State, within a period of not more than four months after the date of notification by the Secretary-General.

THE COMMITTEE OF EXPERTS

Article 11

The Committee of Experts shall be composed of the representatives of the member States.

It shall meet twice a year in regular session and may hold special sessions at the request of the Secretary-General.

Its meetings shall be held in the State in which the Council of Ministers is meeting.

The office of chairman shall be held by the Secretary-General.

The Committee of Experts shall formulate proposals, recommendations or opinions on the questions submitted by the Secretary-General.

It may set up commissions from among its members to draw up proposals or carry out studies on matters concerned with realizing the objectives of the Union.

THE SECRETARY-GENERAL

Article 12

The Secretary-General shall not have any power of decision.

Under the authority of the President of the Council of Ministers, he shall have power to:

perform liaison functions between the member States of the Union and with bodies of similar status;

transmit information to the various States and notify them of the action taken to put the decisions of the Council into effect;

carry out studies on the common external tariff;

study the problems of achieving uniformity in customs laws and regulations;

make preparations for the proceedings of the Council of Ministers and the Committee of Experts.

The Secretary-General shall ensure that the decisions of the Council are carried out and shall report thereon, as necessary, to the President of the Council.

The status of the Secretary-General and of the Secretariat staff and the composition of the General Secretariat shall be determined by decision of the Council.

The Secretary-General shall be appointed by the Council of Ministers, on the proposal of the member States, for a three-year term, which shall be renewable.

The headquarters and the budget of the General Secretariat shall be determined by decision of the Council.

TITLE III

FINAL PROVISIONS

Article 13

Subject to the authorization of the Council of Ministers, the member States of the Union may constitute themselves an economic union and grant each other advantages more favorable than those provided for in this Convention.

Article 14

The present Convention shall come into force thirty days after the date on which the instruments of ratification or acceptance of at least five States have been deposited with the Chairman in office of the Customs Union Committee established by the Convention of June 9, 1959.

The Convention of June 9, 1959, shall terminate upon the entry into force of the present Convention.

CHAPTER SEVEN

Arab Common Market

Arab economic cooperation attempts go back to 1945, when the League of Arab States was created. One objective of the League was to foster close cooperation among member countries in economic and financial fields, especially in relation to trade, currency, and agricultural and industrial development. These matters were expected to be handled with the assistance of the Economic and Financial Committee of the League, but the committee has never advanced beyond the stage of presenting general recommendations.

In April 1950, in response to the emergence of Israel as an independent state, Egypt, Iraq, Jordan, Lebanon, Saudi Arabia, Syria, and Yemen signed the Treaty of Joint Defense and Economic Cooperation among the States of the Arab League. In addition to its military clauses, the treaty provided for cooperation in the exploitation of natural resources, expansion of mutual trade, and coordination of economic activities. The treaty established an Economic Council, consisting of the ministers in charge of economic affairs or their representatives. With the assistance of the Economic and Financial Committee of the League of Arab States, the Economic Council was to elaborate and submit to the governments of the signatory countries specific recommendations in the field of economic cooperation.

At a conference of Arab Ministers of Finance and National Economy in May 1953, an agreement in principle was reached that early measures should be taken to create an Arab common market, which, among other things, was to facilitate the eventual establishment of a united Arab state, increase the area's military potential vis-à-vis Israel, lead to regional specialization of production, permit utilization of advantages arising from mass production methods and economies of scale, and, finally, make possible a unified policy with respect to the oil exploitation controlled by extraregional economic interests. The 1953 conference led to the negotiation and signature in the same year of the Convention for Facilitating Trade and Regulating Transit Trade Between States of the Arab League, which was replaced in 1957 by the Agreement for Economic Unity among Arab League States.

The 1957 Agreement envisaged the creation of an economic area within which the movement of people, capital, and trade would be free, and the rights of residence and employment, transit, ownership, trusteeship, and inheritance would be recognized throughout the region. The Council for Arab Economic Unity established by the 1957 Agreement was to propose to the member countries operative measures aimed at unifying their policies on foreign trade, customs duties, foreign exchange regulations, payments arrangements, taxation, development programs, and other matters. By the end of 1963, seven Arab countries (Iraq, Jordan, Kuwait, Morocco, Syria, the UAR, and Yemen) had signed the Agreement, which became effective in early 1964, when five countries (Iraq, Jordan, Kuwait, Syria, and the UAR) had ratified it.

In the summer of 1964 the Council for Arab Economic Unity elaborated a set of "Decisions and Recommendations" calling for the gradual establishment of an Arab common market beginning in January 1965. Although the agreement did not take the form of a multilateral treaty, it was subsequently ratified by Iraq, Jordan, Syria, and the UAR and entered into force on January 1, 1965. Participation in the arrangement, which in fact establishes not a common market but a free trade zone, was left open to the other eight members of the Arab League. The agreement stipulates the gradual elimination, over periods ranging from five to ten years, of customs duties and quantitative restrictions on products originating in the area. It does not, however, call for the concurrent establishment of a common external tariff. The settlement of outstanding trade balances is to be made through bilateral payment agreements or, in their absence, in convertible currencies. Commitments undertaken by member countries are considerably weakened by the content of Article 14 of the Decisions and Recommendations, which gives each member country the right to apply to the Council for Arab Economic Unity "for the exclusion of certain products from the duty and tax exemption or reductions applied, and from the removal of quantitative restrictions by reasons of real and justifiable causes." The duration of the exceptions cannot, however, exceed that of the stages of trade liberalization provided for in the 1957 Agreement for Economic Unity.

Trade among the five signatories of the 1957 Agreement expanded from $60 million in 1961 to $72 million in 1965 despite the virtual disappearance of trade between the Egyptian and the Syrian parts of what in 1961 was still the United Arab Republic. If the trade flows between the UAR (Egypt) and Syria are left aside, the remaining intraregional trade grew between 1961 and 1965 from $25 million to $70 million, or almost threefold, reflecting the steady increase of exports from the entire area to Kuwait, from the UAR to Jordan, and from Kuwait to the UAR. Trade continues to be composed mainly of petroleum and agricultural products and fluctuates between 5 and 10 per cent of the total export trade of the five republics. The magnitude of these fluctuations points to the weakness of the scheme.

In the fall of 1964, after they had signed the Arab common market agreement, Iraq, Jordan, Kuwait, Syria, and the UAR also approved several draft agreements providing for the formation of various pan-Arab companies and organizations. The most important of these draft agreements called for the formation of an Arab Financial Organization, capitalized at the equivalent of $70 million, of which Kuwait promised to contribute a substantial part. Another agreement provided for the establishment of an Arab Tanker Company, capitalized at $90 million, to be subscribed equally by all five countries, for the purpose of distributing oil originating in the area throughout the world. A third draft agreement called for a Pan-Arab Airlines Organization to coordinate and supplement the operations of existing national airlines. An Arab Shipping Company also was to be set up with capital of approximately $15 million, of which 30 per cent was to be contributed by the UAR.

Because of Kuwait's reluctance to ratify the Arab common market agreement or to participate financially in the four pan-Arab companies and organizations, and because of political frictions among the member countries, no progress has been reported in the fields of regional development financing, petroleum export, air transport, and shipping cooperation. Neither have any agreements been reached on the coordination of new industrial activity, in which the UAR (Egypt) is very much ahead of the other Arab countries.

Bibliographic References

Dage, Theodor. "The Arabian Common Market — Little Progress on the Road to Economic Integration in the Middle East," *Monthly Review of Economic Policy* (Hamburg), No. 6, June 1965. (English edition of *Wirtschaftdienst,* Hamburgisches Welt-Wirtschafts-Archiv.)

Diab, Muhammed A. "The Arab Common Market," *Journal of Common Market Studies* (Oxford), Vol. IV, No. 3 (May 1966).

————. *Inter-Arab Economic Cooperation, 1951–1960.* Beirut: American University, Economic Research Institute, 1963.

League of Arab States. General Secretariat. Economic Department. *Agreement for Economic Unity among Arab League States.* Cairo, 1962.

————. General Secretariat. *The Arab Financial Institution for Economic Development.* Cairo, 1959.

AGREEMENT FOR ECONOMIC UNITY AMONG ARAB LEAGUE STATES*

The Governments of:

The Hashemite Kingdom of Jordan
The Tunisian Republic
The Republic of Sudan
The Iraqi Republic
The Saudi Arabian Kingdom
The Syrian Arab Republic
The United Arab Republic
The Lebanese Republic
The United Libyan Kingdom
The Yemenite Kingdom
The Kingdom of Morocco
The State of Kuwait

Declare that it is their ardent desire to organize economic relations among the Arab League states, to strengthen these relations on such bases as shall suit the existing natural and historical ties among them to realize the best conditions for the development of their economies, to exploit their wealth, and to secure the welfare of their countries.

They agree to establish a complete unity among themselves and to implement it gradually in the shortest possible time that will guarantee the transfer of their countries from present to future conditions without harming fundamental interests, in accordance with the following provisions.

---

*Drafted on June 3, 1957 and signed by Jordan, Syria, the United Arab Republic, Morocco, and Kuwait in Cairo, June 6, 1962. This is an unofficial translation from the Arabic made by the Economic Department of the General Secretariat of the League of Arab States and published under the same title (Cairo, 1962). [Editor's note.]

CHAPTER ONE: OBJECTIVES AND MEANS

ARTICLE ONE

A complete economic unity shall be established among the Arab League states to guarantee, in particular, for these states and for their citizens on the basis of complete equality:

1. freedom of movement of men and capital,
2. freedom of exchange of national and foreign goods and products,
3. freedom of residence, work, employment and the practice of economic activities,
4. freedom of transport and transit and the use of means of transport, ports, and civil airports,
5. the rights of ownership, donation, and inheritance.

ARTICLE TWO

To achieve the realization of the unity specified in the previous article, the contracting parties agree:

1. to consider their countries a unified customs region subject to a unified administration; and to unify the applied customs tariffs, legislations, and regulations in each of them,
2. to unify the policy and systems of import and export,
3. to unify the transport and transit policies,
4. to conclude commercial and payments agreements with other countries collectively,
5. to coordinate policy regarding agriculture, industry, and internal trade and to unify economic legislation in such a manner as shall guarantee equal opportunities for citizens of the contracting countries engaged in agriculture, industry, commerce, and the professions,
6. to coordinate legislation concerning labor and social security,
7. (a) to coordinate legislation regarding taxes, government and municipal dues, and all other kinds of taxations and duties on agriculture, industry, trade, immovable property, and capital investment in such a way as shall guarantee the principle of equal opportunities for all,
   (b) to prevent double taxation and duties on the citizens of the contracting states,
8. to coordinate financial and monetary policies and regulations in the countries of the contracting parties with a view to unifying their currencies,
9. to unify methods of statistical tabulations and classifications, and,
10. to take any other necessary measures for the implementation of the objectives specified in Articles One and Two.

It is possible to disregard the principle of unification in certain cases and countries provided the approval of the Council for Arab Economic Unity shall be secured. Article Three of this agreement stipulates the formation of this Council.

CHAPTER TWO: MANAGEMENT

ARTICLE THREE

A permanent body to be called "The Council for Arab Economic Unity" shall be established. Its duties and powers are determined in accordance with the stipulations of this agreement.

ARTICLE FOUR

1. The Council shall be formed of one or more full-time representatives of each of the contracting parties.

2. Cairo shall be the permanent seat for the Council for Arab Economic Unity. The Council has the right to convene at any other place it shall determine.

3. The duration of the chairmanship of the Council shall be one year and in a rotating order among the contracting parties.

4. The Council shall pass its decisions by a two-thirds majority vote. Each contracting country has one single vote.

ARTICLE FIVE

1. The Council shall be helped in its duties by economic and administrative committees which function permanently or temporarily under its supervision. The Council determines their duties.

2. The following permanent committees shall be preliminarily formed:
   (a) the Customs Committee, to consider the technical and administrative customs matters,
   (b) the Monetary and Financial Committee, to consider matters relating to currency, banking, taxation, rates, and other financial questions, and
   (c) the Economic Committee, to consider matters relating to agriculture, industry, trade, transport and communications, labor, and social security.
   The Council shall have the right to form other committees when necessary and in accordance with the requirements of the situation.

3. Each of the contracting parties shall appoint its representatives on the above-mentioned permanent committees. Each party shall have one single vote.

ARTICLE SIX

1. A Permanent Technical Advisory Office shall be established for the Council for Arab Economic Unity. It shall be made up of experts appointed by the Council and shall function under its supervision.

2. The Permanent Technical Office shall execute the study and research work in matters referred to it by the Council or any of its committees. The Office shall submit research work and recommendations that will guarantee harmony and coordination in matters within the jurisdiction of the Council.

3. The Council shall establish a central office for statistics. This office shall gather and analyze statistics and publish them when necessary.

ARTICLE SEVEN

1. The Council for Arab Economic Unity, together with its subsidiary organs, shall constitute one single unit enjoying financial and administrative independence and having its own budget.

2. The Council shall draft its own regulations and those for its subsidiary organs.

ARTICLE EIGHT

During a period not exceeding one month as of the date of the implementation of this agreement, the governments of the Contracting parties shall nominate their representatives on the Council and on the committees specified in paragraph 2 of Article Five of this agreement. The Council shall carry out its functions immediately on its formation. Also, the Council shall immediately form its subsidiary organs.

ARTICLE NINE

The Council for Arab Economic Unity shall carry out, in general, all the duties and powers specified in this agreement and its appendices which it shall deem necessary for its implementation. In particular, the Council shall:

1 — In Administration

(a) implement the stipulations of this agreement and its appendices and all the regulations and decisions issued for the implementation of this agreement and its appendices,

(b) supervise the working of the committees and the subsidiary organs, and

(c) appoint the staff and experts for the Council and its subsidiary organs in accordance with the stipulations of this agreement.

2 — In Organization and Legislation

(a) draft tariffs, laws, and regulations which aim at the establishment of an Arab unified customs zone and introduce the essential modifications to them when necessary,

(b) coordinate foreign trade policies with a view to coordinating the economy of the region vis-à-vis the world economy, and to attain the objectives of economic unity specified in this agreement. The signing of trade and payments agreements with other countries shall take place with the approval of the Council for Arab Economic Unity,

(c) coordinate economic development activities and draft plans for the execution of the common Arab development project,

(d) coordinate policies regarding agriculture, industry, and internal trade,

(e) coordinate financial and monetary policies with a view to attaining monetary unity,

(f) draft unified transport regulations in the contracting countries as well as transit regulations and coordinate policy concerning them,

(g) draft unified labor and social security legislation,

(h) coordinate legislation for taxes and rates,

(i) draft other legislation concerning matters specified in this agreement and its appendices which are essential to the implementation of the said agreement and appendices,

(j) draft and approve the budget of the Council and its subsidiary organs.

ARTICLE TEN

Expenditures of the Council and its subsidiary organs shall be covered by common revenues. During the period preceding the realization of such revenues, governments shall participate in these expenditures according to rates fixed by the Council.

ARTICLE ELEVEN

The common revenues of the Council shall be distributed among the governments of the Contracting parties by agreement among them on the basis of the studies carried out by the Council for Economic Unity. These studies shall be made before the realization of the customs unity.

ARTICLE TWELVE

The Council shall perform these and other powers entrusted to it by this agreement and its appendices by decisions to be issued and implemented by the member states in accordance with their own prevailing constitutional principles.

ARTICLE THIRTEEN

The Governments of the Contracting parties undertake not to issue in their territories any laws, regulations, or administrative decisions contradictory to this agreement or its appendices.

CHAPTER THREE: TRANSITIONAL RULES

ARTICLE FOURTEEN

1. The implementation of this agreement shall take place in successive stages and in the shortest possible time.

2. The Council for Arab Economic Unity shall, upon its formation, draft a practical plan indicating the stages of implementation and terming the legislative, administrative, and technical measures necessary for each stage, taking into consideration the appendix concerning ". . . the essential steps for the implementation of Arab Economic Unity . . ." attached to this agreement and constituting an integral part of it.

3. On exercising its duties specified in this agreement, the Council shall take into consideration certain specific circumstances existing in some of the contracting countries. This shall not undermine the objectives of Arab Economic unity.

4. The Council, as well as the contracting parties, shall carry out the measures specified in paragraph 2 of this article according to the terms of this agreement.

ARTICLE FIFTEEN

Any two or more of the contracting parties shall have the right to conclude economic agreements among themselves with the object of realizing a unity, wider in range, than that stipulated by this agreement.

CHAPTER FOUR: RATIFICATION OF, MEMBERSHIP IN, AND WITHDRAWAL FROM THE AGREEMENT

ARTICLE SIXTEEN

This agreement shall be ratified by the signatory states according to their constitutional systems in the shortest possible time. Documents of ratification shall be deposited with the General Secretariat of the League of Arab States who shall prepare the necessary minutes regarding the ratification document of each state and who shall inform the other contracting states of it.

ARTICLE SEVENTEEN

States of the Arab League who are not party to this agreement can join it by an application addressed to the Secretary-General of the League of Arab States who shall announce their membership to the other contracting states.

ARTICLE EIGHTEEN

Arab countries which are not members in the League of Arab States can join this agreement subject to the approval of the contracting states. Such countries shall apply for membership to the Secretary-General of the League of Arab States who shall inform the contracting states and request their approval.

ARTICLE NINETEEN

Any of the contracting parties can withdraw from this agreement after the lapse of five years as from the end of the transitional period. The withdrawal shall be effective after the lapse of one year from the date of the application for withdrawal to the General Secretariat of the League of Arab States.

ARTICLE TWENTY

This agreement shall enter into force three months as from the date of deposit of the ratification documents by three of the signatory states. Regarding other states, the agreement shall enter into force after one month as from the date of deposit of their ratification documents or their application for membership.

In confirmation of the aforementioned stipulations, the delegated members, whose names are specified hereinafter, have signed this agreement on behalf and in the name of their governments.

This agrement is written in Arabic on the third of June 1957.

One original form to be kept with the General Secretariat of the League of Arab States, copies of which shall be given to each of the contracting states to this agreement on joining it.

On the sixth of June 1962, the delegates of the following states have signed this agreement:

1. The Hashemite Kingdom of Jordan
2. The Syrian Arab Republic
3. The United Arab Republic
4. The Kingdom of Morocco
5. The State of Kuwait

SPECIAL APPENDIX RELATING TO THE BILATERAL ECONOMIC AGREEMENTS WITH A COUNTRY OTHER THAN THE CONTRACTING PARTIES TO THIS AGREEMENT

With reference to paragraph 4 of Article Two and to Section 2, paragraph (b), of Article Nine (regarding organization and legislation) of the Agreement for Economic Unity among Arab League States signed

by the Hashemite Kingdom of Jordan, the Syrian Arab Republic, the United Arab Republic, the Kingdom of Morocco, and the State of Kuwait on the sixth of June of 1962

the contracting parties have agreed that the stipulations of this agreement do not affect the right of any of the contracting parties to conclude, individually, bilateral economic agreements for extraordinary political or defense purposes with a country other than the contracting parties to this agreement provided that the objectives of the present agreement shall not be undermined.

SPECIAL APPENDIX REGARDING THE ESSENTIAL STEPS FOR THE IMPLEMENTATION OF ARAB ECONOMIC UNITY

In accordance with paragraph 1 of Article Fourteen of the Arab Economic Unity agreement which stipulates that the implementation of the said agreement shall take place in successive stages in the shortest possible time, the contracting parties have agreed to the following:

First: The Council for Arab Economic Unity stipulated in Article Three of this agreement shall be established within the period fixed in Article Eight of the same agreement.

Second: The said Council shall carry out, during a preparatory stage not exceeding five years, the study of the essential steps for the coordination of policies relating to economic, financial, and social matters contributing to the realization of the following objectives:

(a) freedom of movement of individuals, work, employment, residence, rights of property, guardianship, and inheritance;

(b) unconditional freedom of transit trade without any discrimination in means of transport relating to kind or nationality;

(c) facilitation of the exchange of Arab goods and products;

(d) freedom of the exercise of economic activities, provided the interests of certain of the contracting parties during the transition shall not be endangered;

(e) freedom of the use of ports and civil airports in a manner contributing to their development.

If it deems necessary, the Council can recommend to the governments of the contracting parties to extend this stage for another period not exceeding five additional years.

Third: The Council shall study the necessary steps to the realization of the objectives of Arab unity in its various stages. The Council shall submit its recommendations in this respect to the governments of the contracting parties for approval in accordance with the constitutional systems in force in each of them.

Fourth: Two or more of the contracting parties can agree to end the transitional stage or any of the other stages and to move directly to complete economic unity.

DECISIONS AND RECOMMENDATIONS OF THE COUNCIL FOR ARAB ECONOMIC UNITY AT ITS SECOND ORDINARY SESSION*

THE ARAB COMMON MARKET

According to the rules of the Agreement for Economic Unity among Arab League States,[1] the Council for Arab Economic Unity, desirous to ensure social progress and economic prosperity for contracting parties and to establish the pillars of an economic unity on a solid foundation of a constantly harmonious economic development in line with the existing natural and historical links, wishing to further economic integration among contracting parties, to consolidate the efforts aimed at the attainment of the most favorable environment for the development of their wealth and to raise their living standards and improve working conditions, has decided upon the establishment of the Arab Common Market with the aim of achieving the following main purposes:

1. free movement of persons and capital,

2. free exchange of domestic and foreign products,

3. freedom of settlement, working, employment, and practicing economic activities,

4. freedom of transport, transit and the usage of means of transport utilities and civil airports,

in accordance with the following provisions:

PART ONE
CONCEPTS AND TERMINOLOGY

Article 1

The following concepts, whenever they are referred to, mean:

1. *Contracting parties*: member States of the Council for Arab Economic Unity.

---

* Held in Cairo, August 8–13, 1964. This is an unofficial translation of the original Arabic text issued on August 13, 1964; it was made available to the editor by the General Secretariat of the League of Arab States. [Editor's note.]

1 Signed on various dates between June 6, 1962 and December 17, 1963 and subsequently ratified by Iraq, Jordan, Kuwait, Syria, and the United Arab Republic. [Editor's note.]

2. *Restrictions*: administrative restrictions put by any of the contracting parties on its imports and exports, including the import prohibition and export quotas and any other measure with equivalent effects concerning commercial transactions.

3. *Customs duties and other charges*: customs duties are the duties embodied in the customs tariff schedule, while other charges are all fees and taxes, or whatever else they may be called, on imported goods. The following should not be considered as fees or taxes in the real sense of the word:

(a) All fees, taxes, or payments for services,

(b) All fees or taxes imposed on raw materials imported from contracting parties whenever similar domestic products or raw materials are subject to the same fees and taxes.

4. *Agricultural and animal products and mineral resources*: those which originate in one of the contracting parties and would be imported with the same natural characteristics.

5. *Manufactured goods*: those processed in any of the contracting parties under condition that the added domestic value be not less than 40 per cent of the total cost.

The value of products originating in, and imported from, any of the contracting parties should be considered as part of the domestic cost.

PART TWO
GENERAL PRINCIPLES

Article 2

The free exchange of agricultural and animal products, mineral resources, and manufactured goods shall be ensured among the contracting parties, in accordance with the principles and provisions contained in the following articles.

Article 3

Restrictions, duties, and taxes on imports and exports applied at the present time in the contracting parties shall stay unchanged. This provision shall be carried out by refraining from introduction of new customs duties and taxes, new restrictions, increases in the already imposed customs duties, taxes, and restrictions on the exchange of agricultural and animal products, mineral resources, and manufactured goods.

Article 4

The governments of the contracting parties shall extend to each other the most-favored-nation clause which governs their commercial transactions with nonmember countries of the Agreement for Economic Unity among Arab League States. The provisions of this article shall not apply to the agreements already in effect.

Article 5

Governments of the contracting parties are not authorized to impose customs duties or excises on agricultural and animal products, mineral resources, and manufactured goods exchanged among themselves which may exceed customs duties or excises on similar domestic products or their raw materials.

Article 6

No export duties shall be levied on agricultural and animal products, mineral resources, and manufactured goods exchanged among the contracting parties.

Article 7

1. Re-exportation outside of the Market of agricultural and animal products, mineral resources, and manufactured goods, previously exchanged among the contracting parties, shall be prohibited, unless permission is given by the original exporting country, or after they have undergone a manufacturing process which gives the product the characteristics of the domestic product of the importing country.

2. Re-exportation to any contracting party of agricultural and animal products, mineral resources, and manufactured goods, previously exchanged among member countries, shall be prohibited if the original importing country has granted them subsidies and similar domestic production exists in the country to which these products would be re-exported.

Article 8

Subsidies — contracting parties shall not be authorized to grant any kinds of subsidies whatsoever to domestic products exported to other contracting parties, when there are similar products in the importing countries.

Article 9

Conditions under which concessions and monopolies existing in a contracting party would operate in other contracting parties shall be brought into line with the provisions of the Arab Common Market.

PART THREE
EXCHANGE OF AGRICULTURAL AND ANIMAL PRODUCTS AND MINERAL RESOURCES

Article 10

The following provisions shall be applied until a technical committee, formed by the Council for Economic Unity, sets up a more conclusive schedule for the Arab Common Market:

1. Agricultural and animal products and mineral resources listed in Schedule A, annexed to the Convention for Facilitating Trade and Regulating Transit Trade Between States of the Arab League[2] and its first three amendments, products which originate in one of the contracting parties, shall

[2] Signed by Egypt, Iraq, Jordan, Lebanon, Libya, Saudi Arabia, and Yemen on September 7, 1953 in Cairo. [Editor's note.]

be exempt from customs duties, fees, and other taxes if exchanged among contracting parties.

Those agricultural and animal products and mineral resources which are not listed in the aforementioned schedule are subject to a gradual reduction of all customs duties and taxes by 20 per cent per annum starting with the beginning of 1965.

2. Contracting parties shall undertake the liberation of the said products from all quantitative restrictions at a rate of 20 per cent of the list of products in five annual stages starting with the beginning of 1965.

PART FOUR
EXCHANGE OF MANUFACTURED GOODS

Article 11

The following stipulations shall be applied until a technical committee, formed by the Council for Economic Unity, sets up conclusive schedules for the Arab Common Market:

1. Customs duties, and all other duties on manufactured goods, originating in a contracting party, shall be subject to a reduction of 10 per cent per annum starting with the beginning of 1965.

Regarding manufactured goods which are listed in Schedule B, annexed to the Convention for Facilitating Trade and Regulating Transit Trade Between States of the Arab League and its first three amendments, and which enjoy at the present a reduction of 25 per cent in customs duties, and manufactured goods which are listed in Schedule E, and which enjoy a reduction of 50 per cent in customs duties, the enforced duty reduction shall be as follows:

Date of Reduction	Reduction in Customs Duties and All Other Duties on Manufactured Goods Listed in Schedule B (per cent)	Reduction in Customs Duties and All Other Duties on Products Listed in Schedule E (per cent)
1/1/1965	35	60
1/1/1966	45	70
1/1/1967	55	80
1/1/1968	65	90
1/1/1969	75	100
1/1/1970	85	
1/1/1971	95	
1/7/1971	100	

2. The contracting parties shall undertake among themselves the exemption from quantitative restrictions on these manufactured goods at the rate of 10 per cent of the number of such commodities in ten annual stages, commencing with the beginning of 1965.

PART FIVE
GENERAL PROVISIONS

Article 12

Two months before the start of each annual stage of the Arab Common Market, all contracting parties are to submit to the Council for Economic Unity:

1. A list of the agricultural and animal products and mineral resources which will actually be freed from restrictions during the forthcoming stage, and which represent 20 per cent of the said products.

2. A list of the manufactured goods which will actually be freed from restrictions during each coming stage and which account for 10 per cent of the said products.

Article 13

All contracting parties shall submit the following lists to the Council for Economic Unity within a period not exceeding the first of November 1964:

1. A complete schedule of all restrictions put on the imports or exports of:

agricultural and animal products, and mineral resources,

manufactured goods.

2. A complete schedule listing all other customs duties, fees, and taxes imposed on imports and exports.

3. A complete schedule listing all excises and taxes levied on domestic manufactured goods, agricultural and animal products.

4. A complete schedule listing all charges levied on services.

5. A complete schedule listing all domestic products which enjoy any subsidies whatsoever and their magnitude. The Council for Economic Unity shall be informed about any later changes.

Article 14

Each contracting party shall have the right to apply to the Council for Economic Unity for the exclusion of certain products from the duty and tax exemption or reductions applied, and from the removal of quantitative restrictions by reasons of real and justifiable causes. The Council for Economic Unity shall have the power to approve such exceptions and shall determine their duration for specific periods of time which shall not exceed the stages stipulated.

Article 15

Certificate of origin: Every product that enjoys the exemption or the customs preference shall be accompanied by a certificate of origin issued by the authority concerned. The certificate of origin for manufactured goods shall have the following form:

I certify, that the goods mentioned here are of . . . . origin and that the local production cost, including the Arab material, originated in one of the contracting parties of the Arab Common Market, amounts to at least 40 per cent of the total production cost.

Customs officials in each of the contracting parties shall establish necessary procedures for the purpose of ensuring the conformity of the goods with the certificate of origin.

PART SIX
SETTLEMENT OF CURRENT TRANSACTIONS AMONG CONTRACTING PARTIES

Article 16

Until the establishment of an Arab Payments Union and an Arab Monetary Fund for the contracting parties whicth would make possible the convertibility of their currencies, the following provisions shall be applied:

1. Payments covering the value of the goods and services exchanged among the contracting parties shall be settled according to the bilateral payments agreements concluded among these countries.

2. In case of the absence of a bilateral payments agreement between two contracting parties, settlement of the payments covered by this article shall be made in U.S. dollars, pounds sterling, or any other convertible currency acceptable to the two parties involved. The two countries shall pledge, in such case, granting permits for transfer without any delay of all the outstanding balances due to the exporting country.

PART SEVEN
IMPLEMENTING PROVISIONS

Article 17

Following the rules of Article Twelve of the Agreement for Economic Unity among Arab League States, the contracting parties shall carry out the provisions set up in this agreement, in accordance with the principles incorporated in their respective constitutions.

Issued in Cairo on Thursday the 13th of August 1964 by the Council for Arab Economic Unity at its second ordinary session.

APPENDIX: OFFICIAL SUMMARY OF THE CONVENTION FOR FACILITATING TRADE AND REGULATING TRANSIT TRADE BETWEEN STATES OF THE ARAB LEAGUE

The countries of Jordan, Syria, Iraq, Saudi Arabia, Lebanon, Lybia, Egypt, and Yemen, desirous to develop economic links among the Arab League States, have agreed, among others, upon the following:

Article One

A. Agricultural and animal products and natural resources listed in Appendix A annexed to this agreement are to be exempted from customs duties on imports, provided their origin be one of the contracting parties.

B. The Arab manufactured goods listed in Appendix B annexed to this agreement, whose origin is one of the contracting parties, are to enjoy a special concession, thus are subjected to a reduction of 25 per cent on the normal customs tariffs applied at present in the Arab importing country.

C. Agricultural, animal, and manufactured goods produced in one of the contracting parties, which may be imported to another party country, are not subjected to excise duties higher than those imposed on similar domestic products.

Article Three

Those goods whose exchange among the contracting parties is, or will be, prohibited under the provisions of this agreement, are liable to confiscation whenever imported, unless having a previous permission.

Article Four

The contracting parties are to undertake facilitating the movement of transit within their boundaries.

Cairo   *September 7, 1953*

SUMMARY OF ARTICLES EXEMPT FROM CUSTOMS DUTIES[3]

Chapter 1   Living animals, poultry, and bees.
Chapter 2   Meat, fresh, chilled, or frozen.
Chapter 3   Fish, crustaceans, and mollusks.
Chapter 4   Dairy products, eggs, and honey.
Chapter 5   Animal raw material and other products.
Chapter 6   Living plants and products of floriculture.
Chapter 7   Edible vegetables and certain roots and tubers.
Chapter 8   Dried dates, and other fresh and dried fruit.
Chapter 9   Coffee beans not roasted.
Chapter 10 Cereals (wheat, barley, white maize, yellow maize, rice, and other cereals).
Chapter 11 Oilseeds and oleaginous fruit, miscellaneous grains, seeds and fruit, industrial and medical plants, straw, and fodder (with the exception of tobacco).
Chapter 12 Raw material for dyeing and tanning, gums, resins, and other saps and juices.
Chapter 13 Vegetable plaiting and carving materials and other vegetable products.

[3] Appendix A to the 1953 Convention for Facilitating Trade. [Editor's note.]

Chapter 14 Earth, stones, and lime in its natural condition.
Chapter 15 Raw wood (fuel wood and raw log wood).
Chapter 16 Raw hides and skins, silk worms, cocoons, raw wool, and raw animal hair.
Chapter 17 Yarn fibers (cotton, flax, and hemp).

SUMMARY OF THE MANUFACTURED GOODS ENJOYING SPECIAL CONCESSION[4]

Chapter 4 Dairy products.
Chapter 8 Kamar el dine.[5]
Chapter 9 Roasted, ground, and canned coffee.
Chapter 11 Cereal of flour, potato starch, and cereals starch.
Chapter 15 Cottonseed oil, sesame oil, olive oil, and linseed oil.
Chapter 16 Meat and fish products and their preservatives (including port).
Chapter 17 Glucose, molasses, and sugar products.
Chapter 19 Macaroni and pastry.
Chapter 20 Canned edible vegetables and fruits.
Chapter 22 Ethyl alcohol.
Chapter 23 Sugar beets and molasses.
Chapter 25 Cement (with the exception of white and colored cement).
Chapter 28 Gaseous hydrocarbonic acid, pressed or liquid oxygen, sulfuric acid, glycerine, and pharmaceutical products.
Chapter 30, 32, 34, 35 Varnishes and paints, soap, matches, and fertilizers.
Chapter 36, 37 All kinds of skins and skin products.
Chapter 40, 44 Wood and ordinary cardboard.
Chapter 46, 47, 48, 50, 51, 52 All kinds of yarn, textiles, and cloth.
Chapter 54 Shoes of all types made of Arab-origin leather.
Chapter 58 All kinds of Arab marble, alabaster products, cement or concrete cement products.
Chapter 59, 60 Refractory bricks, sanitary fittings, china, porcelain, glass and crystal.
Chapter 62 Stoves and heaters.
Chapter 82 Shell works.

[4] Appendix B to the 1953 Convention for Facilitating Trade. [Editor's note.]
[5] A dried apricot product.

CHAPTER EIGHT

Economic Cooperation among Maghrib Countries

The possibility of regional economic cooperation among the Maghrib countries — Morocco, Algeria, Tunisia, and Lybia — has been informally discussed in the area since Algeria became an independent state. One of the first supporters of the idea was President Habib Bourguiba of Tunisia, a representative of the school of thought maintaining that any African economic cooperation on a continental scale — such as the model advocated by Kwame Nkrumah — must be preceded by subregional arrangements harmonizing the economic and social development programs of small groups of neighboring African countries. This approach was defended by Bourguiba and a small minority of African political leaders at the 1960 Addis Ababa Summit Conference of African Heads of State that led to the foundation of the Organization of African Unity. The first steps toward Maghrib economic cooperation were taken in early 1964, when Tunisia and Morocco signed a series of agreements on commercial cooperation, and Tunisia and Lybia agreed to establish a joint shipping line.

On Tunisia's initiative, the Ministers of Economic Affairs of the four countries met in Tunis at the end of September 1964 and negotiated the protocol of the agreement establishing the Maghrib Standing Consultative Committee. This committee was to promote the coordination of development plans in the region with special emphasis on industrial harmonization, cooperation in the fields of energy and mining, the preparation of a basis for multilateral preferential trade, the training of manpower, and a common approach toward the problems of development financing.

A number of Maghrib cooperation institutions subsequently were established: the Council of Ministers of Economic Affairs, which holds authority over the work of the Standing Consultative Committee; the Consultative Committee — with headquarters in Tunis — charged with the preparation of initiatives for economic cooperation; a Secretariat charged with the collection of statistical data and documentation; a Center for Industrial Studies in Tripoli, Libya; and specialized commissions on industry, trade, transport, tourism, statistics, and national accounts.

The Council of Ministers of Economic Affairs met twice before the end of 1965. At the first meeting, held in Tangier, Morocco, in November 1964, the statutes of the Standing Consultative Committee were agreed upon in detail, and decisions were taken calling for continuous cooperation with the United Nations Economic Commission for Africa (ECA) and for the establishment of a Center for Industrial Studies with the financial assistance of the United Nations Special Fund. At the second meeting of the Council, held in Tripoli in May 1965, discussions took place on specific aspects of economic cooperation, the coordination of agricultural exports from the area, and the question of the region's future association with the European Economic Community (EEC). The Standing Consultative Committee also held several meetings between 1964 and 1966 and carried out feasibility studies on the iron, steel, and glass industries of the region as well as on trade relations between the Maghrib countries and the EEC.

Although the work of the Maghrib Council of Ministers and of the Standing Consultative Committee was hailed as constituting "the basis for the economic cooperation of the region" and "the first milestone on the road to the final goal of African and Arab unity" at a June 1966 ECA subregional meeting on economic cooperation in North Africa, the actual results have been extremely meager. They consist of studies and periodic contacts on the technical and political level and include no formal commitment with respect to the implementation of proposals.

Any meaningful economic cooperation is hampered by considerable differences in the political structure of the member countries — among which are two traditional monarchies, one Western-type parliamentary democracy, and one semisocialist state — as well as by the absence of economic complementarity and by strong economic links between individual countries and Western Europe.

Trade among the Maghrib countries in the mid-1960s was estimated at less than 3 per cent of their total foreign trade and consisted mostly of commercial transactions between Algeria and its neighbors, Morocco and Tunisia. Trade flows between Morocco and Tunisia or between Libya and the rest of the Maghrib states are practically nonexistent. Domestic economic and political difficulties and the autarkic development policy of Algeria and the steep decline in the role of traditional European merchant communities throughout the region led to the actual decline of intra-Maghrib trade from close to $60 million in 1961 to some $30 million in 1964 — the last year for which detailed statistics on the direction of foreign trade are available for the four countries.

The Maghrib countries still are not cooperating in the distribution of new regional industries throughout the region, in the establishment of jointly owned industrial projects serving the whole area, or in the co-ordination of industrial investment policies — as was suggested by the ECA Industrial Mission that visited Algeria, Libya, Morocco, and Tunisia in January 1964. The only areas in which regional cooperation seems to be offering some immediate results are transport and communications, the tourist industry, and a joint policy in the negotiation of a special trade link with the European Economic Community.

Bibliographic References

Economic Commission for Africa. *Report of the ECA Industrial Coordination Mission to Algeria, Libya, Morocco and Tunisia.* (E/CN.14/248.) Addis Ababa, February 5, 1964. Mimeographed.
———. *Report of the Sub-Regional Meeting on Economic Cooperation in North Africa.* (E/CN.14/354.) Tangier, June 24, 1966. Mimeographed.
"The Maghreb Is on the March," *The Financial Times* (London), May 27, 1965.
Maghrib Ministerial Conference, Tripoli, Libya, November 26, 1964. *Proceedings.* Mimeographed.

PROTOCOL OF THE AGREEMENT BETWEEN THE KINGDOM OF LIBYA, THE TUNISIAN REPUBLIC, THE PEOPLE'S DEMOCRATIC REPUBLIC OF ALGERIA, AND THE KINGDOM OF MOROCCO*

I: PLANNING

The Ministers of Economic Affairs of the Maghrib recommend that the Standing Consultative Committee arrange the necessary meetings to promote the coordination of development plans.

II: INDUSTRIAL HARMONIZATION

In order to prepare the conditions for far-reaching industrial harmonization, the Conference of Ministers of Economic Affairs of the Maghrib has decided:

1. To recommend that the Economic Commission for Africa establish contact with the Permanent Consultative Committee, and to provide the latter as soon as possible wih the following studies:

(a) A detailed comparative study of existing industrial potentialities, in particular from the viewpoint of production capacities, volumes of production and their uses, as well as prime costs, etc.

(b) A detailed comparative study of the requirements of the Maghrib countries for industrial products.

(c) A comparative study of agricultural production, in particular from the viewpoint of quantities and their uses, locations, and production periods. This study should be supplemented by a study of development potentialities, especially for industrial cultivation.

(d) A preliminary feasibility study on the coordination of industrial standardization.

2. To give the Standing Consultative Committee the task of considering

* Signed by Libya, Tunisia, Algeria, and Morocco in Tunis, October 1, 1964. The text given here is an unofficial translation from the French prepared by the United Nations Economic Commission for Africa (ECA) and made available to the editor. [Editor's note.]

the type of study required, and the criteria to be adopted in considering harmonization in the different industrial branches;

To recommend that the Standing Consultative Committee consider the conditions for coordination and harmonization, taking into account the urgent needs for simultaneous industrialization in the countries of the Maghrib;

To entrust the Standing Consultative Committee, at its forthcoming meeting, with a concrete study on specific projects of industrial coordination and harmonization, in those sectors where such coordination and harmonization may prove possible forthwith.

3. To establish a Center for Industrial Studies, in regard to which a request to the United Nations Special Fund has been prepared, and to give the Standing Consultative Committee the task of preparing the Statutes for submission to the Governments for their approval.

III: MINES AND ENERGY

The Ministers of Economic Affairs of the Maghrib agree to refer to the Standing Consultative Committee the problems relating to coordination and cooperation in the fields of energy and mining, and give it the task of making proposals to the Governments, beginning with electrical energy.

IV: COMMERCIAL RELATIONS AND SERVICES

Simultaneously with the mission entrusted to the Standing Consultative Committee at the Tunis Conference relating to intra-Maghrib commercial exchanges, the Ministers of Economic Affairs give the Standing Consultative Committee the task of defining the basis and general conditions for establishing a multilateral framework of privileged commercial exchanges.

The Conference of the Ministers of Economic Affairs of the Maghrib recommend the holding, under the auspices of the Standing Consultative Committee, of:

1. A meeting of the appropriate agencies of each country with a view to drawing up a list of products of significance to their balances of payments, where coordination in imports and exports can be set in train, and to defining the practical terms and conditions of this coordination.

2. A meeting of the national agencies concerned to define means of coordinating tourism for the Maghrib as a whole.

3. A meeting of the national agencies concerned with a view to producing a report on the harmonization of the policies of the four Maghrib countries in air transport, and on the closest coordination possible between their airway companies.

4. A meeting of experts of the four Maghrib countries with a view to considering the problems of coordinating rail and road transport, and to examining the terms and conditions for implementing this coordination.

5. A meeting of the national agencies concerned to study the respective

positions of the merchant navies of the four countries of the Maghrib and the prospects for cooperation and coordination.

6. A meeting of posts and telecommunications experts for the four Maghrib countries to define the terms and conditions for cooperation and coordination in these fields.

V: MANPOWER

The Ministers of Economic Affairs of the Maghrib give the Standing Consultative Committee the task of considering the problems of training Maghribian manpower, and of its employment inside and outside the Maghrib, in conjunction with the Economic Commission for Africa and the other appropriate international agencies.

VI: FINANCING OF DEVELOPMENT

The Ministers of Economic Affairs of the Maghrib give the Standing Consultative Committee the task of studying, in cooperation with the Maghribian and foreign financial agencies, the problems connected with the financing of development projects.

STATUTES OF THE STANDING
CONSULTATIVE COMMITTEE*

In accordance with the Protocol of the Agreement signed in Tunis on October 1, 1964 by the Ministers of Economic Affairs of the Maghrib,

In accordance with the decision of the Ministers to set up a Standing Consultative Committee responsible for considering all those problems relating to economic cooperation in the four countries, and for proposing to the Council of Ministers of Economic Affairs of the Maghrib, for their decision, all measures to be taken to harmonize and coordinate economic policies,

In accordance with the decisions taken by the Ministers of Economic Affairs during the meeting held in Tangier from November 26 to 28, 1964,

The Statutes of the Standing Consultative Committee shall be laid down as follows:

ARTICLE 1

The Standing Consultative Committee shall be an agency comprising the representatives of the four Maghrib countries. It shall be composed of a Chairman and eight members, four of whom shall be permanent members and four alternates.

ARTICLE 2

The Chairman of the Standing Consultative Committee shall be of the rank of Minister. The chairmanship shall be held in turn by each of the member countries for a period of one year.

* Signed by Libya, Tunisia, Algeria, and Morocco in Tangier, Morocco, on November 28, 1964. The text given here is an unofficial translation from the French prepared by the United Nations Economic Commission for Africa (ECA) and made available to the editor. [Editor's note.]

ARTICLE 3

The Chairman shall be entitled to have the assistance of a Vice-Chairman, who shall be the permanent representative of the country holding the chairmanship.

ARTICLE 4

The Government of each of the Maghrib countries shall designate a permanent member, and an alternate member holding the rank of director in the central administration.

The representatives of each country shall be entitled to the assistance, as need arises, of experts.

ARTICLE 5

The Standing Consultative Committee shall be endowed with a permanent Secretariat headed by an Administrative Secretary designated by the Chairman. The seat of the permanent Secretariat shall provisionally be located at the headquarters of the Chairman in office.

ARTICLE 6

The Standing Consultative Committee shall have correspondents, designated by the government concerned, in each member country. These correspondents shall be officials of a central administration, and preferably of agencies and departments responsible for planning.

ARTICLE 7

The Standing Consultative Committee shall meet at least once every three months when convened by the Chairman. The Chairman shall communicate to the members of the Committee, at the same time that he convenes the meeting, a draft agenda which shall take into account the proposals received from member countries.

ARTICLE 8

The proceedings of every session of the Standing Consultative Committee shall be recorded in minutes: the Chairman shall be responsible for ensuring that such minutes are kept. The minutes shall be required to receive the unanimous approval of the members of the Committee.

ARTICLE 9

The Chairman shall communicate to each member of the Committee copies of all the documents deposited with him, as well as all documentation of potential interest to the Committee.

ARTICLE 10

The Chairman shall submit to the Council of Ministers of Economic Affairs of the Maghrib for approval the draft budget designed to cover the expenses of the Committee.

CHAPTER NINE

Regional Cooperation for Development among Pakistan, Iran, and Turkey

The decision to set up a regional cooperation scheme with participation by Pakistan, Iran, and Turkey was reached at a meeting of the heads of state in Istanbul in July 1964, after the preparatory work undertaken earlier that year by the foreign ministers and economic experts of the three countries involved had been completed. The scheme is known as Regional Cooperation for Development (RCD) and calls for broad cooperation in trade, industrial development, transport, banking and insurance, tourism, and technical assistance. The outstanding characteristic of RCD is that it gives highest priority to the coordination of industrial development programs through the establishment of a number of jointly owned industrial enterprises and their equitable distribution throughout the area. This approach takes into consideration what other regional cooperation schemes seem to forget: in the context of underdevelopment, the possibilities of trade expansion in traditional products are rapidly exhausted, and autonomous industrial development in member countries in the long run creates obstacles to the expansion of intraregional trade instead of fomenting commercial exchange.

Soon after its establishment RCD determined, in principle, to seek industrial complimentarity in some twenty branches of industry, including electronics, pharmaceuticals, petrochemicals, iron and steel, coal mining, motor vehicles, electrical equipment, agricultural machinery, railway equipment, shipbuilding, cement, and aluminum. All of these industrial branches are either nonexistent in the area or represented by small and antiquated plants. The member countries distributed feasibility studies among themselves according to factor endowments, with the understanding that these studies are to be undertaken on a regional basis and that each enterprise is to be established with joint equity participation by all member countries.

It is expected that the expansion of intraregional trade will follow rather than precede the building up of regional industrial enterprises. Traditional intraregional trade is still very small, and its bulk is represented by Iran's exports to Turkey and Pakistan. Moreover, even that trade is still negligible. As in other parts of the developing world, national policies of import substitution preceding the emergence of RCD caused commercial transactions among the three countries to decline from about $45 million in 1961 (in terms of exports) to $30 million in 1965. Trade between Pakistan, Iran, and Turkey amounted to less than 1.5 per cent of their total foreign trade in 1965. According to the most recent data available from the RCD Secretariat, this declining trend was reversed in 1966.

The work of RCD is carried out by a number of agencies: a Ministerial Council, a Regional Planning Committee, thirteen Permanent Committees (air transportation, shipping, roads and railways, post and telecommunications, banking and insurance, petroleum, petrochemicals, joint-purpose enterprises, technical cooperation and public administration, trade, tourism, cultural cooperation, and information), and a Secretariat (headed by Fuad Rouhani, an Iranian). The RCD Secretariat headquarters are in Teheran, Iran, and the meetings of the executive organs are held in the capitals of the three members on a rotating basis. Between mid-1964 and the end of 1966 the RCD Ministerial Council met six times; each meeting was preceded by a meeting of the Regional Planning Committee. To mobilize the support and participation of the private sector of the economies of the member countries, an RCD Chamber of Commerce and Industry was created in August 1965.

RCD appears to have made considerable progress on various fronts. By the end of 1966 the majority of the nineteen industry feasibility studies had been completed, and three industrial projects serving the region — aluminum, carbon black, and bank note paper plants jointly owned by the three member countries — had been approved by the Ministerial Council. Joint ventures for petroleum exploration, exploitation, and refining are in an advanced stage of elaboration. A joint shipping conference — RCD Shipping Services — started operating between the region and the United States in mid-1966. An agreement was reached on the exchange of petrochemicals. Bilateral trade treaties were signed by Pakistan and Turkey and by Pakistan and Iran. Three RCD reinsurance pools (accident, marine, and fire) have been set up, and a study of a regional payments mechanism is under way. Finally, national road and rail expansion programs are being coordinated, with the end of 1968 set as the target date for the completion of major road and rail links among the three participating countries.

Bibliographic References

Islam, Nurul. "Regional Co-operation for Development: Pakistan, Iran and Turkey," *Journal of Common Market Studies* (Oxford), Vol. V, No. 3 (March 1967).

Kashefi, R., ed. *Report on First Two Years of RCD*. Teheran: RCD Secretariat, Information Department, July 1966.

Regional Co-operation for Development, Secretariat. *RCD Anniversary Publication*. Teheran, July 21, 1965.

———. Secretariat. *Report on the Inaugural Meeting of the Chamber of Commerce and Industry — Iran, Pakistan and Turkey*. Teheran, 1965.

JOINT STATEMENT BY THE HEADS OF STATE OF IRAN, PAKISTAN, AND TURKEY*

The Heads of State of Iran, Pakistan and Turkey, His Imperial Majesty Mohammad Reza Shah Pahlavi, Shahinshah of Iran, His Excellency Field Marshal Mohammad Ayub Khan, President of Pakistan and His Excellency Cemal Gursel, President of the Republic of Turkey met on 20th and 21st of July, 1964, in Istanbul.

The Heads of State reaffirmed their belief that regional co-operation is an essential factor in accelerating the pace of national development and in contributing to peace and stability.

They expressed their conviction that the strong cultural and historical ties which bind the peoples of their countries and have already provided them with a solid basis for collaboration should be strengthened further and developed for the common benefit of the peoples of the entire region.

To this end, the Heads of State resolved that appropriate ways and means should be adopted to enlarge and develop further co-operation in their existing relations in all fields.

They unanimously expressed the belief that this new collaboration should be carried out in a spirit of regional co-operation notwithstanding their activities as members of other organizations of a regional character.

The three countries would be pleased to consider the participation of other countries of the region in this co-operation.

Having reviewed the practical steps taken by the Foreign Ministers in the field of co-operation among the three countries, during their meeting on 3rd and 4th of July, 1964, in Ankara, the Heads of State expressed their full appreciation for the progress already achieved in this respect. They endorsed the recommendations made by the Ministerial Pre-Summit meeting of the three countries held in Ankara on July 18 and 19, 1964 on subjects of common and regional interest.

The Heads of State noted with approval the creation of a Ministerial Council composed of the Foreign Ministers with the participation of other

---

* Issued at Istanbul, Turkey, on July 21, 1964. This is the official text published in Regional Co-operation for Development, Secretariat, *RCD Anniversary Publication* (Teheran, July 21, 1965). [Editor's note.]

Ministers of their respective governments in order to take and implement appropriate decisions on matters of common interest.

They noted with satisfaction the decision of the three Heads of Government to establish a Regional Planning Committee composed of the Heads of the three Plan Organizations, dealing with work relating to regional collaboration and harmonization of development plans. To this end, they have agreed to establish Secretarial arrangements to serve the Regional Planning Committee and the Ministerial Council.

They agreed in principle:

1. To a free or freer movement of goods through all practical means such as the conclusion of trade agreements.

2. To establish closer collaboration amongst existing Chambers of Commerce and eventually a joint Chamber of Commerce.

3. To the formulation and implementation of joint proposed projects.

4. To reduce the postal rates between the three countries to the level of internal rates.

5. To improve the air transport services within the region and the eventual establishment of a strong and competitive international air line among the three countries.

6. To investigate the possibilities of securing a close co-operation in the field of shipping including the establishment of a joint maritime line or "conference" arrangements.

7. To undertake necessary studies for construction and improvement of rail and road links.

8. To sign at an early date an agreement with a view to promoting tourism.

9. To abolish visa formalities among the three countries for travel purposes.

10. To provide technical assistance to each other in the form of experts and training facilities.

Furthermore, the Heads of State have directed to explore all the possibilities for expanding co-operation in the cultural field among the countries of the region. Cultural relations should be particularly oriented towards creating mass consciousness of the common cultural heritage, disseminating information about the history, civilization and culture of the peoples of the region, *inter alia* through the establishment of chairs in universities, the exchange of students, the grant of scholarships, the establishment of cultural centres and the joint sponsoring of an Institute for initiating studies and research on their common cultural heritage.

The activities planned within the present scheme of collaboration shall be carried out under the name of "Regional Co-operation for Development."

The Heads of State expressed the hope that the spirit of perfect harmony and of regional solidarity which prevailed throughout the deliberations of the Istanbul Conference would ensure the attainment of the objectives formulated at this Conference.

They are confident that the combined efforts of their peoples to this end will open new vistas of hope and opportunity for them and thus contribute to world peace and to the prosperity of the whole region.

Part II

MONETARY COOPERATION ARRANGEMENTS

CHAPTER TEN

Central American Clearing House

Periodic meetings of the monetary authorities of Costa Rica, El Salvador, Guatemala, Honduras, and Nicaragua on the subject of multilateral monetary and financial cooperation were initiated in 1952. Six of these meetings were held between that year and 1961 to discuss the broad range of subjects pertaining to money and banking in the region. Although several proposals were made for setting up an intraregional payments clearing system, no agreement was reached even on basic issues. It was not until the end of the 1950s, during the time of the preparatory work on the General Treaty on Central American Economic Integration, that the region's five central banks first gave serious consideration to the need for a formal arrangement to facilitate the settlement of balances arising from intraregional payments and the consequent need to encourage the use of Central American currencies in transactions within the proposed common market. An agreement establishing the Central American Clearing House was signed by the monetary authorities of the five countries in July 1961 and entered into force in September of the same year. El Salvador, Guatemala, and Honduras were participants in the Clearing House when it began operations in October 1961; Nicaragua joined the scheme in May 1962 and Costa Rica a year later.

The Clearing House, which is the only system of its kind involving a group of developing countries with separate national monetary systems, is voluntary for the commercial banks of member countries. These banks may choose to channel documents covering all kinds of intrazonal financial transactions to their respective central banks, which in turn transmit them to the central banks of the countries in whose currency the payments are expressed. Upon receipt of records of remittances, the Clearing House processes them through the central accounting system.

Under the 1961 agreement the operations of the Clearing House were backed by capital subscriptions of $300,000 from each member bank. Under the 1964 agreement, which supersedes the 1961 agreement, each central bank grants the others a global automatic credit equivalent to $500,000. Balances within this limit are settled twice a year in United States dollars or in any other fully convertible currency. Any excess over the global credit line can be collected by a surplus country at any time, also in fully convertible currencies. For this purpose the Central American Clearing House calculates weekly the credit or debit positions of member central banks and, on request, issues instructions to the debtors for the payment of balances due. In practice, apart from the global settlements arranged automatically twice a year, the collection of credit surpluses depends on the actual over-all liquidity needs of the region's central banks. This practice of extending credits exceeding the global automatic credit to debtor countries is fostered by a provision in the Clearing House agreement for the payment of interest on all credits resulting from current transactions among member banks. The interest rate on these credits is informally linked to the current rate for the prime grade of commercial paper in the New York money market.

During the early stages of its existence, many reservations were expressed concerning the ability of the Clearing House to cope with problems arising from temporary external payment restrictions introduced in a member country except by extending restrictions to the whole area. The scheme successfully resolved such difficulties, however, when temporary exchange restrictions were introduced in Guatemala and El Salvador in 1961 and 1962, respectively. Total clearings through the mechanism rose from less than 10 per cent of intraregional current financial transactions in 1961 to 49 per cent in 1962 and almost 87 per cent in 1966. In absolute terms, total settlements through the mechanism rose from less than $25 million in 1962 to over $153 million in 1966, reflecting the rapid expansion of intra–Central American trade.

The multilateral clearing system brought about a substantial reduction in the use of nonregional currencies; final settlements in dollars were about 30 per cent of total clearing operations in 1962, but only about 12 per cent in 1966. The settlements through the debit and credit operations of the Clearing House have gradually increased and have replaced what formerly was accomplished by using each central bank's dollar working balances and thus have brought about considerable savings to the respective national monetary authorities. The satisfactory experience of this regional payments arrangement led the area's central banks toward closer cooperation, which in February 1964 translated itself into the signing of an agreement to gradually implement a Central American Monetary Union.

Bibliographic Reference

Angulo, Enrique. "Los acuerdos de créditos y compensación en Centroamérica y en la ALALC," *Boletín Mensual del CEMLA* (Mexico City), Vol. XII, No. 8 (August 1966).

Cámara de Compensación Centroamericana. *Informes de Labores* (Tegucigalpa, Honduras). Annual reports, the last corresponding to the year 1965. Mimeographed.

González del Valle, Jorge. "The Intra-Central American Payments System and Trade." In Miguel S. Wionczek, ed., *Latin American Economic Integration: Experiences and Prospects.* New York: Frederick A. Praeger, 1966.

Young, John Parke. *Central American Monetary Union.* Guatemala City: U.S. Department of State, Agency for International Development, Regional Office for Central America and Panama Affairs, [1965].

DOCUMENT 18

AGREEMENT GOVERNING THE CENTRAL AMERICAN CLEARING HOUSE*

The Central Bank of Costa Rica, the Central Reserve Bank of El Salvador, the Bank of Guatemala, the Central Bank of Honduras, and the Central Bank of Nicaragua

Whereas an Agreement creating the Central American Clearing House was signed by them in Tegucigalpa, Honduras, on July 28, 1961;

Whereas parts of this Agreement were amended in January 1963, expanding the functions of the Central American Clearing House and modifying its organization;

Whereas experience has shown the advisability of giving the Clearing House greater flexibility in the development of its functions; and

Whereas in order to achieve the desired objectives, it is necessary to modify the Agreement creating the Clearing House together with its amendments;

Therefore agree to sign the following Agreement, which will govern the Central American Clearing House henceforth.

CHAPTER I: PURPOSE AND HEADQUARTERS

ARTICLE 1

The purpose of the Central American Clearing House will be:

a. To promote in an orderly way the use of Central American currencies in transactions among the countries of the Isthmus;

b. To coordinate activities directed towards ensuring, in a continuous and permanent fashion, the monetary and exchange cooperation envisaged in Article X of the General Treaty on Central American Economic Integration; and

c. To act as a Permanent Secretariat for the meetings of the Central American Central Banks.

* Signed in San Salvador, El Salvador, on May 5, 1964. The text given here is an unofficial translation from the original Spanish prepared at the International Monetary Fund. [Editor's note.]

ARTICLE 2

The Clearing House will have its Headquarters at the Main Office of the Central Bank of Honduras.

CHAPTER II: TERMS

ARTICLE 3

In the text of this Agreement the following terms will be used: "Agreement" for Agreement on the Central American Clearing House; "Clearing House" for Central American Clearing House; and "member Bank" for Central Bank Member of the Central American Clearing House.

CHAPTER III: CREDIT, UNIT OF ACCOUNT, AND PARITY RATE

ARTICLE 4

Each member Bank will grant a credit in its own currency to the other member Banks for an amount equivalent to up to five hundred thousand U.S. dollars ($500,000.00).

ARTICLE 5

Any member Bank may, on its own initiative or at the proposal of the Board of Directors of the Clearing House, increase the amount of the credit referred to in the foregoing article.

ARTICLE 6

All operations recorded by the Clearing House will be expressed in terms of a unit of account called "Central American Peso" ($CA), equivalent to U.S. $1.00 at the rate of parity declared by each member Bank in respect of its own currency.

ARTICLE 7

Any change in the parity rate declared by a member Bank in accordance with the foregoing article must be reported immediately to the Clearing House and to the other member Banks so that appropriate adjustments may be made.

ARTICLE 8

The member Banks guarantee convertibility to U.S. dollars, at their declared parity rates, of the amounts represented by their net position as recorded by the Clearing House. The "net position" of a member Bank will be understood to mean the difference between the balance of its account with the Clearing House, and the amount of credit granted in its own currency in accordance with Articles 4 and 5 of this Agreement.

ARTICLE 9

Guarantees offered by each member Bank in accordance with Articles 7 and 8 above will be applicable to remittances in transit and to holdings, in payable notes, of the banking systems of the other member Banks.

CHAPTER IV: OPERATIONS

ARTICLE 10

The member Banks will conduct operations among themselves using documents and payable notes, simultaneously reporting such operations to the Clearing House. These operations will be recorded by the Clearing House in individual accounts for each of the member Banks, based on notices received from the latter and in accordance with the pertinent regulations.

ARTICLE 11

At the end of each week the Clearing House will calculate, within its multilateral clearing, the net position of each member Bank. The result of this calculation will be communicated immediately and by the quickest means to all member Banks.

ARTICLE 12

The member Banks may request, through the Clearing House, the return in U.S. dollars of whatever credit they may have granted in excess of the credit amounts stipulated in Articles 4 and 5 of this Agreement.

ARTICLE 13

The debtor Banks will reimburse the credit referred to in the foregoing article to the creditor Banks, in accordance with payment instructions received from the Clearing House. Payment will be made within three working days after the date of receipt of instructions, and the Clearing House will be notified at the time of payment.

ARTICLE 14

With a view to stabilizing the movement of funds deriving from the operations of the Clearing House, creditor member Banks after clearing may invest the balances in their favor in bonds offered to them by debtor member Banks.

CHAPTER V: SETTLEMENTS AND INTEREST

ARTICLE 15

The Clearing House will effect an ordinary settlement of clearing operations once every six months so that the utilized credits, referred to in Articles 4 and 5, may be paid off.

Within eight working days after the date of receipt of the settlement sheet, the debtor member Banks will pay the creditor member Banks, in U.S. dollars, the amounts charged to them as per the settlement, simultaneously notifying the Clearing House thereof.

ARTICLE 16

For payment purposes member Banks will accept the settlement as submitted to them by the Clearing House. Should they be unsatisfied, they will have a fifteen-day period as of the date of receipt of the settlement sheet to submit their claims.

ARTICLE 17

On the date of each ordinary settlement, the Clearing House will charge or pay interest on the daily credit balances received or granted by each of the member Banks.

ARTICLE 18

Interest referred to in the foregoing article will be computed at a uniform rate, which will be determined in accordance with rules to be established by the Board of Directors of the Clearing House.

CHAPTER VI: ORGANIZATION AND ADMINISTRATION

ARTICLE 19

The Board of Directors and the Management are organs of the Clearing House.

ARTICLE 20

The Clearing House will be directed by its Board of Directors, which will be formed by titular representatives, one to be appointed by each of the member Banks. The member Banks will also appoint substitute representatives to replace their respective titular representatives in cases of absence or impediments.

ARTICLE 21

The Board of Directors will be empowered:

a. To interpret the terms of this Agreement;

d. To elect and remove the Manager of the Clearing House;
operations of the Clearing House;

c. To propose to the member Banks for their approval an annual plan of the income and expenses of the Clearing House, and appropriate rules for budgetary implementation;

d. To elect and remove the Manager of the Clearing House;

e. To appoint and remove the Head of the Clearing House at the proposal of the Manager;

f. To appoint an Auditing Commission once a year;

g. To approve the financial statements and the annual report of the Clearing House;

h. To establish periodically the interest rate referred to in Article 18 of this Agreement;

i. To propose to the member Banks measures and provisions for the achievement of the objectives of the Clearing House; and

j. To perform any other duties incumbent upon it.

ARTICLE 22

At its regular meetings the Board of Directors will elect a President from among the titular representatives of the member Central Banks, in rotation, who will exercise his functions until the next regular meeting.

In the case of absence or a temporary impediment, the President will be replaced in respect of all his functions by his substitute representative.

ARTICLE 23

The terms of reference of the President will be:

a. To convene the Board of Directors for regular and special meetings, and preside over its sessions; and

b. Any others assigned to him by this Agreement, the bylaws of the Clearing House, and the resolutions of the Board of Directors.

ARTICLE 24

The Board of Directors of the Clearing House will meet with the attendance of at least three of its member representatives, ordinarily once a year and extraordinarily when convened by the President at the request of any of the representatives.

The President will inform the other representatives of the purposes of the extraordinary meetings at least eight days in advance.

ARTICLE 25

The resolutions of the Board of Directors will be adopted with affirmative votes on the part of at least three of the representatives. Each representative will be entitled to one vote, and in the case of a tie the President will cast the deciding one.

ARTICLE 26

The Manager will be in charge of the coordination, execution, and supervision of the activities and operations of the Clearing House; he must be a citizen of one of any of the countries of the member Banks, will perform his duties for three years, and may be re-elected.

The Manager may be removed only for manifest incompetence or if, in the judgment of the Board of Directors of the Clearing House, his behavior is incompatible with the dignity of his post.

ARTICLE 27

The Manager will act in accordance with this Agreement, the respective bylaws, and the resolutions of the Board of Directors of the Clearing House. He will have a voice but no vote in the meetings of the Board of Directors of the Clearing House.

The Manager will appoint and remove the administrative personnel, with the exception of the Head of the Clearing House.

ARTICLE 28

The Central Bank of Honduras will be in charge of:

a. Attending to all matters regarding the collection, management, and settlement of its funds;

b. Ensuring that the operations of the Clearing House are conducted in accordance with this Agreement, the respective bylaws, and the resolutions of the Board of Directors;

c. Becoming a party to actions and contracts, as proposed to it by the Board of Directors or the Manager of the Clearing House.

d. Performing all other functions entrusted to it by the Board of Directors, within the limits of this Agreement.

ARTICLE 29

The budget of the Clearing House will become effective upon its approval by all the member Banks; administration expenses will be shared equally.

CHAPTER VII: WITHDRAWAL AND DISSOLUTION

ARTICLE 30

Should a member Bank wish to denounce this Agreement, it must so notify the Clearing House and the other member Banks at least thirty days in advance. The Clearing House will effect a special settlement to determine the debtor or creditor position of the denouncing member Bank at the date of withdrawal. Payments resulting from this settlement must be made in accordance with the provisions of Article 13 of this Agreement.

ARTICLE 31

The Clearing House will be dissolved:
a. Upon the unanimous decision of the member Central Banks; or
b. When only two of them remain as parties to this Agreement.
The Board of Directors will determine the terms on which the Clearing House will liquidate its operations.

CHAPTER VIII: GENERAL PROVISIONS

ARTICLE 32

Those member Banks whose countries practice exchange restrictions will adopt measures within their exchange control systems to facilitate the performance of the Clearing House. Such measures will be reported immediately to the Clearing House and the other member Banks, who will cooperate closely in order to make their application effective.

ARTICLE 33

The member Banks may enter into and sign jointly treaties, agreements and special arrangements for reciprocal clearing and credit with the central banks of other Latin American countries.

CHAPTER IX: FINAL PROVISIONS

ARTICLE 34

This Convention will replace the "Agreement creating the Central American Clearing House," signed in Tegucigalpa, Honduras, on July 28, 1961, and its amendments.

ARTICLE 35

The Board of Directors will determine the date on which this Agreement will go into effect, for which it must be ratified by all of the member Banks.

CHAPTER X: TEMPORARY PROVISIONS

ARTICLE 36

The amounts recorded at present as contributions of the member Banks to the Current Operations Fund of the Clearing House, in accordance with the Agreement dated July 28, 1961, may form part of the credit in national currency referred to in Article 4 of this Agreement.

ARTICLE 37

Contributions in U.S. dollars made by member Banks to constitute the Guarantee Fund of the Clearing House, in accordance with the Agreement dated July 28, 1961, will be reimbursed with interest on the date when this Agreement enters into effect.

CHAPTER ELEVEN

Central American Monetary Union

The success of the Central American Clearing House, in operation since the fall of 1961, prompted the five central banks in the region to seek other avenues of monetary cooperation and financial integration within the framework of the Central American Common Market. Some ideas in this respect had been advanced in 1963, leading to a recommendation to prepare a formal regional treaty defining the legal commitments of each of the Central American republics with regard to the coordination of monetary policies, which eventually was to lead to the adoption of common internal and external financial policies. Although it is held in many quarters in Central America that the implementation of such proposals was made impossible by insurmountable legal obstacles, the failure of this initiative can also be attributed to the fact that the central banks in the region proved unable and unwilling to surrender their political and administrative independence, a necessary precondition for such an ambitious and far-reaching joint enterprise.

Under these circumstances the central banks of Costa Rica, El Salvador, Guatemala, Honduras, and Nicaragua signed the Agreement for Establishment of the Central American Monetary Union in February 1964. The Agreement does not represent a formal commitment but, rather, an informal arrangement defining ways and means for voluntary monetary and financial cooperation among five independent monetary authorities. It establishes a Central American Monetary Council, several consultative committees, and an Executive Secretariat. The headquarters of the Monetary Union are in Guatemala City.

The main objective of the Agreement is to promote the coordination of the monetary, exchange, and credit policies of the Central American countries and to create progressively a basis for the Central American Monetary Union. Such a basis is to be created, *inter alia*, through the promotion of uniformity of exchange systems, the strengthening of the multilateral payments system, and mutual financial assistance among member countries in case of temporary balance-of-payments disequilibria.

The Central American Monetary Council has held several meetings since its inception. Before the middle of 1966 its chief concern was the functioning of the Clearing House. It was under the Council's influence that some adjustments in the operative and administrative techniques of the multilateral payments scheme were introduced in 1965/66. In the spring of 1966 the Monetary Council turned to examining the possibility of establishing a regional common reserve fund with the double function of providing short-term financial help to member countries suffering temporary balance-of-payments difficulties and of adopting a common policy concerning the investment of the portion of international reserves that is composed of assets other than gold. It was reported in late 1966 that work on the establishment of a common reserve fund (possibly with the participation of some other Latin American countries) had advanced considerably. The Monetary Council has not yet registered any progress, however, in the harmonization of monetary and financial legislation or in formal consultations and common decisions relating to the regional coordination of monetary and financial activities.

Bibliographic References

Angulo, Enrique. "Los acuerdos de créditos y compensación en Centroamérica y en la ALALC." *Boletín Mensual del CEMLA* (Mexico City), Vol. XII, No. 8 (August 1966).

Consejo Monetario Centroamericano. *Primer Informe de Labores.* Reproduced in *Boletín Mensual del CEMLA* (Mexico City), Vol. XII, No. 7 (July 1966).

Young, John Parke. *Central American Monetary Union.* Guatemala City: U.S. Department of State, Agency for International Development, Regional Office for Central America and Panama Affairs, [1965].

AGREEMENT FOR ESTABLISHMENT OF THE CENTRAL AMERICAN MONETARY UNION*

The Central Bank of Costa Rica, the Central Reserve Bank of El Salvador, the Bank of Guatemala, the Central Bank of Honduras, and the Central Bank of Nicaragua:

Whereas

First. The General Treaty on Central American Economic Integration, in its Article X, entrusts to the Central Banks of the Member States the necessary cooperation to "prevent any currency speculation that might affect the rates of exchange and to maintain the convertibility of the currencies of the respective countries on a basis which, in normal conditions, shall guarantee the freedom, uniformity and stability of exchange."

Second. The Central American Economic Council, in its Second Special Meeting of August 16, 1962, agreed "to declare that it is in the best interests of the Central American Economic Integration Program, to create the means or mechanisms necessary to assure a continuous and permanent coordination of monetary and exchange policies of the Member States, including the expansion and improvement of the present system of multilateral clearing of payments"; and "to request from the Central Banks of the Member States, the prompt study of the above mechanisms, as well as the submission to the Executive Council of the General Treaty, of concrete proposals for an agreement necessary for the full achievement of the above-mentioned objectives."

Third. At a meeting held in San José, Costa Rica, on March 19, 1963, the Presidents of the Central American States committed themselves before their people, "to establish a monetary union and a common policy concerning fiscal, economic, and social matters, within the Economic Integration Program"; and

Fourth. The above-mentioned agreements and pronouncements of the Central American Governments; and the progress achieved within the Program of

---

* Signed by Costa Rica, El Salvador, Guatemala, Honduras, and Nicaragua in San Salvador, El Salvador, February 25, 1964. The text reproduced here is an unofficial translation from the Spanish, published in John Parke Young, *Central American Monetary Union* (Guatemala: U.S. Department of State, Agency for International Development, Regional Office for Central America and Panama Affairs, [1965]). [Editor's note.]

Central American Economic Integration, and within the mechanisms of cooperation established by the Central Banks; as well as the monetary conditions prevailing in the countries of the area, indicate the need and opportunity to adopt measures tending to achieve by stages the monetary integration of Central America.

Agree to enter into the following

AGREEMENT FOR ESTABLISHMENT OF THE CENTRAL AMERICAN MONETARY UNION

ARTICLE I

The objective of this Agreement is to promote the coordination of monetary, exchange, and credit policies of the Central American countries, and to create progressively the basis for the Central American Monetary Union.

To this end, the Central Banks of Central America agree on the following goals:

1. To promote uniformity of the Central American exchange systems, as well as the stability and convertibility of the currencies of the area;

2. To expand the multilateral clearings system of Central America, and to stimulate the use of national currencies in all transactions among the Central American countries;

3. To promote financial assistance designed to correct temporary disturbances in the balance of payments, and to prevent unfavorable trends in the Central American exchange systems;

4. To obtain a high degree of uniformity in legislation, as well as in the monetary, exchange, and credit structures and conditions of the Central American countries;

5. To create appropriate conditions to foster the coordination of monetary and fiscal policies; and

6. To establish a permanent system of information and consultation, in order to bring about common means of action and instruments of monetary, exchange, and credit policies.

ARTICLE II

The goals of monetary integration set forth in this Agreement will be achieved gradually and progressively through the following means:

1. Exchange of information, specific research and regular consultation in the monetary, exchange, and credit fields;

2. Technical investigation relating to the legislation, institutional structure, conditions of development, and nature of the instruments of monetary, exchange, and credit policies of the Central American countries;

3. Consultation at a high executive and technical level, on a voluntary and strictly confidential basis, with respect to the domestic and foreign policies of the Central Banks;

4. Specific mechanisms designed to provide financial assistance adequate to prevent unfavorable trends in the exchange systems, lessen the effects of temporary disturbances in the balance of payments, and to further the free flow of capital in Central America; and

5. Consultation and studies designed to achieve favorable conditions to coordinate the monetary and fiscal policies.

On the basis of such progress as may be accomplished, will be determined the appropriate time to formulate and propose agreements that may be necessary to create the Central American Monetary Union.

ARTICLE III

The execution of this Agreement will be in charge of the Central Banks System of Central America, through the following bodies:
1. The Central American Monetary Council;
2. The Committees for consultation or action; and
3. The Executive Secretariat.

ARTICLE IV

The Central American Monetary Council will consist of the Presidents of the Central Banks of El Salvador, Guatemala, Honduras, and Nicaragua, and the Manager of the Central Bank of Costa Rica, as members.

Each Central Bank will appoint a permanent alternate member of the Council, selected from their high executive officials.

ARTICLE V

The Central American Monetary Council will have the following functions:
1. To hold periodic consultations on the general aspects of the monetary, exchange and credit policies of the Central American countries, and to agree or recommend adequate measures to arrive at common policies;
2. To maintain the necessary relations and hold consultations with the governmental authorities of Central America in order to coordinate the monetary and fiscal policies;
3. To determine the scope and procedures for achievement of the program set forth in this Agreement;
4. To agree on the measures needed to enlarge and improve the Central American system of multilateral clearings;
5. To establish consultative or executive Committees that the Council considers necessary in order to fulfill all functions related to the achievement of the program set forth in this Agreement. The Council will determine the functions and obligations of these Committees;
6. To appoint the Executive Secretary;
7. To approve the rules and regulations that will govern the Committees and Executive Secretariat;
8. To approve the budget of all bodies comprising the System of Central Banks of Central America;

9. To submit drafts of agreements whose approval at a governmental level may be necessary to achieve the Central American Monetary Union;

10. To interpret the terms and conditions of this Agreement; and

11. All other functions that may be necessary to meet the objectives of this Agreement.

ARTICLE VI

Annually the Council will elect a President from among its members in rotation.

The Council will hold meetings as follows:

1. One regular annual meeting, and special meetings whenever called by the Council or the President, or requested by any one of its members.

2. Its resolutions will be by a majority of votes of all members; they will be binding only on such Central Banks whose representative subscribed to them, or adhered to such resolutions at a later date.

3. The Executive Secretary will participate in the discussions of the Council, without vote. The alternate members of the Council may participate in the same manner.

ARTICLE VII

There will be, at least, the following Committees:

1. Committee on Monetary Policy;

2. Committee on Exchange and Clearing Policies;

3. Committee on Financial Operations; and

4. Committee on Legal Studies.

The Council will establish these Committees or any others that circumstances may require.

ARTICLE VIII

Each Central Bank will participate in all Committees through a representative and an alternate member.

ARTICLE IX

The Executive Secretariat will be in charge of a Secretary, who is a Central American officer, elected by the Monetary Council for a term of two years, eligible for re-election, and must be a person of well-known professional competence in central banking matters and international finance.

The Executive Secretary will be responsible exclusively to the Central American Monetary Council.

ARTICLE X

The Executive Secretariat will be responsible for the preparation of all necessary technical studies and will coordinate the activities of the Committees.

At the same time, it will provide clerical services for conferences and meetings of the Central Banks System. It will be governed by this Agreement and the regulations and decisions adopted by the Central American Monetary Council.

Headquarters of the Executive Secretariat will be rotated every two years among the Central Banks, as determined by the Monetary Council.

ARTICLE XI

The officers and employees of the Executive Secretariat must be nationals of the Central American countries.

ARTICLE XII

The Central American Monetary Council will determine the provision of funds for operating expenses of the organs of the System.

ARTICLE XIII

Through the Executive Secretary, the different organs of the System will operate in close collaboration and coordination of activities with other organizations and entities of the Central American Economic Integration Program.

ARTICLE XIV

This Agreement will have indefinite life, and may be amended by unanimous decision of the Central Banks.

ARTICLE XV

This Agreement will be subject to ratification by the Central Banks. Such ratification will be notified by each Central Bank to the Permanent Secretariat of the General Treaty on Central American Economic Integration, and simultaneously to the other Central Banks of Central America.

ARTICLE XVI

This Agreement will become effective eight days after the date of notification of the ratification. It will be binding only on those Central Banks which have ratified it.

ARTICLE XVII

The Committee on Exchange and Clearing Policies, mentioned in Article VII, will act as a consultative body for exchange policy and, when this Agreement has been ratified by the five Central Banks, will also be responsible for the execution of the Central American Clearing House Agreement, as well as for any other clearing or credit arrangements that may be signed with countries outside the area.

ARTICLE XVIII

The Central American Monetary Council will hold its first meeting within sixty days from the date when this Agreement becomes effective. It will be convened by the Central Reserve Bank of El Salvador, in consultation with the other Central Banks.

Measures will be taken at such meeting with regard to the organization and establishment of the different organs of the System.

In witness whereof, the representatives of the Central Banks of Central America, have signed this instrument in five copies, in the city of San Salvador, Republic of El Salvador, on February 25, 1964.

GENERAL REGULATIONS OF THE COMMITTEES AND OF THE EXECUTIVE SECRETARIAT OF THE AGREEMENT FOR ESTABLISHMENT OF THE CENTRAL AMERICAN MONETARY UNION*

TITLE ONE: THE COMMITTEES

CHAPTER I
GENERAL PROVISIONS

ARTICLE I

The Committees created by the Agreement for Establishment of the Central American Monetary Union are consultative and executive bodies of the Central American Central Banks System. As such, these Committees will act on request of the Monetary Council or the Executive Secretary, in accordance with these Regulations.

ARTICLE 2

The duties of the Committees consist of preparing proposals for the Monetary Council regarding the adoption of measures designed to realize progressively the objectives of the Agreement for Establishment of the Central American Monetary Union.

ARTICLE 3

Each Committee will consist of one member and one alternate member appointed by each Central Bank, for indefinite periods. Appointments will be notified through letter addressed to the Executive Secretary, with copies to the other Central Banks. The alternate member will act only in the absence of the member.

* Approved by the Central American Monetary Council in San José, Costa Rica, on May 19, 1964. The text reproduced here is an unofficial translation from the Spanish, published in John Parke Young, *Central American Monetary Union* (Guatemala: U.S. Department of State, Agency for International Development, Regional Office for Central America and Panama Affairs, [1965]). [Editor's note.]

ARTICLE 4

The Central Banks will endeavor to nominate officers for the different Committees whose activities are related to their duties in the respective Committee.

ARTICLE 5

Every two years, the Commitees will elect a Chairman from among their respective members, who will discharge the following duties:

a. to call and preside at meetings of the Committee;
b. to direct, supervise, and coordinate the activities of the Committee; and
c. to represent the Committee in its external relations.

In case of absence of the Chairman, the respective alternate member will act as substitute.

The chairmanship of each Committee will be discharged in rotation by the members of every Central Bank, and the respective elections will endeavor to achieve geographical distribution, in order that all Central Banks may share in the responsibilities assigned to the Committees.

A project undertaken by a Central Bank must be completed by this bank, even when the chairmanship has passed to another bank.

ARTICLE 6

The Committees will hold all meetings necessary to complete their work programs, meeting at least once a year. Meetings will be called by the Chairman of the Committee whenever he deems convenient, or at the request of the Executive Secretary or of any of its Members.

ARTICLE 7

The attendance of three members of a Committee (members or alternate members) will constitute a quorum. However, the Chairman will endeavor to obtain the participation of all members, in order to expedite proceedings related to resolutions adopted by the Committee.

ARTICLE 8

All Committee decisions will be taken through a majority of at least three votes.

All dissenting votes and the opinions of the minority shall be recorded in the minutes.

ARTICLE 9

The Executive Secretary or his representative will participate in the meetings of the Committees, without vote. Advisers appointed by the Central Banks, will participate in the same manner.

ARTICLE 10

The Executive Secretary and the Chairman of the respective Committee will be in charge of the organization of the meetings, and will coordinate the preparation of work presented to the Committees.

ARTICLE 11

At the end of each meeting, a minute will be prepared summing up the discussions and recommendations. The original of this minute will be signed by all attendant members, remaining in the custody of the Executive Secretary, who will send a copy to the President of the Central American Monetary Council, and to all other Members.

ARTICLE 12

Copies of all documents received or dispatched by every Committee will be sent to the Executive Secretary.

CHAPTER II
SPECIAL PROVISIONS

Committee on Monetary Policy

ARTICLE 13

The Committee on Monetary Policy will study and recommend measures considered appropriate to coordinate and harmonize the monetary and financial policies of the Central Banks.

ARTICLE 14

In fulfillment of its objectives, this Committee will discharge the following functions and duties:

a. development of a permanent system of exchange of information and of periodic consultation on the decisions, activities, and instruments of monetary and financial policies;

b. elaboration of standard statistics to permit greater comparability and facility of analysis in the fields of national income, money and banking, balance of payments, public finances, foreign trade and prices;

c. study of the institutional structure, stage of development, and nature of the instruments of monetary, exchange, and credit policies;

d. preparation of studies designed to harmonize the monetary policies of the Central Banks with the fiscal policies of the Central American countries; and

e. all other functions and duties recommended by the Central American Monetary Council.

Committee on Financial Operations

ARTICLE 15

The Committee on Financial Operations will study and recommend measures considered appropriate to facilitate financial operations among the Central Banks of Central America, and among these and other institutions.

ARTICLE 16

To fulfill its objectives this Committee will have as functions and duties the study and recommendation of:

a. measures tending to accelerate the expansion and development of the market for securities in the Central American countries;

b. mechanisms to facilitate financing of trade in the area, including the development of a market for bank acceptances;

c. common policies to finance Central American exports to the rest of the world;

d. concrete measures to develop mechanisms designed to facilitate mutual financial assistance among the Central Banks;

e. measures to improve and standardize the practices of financial operations of the Central Banks;

f. measures to standardize the practices and uses of credit instruments, in order to facilitate their negotiation in the Central American countries;

g. joint action of the Central Banks to gain better terms in negotiations undertaken with foreign financial institutions.

The Committee on Financial Operations will fulfill all other functions and duties assigned by the Central American Monetary Council.

Committee on Legal Studies

ARTICLE 17

The Committee on Legal Studies will consider the legal aspects and institutions related to the execution of the Agreement for Establishment of the Central American Monetary Union.

ARTICLE 18

In fulfillment of its objectives, this Committee will discharge the following functions and duties:

a. to prepare studies and suggest measures to bring up to date and co-ordinate the monetary, banking, and financial legislation of the Central American countries;

b. to keep under permanent analysis the legal instruments of the Central American Monetary Union, and to propose the necessary agreements or arrangements to achieve their improvement;

c. to give an opinion on matters of a legal character having to do with the Central American Monetary Council, the Executive Secretary and the other Committees; and

d. all other functions and duties assigned by the Central American Monetary Council.

Committee on Exchange and Clearing Policies

ARTICLE 19

The Committee on Exchange and Clearing Policies will study and recommend measures designed to coordinate the exchange practices and to improve the system of Central American multilateral clearings.

ARTICLE 20

This Committee will have the following functions and duties.

a. to propose to the Central American Monetary Council regulations to govern the operations of the Central American Clearing House;

b. to give an opinion on matters relative to the interpretation of the Agreement, of the Clearing House and its regulations;

c. to appoint annually an Auditing Commission in rotation among the Member Banks, designed to review the operations of the Clearing House, and to consider the reports of such Commission;

d. to submit to the Central American Monetary Council, together with its opinion, the annual report and financial statements of the Clearing House presented by the Executive Secretary;

e. to determine the means of fixing the uniform rate of interest mentioned in the Clearing House Agreement;

f. to propose to the Monetary Council the method of settlement of Clearing House operations in case of its dissolution;

g. to propose to the Executive Secretariat measures intended to prevent exchange speculation;

h. to propose to the Executive Secretariat measures intended to stimulate and extend the use of the Central American currencies in payments within the area, including the execution of information programs;

i. to direct and supervise, within the specific regulations approved by the Monetary Council, the activities concerning the multilateral clearing agreements signed among the Central American Central Banks and other foreign financial institutions; and

j. all other functions and duties assigned by the Monetary Council.

TITLE TWO: EXECUTIVE SECRETARIAT

ARTICLE 21

The Executive Secretariat will be in charge of a Secretary, a Central American officer elected by the Monetary Council for a term of two years, who may be re-elected. The Secretary must be a person of well-known professional competence in matters of central banking and international finance.

The Executive Secretary will be responsible exclusively to the Central American Monetary Council. He will act as a full time officer and may not accept another post, except when expressly authorized by the Monetary Council.

ARTICLE 22

The Executive Secretary will be responsible for the execution of resolutions of the Central American Monetary Council; for the coordination of activities of the different Committees of the Central American Central Banks System; and of all studies necessary to achieve the objectives mentioned in the Agreement for Establishment of the Central American Monetary Union.

ARTICLE 23

The Executive Secretary will have the following functions and duties:

a. to prepare all technical studies necessary in order to carry out the work programs approved by the Central American Monetary Council;

b. to organize the meetings of the Central American Monetary Council, to participate in these, and to maintain records and minutes;

c. to manage the Central American Clearing House;

d. to coordinate the activities of the different Committees; to submit to the Central American Monetary Council drafts of work programs; and to recommend respective priorities;

e. to collaborate with the different Committee Chairmen regarding the organization of their meetings; to participate or be represented in such meetings; and to communicate to the Central American Monetary Council all recommendations adopted;

f. to give technical and material assistance in the preparation of work agreed by the Committees;

g. to maintain a record and file of the technical studies, as well as of the statistical data published by the Central American Central Banks;

h. to prepare and publish regularly a statistical bulletin containing information of the Central American countries, of a monetary, exchange, credit, and fiscal character;

i. to submit to the Regular Meeting of the Central American Monetary Council an annual report, which will be distributed among the Members of the Council at least 15 days before the meeting; and

j. to perform all other functions specially recommended by the Central American Monetary Council.

ARTICLE 24

The Executive Secretary will be directly responsible for the operation of the Executive Secretariat; he will appoint and remove the personnel, and submit a budget annually to the Central American Monetary Council.

ARTICLE 25

The officers and employees of the Executive Secretariat must be nationals of Central American countries.

TITLE THREE: MISCELLANEOUS PROVISIONS

ARTICLE 26

All technical assistance programs concerning the achievement of objectives of the Agreement for Establishment of the Central American Monetary Union require the approval of the Central American Monetary Council, which will act on these after considering opinions submitted by the respective Committee.

ARTICLE 27

The Central American Monetary Council will decide on matters not considered in these Regulations.

ARTICLE 28

These Regulations become effective on May 21, 1964.

CHAPTER TWELVE

Multilateral Payments Clearing Agreement
among LAFTA Central Banks

The need for a regional payments mechanism in Latin America was recognized by ECLA in the mid-1950s, and various proposals for an appropriate mechanism — ranging from a simple clearing house to a Latin American payments union — were discussed in many inter–Latin American and hemispheric meetings for almost a decade. However, the orthodox attitudes of certain international financial agencies and many central banks in the area, the opposition of private banking interests outside the region, and general unwillingness to provide the necessary working capital for a regional payments mechanism for a long time prevented the establishment of any form of monetary cooperation in Latin America.

An agreement on multilateral clearings, signed in Mexico City in September 1965 by the central banks of the member countries of the Latin American Free Trade Association (LAFTA), is considered a significant, though extremely cautious, step toward a regional payments system that will, it is hoped, one day cover the whole of Latin America. Although a resolution calling for the preparation of studies on credit and payments problems with specific proposals on ways of facilitating intraregional trade and service transactions had been appended to the Montevideo Treaty establishing LAFTA at the time of its signing in December 1960, it was only in 1964 that the LAFTA Advisory Commission on Monetary Affairs reopened discussion of this subject.

A Technical Group composed of experts from the central banks of some LAFTA members and set up by the Advisory Commission submitted in mid-1965 a series of proposals that were considered initial steps toward more advanced forms of regional financial cooperation. These proposals, somewhat similar to a scheme elaborated in late 1958 under ECLA auspices by a Working Group of Latin American Central Banks,

called for the establishment of a multilateral compensation and reciprocal credit mechanism based primarily upon bilateral agreements among
the nine participating central banks. Such agreements provide for reciprocal credit, expressed in United States dollars, with a maximum limit
to be designated in each of the respective bilateral agreements. The outstanding balances within the lines of bilateral credits are to be settled and
multilaterally cleared in United States dollars every two months. Any
surplus over the agreed credit limits established between each pair of
central banks must immediately be settled by the debtor in United States
currency. The channeling of payments through the system is voluntary.
The agreement provides that the participating central banks may, in
addition to the ordinary lines of credit, negotiate extraordinary credits
among themselves. The Central Reserve Bank of Peru acts as the system's
agent, and outstanding balances are cleared through the Federal Reserve
Bank of New York.

Prior to October 31, 1967, sixteen bilateral agreements involving reciprocal lines of credit were signed by seven central banks of LAFTA
countries. Upon completion of the scheme, fifty-five agreements will be in
force between eleven central banks. Credits available under the first sixteen
agreements amounted to $50.7 million (in both directions). The Sixth
Conference of LAFTA Contracting Parties, held in Montevideo in December 1966, agreed to admit to this rudimentary clearing system the central banks of the Latin American countries that had not yet joined
LAFTA.

Bibliographic References

Angulo, Enrique. "Los acuerdos de créditos y compensación en Centroamérica y en
    la ALALC," *Boletín Mensual del CEMLA* (Mexico City), Vol. XII, No. 8 (Au-
    gust 1966).
Asociación Latinoamericana de Libre Comercio. *Informe final de la Segunda Reunión
    de la Comisión Asesora de Asuntos Monetarios.* (ALALC/CMA/II/Informe.)
    Montevideo, March 19, 1965.
Centro de Estudios Monetarios Latinoamericanos (CEMLA). *Problemas de pagos en
    América Latina.* Mexico City, 1964.
Comisión Económica para América Latina (CEPAL). "Payments and Credits in the
    Free Trade Area: Possible Systems." In Economic Commission for Latin Amer-
    ica, *Multilateral Economic Co-operation in Latin America*, Vol. I: *Texts and
    Documents.* (United Nations Publication, Sales No. 62.II.G.3.) New York:
    United Nations, Department of Economic and Social Affairs, 1962.
———. *Principales objetivos y posibles características de una unión de pagos lati-
    noamericana.* (E/CN.12/CI/WG1/9.) Santiago de Chile, September 1958.
    Mimeographed.

Keesing, F. A. G., and P. J. Brand. "Possible Role of a Clearing House in the Latin American Regional Market," *IMF Staff Papers* (Washington, D.C.), Vol. X, No. 3 (November 1963).

Siegel, Barry N. "Payments Systems for the Latin American Free Trade Association." In Miguel S. Wionczek, ed., *Latin American Economic Integration: Experiences and Prospects.* New York: Frederick A. Praeger, 1966.

Triffin, Robert. "International Monetary Arrangements, Capital Markets and Economic Integration in Latin America," *Journal of Common Market Studies* (Oxford), Vol. IV, No. 1 (October 1965).

———. "Una cámara de compensación y unión latinoamericana." In CEMLA, *Cooperación financiera en América Latina.* Mexico City, 1963.

AGREEMENT BETWEEN THE CENTRAL BANKS OF MEMBER COUNTRIES OF LAFTA*

Banco Central de la República Argentina, Banco Central de la República de Brasil, Banco de la República de Colombia, Banco Central de Chile, Banco Central del Ecuador, Banco de México, S. A., Banco Central del Paraguay, Banco Central de Reserva del Perú, and Banco de la República Oriental del Uruguay

Considering:

that the monetary stability and the multilateral mechanism of payments in convertible and freely transferable currencies constitute an effective means of increasing trade and settlement;

that they should make the greatest efforts to counteract inflationary pressures and to correct disequilibria in their balance of payments;

that they should also endeavor as much as possible to eliminate restrictions, prohibitions, and surcharges of a monetary and financial character which obstruct trade within the area;

that these efforts will bring about closer relationships between private financial institutions in the Zone and will facilitate the granting of reciprocal lines of credit among them;

that it is necessary to begin at once formal multilateral cooperation between banks of the region in order to achieve, in successive stages, monetary and financial integration through the formation of financing agencies that may establish more advanced cooperation, such as a clearing house and a guarantee fund;

that while the appropriate measures are being adopted and the competent bodies are laying down the legal provisions for organizing more elaborate forms of financial and monetary cooperation, it is essential to establish initial conditions or bases which will both prepare the way for achieving such advances and signify important progress in this field, and

that as a result of the foregoing, it is necessary to initiate cooperation in the

---

* Signed by representatives of the central banks of Argentina, Brazil, Colombia, Chile, Ecuador, Mexico, Paraguay, Peru, and Uruguay in Mexico City on September 22, 1965. The text presented here is an unofficial translation prepared at the International Monetary Fund from the original Spanish, published by Asosiación Latinoamericana de Libre Comercio, *Informe final de la Segunda Reunión del Consejo de Política Financiera y Monetaria de la ALALC* (Mexico City, September 22, 1965; mimeographed). [Editor's note.]

monetary and financial sphere by the establishment of a mechanism of multilateral compensation and of reciprocal credits between the Central Banks of LAFTA member countries, which could stimulate financial relationships, increase the expansion of their reciprocal trade, and systematize joint consultations in monetary, foreign exchange, and payments matters.

Agree:

to create among the Central Banks of LAFTA a mechanism of multilateral clearing and reciprocal credits, in convertible currencies, in accordance with the following working bases:

ARTICLE 1

Each pair of Central Banks shall agree upon the establishment of ordinary lines of reciprocal credit in United States dollars, with maximum limits that shall be assigned in the respective agreements. Preferably, no interest shall be charged for such credits.

ARTICLE 2

The balances of the ordinary lines of credit, throughout the system, shall be settled every two months in the manner and on the terms established in the Regulations.

ARTICLE 3

The balances shown on the accounts at the end of each settlement period shall be cleared multilaterally according to the procedure established in the Regulations.

ARTICLE 4

Without prejudice to the stipulations of Article 2, every surplus over the limit of ordinary credit in the amount of the obligations that the debtor Central Bank has assumed shall be paid by it, immediately, by cabled transfer.

ARTICLE 5

As a supplement to the ordinary lines of credit referred to in Article 1, the Central Banks may mutually negotiate additional extraordinary reciprocal credits in United States dollars.

ARTICLE 6

The additional extraordinary credits shall be settled according as the Central Banks that have negotiated them jointly specify.

ARTICLE 7

The Central Banks shall undertake to guarantee the convertibility of the foreign exchange intended to settle payments channeled through the system, when it is already demandable and is covered by the debtor in local currency.

ARTICLE 8

For payments arising from settlements referred to in Articles 2, 4, 5, and 6, United States dollars shall be used.

ARTICLE 9

The channeling of payments through this system is voluntary. Therefore, this agreement shall not interfere with existing payments and transfer practices in each country of the Zone.

ARTICLE 10

The signatory Central Banks shall encourage as far as possible the expansion of financial relations among the commercial banks of the region. To this end, they may utilize credits that are granted to stimulate the opening of lines of credit between commercial banks.

Transfers of the balances resulting from reciprocal credit agreements that the commercial banks conclude may be made through this system.

ARTICLE 11

The signatory Central Banks shall proceed to appoint from among themselves a bank that shall act as Agent Bank for the system. The Agent Bank shall be responsible for collecting the information the Central Banks provide it with, and shall establish and announce the positions to be cleared.

ARTICLE 12

The operating mechanism between the commercial banks and their respective Central Bank shall be governed by the internal regulations of each country and must be communicated to each signatory Central Bank through the Agent Bank.

ARTICLE 13

Representatives of the Central Banks signing this agreement shall meet periodically for the purpose of examining its development, of effecting the necessary adjustments, and of establishing bases which will enable a clearing house and guaranty fund to be created as soon as possible.

ARTICLE 14

This agreement shall enter into effect for each Central Bank from the date on which it advises the Agent Bank that it has completed the required procedure for its legal and administrative establishment.

In witness whereof, the representatives of the Central Banks proceed to sign the present Agreement on the occasion of the second meeting of the Council for Financial and Monetary Policy, held in Mexico City on September 22, 1965.

Part III

REGIONAL DEVELOPMENT BANKS

CHAPTER THIRTEEN

Inter-American Development Bank

The idea of an inter-American bank gathered support with the emergence of the Inter-American system in the last quarter of the nineteenth century. As early as the First Inter-American Conference in Washington in 1889/90, long before the concepts of central banking and development banking had been accepted throughout the world, a number of Latin American republics recommended the establishment of a regional private commercial bank with a network of agencies in the Western Hemisphere. The purpose of such an institution was to be the provision of facilities for financing inter-American trade. Similar but somewhat more sophisticated proposals were made on a number of occasions in the 1930s at various inter-American economic and political conferences. In the midst of the Great Depression, at the Seventh Inter-American Conference held in Montevideo in 1933, some Latin American countries went so far as to suggest the setting up of an inter-American central bank.

After the Second World War, partly because of Latin America's deep dissatisfaction with the concentration of United States postwar economic aid for reconstruction in Western Europe, several Latin American republics, led by Chile and Mexico, revived the long-dormant proposals to establish a regional development bank. These initiatives, presented for the first time at the Ninth Inter-American Conference in Bogotá in the spring of 1948 and again at the Inter-American Conference of the Ministers of Treasury and Economy in Quintandinha, Brazil, in late 1954, were rejected by the United States on the ground that the bank would duplicate the functions of existing institutions. During the vote on a resolution presented at the Quintandinha meeting and calling for the appointment of a group of experts to prepare a preliminary draft of the Inter-American Bank charter, the United States, joined by the Latin American republics considered to be its closest allies in the hemisphere,

357

abstained. Despite the negative attitude of the United States, such an ad hoc committee was set up, comprising experts from Argentina, Brazil, Chile, Colombia, Costa Rica, Cuba, Haiti, Mexico, and Venezuela, as well as from the ECLA Secretariat. At a meeting held in Santiago, Chile, from mid-February to mid-April 1955, a preliminary charter of the bank was drafted by this group.

This draft charter called for the setting up of an inter-American financial agency with an initial capital of $200 million, half of which was to be provided by the United States. The main purpose of the agency was to act as a regional investment bank, but the Santiago group of experts proposed that it become at the same time a financial agent of the member countries, a correspondent bank of the central banks in the area, and a source of technical assistance for closer regional economic cooperation. The draft was again rejected in August 1955 by the United States as aiming at duplication of the functions of already existing financial agencies such as the IBRD, the Export-Import Bank in Washington, and private banks in the hemisphere.

Three years were to pass before the United States position on the subject changed. At a special meeting of the Inter-American Economic and Social Council of the Organization of American States (IA-ECOSOC) in August 1958, Douglas Dillon (then the United States Undersecretary of State) declared that the United States government was willing to support the establishment of an inter-American development agency. Dillon's declaration followed in the footsteps of proposals for closer hemispheric economic cooperation that originated with Juscelino Kubitschek, then President of Brazil, under the name of Operación Panamericana, the forerunner of the Alliance for Progress. The IA-ECOSOC special commission, officially created in October 1958 for the purpose of drafting and negotiating the charter of an inter-American financial agency, finished its work in April 1959. The new draft charter provided for the establishment of an Inter-American Development Bank (IDB) with ordinary capital resources of $850 million and additional capital resources of $150 million for a Fund for Special Operations. Paid-in capital was set at $400 million and callable capital at $450 million. The Bank officially came into existence on January 1, 1960, when sixteen countries in the hemisphere, accounting for 85 per cent of the Bank's capital, deposited the documents of ratification of its charter with the Pan American Union. IDB started its operations on October 1, 1960. At present, all twenty countries of the pan-American system are members of the institution, whose headquarters are in Washington, D.C. The first annual meeting of the Board of Governors, held in San Salvador, El Salvador, in February 1961, elected Felipe Herrera — formerly Minister of Finance for Chile and president of the Central Bank of Chile — president of IDB. Herrera was subsequently re-elected for a second five-year term in 1966.

The Inter-American Development Bank provides long-term development loans from its ordinary capital at interest rates close to those of the international capital markets, and credits are granted on special terms from its Fund for Special Operations and the Social Progress Trust Fund. The Trust Fund, established in September 1960, consists of resources transferred to IDB by the United States from its general foreign aid funds.

In 1964 the ordinary capital of the Bank was increased by an additional $1,000 million and the resources of its Fund for Special Operations by $73.2 million. In the case of the Fund, a further $900 million increase of resources was determined in the same year at the fifth annual meeting of the Board of Governors. In addition to the $525 million that IDB received from the United States as part of the bilateral arrangements under the Social Progress Trust Fund arrangements, the institution floated bonds in United States private capital markets in 1962 and 1964 for a total of $225 million. Moreover, between 1962 and 1966, IDB mobilized another $230 million, mainly through long-term bond issues, in nonmember countries (Canada, Federal Republic of Germany, Italy, the Netherlands, and the United Kingdom).

During the first six years of operation, IDB granted its Latin American member countries 393 loans totaling $1,913 million. The sources of these loans were ordinary capital resources, $747.2 million; Fund for Special Operations, $656.9 million; Social Progress Trust Fund, $501.2 million; and other resources, $4.7 million. The total credits extended to individual countries through 1966 ranged from $417 million for Brazil to $7 million for Haiti. The conditions under which IDB credits were extended in 1966 varied: loans from ordinary capital resources carried maturity from nine to twenty years at 6 per cent annual interest; those from the Fund for Special Operations carried maturity from five and a half years (in the case of some preinvestment studies) to thirty years, with interest rates ranging from 2.25 to 4 per cent; and those from the Trust Fund carried maturity from twenty to thirty years, with interest rates between 1.25 and 2.75 per cent. The Trust Fund also provides financial resources for technical assistance activities of the Bank.

Since its very beginning, the Bank has given high priority to credit and technical assistance activities aimed at supporting economic integration programs in Latin America within the frameworks of both the Latin American Free Trade Association (LAFTA) and the Central American Common Market. In harmony with this objective, it established two financial mechanisms meant to support regional integration schemes: a program for the financing of trade in capital goods within Latin America, which began operations in early 1964 with initial resources of $30 million, and a preinvestment fund for Latin American integration set up in early 1966 with an endowment of $15 million. For the purpose of training and research in various aspects of Latin American integration, a Latin American Integration Institute (INTAL) was established in Buenos Aires, Argentina, under IDB auspices in December 1964.

IDB Program for Financing Intraregional Exports of Capital Goods

When the treaty establishing the Latin American Free Trade Association and the General Treaty on Central American Economic Integration entered into force in 1961, intraregional trade of capital goods in Latin America was practically nonexistent. This was due not only to the relative underdevelopment of the industrial structure and noncompetitiveness of capital goods produced behind the protectionist walls of the major Latin American countries but also to the lack of facilities for medium- and long-term export financing. In the early 1960s some rudimentary financing mechanisms for exports of manufactures were established by central bank authorities in Argentina, Brazil, and Mexico.

The absence — or the high cost — of export financing for other than traditional commodities, coupled with the interest of the member countries of LAFTA and the Central American Common Market in the expansion of manufactured exports within Latin America, led to the first initiatives in this field in 1961. At the first Conference of Contracting Parties of LAFTA held in Montevideo in the final months of the same year, Argentina formally proposed to establish a $2 million export-supporting fund, composed of equal contributions by Latin America on the one hand and the United States and European countries on the other. It was proposed that this fund, to be administered by the Inter-American Development Bank in close cooperation with LAFTA authorities, rediscount to the region's central banks the commercial paper deriving from exports of manufactures and capital goods. The Argentine proposal, supported by other Latin American republics, was not unrelated to one of the recommendations of the Punta del Este charter that established the

Alliance for Progress in August 1961. This recommendation suggested that in the application of Alliance resources special consideration should be given to "the necessary financing of industrial production, and to the growing expansion of trade in industrial products within Latin America" (Title III, paragraph 6).

The establishment of a regional system of export financing was the subject of a long discussion at the third annual meeting of the IDB Board of Governors in Buenos Aires in April 1962. Recognizing the urgent need for such a scheme, the Board asked the Executive Directors of the Bank to present, before the end of the same year, a report on the various systems or mechanisms appropriate to provide for the financing of such exports and, if pertinent, to submit a concrete proposal for modifying the existing regulations of the Bank's charter. A working group established under the auspices of IDB prepared a technical study of the problem for submission at the following annual meeting of the IDB Board of Governors. At the meetings of the Inter-American Economic and Social Council and of the Center for Latin American Monetary Studies held in the fall of 1962, the preliminary IDB proposals were discussed in detail and supported.

The IDB Board of Governors' fourth annual meeting, held in Caracas in April 1963, approved the content of the report in principle and asked the Executive Directors to adopt, before September 30, 1963, the procedures necessary for the establishment of a program providing funds for financing exports of capital goods within Latin America. The program, endowed with $30 million, began to operate on January 1, 1964. Before the end of 1965 it had extended lines of credit to Argentina, Brazil, Mexico, and Peru for a total of $12 million, of which some $4 million had been effectively utilized by the end of 1966.

Preinvestment Fund for Latin American Integration

The first five years of the operation of the Latin American Free Trade Association and the Central American Common Market proved, at least to the countries participating in the two Latin American economic integration schemes, that trade liberalization alone cannot bring about a reorganization of the structure of the Latin American economies on a regional basis. It gradually became clear that the cooperation and integration process could be accelerated only if investment is both multilateral (whether the investors are private groups or the public sector) and regionally coordinated. These two requirements are especially acute for investment in infrastructure and industry. Experience has also shown that a group of developing countries beset with external and internal difficulties of considerable magnitude is hardly in a position to initiate policies defining investment projects that are either to involve more than one country or to be undertaken at the national level and coordinated with the investment plans of other members of the regional grouping.

These serious limitations have not been surmounted by national planning and programing in Latin America. The Inter-American Committee of the Alliance for Progress and the first LAFTA meeting of foreign ministers held in Montevideo in November 1965 suggested, independently of each other, that the Inter-American Development Bank give high priority to fostering studies of regional or multinational investment projects in the area. The IDB already had been offering technical assistance in this field for some time. It has also started financing global investment projects aimed at the economic integration of the border areas of certain neighboring countries of South America, for example, Colombia and Venezuela. In response to suggestions from various inter-American and regional agencies, the seventh meeting of the Board of Governors of the IDB, held in Mexico City in the spring of 1966, asked the Executive Directors to take, prior to July 31, 1966, the necessary steps to establish a Preinvestment Fund for Latin American Economic Integration. The Fund is to finance initial studies as well as the preparation of projects that will help accelerate the process of Latin American integration. The Preinvestment Fund will obtain initial resources of $15 million from IDB's Fund for Special Operations, which will permit the financing of the feasibility studies at concessional terms.

Simultaneously with the preparatory work on the Preinvestment Fund, the IDB contracted with the Development and Resources Corporation of New York to elaborate a preliminary survey of multinational investment program possibilities in the region. The Corporation's report, released in September 1966, suggested feasibility studies covering a number of fields, including the mining of metallurgical coal in Colombia and Mexico for the Latin American iron and steel industry; the regional availability of potash and phosphates; cooperation in the field of hydroelectric energy generation between Argentina and Uruguay; integrated development of the Bolivian-Chilean-Peruvian border area; joint river development by Ecuador and Peru; potential major electrical interconnections in South America and the interconnection of existing national power systems in Central America; and coordinated rehabilitation and improvement of Latin American harbor facilities. Other multinational project feasibility studies are under preparation or consideration by the IDB Latin American Integration Institute, the LAFTA Advisory Committee on Industrial Development, and a joint study group involving ECLA, the Latin American Economic and Social Planning Institute, and IDB. Since its inception in 1961, the Central American Bank for Economic Integration also has offered to finance feasibility studies of industrial projects of regional interest.

Bibliographic References

INTER-AMERICAN DEVELOPMENT BANK

Almeida, Rómulo, Aldo Ferrer, Eduardo Figueroa, Mauricio Herman, Felipe Herrera, Helio Jaguaribe, Milic Kybal, Raymond Mikesell, Ben Moore, Francisco Pinto, and Raúl Rey Alvarez. *Factores para la integración latinoamericana.* Mexico City and Buenos Aires: Fondo de Cultura Económica, 1966.
Herrera, Felipe. "The Inter-American Development Bank and Latin American Integration." In Miguel S. Wionczek, ed., *Latin American Economic Integration: Experiences and Prospects.* New York: Frederick A. Praeger, 1966.
——. "The Inter-American Development Bank and the Latin American Integration Movement," *Journal of Common Market Studies* (Oxford), Vol. V, No. 2 (December 1966).
Inter-American Development Bank. *Annual Reports,* 1961–1966, Washington, D.C.
——. *Multinational Investment Programs and Latin American Integration.* A report prepared by Development and Resources Corporation. New York, September 1966. Mimeographed.
——. Board of Governors. *Proceedings of the Annual Meeting,* 1960–1966. Washington, D.C.
Maschke, Arturo. *La creación del Banco Interamericano de Desarrollo.* Mexico City: Centro de Estudios Monetarios Latinoamericanos, 1966.
Organización de los Estados Americanos. Comisión Especializada Encargada de la Negociación y Redacción del Instrumento Constitutivo de una Institución Financiera Interamericana (Washington, D.C.), 8 de enero a 8 de abril de 1959. *Acta Final.* (ES–CEIFI–104.) Washington, D.C.: Secretaría General de la Organización de los Estados Americanos. Also published in English.

IDB PROGRAM FOR THE FINANCING OF INTRAREGIONAL EXPORTS
OF CAPITAL GOODS

Centro de Estudios Monetarios Latinoamericanos (CEMLA). *Cooperación financiera en América Latina.* Mexico City, 1963.
Galveas, Ernane. "Financing Latin American Exports." In Miguel S. Wionczek, ed., *Latin American Economic Integration: Experiences and Prospects.* New York: Frederick A. Praeger, 1966.
Inter-American Development Bank. *Medium-Term Financing of Latin American Exports.* (Doc. DED/63/5/Rev.1.) Washington, D.C., February 11, 1963. Mimeographed.
——. *Program for the Financing of Intraregional Exports of Capital Goods.* Washington, D.C., March 1964. Mimeographed.
——. *Study of Export Financing in Latin America.* (Doc. DED/62/133/Rev.3.) Washington, D.C., February 9, 1963. Mimeographed.

PREINVESTMENT FUND FOR LATIN AMERICAN INTEGRATION

Economic Commission for Latin America. *Process of Industrial Development in Latin America.* (United Nations Publication, Sales No. 66.II.G.4.) New York: United Nations, 1965.

Inter-American Development Bank. *Multinational Investment Programs and Latin American Integration.* A report prepared by Development and Resources Corporation. New York, September 1966. Mimeographed.

————. *Possibility of Integration of the Colombian-Venezuelan Frontier Area.* Washington, D.C., 1964. Mimeographed.

————. *Preinvestment Fund for Latin American Integration.* (Memorandum submitted to the Board of Executive Directors by Felipe Herrera, President.) Washington, D.C., May 24, 1966. Mimeographed.

————. *Proceedings of the Seventh Meeting of the Board of Directors, Mexico City, April 23–28, 1966.* Mimeographed.

Perloff, Harvey S., and Rómulo Almeida. "Regional Economic Integration in the Development of Latin America," *Economía Latinoamericana* (Washington, D.C.), Vol. I, No. 2 (November 1963).

AGREEMENT ESTABLISHING THE INTER-AMERICAN DEVELOPMENT BANK*

The countries on whose behalf this Agreement is signed agree to create the Inter-American Development Bank, which shall operate in accordance with the following provisions:

ARTICLE I: PURPOSE AND FUNCTIONS

SECTION 1
PURPOSE

The purpose of the Bank shall be to contribute to the acceleration of the process of economic development of the member countries, individually and collectively.

SECTION 2
FUNCTIONS

(a) To implement its purpose, the Bank shall have the following functions:
 (i) to promote the investment of public and private capital for development purposes;
 (ii) to utilize its own capital, funds raised by it in financial markets, and other available resources, for financing the development of the member countries, giving priority to those loans and guarantees that will contribute most effectively to their economic growth;
 (iii) to encourage private investment in projects, enterprises, and activities contributing to economic development and to supplement private in-

---

* Signed by Argentina, Bolivia, Brazil, Chile, Colombia, Costa Rica, Dominican Republic, Ecuador, El Salvador, Guatemala, Haiti, Honduras, Mexico, Nicaragua, Panama, Paraguay, Peru, United States of America, Uruguay, and Venezuela in Washington, D.C., on April 8, 1959, and adhered to by Trinidad and Tobago on July 10, 1967. Official English text published by the Inter-American Development Bank in a pamphlet under the same title, Washington, D.C., 1965. [Editor's note.]

vestment when private capital is not available on reasonable terms and conditions;

(iv) to cooperate with the member countries to orient their development policies toward a better utilization of their resources, in a manner consistent with the objectives of making their economies more complementary and of fostering the orderly growth of their foreign trade; and

(v) to provide technical assistance for the preparation, financing, and implementation of development plans and projects, including the study of priorities and the formulation of specific project proposals.

(b) In carrying out its functions, the Bank shall cooperate as far as possible with national and international institutions and with private sources supplying investment capital.

ARTICLE II: MEMBERSHIP IN AND CAPITAL OF THE BANK

SECTION 1
MEMBERSHIP

(a) The original members of the Bank shall be those members of the Organization of American States which, by the date specified in Article XV, Section 1 (a), shall accept membership in the Bank.

(b) Membership shall be open to other members of the Organization of American States at such times and in accordance with such terms as the Bank may determine.

SECTION 2
AUTHORIZED CAPITAL

(a) The authorized capital stock of the Bank, together with the initial resources of the Fund for Special Operations established in Article IV (hereinafter called the Fund), shall total one billion dollars ($1,000,000,000) in terms of United States dollars of the weight and fineness in effect on January 1, 1959. Of this sum, eight hundred fifty million dollars ($850,000,000) shall constitute the authorized capital stock of the Bank and shall be divided into 85,000 shares having a par value of $10,000 each, which shall be available for subscription by members in accordance with Section 3 of this article.

(b) The authorized capital stock shall be divided into paid-in shares and callable shares. The equivalent of four hundred million dollars ($400,000,000) shall be paid in, and four hundred fifty million dollars ($450,000,000) shall be callable for the purposes specified in Section 4 (a) (ii) of this article.

(c) The capital stock indicated in (a) of this section shall be increased by five hundred million dollars ($500,000,000) in terms of United States dollars of the weight and fineness existing on January 1, 1959, provided that:

(i) the date for payment of all subscriptions established in accordance with Section 4 of this article shall have passed; and

(ii) a regular or special meeting of the Board of Governors, held as soon as possible after the date referred to in subparagraph (i) of this paragraph, shall have approved the above-mentioned increase of five hundred million dollars ($500,000,000) by a three-fourths majority of the total voting power of the member countries.

(d) The increase in capital stock provided for in the preceding paragraph shall be in the form of callable capital.

(e) Notwithstanding the provisions of paragraphs (c) and (d) of this section, the authorized capital stock may be increased when the Board of Governors deems it advisable and in a manner agreed upon by a two-thirds majority of the total number of governors representing not less than three-fourths of the total voting power of the member countries.

SECTION 3
SUBSCRIPTION OF SHARES

(a) Each member shall subscribe to shares of the capital stock of the Bank. The number of shares to be subscribed by the original members shall be those set forth in Annex A of this Agreement, which specifies the obligation of each member as to both paid-in and callable capital. The number of shares to be subscribed by other members shall be determined by the Bank.

(b) In case of an increase in capital pursuant to Section 2, paragraph (c) or (e) of this article, each member shall have a right to subscribe, under such conditions as the Bank shall decide, to a proportion of the increase of stock equivalent to the proportion which its stock theretofore subscribed bears to the total capital stock of the Bank. No member, however, shall be obligated to subscribe to any part of such increased capital.

(c) Shares of stock initially subscribed by original members shall be issued at par. Other shares shall be issued at par unless the Bank decides in special circumstances to issue them on other terms.

(d) The liability of the member countries on shares shall be limited to the unpaid portion of their issue price.

(e) Shares of stock shall not be pledged or encumbered in any manner, and they shall be transferable only to the Bank.

SECTION 4
PAYMENT OF SUBSCRIPTIONS

(a) Payment of the subscriptions to the capital stock of the Bank as set forth in Annex A shall be made as follows:

(i) Payment of the amount subscribed by each country to the paid-in capital stock of the Bank shall be made in three installments, the first of which shall be 20 per cent, and the second and third each 40 per cent, of such amount. The first installment shall be paid by each country at any time on or after the date on which this Agreement is signed, and the instrument of acceptance or ratification deposited, on its behalf in accordance with Article XV, Section 1, but not later than September 30, 1960. The remaining two installments shall be paid on such dates as are determined by the Bank, but not sooner than September 30, 1961, and September 30, 1962, respectively.

Of each installment, 50 per cent shall be paid in gold and/or dollars and 50 per cent in the currency of the member.

(ii) The callable portion of the subscription for capital shares of the Bank shall be subject to call only when required to meet the obligations of the Bank created under Article III, Section 4 (ii) and (iii) on borrowings of funds for inclusion in the Bank's ordinary capital resources or guarantees chargeable to such resources. In the event of such a call, payment may be made at the option of the member either in gold, in United States dollars, or in the currency required to discharge the obligations of the Bank for the purpose for which the call is made.

Calls on unpaid subscriptions shall be uniform in percentage on all shares.

(b) Each payment of a member in its own currency under paragraph (a) (i) of this section shall be in such amount as, in the opinion of the Bank, is equivalent to the full value in terms of United States dollars of the weight and fineness in effect on January 1, 1959, of the portion of the subscription being paid. The initial payment shall be in such amount as the member considers appropriate hereunder but shall be subject to such adjustment, to be effected within 60 days of the date on which the payment was due, as the Bank shall determine to be necessary to constitute the full dollar value equivalent as provided in this paragraph.

(c) Unless otherwise determined by the Board of Governors by a three-fourths majority of the total voting power of the member countries, the liability of members for payment of the second and third installments of the paid-in portion of their subscriptions to the capital stock shall be conditional upon payment of not less than 90 per cent of the total obligations of the members due for:

(i) the first and second installments, respectively, of the paid-in portion of the subscriptions; and

(ii) the initial payment and all prior calls on the subscription quotas to the Fund.

SECTION 5
ORDINARY CAPITAL RESOURCES

As used in this Agreement, the term "ordinary capital resources" of the Bank shall be deemed to include the following:

(i) authorized capital, including both paid-in and callable shares, subscribed pursuant to Section 2 and 3 of this article;

(ii) all funds raised by borrowings under the authority of Article VII,

Section 1 (i) to which the commitment set forth in Section 4 (a) (ii) of this article is applicable;

(iii) all funds received in repayment of loans made with the resources indicated in (i) and (ii) of this section; and

(iv) all income derived from loans made from the afore-mentioned funds or from guarantees to which the commitment set forth in Section 4 (a) (ii) of this article is applicable.

ARTICLE III: OPERATIONS

SECTION 1
USE OF RESOURCES

The resources and facilities of the Bank shall be used exclusively to implement the purpose and functions enumerated in Article I of this Agreement.

SECTION 2
ORDINARY AND SPECIAL OPERATIONS

(a) The operations of the Bank shall be divided into ordinary operations and special operations.

(b) The ordinary operations shall be those financed from the Bank's ordinary capital resources, as defined in Article II, Section 5, and shall relate exclusively to loans made, participated in, or guaranteed by the Bank which are repayable only in the respective currency or currencies in which the loans were made. Such operations shall be subject to the terms and conditions that the Bank deems advisable, consistent with the provisions of this Agreement.

(c) The special operations shall be those financed from the resources of the Fund in accordance with the provisions of Article IV.

SECTION 3
BASIC PRINCIPLE OF SEPARATION

(a) The ordinary capital resources of the Bank as defined in Article II, Section 5, shall at all times and in all respects be held, used, obligated, invested, or otherwise disposed of entirely separate from the resources of the Fund, as defined in Article IV, Section 3 (h).

The financial statements of the Bank shall show the ordinary operations of the Bank and the operations of the Fund separately, and the Bank shall establish such other administrative rules as may be necessary to ensure the effective separation of the two types of operations.

The ordinary capital resources of the Bank shall under no circumstances be charged with, or used to discharge, losses or liabilities arising out of operations for which the resources of the Fund were originally used or committed.

(b) Expenses pertaining directly to ordinary operations shall be charged to the ordinary capital resources of the Bank. Expenses pertaining directly to special operations shall be charged to the resources of the Fund. Other expenses shall be charged as the Bank determines.

SECTION 4
METHODS OF MAKING OR GUARANTEEING LOANS

Subject to the conditions stipulated in this article, the Bank may make or guarantee loans to any member, or any agency or political subdivision thereof, and to any enterprise in the territory of a member, in any of the following ways:

(i) by making or participating in direct loans with funds corresponding to the unimpaired paid-in capital and, except as provided in Section 13 of this article, to its reserves and undistributed surplus; or with the unimpaired resources of the Fund;

(ii) by making or participating in direct loans with funds raised by the Bank in capital markets, or borrowed or acquired in any other manner for inclusion in the ordinary capital resources of the Bank or the resources of the Fund; and

(iii) by guaranteeing in whole or in part loans made, except in special cases, by private investors.

SECTION 5
LIMITATIONS ON ORDINARY OPERATIONS

(a) The total amount outstanding of loans and guarantees made by the Bank in its ordinary operations shall not at any time exceed the total amount of the unimpaired subscribed capital of the Bank, plus the unimpaired reserves and surplus included in the ordinary capital resources of the Bank, as defined in Article II, Section 5, exclusive of income assigned to the special reserve established pursuant to Section 13 of this article and other income assigned by decision of the Board of Governors to reserves not available for loans or guarantees.

(b) In the case of loans made out of funds borrowed by the Bank to which the obligations provided for in Article II, Section 4 (a) (ii) are applicable, the total amount of principal outstanding and payable to the Bank in a specific currency shall at no time exceed the total amount of principal of the outstanding borrowings by the Bank that are payable in the same currency.

SECTION 6
DIRECT LOAN FINANCING

In making direct loans or participating in them, the Bank may provide financing in any of the following ways:

(a) By furnishing the borrower currencies of members, other than the currency of the member in whose territory the project is to be carried out, that are necessary to meet the foreign exchange costs of the project.

(b) By providing financing to meet expenses related to the purposes of the loan in the territories of the member in which the project is to be carried out.

Only in special cases, particularly when the project indirectly gives rise to an increase in the demand for foreign exchange in that country, shall the financing granted by the Bank to meet local expenses be provided in gold or in currencies other than that of such member; in such cases, the amount of the financing granted by the Bank for this purpose shall not exceed a reasonable portion of the local expenses incurred by the borrower.

SECTION 7
RULES AND CONDITIONS FOR MAKING
OR GUARANTEEING LOANS

(a) The Bank may make or guarantee loans subject to the following rules and conditions:

(i) the applicant for the loan shall have submitted a detailed proposal and the staff of the Bank shall have presented a written report recommending the proposal after a study of its merits. In special circumstances, the Board of Executive Directors, by a majority of the total voting power of the member countries, may require that a proposal be submitted to the Board for decision in the absence of such a report;

(ii) in considering a request for a loan or a guarantee, the Bank shall take into account the ability of the borrower to obtain the loan from private sources of financing on terms which, in the opinion of the Bank, are reasonable for the borrower, taking into account all pertinent factors;

(iii) in making or guaranteeing a loan, the Bank shall pay due regard to prospects that the borrower and its guarantor, if any, will be in a position to meet their obligations under the loan contract;

(iv) in the opinion of the Bank, the rate of interest, other charges and the schedule for repayment of principal are appropriate for the project in question;

(v) in guaranteeing a loan made by other investors, the Bank shall receive suitable compensation for its risk; and

(vi) loans made or guaranteed by the Bank shall be principally for financing specific projects, including those forming part of a national or regional development program. However, the Bank may make or guarantee over-all loans to development institutions or similar agencies of the members in order that the latter may facilitate the financing of specific development projects whose individual financing requirements are not, in the opinion of the Bank, large enough to warrant the direct supervision of the Bank.

(b) The Bank shall not finance any undertaking in the territory of a member if that member objects to such financing.

SECTION 8
OPTIONAL CONDITIONS FOR MAKING
OR GUARANTEEING LOANS

(a) In the case of loans or guarantees of loans to nongovernmental entities, the Bank may, when it deems it advisable, require that the member in whose territory the project is to be carried out, or a public institution or a similar agency of the member acceptable to the Bank, guarantee the repayment of the principal and the payment of interest and other charges on the loan.

(b) The Bank may attach such other conditions to the making of loans or guarantees as it deems appropriate, taking into account both the interests of the members directly involved in the particular loan or guarantee proposal and the interests of the members as a whole.

SECTION 9
USE OF LOANS MADE OR GUARANTEED BY THE BANK

(a) Except as provided in Article V, Section 1, the Bank shall impose no condition that the proceeds of a loan shall be spent in the territory of any particular country nor that such proceeds shall not be spent in the territories of any particular member or members.

(b) The Bank shall take the necessary measures to ensure that the proceeds of any loan made, guaranteed, or participated in by the Bank are used only for the purposes for which the loan was granted, with due attention to considerations of economy and efficiency.

SECTION 10
PAYMENT PROVISIONS FOR DIRECT LOANS

Direct loan contracts made by the Bank in conformity with Section 4 (i) or (ii) of this article shall establish:

(a) All the terms and conditions of each loan, including among others, provision for payment of principal, interest and other charges, maturities, and dates of payment; and

(b) The currency or currencies in which payments shall be made to the Bank.

SECTION 11
GUARANTEES

(a) In guaranteeing a loan the Bank shall charge a guarantee fee, at a rate determined by the Bank, payable periodically on the amount of the loan outstanding.

(b) Guarantee contracts concluded by the Bank shall provide that the Bank may terminate its liability with respect to interest if, upon default by the borrower and by the guarantor, if any, the Bank offers to purchase, at par and interest accrued to a date designated in the offer, the bonds or other obligations guaranteed.

(c) In issuing guarantees, the Bank shall have power to determine any other terms and conditions.

SECTION 12
SPECIAL COMMISSION

On all loans, participations, or guarantees made out of or by commitment of the ordinary capital resources of the Bank, the latter shall charge a special commission. The special commission, payable periodically, shall be computed on the amount outstanding on each loan, participation, or guarantee and shall be at the rate of one per cent per annum, unless the Bank, by a two-thirds majority of the total voting power of the member countries, decides to reduce the rate of commission.

SECTION 13
SPECIAL RESERVE

The amount of commissions received by the Bank under Section 12 of this article shall be set aside as a special reserve, which shall be kept for meeting liabilities of the Bank in accordance with Article VII, Section 3 (b) (i). The special reserve shall be held in such liquid form, permitted under this Agreement, as the Board of Executive Directors may decide.

ARTICLE IV: FUND FOR SPECIAL OPERATIONS

SECTION 1
ESTABLISHMENT, PURPOSE, AND FUNCTIONS

A Fund for Special Operations is established for the making of loans on terms and conditions appropriate for dealing with special circumstances arising in specific countries or with respect to specific projects.

The Fund, whose administration shall be entrusted to the Bank, shall have the purpose and functions set forth in Article I of this Agreement.

SECTION 2
APPLICABLE PROVISIONS

The Fund shall be governed by the provisions of the present article and all other provisions of this Agreement, excepting those inconsistent with the provisions of the present article and those expressly applying only to the ordinary operations of the Bank.

SECTION 3
RESOURCES

(a) The original members of the Bank shall contribute to the resources of the Fund in accordance with the provisions of this section.

(b) Members of the Organization of American States that join the Bank after the date specified in Article XV, Section 1 (a) shall contribute to the Fund with such quotas, and under such terms, as may be determined by the Bank.

(c) The Fund shall be established with initial resources in the amount of one hundred fifty million dollars ($150,000,000) in terms of United States dollars of the weight and fineness in effect on January 1, 1959, which shall be contributed by the original members of the Bank in accordance with the quotas specified in Annex B.

(d) Payment of the quotas shall be made as follows:

(i) Fifty per cent of its quota shall be paid by each member at any time on or after the date on which this Agreement is signed, and the instrument of acceptance or ratification deposited, on its behalf in accordance with Article XV, Section 1, but not later than September 30, 1960.

(ii) The remaining 50 per cent shall be paid at any time subsequent to one year after the Bank has begun operations, in such amounts and at such times as are determined by the Bank; provided, however, that the total amount of all quotas shall be made due and payable not later than the date fixed for payment of the third installment of the subscriptions to the paid-in capital stock of the Bank.

(iii) The payments required under this section shall be distributed among the members in proportion to their quotas and shall be made one half in gold and/or United States dollars, and one half in the currency of the contributing member.

(e) Each payment of a member in its own currency under the preceding paragraph shall be in such amount as, in the opinion of the Bank, is equivalent to the full value, in terms of United States dollars of the weight and fineness in effect on January 1, 1959, of the portion of the quota being paid. The initial payment shall be in such amount as the member considers appropriate hereunder but shall be subject to such adjustment, to be effected within 60 days of the date on which payment was due, as the Bank shall determine to be necessary to constitute the full dollar value equivalent as provided in this paragraph.

(f) Unless otherwise determined by the Board of Governors by a three-fourths majority of the total voting power of the member countries, the liability of members for payment of any call on the unpaid portion of their subscription quotas to the Fund shall be conditional upon payment of not less than 90 per cent of the total obligations of the members for:

(i) the initial payment and all prior calls on such quota subscriptions to the Fund; and

(ii) any installments due on the paid-in portion of the subscriptions to the capital stock of the Bank.

(g) The resources of the Fund shall be increased through additional contributions by the members when the Board of Governors considers it advisable by a three-fourths majority of the total voting power of the member countries. The provisions of Article II, Section 3 (b), shall apply to such increases, in terms of the proportion between the quota in effect for each member and the total amount of the resources of the Fund contributed by members.

(h) As used in this Agreement, the terms "resources of the Fund" shall be deemed to include the following:

   (i) contributions by members pursuant to paragraphs (c) and (g) of this section;

   (ii) all funds raised by borrowing to which the commitment stipulated in Article II, Section 4 (a) (ii) is not applicable, i.e., those that are specifically chargeable to the resources of the Fund;

   (iii) all funds received in repayment of loans made from the resources mentioned above;

   (iv) all income derived from operations using or committing any of the resources mentioned above; and

   (v) any other resources at the disposal of the Fund.

SECTION 4
OPERATIONS

(a) The operations of the Fund shall be those financed from its own resources, as defined in Section 3 (h) of the present article.

(b) Loans made with resources of the Fund may be partially or wholly repayable in the currency of the member in whose territory the project being financed will be carried out. The part of the loan not repayable in the currency of the member shall be paid in the currency or currencies in which the loan was made.

SECTION 5
LIMITATION ON LIABILITY

In the operations of the Fund, the financial liability of the Bank shall be limited to the resources and reserves of the Fund, and the liability of members shall be limited to the unpaid portion of their respective quotas that has become due and payable.

SECTION 6
LIMITATION ON DISPOSITION OF QUOTAS

The rights of members of the Bank resulting from their contributions to the Fund may not be transferred or encumbered, and members shall have no right of reimbursement of such contributions except in cases of loss of the status of membership or of termination of the operations of the Fund.

SECTION 7
DISCHARGE OF FUND LIABILITIES ON BORROWINGS

Payments in satisfaction of any liability on borrowings of funds for inclusion in the resources of the Fund shall be charged:

(i) first, against any reserve established for this purpose; and

(ii) then, against any other funds available in the resources of the Fund.

SECTION 8
ADMINISTRATION

(a) Subject to the provisions of this Agreement, the authorities of the Bank shall have full powers to administer the Fund.

(b) There shall be a Vice President of the Bank in charge of the Fund. The Vice President shall participate in the meetings of the Board of Executive Directors of the Bank, without vote, whenever matters relating to the Fund are discussed.

(c) In the operations of the Fund the Bank shall utilize to the fullest extent possible the same personnel, experts, installations, offices, equipment, and services as it uses for its ordinary operations.

(d) The Bank shall publish a separate annual report showing the results of the Fund's financial operations, including profits or losses. At the annual meeting of the Board of Governors there shall be at least one session devoted to consideration of this report. In addition, the Bank shall transmit to the members a quarterly summary of the Fund's operations.

SECTION 9
VOTING

(a) In making decisions concerning operations of the Fund, each member country of the Bank shall have the voting power in the Board of Governors accorded to it pursuant to Article VIII, Section 4 (a) and (b), and each Director shall have the voting power in the Board of Executive Directors accorded to him pursuant to Article VIII, Section 4 (a) and (c).

(b) All decisions of the Bank concerning the operations of the Fund shall be adopted by a two-thirds majority of the total voting power of the member countries, unless otherwise provided in this article.

SECTION 10
DISTRIBUTION OF NET PROFITS

The Board of Governors of the Bank shall determine what portion of the net profits of the Fund shall be distributed among the members after making provision for reserves. Such net profits shall be shared in proportion to the quotas of the members.

SECTION 11
WITHDRAWAL OF CONTRIBUTIONS

(a) No country may withdraw its contribution and terminate its relations with the Fund while it is still a member of the Bank.

(b) The provisions of Article IX, Section 3, with respect to the settlement of accounts with countries that terminate their membership in the Bank also shall apply to the Fund.

SECTION 12
SUSPENSION AND TERMINATION

The provisions of Article X also shall apply to the Fund with substitution of terms relating to the Fund and its resources and respective creditors for those relating to the Bank and its ordinary capital resources and respective creditors.

ARTICLE V: CURRENCIES

SECTION 1
USE OF CURRENCIES

(a) The currency of any member held by the Bank, either in its ordinary capital resources or in the resources of the Fund, however acquired, may be used by the Bank and by any recipient from the Bank, without restriction by the member, to make payments for goods and services produced in the territory of such member.

(b) Members may not maintain or impose restrictions of any kind upon the use by the Bank or by any recipient from the Bank, for payments in any country, of the following:

(i) gold and dollars received by the Bank in payment of the 50 per cent portion of each member's subscription to shares of the Bank's capital and of the 50 per cent portion of each member's quota for contribution to the Fund, pursuant to the provisions of Article II and Artivle IV, respectively;

(ii) currencies of members purchased with the gold and dollar funds referred to in (i) of this paragraph;

(iii) currencies obtained by borrowings, pursuant to the provisions of ArticleVII, Section 1 (i), for inclusion in the ordinary capital resources of the Bank;

(iv) gold and dollars received by the Bank in payment on account of principal, interest, and other charges, of loans made from the gold and dollar funds referred to in (i) of this paragraph; currencies received in payment of principal, interest, and other charges, of loans made from currencies referred to in (ii) and (iii) of this paragraph; and currencies received in payment of commissions and fees on all guarantees made by the Bank; and

(v) currencies, other than the member's own currency, received from the Bank pursuant to Article VII, Section 4 (c) and Article IV, Section 10, in distribution of net profits.

(c) A member's currency held by the Bank, either in its ordinary capital resources or in the resources of the Fund, not covered by paragraph (b) of this section, also may be used by the Bank or any recipient from the Bank for payments in any country without restriction of any kind, unless the member notifies the Bank of its desire that such currency or a portion thereof be restricted to the uses specified in paragraph (a) of this section.

(d) Members may not place any restrictions on the holding and use by the Bank, for making amortization payments or anticipating payment of, or repurchasing part or all of, the Bank's own obligations, of currencies received by the Bank in repayment of direct loans made from borrowed funds included in the ordinary capital resources of the Bank.

(e) Gold or currency held by the Bank in its ordinary capital resources or in the resources of the Fund shall not be used by the Bank to purchase other currencies unless authorized by a two-thirds majority of the total voting power of the member countries.

SECTION 2
VALUATION OF CURRENCIES

Whenever it shall become necessary under this Agreement to value any currency in terms of another currency, or in terms of gold, such valuation shall be determined by the Bank after consultation with the International Monetary Fund.

SECTION 3
MAINTENANCE OF VALUE OF THE CURRENCY HOLDINGS OF THE BANK

(a) Whenever the par value in the International Monetary Fund of a member's currency is reduced or the foreign exchange value of a member's currency has, in the opinion of the Bank, depreciated to a significant extent, the member shall pay to the Bank within a reasonable time an additional amount of its own currency sufficient to maintain the value of all the currency of the member held by the Bank in its ordinary capital resources, or in the resources of the Fund, excepting currency derived from borrowings by the Bank. The standard of value for this purpose shall be the United States dollar of the weight and fineness in effect on January 1, 1959.

(b) Whenever the par value in the International Monetary Fund of a member's currency is increased or the foreign exchange value of such member's currency has, in the opinion of the Bank, appreciated to a significant extent, the Bank shall return to such member within a reasonable time an amount of that member's currency equal to the increase in the value of the amount of such currency which is held by the Bank in its ordinary capital resources or in the resources of the Fund, excepting currency derived from borrowings by the Bank. The standard of value for this purpose shall be the same as that established in the preceding paragraph.

(c) The provisions of this section may be waived by the Bank when a uniform proportionate change in the par value of the currencies of all the Bank's members is made by the International Monetary Fund.

SECTION 4
METHODS OF CONSERVING CURRENCIES

The Bank shall accept from any member promissory notes or similar securities issued by the government of the member, or by the depository designated by such member, in lieu of any part of the currency of the member representing the 50 per cent portion of its subscription to the Bank's authorized capital and the 50 per cent portion of its subscription to the resources of the Fund, which, pursuant to the provisions of Article II and Article IV, respectively, are payable by each member in its national currency, provided such currency is not required by the Bank for the conduct of its operations. Such promissory notes or securities shall be non-negotiable, non-interest-bearing, and payable to the Bank at their par value on demand.

ARTICLE VI: TECHNICAL ASSISTANCE

SECTION 1
PROVISION OF TECHNICAL ADVICE AND ASSISTANCE

The Bank may, at the request of any member or members, or of private firms that may obtain loans from it, provide technical advice and assistance in its field of activity, particularly on:

(i) the preparation, financing, and execution of development plans and projects, including the consideration of priorities, and the formulation of loan proposals on specific national or regional development projects; and

(ii) the development and advanced training, through seminars and other forms of instruction, of personnel specializing in the formulation and implementation of development plans and projects.

SECTION 2
COOPERATIVE AGREEMENTS ON TECHNICAL ASSISTANCE

In order to accomplish the purposes of this article, the Bank may enter into agreements on technical assistance with other national or international institutions, either public or private.

SECTION 3
EXPENSES

(a) The Bank may arrange with member countries or firms receiving technical assistance, for reimbursement of the expenses of furnishing such assistance on terms which the Bank deems appropriate.

(b) The expenses of providing technical assistance not paid by the recipients shall be met from the net income of the Bank or of the Fund. However, during the first three years of the Bank's operations, up to three per cent, in total, of the initial resources of the Fund may be used to meet such expenses.

ARTICLE VII: MISCELLANEOUS POWERS AND DISTRIBUTION OF PROFITS

SECTION 1
MISCELLANEOUS POWERS OF THE BANK

In addition to the powers specified elsewhere in this Agreement, the Bank shall have the power to:

(i) borrow funds and in that connection to furnish such collateral or other security therefor as the Bank shall determine, provided that, before making a sale of its obligations in the markets of a country, the Bank shall have obtained the approval of that country and of the member in whose currency the obligations are denominated. In addition, in the case of borrowings of funds to be included in the Bank's ordinary capital resources, the Bank shall obtain agreement of such countries that the proceeds may be exchanged for the currency of any other country without restriction;

(ii) buy and sell securities it has issued or guaranteed or in which it has invested, provided that the Bank shall obtain the approval of the country in whose territories the securities are to be bought or sold;

(iii) with the approval of a two-thirds majority of the total voting power of the member countries, invest funds not needed in its operations in such obligations as it may determine;

(iv) guarantee securities in its portfolio for the purpose of facilitating their sale; and

(v) exercise such other powers as shall be necessary or desirable in further-ance of its purpose and functions, consistent with the provisions of this Agreement.

SECTION 2
WARNING TO BE PLACED ON SECURITIES

Every security issued or guaranteed by the Bank shall bear on its face a conspicuous statement to the effect that it is not an obligation of any govern-ment, unless it is in fact the obligation of a particular government, in which case it shall so state.

SECTION 3
METHODS OF MEETING LIABILITIES OF THE BANK IN CASE OF DEFAULTS

(a) The Bank, in the event of actual or threatened default on loans made or guaranteed by the Bank using its ordinary capital resources, shall take such action as it deems appropriate with respect to modifying the terms of the loan, other than the currency of repayment.

(b) The payments in discharge of the Bank's liabilities on borrowings or guarantees under Article III, Section 4 (ii) and (iii) chargeable against the ordinary capital resources of the Bank shall be charged:

(i) first, against the special reserve provided for in Article III, Section 13; and

(ii) then, to the extent necessary and at the discretion of the Bank, against the other reserves, surplus, and funds corresponding to the capital paid in for shares.

(c) Whenever necessary to meet contractual payments of interest, other charges, or amortization on the Bank's borrowings, or to meet the Bank's liabilities with respect to similar payments on loans guaranteed by it chargeable to its ordinary capital resources, the Bank may call upon the members to pay an appropriate amount of their callable capital subscriptions, in accordance with Article II, Section 4 (a) (ii). Moreover, if the Bank believes that a default may be of long duration, it may call an additional part of such subscriptions not to exceed in any one year one per cent of the total subscriptions of the members, for the following purposes:

(i) to redeem prior to maturity, or otherwise discharge its liability on, all or part of the outstanding principal of any loan guaranteed by it in respect of which the debtor is in default; and

(ii) to repurchase, or otherwise discharge its liability on, all or part of its own outstanding obligations.

SECTION 4
DISTRIBUTION OF NET PROFITS AND SURPLUS

(a) The Board of Governors may determine periodically what part of the net profits and of the surplus shall be distributed. Such distributions may be made only when the reserves have reached a level which the Board of Governors considers adequate.

(b) The distributions referred to in the preceding paragraph shall be made in proportion to the number of shares held by each member.

(c) Payments shall be made in such manner and in such currency or currencies as the Board of Governors shall determine. If such payments are made to a member in currencies other than its own, the transfer of such currencies and their use by the receiving country shall be without restriction by any member.

ARTICLE VIII: ORGANIZATION AND MANAGEMENT

SECTION 1
STRUCTURE OF THE BANK

The Bank shall have a Board of Governors, a Board of Executive Directors, a President, an Executive Vice President, a Vice President in charge of the Fund, and such other officers and staff as may be considered necessary.

SECTION 2
BOARD OF GOVERNORS

(a) All the powers of the Bank shall be vested in the Board of Governors. Each member shall appoint one governor and one alternate, who shall serve for five years, subject to termination of appointment at any time, or to reappointment, at the pleasure of the appointing member. No alternate may vote except in the absence of his principal. The Board shall select one of the governors as Chairman, who shall hold office until the next regular meeting of the Board.

(b) The Board of Governors may delegate to the Board of Executive Directors all its powers except power to:

 (i) admit new members and determine the conditions of their admission;

 (ii) increase or decrease the authorized capital stock of the Bank and contributions to the Fund;

 (iii) elect the President of the Bank and determine his remuneration;

 (iv) suspend a member, pursuant to Article IX, Section 2;

 (v) determine the remuneration of the executive directors and their alternates;

 (vi) hear and decide any appeals from interpretations of this Agreement given by the Board of Executive Directors;

 (vii) authorize the conclusion of general agreements for cooperation with other international organizations;

 (viii) approve, after reviewing the auditors' report, the general balance sheet and the statement of profit and loss of the institution;

 (ix) determine the reserves and the distribution of the net profits of the Bank and of the Fund;

 (x) select outside auditors to certify to the general balance sheet and the statement of profit and loss of the institution;

 (xi) amend this Agreement; and

 (xii) decide to terminate the operations of the Bank and to distribute its assets.

(c) The Board of Governors shall retain full power to exercise authority over any matter delegated to the Board of Executive Directors under paragraph (b) above.

(d) The Board of Governors shall, as a general rule, hold a meeting annually. Other meetings may be held when the Board of Governors so provides or when called by the Board of Executive Directors. Meetings of the Board of Governors also shall be called by the Board of Executive Directors whenever requested by five members of the Bank or by members having one fourth of the total voting power of the member countries.

(c) The Board of Governors shall retain full power to exercise authority solute majority of the total number of governors, representing not less than two thirds of the total voting power of the member countries.

(f) The Board of Governors may establish a procedure whereby the Board of Executive Directors, when it deems such action appropriate, may submit a specific question to a vote of the governors without calling a meeting of the Board of Governors.

(g) The Board of Governors, and the Board of Executive Directors to the extent authorized, may adopt such rules and regulations as may be necessary or appropriate to conduct the business of the Bank.

(h) Governors and alternates shall serve as such without compensation from the Bank, but the Bank may pay them reasonable expenses incurred in attending meetings of the Board of Governors.

SECTION 3
BOARD OF EXECUTIVE DIRECTORS

(a) The Board of Executive Directors shall be responsible for the conduct of the operations of the Bank, and for this purpose may exercise all the powers delegated to it by the Board of Governors.

(b) There shall be seven executive directors, who shall not be governors, and of whom:

(i) one shall be appointed by the member having the largest number of shares in the Bank;

(ii) six shall be elected by the governors of the remaining members pursuant to the provisions of Annex C of this Agreement.

Executive directors shall be appointed or elected for terms of three years and may be reappointed or re-elected for successive terms. They shall be persons of recognized competence and wide experience in economic and financial matters.

(c) Each executive director shall appoint an alternate who shall have full power to act for him when he is not present. Directors and alternates shall be citizens of the member countries. None of the elected directors and their alternates may be of the same citizenship. Alternates may participate in meetings but may vote only when they are acting in place of their principals.

(d) Directors shall continue in office until their successors are appointed or elected. If the office of an elected director becomes vacant more than 180 days before the end of his term, a successor shall be elected for the remainder of the term by the governors who elected the former director. An absolute majority of the votes cast shall be required for election. While the office remains vacant, the alternate shall have all the powers of the former director except the power to appoint an alternate.

(e) The Board of Executive Directors shall function in continuous session at the principal office of the Bank and shall meet as often as the business of the Bank may require.

(f) A quorum for any meeting of the Board of Executive Directors shall be an absolute majority of the total number of directors representing not less than two thirds of the total voting power of the member countries.

(g) A member of the Bank may send a representative to attend any meeting of the Board of Executive Directors when a matter especially affecting that member is under consideration. Such right of representation shall be regulated by the Board of Governors.

(h) The Board of Executive Directors may appoint such committees as it deems advisable. Membership of such committees need not be limited to governors, directors, or alternates.

(i) The Board of Executive Directors shall determine the basic organization of the Bank, including the number and general responsibilities of the chief administrative and professional positions of the staff, and shall approve the budget of the Bank.

SECTION 4
VOTING

(a) Each member country shall have 135 votes plus one vote for each share of capital stock of the Bank held by that country.

(b) In voting in the Board of Governors, each governor shall be entitled to cast the votes of the member country which he represents. Except as otherwise specifically provided in this Agreement, all matters before the Board of Governors shall be decided by a majority of the total voting power of the member countries.

(c) In voting in the Board of Executive Directors:

(i) the appointed director shall be entitled to cast the number of votes of the member country which appointed him;

(ii) each elected director shall be entitled to cast the number of votes that counted toward his election, which votes shall be cast as a unit; and

(iii) except as otherwise specifically provided in this Agreement, all matters before the Board of Executive Directors shall be decided by a majority of the total voting power of the member countries.

SECTION 5
PRESIDENT, EXECUTIVE VICE PRESIDENT, AND STAFF

(a) The Board of Governors, by an absolute majority of the total number of governors representing not less than a majority of the total voting power of the member countries, shall elect a President of the Bank who, while holding office, shall not be a governor or an executive director or alternate for either.

Under the direction of the Board of Executive Directors, the President of the Bank shall conduct the ordinary business of the Bank and shall be chief of its staff. He also shall be the presiding officer at meetings of the Board of Executive Directors, but shall have no vote, except that it shall be his duty to cast a deciding vote when necessary to break a tie.

The President of the Bank shall be the legal representative of the Bank. The term of office of the President of the Bank shall be five years, and he may be reelected to successive terms. He shall cease to hold office when the Board of Governors so decides by a majority of the total voting power of the member countries.

(b) The Executive Vice President shall be appointed by the Board of Executive Directors on the recommendation of the President of the Bank. Under the direction of the Board of Executive Directors and the President of the

Bank, the Executive Vice President shall exercise such authority and perform such functions in the administration of the Bank as may be determined by the Board of Executive Directors. In the absence or incapacity of the President of the Bank, the Executive Vice President shall exercise the authority and perform the functions of the President.

The Executive Vice President shall participate in meetings of the Board of Executive Directors but shall have no vote at such meetings, except that he shall cast the deciding vote, as provided in paragraph (a) of this section, when he is acting in place of the President of the Bank.

(c) In addition to the Vice President referred to in Article IV, Section 8 (b), the Board of Executive Directors may, on recommendation of the President of the Bank, appoint other Vice Presidents who shall exercise such authority and perform such functions as the Board of Executive Directors may determine.

(d) The President, officers, and staff of the Bank, in the discharge of their offices, owe their duty entirely to the Bank and shall recognize no other authority. Each member of the Bank shall respect the international character of this duty.

(e) The paramount consideration in the employment of the staff and in the determination of the conditions of service shall be the necessity of securing the highest standards of efficiency, competence, and integrity. Due regard shall be paid to the importance of recruiting the staff on as wide a geographical basis as possible.

(f) The Bank, its officers, and employees shall not interfere in the political affairs of any member, nor shall they be influenced in their decisions by the political character of the member or members concerned. Only economic considerations shall be relevant to their decisions, and these considerations shall be weighed impartially in order to achieve the purpose and functions stated in Article I.

SECTION 6
PUBLICATION OF REPORTS AND PROVISION OF INFORMATION

(a) The Bank shall publish an annual report containing an audited statement of the accounts. It shall also transmit quarterly to the members a summary statement of the financial position and a profit-and-loss statement showing the results of its ordinary operations.

(b) The Bank may also publish such other reports as it deems desirable to carry out its purpose and functions.

ARTICLE IX: WITHDRAWAL AND SUSPENSION OF MEMBERS

SECTION 1
RIGHT TO WITHDRAW

Any member may withdraw from the Bank by delivering to the Bank at its principal office written notice of its intention to do so. Such withdrawal shall become finally effective on the date specified in the notice but in no event less than six months after the notice is delivered to the Bank. However, at any time before the withdrawal becomes finally effective, the member may notify the Bank in writing of the cancellation of its notice of intention to withdraw.

After withdrawing, a member shall remain liable for all direct and contingent obligations to the Bank to which it was subject at the date of delivery of the withdrawal notice, including those specified in Section 3 of this article. However, if the withdrawal becomes finally effective, the member shall not incur any liability for obligations resulting from operations of the Bank effected after the date on which the withdrawal notice was received by the Bank.

SECTION 2
SUSPENSION OF MEMBERSHIP

If a member fails to fulfill any of its obligations to the Bank, the Bank may suspend its membership by decision of the Board of Governors by a two-thirds majority of the total number of governors representing not less than three fourths of the total voting power of the member countries.

The member so suspended shall automatically cease to be a member of the Bank one year from the date of its suspension unless the Board of Governors decides by the same majority to terminate the suspension.

While under suspension, a member shall not be entitled to exercise any rights under this Agreement, except the right of withdrawal, but shall remain subject to all its obligations.

SECTION 3
SETTLEMENT OF ACCOUNTS

(a) After a country ceases to be a member, it no longer shall share in the profits or losses of the Bank, nor shall it incur any liability with respect to loans and guarantees entered into by the Bank thereafter. However, it shall remain liable for all amounts it owes the Bank and for its contingent liabilities to the Bank so long as any part of the loans or guarantees contracted by the Bank before the date on which the country ceased to be a member remains outstanding.

(b) When a country ceases to be a member, the Bank shall arrange for the repurchase of such country's capital stock as a part of the settlement of accounts pursuant to the provisions of this section; but the country shall have no other rights under this Agreement except as provided in this section and in Article XIII, Section 2.

(c) The Bank and the country ceasing to be a member may agree on the repurchase of the capital stock on such terms as are deemed appropriate in the circumstances, without regard to the provisions of the following paragraph. Such agreement may provide, among other things, for a final settlement of all obligations of the country to the Bank.

(d) If the agreement referred to in the preceding paragraph has not been consummated within six months after the country ceases to be a member or such other time as the Bank and such country may agree upon, the repurchase price of such country's capital stock shall be its book value, according to the books of the Bank, on the date when the country ceased to be a member. Such repurchase shall be subject to the following conditions:

(i) As a prerequisite for payment, the country ceasing to be a member shall surrender its stock certificates, and such payment may be made in such installments, at such times and in such available currencies as the Bank determines, taking into account the financial position of the Bank.

(ii) Any amount which the Bank owes the country for the repurchase of its capital stock shall be withheld to the extent that the country or any of its subdivisions or agencies remains liable to the Bank as a result of loan or guarantee operations. The amount withheld may, at the option of the Bank, be applied on any such liability as it matures. However, no amount shall be withheld on account of the country's contingent liability for future calls on its subscription pursuant to Article II, Section 4 (a) (ii).

(iii) If the Bank sustains net losses on any loans or participations, or as a result of any guarantees, outstanding on the date the country ceased to be a member, and the amount of such losses exceeds the amount of the reserves provided therefor on such date, such country shall repay on demand the amount by which the repurchase price of its shares would have been reduced, if the losses had been taken into account when the book value of the shares, according to the books of the Bank, was determined. In addition, the former member shall remain liable on any call pursuant to Article II, Section 4 (a) (ii), to the extent that it would have been required to respond if the impairment of capital had occurred and the call had been made at the time the repurchase price of its shares had been determined.

(e) In no event shall any amount due to a country for its shares under this section be paid until six months after the date upon which the country ceases to be a member. If within that period the Bank terminates operations all rights of such country shall be determined by the provisions of Article X, and such country shall be considered still a member of the Bank for the purposes of such article except that it shall have no voting rights.

ARTICLE X: SUSPENSION AND TERMINATION OF OPERATIONS

SECTION 1
SUSPENSION OF OPERATIONS

In an emergency the Board of Executive Directors may suspend operations in respect of new loans and guarantees until such time as the Board of Governors may have an opportunity to consider the situation and take pertinent measures.

SECTION 2
TERMINATION OF OPERATIONS

The Bank may terminate its operations by a decision of the Board of Governors by a two-thirds majority of the total number of governors representing not less than three fourths of the total voting power of the member countries. After such termination of operations the Bank shall forthwith cease all activities, except those incident to the conservation, preservation, and realization of its assets and settlement of its obligations.

SECTION 3
LIABILITY OF MEMBERS AND PAYMENT OF CLAIMS

(a) The liability of all members arising from the subscriptions to the capital stock of the Bank and in respect to the depreciation of their currencies shall continue until all direct and contigent obligations shall have been discharged.

(b) All creditors holding direct claims shall be paid out of the assets of the Bank and then out of payments to the Bank on unpaid or callable subscriptions. Before making any payments to creditors holding direct claims, the Board of Executive Directors shall make such arrangements as are necessary, in its judgment, to ensure a pro rata distribution among holders of direct and contingent claims.

SECTION 4
DISTRIBUTION OF ASSETS

(a) No distribution of assets shall be made to members on account of their subscriptions to the capital stock of the Bank until all liabilities to creditors shall have been discharged or provided for. Moreover, such distribution must be approved by a decision of the Board of Governors by a two-thirds majority of the total number of governors representing not less than three fourths of the total voting power of the member countries.

(b) Any distribution of the assets of the Bank to the members shall be in proportion to capital stock held by each member and shall be effected at such times and under such conditions as the Bank shall deem fair and equitable. The shares of assets distributed need not be uniform as to type of assets. No member shall be entitled to receive its share in such a distribution of assets until it has settled all of its obligations to the Bank.

(c) Any member receiving assets distributed pursuant to this article shall enjoy the same rights with respect to such assets as the Bank enjoyed prior to their distribution.

ARTICLE XI: STATUS, IMMUNITIES, AND PRIVILEGES

SECTION 1
SCOPE OF ARTICLE

To enable the Bank to fulfill its purpose and the functions with which it is entrusted, the status, immunities, and privileges set forth in this article shall be accorded to the Bank in the territories of each member.

SECTION 2
LEGAL STATUS

The Bank shall possess juridical personality and, in particular, full capacity:
(a) to contract;
(b) to acquire and dispose of immovable and movable property; and
(c) to institute legal procedings.

SECTION 3
JUDICIAL PROCEEDINGS

Actions may be brought against the Bank only in a court of competent jurisdiction in the territories of a member in which the Bank has an office, has appointed an agent for the purpose of accepting service or notice of process, or has issued or guaranteed securities.

No action shall be brought against the Bank by members or persons acting for or deriving claims from members. However, member countries shall have recourse to such special procedures to settle controversies between the Bank and its members as may be prescribed in this Agreement, in the bylaws and regulations of the Bank, or in contracts entered into with the Bank.

Property and assets of the Bank shall, wheresoever located and by whomsoever held, be immune from all forms of seizure, attachment, or execution before the delivery of final judgment against the Bank.

SECTION 4
IMMUNITY OF ASSETS

Property and assets of the Bank, wheresoever located and by whomsoever held, shall be considered public international property and shall be immune from search, requisition, confiscation, expropriation, or any other form of taking or foreclosure by executive or legislative action.

SECTION 5
INVIOLABILITY OF ARCHIVES

The archives of the Bank shall be inviolable.

SECTION 6
FREEDOM OF ASSETS FROM RESTRICTIONS

To the extent necessary to carry out the purpose and functions of the Bank and to conduct its operations in accordance with this Agreement, all property and other assets of the Bank shall be free from restrictions, regulations, controls, and moratoria of any nature, except as may otherwise be provided in this Agreement.

SECTION 7
PRIVILEGE FOR COMMUNICATIONS

The official communications of the Bank shall be accorded by each member the same treatment that it accords to the official communications of other members.

SECTION 8
PERSONAL IMMUNITIES AND PRIVILEGES

All governors, executive directors, alternates, officers, and employees of the Bank shall have the following privileges and immunities:

(a) Immunity from legal process with respect to acts performed by them in their official capacity, except when the Bank waives this immunity.

(b) When not local nationals, the same immunities from immigration restrictions, alien registration requirements, and national service obligations and the same facilities as regards exchange provisions as are accorded by members to the representatives, officials, and employees of comparable rank of other members.

(c) The same privileges in respect of traveling facilities as are accorded by members to representatives, officials, and employees of comparable rank of other members.

SECTION 9
IMMUNITIES FROM TAXATION

(a) The Bank, its property, other assets, income, and the operations and transactions it carries out pursuant to this Agreement shall be immune from all taxation and from all customs duties. The Bank shall also be immune from any obligation relating to the payment, withholding, or collection of any tax, or duty.

(b) No tax shall be levied on or in respect of salaries and emoluments paid by the Bank to executive directors, alternates, officials, or employees of the Bank who are not local citizens or other local nationals.

(c) No tax of any kind shall be levied on any obligation or security issued by the Bank, including any dividend or interest thereon, by whomsoever held:

(i) which discriminates against such obligation or security solely because it is issued by the Bank; or

(ii) if the sole jurisdictional basis for such taxation is the place or currency in which it is issued, made payable or paid, or the location of any office or place of business maintained by the Bank.

(d) No tax of any kind shall be levied on any obligation or security guaranteed by the Bank, including any dividend or interest thereon, by whomsoever held:

(i) which discriminates against such obligation or security solely because it is guaranteed by the Bank; or

(ii) if the sole jurisdictional basis for such taxation is the location of any office or place of business maintained by the Bank.

SECTION 10
IMPLEMENTATION

Each member, in accordance with its juridical system, shall take such action as is necessary to make effective in its own territories the principles set forth in this article, and shall inform the Bank of the action which it has taken on the matter.

ARTICLE XII: AMENDMENTS

(a) This Agreement may be amended only by decision of the Board of Governors by a two-thirds majority of the total number of governors representing not less than three fourths of the total voting power of the member countries.

(b) Notwithstanding the provisions of the preceding paragraph, the unanimous agreement of the Board of Governors shall be required for the approval of any amendment modifying:

(i) the right to withdraw from the Bank as provided in Article IX, Section 1;

(ii) the right to purchase capital stock of the Bank and to contribute to the Fund as provided in Article II, Section 3 (b) and in Article IV, Section 3 (g), respectively; and

(iii) the limitation on liability as provided in Article II, Section 3 (d) and Article IV, Section 5.

(c) Any proposal to amend this Agreement, whether emanating from a member or the Board of Executive Directors, shall be communicated to the Chairman of the Board of Governors, who shall bring the proposal before the Board of Governors. When an amendment has been adopted, the Bank shall so certify in an official communication addressed to all members. Amendments shall enter into force for all members three months after the date of the official communication unless the Board of Governors shall specify a different period.

ARTICLE XIII: INTERPRETATION AND ARBITRATION

SECTION 1
INTERPRETATION

(a) Any question of interpretation of the provisions of this Agreement arising between any member and the Bank or between any members of the Bank shall be submitted to the Board of Executive Directors for decision.

Members especially affected by the question under consideration shall be entitled to direct representation before the Board of Executive Directors as provided in Article VIII, Section 3 (g).

(b) In any case where the Board of Executive Directors has given a decision under (a) above, any member may require that the question be submitted to the Board of Governors, whose decision shall be final. Pending the decision of the Board of Governors, the Bank may, so far as it deems it necessary, act on the basis of the decision of the Board of Executive Directors.

SECTION 2
ARBITRATION

If a disagreement should arise between the Bank and a country which has ceased to be a member, or between the Bank and any member after adoption of a decision to terminate the operation of the Bank, such disagreement shall be submitted to arbitration by a tribunal of three arbitrators. One of the arbitrators shall be appointed by the Bank, another by the country concerned, and the third, unless the parties otherwise agree, by the Secretary General of the Organization of American States. If all efforts to reach a unanimous agreement fail, decisions shall be made by a majority vote of the three arbitrators.

The third arbitrator shall be empowered to settle all questions of procedure in any case where the parties are in disagreement with respect thereto.

ARTICLE XIV: GENERAL PROVISIONS

SECTION 1
PRINCIPAL OFFICE

The principal office of the Bank shall be located in Washington, District of Columbia, United States of America.

SECTION 2
RELATIONS WITH OTHER ORGANIZATIONS

The Bank may enter into arrangements with other organizations with respect to the exchange of information or for other purposes consistent with this Agreement.

SECTION 3
CHANNEL OF COMMUNICATION

Each member shall designate an official entity for purposes of communication with the Bank on matters connected with this Agreement.

SECTION 4
DEPOSITORIES

Each member shall designate its central bank as a depository in which the Bank may keep its holdings of such member's currency and other assets of the Bank. If a member has no central bank, it shall, in agreement with the Bank, designate another institution for such purpose.

ARTICLE XV: FINAL PROVISIONS

SECTION 1
SIGNATURE AND ACCEPTANCE

(a) This Agreement shall be deposited with the General Secretariat of the Organization of American States, where it shall remain open until December 31, 1959, for signature by the representatives of the countries listed in Annex A. Each signatory country shall deposit with the General Secretariat of the Organization of American States an instrument setting forth that it has accepted or ratified this Agreement in accordance with its own laws and has taken the steps necessary to enable it to fulfill all of its obligations under this Agreement.

(b) The General Secretariat of the Organization of American States shall send certified copies of this Agreement to the members of the Organization and duly notify them of each signature and deposit of the instrument of acceptance or ratification made pursuant to the foregoing paragraph, as well as the date thereof.

(c) At the time the instrument of acceptance or ratification is deposited on its behalf, each country shall deliver to the General Secretariat of the Organization of American States, for the purpose of meeting administrative expenses of the Bank, gold or United States dollars equivalent to one tenth of one per cent of the purchase price of the shares of the Bank subscribed by it and of its quota in the Fund. This payment shall be credited to the member on account of its subcription and quota prescribed pursuant to Articles II, Section 4 (a) (i), and IV, Section 3 (d) (i). At any time on or after the date on which its instrument of acceptance or ratification is deposited, any member may make additional payments to be credited to the member on account of its subscription and quota prescribed pursuant to Articles II and IV. The General Secretariat of the Organization of American States shall hold all funds paid under this paragraph in a special deposit account or accounts and shall make such funds available to the Bank not later than the time of the first meeting of the Board of Governors held pursuant to Section 3 of this article. If this Agreement has not come into force by December 31, 1959, the General Secretariat of the Organization of American States shall return such funds to the countries that delivered them.

(d) On or after the date on which the Bank commences operations, the General Secretariat of the Organization of American States may receive the signature and the instrument of acceptance or ratification of this Agreement from any country whose membership has been approved in accordance with Article II, Section 1 (b).

SECTION 2
ENTRY INTO FORCE

(a) This Agreement shall enter into force when it has been signed and instruments of acceptance or ratification have been deposited, in accordance with Section 1 (a) of this article, by representatives of countries whose subscriptions comprise not less than 85 per cent of the total subscriptions set forth in Annex A.

(b) Countries whose instruments of acceptance or ratification were deposited prior to the date on which the agreement entered into force shall become members on that date. Other countries shall become members on the dates on which their instruments of acceptance or ratification are deposited.

SECTION 3
COMMENCEMENT OF OPERATIONS

(a) The Secretary General of the Organization of American States shall call the first meeting of the Board of Governors as soon as this Agreement enters into force under Section 2 of this article.

(b) At the first meeting of the Board of Governors arrangements shall be made for the selection of the executive directors and their alternates in accordance with the provisions of Article VIII, Section 3, and for the determination of the date on which the Bank shall commence operations. Notwithstanding the provisions of Article VIII, Section 3, the governors, if they deem it desirable, may provide that the first term to be served by such directors may be less than three years.

Done at the city of Washington, District of Columbia, United States of America, in a single original, dated April 8, 1959, whose English, French, Portuguese, and Spanish texts are equally authentic.

ANNEX A

ORIGINAL SUBSCRIPTIONS TO AUTHORIZED CAPITAL STOCK OF THE BANK

(in shares of U.S. $10,000 each)

Country	Paid-in Capital Shares	Callable Shares	Total Subscription
Argentina	5,157	5,157	10,314
Bolivia	414	414	828
Brazil	5,157	5,157	10,314
Chile	1,416	1,416	2,832
Colombia	1,415	1,415	2,830
Costa Rica	207	207	414
Cuba*	1,842	1,842	3,684
Dominican Republic	276	276	552
Ecuador	276	276	552
El Salvador	207	207	414
Guatemala	276	276	552
Haiti	207	207	414
Honduras	207	207	414
Mexico	3,315	3,315	6,630
Nicaragua	207	207	414
Panama	207	207	414
Paraguay	207	207	414
Peru	691	691	1,382
United States of America	15,000	20,000	35,000
Uruguay	553	553	1,106
Venezeula	2,763	2,763	5,526
Total	40,000	45,000	85,000

* Cuba did not join the Bank. [Editor's note.]

ANNEX B

ORIGINAL CONTRIBUTION QUOTAS FOR THE FUND FOR SPECIAL OPERATIONS

(in thousands of U.S. $)

Country	Quota
Argentina	10,314
Bolivia	828
Brazil	10,314
Chile	2,832
Colombia	2,830
Costa Rica	414
Cuba*	3,684
Dominican Republic	552
Ecuador	552
El Salvador	414
Guatemala	552
Haiti	414
Honduras	414
Mexico	6,630
Nicaragua	414
Panama	414
Paraguay	414
Peru	1,382
United States of America	100,000
Uruguay	1,106
Venezuela	5,526
Total	150,000

* By not joining the Bank, Cuba also did not subscribe to its Fund for Special Operations. [Editor's note.]

ANNEX C

ELECTION OF EXECUTIVE DIRECTORS

a. The six executive directors referred to in Article VIII, Section 3 (b) (ii) shall be elected by the governors eligible to vote for that purpose.

b. Each governor shall cast in favor of a single person all the votes to which the member he represents is entitled under Article VIII, Section 4.

c. In the first place, as many ballots as are necessary shall be taken until each of four candidates receives a number of votes that represents a percentage not less than the sum of the percentages appertaining to the country with the greatest voting power and to the country with the least voting power. For the purposes of this paragraph, the total voting power of the countries entitled to participate in the voting provided for under this annex shall be counted as 100 per cent.

d. In the second place, governors whose votes have not been cast in favor of any of the directors elected under paragraph (c) of this annex shall elect the other two directors on the basis of one vote for each governor. The two candidates who each receive a greater number of votes than any other candidate, on the same ballot, shall be elected executive directors, and the balloting shall be repeated until this occurs. After the balloting has been completed, each governor who did not vote for either of the candidates elected shall assign his vote to one of them.

The number of votes under Article VIII, Section 4, of each governor who has voted for or assigned his vote to a candidate elected hereunder shall be deemed for the purposes of Article VIII, Section 4 (c) (ii) to have counted toward the election of such candidate.

REGULATIONS FOR THE FINANCING OF EXPORTS OF CAPITAL GOODS*

CHAPTER I: PURPOSES

ARTICLE 1

It is the purpose of these Regulations to establish the basic rules to put into effect a program for the medium-term financing of intraregional exports of capital goods among the Latin American member countries of the Bank (hereinafter called "the Program"), with a view to promoting the integration and economic development of the region by expanding and diversifying its commerce.

CHAPTER II: PARTICIPATING COUNTRIES

ARTICLE 2

There may participate in the Program, in their capacity as exporters, those Latin American member countries of the Bank which have designated a national agency as provided for in Chapter V of these Regulations, whose attributes and objectives are, in the Bank's opinion, appropriately related to the purpose of the Program.

CHAPTER III: ELIGIBLE GOODS

ARTICLE 3

Exports Eligible for Financing

The Program shall be limited exclusively to the financing of intraregional exports of capital goods which, for the purpose of these Regulations, shall be

* Approved by the IDB Board of Executive Directors, September 30, 1963. Official text published in Inter-American Development Bank, *Program for the Financing of Intraregional Exports of Capital Goods* (Washington, D.C., March 1964; mimeographed). [Editor's note.]

understood to be those goods, which, either by their nature or their use, are generally considered in international trade practice to be capital goods and which are normally subject to medium-term financing. These goods shall be set forth in the list specified in Article 6.

The financing may include, in conformance with customary international trade practices and within the percentages set by the Bank, exports of spare parts for goods specified in the list, provided such exportation forms part of a transaction financed under this Program.

ARTICLE 4

Origin of Goods

The Program shall be limited to the financing of exports of capital goods originating in the Latin American member countries of the Bank. Goods shall be considered to have originated in such a country when they are produced or manufactured therein from raw materials or parts coming from that country, or any other Latin American member country of the Bank. Goods incorporating imported components not originating in Latin American member countries also shall be considered to have originated in a member country when they meet the following requirements:

a. That there has been effected in the exporting country the last process which substantially altered the character of the goods provided that the c.i.f. value of the imported component not originating in Latin American member countries of the Bank is less than 50% of the total f.o.b. price of the item. The Bank shall follow the policy of diminishing this percentage for specific categories of goods when in its judgment there exists in the intraregional commerce a reasonable supply of such goods with a smaller component imported from outside the region.

b. That the imported components originate in countries where the Bank's ordinary capital resources may be expended, with the understanding, however, that imported components not exceeding in the aggregate more than 10% of the f.o.b. price of the item may originate in other countries.

ARTICLE 5

Exports Not Eligible for Financing

The Program shall not finance: (a) exports of goods which, in the judgment of the Bank, will not promote the economic development of the importing country; (b) exports of used goods; (c) re-exportations; (d) export transactions which depart from normal commercial practice.

ARTICLE 6

List of Goods

The Bank shall distribute to the national agencies a list of the goods whose exportation may be financed under the Program. The list may be revised when deemed appropriate, particularly for the purpose of including new capital goods that the Latin American member countries may be in a position to export.

CHAPTER IV: OPERATING PRINCIPLES

ARTICLE 7

Types of Operations

In the execution of the Program, the Bank may conduct loan operations through the following procedures: (a) granting global loans to the national agencies to which Chapter V refers; (b) concluding line-of-credit agreements with those agencies, either for acquiring credit documents which they may issue or for discounting credit documents which such agencies may have acquired; (c) effecting such other operations as the Bank may determine.

ARTICLE 8

Periods of Financing

The Program shall finance export credit transactions considered to be at medium term, that is, between 180 days and, in general, 5 years. In establishing the periods, there shall be taken into consideration the conditions and practices customarily available in international financing for the respective goods.

The Bank shall establish maximum payment periods taking into account the type of goods, their unit values, and the total amounts of the respective transactions. Such periods may extend beyond 5 years in order to allow the member countries to adjust to the variations which may exist in international competition. The periods shall normally be determined from the date of shipment of the goods.

ARTICLE 9

Percentage of Financing

The Bank may finance up to 70% of the invoice value of the export.

ARTICLE 10

Conditions of Financing

To qualify an exportation for financing under the Program, it shall be requisite that: (a) the importer, at the time of delivery of the shipping documents or prior thereto, shall have made a cash payment of not less than 20% of the invoice value of the export or a lesser percentage which in special cases the Bank deems acceptable to adjust to international competition; (b) the exporter has assumed and continues to assume the financial responsibility for at least 15% of the amount owed by the importer; (c) the periods of amortization and interest charges applied to the portion not financed by the Bank shall be consistent with the practices of international competition in export financing; (d) the importer's obligation shall be payable in United States dollars; (e) reliable evidence shall be furnished to the Bank that the goods in question have been shipped with the necessary documentation and protected by the insurance customary in commercial practice; (f) in the case of exportations which are to be effected through partial deliveries, the special requirements which the Bank may establish shall have been fulfilled, and (g) all other provisions which the Bank may establish in connection with the Program have been fulfilled.

ARTICLE 11

Global Loans

The global loans granted by the Bank to the national agencies under the Program shall conform to the following provisions: (a) the Bank may charge a commitment fee on undisbursed balances of the loan; (b) the period of the loan shall be in keeping with the objectives of the Program; (c) the respective contract shall contain all the provisions necessary to ensure that the national agency concerned shall utilize the funds in accordance with the purposes of the Program, the provisions of these Regulations, and the principles and practices of international trade.

ARTICLE 12

Credit Documents

The credit documents which the Bank may acquire or discount under these Regulations shall: (a) be payable in United States dollars; (b) have been prepared in the form and in compliance with requirements stipulated by the Bank; (c) provide for payment of interest in semiannual installments; (d) have been issued or unconditionally guaranteed by the national agency or such other institution of the exporting country as approved by the Bank; (e) be accompanied by such documents and other proof as the Bank may deem appropriate. (As amended April 1, 1964.)

ARTICLE 13

Interest Rate and Guarantee

In the operations financed under the Program, the Bank shall charge a rate of interest which may in no case be less than the rate which it applies in its other operations from the ordinary capital resources, and the Bank may require the guarantee of the government of the exporting country or of a financing institution of that country acceptable to the Bank.

CHAPTER V: NATIONAL AGENCIES

ARTICLE 14

Designation

The Program shall be carried out through National Agencies appointed by the member countries for that purpose, which agencies, in the opinion of the Bank, shall have legal and financial capacity for the execution of the Program.

ARTICLE 15

Powers of the National Agencies

The National Agencies shall be empowered to perform those of the following functions which the Bank determines are necessary to conduct the transactions under these Regulations: (a) enter into agreements and loan contracts with the Bank for the purpose of executing the Program; (b) discount credit documents deriving from exports included under the Program; (c) issue credit documents in favor of the Bank resulting from the financing of exports eligible under the Program; (d) rediscount with the Bank, with its full and unconditional guarantee or that of such other institution satisfactory to the Bank, credit documents which it has acquired through the financing of exports eligible under the Program; (e) verify that the exports financed under the Program are in keeping with its purposes, the provisions of these Regulations, and the instructions issued by the Bank; (f) issue or authenticate certificates as to the origin and the dates of shipment of the goods, as well as certify the fulfillment of the legal and other formalities pertaining to the exportation, and (g) perform all other functions which are their responsibility to fulfill in the implementation of the Program.

CHAPTER VI: RESOURCES

ARTICLE 16

Resources of the Program

The Program will be financed with the ordinary capital resources of the Bank. There shall also be utilized for the Program such resources as the Bank may obtain in the capital market without giving its guarantee, through the sale of credit documents or participations in such documents or in the global loan contracts resulting from operations financed under the Program.

CHAPTER VII: APPLICATION OF THESE REGULATIONS

ARTICLE 17

Criteria for Application of the Regulations

The provisions of these Regulations are to be applied with due consideration in each case of the transaction as a whole, the norms of international competition in the field of export financing, the regional content of the goods, the need for placing the Latin American exporter who lacks other adequate sources of financing on an equal footing relative to international competition, and the extent to which the economic and social development of the member countries will be furthered.

ARTICLE 18

Discretionary Power of the Bank

None of the provisions of these Regulations shall limit or restrict the Bank's power to accept or reject any of the operations envisaged in the Program and to determine the legality or propriety of the export transactions.

ARTICLE 19

Coordination of Financing Practices

In order to attain the greatest possible coordination and uniformity in export financing practices, the Bank shall maintain liaison with the extra-regional organizations concerned with the subject, as well as stimulate and facilitate contacts among the National Agencies themselves.

ARTICLE 20

Additional Instructions

The Bank shall issue such additional instructions as may be necessary to ensure the quickest and most effective execution of the Program.

CHAPTER VIII: TRANSITORY PROVISION

The Bank shall begin the execution of this Program not later than January 1, 1964; it may, however, finance exports initiated not more than 90 days prior to the date on which the Program shall have been initiated, provided they are consonant with the terms and purposes of these Regulations.

ANNEX 2

PROVISIONAL LIST OF CAPITAL GOODS
ELIGIBLE FOR FINANCING

I. *Machinery and equipment for power generating (except electric), such as*:

Steam-generating boilers.

Boiler-house plants, including economizers, superheaters, condensers, soot-removers, gas-recoverers, and related items.

Steam engines, including steam tractors and steam engines with self-contained boilers (generally known as locomobiles), and steam turbines.

Aircraft engines, including jet propulsion engines.

Internal combustion, diesel, and semidiesel engines for industrial use.

Wind engines, hot-air engines, water wheels and water turbines, and gas turbines, for industrial use.

II. *Machinery and mechanical equipment for agriculture, such as*:

Agricultural machinery and appliances for preparing and cultivating the soil.

Agricultural machinery and appliances for harvesting, threshing, and sorting.

Milking machines, cream separators, and other dairy-farm equipment.

Machinery and equipment for aviculture.

III. *Tractors*

IV. *Office machinery and apparatus, such as*:

Accounting, bookkeeping, calculating machines, and cash registers.

V. *Metalworking machinery and equipment, such as*:

Machine tools for boring, drilling, milling, planing, grinding, and cutting.

Rolling mills, forging, wire drawing, bending and forming machinery, and foundry equipment.

VI. *Machinery and equipment for mining, construction, and other industrial uses, such as*:

Machinery for conveying, hoisting, excavating, road construction, and mining.

Machinery and equipment for the textile industry.

Machinery and equipment for the hide and leather industry.

Machinery and equipment for the manufacture of paper and pulp and for paper manufactures.

Machinery and equipment for the rubber and plastics industries.

Machinery and equipment for working wood, cork, bones, and ebonite.

Machinery and equipment for the glass industry.

Machinery and equipment for the food products industry.

Machinery and equipment for the printing industry.

Machinery and equipment for the fish meal industry.

Sewing machines for industrial use.

VII. *Electric machinery and apparatus, such as*:
Generators, motors, converters, and the like for industrial use.
Apparatus for telecommunications.
Electrical equipment for internal combustion motors and for vehicles appearing on this list.
Electromechanical machines and tools.
Apparatus for measuring and controlling electric energy.
Electrical apparatus and equipment for refrigeration and air-conditioning for industrial and commercial use.
Batteries and electrical accumulators, for industrial use.

VIII. *Railway material, such as*:
Railway locomotives.
Self-propelled railway and tramway cars.
Railway and tramway passenger cars without power equipment.
Railway and tramway freight and maintenance cars without power equipment.
Rails.

IX. *Automotive vehicles for industrial and commercial use, such as*:
Buses and trucks.
Automotive vehicles for special uses, such as irrigation trucks, crane trucks, and concrete-mixer trucks.
Other industrial vehicles.
Chassis for the above-mentioned vehicles.

X. *Road vehicles other than motor vehicles, such as*:
Trailers for industrial and commercial use.

XI. *Aircraft*

XII. *Ships and other vessels, such as*:
Ships for industrial and commercial use in the transportation of freight and passengers.
Boats for industrial and commercial use, whether or not self-propelled.
Boats for commercial fishing.
Towboats, lightships, pump boats, and dredges.

XIII. *Prefabricated buildings for industrial use, of any material*

XIV. *Other apparatus and materials for the use of agriculture, industry, mining, trade, and transportation, such as*:
Tanks and containers of any material.
Tubes for hydroelectric power stations, water and sewerage systems, and irrigation.
Iron and steel cables and structures for bridges.

XV. *Manufactured components to be used in the production of goods listed above.*

FUND FOR PREINVESTMENT STUDIES IN ASPECTS
OF LATIN AMERICAN ECONOMIC INTEGRATION*

Whereas:

A communication of August 10, 1965 from the Inter-American Committee of the Alliance for Progress (CIAP) to the Heads of State of the American Republics advised that the President of CIAP had been asked "to explore the possibilities of support by governments of the Hemisphere and of the external financing agencies for a revolving fund which would finance project preparation and feasibility studies related to regional integration, the fund to be replenished from the loans flowing from these studies";

This suggestion accords with the Charter of Punta del Este, which in Title III establishes that "in the application of resources under the Alliance for Progress, special attention should be given not only to investments for multinational projects that will contribute to strengthening the integration process in all its aspects, but also to the necessary financing of industrial production and to the growing expansion of trade in industrial products within Latin America"; and that there should be sought "the cooperation of the Inter-American Development Bank in channeling extraregional contributions which may be granted for these purposes";

In response to the communication of the President of CIAP, the President of the United States of America, in a speech of August 17, 1965, on the fourth anniversary of the Charter of Punta del Este, stated that "the United States will, as CIAP suggests, contribute from its Alliance resources to the creation of a new fund for preparing multinational projects";

In his message on foreign aid submitted to the United States Congress on February 1, 1966, President Johnson reiterated these concepts when he said that the United States would support the proposal of the Inter-American Committee of the Alliance for Progress and the Inter-American Development

---

* Resolution AG–7/66. Approved in the Fourth Plenary Session, Seventh Annual Meeting of the Board of Governors of the Inter-American Development Bank, Mexico City, April 28, 1966. This is the official English text published in Inter-American Development Bank, *Proceedings: Seventh Meeting of the Board of Governors* (Washington, D.C., April 1966). [Editor's note.]

Bank to establish a new fund for feasibility studies of multinational projects;

In a resolution adopted in Montevideo on November 6, 1965, the Foreign Ministers of the Latin American Free Trade Association (LAFTA) member countries agreed "to recommend that the Inter-American Development Bank establish, as soon as possible, a fund on which LAFTA may draw to finance preinvestment studies proposed for the Association on programs and projects of interest to regional integration, particularly in the fields of physical infrastructure, basic industry development, the prospecting and exploitation of the natural resources of major importance to industrial development, and the development of geoeconomic regions affecting two or more countries";

The Second Extraordinary Inter-American Conference meeting at Rio de Janeiro on November 17–30, 1965, approved the Socio-Economic Act of Rio de Janeiro, in which Chapter V provides that "with the objective of strengthening and accelerating integration in all its aspects, special priority must be given to the preparation and execution of multinational projects, and to the financing thereof, and the already existing economic integration agencies should coordinate their activities with a view to the earliest possible establishment of the Latin American Common Market. Likewise, the economic and financial institutions of the region should continue to give their fullest support to the organization for regional integration";

At the Ninth Meeting of the Committee for Economic Cooperation on the Central American Isthmus, its Chairman offered the broadest support of the Central American countries to the negotiations for the establishment of a regional preinvestment fund;

At its Ninth Meeting, held at Asunción in April 1965, the Board of Governors of the Bank adopted a resolution which, after stressing and giving the most complete support to the efforts of the Bank to facilitate and promote the process of Latin American integration, recommends "that the Board of Executive Directors request the Management to formulate programs of technical and financial assistance, and to study, in coordination with other agencies participating in the process of Latin American integration, all aspects of that process relating to the purposes for which the Bank was established";

At the Meeting mentioned in the above paragraph, the Board of Governors gave full support to the creation of the Institute for Latin American Integration as a dependency of the Bank;

The Board of Governors

Resolves:

1. That the Board of Executive Directors is requested to take, prior to July 31, 1966, the necessary steps to establish a Preinvestment Fund for Latin American Integration destined to finance studies and the preparation of projects which may help to accelerate the process of Latin American integration.

2. That for the establishment of the Fund referred to in the preceding paragraph, to be used in conformity with the basic rules and mechanisms provided in the Agreement Establishing the Bank, it is recommended that the Board of Executive Directors earmark a suitable sum from the Fund for Spe-

cial Operations, such sum not to affect in any case the other activities financed by said Fund.

3. That the regional preinvestment studies which may be financed on a nonreimbursable or contingent recovery basis with Bank resources allocated through the Bank's Technical Assistance Budget, may be included in the annual work program of the Preinvestment Fund referred to in the present resolution.

4. That the Bank may also receive contributions for the purpose of the Pre-investment Fund from member and nonmember countries and from other national and international institutions and agencies.

5. Except to the extent that other possibilities are established in documents providing contributions to the Fund, its resources shall be utilized to grant loans for the financing of studies, chiefly in the following fields:

(a) Multinational infrastructure works, such as highway systems, air transport, marine and river transport, communications, and the promotion of related services on a regional scale.

(b) The integrated development of geoeconomic zones embracing areas in more than one country, as in the joint development of international river basins, including energy sources, river navigation, irrigation, land settlement, and forest resources.

(c) Basic industry on a regional scale operating in a market combining the consumer requirements of several countries.

(d) Other activities oriented toward integration, such as studies and programs for the joint exploitation of natural resources, the establishment of multinational agencies and enterprises, research and the exchange of scientific and technical knowledge, the study of the legal and institutional infrastructure of integration, the training of technical personnel, and, in general, the mobilization of human resources.

6. That, whenever possible, the Bank, in granting loans resulting from studies financed with the Fund, whether granted out of its own resources or from funds entrusted to it for administration, shall endeavor as far as possible to include in such loans the entire cost of those studies, including the cost of related studies performed previously as nonreimbursable technical assistance.

7. That the Bank shall prepare annual work programs for regional preinvestment matters, taking into account the projects and studies that the Latin American Free Trade Association (LAFTA) and the Secretariat for Central American Economic Integration (SIECA) may have under consideration. These programs shall be presented by the Bank to the Inter-American Committee of the Alliance for Progress (CIAP) for consultation, in order that they may be evaluated with the participation of representatives of LAFTA and SIECA.

8. That the existence of the Fund shall not prejudice the right of the Bank to make either national or multinational preinvestment loans in keeping with the provisions of its constituent Agreement, utilizing only its own resources or acting in collaboration with other multilateral or governmental sources of financing.

CHAPTER FOURTEEN

African Development Bank

The first call for the establishment of a regional development bank in Africa was raised at the Summit Conference of the Heads of State and Government of twelve independent African States held in Addis Ababa, Ethiopia, in June 1960 — shortly before the acceleration of the decolonization process in Africa. At the same conference a number of other resolutions with a heavy anticolonial tinge were passed, calling for, among other things, the formation of a council for African economic cooperation to "organize, coordinate, implement and maintain African economic unity" and warning against the introduction of new forms of colonialism under the guise of economic, financial, and technical assistance offered by the former European colonial powers.

At its third session, held in February 1961, the United Nations Economic Commission for Africa (ECA) adopted a resolution requesting the Executive Secretary of ECA to undertake a detailed study of the possibility of forming an African Development Bank and to report to the next session of the Commission. This study, prepared by an ad hoc group of experts, was examined at the fourth session of ECA (February and March 1962), which accepted the principle of the establishment of the Bank, subject to further investigations. To implement the decision, ECA set up a committee composed of the representatives of nine member governments: Cameroon, Ethiopia, Guinea, Liberia, Mali, Nigeria, Sudan, Tanganyika, and Tunisia. The Committee of Nine was to undertake a comprehensive study of the financial and administrative structure of the proposed agency and of the nature and extent of its operations and to draft a charter for the Bank. The Committee fulfilled its mandate in January 1963.

In July 1963 the ECA Executive Secretary convened the Conference of African Finance Ministers in Khartoum, Sudan, which approved the final text of the Agreement Establishing the African Development Bank and opened it for signature. By the end of 1963, thirty African governments had acceded to the Agreement. The governments of Chad, Gabon, and Madagascar did not sign, but they informed the Secretary-General of the United Nations that they might accede at a later date. The Agreement entered into force in September 1964 after twenty signatories had deposited their instruments of ratification, with the aggregate amount of initial subscriptions at that point exceeding 65 per cent of the authorized capital stock of the African Development Bank. By the end of 1965, twenty-seven African states had fulfilled all legal requirements to become members of the Bank.

The inaugural meeting of the African Development Bank was held in Lagos, Nigeria, in November 1964. Mamoun Beheiry, the former Governor of the Central Bank of Sudan and Chairman of the Preparatory Meeting of the Conference of Finance Ministers on the establishment of the African Development Bank, was elected the Bank's president. The nine members of the Board of Directors are nationals of Algeria, Dahomey, Ethiopia, Ghana, Liberia, Morocco, Nigeria, Tanzania, and the United Arab Republic. In the spring of 1965 the Bank moved from its temporary site in Addis Ababa to permanent headquarters in Abidjan, Ivory Coast. The capital funds paid by the member states by the end of 1965 amounted to the equivalent of $31.2 million toward the total authorized capital of $250 million, $200 million of which has been subscribed by the twenty-seven member countries (one half payable in specified installments and another half payable on call).

Unlike the membership of the Inter-American Development Bank or the Asian Development Bank, that of the African Bank is limited to countries within the region. At the time of the Bank's establishment it was widely believed in Africa that the Bank, by restricting participation to independent African states, could avoid certain practical difficulties and undesirable political complications that might arise. The formula finally adopted aims to insulate the regional bank from outside "neocolonialist interference."

The Agreement setting up the Bank also provides for means of cooperation other than equity participation: potential nonregional provision of financial resources through the establishment of a multilateral Special Fund administered by the Bank. The creation of additional special funds on a bilateral basis may also be considered. The Bank's charter gives considerable flexibility to management with respect to conditions under which it may offer loans to member countries either directly or through national development banks. It is understood that, in principle, credits may be extended only for projects in which the borrower has made or expects to make a 50 per cent contribution toward the total cost. Especially for the least developed member countries, however, some consideration will be given to requests for global loans related to national development plans. Rates of interest will differ according to the degree to which projects will be self-liquidating and directly productive. In procuring goods and services with the Bank's resources, preference will be given to bids from any African member country, provided that prices are not considered excessive. This policy is motivated by the desire to encourage local production and employment.

Amortization terms normally will vary between five and twenty years, depending on the projects. Limitations on the size of loans have been set at a minimum of $100,000 (except for preinvestment studies) and a maximum of $3 million for national projects and $8 million for multinational projects. These limits, however, will not preclude the Bank from joining with local and foreign lending agencies to finance larger projects. In its ordinary loan operations the Bank will attempt to set interest rates in such a way that non-African banks may become interested in direct participation and that the Bank itself may be able to mobilize additional resources by borrowing from the private capital markets of the major capital-exporting advanced countries. At present, however, the floating of bonds in private capital markets outside of Africa is not considered feasible.

At the end of 1966 the African Development Bank had a score of requests for loans under study. Its first credit operations were expected to take place in 1967.

Bibliographic References

African Development Bank. *Financial Regulations of the African Development Bank.* Abidjan, 1965.
——. *First Annual Report (10 September 1964–31 December 1965).* Abidjan, 1966.
Economic Commission for Africa. *Agreement Establishing the African Development Bank (Preparatory Work Including Summary Records of the Conference of Finance Ministers).* (United Nations Publication, Sales No. 64.II.K.6.) New York: United Nations, 1964.
——. *Report on the Establishment of the African Development Bank (submitted to the seventh session of ECA, Nairobi, 9–23 February 1965).* (E/CN.14/310.) Addis Ababa, December 4, 1964. Mimeographed.
——. *A Report on the Possibility of Establishing an African Development Bank.* (E/CN.14/129.) Addis Ababa, 1961. Mimeographed.

AGREEMENT ESTABLISHING THE AFRICAN DEVELOPMENT BANK*

PREAMBLE

The Governments on whose behalf this Agreement is signed;

Determined to strengthen African solidarity by means of economic cooperation between African States;

Considering the necessity of accelerating the development of the extensive human and natural resources of Africa in order to stimulate economic development and social progress in that region;

Realizing the importance of co-ordinating national plans of economic and social development for the promotion of the harmonious growth of African economies as a whole and the expansion of African foreign trade and, in particular, inter-African trade;

Recognizing that the establishment of a financial institution common to all African countries would serve these ends;

Have agreed to establish hereby the African Development Bank (hereinafter called the "Bank") which shall be governed by the following provisions:

---

* Signed in Khartoum, August 4, 1963, by Algeria, Burundi, Central African Republic, Congo (Kinshasa), Ethiopia, Ghana, Guinea, Ivory Coast, Kenya, Liberia, Mali, Mauritania, Morocco, Nigeria, Sierra Leone, Somalia, Sudan, Tanganyika, Tunisia, Uganda, and United Arab Republic, and adhered to between October 8 and December 18, 1963, by Cameroon, Dahomey, Togo, Upper Volta, Congo (Brazzaville), Senegal, and Rwanda. The Agreement remained open to signature until December 31, 1963. The governments of Chad, Gabon, and Madagascar did not sign it but informed the Secretary-General of the United Nations, the depository of the Agreement, that they would accede at a later date. This is the official English text, which was published under the same title as a United Nations document (Sales No. 64.II.K.5; New York, 1964). [Editor's note.]

CHAPTER I: PURPOSE, FUNCTIONS, MEMBERSHIP AND STRUCTURE

ARTICLE 1
PURPOSE

The purpose of the Bank shall be to contribute to the economic development and social progress of its members — individually and jointly.

ARTICLE 2
FUNCTIONS

1. To implement its purpose, the Bank shall have the following functions:
(a) to use the resources at its disposal for the financing of investment projects and programmes relating to the economic and social development of its members, giving special priority to:
  (i) projects or programmes which by their nature or scope concern several members; and
  (ii) projects or programmes designed to make the economies of its members increasingly complementary and to bring about an orderly expansion of their foreign trade;
(b) to undertake, or participate in, the selection, study and preparation of projects, enterprises and activities contributing to such development;
(c) to mobilize and increase in Africa, and outside Africa, resources for the financing of such investment projects and programmes;
(d) generally, to promote investment in Africa of public and private capital in projects or programmes designed to contribute to the economic development or social progress of its members;
(e) to provide such technical assistance as may be needed in Africa for the study, preparation, financing and execution of development projects or programmes; and
(f) to undertake such other activities and provide such other services as may advance its purpose.

2. In carrying out its functions, the Bank shall seek to co-operate with national, regional and sub-regional development institutions in Africa. To the same end, it should co-operate with other international organizations pursuing a similar purpose and with other institutions concerned with the development of Africa.

3. The Bank shall be guided in all its decisions by the provisions of Articles 1 and 2 of this Agreement.

ARTICLE 3
MEMBERSHIP AND GEOGRAPHICAL AREA

1. Any African country which has the status of an independent State may become a member of the Bank. It shall acquire membership in accordance with paragraph 1 or paragraph 2 of Article 64 of this Agreement.

2. The geographical area to which the membership and development activities of the Bank may extend (referred to in this Agreement as "Africa" or "African," as the case may be) shall comprise the continent of Africa and African islands.

ARTICLE 4
STRUCTURE

The Bank shall have a Board of Governors, a Board of Directors, a President, at least one Vice-President and such other officers and staff to perform such duties as the Bank may determine.

CHAPTER II: CAPITAL

ARTICLE 5
AUTHORIZED CAPITAL

1. (a) The authorized capital stock of the Bank shall be 250,000,000 units of account. It shall be divided into 25,000 shares of a par value of 10,000 units of account each share, which shall be available for subscription by members.
   (b) The value of the unit of account shall be 0.88867088 gramme of fine gold.
2. The authorized capital stock shall be divided into paid-up shares and callable shares. The equivalent of 125,000,000 units of account shall be paid up, and the equivalent of 125,000,000 units of account shall be callable for the purpose defined in paragraph 4 (a) of Article 7 of this Agreement.
3. The authorized capital stock may be increased as and when the Board of Governors deems it advisable. Unless that stock is increased solely to provide for the initial subscription of a member, the decision of the Board shall be adopted by a two-thirds majority of the total number of Governors, representing not less than three-quarters of the total voting power of the members.

ARTICLE 6
SUBSCRIPTION OF SHARES

1. Each member shall initially subscribe shares of the capital stock of the Bank. The initial subscription of each member shall consist of an equal number of paid-up and callable shares. The initial number of shares to be subscribed by a State which acquires membership in accordance with paragraph 1 of Article 64 of this Agreement, shall be that set forth in its respect in annex A to this Agreement, which shall form an integral part thereof. The initial number of shares to be subscribed by other members shall be determined by the Board of Governors.
2. In the event of an increase of the capital stock for a purpose other than solely to provide for an initial subscription of a member, each member shall

have the right to subscribe, on such uniform terms and conditions as the Board of Governors shall determine, a proportion of the increase of stock equivalent to the proportion which its stock theretofore subscribed bears to the total capital stock of the Bank. No member, however, shall be obligated to subscribe to any part of such increased stock.

3. A member may request the Bank to increase its subscription on such terms and conditions as the Board of Governors may determine.

4. Shares of stock initially subscribed by States which acquire membership in accordance with paragraph 1 of Article 64 of this Agreement shall be issued at par. Other shares shall be issued at par unless the Board of Governors by a majority of the total voting power of the members decides in special circumstances to issue them on other terms.

5. Liability on shares shall be limited to the unpaid portion of their issue price.

6. Shares shall not be pledged nor encumbered in any manner. They shall be transferable only to the Bank.

ARTICLE 7
PAYMENT OF SUBSCRIPTION

1. (a) Payment of the amount initially subscribed to the paid-up capital stock of the Bank by a member which acquires membership in accordance with paragraph 1 of Article 64, shall be made in six instalments, the first of which shall be five per cent, the second thirty-five per cent, and the remaining four instalments each fifteen per cent of that amount.

   (b) The first instalment shall be paid by the Government concerned on or before the date of deposit, on its behalf, of the instrument of ratification or acceptance of this Agreement in accordance with paragraph 1 of Article 64. The second instalment shall become due on the last day of a period of six months from the entry into force of this Agreement or on the day of the said deposit, whichever is the later day. The third instalment shall become due on the last day of a period of eighteen months from the entry into force of this Agreement. The remaining three instalments shall become due successively each on the last day of a period of one year immediately following the day on which the preceding instalment becomes due.

2. Payments of the amounts initially subscribed by the members of the Bank to the paid-up capital stock shall be made in gold or convertible currency. The Board of Governors shall determine the mode of payment of other amounts subscribed by the members to the paid-up capital stock.

3. The Board of Governors shall determine the dates for the payment of amounts subscribed by the members of the Bank to the paid-up capital stock to which the provisions of paragraph 1 of this Article do not apply.

4. (a) Payment of the amounts subscribed to the callable capital stock of the Bank shall be subject to call only as and when required by the

Bank to meet its obligations incurred, pursuant to paragraph 1 (b) and (d) of Article 14, on borrowing of funds for inclusion in its ordinary capital resources or guarantees chargeable to such resources.

(b) In the event of such calls, payment may be made at the option of the member concerned in gold, convertible currency or in the currency required to discharge the obligation of the Bank for the purpose of which the call is made.

(c) Calls on unpaid subscriptions shall be uniform in percentage on all callable shares.

5. The Bank shall determine the place for any payment under this Article provided that, until the first meeting of its Board of Governors provided in Article 66 of this Agreement, the payment of the first instalment referred to in paragraph 1 of this Article shall be made to the Trustee referred to in Article 66.

ARTICLE 8
SPECIAL FUNDS

1. The Bank may establish, or be entrusted with the administration of, Special Funds which are designed to serve its purpose and come within its functions. It may receive, hold, use, commit or otherwise dispose of, resources appertaining to such special funds.

2. The resources of such special funds shall be kept separate and apart from the ordinary capital resources of the Bank in accordance with the provisions of Article 11 of this Agreement.

3. The Bank shall adopt such special rules and regulations as may be required for the administration and use of each Special Fund; provided always that:

(a) such special rules and regulations shall be subject to paragraph 4 of Article 7, Article 9 to 11, and those provisions of this Agreement which expressly apply to the ordinary capital resources or ordinary operations of the Bank;

(b) such special rules and regulations must be consistent with provisions of this Agreement which expressly apply to special resources or special operations of the Bank; and that

(c) where such special rules and regulations do not apply, the Special Funds shall be governed by the provisions of this Agreement.

ARTICLE 9
ORDINARY CAPITAL RESOURCES

For the purposes of this Agreement, the expression "ordinary capital resources" of the Bank shall include:

(a) authorized capital stock of the Bank subscribed pursuant to the provisions of Article 6 of this Agreement;

(b) funds raised by borrowing of the Bank, by virtue of powers conferred in paragraph (a) of Article 23 of this Agreement, to which the commitment to calls provided for in paragraph 4 of Article 7 of this Agreement applies;

(c) funds received in repayment of loans made with resources referred to in paragraphs (a) and (b) of this Article; and

(d) income derived from loans made from the aforementioned funds; income from guarantees to which the commitment to calls provided for in paragraph 4 of Article 7 of this Agreement applies; as well as

(e) any other funds or income received by the Bank which do not form part of its special resources.

ARTICLE 10
SPECIAL RESOURCES

1. For the purposes of this Agreement, the expression "special resources" shall refer to the resources of Special Funds and shall include:

(a) resources initially contributed to any Special Fund;

(b) funds borrowed for the purposes of any Special Fund, including the Special Fund provided for in paragraph 6 of Article 24 of this Agreement;

(c) funds repaid in respect of loans or guarantees financed from the resources of any Special Fund which, under the rules and regulations governing that Special Fund, are received by that Special Fund;

(d) income derived from operations of the Bank by which any of the aforementioned resources or funds are used or committed if, under the rules and regulations governing the Special Fund concerned, that income accrues to the said Special Fund; and

(e) any other resources at the disposal of any Special Fund.

2. For the purposes of this Agreement, the expression "special resources appertaining to a Special Fund" shall include the resources, funds and income which are referred to in the preceding paragraph and are — as the case may be — contributed to, borrowed or received by, accruing to, or at the disposal of, the Special Fund concerned in conformity with the rules and regulations governing that Special Fund.

ARTICLE 11
SEPARATION OF RESOURCES

1. The ordinary capital resources of the Bank shall at all times and in all respects be held, used, committed, invested or otherwise disposed of, entirely separate from special resources. Each Special Fund, its resources and accounts shall be kept entirely separate from other Special Funds, their resources and accounts.

2. The ordinary capital resources of the Bank shall under no circumstances be charged with, or used to discharge, losses or liabilities arising out of operations or other activities of any Special Fund. Special resources appertaining to any Special Fund shall under no circumstances be charged with, or

used to discharge, losses or liabilities arising out of operations or other activities of the Bank financed from its ordinary capital resources or from special resources appertaining to any other Special Fund.

3. In the operations and other activities of any Special Fund, the liability of the Bank shall be limited to the special resources appertaining to that Special Fund which are at the disposal of the Bank.

CHAPTER III: OPERATIONS

ARTICLE 12
USE OF RESOURCES

The resources and facilities of the Bank shall be used exclusively to implement the purpose and functions set forth in Articles 1 and 2 of this Agreement.

ARTICLE 13
ORDINARY AND SPECIAL OPERATIONS

1. The operations of the Bank shall consist of ordinary operations and of special operations.

2. The ordinary operations shall be those financed from the ordinary capital resources of the Bank.

3. The special operations shall be those financed from the special resources.

4. The financial statements of the Bank shall show the ordinary operations and the special operations of the Bank separately. The Bank shall adopt such other rules and regulations as may be required to ensure the effective separation of the two types of its operations.

5. Expenses appertaining directly to ordinary operations shall be charged to the ordinary capital resources of the Bank; expenses appertaining directly to special operations shall be charged to the appropriate special resources. Other expenses shall be charged as the Bank shall determine.

ARTICLE 14
RECIPIENTS AND METHODS OF OPERATIONS

1. In its operations, the Bank may provide or facilitate financing for any member, political sub-division or any agency thereof or for any institution or undertaking in the territory of any member as well as for international or regional agencies or institutions concerned with the development of Africa. Subject to the provisions of this Chapter, the Bank may carry out its operations in any of the following ways:

(a) by making or participating in, direct loans out of:
    (i) funds corresponding to its unimpaired subscribed paid-up capital and, except as provided in Article 20 of this Agreement, to its reserves and undistributed surplus; or out of
    (ii) funds corresponding to special resources; or

(b) by making or participating in, direct loans out of funds borrowed or otherwise acquired by the Bank for inclusion in its ordinary capital resources or in special resources; or

(c) by investment of funds referred to in sub-paragraph (a) or (b) of this paragraph in the equity capital of an undertaking or institution; or

(d) by guaranteeing, in whole or in part, loans made by others.

2. The provisions of this Agreement applying to direct loans which the Bank may make pursuant to sub-paragraph (a) or (b) of the preceding paragraph shall also apply to its participation in any direct loan undertaken pursuant to any of those sub-paragraphs. Equally, the provisions of this Agreement applying to guarantees of loans undertaken by the Bank pursuant to sub-paragraph (d) of the preceding paragraph shall apply where the Bank guarantees part of such a loan only.

ARTICLE 15
LIMITATIONS ON OPERATIONS

1. The total amount outstanding in respect of the ordinary operations of the Bank shall not at any time exceed the total amount of its unimpaired subscribed capital, reserves and surplus included in its ordinary capital resources excepting, however, the special reserve provided for in Article 20 of this Agreement.

2. The total amount outstanding in respect of the special operations of the Bank relating to any Special Fund shall not at any time exceed the total amount of the unimpaired special resources appertaining to that Special Fund.

3. In the case of loans made out of funds borrowed by the Bank to which the commitment to calls provided for in paragraph 4 of Article 7 of this Agreement applies, the total amount of principal outstanding and payable to the Bank in a specific currency shall not at any time exceed the total amount of principal outstanding in respect of funds borrowed by the Bank that are payable in the same currency.

4. (a) In the case of investments made by virtue of paragraph 1 (c) of Article 14 of this Agreement out of the ordinary capital resources of the Bank, the total amount outstanding shall not at any time exceed ten per cent of the aggregate amount of the paid-up capital stock of the Bank together with the reserves and surplus included in its ordinary capital resources excepting, however, the special reserve provided for in Article 20 of this Agreement.

(b) At the time it is made, the amount of any specific investment referred to in the preceding sub-paragraph shall not exceed a percentage of equity capital of the institution or undertaking concerned, which the Board of Governors shall have fixed for any investment to be made by virtue of paragraph 1 (c) of Article 14 of this Agreement. In no event shall the Bank seek to obtain by such an investment a controlling interest in the institution or undertaking concerned.

ARTICLE 16
PROVISION OF CURRENCIES FOR DIRECT LOANS

In making direct loans, the Bank shall furnish the borrower with currencies other than the currency of the member in whose territory the project concerned is to be carried out (the latter currency hereinafter to be called "local currency"), which are required to meet foreign exchange expenditure on that project; provided always that the Bank may, in making direct loans, provide financing to meet local expenditure on the project concerned:

(a) where it can do so by supplying local currency without selling any of its holdings in gold or convertible currencies; or

(b) where, in the opinion of the Bank, local expenditure on that project is likely to cause undue loss or strain on the balance of payments of the country where that project is to be carried out and the amount of such financing by the Bank does not exceed a reasonable portion of the total local expenditure incurred on that project.

ARTICLE 17
OPERATIONAL PRINCIPLES

1. The operations of the Bank shall be conducted in accordance with the following principles:

(a) (i) The operations of the Bank shall, except in special circumstances, provide for the financing of specific projects, or groups of projects, particularly those forming part of a national or regional development programme urgently required for the economic or social development of its members. They may, however, include global loans to, or guarantees of loans made to, African national development banks or other suitable institutions, in order that the latter may finance projects of a specified type serving the purpose of the Bank within the respective fields of activities of such banks or institutions;

(ii) In selecting suitable projects, the Bank shall always be guided by the provisions of paragraph 1 (a) of Article 2 of this Agreement and by the potential contribution of the project concerned to the purpose of the Bank rather than by the type of the project. It shall, however, pay special attention to the selection of suitable multinational projects;

(b) The Bank shall not provide for the financing of a project in the territory of a member if that member objects thereto;

(c) The Bank shall not provide for the financing of a project to the extent that in its opinion the recipient may obtain the finance or facilities elsewhere on terms that the Bank considers are reasonable for the recipient;

(d) Subject to the provisions of Articles 16 and 24 of this Agreement, the Bank shall not impose conditions enjoining that the proceeds of any financing undertaken pursuant to its ordinary operations shall be spent in the territory of any particular country nor that such proceeds shall not be spent in the territory of any particular country;

(e) In making or guaranteeing a loan, the Bank shall pay due regard to the prospects that the borrower and the guarantor, if any, will be in a position to meet their obligations under the loan;

(f) In making or guaranteeing a loan, the Bank shall be satisfied that the rate of interest and other charges are reasonable and such rate, charges and the schedule for the repayment of principal are appropriate for the project concerned;

(g) In the case of a direct loan made by the Bank, the borrower shall be permitted by the Bank to draw its funds only to meet expenditure in connexion with the project as it is actually incurred;

(h) The Bank shall make arrangements to ensure that the proceeds of any loan made or guaranteed by it are used only for the purposes for which the loan was granted, with due attention to considerations of economy and efficiency;

(i) The Bank shall seek to maintain a reasonable diversification in its investments in equity capital;

(j) The Bank shall apply sound banking principles to its operations and, in particular, to its investments in equity capital. It shall not assume responsibility for managing any institution or undertaking in which it has an investment; and

(k) In guaranteeing a loan made by other investors, the Bank shall receive suitable compensation for its risk.

2. The Bank shall adopt such rules and regulations as are required for the consideration of projects submitted to it.

ARTICLE 18
TERMS AND CONDITIONS FOR DIRECT LOANS AND GUARANTEES

1. In the case of direct loans made by the Bank, the contract:

(a) shall establish, in conformity with the operational principles set forth in paragraph 1 of Article 17 of this Agreement and subject to the other provisions of this Chapter, all the terms and conditions for the loan concerned, including those relating to amortization, interest and other charges, and to maturities and dates of payment; and, in particular

(b) shall provide that — subject to paragraph 3 (c) of this Article — payments to the Bank of amortization, interest, commission and other charges shall be made in the currency loaned, unless — in the case of a direct loan made as part of special operations — the rules and regulations provide otherwise.

2. In the case of loans guaranteed by the Bank, the contract of guarantee:

(a) shall establish, in conformity with the operational principles set forth in paragraph 1 of Article 17 of this Agreement and subject to the other provisions of this Chapter, all the terms and conditions of the guarantee concerned including those relating to the fees, commission, and other charges of the Bank; and, in particular

(b) shall provide that — subject to paragraph 3 (c) of this Article — all payments to the Bank under the guarantee contract shall be made in the currency loaned, unless — in the case of a loan guaranteed as part of special operations — the rules and regulations provide otherwise; and

(c) shall also provide that the Bank may terminate its liability with respect to interest if, upon default by the borrower and the guarantor, if any, the Bank offers to purchase, at par and interest accrued to a date designated in the offer, the bonds or other obligations guaranteed.

3. In the case of direct loans made or loans guaranteed by the Bank, the Bank:

(a) in determining the terms and conditions for the operation, shall take due account of the terms and conditions on which the corresponding funds were obtained by the Bank;

(b) where the recipient is not a member, may, when it deems it advisable, require that the member in whose territory the project concerned is to be carried out, or a public agency or institution of that member acceptable to the Bank, guarantee the repayment of the principal and the payment of interest and other charges on the loan;

(c) shall expressly state the currency in which all payments to the Bank under the contract concerned shall be made. At the option of the borrower, however, such payments may always be made in gold or convertible currency or, subject to the agreement of the Bank in any other currency; and

(d) may attach such other terms or conditions, as it deems appropriate, taking into account both the interest of the member directly concerned in the project and the interests of the members as a whole.

ARTICLE 19
COMMISSION AND FEES

1. The Bank shall charge a commission on direct loans made and guarantees given as part of its ordinary operations. This commission, payable periodically, shall be computed on the amount outstanding on each loan or guarantee and shall be at the rate of not less than one per cent per annum, unless the Bank, after the first ten years of its operations, decides to change this minimum rate by a majority of two-thirds of its members representing not less than three-quarters of the total voting power of the members.

2. In guaranteeing a loan as part of its ordinary operations, the Bank shall charge a guarantee fee, at a rate determined by the Board of Directors, payable periodically on the amount of the loan outstanding.

3. Other charges of the Bank in its ordinary operations and the commission, fees and other charges in its special operations shall be determined by the Board of Directors.

ARTICLE 20
SPECIAL RESERVE

The amount of commissions received by the Bank pursuant to Article 19 of this Agreement shall be set aside as a special reserve which shall be kept for meeting liabilities of the Bank in accordance with its Article 21. The special reserve shall be held in such liquid form, permitted under this Agreement, as the Board of Directors may decide.

ARTICLE 21
METHODS OF MEETING LIABILITIES OF THE BANK
(Ordinary Operations)

1. Whenever necessary to meet contractual payments of interest, other charges or amortization on the borrowing of the Bank, or to meet its liabilities with respect to similar payments in respect of loans guaranteed by it and chargeable to its ordinary capital resources, the Bank may call an appropriate amount of the unpaid subscribed callable capital in accordance with paragraph 4 of Article 7 of this Agreement.

2. In cases of default in respect of a loan made out of borrowed funds or guaranteed by the Bank as part of its ordinary operations, the Bank may, if it believes that the default may be of long duration, call an additional amount of such callable capital not to exceed in any one year one per cent of the total subscriptions of the members, for the following purposes:

(a) To redeem before maturity, or otherwise discharge, its liability on all or part of the outstanding principal of any loan guaranteed by it in respect of which the debtor is in default; and

(b) To repurchase, or otherwise discharge, its liability on all or part of its own outstanding borrowing.

ARTICLE 22
METHODS OF MEETING LIABILITIES OF THE BANK ON
BORROWINGS FOR SPECIAL FUNDS

Payments in satisfaction of any liability in respect of borrowings of funds for inclusion in the special resources appertaining to a Special Fund shall be charged:

(i) first, against any reserve established for this purpose for or within the Special Fund concerned; and

(ii) then, against any other assets available in the special resources appertaining to that Special Fund.

CHAPTER IV: BORROWING AND OTHER
ADDITIONAL POWERS

ARTICLE 23
GENERAL POWERS

In addition to the powers provided elsewhere in this Agreement, the Bank shall have power to:

(a) borrow funds in member countries or elsewhere, and in that connexion to furnish such collateral or other security as it shall determine provided always that:

(i) before making a sale of its obligations in the market of a member, the Bank shall have obtained its approval;

(ii) where the obligations of the Bank are to be denominated in the currency of a member, the Bank shall have obtained its approval; and

(iii) where the funds to be borrowed are to be included in its ordinary capital resources, the Bank shall have obtained, where appropriate, the approval of the members referred to in sub-paragraphs (i) and (ii) of this paragraph that the proceeds may be exchanged for any other currency without any restrictions;

(b) buy and sell securities the Bank has issued or guaranteed or in which it has invested provided always that it shall have obtained the approval of any member in whose territory the securities are to be bought or sold;

(c) guarantee or underwrite securities in which it has invested in order to facilitate their sale:

(d) invest funds not needed in its operations in such obligations as it may determine and invest funds held by the Bank for pensions or similar purposes in marketable securities;

(e) undertake activities incidental to its operations such as, among others, the promotion of consortia for financing which serves the purpose of the Bank and comes within its functions;

(f) (i) provide all technical advice and assistance which serve its purpose and come within its functions; and

(ii) where expenditure incurred by such a service is not reimbursed, charge the net income of the Bank therewith and, in the first five years of its operations, use up to one per cent of its paid-up capital on such expenditure; provided always that the total expenditure of the Bank on such services in each year of that period does not exceed one-fifth of that percentage; and

(g) exercise such other powers as shall be necessary or desirable in furtherance of its purpose and functions, consistent with the provisions of this Agreement.

ARTICLE 24
SPECIAL BORROWING POWERS

1. The Bank may request any member to loan amounts of its currency to the Bank in order to finance expenditure in respect of goods or services produced in the territory of that member for the purpose of a project to be carried out in the territory of another member.

2. Unless the member concerned invokes economic and financial difficulties which, in its opinion, are likely to be provoked or aggravated by the granting of such a loan to the Bank, that member shall comply with the request of the Bank. The loan shall be made for a period to be agreed with the Bank, which shall be in relation to the duration of the project which the proceeds of that loan are designed to finance.

3. Unless the member agrees otherwise, the aggregate amount outstanding in respect of its loans made to the Bank pursuant to this Article shall not, at any time, exceed the equivalent of the amount of its subscription to the capital stock of the Bank.

4. Loans to the Bank made pursuant to this Article shall bear interest, payable by the Bank to the lending member, at a rate which shall correspond to the average rate of interest paid by the Bank on its borrowings for Special Funds during a period of one year preceding the conclusion of the loan agreement. This rate shall in no event exceed a maximum rate which the Board of Governors shall determine from time to time.

5. The Bank shall repay the loan, and pay the interest due in respect thereof, in the currency of the lending member or in a currency acceptable to the latter.

6. All resources obtained by the Bank by virtue of the provisions of this Article shall constitute a Special Fund.

ARTICLE 25
WARNING TO BE PLACED ON SECURITIES

Every security issued or guaranteed by the Bank shall bear on its face a conspicuous statement to the effect that it is not an obligation of any Government unless it is in fact the obligation of a particular Government in which case it shall so state.

ARTICLE 26
VALUATION OF CURRENCIES AND DETERMINATION OF CONVERTIBILITY

Whenever it shall become necessary under this Agreement:
(i) to value any currency in terms of another currency, in terms of gold or of the unit of account defined in paragraph 1 (b) of Article 5 of this Agreement; or
(ii) to determine whether any currency is convertible,

such valuation or determination, as the case may be, shall be reasonably made by the Bank after consultation with the International Monetary Fund.

ARTICLE 27
USE OF CURRENCIES

1. Members may not maintain or impose any restrictions on the holding or use by the Bank or by any recipient from the Bank, for payments anywhere, of the following:

(a) gold or convertible currencies received by the Bank in payment of subscriptions to the capital stock of the Bank from its members;

(b) currencies of members purchased with the gold or convertible currencies referred to in the preceding sub-paragraph;

(c) currencies obtained by the Bank by borrowing, pursuant to paragraph 2 of Article 23 of this Agreement, for inclusion in its ordinary capital resources;

(d) gold or currencies received by the Bank in payment on account of principal, interest, dividends or other charges in respect of loans or investments made out of any of the funds referred to in sub-paragraphs (a) to (c) or in payment of commissions or fees in respect of guarantees issued by the Bank; and

(e) currencies, other than its own, received by a member from the Bank in distribution of the net income of the Bank in accordance with Article 42 of this Agreement.

2. Members may not maintain or impose any restrictions on the holding or use by the Bank or by any recipient from the Bank, for payments anywhere, of currency of a member received by the Bank which does not come within the provisions of the preceding paragraph, unless:

(a) that member declares that it desires the use of such currency to be restricted to payment for goods or services produced in its territory; or

(b) such currency forms part of the special resources of the Bank and its use is subject to special rules and regulations.

3. Members may not maintain or impose any restrictions on the holding or use by the Bank, for making amortization or anticipatory payments or for repurchasing — in whole or in part — its obligations, of currencies received by the Bank in repayment of direct loans made out of its ordinary capital resources.

4. The Bank shall not use gold or currencies which it holds for the purchase of other currencies of its members except:

(a) in order to meet its existing obligations; or

(b) pursuant to decision of the Board of Directors adopted by a two-thirds majority of the total voting power of the members.

ARTICLE 28
MAINTENANCE OF VALUE OF THE CURRENCY HOLDINGS OF THE BANK

1. Whenever the par value of the currency of a member is reduced in terms of the unit of account defined in paragraph 1 (b) of Article 5 of this Agree-

ment, or its foreign exchange value has, in the opinion of the Bank, depreciated to a significant extent, that member shall pay to the Bank within a reasonable time an amount of its currency required to maintain the value of all such currency held by the Bank excepting currency derived by the Bank from its borrowing.

2. Whenever the par value of the currency of a member is increased in terms of the said unit of account, or its foreign exchange value has, in the opinion of the Bank appreciated to a significant extent, the Bank shall pay to that member within a reasonable time an amount of that currency required to adjust the value of all such currency held by the Bank, excepting currency derived by the Bank from its borrowing.

3. The Bank may waive the provisions of this Article where a uniform proportionate change in the par value of the currencies of all its members takes place.

CHAPTER V: ORGANIZATION AND MANAGEMENT

ARTICLE 29
BOARD OF GOVERNORS: POWERS

1. All the powers of the Bank shall be vested in the Board of Governors. In particular, the Board shall issue general directives concerning the credit policy of the Bank.

2. The Board of Governors may delegate to the Board of Directors all its powers except the power to:

(a) decrease the authorized capital stock of the Bank;

(b) establish or accept the administration of Special Funds;

(c) authorize the conclusion of general arrangements for co-operation with the authorities of African countries which have not yet attained independent status or of general agreements for co-operation with African governments which have not yet acquired membership of the Bank, as well as of such agreements with other governments and with other international organizations;

(d) determine the remuneration of directors and their alternates;

(e) select outside auditors to certify the general balance sheet and the statement of profit and loss of the bank and to select such other experts as may be necessary to examine and report on the general management of the Bank;

(f) approve, after reviewing the report of the auditors, the general balance sheet and statement of profit and loss of the Bank; and

(g) exercise such other powers as are expressly provided for that Board in this Agreement.

3. The Board of Governors shall retain full powers to exercise authority over any matter delegated to the Board of Directors pursuant to paragraph 2 of this Article.

ARTICLE 30
BOARD OF GOVERNORS: COMPOSITION

1. Each member shall be represented on the Board of Governors and shall appoint one governor and one alternate governor. They shall be persons of the highest competence and wide experience in economic and financial matters and shall be nationals of the member States. Each governor and alternate shall serve for five years, subject to termination of appointment at any time, or to reappointment, at the pleasure of the appointing member. No alternate may vote except in the absence of his principal. At its annual meeting, the Board shall designate one of the governors as Chairman who shall hold office until the election of the Chairman at the next annual meeting of the Board.

2. Governors and alternates shall serve as such without remuneration from the Bank, but the Bank may pay them reasonable expenses incurred in attending meetings.

ARTICLE 31
BOARD OF GOVERNORS: PROCEDURE

1. The Board of Governors shall hold an annual meeting and such other meetings as may be provided for by the Board or called by the Board of Directors. Meetings of the Board of Governors shall be called, by the Board of Directors, whenever requested by five members of the Bank, or by members having one-quarter of the total voting power of the members.

2. A quorum for any meeting of the Board of Governors shall be a majority of the total number of Governors or their alternates, representing not less than two-thirds of the total voting power of the members.

3. The Board of Governors may by regulation establish a procedure whereby the Board of Directors may, when it deems such action advisable, obtain a vote of the governors on a specific question without calling a meeting of the Board.

4. The Board of Governors, and the Board of Directors to the extent authorized, may establish such subsidiary bodies and adopt such rules and regulations as may be necessary or appropriate to conduct the business of the Bank.

ARTICLE 32
BOARD OF DIRECTORS: POWERS

Without prejudice to the powers of the Board of Governors as provided in Article 29 of this Agreement, the Board of Directors shall be responsible for the conduct of the general operations of the Bank and for this purpose shall, in addition to the powers provided for it expressly in this Agreement, exercise all the powers delegated to it by the Board of Governors, and in particular:

    (a) elect the President and on his recommendation, one or more Vice-Presidents of the Bank and determine their terms of service;

(b) prepare the work of the Board of Governors;

(c) in conformity with the general directives of the Board of Governors, take decisions concerning particular direct loans, guarantees, investments in equity capital and borrowing of funds by the Bank;

(d) determine the rates of interest for direct loans and of commissions for guarantees;

(e) submit the accounts for each financial year and an annual report for approval to the Board of Governors at each annual meeting; and

(f) determine the general structure of the services of the Bank.

ARTICLE 33
BOARD OF DIRECTORS: COMPOSITION

1. The Board of Directors shall be composed of nine members who shall not be governors or alternate governors. They shall be elected by the Board of Governors in accordance with annex B to this Agreement, which shall form an integral part thereof. In electing the Board of Directors, the Board of Governors shall have due regard to the high competence in economic and financial matters required for the office.

2. Each director shall appoint an alternate who shall act for him when he is not present. Directors and their alternates shall be nationals of member States; but no alternate may be of the same nationality as his director. An alternate may participate in meetings of the Board but may vote only when he is acting in place of his director.

3. Directors shall be elected for a term of three years and may be re-elected. They shall continue in office until their successors are elected. If the office of a director becomes vacant more than 180 days before the end of his term, a successor shall be elected in accordance with annex B to this Agreement, for the remainder of the term by the Board of Governors at its next session. While the office remains vacant the alternate of the former director shall exercise the powers of the latter except that of appointing an alternate.

ARTICLE 34
BOARD OF DIRECTORS: PROCEDURE

1. The Board of Directors shall function in continuous session at the principal office of the Bank and shall meet as often as the business of the Bank may require.

2. A quorum for any meeting of the Board of Directors shall be a majority of the total number of directors representing not less than two-thirds of the total voting power of the members.

3. The Board of Governors shall adopt regulations under which, if there is no director of its nationality, a member may be represented at a meeting of the Board of Directors when a request made by, or a matter particularly affecting, that member is under consideration.

ARTICLE 35
VOTING

1. Each member shall have 625 votes and, in addition, one vote for each share of the capital stock of the Bank held by that member.

2. In voting in the Board of Governors, each governor shall be entitled to cast the votes of the member he represents. Except as otherwise expressly provided in this Agreement, all matters before the Board of Governors shall be decided by a majority of the voting power represented at the meeting.

3. In voting in the Board of Directors, each director shall be entitled to cast the number of votes that counted towards his election, which votes shall be cast as a unit. Except as otherwise provided in this Agreement, all matters before the Board of Directors shall be decided by a majority of the voting power represented at the meeting.

ARTICLE 36
THE PRESIDENT: APPOINTMENT

The Board of Directors, by a majority of the total voting power of the members, shall elect the President of the Bank. He shall be a person of the highest competence in matters pertaining to the activities, management and administration of the Bank and shall be a national of a member State. While holding office, neither he nor any Vice-President shall be a governor or a director or alternate for either. The term of office of the President shall be five years. It may be renewed. He shall, however, cease to hold office if the Board of Directors so decides by a two-thirds majority of the voting power of the members.

ARTICLE 37
THE OFFICE OF THE PRESIDENT

1. The President shall be Chairman of the Board of Directors but shall have no vote except a deciding vote in case of an equal division. He may participate in meetings of the Board of Governors but shall not vote.

2. The President shall be chief of the staff of the Bank and shall conduct under the direction of the Board of Directors, the current business of the Bank. He shall be responsible for the organization of the officers and staff of the Bank whom he shall appoint and release in accordance with regulations adopted by the Bank. He shall fix the terms of their employment in accordance with rules of sound management and financial policy.

3. The President shall be the legal representative of the Bank.

4. The Bank shall adopt regulations which shall determine who shall legally represent the Bank and perform the other duties of the President in the event that he is absent or that his office should become vacant.

5. In appointing the officers and staff, the President shall make it his foremost consideration to secure the highest standards of efficiency, technical

competence and integrity. He shall pay full regard to the recruitment of personnel among nationals of African countries, especially as far as senior posts of an executive nature are concerned. He shall recruit them on as wide a geographical basis as possible.

ARTICLE 38
PROHIBITION OF POLITICAL ACTIVITY, THE INTERNATIONAL CHARACTER OF THE BANK

1. The Bank shall not accept loans or assistance that could in any way prejudice, limit, deflect or otherwise alter its purpose or functions.

2. The Bank, its President, Vice-President, officers and staff shall not interfere in the political affairs of any member; nor shall they be influenced in their decisions by the political character of the member concerned. Only economic considerations shall be relevant to their decisions. Such considerations shall be weighed impartially in order to achieve and carry out the functions of the Bank.

3. The President, Vice-Presidents, officers and staff of the Bank, in discharge of their offices, owe their duty entirely to the Bank and to no other authority. Each member of the Bank shall respect the international character of this duty and shall refrain from all attempts to influence any of them in the discharge of their duties.

ARTICLE 39
OFFICES OF THE BANK

1. The principal office of the Bank shall be located in the territory of a member State. The choice of the location of the principal office of the Bank shall be made by the Board of Governors at its first meeting, taking into account the availability of facilities for the proper functioning of the Bank.

2. Notwithstanding the provisions of Article 35 of this Agreement, the choice of the location of the principal office of the Bank shall be made by the Board of Governors in accordance with the conditions that applied to the adoption of this Agreement.

3. The Bank may establish branch offices or agencies elsewhere.

ARTICLE 40
CHANNEL OF COMMUNICATIONS, DEPOSITORIES

1. Each member shall designate an appropriate authority with which the Bank may communicate in connexion with any matter arising under this Agreement.

2. Each member shall designate its central bank or such other institution as may be agreed by the Bank, as a depository with which the Bank may keep its holdings of currency of that member as well as other assets of the Bank.

3. The Bank may hold its assets, including gold and convertible currencies, with such depositories as the Board of Directors shall determine.

ARTICLE 41
PUBLICATION OF THE AGREEMENT, WORKING LANGUAGES, PROVISION OF INFORMATION AND REPORTS

1. The Bank shall endeavour to make available the text of this Agreement and all its important documents in the principal languages used in Africa. The working languages of the Bank shall be, if possible, African languages, English and French.

2. Members shall furnish the Bank with all information it may request of them in order to facilitate the performance of its functions.

3. The Bank shall publish and transmit to its members an Annual Report containing an audited statement of the accounts. It shall also transmit quarterly to the members a summary statement of its financial position and a profit and loss statement showing the results of its operations. The Annual Report and the Quarterly Statements shall be drawn up in accordance with the provisions of paragraph 4 of Article 13 of this Agreement.

4. The Bank may also publish such other reports as it deems desirable to carry out its purpose and functions. They shall be transmitted to the members of the Bank.

ARTICLE 42
ALLOCATION OF NET INCOME

1. The Board of Governors shall determine annually what part of the net income of the Bank, including the net income accruing to its Special Funds, shall be allocated — after making provision for reserves — to surplus and what part, if any, shall be distributed.

2. The distribution referred to in the preceding paragraph shall be made in proportion to the number of shares held by each member.

3. Payments shall be made in such manner and in such currency as the Board of Governors shall determine.

CHAPTER VI: WITHDRAWAL AND SUSPENSION OF MEMBERS, TEMPORARY SUSPENSION AND TERMINATION OF OPERATIONS OF THE BANK

ARTICLE 43
WITHDRAWAL

1. Any member may withdraw from the Bank at any time by transmitting a notice in writing to the Bank at its principal office.

2. Withdrawal by a member shall become effective on the date specified in its notice in but no event less than six months after the date that notice has been received by the Bank.

ARTICLE 44
SUSPENSION

1. If it appears to the Board of Directors that a member fails to fulfil any of its obligations to the Bank, that member shall be suspended by that Board unless the Board of Governors at a subsequent meeting, called by the Board of Directors for that purpose, decides otherwise by a decision taken by a majority of the Governors exercising a majority of the total voting power of the members.

2. A member so suspended shall automatically cease to be a member of the Bank one year from the date of suspension unless a decision is taken by the Board of Governors by the same majority to restore the member to good standing.

3. While under suspension, a member shall not be entitled to exercise any rights under this Agreement, except the right of withdrawal, but shall remain subject to all obligations.

ARTICLE 45
SETTLEMENT OF ACCOUNTS

1. After the date on which a State ceases to be a member (hereinafter in this Article called the "termination date"), the member shall remain liable for its direct obligations to the Bank and for its contingent liabilities to the Bank so long as any part of the loans or guarantees contracted before the termination date is outstanding; but it shall cease to incur liabilities with respect to loans and guarantees entered into thereafter by the Bank and to share either in the income or the expenses of the Bank.

2. At the time a State ceases to be a member, the Bank shall arrange for the repurchase of its shares as a part of the settlement of accounts with that State in accordance with the provisions of paragraphs 3 and 4 of this Article. For this purpose, the repurchase price of the shares shall be the value shown by the books of the Bank on the termination date.

3. The payment for shares repurchased by the Bank under this Article shall be governed by the following conditions:

(a) Any amount due to the State concerned for its shares shall be withheld so long as that State, its central Bank or any of its agencies remains liable, as borrower or guarantor, to the Bank and such amount may, at the option of the Bank, be applied on any such liability as it matures. No amount shall be withheld on account of the liability of the State resulting from its subscription for shares in accordance with paragraph 4 of Article 7 of this Agreement. In any event, no amount due to a member for its shares shall be paid until six months after the termination date.

(b) Payments for shares may be made from time to time, upon their surrender by the Government of the State concerned, to the extent by which the amount due as the repurchase price in accordance with paragraph 2 of this Article exceeds the aggregate amount of liabilities on loans and guarantees referred to in sub-paragraph (a) of this paragraph until the former member has received the full repurchase price.

(c) Payments shall be made in the currency of the State receiving payment or, if such currency is not available, in gold or convertible currency.

(d) If losses are sustained by the Bank on any guarantees or loans which were outstanding on the termination date and the amount of such losses exceeds the amount of the reserve provided against losses on that date, the State concerned shall repay, upon demand, the amount by which the repurchase price of its shares would have been reduced, if the losses had been taken into account when the repurchase price was determined. In addition, the former member shall remain liable on any call for unpaid subscriptions in accordance with paragraph 4 of Article 7 of this Agreement, to the extent that it would have been required to respond if the impairment of capital had occurred and the call had been made at the time the repurchase price of its shares was determined.

4. If the Bank terminates its operations pursuant to Article 47 of this Agreement within six months of the termination date, all rights of the State concerned shall be determined in accordance with the provisions of its Articles 47 to 49.

ARTICLE 46
TEMPORARY SUSPENSION OF OPERATIONS

In an emergency, the Board of Directors may suspend temporarily operations in respect of new loans and guarantees pending an opportunity for further consideration and action by the Board of Governors.

ARTICLE 47
TERMINATION OF OPERATIONS

1. The Bank may terminate its operations in respect of new loans and guarantees by a decision of the Board of Governors exercising a majority of the total voting power of the members.

2. After such termination, the Bank shall forthwith cease all activities, except those incident to the orderly realization, conservation and preservation of its assets and settlement of its obligations.

ARTICLE 48
LIABILITY OF MEMBERS AND PAYMENT OF CLAIMS

1. In the event of termination of the operations of the Bank, the liability of all members for uncalled subscriptions to the capital stock of the Bank and in respect of the depreciation of their currencies shall continue until all claims of creditors, including all contingent claims, shall have been discharged.

2. All creditors holding direct claims shall be paid out of the assets of the Bank and then out of payments to the Bank on calls on unpaid subscriptions. Before making any payments to creditors holding direct claims, the Board of Directors shall make such arrangements as are necessary, in its judgment, to ensure a *pro rata* distribution among holders of direct and contingent claims.

ARTICLE 49

1. In the event of termination of operations of the Bank, no distribution shall be made to members on account of their subscriptions to the capital stock of the Bank until:
   (i) All liabilities to creditors have been discharged or provided for; and
   (ii) the Board of Governors has taken a decision to make a distribution. This decision shall be taken by the Board exercising a majority of the total voting power of the members.

2. After a decision to make a distribution has been taken in accordance with the preceding paragraph, the Board of Directors may by a two-thirds majority vote make successive distributions of the assets of the Bank to members until all assets have been distributed. This distribution shall be subject to the prior settlement of all outstanding claims of the Bank against each member.

3. Before any distribution of assets is made, the Board of Directors shall fix the proportionate share of each member according to the ratio of its shareholding to the total outstanding shares of the Bank.

4. The Board of Directors shall value the assets to be distributed at the date of distribution and then proceed to distribute in the following manner:
   (a) There shall be paid to each member in its own obligations or those of its official agencies or legal entities within its territories, to the extent that they are available for distribution, an amount equivalent in value to its proportionate share of the total amount to be distributed.
   (b) Any balance due to a member after payment has been made in accordance with the preceding sub-paragraph, shall be paid in its currency, to the extent that it is held by the Bank, up to an amount equivalent in value to such balance.
   (c) Any balance due to a member after payment has been made in accordance with sub-paragraphs (a) and (b) of this paragraph shall be paid in gold or currency acceptable to that member, to the extent that they are held by the Bank, up to an amount equivalent in value to such balance.
   (d) Any remaining assets held by the Bank after payments have been made to members in accordance with sub-paragraphs (a) to (c) of this paragraph shall be distributed *pro rata* among the members.

5. Any member receiving assets distributed by the Bank in accordance with the preceding paragraph, shall enjoy the same rights with respect to such assets as the Bank enjoyed before their distribution.

CHAPTER VII: STATUS, IMMUNITIES, EXEMPTIONS AND PRIVILEGES

ARTICLE 50
STATUS

To enable it to fulfil its purpose and the functions with which it is entrusted, the Bank shall possess full international personality. To those ends, it may enter into agreements with members, non-member States and other international organizations. To the same ends, the status, immunities, exemptions and privileges set forth in this Chapter shall be accorded to the Bank in the territory of each member.

ARTICLE 51
STATUS IN MEMBER COUNTRIES

In the territory of each member the Bank shall possess full juridical personality and, in particular, full capacity:
  (a) to contract;
  (b) to acquire, and dispose of, immovable and movable property; and
  (c) to institute legal proceedings.

ARTICLE 52
JUDICIAL PROCEEDINGS

1. The Bank shall enjoy immunity from every form of legal process except in cases arising out of the exercise of its borrowing powers when it may be used only in a court of competent jurisdiction in the territory of a member in which the Bank has its principal office, or in the territory of a member or non-member State where it has appointed an agent for the purpose of accepting service or notice of process or has issued guaranteed securities. No actions shall, however, be brought by members or persons acting for or deriving claims from members.

2. The property and assets of the Bank shall, wherever located and by whomsoever held, be immune from all forms of seizure, attachment or execution before the delivery of final judgement against the Bank.

ARTICLE 53
IMMUNITY OF ASSETS AND ARCHIVES

1. Property and assets of the Bank, wherever located and by whomsoever held, shall be immune from search, requisition, confiscation, expropriation or any other form of taking or foreclosure by executive or legislative action.

2. The archives of the Bank and, in general, all documents belonging to it, or held by it, shall be inviolable, wherever located.

ARTICLE 54
FREEDOM OF ASSETS FROM RESTRICTION

To the extent necessary to carry out the purpose and functions of the Bank and subject to the provisions of this Agreement, all property and other assets of the Bank shall be exempt from restrictions, regulations, controls and moratoria of any nature.

ARTICLE 55
PRIVILEGE FOR COMMUNICATIONS

Official communications of the Bank shall be accorded by each member the same treatment that it accords to the official communications of other members.

ARTICLE 56
PERSONAL IMMUNITIES AND PRIVILEGES

1. All governors, directors, alternates, officers and employees of the Bank:
   (i) Shall be immune from legal process with respect to acts performed by them in their official capacity;
   (ii) Where they are not local nationals, shall be accorded the same immunities from immigration restrictions, alien registration requirements and national service obligations, and the same facilities as regards exchange regulations as are accorded by members to the representatives, officials and employees of comparable rank of other members; and
   (iii) Shall be granted the same treatment in respect of travelling facilities as is accorded by members to representatives, officials and employees of comparable rank of other members.

2. Experts and consultants performing missions for the Bank shall be accorded such immunities and privileges as are, in the opinion of the Bank, necessary for the independent exercise of their functions during the period of their mission, including the time spent on journeys in connexion therewith.

ARTICLE 57
EXEMPTION FROM TAXATION

1. The Bank, its property, other assets, income and its operations and transactions, shall be exempt from all taxation and from all customs duties. The Bank shall also be exempt from any obligation relating to the payment, withholding or collection of any tax or duty.

2. No tax shall be levied on or in respect of salaries and emoluments paid by the Bank to directors, alternates, officers and other professional staff of the Bank.

3. No tax of any kind shall be levied on any obligation or security issued by the Bank, including any dividend or interest thereon, by whomsoever held:

(i) which discriminates against such obligation or security solely because it is issued by the Bank; or

(ii) if the sole jurisdictional basis for such taxation is the place or currency in which it is issued, made payable or paid, or the location of any office or place of business maintained by the Bank.

4. No tax of any kind shall be levied on any obligation or security guaranteed by the Bank, including any dividend or interest thereon, by whomsoever held:

(i) which discriminates against such obligation or security solely because it is guaranteed by the Bank; or

(ii) if the sole jurisdictional basis for such taxation is the location of any office or place of business maintained by the Bank.

ARTICLE 58
NOTIFICATION OF IMPLEMENTATION

Each member shall promptly inform the Bank of the specific action which it has taken to make effective in its territory the provisions of this Chapter.

ARTICLE 59
APPLICATION OF IMMUNITIES, EXEMPTIONS AND PRIVILEGES

The immunities, exemptions and privileges provided in this Chapter are granted in the interests of the Bank. The Board of Directors may waive, to such extent and upon such conditions as it may determine, the immunities and exemptions provided in Articles 52, 54, 56, and 57 of this Agreement in cases where its action would in its opinion, further the interests of the Bank. The President shall have the duty to waive the immunity of any official in cases where, in his opinion, the immunity would impede the course of justice and can be waived without prejudice to the interests of the Bank.

CHAPTER VIII: AMENDMENTS, INTERPRETATION, ARBITRATION

ARTICLE 60
AMENDMENTS

1. Any proposal to introduce modifications to this Agreement, whether emanating from a member, a governor or the Board of Directors, shall be communicated to the Chairman of the Board of Governors, who shall bring the proposal before that Board. If the proposed amendment is approved by the Board, the Bank shall, by circular letter or telegram, ask the members whether they accept the proposed amendment. When two-thirds of the members having three-quarters of the total voting power of the members, have accepted the proposed amendment, the Bank shall certify the fact by formal communication addressed to the members.

2. Notwithstanding paragraph 1 of this Article, acceptance by all the members is required for any amendment modifying:

(i) the right secured by paragraph 2 of Article 6 of this Agreement;
(ii) the limitation on liability provided in paragraph 5 of that Article; and
(iii) the right to withdraw from the Bank provided in Article 43 of this Agreement.

3. Amendments shall enter into force for all members three months after the date of the formal communication provided for in paragraph 1 of this Article unless the Board of Governors specifies a different period.

4. Notwithstanding the provisions of paragraph 1 of this Article, three years at the latest after the entry into force of this Agreement and in the light of the experience of the Bank, the rule according to which each member should have one vote shall be examined by the Board of Governors or at a meeting of Heads of State of the member countries in accordance with the conditions that applied to the adoption of this Agreement.

ARTICLE 61
INTERPRETATION

1. The English and French texts of this Agreement shall be regarded as equally authentic.

2. Any question of interpretation of the provisions of this Agreement arising between any member and the Bank or between any members of the Bank shall be submitted to the Board of Directors for decision. If there is no director of its nationality on that Board, a member particularly affected by the question under consideration shall be entitled to direct representation in such cases. Such right of representation shall be regulated by the Board of Governors.

3. In any case where the Board of Directors has given a decision under paragraph 2 of this Article, any member may require that the question be referred to the Board of Governors, whose decision shall be sought — under a procedure to be established in accordance with paragraph 3 of Article 31 of this Agreement — within three months. That decision shall be final.

ARTICLE 62
ARBITRATION

In the case of a dispute between the Bank and the Government of a State which has ceased to be a member, or between the Bank and any member upon the termination of the operations of the Bank, such dispute shall be submitted to arbitration by a tribunal of three arbitrators. One of the arbitrators shall be appointed by the Bank, another by the Government of the State concerned, and the third arbitrator, unless the parties otherwise agree, shall be appointed by such other authority as may have been prescribed by regulations adopted by the Board of Governors. The third arbitrator shall have full power to settle all questions of procedure in any case where the parties are in disagreement with respect thereto.

CHAPTER IX: FINAL PROVISIONS

ARTICLE 63
SIGNATURE AND DEPOSIT

1. This Agreement, deposited with the Secretary-General of the United Nations (hereinafter called the "Depository"), shall remain open until 31 December 1963 for signature by the Governments of States whose names are set forth in annex A to this Agreement.

2. The Depository shall communicate certified copies of this Agreement to all the Signatories.

ARTICLE 64
RATIFICATION, ACCEPTANCE, ACCESSION AND
ACQUISITION OF MEMBERSHIP

1. (a) This Agreement shall be subject to ratification or acceptance by the Signatories. Instruments of ratification or acceptance shall be deposited by the signatory Governments with the Depository before 1 July 1965. The Depository shall notify each deposit and the date thereof to the other Signatories.

   (b) A State whose instrument of ratification or acceptance is deposited before the date on which this Agreement enters into force, shall become a member of the Bank on that date. Any other Signatory which complies with the provisions of the preceding paragraph, shall become a member on the date on which its instrument of ratification or acceptance is deposited.

2. States which do not acquire membership of the Bank in accordance with the provisions of paragraph 1 of this Article, may become members — after the Agreement has entered into force — by accession thereto on such terms as the Board of Governors shall determine. The Government of any such State shall deposit, on or before a date appointed by that Board, an instrument of accession with the Depository, who shall notify such deposit and the date thereof to the Bank and to the Parties to this Agreement. Upon the deposit, the State shall become member of the Bank on the appointed date.

ARTICLE 65
ENTRY INTO FORCE

This Agreement shall enter into force upon the deposit of instruments of ratification or acceptance by twelve signatory Governments whose initial subscriptions, as set forth in annex A to this Agreement, in aggregate comprise not less than sixty-five per cent of the authorized capital stock[1] of the Bank;

---

[1] The words "authorized capital stock of the Bank" shall be understood to refer to such authorized capital stock of the Bank as is equivalent to 211.2 million units of account and as corresponds to the aggregate initial number of shares to be subscribed by the States that

provided always that 1 January 1964 shall be the earliest date on which this Agreement may enter into force in accordance with the provisions of this Article.

ARTICLE 66
COMMENCEMENT OF OPERATIONS

1. As soon as this Agreement enters into force, each member shall appoint a Governor, and the Trustee appointed for this purpose and for the purpose indicated in paragraph 5 of Article 7 of this Agreement shall call the first meeting of the Board of Governors.

2. At its first meeting, the Board of Governors:
   (a) shall elect nine directors of the Bank in accordance with paragraph 1 of Article 33 of this Agreement; and
   (b) shall make arrangements for the determination of the date on which the Bank shall commence its operations.

3. The Bank shall notify its members of the date of the commencement of its operations.

Done in Khartoum, this fourth day of August, Nineteen Hundred and Sixty-Three, in a single copy in the English and French languages.

ANNEX A: INITIAL SUBSCRIPTIONS TO THE AUTHORIZED CAPITAL STOCK OF THE BANK*

Member	Paid-up Shares	Callable Shares	Total Subscription (in millions of units of account)
1. Algeria	1,225	1,225	24.50
2. Burundi	60	60	1.20
3. Cameroun	200	200	4.00
4. Central African Republic	50	50	1.00
5. Chad	80	80	1.60
6. Congo (Brazzaville)	75	75	1.50
7. Congo (Leopoldville)	650	650	13.00
8. Dahomey	70	70	1.40
9. Ethiopia	515	515	10.30
10. Gabon	65	65	1.30
11. Ghana	640	640	12.80
12. Guinea	125	125	2.50
13. Ivory Coast	300	300	6.00
14. Kenya	300	300	6.00
15. Liberia	130	130	2.60

may acquire its membership in accordance with paragraph 1 of Article 64 of the Agreement; see the Memorandum by the Executive Secretary of the United Nations Economic Commission for Africa on the interpretation of Article 65 of the Agreement Establishing the African Development Bank, attached to the Final Act of the Conference.

Member	Paid-up Shares	Callable Shares	Total Subscription (in millions of units of account)
16. Libya	95	95	1.90
17. Madagascar	260	260	5.20
18. Mali	115	115	2.30
19. Mauritania	55	55	1.10
20. Morocco	755	755	15.10
21. Niger	80	80	1.60
22. Nigeria	1,205	1,205	24.10
23. Rwanda	60	60	1.20
24. Senegal	275	275	5.50
25. Sierra Leone	105	105	2.10
26. Somalia	110	110	2.20
27. Sudan	505	505	10.10
28. Tanganyika	265	265	5.30
29. Togo	50	50	1.00
30. Tunisia	345	345	6.90
31. Uganda	230	230	4.60
32. U.A.R. (Egypt)	1,500	1,500	30.00
33. Upper Volta	65	65	1.30

* As approved and adopted by the Conference of Finance Ministers at Khartoum. Chad, Gabon, and Madagascar did not adhere to the Agreement. Three signatory governments — Burundi, the Central African Republic, and Libya — had not deposited the instruments of accession as of June 30, 1965, the time limit for acquisition of membership. [Editor's note.]

ANNEX B: ELECTION OF DIRECTORS

1. At the election of directors each governor shall cast all votes of the member he represents for a single person.

2. The nine persons receiving the highest number of votes shall be directors, except that no person who receives less than ten per cent of the total voting power of the members shall be considered as elected.

3. If nine persons are not elected at the first ballot, a second ballot shall be held in which the person who received the lowest number of votes in the preceding ballot shall be ineligible and in which votes shall be cast only by:

    (a) governors who voted in the preceding ballot for a person who is not elected; and

    (b) governors whose votes for a person who is elected are deemed, in accordance with paragraph 4 of this annex, to have raised the votes cast for that person above twelve per cent of the total voting power of the members.

4. (a) In determining whether the votes cast by a governor shall be deemed to have raised the total number of votes for any person above twelve per cent, the said twelve per cent shall be deemed to include, first, the votes of the governor casting the highest number of votes for

that person, and then, in diminishing order, the votes of each governor casting the next highest number until twelve per cent is attained.

(b) Any governor part of whose votes must be counted in order to raise the votes cast for any person above ten per cent shall be considered as casting all his votes for that person even if the total number of votes cast for that person thereby exceeds twelve per cent.

5. If, after the second ballot, nine persons are not elected, further ballots shall be held in conformity with the principle laid down in this annex, provided that after eight persons are elected, the ninth may be elected — notwithstanding the provisions of paragraph 2 of this annex — by a simple majority of the remaining votes. All such remaining votes shall be deemed to have counted towards the election of the ninth director.

CHAPTER FIFTEEN

Asian Development Bank

Regional economic cooperation in the form of subregional common markets and free trade arrangements has never gotten off the ground in Asia, mainly because of highly unsettled political conditions. The Asian Development Bank that was put into operation in December 1966 seems, however, to offer greater hope for the future, especially if the Vietnam conflict is solved.

Proposals for the establishment of the Asian development agency first emerged informally within the United Nations Economic Commission for Asia and the Far East (ECAFE) in the early 1960s in response to the creation of the Inter-American Development Bank. An ECAFE paper prepared for the first session of the Conference of Asian Economic Planners, held in New Delhi in 1961, offered arguments that an Asian development bank with a more intimate acquaintance with the economic problems and opportunities of the region would make possible a more efficient use of funds by the countries in the region and that such an agency would make a substantial contribution to the coordinated development of the Asian economies, assuming that the establishment of the Bank would at the same time bring more rational and multilateral allocations of foreign capital assistance to the countries of South and Southeast Asia.

The idea of a regional bank was discussed at the Preparatory Meeting for a Special Conference on Asian Economic Cooperation (Bangkok, October 1963), which considered a report, prepared by a working group of experts, on measures for economic cooperation in the ECAFE region. The expert group suggested that there was a great need in the area for an agency that would pool part of the savings available in different countries and direct them from national to more essential regional uses. Such a body, it was stressed, might augment local savings with capital from outside the region for financing the development of industrial and general projects requiring enlarged markets to function effectively and fitting into patterns of coordinated industrial development. The group suggested that, in addition to financing industrial and mineral development projects of regional interest, the proposed regional financial agency might also help finance intraregional export trade. It was furthermore proposed that one half of the contributions of Asian member countries be made in foreign exchange and the other half in local currencies and that the Bank undertake to finance, as far as possible, only the external costs of development projects. It was assumed that the Bank's capital would be contributed by the countries of the region, but the expert group expressed the hope that this capital perhaps could be augmented by loans from outside the region.

At the Ministerial Conference on Asian Economic Cooperation in Manila in December 1963, the twenty-one participating countries of Asia and Oceania agreed, *inter alia,* to proceed with the setting up of an ad hoc committee that would recommend the institutional arrangements necessary to establish an Asian Development Bank. Consultations on a possible draft of the charter of the Bank were held in Bangkok under ECAFE auspices in June 1965 — shortly after the United States reversed its negative attitude toward the proposed Asian agency. On that occasion, and in view of the United States offer to contribute $200 million toward the initial capitalization of the Bank and to give additional resources for a special fund for development loans on concessional terms, it was agreed in principle that the initial capital of the agency would be $1,000 million, with 60 per cent subscribed by Asian countries and the rest by the industrial powers. In the latter part of 1965 and early 1966 the charter of the Bank was drafted by a preparatory committee headed by Cornelio Balmaceda of the Philippines. It was signed by thirty-one (nineteen Asian and twelve non-Asian) countries during the spring 1966 session of ECAFE in New Delhi. Asian countries offered to subscribe 65 per cent of the previously agreed initial capital, and the advanced non-Asian powers pledged to provide the rest. The largest Asian contribution — equal to that of the United States — came from Japan. The proposed subscription quotas of other Asian countries range from less than $100,000 for Western Samoa to $93 million for India, and for other non-Asian countries from $5 to $30 million.

The inaugural meeting of the Board of Governors of the Asian Development Bank was held in Tokyo at the end of November 1966. An adviser to Japan's Finance Ministry and a former executive director of the

International Monetary Fund and the International Bank for Reconstruction and Development, Takeshi Watanabe, was elected the Bank's first president. The ten members of the Board of Directors represent, respectively, Australia, India, Indonesia, Japan, Malaysia, the Philippines, South Korea, Canada, the United States, and the Federal Republic of Germany. After having admitted Switzerland as the Bank's thirty-second member, the Board of Governors adopted a resolution inviting Burma, France, and the Soviet Union to join. Another resolution raised the authorized capital to $1,100 million — in view of the increased contributions pledged by a number of members.

The headquarters of the Asian Development Bank are in Manila, Philippines. The Bank started its activities on December 19, 1966 with initial cash resources of close to $100 million in paid-in subscriptions, of which some $65 million is available in convertible currencies. Another $100 million was to be paid in by member countries in 1967.

Bibliographic References

Cullison, A. E. "Asian Bank Inaugural: Milestone for Far East," and "Asian Bank's Success Seen in Its Policy Role," *The Journal of Commerce* (New York), November 9 and 10, 1966.

Economic Commission for Asia and the Far East (ECAFE). *Regional Economic Co-operation in Asia and the Far East* (*Report of the Ministerial Conference on Asian Economic Co-operation, Manila, Philippines, 3 to 6 December 1963*). (United Nations Publication, Sales No. 64.II.F.14.) New York, 1964.

———. "Regional Trade Co-operation: An Exploratory Study with Special Reference to Asia and the Far East," *Economic Bulletin for Asia and the Far East* (Bangkok), Vol. XII, No. 1 (June 1961).

———. "The Scope for Regional Economic Co-operation in Asia and the Far East," *Economic Bulletin for Asia and the Far East*, Vol. XII, No. 3 (December 1961).

———. Working Group Report, Bangkok, September 9, 1963, for Preparatory Meeting for Special Conference on Asian Economic Co-operation, Bangkok, Thailand, October 21–26, 1963, "Measures for Economic Co-operation in the ECAFE Region." Reproduced in ECAFE, *Regional Economic Co-operation*.

Geylin, Philip. "Asian Marshall Plan," *The Wall Street Journal* (New York), June 30, 1965.

Kitamura, Hiroshi. "Economic Theory and Regional Economic Integration in Asia," *Pakistan Development Review* (Karachi), Vol. 2 (1962), No. 4.

Wightman, David. *Toward Economic Cooperation in Asia* (*The United Nations Economic Commission for Asia and the Far East*). New Haven, Conn.: Published for the Carnegie Endowment for International Peace by the Yale University Press, 1963.

AGREEMENT ESTABLISHING THE ASIAN
DEVELOPMENT BANK*

Considering the importance of closer economic co-operation as a means for achieving the most efficient utilization of resources and for accelerating the economic development of Asia and the Far East;

Realizing the significance of making additional development financing available for the region by mobilizing such funds and other resources both from within and outside the region, and by seeking to create and foster conditions conducive to increased domestic savings and greater flow of development funds into the region;

Recognizing the desirability of promoting the harmonious growth of the economies of the region and the expansion of external trade of member countries;

Convinced that the establishment of a financial institution that is Asian in its basic character would serve these ends;

Have agreed to establish hereby the Asian Development Bank (hereinafter called the "Bank") which shall operate in accordance with the following *Articles of Agreement.*

CHAPTER I: PURPOSE, FUNCTIONS AND MEMBERSHIP

ARTICLE 1
PURPOSE

The purpose of the Bank shall be to foster economic growth and co-operation in the region of Asia and the Far East (hereinafter referred to as the "region") and to contribute to the acceleration of the process of economic

---

* Signed in Manila, the Philippines, on October 4, 1965 by Afghanistan, Australia, Cambodia, Canada, Ceylon, China (Taiwan), the Federal Republic of Germany, India, Iran, Japan, Laos, Malaysia, Nepal, Netherlands, New Zealand, Pakistan, the Philippines, the Republic of Korea, Thailand, the United Kingdom, and Western Samoa, and (also in Manila) by Belgium, Denmark, Italy, the Republic of Viet-Nam, Singapore, Finland, Norway, Austria, and Sweden between January 28 and 31, 1966. This is the official text as released by the United Nations in New York in February 1966. [Editor's note.]

development of the developing member countries in the region, collectively and individually. Wherever used in this Agreement, the terms "region of Asia and the Far East" and "region" shall comprise the territories of Asia and the Far East included in the Terms of Reference of the United Nations Economic Commission for Asia and the Far East.

ARTICLE 2
FUNCTIONS

To fulfil its purpose, the Bank shall have the following functions:
  (i) to promote investment in the region of public and private capital for development purposes;
 (ii) to utilize the resources at its disposal for financing development of the developing member countries in the region, giving priority to those regional, sub-regional as well as national projects and programmes which will contribute most effectively to the harmonious economic growth of the region as a whole, and having special regard to the needs of the smaller or less developed member countries in the region;
(iii) to meet requests from members in the region to assist them in the co-ordination of their development policies and plans with a view to achieving better utilization of their resources, making their economies more complementary, and promoting the orderly expansion of their foreign trade, in particular, intra-regional trade;
 (iv) to provide technical assistance for the preparation, financing and execution of development projects and programmes, including the formulation of specific project proposals;
  (v) to co-operate, in such manner as the Bank may deem appropriate, within the terms of this Agreement, with the United Nations, its organs and subsidiary bodies including, in particular, the Economic Commission for Asia and the Far East, and with public international organizations and other international institutions, as well as national entities whether public or private, which are concerned with the investment of development funds in the region, and to interest such institutions and entities in new opportunities for investment and assistance; and
 (vi) to undertake such other activities and provide such other services as may advance its purpose.

ARTICLE 3
MEMBERSHIP

1. Membership in the Bank shall be open to: (i) members and associate members of the United Nations Economic Commission for Asia and the Far East; and (ii) other regional countries and non-regional developed countries which are members of the United Nations or of any of its specialized agencies.

2. Countries eligible for membership under paragraph 1 of this Article which do not become members in accordance with Article 64 of this Agree-

ment may be admitted, under such terms and conditions as the Bank may determine, to membership in the Bank upon the affirmative vote of two-thirds of the total number of Governors, representing not less than three-fourths of the total voting power of the members.

3. In the case of associate members of the United Nations Economic Commission for Asia and the Far East which are not responsible for the conduct of their international relations, application for membership in the Bank shall be presented by the member of the Bank responsible for the international relations of the applicant and accompanied by an undertaking by such member that, until the applicant itself assumes such responsibility, the member shall be responsible for all obligations that may be incurred by the applicant by reason of admission to membership in the Bank and enjoyment of the benefits of such membership. "Country" as used in this Agreement shall include a territory which is an associate member of the United Nations Economic Commission for Asia and the Far East.

CHAPTER II: CAPITAL

ARTICLE 4
AUTHORIZED CAPITAL

1. The authorized capital stock of the Bank shall be one billion dollars ($1,000,000,000) in terms of United States dollars of the weight and fineness in effect on 31 January 1966. The dollar wherever referred to in this Agreement shall be understood as being a United States dollar of the above value. The authorized capital stock shall be divided into one hundred thousand (100,000) shares having a par value of ten thousand dollars ($10,000) each, which shall be available for subscription only by members in accordance with the provisions of Article 5 of this Agreement.

2. The original authorized capital stock shall be divided into paid-in shares and callable shares. Shares having an aggregate par value of five hundred million dollars ($500,000,000) shall be paid-in shares, and shares having an aggregate par value of five hundred million dollars ($500,000,000) shall be callable shares.

3. The authorized capital stock of the Bank may be increased by the Board of Governors, at such time and under such terms and conditions as it may deem advisable, by a vote of two-thirds of the total number of Governors, representing not less than three-fourths of the total voting power of the members.

ARTICLE 5
SUBSCRIPTION OF SHARES

1. Each member shall subscribe to shares of the capital stock of the Bank. Each subscription to the original authorized capital stock shall be for paid-in shares and callable shares in equal parts. The initial number of shares to be

subscribed by countries which become members in accordance with Article 64 of this Agreement shall be that set forth in Annex A hereof. The initial number of shares to be subscribed by countries which are admitted to membership in accordance with paragraph 2 of Article 3 of this Agreement shall be determined by the Board of Governors; provided, however, that no such subscription shall be authorized which would have the effect of reducing the percentage of capital stock held by regional members below sixty (60) per cent of the total subscribed capital stock.

2. The Board of Governors shall at intervals of not less than five (5) years review the capital stock of the Bank. In case of an increase in the authorized capital stock, each member shall have a reasonable opportunity to subscribe, under such terms and conditions as the Board of Governors shall determine, to a proportion of the increase of stock equivalent to the proportion which its stock theretofore subscribed bears to the total subscribed capital stock immediately prior to such increase; provided, however, that the foregoing provision shall not apply in respect of any increase or portion of an increase in the authorized capital stock intended solely to give effect to determinations of the Board of Governors under paragraphs 1 and 3 of this Article. No member shall be obligated to subscribe to any part of an increase of capital stock.

3. The Board of Governors may, at the request of a member, increase the subscription of such member on such terms and conditions as the Board may determine; provided, however, that no such increase in the subscription of any member shall be authorized which would have the effect of reducing the percentage of capital stock held by regional members below sixty (60) per cent of the total subscribed capital stock. The Board of Governors shall pay special regard to the request of any regional member having less than six (6) per cent of the subscribed capital stock to increase its proportionate share thereof.

4. Shares of stock initially subscribed by members shall be issued at par. Other shares shall be issued at par unless the Board of Governors by a vote of a majority of the total number of Governors, representing a majority of the total voting power of the members, decides in special circumstances to issue them on other terms.

5. Shares of stock shall not be pledged or encumbered in any manner whatsoever, and they shall not be transferable except to the Bank in accordance with Chapter VII of this Agreement.

6. The liability of the members on shares shall be limited to the unpaid portion of their issue price.

7. No member shall be liable, by reason of its membership, for obligations of the Bank.

ARTICLE 6
PAYMENT OF SUBSCRIPTIONS

1. Payment of the amount initially subscribed by each Signatory to this Agreement which becomes a member in accordance with Article 64 to the paid-in capital stock of the Bank shall be made in five (5) instalments, of

twenty (20) per cent each of such amount. The first instalment shall be paid by each member within thirty (30) days after entry into force of this Agreement, or on or before the date of deposit on its behalf of its instrument of ratification or acceptance in accordance with paragraph 1 of Article 64, whichever is later. The second instalment shall become due one (1) year from the entry into force of this Agreement. The remaining three instalments shall each become due successively one (1) year from the date on which the preceding instalment becomes due.

2. Of each instalment for the payment of initial subscriptions to the original paid-in capital stock:

(a) fifty (50) per cent shall be paid in gold or convertible currency; and

(b) fifty (50) per cent in the currency of the member.

3. The Bank shall accept from any member promissory notes or other obligations issued by the Government of the member, or by the depository designated by such member, in lieu of the amount to be paid in the currency of the member pursuant to paragraph 2 (b) of this Article, provided such currency is not required by the Bank for the conduct of its operations. Such notes or obligations shall be non-negotiable, non-interest-bearing, and payable to the Bank at par value upon demand. Subject to the provisions of paragraph 2 (ii) of Article 24, demands upon such notes or obligations payable in convertible currencies shall, over reasonable periods of time, be uniform in percentage on all such notes or obligations.

4. Each payment of a member in its own currency under paragraph 2 (b) of this Article shall be in such amount as the Bank, after such consultation with the International Monetary Fund as the Bank may consider necessary and utilizing the par value established with the International Monetary Fund, if any, determines to be equivalent to the full value in terms of dollars of the portion of the subscription being paid. The initial payment shall be in such amount as the member considers appropriate hereunder but shall be subject to such adjustment, to be effected within ninety (90) days of the date on which such payment was due, as the Bank shall determine to be necessary to constitute the full dollar equivalent of such payment.

5. Payment of the amount subscribed to the callable capital stock of the Bank shall be subject to call only as and when required by the Bank to meet its obligations incurred under sub-paragraphs (ii) and (iv) of Article 11 on borrowings of funds for inclusion in its ordinary capital resources or on guarantees chargeable to such resources.

6. In the event of the call referred to in paragraph 5 of this Article, payment may be made at the option of the member in gold, convertible currency or in the currency required to discharge the obligations of the Bank for the purpose of which the call is made. Calls on unpaid subscriptions shall be uniform in percentage on all callable shares.

7. The Bank shall determine the place for any payment under this Article, provided that, until the inaugural meeting of its Board of Governors, the payment of the first instalment referred to in paragraph 1 of this Article shall be made to the Secretary-General of the United Nations, as Trustee for the Bank.

ARTICLE 7
ORDINARY CAPITAL RESOURCES

As used in this Agreement, the term "ordinary capital resources" of the Bank shall include the following:

  (i) authorized capital stock of the Bank, including both paid-in and callable shares, subscribed pursuant to Article 5 of this Agreement, except such part thereof as may be set aside into one or more Special Funds in accordance with paragraph 1 (i) of Article 19 of this Agreement;

 (ii) funds raised by borrowings of the Bank by virtue of powers conferred by sub-paragraph (i) of Article 21 of this Agreement, to which the commitment to calls provided for in paragraph 5 of Article 6 of this Agreement is applicable;

(iii) funds received in repayment of loans or guarantees made with the resources indicated in (i) and (ii) of this Article;

 (iv) income derived from loans made from the aforementioned funds or from guarantees to which the commitment to calls set forth in paragraph 5 of Article 6 of this Agreement is applicable; and

  (v) any other funds or income received by the Bank which do not form part of its Special Funds resources referred to in Article 20 of this Agreement.

CHAPTER III: OPERATIONS

ARTICLE 8
USE OF RESOURCES

The resources and facilities of the Bank shall be used exclusively to implement the purpose and functions set forth respectively in Articles 1 and 2 of this Agreement.

ARTICLE 9
ORDINARY AND SPECIAL OPERATIONS

1. The operations of the Bank shall consist of ordinary operations and special operations.

2. Ordinary operations shall be those financed from the ordinary capital resources of the Bank.

3. Special operations shall be those financed from the Special Funds resources referred to in Article 20 of this Agreement.

ARTICLE 10
SEPARATION OF OPERATIONS

1. The ordinary capital resources and the Special Funds resources of the Bank shall at all times and in all respects be held, used, committed, invested

or otherwise disposed of entirely separate from each other. The financial statements of the Bank shall show the ordinary operations and special operations separately.

2. The ordinary capital resources of the Bank shall under no circumstances be charged with, or used to discharge, losses or liabilities arising out of special operations or other activities for which Special Funds resources were originally used or committed.

3. Expenses appertaining directly to ordinary operations shall be charged to the ordinary capital resources of the Bank. Expenses appertaining directly to special operations shall be charged to the Special Funds resources. Any other expenses shall be charged as the Bank shall determine.

ARTICLE 11
RECIPIENTS AND METHODS OF OPERATION

Subject to the conditions stipulated in this Agreement, the Bank may provide or facilitate financing to any member, or any agency, instrumentality or political subdivision thereof, or any entity or enterprise operating in the territory of a member, as well as to international or regional agencies or entities concerned with economic development of the region. The Bank may carry out its operations in any of the following ways:

(i) by making or participating in direct loans with its unimpaired paid-in capital and, except as provided in Article 17 of this Agreement, with its reserves and undistributed surplus; or with the unimpaired Special Funds resources;

(ii) by making or participating in direct loans with funds raised by the Bank in capital markets or borrowed or otherwise acquired by the Bank for inclusion in its ordinary capital resources;

(iii) by investment of funds referred to in (i) and (ii) of this Article in the equity capital of an institution or enterprise, provided no such investment shall be made until after the Board of Governors, by a vote of a majority of the total number of Governors, representing a majority of the total voting power of the members, shall have determined that the Bank is in a position to commence such type of operations; or

(iv) by guaranteeing, whether as primary or secondary obligor, in whole or in part, loans for economic development participated in by the Bank.

ARTICLE 12
LIMITATIONS ON ORDINARY OPERATIONS

1. The total amount outstanding of loans, equity investments and guarantees made by the Bank in its ordinary operations shall not at any time exceed the total amount of its unimpaired subscribed capital, reserves and surplus included in its ordinary capital resources, exclusive of the special reserve provided for by Article 17 of this Agreement and other reserves not available for ordinary operations.

2. In the case of loans made with funds borrowed by the Bank to which

the commitment to calls provided for by paragraph 5 of Article 6 of this Agreement is applicable, the total amount of principal outstanding and payable to the Bank in a specific currency shall not at any time exceed the total amount of the principal of outstanding borrowings by the Bank that are payable in the same currency.

3. In the case of funds invested in equity capital out of the ordinary capital resources of the Bank, the total amount invested shall not exceed ten (10) per cent of the aggregate amount of the unimpaired paid-in capital stock of the Bank actually paid up at any given time together with the reserves and surplus included in its ordinary capital resources, exclusive of the special reserve provided for in Article 17 of this Agreement.

4. The amount of any equity investment shall not exceed such percentage of the equity capital of the entity or enterprise concerned as the Board of Directors shall in each specific case determine to be appropriate. The Bank shall not seek to obtain by such an investment a controlling interest in the entity or enterprise concerned, except where necessary to safeguard the investment of the Bank.

ARTICLE 13
PROVISION OF CURRENCIES FOR DIRECT LOANS

In making direct loans or participating in them, the Bank may provide financing in any of the following ways:

(i) by furnishing the borrower with currencies other than the currency of the member in whose territory the project concerned is to be carried out (the latter currency hereinafter to be called "local currency"), which are necessary to meet the foreign exchange costs of such project; or

(ii) by providing financing to meet local expenditures on the project concerned, where it can do so by supplying local currency without selling any of its holdings in gold or convertible currencies. In special cases when, in the opinion of the Bank, the project causes or is likely to cause undue loss or strain on the balance of payments of the member in whose territory the project is to be carried out, the financing granted by the Bank to meet local expenditures may be provided in currencies other than that of such member; in such cases, the amount of the financing granted by the Bank for this purpose shall not exceed a reasonable portion of the total local expenditure incurred by the borrower.

ARTICLE 14
OPERATING PRINCIPLES

The operations of the Bank shall be conducted in accordance with the following principles:

(i) The operations of the Bank shall provide principally for the financing of specific projects, including those forming part of a national, sub-regional or regional development programme. They may, however, include loans to, or guarantees of loans made to, national development banks or other suitable entities, in order that the latter may finance specific development projects whose individual financing requirements are not, in the opinion of the Bank, large enough to warrant the direct supervision of the Bank;

(ii) In selecting suitable projects, the Bank shall always be guided by the provisions of paragraph (ii) of Article 2 of this Agreement;

(iii) The Bank shall not finance any undertaking in the territory of a member if that member objects to such financing;

(iv) Before a loan is granted, the applicant shall have submitted an adequate loan proposal and the President of the Bank shall have presented to the Board of Directors a written report regarding the proposal, together with his recommendations, on the basis of a staff study;

(v) In considering an application for a loan or guarantee, the Bank shall pay due regard to the ability of the borrower to obtain financing or facilities elsewhere on terms and conditions that the Bank considers reasonable for the recipient, taking into account all pertinent factors;

(vi) In making or guaranteeing a loan, the Bank shall pay due regard to the prospects that the borrower and its guarantor, if any, will be in a position to meet their obligations under the loan contract;

(vii) In making or guaranteeing a loan, the rate of interest, other charges and the schedule for repayment of principal shall be such as are, in the opinion of the Bank, appropriate for the loan concerned;

(viii) In guaranteeing a loan made by other investors, or in underwriting the sale of securities, the Bank shall receive suitable compensation for its risk;

(ix) The proceeds of any loan, investment or other financing undertaken in the ordinary operations of the Bank or with Special Funds established by the Bank pursuant to paragraph 1 (i) of Article 19, shall be used only for procurement in member countries of goods and services produced in member countries, except in any case in which the Board of Directors, by a vote of the Directors representing not less than two-thirds of the total voting power of the members, determines to permit procurement in a non-member country or of goods and services produced in a non-member country in special circumstances making such procurement appropriate, as in the case of a non-member country in which a significant amount of financing has been provided to the Bank;

(x) In the case of a direct loan made by the Bank, the borrower shall be permitted by the Bank to draw its funds only to meet expenditures in connexion with the project as they are actually incurred;

(xi) The Bank shall take the necessary measures to ensure that the proceeds of any loan made, guaranteed or participated in by the Bank

are used only for the purposes for which the loan was granted and
with due attention to considerations of economy and efficiency;

(xii) The Bank shall pay due regard to the desirability of avoiding a dis-
proportionate amount of its resources being used for the benefit of
any member;

(xiii) The Bank shall seek to maintain reasonable diversification in its investments in equity capital; it shall not assume responsibility for
managing any entity or enterprise in which it has an investment,
except where necessary to safeguard its investments; and

(xiv) The Bank shall be guided by sound banking principles in its operations.

ARTICLE 15
TERMS AND CONDITIONS FOR DIRECT LOANS AND GUARANTEES

1. In the case of direct loans made or participated in or loans guaranteed by
the Bank, the contract shall establish, in conformity with the operating principles set forth in Article 14 of this Agreement and subject to the other provisions
of this Agreement, the terms and conditions for the loan or the guarantee
concerned, including those relating to payment of principal, interest and other
charges, maturities, and dates of payment in respect of the loan, or the fees
and other charges in respect of the guarantee, respectively. In particular, the
contract shall provide that, subject to paragraph 3 of this Article, all payments
to the Bank under the contract shall be made in the currency loaned, unless,
in the case of a direct loan made or a loan guaranteed as part of special
operations with funds provided under paragraph 1 (ii) of Article 19, the
rules and regulations of the Bank provide otherwise. Guarantees by the Bank
shall also provide that the Bank may terminate its liability with respect to
interest if, upon default by the borrower and the guarantor, if any, the
Bank offers to purchase, at par and interest accrued to a date designated in
the offer, the bonds or other obligations guaranteed.

2. Where the recipient of loans or guarantees of loans is not itself a member,
the Bank may, when it deems it advisable, require that the member in whose
territory the project concerned is to be carried out, or a public agency or any
instrumentality of that member acceptable to the Bank, guarantee the repayment of the principal and the payment of interest and other charges on the
loan in accordance with the terms thereof.

3. The loan or guarantee contract shall expressly state the currency in which
all payments to the Bank thereunder shall be made. At the option of the
borrower, however, such payments may always be made in gold or convertible
currency.

ARTICLE 16
COMMISSION AND FEES

1. The Bank shall charge, in addition to interest, a commission on direct
loans made or participated in as part of its ordinary operations. This com-

mission, payable periodically, shall be computed on the amount outstanding on each loan or participation and shall be at the rate of not less than one (1) per cent per annum, unless the Bank, after the first five (5) years of its operations, decides to reduce this minimum rate by a two-thirds majority of its members, representing not less than three-fourths of the total voting power of the members.

2. In guaranteeing a loan as part of its ordinary operations, the Bank shall charge a guarantee fee, at a rate determined by the Board of Directors, payable periodically on the amount of the loan outstanding.

3. Other charges of the Bank in its ordinary operations and any commission, fees or other charges in its special operations shall be determined by the Board of Directors.

ARTICLE 17
SPECIAL RESERVE

The amount of commissions and guarantee fees received by the Bank pursuant to Article 16 of this Agreement shall be set aside as a special reserve which shall be kept for meeting liabilities of the Bank in accordance with Article 18 of this Agreement. The special reserve shall be held in such liquid form as the Board of Directors may decide.

ARTICLE 18
METHODS OF MEETING LIABILITIES OF THE BANK

1. In cases of default on loans made, participated in or guaranteed by the Bank in its ordinary operations, the Bank shall take such action as it deems appropriate with respect to modifying the terms of the loan, other than the currency of repayment.

2. The payments in discharge of the Bank's liabilities on borrowings or guarantees under sub-paragraphs (ii) and (iv) of Article 11 chargeable to the ordinary capital resources shall be charged:

   (i) First, against the special reserve provided for in Article 17;
   (ii) Then, to the extent necessary and at the discretion of the Bank, against the other reserves, surplus and capital available to the Bank.

3. Whenever necessary to meet contractual payments of interest, other charges or amortization on borrowings of the Bank in its ordinary operations, or to meet its liabilities with respect to similar payments in respect of loans guaranteed by it, chargeable to its ordinary capital resources, the Bank may call an appropriate amount of the uncalled subscribed callable capital in accordance with paragraphs 6 and 7 of Article 6 of this Agreement.

4. In cases of default in respect of a loan made from borrowed funds or guaranteed by the Bank as part of its ordinary operations, the Bank may, if it believes that the default may be of long duration, call an additional amount of such callable capital not to exceed in any one (1) year one (1) per cent of the total subscriptions of the members to such capital, for the following purposes:

   (i) To redeem before maturity, or otherwise discharge, the Bank's liability on all or part of the outstanding principal of any loan guaranteed by it in respect of which the debtor is in default; and

(ii) To repurchase, or otherwise discharge, the Bank's liability on all or part of its own outstanding borrowing.

5. If the Bank's subscribed callable capital stock shall be entirely called pursuant to paragraphs 3 and 4 of this Article, the Bank may, if necessary for the purposes specified in paragraph 3 of this Article, use or exchange the currency of any member without restriction, including any restriction imposed pursuant to paragraphs 2 (i) and (ii) of Article 24.

ARTICLE 19
SPECIAL FUNDS

1. The Bank may:

(i) set aside, by a vote of two-thirds of the total number of Governors, representing at least three-fourths of the total voting power of the members, not more than ten (10) per cent each of the portion of the unimpaired paid-in capital of the Bank paid by members pursuant to paragraph 2 (a) of Article 6 and of the portion thereof paid pursuant to paragraph 2 (b) of Article 6, and establish therewith one or more Special Funds; and

(ii) accept the administration of Special Funds which are designed to serve the purpose and come within the functions of the Bank.

2. Special Funds established by the Bank pursuant to paragraph 1 (i) of this Article may be used to guarantee or make loans of high developmental priority, with longer maturities, longer deferred commencement of repayment and lower interest rates than those established by the Bank for its ordinary operations. Such Funds may also be used on such other terms and conditions, not inconsistent with the applicable provisions of this Agreement nor with the character of such Funds as revolving funds, as the Bank in establishing such Funds may direct.

3. Special Funds accepted by the Bank under paragraph 1 (ii) of this Article may be used in any manner and on any terms and conditions not inconsistent with the purpose of the Bank and with the agreement relating to such Funds.

4. The Bank shall adopt such special rules and regulations as may be required for the establishment, administration and use of each Special Fund. Such rules and regulations shall be consistent with the provisions of this Agreement, excepting those provisions expressly applicable only to ordinary operations of the Bank.

ARTICLE 20
SPECIAL FUNDS RESOURCES

As used in this Agreement, the term "Special Funds resources" shall refer to the resources of any Special Fund and shall include:

(a) resources set aside from the paid-in capital to a Special Fund or otherwise initially contributed to any Special Fund;

(b) funds accepted by the Bank for inclusion in any Special Fund;

(c) funds repaid in respect of loans or guarantees financed from the resources of any Special Fund which, under the rules and regulations of
the Bank governing that Special Fund, are received by such Special
Fund;

(d) income derived from operations of the Bank in which any of the aforementioned resources or funds are used or committed if, under the rules
and regulations of the Bank governing the Special Fund concerned, that
income accrues to such Special Fund; and

(e) any other resources placed at the disposal of any Special Fund.

CHAPTER IV: BORROWING AND OTHER MISCELLANEOUS POWERS

ARTICLE 21
GENERAL POWERS

In addition to the powers specified elsewhere in this Agreement, the Bank
shall have the power to:

(i) borrow funds in member countries or elsewhere, and in this connexion
to furnish such collateral or other security therefor as the Bank shall
determine, provided always that:

(a) before making a sale of its obligations in the territory of a country, the Bank shall have obtained its approval;

(b) where the obligations of the Bank are to be denominated in the
currency of a member, the Bank shall have obtained its approval;

(c) the Bank shall obtain the approval of the countries referred to
in sub-paragraphs (a) and (b) of this paragraph that the proceeds may be exchanged for the currency of any member without
restriction; and

(d) before determining to sell its obligations in a particular country,
the Bank shall consider the amount of previous borrowing, if
any, in that country, the amount of previous borrowing in other
countries, and the possible availability of funds in such other
countries; and shall give due regard to the general principle that
its borrowings should to the greatest extent possible be diversified
as to country of borrowing;

(ii) buy and sell securities the Bank has issued or guaranteed or in which
it has invested, provided always that it shall have obtained the approval of any country in whose territory the securities are to be bought
or sold;

(iii) guarantee securities in which it has invested in order to facilitate their
sale;

(iv) underwrite, or participate in the underwriting of, securities issued by
any entity or enterprise for purposes consistent with the purpose of
the Bank;

    (v) invest funds, not needed in its operations, in the territories of members in such obligations of members or nationals thereof as it may determine, and invest funds held by the Bank for pensions or similar purposes in the territories of members in marketable securities issued by members or nationals thereof;

  (vi) provide technical advice and assistance which serve its purpose and come within its functions, and where expenditures incurred in furnishing such services are not reimbursable, charge the net income of the Bank therewith; in the first five (5) years of its operations, the Bank may use up to two (2) per cent of its paid-in capital for furnishing such services on a non-reimbursable basis; and

 (vii) exercise such other powers and establish such rules and regulations as may be necessary or appropriate in furtherance of its purpose and functions, consistent with the provisions of this Agreement.

ARTICLE 22
NOTICE TO BE PLACED ON SECURITIES

Every security issued or guaranteed by the Bank shall bear on its face a conspicuous statement to the effect that it is not an obligation of any Government, unless it is in fact the obligation of a particular Government, in which case it shall so state.

CHAPTER V: CURRENCIES

ARTICLE 23
DETERMINATION OF CONVERTIBILITY

Whenever it shall become necessary under this Agreement to determine whether any currency is convertible, such determination shall be made by the Bank after consultation with the International Monetary Fund.

ARTICLE 24
USE OF CURRENCIES

  1. Members may not maintain or impose any restrictions on the holding or use by the Bank or by any recipient from the Bank, for payments in any country, of the following:

    (i) gold or convertible currencies received by the Bank in payment of subscriptions to its capital stock, other than that paid to the Bank by members pursuant to paragraph 2 (b) of Article 6 and restricted pursuant to paragraphs 2 (i) and (ii) of this Article;

  (ii) currencies of members purchased with the gold or convertible currencies referred to in the preceding sub-paragraph;

 (iii) currencies obtained by the Bank by borrowing, pursuant to sub-paragraph (i) of Article 21 of this Agreement, for inclusion in its ordinary capital resources;

 (iv) gold or currencies received by the Bank in payment on account of principal, interest, dividends or other charges in respect of loans or investments made out of any of the funds referred to in sub-paragraphs (i) to (iii) of this paragraph or in payment of fees in respect of guarantees made by the Bank; and

(v) currencies, other than the member's own currency, received by the member from the Bank in distribution of the net income of the Bank in accordance with Article 40 of this Agreement.

2. Members may not maintain or impose any restriction on the holding or use by the Bank or by any recipient from the Bank, for payments in any country, of currency of a member received by the Bank which does not come within the provisions of the preceding paragraph, unless:

(i) a developing member country, after consultation with and subject to periodic review by the Bank, restricts in whole or in part the use of such currency to payments for goods or services produced and intended for use in its territory; or

(ii) any other member whose subscription has been determined in Part A of Annex A hereof and whose exports of industrial products do not represent a substantial proportion of its total exports, deposits with its instrument of ratification or acceptance a declaration that it desires the use of the portion of its subscription paid pursuant to paragraph 2 (b) of Article 6 to be restricted, in whole or in part, to payments for goods or services produced in its territory, provided that such restrictions be subject to periodic review by and consultation with the Bank and that any purchases of goods or services in the territory of that member, subject to the usual consideration of competitive tendering, shall be first charged against the portion of its subscription paid pursuant to paragraph 2 (b) of Article 6; or

(iii) such currency forms part of the Special Funds resources of the Bank available under paragraph 1 (ii) of Article 19 and its use is subject to special rules and regulations.

3. Members may not maintain or impose any restrictions on the holding or use by the Bank, for making amortization payments or anticipatory payments or for repurchasing in whole or in part the Bank's own obligations, of currencies received by the Bank in repayment of direct loans made out of its ordinary capital resources, provided, however, that until the Bank's subscribed callable capital stock has been entirely called, such holding or use shall be subject to any limitations imposed pursuant to paragraph 2 (i) of this Article except in respect of obligations payable in the currency of the member concerned.

4. Gold or currencies held by the Bank shall not be used by the Bank to purchase other currencies of members or non-members except:

(i) in order to meet its obligations in the ordinary course of its business; or

(ii) pursuant to a decision of the Board of Directors adopted by a vote of the Directors representing not less than two-thirds of the total voting power of the members.

5. Nothing herein contained shall prevent the Bank from using the currency of any member for administrative expenses incurred by the Bank in the territory of such member.

ARTICLE 25
MAINTENANCE OF VALUE OF THE CURRENCY HOLDINGS OF THE BANK

1. Whenever (a) the par value in the International Monetary Fund of the currency of a member is reduced in terms of the dollar defined in Article 4 of this Agreement, or (b) in the opinion of the Bank, after consultation with the International Monetary Fund, the foreign exchange value of a member's currency has depreciated to a significant extent, that member shall pay to the Bank within a reasonable time an additional amount of its currency required to maintain the value of all such currency held by the Bank, excepting (a) currency derived by the Bank from its borrowings and (b) unless otherwise provided in the agreement establishing such Funds, Special Funds resources accepted by the Bank under paragraph 1 (ii) of Article 19.

2. Whenever (a) the par value in the International Monetary Fund of the currency of a member is increased in terms of the said dollar, or (b) in the opinion of the Bank, after consultation with the International Monetary Fund, the foreign exchange value of a member's currency has appreciated to a significant extent, the Bank shall pay to that member within a reasonable time an amount of that currency required to adjust the value of all such currency held by the Bank excepting (a) currency derived by the Bank from its borrowings, and (b) unless otherwise provided in the agreement establishing such Funds, Special Funds resources accepted by the Bank under paragraph 1 (ii) of Article 19.

3. The Bank may waive the provisions of this Article when a uniform proportionate change in the par value of the currencies of all its members takes place.

CHAPTER VI: ORGANIZATION AND MANAGEMENT

ARTICLE 26
STRUCTURE

The Bank shall have a Board of Governors, a Board of Directors, a President, one or more Vice-Presidents and such other officers and staff as may be considered necessary.

ARTICLE 27
BOARD OF GOVERNORS: COMPOSITION

1. Each member shall be represented on the Board of Governors and shall appoint one Governor and one alternate. Each Governor and alternate shall serve at the pleasure of the appointing member. No alternate may vote except in the absence of his principal. At its annual meeting, the Board shall designate

one of the Governors as Chairman who shall hold office until the election of the next Chairman and the next annual meeting of the Board.

2. Governors and alternates shall serve as such without remuneration from the Bank, but the Bank may pay them reasonable expenses incurred in attending meetings.

ARTICLE 28
BOARD OF GOVERNORS: POWERS

1. All the powers of the Bank shall be vested in the Board of Governors.

2. The Board of Governors may delegate to the Board of Directors any or all its powers, except the power to:

(i) admit new members and determine the conditions of their admission;

(ii) increase or decrease the authorized capital stock of the Bank;

(iii) suspend a member;

(iv) decide appeals from interpretations or applications of this Agreement given by the Board of Directors;

(v) authorize the conclusion of general agreements for co-operation with other international organizations;

(vi) elect the Directors and the President of the Bank;

(vii) determine the remuneration of the Directors and their alternates and the salary and other terms of the contract of service of the President;

(viii) approve, after reviewing the auditors' report, the general balance sheet and the statement of profit and loss of the Bank;

(ix) determine the reserves and the distribution of the net profits of the Bank;

(x) amend this Agreement;

(xi) decide to terminate the operations of the Bank and to distribute its assets; and

(xii) exercise such other powers as are expressly assigned to the Board of Governors in this Agreement.

3. The Board of Governors shall retain full power to exercise authority over any matter delegated to the Board of Directors under paragraph 2 of this Article.

4. For the purposes of this Agreement, the Board of Governors may, by a vote of two-thirds of the total number of Governors, representing not less than three-fourths of the total voting power of the members, from time to time determine which countries or members of the Bank are to be regarded as developed or developing countries or members, taking into account appropriate economic considerations.

ARTICLE 29
BOARD OF GOVERNORS: PROCEDURE

1. The Board of Governors shall hold an annual meeting and such other meetings as may be provided for by the Board or called by the Board of

Directors. Meetings of the Board of Governors shall be called, by the Board of Directors, whenever requested by five (5) members of the Bank.

2. A majority of the Governors shall constitute a quorum for any meeting of the Board of Governors, provided such majority represents not less than two-thirds of the total voting power of the members.

3. The Board of Governors may by regulation establish a procedure whereby the Board of Directors may, when the latter deems such action advisable, obtain a vote of the Governors on a specific question without calling a meeting of the Board of Governors.

4. The Board of Governors, and the Board of Directors to the extent authorized, may establish such subsidiary bodies as may be necessary or appropriate to conduct the business of the Bank.

ARTICLE 30
BOARD OF DIRECTORS: COMPOSITION

1. (i) The Board of Directors shall be composed of ten (10) members who shall not be members of the Board of Governors, and of whom:
   (a) seven (7) shall be elected by the Governors representing regional members; and
   (b) three (3) by the Governors representing non-regional members. Directors shall be persons of high competence in economic and financial matters and shall be elected in accordance with Annex B hereof.
   (ii) At the Second Annual Meeting of the Board of Governors after its inaugural meeting, the Board of Governors shall review the size and composition of the Board of Directors, and shall increase the number of Directors as appropriate, paying special regard to the desirability, in the circumstances at that time, of increasing representation in the Board of Directors of smaller less developed member countries. Decisions under this paragraph should be made by a vote of majority of the total number of Governors, representing not less than two-thirds of the total voting power of the members.

2. Each Director shall appoint an alternate with full power to act for him when he is not present. Directors and alternates shall be nationals of member countries. No two or more Directors may be of the same nationality nor may any two or more alternates be of the same nationality. An alternate may participate in meetings of the Board but may vote only when he is acting in place of his principal.

3. Directors shall hold office for a term of two (2) years and may be re-elected. They shall continue in office until their successors shall have been chosen and qualified. If the office of a Director becomes vacant more than one hundred and eighty (180) days before the end of his term, a successor shall be chosen in accordance with Annex B hereof, for the remainder of the term, by the Governors who elected the former Director. A majority of the votes cast by such Governors shall be required for such election. If the office of a Director becomes vacant one hundred and eighty (180) days or less before the

end of his term, a successor may similarly be chosen for the remainder of the term, by the Governors who elected the former Director, in which election a majority of the votes cast by such Governors shall be required. While the office remains vacant, the alternate of the former Director shall exercise the powers of the latter, except that of appointing an alternate.

ARTICLE 31
BOARD OF DIRECTORS: POWERS

The Board of Directors shall be responsible for the direction of the general operations of the Bank and, for this purpose, shall, in addition to the powers assigned to it expressly by this Agreement, exercise all the powers delegated to it by the Board of Governors, and in particular:

  (i) prepare the work of the Board of Governors;
 (ii) in conformity with the general directions of the Board of Governors, take decisions concerning loans, guarantees, investments in equity capital, borrowing by the Bank, furnishing of technical assistance and other operations of the Bank;
(iii) submit the accounts for each financial year for approval of the Board of Governors at each annual meeting; and
 (iv) approve the budget of the Bank.

ARTICLE 32
BOARD OF DIRECTORS: PROCEDURE

1. The Board of Directors shall normally function at the principal office of the Bank and shall meet as often as the business of the Bank may require.

2. A majority of the Directors shall constitute a quorum for any meeting of the Board of Directors, provided such majority represents not less than two-thirds of the total voting power of the members.

3. The Board of Governors shall adopt regulations under which, if there is no Director of its nationality, a member may send a representative to attend, without right to vote, any meeting of the Board of Directors when a matter particularly affecting that member is under consideration.

ARTICLE 33
VOTING

1. The total voting power of each member shall consist of the sum of its basic votes and proportional votes.

  (i) The basic votes of each member shall consist of such number of votes as results from the equal distribution among all the members of twenty (20) per cent of the aggregate sum of the basic votes and proportional votes of all the members.

(ii) The number of the proportional votes of each member shall be equal to the number of shares of the capital stock of the Bank held by that member.

2. In voting in the Board of Governors, each Governor shall be entitled to cast the votes of the member he represents. Except as otherwise expressly provided in this Agreement, all matters before the Board of Governors shall be decided by a majority of the voting power represented at the meeting.

3. In voting in the Board of Directors, each Director shall be entitled to cast the number of votes that counted towards his election which votes need not be cast as a unit. Except as otherwise expressly provided in this Agreement, all matters before the Board of Directors shall be decided by a majority of the voting power represented at the meeting.

ARTICLE 34
THE PRESIDENT

1. The Board of Governors, by a vote of a majority of the total number of Governors, representing not less than a majority of the total voting power of the members, shall elect a President of the Bank. He shall be a national of a regional member country. The President, while holding office, shall not be a Governor or a Director or an alternate for either.

2. The term of office of the President shall be five (5) years. He may be re-elected. He shall, however, cease to hold office when the Board of Governors so decides by a vote of two-thirds of the total number of Governors, representing not less than two-thirds of the total voting power of the members. If the office of the President for any reason becomes vacant more than one hundred and eighty (180) days before the end of his term, a successor shall be elected for the unexpired portion of such term by the Board of Governors in accordance with the provisions of paragraph 1 of this Article. If such office for any reason becomes vacant one hundred and eighty (180) days or less before the end of the term, a successor may similarly be elected for the unexpired portion of such term by the Board of Governors.

3. The President shall be Chairman of the Board of Directors but shall have no vote, except a deciding vote in case of an equal division. He may participate in meetings of the Board of Governors but shall not vote.

4. The President shall be the legal representative of the Bank.

5. The President shall be chief of the staff of the Bank and shall conduct, under the direction of the Board of Directors, the current business of the Bank. He shall be responsible for the organization, appointment and dismissal of the officers and staff in accordance with regulations adopted by the Board of Directors.

6. In appointing the officers and staff, the President shall, subject to the paramount importance of securing the highest standards of efficiency and technical competence, pay due regard to the recruitment of personnel on as wide a regional geographical basis as possible.

ARTICLE 35
VICE-PRESIDENT(S)

1. One or more Vice-Presidents shall be appointed by the Board of Directors on the recommendation of the President. Vice-President(s) shall hold office for such term, exercise such authority and perform such functions in the administration of the Bank, as may be determined by the Board of Directors. In the absence or incapacity of the President, the Vice-President or, if there be more than one, the ranking Vice-President, shall exercise the authority and perform the functions of the President.

2. Vice-President(s) may participate in meetings of the Board of Directors but shall have no vote at such meetings, except that the Vice-President or ranking Vice-President, as the case may be, shall cast the deciding vote when acting in place of the President.

ARTICLE 36
PROHIBITION OF POLITICAL ACTIVITY: THE INTERNATIONAL CHARACTER OF THE BANK

1. The Bank shall not accept loans or assistance that may in any way prejudice, limit, deflect or otherwise alter its purpose or functions.

2. The Bank, its President, Vice-President(s), officers and staff shall not interfere in the political affairs of any member, nor shall they be influenced in their decisions by the political character of the member concerned. Only economic considerations shall be relevant to their decisions. Such considerations shall be weighed impartially in order to achieve and carry out the purpose and functions of the Bank.

3. The President, Vice-President(s), officers and staff of the Bank, in the discharge of their offices, owe their duty entirely to the Bank and to no other authority. Each member of the Bank shall respect the international character of this duty and shall refrain from all attempts to influence any of them in the discharge of their duties.

ARTICLE 37
OFFICE OF THE BANK

1. The principal office of the Bank shall be located in Manila, Philippines.

2. The Bank may establish agencies or branch offices elsewhere.

ARTICLE 38
CHANNEL OF COMMUNICATIONS, DEPOSITORIES

1. Each member shall designate an appropriate official entity with which the Bank may communicate in connexion with any matter arising under this Agreement.

2. Each member shall designate its central bank, or such other agency as may be agreed upon with the Bank, as a depository with which the Bank may keep its holdings of currency of that member as well as other assets of the Bank.

ARTICLE 39
WORKING LANGUAGE, REPORTS

1. The working language of the Bank shall be English.

2. The Bank shall transmit to its members an Annual Report containing an audited statement of its accounts and shall publish such Report. It shall also transmit quarterly to its members a summary statement of its financial position and a profit and loss statement showing the results of its operations.

3. The Bank may also publish such other reports as it deems desirable in the carrying out of its purpose and functions. Such reports shall be transmitted to the members of the Bank.

ARTICLE 40
ALLOCATION OF NET INCOME

1. The Board of Governors shall determine annually what part of the net income of the Bank, including the net income accruing to Special Funds, shall be allocated, after making provision for reserves, to surplus and what part, if any, shall be distributed to the members.

2. The distribution referred to in the preceding paragraph shall be made in proportion to the number of shares held by each member.

3. Payments shall be made in such manner and in such currency as the Board of Governors shall determine.

CHAPTER VII: WITHDRAWAL AND SUSPENSION OF MEMBERS, TEMPORARY SUSPENSION AND TERMINATION OF OPERATIONS OF THE BANK

ARTICLE 41
WITHDRAWAL

1. Any member may withdraw from the Bank at any time by delivering a notice in writing to the Bank at its principal office.

2. Withdrawal by a member shall become effective, and its membership shall cease, on the date specified in its notice but in no event less than six (6) months after the date that notice has been received by the Bank. However, at any time before the withdrawal becomes finally effective, the member may notify the Bank in writing of the cancellation of its notice of intention to withdraw.

3. A withdrawing member shall remain liable for all direct and contingent obligations to the Bank to which it was subject at the date of delivery of the withdrawal notice. If the withdrawal becomes finally effective, the member shall not incur any liability for obligations resulting from operations of the Bank effected after the date on which the withdrawal notice was received by the Bank.

ARTICLE 42
SUSPENSION OF MEMBERSHIP

1. If a member fails to fulfil any of its obligations to the Bank, the Board of Governors may suspend such member by a vote of two-thirds of the total number of Governors, representing not less than three-fourths of the total voting power of the members.

2. The member so suspended shall automatically cease to be a member of the Bank one (1) year from the date of its suspension unless the Board of Governors, during that one-year period, decides by the same majority necessary for suspension to restore the member to good standing.

3. While under suspension, a member shall not be entitled to exercise any rights under this Agreement, except the right of withdrawal, but shall remain subject to all its obligations.

ARTICLE 43
SETTLEMENT OF ACCOUNTS

1. After the date on which a country ceases to be a member, it shall remain liable for its direct obligations to the Bank and for its contingent liabilities to the Bank so long as any part of the loans or guarantees contracted before it ceased to be a member is outstanding; but it shall not incur liabilities with respect to loans and guarantees entered into thereafter by the Bank nor share either in the income or the expenses of the Bank.

2. At the time a country ceases to be a member, the Bank shall arrange for the repurchase of such country's shares by the Bank as a part of the settlement of accounts with such country in accordance with the provisions of paragraphs 3 and 4 of this Article. For this purpose, the repurchase price of the shares shall be the value shown by the books of the Bank on the date the country ceases to be a member.

3. The payment for shares repurchased by the Bank under this Article shall be governed by the following conditions:

(i) Any amount due to the country concerned for its shares shall be withheld so long as that country, its central bank or any of its agencies, instrumentalities or political subdivisions remains liable, as borrower or guarantor, to the Bank and such amount may, at the option of the Bank, be applied on any such liability as it matures. No amount shall be withheld on account of the contingent liability of the country for future calls on its subscription for shares in accordance with paragraph 5 of Article 6 of this Agreement. In any event, no amount due to a member for its shares shall be paid until six (6) months after the date on which the country ceases to be a member.

(ii) Payments for shares may be made from time to time, upon surrender of the corresponding stock certificates by the country concerned, to the extent by which the amount due as the repurchase price in accordance with paragraph 2 of this Article exceeds the aggregate amount of liabilities on loans and guarantees referred to in subparagraph (i) of this paragraph, until the former member has received the full repurchase price.

(iii) Payments shall be made in such available currencies as the Bank determines, taking into account its financial position.

(iv) If losses are sustained by the Bank on any guarantees or loans which were outstanding on the date when a country ceased to be a member and the amount of such losses exceeds the amount of the reserve provided against losses on that date, the country concerned shall repay, upon demand, the amount by which the repurchase price of its shares would have been reduced if the losses had been taken into account when the repurchase price was determined. In addition, the former member shall remain liable on any call for unpaid subscriptions in accordance with paragraph 5 of Article 6 of this Agreement, to the same extent that it would have been required to respond if the impairment of capital had occurred and the call had been made at the time the repurchase price of its shares was determined.

4. If the Bank terminates its operations pursuant to Article 45 of this Agreement within six (6) months of the date upon which any country ceases to be a member, all rights of the country concerned shall be determined in accordance with the provisions of Articles 45 to 47 of this Agreement. Such country shall be considered as still a member for purposes of such Articles but shall have no voting rights.

ARTICLE 44
TEMPORARY SUSPENSION OF OPERATIONS

In an emergency, the Board of Directors may temporarily suspend operations in respect of new loans and guarantees, pending an opportunity for further consideration and action by the Board of Governors.

ARTICLE 45
TERMINATION OF OPERATIONS

1. The Bank may terminate its operations by a resolution of the Board of Governors approved by a vote of two-thirds of the total number of Governors, representing not less than three-fourths of the total voting power of the members.

2. After such termination, the Bank shall forthwith cease all activities, except those incident to the orderly realization, conservation and preservation of its assets and settlement of its obligations.

ARTICLE 46
LIABILITY OF MEMBERS AND PAYMENT OF CLAIMS

1. In the event of termination of the operations of the Bank, the liability of all members for uncalled subscriptions to the capital stock of the Bank and in respect of the depreciation of their currencies shall continue until all claims of creditors, including all contingent claims, shall have been discharged.

2. All creditors holding direct claims shall first be paid out of the assets of the Bank and then out of payments to the Bank on unpaid or callable subscriptions. Before making any payments to creditors holding direct claims, the Board of Directors shall make such arrangements as are necessary, in its judgment, to ensure a *pro rata* distribution among holders of direct and contingent claims.

ARTICLE 47
DISTRIBUTION OF ASSETS

1. No distribution of assets shall be made to members on account of their subscriptions to the capital stock of the Bank until all liabilities to creditors shall have been discharged or provided for. Moreover, such distribution must be approved by the Board of Governors by a vote of two-thirds of the total number of Governors, representing not less than three-fourths of the total voting power of the members.

2. Any distribution of the assets of the Bank to the members shall be in proportion to the capital stock held by each member and shall be effected at such times and under such conditions as the Bank shall deem fair and equitable. The shares of assets distributed need not be uniform as to type of asset. No member shall be entitled to receive its share in such a distribution of assets until it has settled all of its obligations to the Bank.

3. Any member receiving assets distributed pursuant to this Article shall enjoy the same rights with respect to such assets as the Bank enjoyed prior to their distribution.

CHAPTER VIII: STATUS, IMMUNITIES, EXEMPTIONS AND PRIVILEGES

ARTICLE 48
PURPOSE OF CHAPTER

To enable the Bank effectively to fulfil its purpose and carry out the functions entrusted to it, the status, immunities, exemptions and privileges set forth in this Chapter shall be accorded to the Bank in the territory of each member.

ARTICLE 49
LEGAL STATUS

The Bank shall possess full juridical personality and, in particular, full capacity:
  (i) to contract;
 (ii) to acquire, and dispose of, immovable and movable property; and
(iii) to institute legal proceedings.

ARTICLE 50
IMMUNITY FROM JUDICIAL PROCEEDINGS

1. The Bank shall enjoy immunity from every form of legal process, except in cases arising out of or in connexion with the exercise of its powers to borrow money, to guarantee obligations, or to buy and sell or underwrite the sale of securities, in which cases actions may be brought against the Bank in a court of competent jurisdiction in the territory of a country in which the Bank has its principal or a branch office, or has appointed an agent for the purpose of accepting service or notice of process, or has issued or guaranteed securities.

2. Notwithstanding the provisions of paragraph 1 of this Article, no action shall be brought against the Bank by any member, or by any agency or instrumentality of a member, or by any entity or person directly or indirectly acting for or deriving claims from a member or from any agency or instrumentality of a member. Members shall have recourse to such special procedures for the settlement of controversies between the Bank and its members as may be prescribed in this Agreement, in the by-laws and regulations of the Bank, or in contracts entered into with the Bank.

3. Property and assets of the Bank shall, wheresoever located any by whomsoever held, be immune from all forms of seizure, attachment or execution before the delivery of final judgment against the Bank.

ARTICLE 51
IMMUNITY OF ASSETS

Property and assets of the Bank, wheresoever located and by whomsoever held, shall be immune from search, requisition, confiscation, expropriation or any other form of taking or foreclosure by executive or legislative action.

ARTICLE 52
IMMUNITY OF ARCHIVES

The archives of the Bank and, in general, all documents belonging to it, or held by it, shall be inviolable, wherever located.

ARTICLE 53
FREEDOM OF ASSETS FROM RESTRICTIONS

To the extent necessary to carry out the purpose and functions of the Bank effectively, and subject to the provisions of this Agreement, all property and assets of the Bank shall be free from restrictions, regulations, controls and moratoria of any nature.

ARTICLE 54
PRIVILEGE FOR COMMUNICATIONS

Official communications of the Bank shall be accorded by each member treatment not less favourable than that it accords to the official communications of any other member.

ARTICLE 55
IMMUNITIES AND PRIVILEGES OF BANK PERSONNEL

All Governors, Directors, alternates, officers and employees of the Bank, including experts performing missions for the Bank:
- (i) shall be immune from legal process with respect to acts performed by them in their official capacity, except when the Bank waives the immunity;
- (ii) where they are not local citizens or nationals, shall be accorded the same immunities from immigration restrictions, alien registration requirements and national service obligations, and the same facilities as regards exchange regulations, as are accorded by members to the representatives, officials and employees of comparable rank of other members; and
- (iii) shall be granted the same treatment in respect of travelling facilities as is accorded by members to representatives, officials and employees of comparable rank of other members.

ARTICLE 56
EXEMPTION FROM TAXATION

1. The Bank, its assets, property, income and its operations and transactions, shall be exempt from all taxation and from all customs duties. The Bank shall also be exempt from any obligation for the payment, withholding or collection of any tax or duty.

2. No tax shall be levied on or in respect of salaries and emoluments paid by the Bank to Directors, alternates, officers or employees of the Bank, including experts performing missions for the Bank, except where a member deposits with its instrument of ratification or acceptance a declaration that such member retains for itself and its political subdivisions the right to tax salaries and emoluments paid by the Bank to citizens or nationals of such member.

3. No tax of any kind shall be levied on any obligation or security issued by the Bank, including any dividend or interest thereon, by whomsoever held:

(i) which discriminates against such obligation or security solely because it is issued by the Bank; or

(ii) if the sole jurisdictional basis for such taxation is the place or currency in which it is issued, made payable or paid, or the location of any office or place of business maintained by the Bank.

4. No tax of any kind shall be levied on any obligation or security guaranteed by the Bank, including any dividend or interest thereon, by whomsoever held:

(i) which discriminates against such obligation or security solely because it is guaranteed by the Bank; or

(ii) if the sole jurisdictional basis for such taxation is the location of any office or place of business maintained by the Bank.

ARTICLE 57
IMPLEMENTATION

Each member, in accordance with its juridical system, shall promptly take such action as is necessary to make effective in its own territory the provisions set forth in this Chapter and shall inform the Bank of the action which it has taken on the matter.

ARTICLE 58
WAIVER OF IMMUNITIES, EXEMPTIONS AND PRIVILEGES

The Bank at its discretion may waive any of the privileges, immunities and exemptions conferred under this Chapter in any case or instance, in such manner and upon such conditions as it may determine to be appropriate in the best interests of the Bank.

CHAPTER IX: AMENDMENTS, INTERPRETATION, ARBITRATION

ARTICLE 59
AMENDMENTS

1. This Agreement may be amended only by a resolution of the Board of Governors approved by a vote of two-thirds of the total number of Governors, representing not less than three-fourths of the total voting power of the members.

2. Notwithstanding the provisions of paragraph 1 of this Article, the unanimous agreement of the Board of Governors shall be required for the approval of any amendment modifying:

(i) the right to withdraw from the Bank;

(ii) the limitations on liability provided in paragraphs 6 and 7 of Article 5; and

(iii) the rights pertaining to purchase of capital stock provided in paragraph 2 of Article 5.

3. Any proposal to amend this Agreement, whether emanating from a member or the Board of Directors, shall be communicated to the Chairman of the Board of Governors, who shall bring the proposal before the Board of Governors. When an amendment has been adopted, the Bank shall so certify in an official communication addressed to all members. Amendments shall enter into force for all members three (3) months after the date of the official communication unless the Board of Governors specifies therein a different period.

ARTICLE 60
INTERPRETATION OR APPLICATION

1. Any question of interpretation or application of the provisions of this Agreement arising between any member and the Bank, or between two or more members of the Bank, shall be submitted to the Board of Directors for decision. If there is no Director of its nationality on that Board, a member particularly affected by the question under consideration shall be entitled to direct representation in the Board of Directors during such consideration; the representative of such member shall, however, have no vote. Such right of representation shall be regulated by the Board of Governors.

2. In any case where the Board of Directors has given a decision under paragraph 1 of this Article, any member may require that the question be referred to the Board of Governors, whose decision shall be final. Pending the decision of the Board of Governors, the Bank may, so far as it deems it necessary, act on the basis of the decision of the Board of Directors.

ARTICLE 61
ARBITRATION

If a disagreement should arise between the Bank and a country which has ceased to be a member, or between the Bank and any member, after adoption of a resolution to terminate the operations of the Bank, such disagreement shall be submitted to arbitration by a tribunal of three arbitrators. One of the arbitrators shall be appointed by the Bank, another by the country concerned, and the third, unless the parties otherwise agree, by the President of the International Court of Justice or such other authority as may have been prescribed by regulations adopted by the Board of Governors. A majority vote of the arbitrators shall be sufficient to reach a decision which shall be final and binding upon the parties. The third arbitrator shall be empowered to settle all questions of procedure in any case where the parties are in disagreement with respect thereto.

ARTICLE 62
APPROVAL DEEMED GIVEN

Whenever the approval of any member is required before any act may be done by the Bank, approval shall be deemed to have been given unless the member presents an objection within such reasonable period as the Bank may fix in notifying the member of the proposed act.

CHAPTER X: FINAL PROVISIONS

ARTICLE 63
SIGNATURE AND DEPOSIT

1. The original of this Agreement in a single copy in the English language shall remain open for signature at the United Nations Economic Commission for Asia and the Far East, in Bangkok, until 31 January 1966 by Governments of countries listed in Annex A to this Agreement. This document shall thereafter be deposited with the Secretary-General of the United Nations (hereinafter called the "Depository").

2. The Depository shall send certified copies of this Agreement to all the Signatories and other countries which become members of the Bank.

ARTICLE 64
RATIFICATION OR ACCEPTANCE

1. This Agreement shall be subject to ratification or acceptance by the Signatories. Instruments of ratification or acceptance shall be deposited with the Depository not later than 30 September 1966. The Depository shall duly notify the other Signatories of each deposit and the date thereof.

2. A Signatory whose instrument of ratification or acceptance is deposited before the date on which this Agreement enters into force, shall become a member of the Bank on that date. Any other Signatory which complies with the provisions of the preceding paragraph, shall become a member of the Bank on the date on which its instrument of ratification or acceptance is deposited.

ARTICLE 65
ENTRY INTO FORCE

This Agreement shall enter into force when instruments of ratification or acceptance have been deposited by at least fifteen (15) Signatories (including not less than ten [10] regional countries) whose initial subscriptions, as set forth in Annex A to this Agreement, in the aggregate comprise not less than sixty-five (65) per cent of the authorized capital stock of the Bank.

ARTICLE 66
COMMENCEMENT OF OPERATIONS

1. As soon as this Agreement enters into force, each member shall appoint a Governor, and the Executive Secretary of the United Nations Economic Com-

mission for Asia and the Far East shall call the inaugural meeting of the Board of Governors.

2. At its inaugural meeting, the Board of Governors:
  (i) shall make arrangements for the election of Directors of the Bank in accordance with paragraph 1 of Article 30 of this Agreement; and
  (ii) shall make arrangements for the determination of the date on which the Bank shall commence its operations.

3. The Bank shall notify its members of the date of the commencement of its operations.

Done at the City of Manila, Philippines, on 4 December 1965, in a single copy in the English language which shall be brought to the United Nations Economic Commission for Asia and the Fart East, Bangkok, and thereafter deposited with the Secretary-General of the United Nations, New York, in accordance with Article 63 of this Agreement.

ANNEX A: INITIAL SUBSCRIPTIONS TO THE AUTHORIZED CAPITAL STOCK FOR COUNTRIES WHICH MAY BECOME MEMBERS IN ACCORDANCE WITH ARTICLE 64

PART A. REGIONAL COUNTRIES

I

Country	Amount of subscription (in million U.S. dollars)
1. Afghanistan	3.36
2. Australia	85.00
3. Cambodia	3.00
4. Ceylon	8.52
5. China, Republic of	16.00
6. India	93.00
7. Iran	60.00
8. Japan	200.00
9. Korea, Republic of	30.00
10. Laos	0.42
11. Malaysia	20.00
12. Nepal	2.16
13. New Zealand	22.56
14. Pakistan	32.00
15. Philippines	35.00
16. Republic of Viet-Nam	7.00
17. Singapore	4.00
18. Thailand	20.00
19. Western Samoa	0.06
Total	642.08

II

The following regional countries may become Signatories of this Agreement in accordance with Article 63, provided that at the time of signing, they shall respectively subscribe to the capital stock of the Bank in the following amounts:

Country	Amount of subscription (in million U.S. dollars)
1. Burma	7.74
2. Mongolia	0.18
Total	7.92

PART B. NON-REGIONAL COUNTRIES

I

Country	Amount of subscription (in million U.S. dollars)
1. Belgium	5.00
2. Canada	25.00
3. Denmark	5.00
4. Germany, Federal Republic of	30.00
5. Italy	10.00
6. Netherlands	11.00
7. United Kingdom	10.00
8. United States	200.00
Total	296.00

II

The following non-regional countries which participated in the meeting of the Preparatory Committee on the Asian Development Bank in Bangkok from 21 October to 1 November 1965 and which there indicated interest in membership in the Bank, may become Signatories of this Agreement in accordance with Article 63, provided that at the time of signing, each such country shall subscribe to the capital stock of the Bank in an amount which shall not be less than five million dollars ($5,000,000):

1. Austria
2. Finland
3. Norway
4. Sweden

III

On or before 31 January 1966, any of the non-regional countries listed in Part B (I) of this Annex may increase the amount of its subscription by so informing the Executive Secretary of the United Nations Economic Commission for Asia and the Far East in Bangkok, provided, however, that the total amount of the initial subscriptions of the non-regional countries listed in Part B (I) and (II) of this Annex shall not exceed the amount of three hundred and fifty million dollars ($350,000,000).

ANNEX B: ELECTION OF DIRECTORS

SECTION A. ELECTION OF DIRECTORS BY GOVERNORS REPRESENTING REGIONAL MEMBERS

1. Each Governor representing a regional member shall cast all votes of the member he represents for a single person.

2. The seven (7) persons receiving the highest number of votes shall be Directors, except that no person who receives less than ten (10) per cent of the total voting power of regional members shall be considered as elected.

3. If seven (7) persons are not elected at the first ballot, a second ballot shall be held in which the person who received the lowest number of votes in the preceding ballot shall be ineligible and in which votes shall be cast only by:

   (a) Governors who voted in the preceding ballot for a person who is not elected; and

   (b) Governors whose votes for a person who is elected are deemed, in accordance with paragraph 4 of this Section, to have raised the votes cast for that person above eleven (11) per cent of the total voting power of regional members.

4. (a) In determining whether the votes cast by a Governor shall be deemed to have raised the total number of votes for any person above eleven (11) per cent, the said eleven (11) per cent shall be deemed to include, first, the votes of the Governor casting the highest number of votes for that person, and then, in diminishing order, the votes of each Governor casting the next highest number until eleven (11) per cent is attained.

   (b) Any Governor, part of whose votes must be counted in order to raise the votes cast for any person above ten (10) per cent, shall be considered as casting all his votes for that person even if the total number of votes cast for that person thereby exceeds eleven (11) per cent.

5. If, after the second ballot, seven (7) persons are not elected, further ballots shall be held in conformity with the principles and procedures laid down in this Section, except that after six (6) persons are elected, the seventh may be elected — notwithstanding the provisions of paragraph (2) of this Section — by a simple majority of the remaining votes of regional members. All such remaining votes shall be deemed to have counted towards the election of the seventh Director.

6. In case of an increase in the number of Directors to be elected by Governors representing regional members, the minimum and maximum

percentage, specified in paragraphs (2), (3), and (4) of Section A of this Annex shall be correspondingly adjusted by the Board of Governors.

SECTION B. ELECTION OF DIRECTORS BY GOVERNORS REPRESENTING NON-REGIONAL MEMBERS

1. Each Governor representing a non-regional member shall cast all votes of the member he represents for a single person.

2. The three (3) persons receiving the highest number of votes shall be Directors, except that no person who receives less than twenty-five (25) per cent of the total voting power of non-regional members shall be considered as elected.

3. If three (3) persons are not elected at the first ballot, a second ballot shall be held in which the person who received the lowest number of votes in the preceding ballot shall be ineligible and in which votes shall be cast only by:

    (a) Governors who voted in the preceding ballot for a person who is not elected; and

    (b) Governors whose votes for a person who is elected are deemed, in accordance with paragraph (4) of this Section, to have raised the votes cast for that person above twenty-six (26) per cent of the total voting power of non-regional members.

4. (a) In determining whether the votes cast by a Governor shall be deemed to have raised the total number of votes for any person above twenty-six (26) per cent, the said twenty-six (26) per cent shall be deemed to include, first, the votes of the Governor casting the highest number of votes for that person, and then, in diminishing order, the votes of each Governor casting the next highest number until twenty-six (26) per cent is attained.

    (b) Any Governor, part of whose votes must be counted in order to raise the votes cast for any person above twenty-six (26) per cent, shall be considered as casting all his votes for that person even if the total number of votes cast for that person thereby exceeds twenty-six (26) per cent.

5. If, after the second ballot, three (3) persons are not elected, further ballots shall be held in conformity with the principles and procedures laid down in this Section, except that after two (2) persons are elected, a third may be elected — provided that subscriptions from non-regional members shall have reached a minimum total of $345 million, and notwithstanding the provisions of paragraph (2) of this Section — by a simple majority of the remaining votes. All such remaining votes shall be deemed to have counted towards the election of the third Director.

5. In case of an increase in the number of directors to be elected by Governors representing non-regional members, the minimum and maximum percentages specified in paragraphs (2), (3) and (4) of Section B of this Annex shall be correspondingly adjusted by the Board of Governors.

CHAPTER SIXTEEN

Central American Bank for Economic Integration

In a preliminary report on economic integration and reciprocity in Central America presented to the first meeting of the ECLA-inspired Economic Cooperation Committee of the Ministers of Economy in the Central American Isthmus, held in Tegucigalpa, Honduras, in August 1952, Raúl Prebisch, then Executive Secretary of ECLA, suggested that, in view of the scarcity of investment resources, any form of economic integration in the area would need support from some kind of regional financing mechanism. Such a mechanism would have to channel external resources to domestic banking systems in the area, either through a banking institution counting on the participation of the five Central American countries or through a consortium of existing financial agencies. Although Central American and ECLA representatives discussed this suggestion at various regional meetings over a period of several years, no action was taken until June 1958, when Costa Rica, El Salvador, Guatemala, Honduras, and Nicaragua signed a multilateral treaty setting up a Central American free trade zone — a treaty that was superseded in December 1960 by the General Treaty on Central American Economic Integration presently in force.

The formal initiative to establish a Central American development bank originated with the above-mentioned Committee of the Ministers of Economy, which in September 1959 asked its Secretariat to prepare, in consultation with other national and international agencies, a draft charter for a Central American institution dedicated to financing and promoting integrated economic development in the area. The charter was drafted concurrently with the General Treaty on Central American Economic Integration and signed by five Central American countries at a ministerial meeting held in Managua, Nicaragua, on December 12, 1960. The charter of the Central American Bank for Economic Integration

(CABEI) provides that only the signatories of the General Treaty are eligible for loans and guarantees from the institution. The purpose of CABEI is to promote economic integration and balanced economic development of the member countries. Its field of action covers financing and extending technical assistance for (a) infrastructure projects aiming to link the economies of the area; (b) long-term industrial projects of a regional character that will help the expansion of intraregional trade; (c) coordinated agricultural projects; and (d) the expansion and modernization of existing industries within the framework of the Common Market.

CABEI's headquarters are in Tegucigalpa, Honduras, the choice of location corresponding to the fact that Honduras happens to be the least developed member country. The Bank began its activities on September 1, 1961 and granted its first loan in December of the same year. Only nationals of the five Central American republics are eligible to be members of the CABEI staff. The former Minister of Economy of Nicaragua, Enrique Delgado, was the first president of CABEI; he was succeeded in 1966 by Gustavo A. Guerrero of the same country.

The initial capital of the Bank was set at the equivalent of $16 million, with equal capital subscriptions from each member country. Half of the capital was paid in various installments and the rest is callable upon the decision of the Board of Directors. Capital resources were increased to $20 million upon the accession of Costa Rica in July 1962. Through the International Cooperation Administration — now known as the Agency for International Development (AID) — the United States government in 1961 extended to CABEI financial support amounting to $2 million. An agreement concerning these funds, signed by CABEI and the United States agency in June 1961, provided that they be administered separately through a special account and that their use for CABEI-approved loans in excess of $100,000 would have to be approved by the United States government. Because of United States objections to the Régime for Central American Integration Industries, no United States aid funds could be used for CABEI loans granted to industrial projects falling within the realm of the Régime. Between June 1962 and May 1964 CABEI received additional resources from AID in the form of loans totaling $28.5 million for the financing of specific projects. By the end of 1965 the Inter-American Development Bank had granted CABEI additional funds of $12.5 million, and the Bank of America had extended credits totaling $2 million. When these resources proved to be insufficient for CABEI's accelerated activities in the mid-1960s, its member countries and the United States government in 1965 agreed to establish a central American Integration Fund to be administered by the Bank. The United States committed itself to provide $35 million to the Fund, while a total of $7 million was to be subscribed in equal parts by the five Central American countries. Thus by the end of 1965 CABEI was able to mobilize a total of $105 million, or more than five times its initial capital. This sum does not include a purchase of $1 million in CABEI long-term bonds by Mexico or credits from Spain that were under negotiation in 1966.

Between December 1, 1961 and June 30, 1966 CABEI granted a total of $80.0 million in the form of 133 loans. The largest part of its credit operations was directed to the industrial sector: ninety-eight loans totaling $32.6 million. Honduras, which obtained $19.5 million in CABEI funds, was the largest recipient, and Costa Rica, which obtained $12.9 million, was the smallest. The conditions of the loans vary considerably, partly in accordance with the cost of the resources of the Bank. Thus loans for infrastructure projects of regional interest granted to governmental agencies carry an interest rate of 3.5 to 6.25 per cent annually, with maturity in some cases extending up to forty years, including a grace period of ten years. Industrial loans extended to the private sector are granted at an interest rate of 6.25 to 8 per cent a year with an average maturity of ten years. Interest charged on the financing of industrial feasibility studies — generally small amounts — varies from 4 per cent for loans in United States dollars to 8 per cent when local currencies are used. Recently CABEI has also become involved in direct industrial promotion activity; together with the Central American Institute for Industrial Research, which is located in Guatemala City, it is looking for industrial opportunities within the Common Market and organizing regional meetings of entrepreneurs.

Bibliographic References

Banco Centroamericano de Integración Económica. *Informe de la Comisión Preparatoria del Banco Centroamericano de Integración Económica a la Asamblea de los Gobernadores.* (Doc. BCIE/I-AG/DT-2.) Tegucigalpa, Honduras, May 1961.

―――. *Memorias de Labores* (Primera 1961–1962, Segunda 1962–1963, Tercera 1963–1964, Cuarta 1964–1965, Quinta 1965–1966), Tegucigalpa, Honduras.

Castillo, Carlos. *Growth and Integration in Central America.* New York: Frederick A. Praeger, 1967.

Comisión Económica para América Latina (CEPAL). *Evaluación de la integración económica en Centroamérica* and *Anexo Estadístico* (submitted to the Ninth Meeting of the Economic Cooperation Committee of the Central American Isthmus, Guatemala City, January 25, 1966). (E/CN.12/CEE/327 and E/CN.12/CEE/327/Add.1.) Mimeographed.

————. *Informe preliminar del Secretario Ejecutivo de la CEPAL sobre integración y reciprocidad económicas en Centroamérica* (submitted to the First Meeting of the Economic Cooperation Committee of the Ministers of Economy of the Central American Isthmus, Tegucigalpa, August 23, 1952). (E/CN.12/AC.17/3.) Mimeographed.

Economic Commission for Latin America (ECLA). *Report to the Central American Economic Co-operation Committee* (December 13, 1960–January 29, 1963). (United Nations Publication, Sales No. 66.II.G.12.) New York, 1964.

AGREEMENT ESTABLISHING THE CENTRAL AMERICAN BANK FOR ECONOMIC INTEGRATION*

The Governments of the Republics of Guatemala, El Salvador, Honduras and Nicaragua agree to create, by virtue of the present Agreement, the Central American Bank for Economic Integration, in accordance with the following provisions:

CHAPTER I: NATURE, PURPOSE, AND HEADQUARTERS

ARTICLE 1

The Central American Bank for Economic Integration is an international juridical person and shall perform its functions in conformity with the present Agreement and with its Regulations.

ARTICLE 2

The purpose of the Bank shall be to promote the economic integration and balanced economic development of the member countries. In pursuance of this objective, its activities shall be primarily designed to meet the needs of the following investment sectors:

a. Infrastructural projects to complete existing regional systems or counterbalance disparities in basic sectors which hinder the balanced economic development of Central America. Consequently, the Bank shall not finance infrastructural projects of purely local or national scope which will not contribute to the completion of the said systems or to the counterbalancing of significant disequilibria as between the member countries;

---

* Signed by Guatemala, El Salvador, Honduras, and Nicaragua in Managua, Nicaragua, December 13, 1960, and adhered to by Costa Rica on July 23, 1962. The text given here is an unofficial translation from the Spanish prepared by the United Nations Economic Commission for Latin Ameriica (ECLA) and published in United Nations, Department of Economic and Social Affairs, *Multilateral Economic Co-operation in Latin America*, Vol. I: *Text and Documents* (Sales No. 62.II.G.3; New York, 1962). [Editor's note].

b. Projects for long-term investment in industries of a regional character or of importance for the Central American market, which will help to increase the supply of goods available for intra–Central American trade, or for such trade and the export sector. The Bank's activities shall not include investment in essentially local industries;

c. Co-ordinated agricultural projects aiming at the improvement or expansion of farms or the replacement of less economic by more economic farms and conducive to Central American regional self-sufficiency;

d. Projects for the financing of enterprises that need to expand their operations, modernize their processes, or change the structure of their production in order to improve their efficiency and their competitive capacity within the common market with a view to facilitating free trade among the Central American countries;

e. Projects for financing services vital to the operation of the common market;

f. Other productive projects calculated to create economic complementarity among the member countries and to expand intra–Central American trade.

ARTICLE 3

The Bank shall have its headquarters and head office in the city of Tegucigalpa, in the Republic of Honduras, and shall be empowered to establish branch offices, agencies, and correspondents.

CHAPTER II: CAPITAL, RESERVES, AND RESOURCES

ARTICLE 4

The Bank's initial authorized capital shall be a sum equivalent to sixteen million United States dollars, to which each of the member States shall subscribe four million dollars, payable in its respective national currency.

One half of the capital subscribed by each member State shall be paid as follows: the equivalent of one million dollars within sixty days from the date of entry into force of the present Agreement, and the equivalent of one million dollars within fourteen months of the said date.

The rest of the capital subscribed shall be payable as and when called in by decision of the Board of Governors, with the concurring vote of at least one Governor from each member State.

The Bank shall be empowered to augment its capital if all the members of the Board of Governors adopt a unanimous decision to that effect.

ARTICLE 5

The shares of the member States in the capital of the Bank shall be represented by stock certificates issued in favour of the States concerned. These certificates shall confer upon their holders equal rights and obligations, shall not yield interest or dividends, and shall not be taxable or transferable.

Such net profits as may accrue to the Bank in the course of its operations shall be deposited in a capital reserve fund.

The responsibility of the members of the Bank, as such, shall be confined to the amount of their capital subscription.

The capital contributed in national currency by each of the member States shall enjoy a guarantee of free convertibility at the official exchange rate most favourable to the Bank.

Each of the member States engages to maintain the value in United States dollars of the capital contribution which it has disbursed to the Bank. Should a change take place in the external official exchange rate for any of the national currencies concerned, the Bank's resources in that currency shall be adjusted in the exact proportion required to maintain their value in United States dollars.

ARTICLE 6

In addition to its own capital and reserves, the resources of the Bank shall include the product of loans and credits obtained in capital markets and any other resources received in any legal form.

CHAPTER III: OPERATIONS

ARTICLE 7

The capital, capital reserves and other resources of the Bank shall be used solely for the fulfilment of the purpose set forth in Article 2 of the present Agreement. To this end, the Bank shall be empowered:

a. To study and promote the investment opportunities created by the economic integration of the member States, duly programming its activities and establishing the necessary financing priorities;

b. To make or participate in long- and medium-term loans;

c. To issue bonds of its own, which may or may not be guaranteed by means of sureties, pledges, or mortgages;

d. To participate in the issuance and placing of credit documents of all kinds, related to the fulfilment of its purpose;

e. To obtain loans, credits, and guarantees from Central American, international, and foreign financial institutions;

f. To act as intermediary in the concerting of loans and credits for the Governments, public institutions, and established enterprises of the member States, to which end it shall institute such arrangements for co-operation with other Central American, international, and foreign institutions as it may deem expedient in that connection, and shall be empowered to take part in the preparation of the specific projects concerned;

g. To guarantee the commitments of public institutions or private enterprises up to such amounts and for such periods as the Board of Governors may determine;

h. To obtain guarantees from the member States for the purpose of securing loans and credits from other financial institutions;

i. To provide, using its own resources or those it may obtain for the purpose, executive, administrative, and technical advisory services for the benefit of applicants for credit;

j. To conduct all such additional business as may be necessary, under the terms of the present Agreement and its Regulations, for the furtherance of its purpose and operation.

ARTICLE 8

The Bank shall finance only economically sound and technically feasible projects and shall refrain from making loans or assuming any responsibility whatsoever for the payment or refinancing of earlier commitments.

CHAPTER IV: ORGANIZATION AND ADMINISTRATION

ARTICLE 9

The Bank shall have a Board of Governors, a Board of Directors, a President, and such other officials and employees as may be deemed necessary.

ARTICLE 10

All the powers of the Bank shall be vested in the Board of Governors. Each member country shall provide two Governors, who shall be absolutely independent in the exercise of their functions and shall have separate votes; one of them shall be the Minister of Economic Affairs or his equivalent, and the other shall be the president or manager of each country's Central Bank, or his equivalent. From among the Governors the Board shall elect a President, who shall remain in office until the next regular meeting of the Board.

ARTICLE 11

The Board of Governors shall be at liberty to delegate all its powers to the Board of Directors, except those relating to the following procedures:

a. Calling-in of capital contributions;

b. Augmentation of the authorized capital;

c. Determination of capital reserves on the basis of proposals made by the Board of Directors;

d. Election of the President and determination of his emoluments;

e. Determination of the emoluments of the Directors;

f. Examination of the interpretations placed upon the present Agreement by the Board of Directors and ruling thereon in case of appeal;

g. Authorization of the conclusion of general agreements relating to co-operation with other agencies;

h. Appointment of outside auditors to check financial statements;

i. Adoption and publication, following the auditor's report, of the over-all balance sheet and the statement of profits and losses;

j. Adoption of decisions, in the event of the Bank's terminating its operations, with respect to the distribution of its net assets.

ARTICLE 12

The Board of Governors shall retain full control over all the powers which, in accordance with Article 11, it may delegate to the Board of Directors.

ARTICLE 13

The Board of Governors shall convene in regular session once a year. It shall also be at liberty to meet in special session whenever it so determines or whenever it is convened by the Board of Directors. The Board of Directors shall convene the Board of Governors whenever one of the member States so requests.

ARTICLE 14

At the meetings of the Board of Governors, one half of the total number of Governors plus one shall constitute a quorum. In all cases except that provided for in Article 4, decisions shall be made by the concurring votes of one half of the total number of Governors plus one.

ARTICLE 15

The Board of Directors shall be responsible for the conduct of the operations of the Bank and to this end shall be entitled to exercise all the powers delegated to it by the Board of Governors.

ARTICLE 16

There shall be one Director for each State member of the Bank, elected by the Board of Governors. The Directors shall be appointed for a term of five years and shall be eligible for re-election for successive periods. They shall be citizens of the member States and persons of acknowledged capacity and wide experience in economic, financial, and banking affairs.

ARTICLE 17

The Directors shall remain in office until their successors are appointed or elected. When a Director's post falls vacant, the Governors shall proceed to appoint a deputy for the remainder of the period.

In the event of a Director's absence for legitimate reasons, the Board of Directors shall be empowered to appoint his temporary substitute.

ARTICLE 18

The Directors shall work full time in the Bank and shall, in addition, discharge such functions as the President may assign to them.

ARTICLE 19

The Board of Directors shall be of a permanent character and shall operate at the headquarters of the Bank.

The Board of Directors shall determine the basic organization of the Bank, including the number of major administrative and professional posts and the general responsibilities attaching, shall adopt the budget, and shall lay before the Board of Governors proposals for the establishment of reserves.

ARTICLE 20

The Board of Governors shall elect from among the Directors the President of the Bank, who shall be its legal representative. Similarly, it shall appoint the person who, should the President himself be prevented from so doing, shall exercise his authority and his functions. The President shall take the chair at the meetings of the Board of Directors and shall conduct the ordinary business of the Bank. His vote shall carry the same weight as that of the other members, except in the event of a tie, in which case he shall have two votes.

ARTICLE 21

There shall be an Executive Vice-President who shall be appointed by the Board of Directors on the proposal of the President of the Bank. He shall exercise the authority and discharge the administrative functions determined by the Board of Directors.

The Executive Vice-President shall attend the meetings of the Board of Directors, but without the right to vote.

ARTICLE 22

In the discharge of their functions, the President, officials, and employees of the Bank shall be answerable to it alone and shall acknowledge no other authority. The member States shall respect the international character of this obligation.

ARTICLE 23

The primary consideration to be born in mind by the Bank in appointing its staff and determining their conditions of service shall be the need to ensure the highest possible degree of efficiency, competence, and integrity. Staff shall also be recruited with due regard to equitable geographical distribution.

ARTICLE 24

The Bank, its officials and its employees — with the exception of the Governors in their respective countries — shall be debarred from taking active part in political affairs.

CHAPTER V: INTERPRETATION AND ARBITRATION

ARTICLE 25

Any difference of opinion as to the interpretation of the provisions of the present Agreement which may arise between any member and the Bank or among member States shall be submitted for a ruling to the Board of Directors.

The member States especially affected by the difference in question shall have the right to direct representation before the Board of Directors.

Any member State shall be entitled to demand that the solution proposed by the Board of Directors in accordance with the first paragraph of this article shall be submitted to the Board of Governors, whose decision shall be final. Pending the Board's decision, the Bank shall be empowered to take such action as it may deem necessary on the basis of the decision reached by the Board of Directors.

ARTICLE 26

Should any disagreement arise between the Bank and a State which has ceased to be a member, or between the Bank and one of its members after it has been agreed that the operations of the institution shall be terminated, the controversy shall be submitted for arbitration to a tribunal composed of three persons. The Bank and the State concerned shall each appoint one of the arbiters, and shall jointly appoint a third and disinterested party. Should agreement not be reached with respect to the last mentioned appointment, the third member shall be chosen by lot from among the Presidents of the Supreme Courts of Justice of the member States, with the exception of that of the country concerned.

The third arbiter shall be empowered to decide upon all questions of procedure in cases where the parties are not in agreement.

CHAPTER VI: IMMUNITIES, EXEMPTIONS, AND PRIVILEGES

ARTICLE 27

The Bank, in the discharge of its functions and in conformity with its purposes, shall enjoy in the territory of the member States the immunities, exemptions and privileges which are set forth in this chapter or which may be otherwise granted to it.

ARTICLE 28

It shall be possible to institute judicial proceedings against the Bank only before a competent tribunal in the territory of a member State where the Bank shall have established an office, or where it shall have appointed an agent or legal representative empowered to accept the writ or notice of a judicial complaint, or where it shall have issued or guaranteed securities.

ARTICLE 29

The Bank's property and other assets, wheresoever situated and whosoever be the holder thereof, shall enjoy immunity from attachment, sequestration, embargo, distraint, auction, adjudication, or any other form of seizure or alienation or forfeiture, so long as no definitive judgment has been pronounced against the Bank.

The property and other assets of the Bank shall be deemed to be international public property and shall enjoy immunity in respect of investigation, requisition, confiscation, expropriation, or any other form of seizure or forfeiture by executive or legislative action.

The Bank's property and other assets shall be exempt from restrictions, regulations, controls, and moratoria of every kind, except as otherwise provided in the present Agreement.

ARTICLE 30

The files and records of the Bank shall be inviolable and shall enjoy absolute immunity.

ARTICLE 31

In territories of the member States the Bank's communications shall be entitled to the same franchises as are granted to official communications.

ARTICLE 32

The personnel of the Bank, whatever their category, shall enjoy the following privileges and immunities:

a. Immunity in respect of judicial, administrative, and legislative proceedings relating to acts performed by them in their official capacity, unless the Bank waives such immunity;

b. In the case of nonnationals of the member State concerned, the same immunities and privileges in respect of immigration restrictions, registration of aliens, and military service requirements, and other facilities relating to exchange and travel regulations, which the State grants to other member States in respect of personnel of comparable rank.

ARTICLE 33

a. The Bank, its income, property, and other assets, as well as any operations and transactions which it may effect in accordance with the present Agreement, shall be exempt from taxes of every kind and from customs duties and other charges of a similar nature. The Bank shall likewise be exempt from all responsibility in connection with the payment, withholding, or collection of any tax, impost, or duty;

b. The bonds or securities issued or guaranteed by the Bank, including dividends or interest thereon, whosoever be their holder, shall not be subject to duties or taxes of any kind;

c. The salaries and emoluments paid by the Bank to its personnel of whatsoever category shall be exempt from taxation.

CHAPTER VII: REQUIREMENTS FOR OBTAINING GUARANTEES OR LOANS

ARTICLE 34

It is hereby established that the members of the Bank shall not be entitled to obtain guarantees or loans from the said institution unless they have previously deposited the instruments of ratification of the following international agreements:

General Treaty on Central American Economic Integration, signed on the same date as the present Agreement;

Multilateral Treaty on Free Trade and Central American Economic Integration, signed on June 10, 1958;

Agreement on the Régime for Central American Integration Industries, signed on June 10, 1958;

Central American Agreement on the Equalization of Import Duties and Charges, signed on September 1, 1959, and the *Protocol* signed on the same date as the present Agreement.

CHAPTER VIII: ACCESSION OF NEW MEMBERS

ARTICLE 35

Central American States not signatories of the present Agreement shall be entitled to accede to it at any time.

CHAPTER IX: DISSOLUTION AND LIQUIDATION

ARTICLE 36

The Bank shall be dissolved:

a. By unanimous decision of the member States; or

b. When only one of the Parties continues to uphold the present Agreement.

In the event of dissolution, the Board of Governors shall determine the conditions under which the Bank shall terminate its operations, liquidate its obligations, and distribute among the member States the surplus capital and reserves remaining after the discharge of the obligations in question.

CHAPTER X: GENERAL PROVISIONS

ARTICLE 37

The present Agreement shall be of unlimited duration and cannot be denounced earlier than twenty years from the date of its entry into force. Denunciation shall become effective five years after its presentation. The Agreement shall remain in force if at least two countries continue to uphold it.

ARTICLE 38

The present Agreement shall enter into force as from the date on which the third instrument of ratification is deposited with the General Secretariat of the Organization of Central American States. For Central American countries acceding to it subsequently, it shall enter into force from the date of deposit of the pertinent instrument with the said Secretariat.

ARTICLE 39

In the event of a signatory State's separation from the Bank, the State shall continue to be responsible for its obligations to the Bank, whether direct or deriving from loans, credits, or guarantees obtained prior to the date on which the State ceases to be a member. However, it shall not be responsible in respect of loans, credits, or guarantees effected subsequently to its withdrawal.

The rights and obligations of the seceding State shall be determined in conformity with the Special Liquidation Balance Sheet which shall be drawn up for the purpose on the date on which the country's separation becomes effective.

ARTICLE 40

The Bank shall be empowered to make its facilities available for the organization and operation of a clearing house on behalf of the Central Banks if and when they so request.

ARTICLE 41

The General Secretariat of the Organization of Central American States shall be the depository of the present Agreement and shall transmit certified copies thereof to the Ministry of Foreign Affairs of each of the Contracting States, which it shall immediately notify of the deposit of each of the instruments of ratification, as well as of any denunciation which may be presented. On the entry into force of the Agreement, it shall also transmit a certified copy thereof to the United Nations Secretariat for registration purposes in conformity with Article 102 of the United Nations Charter.

ARTICLE 42

The Bank constituted by virtue of the present Agreement is the institution referred to in resolutions 84 and 101 of the Central American Economic Co-operation Committee, and, in founding it, Guatemala, El Salvador, and Honduras are complying with the provisions respecting the establishment of the Development and Assistance Fund laid down in the Economic Association Treaty and the Protocol concluded by them on June 8, 1960.

PROVISIONAL ARTICLE

The amounts advanced by the Governments for the initial expenditure arising from the establishment of the Bank shall be deemed to constitute part of their capital contributions to the Bank.

PROVISIONAL ARTICLE

The first meeting of the Board of Governors of the Bank shall be convened by the Ministry of Foreign Affairs of the Republic of Honduras at the earliest opportunity and not later than sixty days from the date of entry into force of the present Agreement.

In witness whereof the respective plenipotentiaries sign the present Agreement in the city of Managua, capital of the Republic of Nicaragua, this thirteenth day of the month of December, nineteen hundred and sixty.

CHAPTER SEVENTEEN

East African Development Bank

The equitable distribution of gains from economic integration, which cannot be assured through the liberalization of trade among participating countries alone, seems to be the core difficulty in all regional integration schemes undertaken in the developing world. On the theoretical level, there is now widespread agreement that no single device to cope with this issue exists because the concept of balanced economic development within a scheme involving the participation of a number of sovereign countries has political and psychological as well as economic aspects. When an integration program includes states with very different development levels, the problem of the distribution of gains becomes even more complicated. In the longer run, the achievement of balanced regional growth in such a situation involves a large degree of agreement on regional investment policies and the willingness of the more developed members to grant preferential measures in commercial and other fields to the other members. In some cases, direct compensation for initial losses of the poorer countries from integration may be in order. In the absence of a unified region-oriented financial aid policy on the part of the outside world, the burden of compensation and other adjustments must fall upon the more advanced members of the regional integration program. Despite the fact that trade liberalization brings them relatively large benefits, however, the more advanced countries face great internal political obstacles when asked to commit themselves to compensating the less developed participants in the integration scheme for their possible trade and fiscal revenue losses. The difficulties encountered are even greater if a need arises to devise a regional mechanism to provide for the transfer of additional resources to the poorer members to accelerate their growth and diminish the existing gap in development levels within the area.

The most recent developments in East Africa prove, however, that when the possibility of a breakdown that would seriously affect the more advanced country arises in the existing common market arrangements, some operative formula to satisfy the poorer participants can be found. In East Africa the unequal distribution of gains from the common market arrangement was formally recognized in the late 1950s, on the eve of the independence of the three British territories — Kenya, Uganda, and Tanganyika — which had been participating in a common market since before the Second World War. Consequently, a Distributable Pool Fund was established in 1960 upon the recommendation of the Economic and Fiscal Commission for East Africa (the Raisman Commission). After the deduction of expenditures for regional common services, the Fund's revenue, originating from corporate income taxes and customs and excise duties collected on a regional basis, was distributed to the three countries in equal shares. Thus, given the relative advancement and the magnitude of Kenya's economy vis-à-vis the two other members, the system in practice provided for a transfer of some net (albeit small) financial resources from Kenya to Uganda and Tanganyika. In view of the dissatisfaction with this redistributive formula in Uganda and Tanganyika and the persistence of trade disequilibria favoring Kenya, shortly after independence an attempt was made to elaborate a regional industrialization policy through distribution of new industries, offering some preferential treatment to the two less developed countries. The scheme did not succeed, however, because each country gave high priority to its own industrial development. When the danger of the breakdown of the East African common market made itself felt in 1964–1965, the issue of the equal distribution of benefits from integration, or, in other words, the problem of balanced regional growth, was by common agreement thrown into the lap of the Philip Commission, established in 1965 and charged with the complete overhauling of preindependence economic cooperation arrangements involving the three independent East African states.

Although the Philip Commission successfully revamped the common market mechanism, it was unable to find an acceptable formula for a common industrialization policy involving the distribution of new region-oriented industries among the three states. Neither was it possible to design a common investment policy. Instead, the Commission recommended the establishment, at an early date, of a regional development bank with the double purpose of providing the necessary resources and technical assistance for expanding the region's industrial capacity and partially alleviating the problem of the relative economic backwardness of Uganda and Tanzania.

The Treaty for East African Co-operation, the outcome of almost two years of negotiations under the auspices of the Philip Commission, provides for the establishment of the East African Development Bank. The Bank's Charter is one of the annexes to the Treaty. The aim of the Bank is to offer financial and technical assistance to promote the industrial development of member states, with special priority "to industrial development in the relatively less industrially developed Partner States, thereby endeavouring to reduce the substantial industrial imbalances between them." Another objective of the regional development institution is to finance, whenever possible, "projects designed to make the economies of the Partner States increasingly complementary in the industrial field." It may be worth recording that one basic difference between the East African Development Bank and the only other existing subregional development agency, the Central American Bank for Economic Integration, is the strict limitation of the field of action of the former to industrial promotion. Thus that Bank is in fact a regional industrial corporation and not a regional development bank.

The authorized capital of the East African Bank was set at £12 million ($33.6 million), with an initial subscription of £6 million payable by the three East African governments in four installments. At the insistence of Uganda and Tanzania and after protracted negotiations, it was agreed that while subscription quotas were to be equal for each member country, a high proportion of the total loans and investments from the ordinary and special funds would be extended to Uganda (38¾ per cent) and to Tanzania (38¾ per cent). The investment flows to receiving countries are to be measured every five years, with the understanding that after ten years of the Bank's operation the member countries will review the agreed upon percentages. The Bank is authorized not only to make and to participate in direct loans for industrial development but also to guarantee loans made by other parties and to invest its capital and supplementary funds in the equity capital of East African industrial enterprises — whether public or private. The agency can operate directly or through the national development agencies as long as its resources are used for specific projects approved beforehand by the Bank. The Charter also provides that the Bank will undertake studies and promote investment opportunities in the region as well as engage in special feasibility studies related to its objectives. In addition to its ordinary capital resources, the East African Development Bank may accept for administration special funds borrowed in the territories of the member states and in third countries. It may also operate with securities that it has issued or guaranteed and invest idle financial resources in marketable securities.

Considering the magnitude of its ordinary capital resources, the East African Development Bank's contribution to the more equal distribution of benefits from economic integration will at first be very limited. It is assumed in the region, however, that through its special funds the Bank will be able to channel into the area additional sizable resources originating in international financial agencies and in bilateral aid. The agreement on preferential treatment for Uganda and Tanzania applies to *all* operations undertaken with the Bank's participation. Furthermore, the role of the agency as a promoter of more balanced development in the region must be considered together with other equalizing devices agreed upon under the Treaty for East African Co-operation. These consist principally of three measures: the reorganization of the Distributable Pool Fund established in 1960, the continuation of the industrial licensing scheme agreed upon in 1964, and the introduction of a transfer tax on imports from the area in case of persistent intraregional trade disequilibria.

Bibliographic References

East African Common Services Organization. *Treaty for East African Co-operation.* Nairobi: Government Printer, 1967.
Ndegwa, Philip. *The Common Market and Development in East Africa.* Nairobi: East African Publishing House, 1965.

THE CHARTER OF THE EAST AFRICAN
DEVELOPMENT BANK*

Whereas the Governments of the United Republic of Tanzania, the Sovereign State of Uganda and the Republic of Kenya, who are referred to in the Treaty and this Charter as "the Partner States," have in Article 21 of the Treaty agreed to establish a Development Bank to be known as the East African Development Bank:

And whereas the said Governments have agreed in Article 22 of the Treaty that the Charter of the East African Development Bank shall be set out in an Annex to the Treaty:

Now therefore it is agreed that the East African Development Bank (hereinafter referred to as "the Bank") be established and operate in accordance with the following provisions:

CHAPTER I
OBJECTIVES AND MEMBERSHIP

Article 1: Objectives of the Bank

1. The objectives of the Bank shall be:
(a) to provide financial and technical assistance to promote the industrial development of the Partner States;
(b) to give priority, in accordance with the operating principles contained in this Charter, to industrial development in the relatively less industrially developed Partner States, thereby endeavouring to reduce the substantial industrial imbalances between them;
(c) to further the aims of the East African Community by financing, wherever possible, projects designed to make the economies of the Partner States increasingly complementary in the industrial field;
(d) to supplement the activities of the national development agencies of the

* This document appears as Annex VI to the Treaty for East African Co-operation (Document 8), signed by Tanzania, Uganda, and Kenya in Kampala, Uganda, June 6, 1967. [Editor's note.]

Partner States by joint financing operations and by the use of such agencies as channels for financing specific projects;

(e) to co-operate, within the terms of this Charter, with other institutions and organizations, public or private, national or international, which are interested in the industrial development of the Partner States; and

(f) to undertake such other activities and provide such other services as may advance the objectives of the Bank.

2. In paragraph 1 of this Article, "industry" with its grammatical variations and cognate expressions means manufacturing, assembling and processing industries including processing associated with the agricultural, forestry and fishing industries but does not include the building, transport and tourist industries.

Article 2: Membership in the Bank

1. The original members of the Bank shall be the Partner States and such bodies corporate, enterprises or institutions who with the approval of the Governments of the Partner States become members on or before the date specified in Article 55 of this Charter.

2. Upon an affirmative decision of the Board of Directors by a majority of the voting power, any body corporate, enterprise or institution, which has not become a member under paragraph 1 of this Article, may, with the approval of the Authority, be admitted to membership of the Bank under such terms and conditions as the Bank may determine.

CHAPTER II
CAPITAL

Article 3: Authorized Capital

1. The authorized capital stock of the Bank shall be 400,000,000 units of account and the value of the unit of account shall be 0.124414 grams of fine gold.

2. The authorized capital stock of the Bank shall be divided into 4,000 shares having a par value of 100,000 units of account each which shall be available for subscription only by members in accordance with Article 4 of this Charter.

3. The original authorized capital stock of the Bank shall be divided equally into paid-in shares and callable shares.

4. The authorized capital stock of the Bank may, after consultation with the Board of Directors, be increased by the Authority.

Article 4: Subscription of Shares

1. Each member of the Bank shall subscribe to shares of the capital stock of the Bank.

2. Each subscription to the original authorized capital stock of the Bank shall be for paid-in shares and callable shares in equal parts.

3. The initial subscription of each of the Partner States to the original authorized capital stock of the Bank shall be 800 shares and the initial subscriptions of other original members to the original authorized capital stock of the Bank shall be as determined by the Governments of the Partner States.

4. The initial subscriptions of members, other than original members, to the original authorized capital stock of the Bank shall be determined by the Bank but no subscription shall be authorized which would have the effect of reducing the percentage of capital stock held by the Partner States below 51 per cent of the total subscribed capital stock.

5. If the authorized capital stock of the Bank is increased, the following provisions shall apply:

(a) subject to this Article, subscriptions to any increase of the authorized capital stock shall be subject to such terms and conditions as the Bank shall determine;

(b) the Partner States shall subscribe to equal parts only of the increased capital stock; and

(c) each member, other than a Partner State, shall be given a reasonable opportunity to subscribe to a proportion of the increase of stock equivalent to the proportion which its stock theretofore subscribed bears to the total subscribed capital stock immediately prior to such increase:

Provided that no such member shall be obligated to subscribe to any part of an increase of capital stock; and

Provided further that subscriptions shall be restricted proportionately to the extent necessary to ensure that the percentage of capital stock held by the Partner States remains not less than 51 per cent of the total subscribed capital stock.

6. Shares of stock initially subscribed for by the original members shall be issued at par. Other shares shall be issued at par unless the Bank, by a vote representing a majority of the total voting power of members, decides in special circumstances to issue them on other terms.

7. Shares of stock shall not be pledged or encumbered in any manner whatsoever and they shall not be transferable except to the Bank:

Provided that if any shares of stock which are transferred to the Bank are subsequently subscribed for by or otherwise transferred to the Partner States, they shall take up such shares in equal parts only.

8. The liability of the members on shares shall be limited to the unpaid portion of the issue price of the shares.

9. No member shall be liable, by reason of its membership in the Bank, for obligations of the Bank.

Article 5: Payment of Subscriptions

1. Payment of the amount initially subscribed by the original members to the paid-in capital stock of the Bank shall be made in four instalments the

first of which shall be 10 per cent of such amount and the remaining instalments shall each be 30 per cent of such amount. The first instalment payable by each Partner State shall be paid within 30 days after the coming into force of the Treaty to which this Charter is annexed and in the case of original members other than the Partner States, the first instalment shall be paid within 30 days of their becoming a member. The second instalment shall be paid six calendar months after the date on which the Treaty comes into force. The remaining two instalments shall each be paid successively six calendar months from the date on which the preceding instalment becomes due under this paragraph.

2. Notwithstanding the provisions of paragraph 1 of this Article, in respect of any instalment, other than the first instalment, of the initial subscriptions to the original paid-in capital stock, the Bank shall, if the funds are not immediately required either defer the due date for payment of such instalment or require that part only of such instalment be payable on the due date and at the same time prescribe a due date for the remainder of such instalment.

3. Of each instalment for the payment of subscriptions by each of the Partner States to the original paid-in capital stock:

(a) 50 per cent shall be paid in convertible currency;

(b) 50 per cent shall be paid in the currency of the Partner State concerned.

4. Each payment of a Partner State in its own currency under sub-paragraph (b) of paragraph 3 of this Article shall be in such amount as the Bank, after such consultation with the International Monetary Fund as the Bank may consider necessary, determines to be equivalent to the full value in terms of the unit of account as expressed in paragraph 1 of Article 3 of this Charter of the portion of the subscription being paid.

5. The initial payment of a Partner State under sub-paragraph (b) of paragraph 3 of this Article shall be in such amount as the member considers appropriate but shall be subject to such adjustment, to be effected within 90 days of the date on which such payment was made, as the Bank shall determine to be necessary to constitute the full value of such payment in terms of the unit of account as expressed in paragraph 1 of Article 3 of this Charter.

6. Each instalment for the payment of subscriptions by members other than Partner States to the original paid-in capital stock shall be paid in convertible currency.

7. Payment of the amount subscribed to the callable capital stock of the Bank shall be subject to call only as and when required by the Bank to meet its obligations incurred under paragraphs (b) and (d) of Article 10 of this Charter on borrowings of funds for inclusion in its ordinary capital resources or on guarantees chargeable to such resources.

8. In the event of a call being made in terms of paragraph 7 of this Article, payment may be made at the option of the member in convertible currency or in the currency required to discharge the obligations of the Bank for the purposes for which the call is made. Calls on unpaid subscriptions shall be uniform in percentage on all callable shares.

9. The Bank shall determine the place for any payment of subscriptions,

provided that, until the first meeting of its Board of Directors, the payment of the first instalment referred to in paragraph 1 of this Article shall be made to the Bank of Uganda as Trustee for the Bank.

CHAPTER III
ORDINARY CAPITAL RESOURCES AND SPECIAL FUNDS

Article 6: Ordinary Capital Resources

In the context of this Chapter, the term "ordinary capital resources" of the Bank shall include:

(a) the authorized capital stock of the Bank including both paid-in and callable shares subscribed pursuant to Article 4 of this Charter;

(b) funds raised by borrowings of the Bank by virtue of powers conferred by Article 19 of this Charter to which the commitment to calls provided for in paragraph 7 of Article 5 of this Charter is applicable;

(c) funds received in repayment of loans or guarantees made with the resources specified in paragraphs (a) and (b) of this Article;

(d) income derived from loans made from the above-mentioned funds or from guarantees to which the commitment to calls provided for in paragraph 7 of Article 5 of this Charter is applicable; and

(e) any other funds or income received by the Bank which do not form part of its Special Funds referred to in Article 7 of this Charter.

Article 7: Special Funds

1. The Bank may accept for administration, from such sources as it considers appropriate, Special Funds which are designed to promote the objectives of the Bank.

2. Special Funds accepted by the Bank under paragraph 1 of this Article shall be used in such manner and on such terms and conditions as are not inconsistent with the objectives of the Bank and the agreement under which such funds are accepted by the Bank for administration.

3. The Board of Directors shall make such regulations as may be necessary for the administration and use of each Special Fund. Such regulations shall be consistent with the provisions of this Charter, other than those provisions which expressly relate only to the ordinary operations of the Bank.

4. The term "Special Funds" as used in this Charter shall refer to the resources of any Special Fund and shall include:

(a) funds accepted by the Bank in any Special Fund;

(b) funds repaid in respect of loans or guarantees financed from any Special Fund which, under the regulations of the Bank covering that Special Fund, are received by such Special Fund; and

(c) income derived from operations of the Bank in which any of the above-mentioned resources or funds are used or committed if, under the regulations of the Bank covering the Special Fund concerned, that income accrues to such Special Fund.

CHAPTER IV
OPERATIONS OF THE BANK

Article 8: Use of Resources

The resources and facilities of the Bank shall be used exclusively to implement the objectives of the Bank as set forth in Article 1 of this Charter.

Article 9: Ordinary and Special Operations

1. The operations of the Bank shall consist of ordinary operations and special operations. Ordinary operations shall be those financed from the ordinary capital resources of the Bank and special operations shall be those financed from the Special Funds referred to in Article 7 of this Charter.

2. The ordinary capital resources and the Special Funds of the Bank shall at all times and in all respects be held, used, committed, invested or otherwise disposed of entirely separately from each other.

3. The ordinary capital resources of the Bank shall not be charged with, or used to discharge, losses or liabilities arising out of special operations for which Special Funds were originally used or committed.

4. Expenses relating directly to ordinary operations shall be charged to ordinary capital resources of the Bank and those relating to special operations shall be charged to the Special Funds. Any other expenses shall be charged as the Bank shall determine.

Article 10: Methods of Operation

Subject to the conditions set forth in this Charter, the Bank may provide finances or facilitate financing in any of the following ways to any agency, entity or enterprise operating in the territories of the Partner States:

(a) by making or participating in direct loans with its unimpaired paid-in capital and, except in the case of its Special Reserve as defined in Article 17 of this Charter, with its reserves and undistributed surplus or with the unimpaired Special Funds;

(b) by making or participating in direct loans with funds raised by the Bank in capital markets or borrowed or otherwise acquired by the Bank for inclusion in its ordinary capital resources;

(c) by investment of funds referred to in paragraphs (a) and (b) of this Article in the equity capital of an institution or enterprise; or

(d) by guaranteeing, in whole or in part, loans made by others for industrial development.

Article 11: Limitations on Operations

1. The total amount outstanding of loans, equity investments and guarantees made by the Bank in its ordinary operations shall not at any time exceed one and a half times the total amount of its unimpaired subscribed capital, reserves and surplus included in its ordinary capital resources, excluding the

Special Reserve and any other reserves not available for ordinary operations.

2. The total amount outstanding in respect of the special operations of the Bank relating to any Special Fund shall not at any time exceed the total amount of the unimpaired special resources appertaining to that Special Fund.

3. In the case of loans made with funds borrowed by the Bank to which the commitment to calls provided for in paragraph 7 of Article 5 of this Charter is applicable, the total amount of principal outstanding and payable to the Bank in a specific currency shall not at any time exceed the total amount of the principal of outstanding borrowings by the Bank that are payable in the same currency.

4. In the case of funds invested in equity capital out of the ordinary capital resources of the Bank, the total amount invested shall not exceed 10 per cent of the aggregate amount of the unimpaired paid-in capital stock of the Bank actually paid up at any given time together with the reserves and surplus included in its ordinary capital resources, excluding the Special Reserve.

5. The amount of any equity investment in any entity or enterprise shall not exceed such percentage of the equity capital of that entity or enterprise as the Board of Directors shall in each specific case determine to be appropriate. The Bank shall not seek to obtain by such investment a controlling interest in the entity or enterprise concerned, except where necessary to safeguard the investment of the Bank.

6. In the case of guarantees given by the Bank in the course of its ordinary operations, the total amount guaranteed shall not exceed 10 per cent of the aggregate amount of the unimpaired paid-in capital stock of the Bank actually paid up at any given time together with the reserves and surplus included in its ordinary capital resources excluding the Special Reserve.

Article 12: Provision of Currencies for Direct Loans

In making direct loans or participating in them, the Bank may provide finance in the following ways:

(a) by furnishing the borrower with currencies other than the currency of the Partner State in whose territory the project is located, which are needed by the borrower to meet the foreign exchange costs of the project; or

(b) by providing, when local currency required for the purposes of the loan cannot be raised by the borrower on reasonable terms, local currency but not exceeding a reasonable portion of the total local expenditure to be incurred by the borrower.

Article 13: Operating Principles

The operations of the Bank shall be conducted in accordance with the following principles:

(a) the Bank shall be guided by sound banking principles in its operations and shall finance only economically sound and technically feasible projects, and shall not make loans or undertake any responsibility for the discharge or re-financing of earlier commitments by borrowers;

(b) in selecting projects, the Bank shall always be guided by the need to pursue the objectives set forth in Article 1 of this Charter;

(c) subject to this Article, the Bank shall ensure that, taken over consecutive periods of five years, the first of which shall begin upon the commencement of the operations of the Bank, it shall so conduct its operations that it shall have loaned, guaranteed or otherwise invested, as nearly as is possible, in the United Republic of Tanzania $38\frac{3}{4}$ per cent of the total sum which it has loaned, guaranteed or otherwise invested of its ordinary capital resources and the Special Funds, in the Sovereign State of Uganda $38\frac{3}{4}$ per cent thereof and in the Republic of Kenya $22\frac{1}{2}$ per cent thereof:

Provided that, after a period of ten years from the commencement of operations of the Bank, the Partner States shall review the percentages specified in this paragraph and thereafter the Authority, after consultation with the Board of Directors, may by order published in the Gazette of the Community alter the percentages specified in this paragraph;

(d) the operations of the Bank shall provide principally for the financing directly of specific projects within the Partner States but may include loans to or guarantees of loans made to the national development agencies of the Partner States so long as such loans or guarantees are in respect of and used for specific projects which are agreed to by the Bank;

(e) the Bank shall seek to maintain a reasonable diversification in its investments;

(f) the Bank shall seek to revolve its funds by selling its investments in equity capital to other investors wherever it can appropriately do so on satisfactory terms;

(g) the Bank shall not finance any undertaking in the territory of a Partner State if that Partner State objects to such financing;

(h) before a loan is granted or guaranteed or an investment made, the applicant shall have submitted an adequate proposal to the Bank, and the Director-General of the Bank shall have presented to the Board of Directors a written report regarding the proposal, together with his recommendations;

(i) in considering an application for a loan or guarantee, the Bank shall pay due regard to the ability of the borrower to obtain finance or facilities elsewhere on terms and conditions that the Bank considers reasonable for the recipient, taking into account all pertinent factors;

(j) in making or guaranteeing a loan, the Bank shall pay due regard to the prospects that the borrower and its guarantor, if any, will be able to meet their obligations under the loan contract;

(k) in making or guaranteeing a loan, the rate of interest, other charges and the schedule for repayment of principal shall be such as are, in the opinion of the Bank, appropriate for the loan concerned;

(l) in guaranteeing a loan made by other investors, the Bank shall charge a suitable fee or commission for its risk;

(m) in the case of a direct loan made by the Bank, the borrower shall be permitted by the Bank to draw the loan funds only to meet payments in connection with the project as they fall due;

(n) the Bank shall take all necessary measures to ensure that the proceeds of any loan made, guaranteed or participated in by the Bank are used only for the purposes for which the loan was granted and with due attention to considerations of economy and efficiency; and

(o) the Bank shall ensure that every loan contract entered into by it shall enable the Bank to exercise all necessary powers of entry, inspection and supervision of operations in connection with the project and shall further enable the Bank to require the borrower to provide information and to allow inspection of its books and records during such time as any part of the loan remains outstanding.

Article 14: Prohibition of Political Activity

1. The Bank shall not accept loans, Special Funds or assistance that may in any way prejudice, limit, deflect or otherwise alter its objectives or functions.

2. The Bank, its Director-General and officers and staff shall not interfere in the political affairs of any Partner State, nor shall they be influenced in their decisions by the political character of a Partner State. Only economic considerations shall be relevant to their decisions and such considerations shall be weighed impartially to achieve and carry out the objectives and functions of the Bank.

Article 15: Terms and Conditions for Direct Loans and Guarantees

1. In the case of direct loans made or participated in or loans guaranteed by the Bank, the contract shall establish, in conformity with the operating principles set out above and subject to the other provisions of this Charter, the terms and conditions for the loan or the guarantee concerned, including payment of principal, interest, commitment fee and other charges, maturities and dates of payment in respect of the loan, or the fees and other charges in respect of the guarantee, respectively.

2. The contract shall provide that all payments to the Bank under the contract shall be made in the currency loaned, unless, in the case of a loan made or guaranteed as part of special operations, the regulations of the Bank provide otherwise.

3. Guarantees by the Bank shall also provide that the Bank may terminate its liability with respect to interest if, upon default by the borrower or any other guarantor, the Bank offers to purchase, at par and interest accrued to a date designated in the offer, the bonds or other obligations guaranteed.

4. Whenever it considers it appropriate, the Bank may require as a condition of granting or participating in a loan that the Partner State in whose territory a project is to be carried out, or a public agency or instrumentality of that Partner State acceptable to the Bank, guarantee the repayment of the

principal and the payment of interest and other charges on the loan in accordance with the terms thereof.

5. The loan or guarantee contract shall specifically state the currency in which all payments to the Bank thereunder shall be made.

Article 16: Commission and Fees

1. In addition to interest, the Bank shall charge a commission on direct loans made or participated in as part of its ordinary operations at a rate to be determined by the Board of Directors and computed on the amount outstanding on each loan or participation.

2. In guaranteeing a loan as part of its ordinary operations, the Bank shall charge a guarantee fee at a rate determined by the Board of Directors payable periodically on the amount of the loan outstanding.

3. Other charges, including commitment fee, of the Bank in its ordinary operations and any commission, fees or other charges in relation to its special operations shall be determined by the Board of Directors.

Article 17: Special Reserve

The amount of commissions and guarantee fees received by the Bank under the provisions of Article 16 of this Charter shall be set aside as a Special Reserve which shall be kept for meeting liabilities of the Bank in accordance with Article 18 of this Charter. The Special Reserve shall be held in such liquid form as the Board of Directors may decide but the Board of Directors shall ensure that any part of the Special Reserve which it may decide to invest in the territories of the Partner States shall be invested, as nearly as possible, in equal proportions in each Partner State.

Article 18: Defaults on Loans and Methods of Meeting Liabilities of the Bank

1. In cases of default on loans made, participated in or guaranteed by the Bank in its ordinary operations, the Bank shall take such action as it considers appropriate to conserve its investment including modification of the terms of the loan, other than any term as to the currency of repayment.

2. Payments in discharge of the Bank's liabilities on borrowings or guarantees chargeable to the ordinary capital resources shall be charged firstly against the Special Reserve and then, to the extent necessary and at the discretion of the Bank, against other reserves, surplus and capital available to the Bank.

3. Whenever necessary to meet contractual payments of interest, other charges or amortization on borrowings of the Bank in its ordinary operations, or to meet its liabilities with respect to similar payments in relation to loans guaranteed by it, chargeable to its ordinary capital resources, the Bank may call an appropriate amount of the uncalled subscribed callable capital in accordance with paragraphs 7 and 8 of Article 5 of this Charter.

CHAPTER V
MISCELLANEOUS POWERS AND DUTIES OF THE BANK

Article 19: Miscellaneous Powers

In addition to the powers specified elsewhere in this Charter, the Bank shall be empowered:

(a) to borrow funds in the territories of the Partner States, or elsewhere, and in this connection to furnish such collateral or other security therefor as the Bank shall determine:

Provided that:

(i) before selling its obligations or otherwise borrowing in the territory of a country, the Bank shall obtain the approval of the Government of that country to the sale; and

(ii) before deciding to sell its obligations or otherwise borrowing in a particular country, the Bank shall consider the amount of previous borrowing, if any, in that country with a view to diversifying its borrowing to the maximum extent possible;

(b) to buy and sell securities which the Bank has issued or guaranteed or in which it has invested;

(c) to guarantee securities in which it has invested in order to facilitate their sale;

(d) to invest funds not immediately needed in its operations in such obligations as it may determine and invest funds held by the Bank for pensions or similar purposes in marketable securities, but the Bank shall ensure that any funds which it may decide to invest in the territories of the Partner States shall be invested, as nearly as possible, in equal proportions in each Partner State;

(e) to provide technical advice and assistance which may serve its purposes and come within its functions and where appropriate, for example in the case of special feasibility studies, the Bank shall charge for such services; and

(f) to study and promote the investment opportunities within the Partner States.

Article 20: Allocation of Net Income

1. The Board of Directors shall determine annually what part of the net income of the Bank, including the net income accruing to the Special Funds, shall be allocated, after making provision for reserves, to surplus and what part, if any, shall be distributed to the members.

2. Any distributions to members made pursuant to paragraph 1 of this Article shall be in proportion to the number of shares held by each member and payments shall be made in such manner and in such currency as the Board of Directors shall determine.

Article 21: Power to Make Regulations

The Board of Directors may make such regulations, including financial regulations, being consistent with the provisions of this Charter as it considers necessary or appropriate to further the objectives and functions of the Bank.

Article 22: Notice to Be Placed on Securities

Every security issued or guaranteed by the Bank shall bear on its face a conspicuous statement to the effect that it is not an obligation of any Government, unless it is in fact the obligation of a particular Government, in which case it shall so state.

CHAPTER VI
CURRENCIES

Article 23: Determination of Convertibility

Whenever it shall become necessary under this Charter to determine whether any currency is convertible, such determination shall be made by the Bank after consultation with the International Monetary Fund.

Article 24: Use of Currencies

1. The Partner States may not maintain or impose any restriction on the holding or use by the Bank or by any recipient from the Bank for payments in any country of the following:
   (a) currencies received by the Bank in payment of subscriptions to its capital stock;
   (b) currencies purchased with the currencies referred to in sub-paragraph (a) of this paragraph;
   (c) currencies obtained by the Bank by borrowing for inclusion in its ordinary capital resources;
   (d) currencies received by the Bank in payment of principal, interest, dividends or other charges in respect of loans or investments made out of any of the funds referred to in sub-paragraphs (a), (b) and (c) of this paragraph or in payment of fees in respect of guarantees made by the Bank; and
   (e) currencies received from the Bank in distribution of the net income of the Bank in accordance with Article 20 of this Charter.

2. The Partner States may not maintain or impose any restriction on the holding or use by the Bank or by any recipient from the Bank, for payments in any country, of currency received by the Bank which does not come within the provisions of paragraph 1 of this Article unless such currency forms part of the Special Funds of the Bank and its use is subject to special regulations.

3. The Partner States may not maintain or impose any restriction on the holding or use by the Bank, for making amortisation payments or for repurchasing in whole or in part the Bank's own obligations, of currencies received by the Bank in repayment of direct loans made out of its ordinary capital resources.

4. Each Partner State shall ensure, in respect of projects within its territories, that the currencies necessary to enable payments to be made to the Bank in accordance with the provisions of the contracts referred to in Article 15 of this Charter shall be made available in exchange for currency of the Partner State concerned.

Article 25: Maintenance of Value of Currency Holdings

1. Whenever the par value in the International Monetary Fund of the currency of a Partner State is reduced or the foreign exchange value of the currency of a Partner State has, in the opinion of the Bank, depreciated to a significant extent within the territory of that Partner State, such Partner State shall pay to the Bank within a reasonable time an additional amount of its own currency sufficient to maintain the value, as of the time of subscription, of the amount of the currency of such Partner State paid in to the Bank by that Partner State under sub-paragraph (b) of paragraph 3 of Article 5 of this Charter, and currency furnished under the provisions of this paragraph, provided, however, that the foregoing shall apply only so long as and to the extent that such currency shall not have been initially disbursed or exchanged for another currency.

2. Whenever the par value in the International Monetary Fund of the currency of a Partner State is increased, or the foreign exchange value of the currency of a Partner State has, in the opinion of the Bank, appreciated to a significant extent within the territory of that Partner State, the Bank shall return to such Partner State within a reasonable time an amount of the currency of that Partner State equal to the increase in the value of the amount of such currency to which the provisions of paragraph 1 of this Article are applicable.

CHAPTER VII
ORGANIZATION AND MANAGEMENT OF THE BANK

Article 26: Structure

The Bank shall have a Board of Directors, a Director-General and such other officers and staff as it may consider necessary.

Article 27: Board of Directors

1. All the powers of the Bank shall, subject to this Charter, be vested in the Board of Directors.

2. The Board of Directors shall consist of not more than five nor fewer than three members of whom:

(a) three shall be appointed by the Partner States, each of which shall appoint one; and

(b) up to two shall be elected by the members other than the Partner States in accordance with such procedure as the said members shall from time to time decide:

Provided that no single member shall be represented by more than one director.

3. All directors shall be persons possessing high competence and wide experience in economic, financial and banking affairs.

4. Directors shall hold office for a term of three years and shall be eligible for re-appointment or re-election:

Provided that:

(a) of the first directors of the Bank two, who shall be chosen by the directors by lot, shall hold office for two years;

(b) a director shall remain in office until his successor has been appointed or elected;

(c) a director appointed or elected in place of one whose office has become vacant before the end of his term shall hold office only for the remainder of that term;

(d) a director appointed by a Partner State may be required at any time by that Partner State to vacate his office.

5. There shall be appointed or elected, as the case may be, an alternate director in respect of each substantive director and an alternate director shall be appointed or elected in the same manner and for the same term of office as the director to whom he is an alternate; and an alternate director shall remain in office until his successor has been appointed or elected.

6. An alternate director may participate in meetings but may vote only when he is acting in place of and in the absence of the director to whom he is an alternate.

7. While the office of a director is vacant the alternate of the former director shall exercise the powers of that director.

Article 28: Procedure of the Board of Directors

1. The Board of Directors shall normally meet at the principal office of the Bank and shall meet at least once every three months or more frequently if the business of the Bank so requires.

2. Meetings of the Board of Directors shall be convened by the Director-General of the Bank.

3. Four directors, including the three directors appointed by the Partner States, or, if there is no member other than the Partner States, three directors, shall constitute a quorum for any meeting of the Board of Directors:

Provided that if within two hours of the time appointed for the holding of a meeting of the Board of Directors a quorum is not present, the meeting shall automatically stand adjourned to the next day, at the same time and place, or if that day is a public holiday, to the next succeeding day which is not a public holiday at the same time and place, and if at such adjourned meeting a quorum is not present within two hours from the time appointed for the meeting, the directors present shall constitute a quorum and may transact the business for which the meeting was called.

4. The Board of Directors may, by regulation, establish a procedure whereby a decision in writing signed by all the Directors of the Bank shall be as valid and effectual as if it had been made at a meeting of the Board of Directors.

Article 29: Voting

1. The voting power of each member of the Bank shall be equal to the number of shares of the capital stock of the Bank held by that member.

2. In voting in the Board of Directors:
(a) an appointed director shall be entitled to cast the number of votes of the Partner State which appointed him;
(b) each elected director shall be entitled to cast the number of votes of the members of the Bank whom he represents, which votes need not be cast as a unit; and
(c) except as otherwise expressly provided in this Charter, all matters before the Board of Directors shall be decided by a majority of the total voting power of the members of the Bank.

Article 30: Director-General of the Bank

1. There shall be a Director-General of the Bank who shall be appointed by the Authority after consultation with the Board of Directors, and who, while he remains Director-General, may not hold office as a Director or an alternate to a Director.

2. Subject to paragraph 3 of this Article, the Director-General shall hold office for a term of five years and may be re-appointed.

3. The Director-General shall vacate his office if the Authority after consultation with the Board of Directors so decides.

4. If the office of Director-General becomes vacant for any reason, a successor shall be appointed for a new term of five years.

5. The Director-General shall preside at meetings of the Board of Directors but shall have no vote.

6. The Director-General shall be the legal representative of the Bank.

7. The Director-General shall be chief of the staff of the Bank and shall conduct under the direction of the Board of Directors the current business of the Bank. He shall be responsible for the organization, appointment and dismissal of the officers and staff in accordance with regulations adopted by the Board of Directors.

8. In appointing officers and staff the Director-General shall, subject to the paramount importance of securing the highest standards of efficiency and technical competence, pay due regard to the recruitment of citizens of the Partner States.

Article 31: Loyalties of Director-General and Officers and Staff

The Director-General and officers and staff of the Bank, in the discharge of their offices, owe their duty entirely to the Bank and to no other authority. Each member of the Bank shall respect the international character of this duty and shall refrain from all attempts to influence the Director-General or any of the officers and staff in the discharge of their duties.

Article 32: Offices of the Bank

The principal office of the Bank shall be located at Kampala in Uganda and the Bank may establish offices or agencies elsewhere.

Article 33: Channel of Communications, Depositories

1. Each member of the Bank shall designate an appropriate official, entity or person with whom the Bank may communicate in connection with any matter arising under this Charter.

2. Each Partner State shall designate its central bank, or such other agency as may be agreed upon with the Bank, as a depository with which the Bank may keep its holdings of currency and other assets.

Article 34: Working Language

The working language of the Bank shall be English.

Article 35: Accounts and Reports

1. The Board of Directors shall ensure that proper accounts and proper records are kept in relation to the operations of the Bank and such accounts shall be audited in respect of each financial year by auditors of high repute selected by the Board of Directors.

2. The Bank shall prepare and transmit to the Authority and to the members of the Bank, and shall also publish, an annual report containing an audited statement of its accounts.

3. The Bank shall prepare and transmit to its members quarterly a summary statement of its financial position and a profit and loss statement showing the results of its operations.

4. All financial statements of the Bank shall show ordinary operations and the operations of each Special Fund separately.

5. The Bank may also publish such other reports as it considers desirable in carrying out its objectives and functions and such reports shall be transmitted to members of the Bank.

CHAPTER VIII
WITHDRAWAL AND SUSPENSION OF MEMBERS

Article 36: Withdrawal of Members

1. A Partner State may not withdraw from the Bank.

2. Any member, other than a Partner State, may withdraw from the Bank at any time by delivering a notice in writing to the Bank at its principal office.

3. Withdrawal by a member under paragraph 2 of this Article shall become effective, and its membership shall cease, on the date specified in its notice but in no event less than six months after the date that notice has been received by the Bank. However, at any time before the withdrawal becomes finally effective, the member may notify the Bank in writing of the cancellation of its notice of intention to withdraw.

4. A withdrawing member shall remain liable for all direct and contingent obligations to the Bank to which it was subject at the date of delivery of the withdrawal notice. If the withdrawal becomes finally effective, the member shall not incur any liability for obligations resulting from operations of the Bank effected after the date on which the withdrawal notice was received by the Bank.

Article 37: Suspension of Membership

1. If a member of the Bank, other than a Partner State, fails to fulfil any of its obligations to the Bank, the Board of Directors may suspend such member by a majority vote of the total number of Directors representing not less than 75 per cent of the total voting power of the members including the affirmative votes of each of the Partner States.

2. The member so suspended shall automatically cease to be a member of the Bank six months from the date of its suspension unless the Board of Directors decides, within that period and by the same majority necessary for suspension, to restore the member to good standing.

3. While under suspension, a member shall not be entitled to exercise any rights under this Charter but shall remain subject to all its obligations.

Article 38: Settlement of Accounts

1. After the date on which a member ceases to be a member, it shall remain liable for its direct obligations to the Bank and for its contingent liabilities to the Bank so long as any part of the loans or guarantees contracted before it ceased to be a member is outstanding; but it shall not incur liabilities with respect to loans and guarantees entered into thereafter by the Bank nor share either in the income or the expenses of the Bank.

2. At the time a member ceases to be a member, the Bank shall arrange for the repurchase of its shares by the Bank as a part of the settlement of accounts with such member in accordance with the provisions of paragraphs 3 and 4 of this Article. For this purpose, the repurchase price of the shares shall be the value shown by the books of the Bank on the date the member ceases to be a member.

3. The payment for shares repurchased by the Bank under this Article shall be governed by the following conditions:

(a) any amount due to the member concerned for its shares shall be withheld so long as that member remains liable, as a borrower or guarantor, to the Bank and such amount may, at the option of the Bank, be applied on any such liability as it matures. No amount shall be withheld on account of the contingent liability of the member for future calls on its subscription for shares in accordance with paragraph 7 of Article 5 of this Charter. In any event, no amount due to a member for its shares shall be paid until six months after the date on which the member ceases to be a member;

(b) payments for shares may be made from time to time, upon their surrender by the member concerned, to the extent by which the amount due as the repurchase price in accordance with paragraph 2 of this Article exceeds the aggregate amount of liabilities on loans and guarantees referred to in sub-paragraph (a) of this paragraph, until the former member has received the full repurchase price;

(c) payments shall be made in such available currencies as the Bank determines, taking into account its financial position; and

(d) if losses are sustained by the Bank on any guarantees or loans which were outstanding on the date when a member ceased to be a member and the amount of such losses exceeds the amount of the reserve provided against losses on that date, the member concerned shall repay, upon demand, the amount by which the repurchase price of its shares would have been reduced if the losses had been taken into account when the repurchase price was determined. In addition, the former member shall remain liable on any call for unpaid subscriptions in accordance with paragraph 7 of Article 5 of this Charter, to the same extent that it would have been required to respond if the impairment of capital had occurred and the call had been made at the time the repurchase price of its shares was determined.

4. If the Bank terminates its operations pursuant to Article 39 of this Charter within six months of the date upon which any member ceases to be a member, all rights of the member concerned shall be determined in accordance with the provisions of Articles 39 to 41 of this Charter. Such member shall be considered as still a member for the purposes of such Articles but shall have no voting rights.

CHAPTER IX
TERMINATION OF OPERATIONS

Article 39: Termination of Operations

1. The Bank may terminate its operations by resolution of the Board of Directors approved by a vote representing not less than 85 per cent of the total voting power of the members and with the approval also of the Authority.

2. After such termination, the Bank shall forthwith cease all activities, except those incidental to the orderly realization, conservation and preservation of its assets and the settlement of its obligations.

Article 40: Liability of Members and Payment of Claims

1. In the event of termination of the operations of the Bank, the liability of all members for uncalled subscriptions to the capital stock of the Bank

shall continue until all claims of creditors, including all contingent claims, shall have been discharged.

2. All creditors holding direct claims shall first be paid out of the assets of the Bank and then out of payments to the Bank on unpaid or callable subscriptions. Before making any payments to creditors holding direct claims, the Board of Directors shall make such arrangements as are necessary, in its judgment, to ensure a *pro rata* distribution among holders of direct and contingent claims.

Article 41: Distribution of Assets

1. No distribution of assets shall be made to members on account of their subscriptions to the capital stock of the Bank until all liabilities to creditors shall have been discharged or provided for and any such distribution shall be approved by the Board of Directors by a vote representing not less than 85 per cent of the total voting power of the members.

2. Any distribution of the assets of the Bank to the members shall be in proportion to the capital stock held by each member and shall be effected at such times and under such conditions as the Bank shall consider fair and equitable. The shares of assets distributed need not be uniform as to type of asset. No member shall be entitled to receive its share in such a distribution of assets until it has settled all of its obligations to the Bank.

3. Any member receiving assets distributed pursuant to this Article shall enjoy the same rights with respect to such assets as the Bank enjoyed prior to their distribution.

CHAPTER X
STATUS, IMMUNITIES AND PRIVILEGES

Article 42: Purpose of Chapter

To enable the Bank effectively to fulfil its objectives and carry out the functions with which it is entrusted, the status, immunities, exemptions and privileges set forth in this Chapter shall be accorded to the Bank in the territories of each of the Partner States.

Article 43: Legal Status

The Bank shall possess full juridical personality and, in particular, full capacity:

(a) to contract;
(b) to acquire, and dispose of, immovable and movable property; and
(c) to institute legal proceedings.

Article 44: Judicial Proceedings

1. Actions may be brought against the Bank in the territories of the Partner States only in a court of competent jurisdiction in a Partner State in which the Bank has an office, has appointed an agent for the purpose of accepting service or notice of process, or has issued or guaranteed securities.

2. No action shall be brought against the Bank by members or persons acting for or deriving claims from members. However, members shall have recourse to such special procedures for the settlement of controversies between the Bank and its members as may be prescribed in this Charter, in the regulations of the Bank or in contracts entered into with the Bank.

Article 45: Immunity of Assets

1. Property and other assets of the Bank, wheresoever located and by whomsoever held, shall be immune from requisition, confiscation, expropriation or any other form of taking or foreclosure by executive or legislative action and premises used for the business of the Bank shall be immune from search.

2. The Bank shall prevent its premises from becoming refuges for fugitives from justice, or for persons subject to extradition, or persons avoiding service of legal process or a judicial proceeding.

Article 46: Immunity of Archives

The archives of the Bank and all documents belonging to it, or held by it, shall be inviolable wherever located.

Article 47: Freedom of Assets from Restriction

To the extent necessary to carry out the objectives and functions of the Bank and subject to the provisions of this Charter, all property and other assets of the Bank shall be free from restrictions, regulations, controls and moratoria of any nature.

Article 48: Personal Immunities and Privileges

Directors, alternates, officers and employees of the Bank and experts and consultants rendering services to the Bank shall have the immunities and privileges provided for under Article 3 of the Treaty to which this Charter is annexed.

Article 49: Exemption from Taxation

1. The Bank shall be enabled to import free of customs duty any goods required for the purpose of its operations except such goods as are intended for sale, or are sold, to the public.

2. No transfer tax may be imposed upon manufactured goods which are required by the Bank for the purpose of its operations, otherwise than upon such goods as are intended for sale, or are sold, to the public.

3. The Bank shall be exempted from income tax and stamp duty.

Article 50: Implementation

Each Partner State shall promptly take such action as is necessary to make effective within that Partner State the provisions set forth in this Chapter and shall inform the Bank of the action which it has taken on the matter.

Article 51: Waiver of Immunities

1. The Bank at its discretion may waive any of the privileges, immunities and exemptions conferred under this Chapter in any case or instance, in such manner and upon such conditions as it may determine to be appropriate in the best interests of the Bank.

2. The Bank shall take every measure to ensure that the privileges, immunities, exemptions and facilities conferred by this Charter are not abused and for this purpose shall establish such regulations as it may consider necessary and expedient.

CHAPTER XI
AMENDMENT, INTERPRETATION AND ARBITRATION

Article 52: Amendment of the Charter

1. This Charter may be amended only by a resolution of the Board of Directors approved by a vote representing not less than 85 per cent of the total voting power of the members and thereafter approved by the Authority.

2. An amendment to this Charter shall be published as a Legal Notice in the Gazette of the Community and shall enter into force three calendar months after the date of such publication unless the resolution referred to in paragraph 1 of this Article otherwise provides.

3. Notwithstanding the provisions of paragraph 1 of this Article, the unanimous agreement of the Board of Directors shall be required for the approval of any amendment of the Charter modifying:

    (a) the right of a member, other than a Partner State, to withdraw from the Bank as provided in Article 36 of this Charter;

    (b) the right to subscribe to capital stock of the Bank as provided in paragraph 5 of Article 4 of this Charter; and

    (c) the limitation on liability as provided in paragraphs 8 and 9 of Article 4 of this Charter.

Article 53: Interpretation or Application

Any question of interpretation or application of the provisions of this Charter arising between any member and the Bank or between two or more members of the Bank shall be submitted to the Board of Directors for decision.

Article 54: Arbitration

1. If a disagreement shall arise between the Bank and a member or between the Bank and a former member of the Bank including a disagreement in respect of a decision of the Board of Directors under Article 53 of this Charter, such disagreement shall be submitted to arbitration by a tribunal of three arbitrators. One of the arbitrators shall be appointed by the Bank, another by the member or former member concerned and the third, unless the parties otherwise agree, by the Executive Secretary of the Economic

Commission for Africa or such other authority as may have been prescribed by regulations made by the Board of Directors.

2. A majority vote of the arbitrators shall be sufficient to reach a decision which shall be final and binding on the parties and a decision of the arbitrators may include an order as to payment of costs and expenses.

3. The third arbitrator shall be empowered to settle all questions of procedure in any case where the parties are in disagreement with respect thereto.

CHAPTER XII
FINAL PROVISIONS

Article 55: Signature and Deposit

1. Upon the signature of the Treaty to which this Charter is annexed on behalf of all three Partner States, a copy of this Charter shall be deposited with the Secretary General of the Common Services Organization where it shall remain open until the first day of December 1967 for signature by the bodies corporate, enterprises or institutions approved under paragraph 1 of Article 2 of this Charter.

2. Immediately after the first day of December 1967 the Secretary General of the Community shall send certified copies of this Charter to all the Partner States and others who by signing this Charter become members of the Bank.

Article 56: Entry into Force

This Charter shall enter into force at the same time as does the Treaty to which it is annexed.

Article 57: Commencement of Operations

1. As soon as this Charter enters into force, the Directors shall be appointed or elected in accordance with the provisions of Article 27 of this Charter and the Secretary General of the Community shall call the first meeting of the Board of Directors.

2. At its first meeting the Board of Directors shall determine the date on which the Bank shall commence its operations.

3. The Bank shall notify its members of the date of the commencement of its operations.

Article 58: Definitions

In this Charter, unless the context otherwise requires:

"Authority" means the East African Authority established by Article 46 of the Treaty to which this Charter is annexed;

"Board of Directors" means the Board of Directors of the Bank;

"Community" means the East African Community established by Article 1 of the Treaty to which this Charter is annexed;

"Director-General" means the Director-General of the Bank;

"Treaty" means the Treaty for East African Co-operation to which this Charter is annexed.

CHAPTER EIGHTEEN

Andean Development Corporation

A deadlock reached by LAFTA during the first five years of its existence on most issues involving the implementation of commitments contained in the Montevideo Treaty led to the appearance in the mid-sixties of three informal LAFTA member groupings, according to their development levels: the big three (Argentina, Brazil, and Mexico), the middle group (Colombia, Chile, Peru, and Uruguay, joined by Venezuela after its entry into LAFTA in 1966), and the least developed republics (Ecuador, Paraguay, and Bolivia).

On the initiative of the presidents of Chile and Colombia, a meeting of heads of state was held in Bogotá in August 1966 with the participation of Colombia, Chile, Ecuador, Peru, and Venezuela. It resulted in the adoption of the Bogotá Declaration, accompanied by an agreement covering the program for immediate action, which defined the fields in which the signatory countries showed readiness to accelerate economic integration by mutual concessions not extended to other LAFTA members but without abandoning the broader commitments contained in the Montevideo Treaty. It was agreed at the Bogotá meeting that the five republics of the South American Pacific coast would free trade within the subregion before the completion of the free trade zone scheme provided for by the LAFTA agreement; coordinate industrial development policies, especially in new and dynamic sectors; bring about the establishment of multinational industrial enterprises; formulate a subregional program of import substitution; establish a subregional transport and telecommunications policy; and promote mutual technical assistance. It was decided also at Bogotá to set up immediately a Joint Commission to draft the necessary legal agreements and take care of their implementation, and to establish a regional development corporation. Bolivia joined in the agreement in 1967.

The American chiefs of state at their meeting in Punta del Este in April 1967 and the LAFTA Council of Ministers of Foreign Relations, at a meeting held in Asunción, Paraguay, in the fall of the same year, recognized the right of the so-called Andean group to proceed with a subregional integration scheme under the assumption that it would later be absorbed by the future Latin American common market.

Between the final months of 1966 and the beginning of 1968 the work on the Andean subregional integration scheme advanced considerably. The Joint Commission held five meetings with the participation of high-level officials of the five signatory countries of the Bogotá Declaration and Bolivia. During the winter of 1967/68 the Joint Commission drafted the outline of a general subregional agreement, bases for the establishment of common external tariffs and the accelerated trade liberalization program within the area, statutes of the Andean Development Corporation, and the outline of a complementarity agreement covering the petrochemical industry.

The Constitutive Agreement of the Andean Development Corporation was signed by the six countries in early February 1968. The authorized capital of the Corporation was set at $100 million and the paid-in capital at $25 million. Each of the four major members (Colombia, Chile, Peru, and Venezuela) agreed to subscribe shares valued at $5.5 million. The capital participation of the two smaller countries (Bolivia and Ecuador) was fixed at $1.5 million each. The Corporation will provide technical and financial assistance for the establishment of new enterprises and the expansion, modernization, or conversion of those already existing in the subregion, taking into consideration the need for specialization and an equitable distribution of investments within the area and the special needs of the less developed member countries. The Corporation also expects to be able to mobilize additional financial resources through the issue of bonds and other obligations to be placed within the area or in the advanced countries. The constitutive chapter of the Andean Development Corporation is somewhat similar to that of Central American Bank for Economic Integration and the East African Development Bank. The institution differs, however, from these other subregional development banks by circumscribing its field of activity to industrial and service enterprises, whether owned publicly or privately, directly related to the subregional integration process. It is expected that the Andean Development Corporation will start its operations in 1969.

Bibliographic References

Botero, Rodrigo. *La comunidad económica caribe-andina.* Bogotá: Ediciones Tercer Mundo, 1967.

"Convenio Constitutivo de la Corporación Andina de Fomento," *Boletín Mensual del CEMLA* (Mexico City), Vol. XIV, No. 3 (March 1968).

CONSTITUTIVE AGREEMENT OF THE ANDEAN
DEVELOPMENT CORPORATION*

The Governments of the Republics of Ecuador, Bolivia, Colombia, Chile, Peru, and Venezuela, moved by a mutual desire to obtain their countries' economic integration as soon as possible in order to accelerate the economic and social development of their peoples, in accord with the principles established by the Montevideo Treaty, the Charter of Punta del Este, the Declaration undersigned in Bogotá by the Presidents of Colombia, Chile, and Venezuela and by personal representatives of the Presidents of Bolivia, Ecuador, and Peru, and the Punta del Este Declaration of American Presidents;

Express the need that each of the signatory countries of the Bogotá Declaration shall set itself the task of creating more propitious economic conditions for participation in the Latin American Common Market;

Declare that in order to obtain these objectives, difficulties that arise due to different levels of development, different general economic conditions, and, particularly, markets must be resolved so as to achieve the subregion's harmonious and equilibrated growth;

Bear in mind that the Bogotá Declaration set up the Joint Commission and other agencies as organs to promote, guide, and coordinate the policies to be adopted in the different countries of the subregion, and advised the establishment of an organization that would embody and put into practice the measures adopted, particularly with regard to the study and execution of multinational projects that would serve as a galvanizing force in the operation and perfection of a subregional integration agreement;

Consider that for more efficient accomplishment of the different activities that the aforementioned organization shall carry out so as to fulfill its role in the subregion, it is convenient that each of the countries shall proceed to adopt the pertinent legal, regulatory, and administrative measures;

Consider that the participation of subregional, and extrasubregional, public and private sectors, as well as of international finance institutions, is of para-

* Signed in Bogotá, Colombia, February 7, 1968, by Bolivia, Colombia, Chile, Ecuador, Peru, and Venezuela. The text given here is an unofficial translation from the Spanish text published as Annex 4 in Comisión Mixta, Comité de Expertos, *Declaración de Bogotá* (Bogotá, Colombia, January–April 1968; mimeographed). [Editor's note.]

mount importance because of the technical, scientific, financial, and technological assistance they can provide;

Underscore the importance of joint action by the countries of the subregion to achieve equilibrated and harmonious economic development together with the other Latin American nations that, once integrated, will form the Common Market; and

Have resolved to create a development corporation and conclude an Agreement for its constitution, designating to this end Plenipotentiary Representatives who, after having presented their credentials, which were duly accepted, have agreed to constitute the *Andean Development Corporation,* which will be governed by the following dispositions:

CHAPTER I: NAME, LEGAL CHARACTER, HEADQUARTERS, OBJECTIVE, AND FUNCTIONS

ARTICLE 1
NAME AND LEGAL CHARACTER

By the present Agreement, the Contracting Parties constitute the Andean Development Corporation.

The Corporation is a legal person by public international law and is governed by the dispositions contained in the present instrument.

ARTICLE 2
HEADQUARTERS

The Corporation shall have its headquarters in the city of Caracas, Republic of Venezuela.

The Corporation may establish the agencies, offices, or delegations required to conduct its activities in each of the participating countries, or elsewhere.

ARTICLE 3
OBJECTIVE

The Corporation's objective is to foster the subregional integration process. In a spirit of rational specialization and equitable distribution of investments within the area, taking into account the need for efficient action on behalf of the relatively less developed countries, and in effective coordination with the organization in charge of subregional integration, it shall foster the best possible use of opportunities and resources that its sphere of action provides, through the creation of production or service enterprises and the expansion, modernization, or conversion of those already existing.

ARTICLE 4
FUNCTIONS

In order to achieve the objective expressed in Article 3, the Corporation shall have the following functions:

a. effect studies designed to identify investment opportunities and prepare the corresponding projects;

b. make known the results of its research and studies to the countries of the area so as to provide adequate guidance for the investment of available resources;

c. provide, directly or indirectly, the technical and financial aid necessary for the preparation and execution of multinational or complementarity projects;

d. obtain internal or external credits;

e. issue bonds, debentures, and other obligations to be placed within or without the subregion;

f. promote the capture and mobilization of resources.

In the exercise of its functions enumerated in points (e) and (f), the Corporation shall be subject to the laws of the countries in which these activities would take place or in whose currencies the respective obligations are denominated;

g. promote capital and technological contributions under the most advantageous conditions;

h. grant loans and provide sureties, endorsements, and other guarantees;

i. promote guarantees for underwriting stock certificates and grant guarantees in cases that fulfill adequate conditions;

j. promote the organization, expansion, modernization, and conversion of enterprises, and to this end underwrite stock certificates or shares.

The Corporation may transfer the stocks, shares, rights, or debentures that it acquires, offering them primarily to subregional public or private groups or, for want of demand, to third parties interested in the subregion's economic and social development;

k. undertake, in conditions that it shall determine, the specific commissions or negotiations entrusted to it by stockholders or third parties;

l. coordinate its action with that of other national and international agencies in developing the subregion;

m. recommend to subregional agencies or organizations that provide investment resources the necessary instruments of coordination;

n. acquire and dispose of personal property or real estate, initiate or answer legal and administrative action, and generally carry out all kinds of operations, acts, contracts, and agreements required for the fulfillment of its objective.

CHAPTER II: CAPITAL, SHARES, AND SHAREHOLDERS

ARTICLE 5
CAPITAL

The Corporation's authorized capital is one hundred million U.S. dollars (U.S. $100,000,000), distributed in series "A" and "B" shares, besides those of series "C" that may be authorized by the Board of Directors.

Underwritten capital is twenty-five million U.S. dollars (U.S. $25,000,000), distributed in the following series:

a. series "A," made up of six (6) nominative shares with a value of one million U.S. dollars (U.S. $1,000,000) each. One of these shares shall be underwritten by the government of each country of the subregion, or by the public, semipublic, or private agency that it shall designate, and

b. series "B," made up of three thousand eight hundred (3,800) nominative shares with a value of five thousand U.S. dollars (U.S. $5,000) each, which shall be underwritten with the guarantee of each respective Government as follows:

Bolivia	100 shares at U.S. $5,000 each	$ 500,000
Colombia	900 shares at U.S. $5,000 each	4,500,000
Chile	900 shares at U.S. $5,000 each	4,500,000
Ecuador	100 shares at U.S. $5,000 each	500,000
Peru	900 shares at U.S. $5,000 each	$4,500,000
Venezuela	900 shares at U.S. $5,000 each	4,500,000
	3,800 shares at U.S. $5,000 each	$19,000,000

These shares may be effectively subscribed in each country by the respective Government, or by the public, semipublic, or private agency that it shall designate, or by natural or legal persons. In the latter case, the maximum available for subscription shall be forty (40) per cent of the total shares of this series corresponding to each country.

The shares of both series "A" and "B" corresponding to each country shall be distinguished by the name of the respective country.

ARTICLE 6
ISSUES OF SHARES DRAWN ON NOT SUBSCRIBED AUTHORIZED CAPITAL

Not subscribed authorized capital, that is, seventy-five million U.S. dollars (U.S. $75,000,000) may be offered for subscription by the Board of Directors by a favorable vote of at least seven (7) Directors, in the following instances:

a. for the issue of new series "B" shares to be offered preferentially to shareholders in proportion to the certificates they already hold, in relation to total capital;

b. for the issue of shares in the case of affiliation by another country, on which occasion the new member may underwrite, directly or through the organization it designates, one share of series "A" and a number of series "B" shares, in the terms specified in point (b) of Article 5, and those others established by the Board of Directors;

c. for the issue of series "C" shares, the characteristics of which shall be determined by the Board of Directors in each case, reserved for subscription by legal or natural persons from outside the subregion.

ARTICLE 7
SPECIAL SUBSCRIPTION RIGHTS

Notwithstanding the provision contained in point (a) of Article 6, any country holding fewer series "B" shares than other countries may at any time subscribe shares corresponding to authorized capital up to an amount equal to that held by the largest shareholder.

ARTICLE 8
CAPITAL PAYMENT

Series "A" and "B" shares shall be redeemed in five (5) yearly consecutive payments, starting ninety (90) days after this Agreement goes into effect or, should it be the case, thirty (30) days after the date of ratification.

At least fifty (50) per cent of each payment shall be liquidated in U.S. dollars, with the exception of the first, which should be paid entirely in U.S. currency.

The other fifty (50) per cent of the remaining payments may be liquidated in the national currency of each country, provided the complete convertibility and maintenance of value of the currency in question vis-à-vis the U.S. dollar, as of the date this Agreement goes into effect, has been guaranteed to the satisfaction of the Corporation, subject to decision by the Board of Directors.

ARTICLE 9
INCREASE OR DECREASE OF CAPITAL

Capital may be increased or decreased, subject to decision at the Shareholders' meeting.

ARTICLE 10
TRANSFERABILITY OF SHARES

Subject to approval by the respective Government, series "A" shares may be transferred in each country to the public, semipublic, or private agencies that it shall designate. Series "B" shares shall be transferable only to legal or natural persons from the respective countries of the subregion, according to the percentage specified in point (b) of Article 5.

CHAPTER III: SHAREHOLDERS' MEETINGS

ARTICLE 11
SHAREHOLDERS' MEETINGS

Shareholders' meetings may be ordinary or extraordinary. They shall be attended by the shareholders, or their representatives or agents, assembled in the quorum and under conditions established in this Agreement.

ARTICLE 12
ORDINARY AND EXTRAORDINARY MEETINGS

An ordinary meeting shall be called once a year by the Executive President of the Corporation, within ninety (90) days after the end of the fiscal year. Extraordinary meetings may be called by the Executive President of the Corporation, on his own initiative or on that of the Board of Directors, or of two (2) series "A" shareholders, or of shareholders representing at least twenty-five (25) per cent of the paid-up capital. Notice to attend extraordinary meetings shall be given thirty (30) days in advance of the date fixed and shall indicate the reasons for calling it.

ARTICLE 13
ATTRIBUTIONS OF THE ORDINARY MEETING

The attributions of the ordinary meeting shall be:
a. after hearing the outside auditors' report, to consider the Board of Directors' annual report, the general balance sheet and statement of losses and earnings, and to determine the employment of profits;
b. to elect members of the Board of Directors in accordance with the norms established in this Agreement;
c. to designate the outside auditors;
d. to take cognizance of any other matter expressly placed before it that is not in the domain of any other organ of the Corporation.

ARTICLE 14
ATTRIBUTIONS OF THE EXTRAORDINARY MEETING

The attributions of the Extraordinary Meeting shall be:
a. to augment, diminish, or replenish capital stock;
b. to dissolve the Corporation;
c. to change Corporation headquarters on the initiative of the Board of Directors; and
d. to take cognizance of any other matter expressly placed before it that is not in the domain of any other organ of the Corporation.
The extraordinary meeting may deal only with matters expressly stipulated in the notice.

ARTICLE 15
REVISION OF THE AGREEMENT

The extraordinary meeting shall be empowered to modify the dispositions that govern the Corporation in all those administrative and procedural matters necessary for the fulfillment of the proposed objectives.
The extraordinary meeting, by the unanimous vote of the six (6) series "A" shareholders and of one half plus one of the other shares represented at

the meeting, may also modify the structure of the Board of Directors and adopt the pertinent dispositions, always bearing in mind the basic norms of this Agreement.

In those other dispositions relative to the structure of the Corporation itself, the extraordinary meeting may propose amendments that it considers should be submitted to the Contracting Parties for approval.

ARTICLE 16
QUORUM

A quorum for ordinary and extraordinary shareholders' meetings shall consist of a number of persons representing at least four (4) series "A" shares and fifty (50) per cent of the other shares.

In cases of lack of the quorum needed to hold an ordinary or extraordinary meeting, another meeting shall be called on at least thirty (30) days' advance notice, stating that the assembly shall take place regardless of the number of participants.

ARTICLE 17
DECISIONS

Decisions shall be made at ordinary meetings by a majority representing at least three (3) series "A" shares and one half plus one of the other shares represented at the meeting.

The required majority for extraordinary meetings shall be four (4) series "A" shares and one half plus one of the other shares represented at the meeting.

In the case of a second notice, decisions at both ordinary and extraordinary meetings shall be adopted by at least two (2) series "A" shareholders, plus the absolute majority of the other shares represented at the meeting.

ARTICLE 18
VOTING RIGHTS

Shareholders who are behind in the payment of their capital contributions shall be deprived of their voting rights.

ARTICLE 19
REPORTS AND BALANCE STATEMENTS

Each shareholder is entitled to examine the inventory and list of shareholders at Corporation headquarters during the fifteen (15) days prior to the holding of shareholders' meetings, and may request a copy of the general balance statement and auditors' report. At least fifteen (15) days before each meeting, reports and statements shall be remitted to all shareholders at the address registered with the Corporation.

ARTICLE 20
MINUTES

The deliberations and agreements of each meeting shall be recorded in a special book of minutes.

ARTICLE 21
VOTES OF THE BOARD OF DIRECTORS

The Board of Directors and the Executive President may not vote on approval of the balance statement, nor on matters in which their responsibility is involved. Neither may they act at meetings as agents for other shareholders.

ARTICLE 22
BINDING POWER OF DECISIONS

Decisions taken at meetings, within the attributions specified in this Agreement, are binding on all shareholders, including those who did not attend.

CHAPTER IV: BOARD OF DIRECTORS

ARTICLE 23
COMPOSITION

The Board shall be composed of eleven (11) Directors elected for a period of three (3) years, who may be re-elected. Each Director shall have a personal substitute elected for the same term and by the same means as the principal holder.

ARTICLE 24
DESIGNATION AND ELECTION

The Board of Directors shall be elected as follows:

a. one (1) Director and his substitute shall be designated by each of the six (6) series "A" shareholders;

b. the remaining five (5) Directors and their substitutes shall be elected by series "B" shareholders. Each shareholder shall have a number of votes equal to the number of shares he possesses or represents, multiplied by the number of Directors to be elected. Each shareholder may give all his votes to one candidate or distribute them among various candidates. Candidates receiving the highest number of votes shall be elected;

c. the five (5) Directors elected must necessarily have different nationalities;

d. on renewing the Board, a Director of the nationality not included in the previous election shall be included;

e. should one of the countries holding a smaller quota of shares attain sixteen and six tenths per cent (16.6) of the subscribed initial capital, the alternating provision incorporated in point (d) shall be rescinded as of the next election;

f. when each of the countries of the subregion has attained at least sixteen and six tenths (16.6) per cent of the subscribed initial capital, the number of members of the Board of Directors shall be increased to twelve (12);

g. in the case of point (f), the Board of Directors shall call an extraordinary meeting for the purpose of considering and resolving, if considered convenient, the corresponding adjustments in dispositions on quorums and Board decisions.

ARTICLE 25
QUORUM

Board meetings require a quorum of at least six (6) Directors.

ARTICLE 26
RESOLUTIONS

Each Director shall have one vote at Board meetings. Resolutions shall be adopted by a majority of no less than one half plus one of the Directors present. In cases provided for in Article 6 and points (a), (c), (d), (i), (j), (n), and (p) of Article 27, a vote of at least seven (7) Directors is required.

ARTICLE 27
ATTRIBUTIONS OF THE BOARD OF DIRECTORS

The Board of Directors shall have the following attributions:

a. establish and direct the Corporation's financial, credit, and economic policies;

b. annually elect one of the Directors to preside over Board and shareholders' meetings;

c. name and remove the Executive President;

d. name and remove Vice-Presidents of the Corporation on request of the Executive President;

e. determine the remuneration to be received by the Executive President and Vice-Presidents;

f. approve the annual budget of expenditures on request of the Executive President;

g. approve credit operations, investments, or any other operation within the Corporation's objectives proposed by the Executive President;

h. approve the issuance of bonds, debentures, or other financial obligations and determine conditions of emission, grant underwriting guarantees on shares and other securities, operate in participation certificates, authorize trust operations;

i. delegate to an executive committee in other subsidiary agencies that the Board of Directors considers should be created, or to the Executive President, or to other officials the Executive President may recommend, the function to which points (g) and (h) refer, in the case of operations for amounts not exceeding the limit established by the Board itself;

j. resolve and give full interpretation, on request of the Executive President, to questions not provided for in the Agreement, and submit its interpretations to the following shareholders' meeting;

k. present an annual report and balance statement to the shareholders' meeting;

l. propose to the shareholders' meeting the distribution of profits;

m. propose to the shareholders' meeting the formation of reserves;

n. promulgate and modify the Corporation's internal regulations;

o. call ordinary shareholders' meetings as provided for by the Agreement, and extraordinary shareholders' meetings when required by the interests of the Corporation, or when the Board considers it desirable, or when Corporation shareholders request them in compliance with the terms of Article 12 of this Agreement; and

p. propose to the shareholders' meeting a change in headquarters when it is considered a matter of undeniable necessity.

ARTICLE 28
REPLACEMENT

Replacement of a Director because of resignation, incapacitation, or death shall follow these norms:

a. a Director representing series "A" shall be replaced directly by the proprietor of the share, and

b. a Director representing series "B" shares shall be replaced by the Board of Directors with his substitute or, should he too not be available, with another substitute until the following ordinary shareholders' meeting can make the definitive election. The Director thus replaced shall remain in office only to complete the term of his predecessor.

ARTICLE 29
MEETINGS

The Board of Directors shall meet according to a self-imposed calendar, or when called by the President, or on request by three (3) Directors, or when summoned by the Executive President. Meetings shall be held at Corporation headquarters unless decided otherwise by the Board on occasions that it shall determine.

ARTICLE 30
MINUTES

The deliberations and agreements of each meeting shall be recorded in a special book of minutes.

CHAPTER V: EXECUTIVE PRESIDENT AND OTHER OFFICERS

ARTICLE 31
FUNCTIONS OF THE EXECUTIVE PRESIDENT

The Executive President, in his role as supranational functionary, shall be the Corporation's legal representative and have the following attributions:

a. to direct and administer the Corporation;

b. to take charge of and direct all matters not expressly reserved to share-holders' meetings, the Board of Directors, the Executive Committee, or other subsidiary agencies created by the Board, in addition to those matters specifically within his domain.

ARTICLE 32
TERM OF OFFICE

The Executive President's term of office shall be five (5) years. He may be re-elected and shall remain at his post until replaced by his successor.

ARTICLE 33
TEMPORARY LEAVES OF ABSENCE

The Executive President shall be temporarily replaced during leaves of absence by the top-ranking Vice-President or by an officer designated by the Board.

ARTICLE 34
TOTAL REPLACEMENT

Should it be necessary to replace the Executive President definitively, the Board of Directors shall name his successor.

ARTICLE 35
POWERS

The Executive President may confer the powers of representing the Corporation that he considers necessary. He may also confer special powers in the interests of the Corporation.

ARTICLE 36
VICE-PRESIDENTS

On recommendation by the Executive President, the Board of Directors shall designate one or more Vice-Presidents, as the proper functioning of the

Corporation requires, specifying in each case the corresponding attributions, duties, and remuneration. Vice-Presidents shall be chosen so that the different nationalities of the subregion are duly represented.

ARTICLE 37
DESIGNATION OF PERSONNEL

Personnel shall be chosen by the Executive President who shall make known his designations to the Board of Directors at the following meeting, specifying the attributions and duties of each employee, as well as the remuneration that shall be fixed according to budget possibilities.

ARTICLE 38
SELECTION OF PERSONNEL

The selection of personnel shall take into account primarily qualities of efficiency, competence, and honesty, without overlooking the importance of encompassing as broad a geographic scope as possible, with special emphasis on the countries of the subregion.

ARTICLE 39
SUPRANATIONAL CHARACTER OF PERSONNEL

In the fulfillment of its tasks, personnel shall neither seek nor receive instructions from any Government or other authority foreign to the Corporation. Personnel members shall abstain from any act incompatible with their positions as internal functionaries responsible to the Corporation alone.

CHAPTER VI: FISCAL PERIOD, BALANCE SHEET, AND UTILITIES

ARTICLE 40
FISCAL PERIOD

The Corporation's fiscal period shall be annual, commencing on a date that shall be established by the Board of Directors.

ARTICLE 41
BALANCE SHEET AND STATEMENT OF EARNINGS AND LOSSES

Accounts required for the preparation of the annual balance sheet and statement of earnings and losses shall be closed on the last day of the fiscal year.

ARTICLE 42
RESERVES

A quota of at least ten (10) per cent of net earnings shall be put aside each year to form a reserve fund up to an amount not less than fifty (50) per cent of the subscribed capital. Moreover, the shareholders may vote the constitution of the other reserves and the distribution of the remainder as dividends.

ARTICLE 43
AUDITORS

The Corporation shall engage the services of an internationally recognized firm of auditors to certify the annual balance sheet submitted to the ordinary shareholders' meeting.

CHAPTER VII: LIQUIDATION AND ARBITRATION

ARTICLE 44
LIQUIDATION

Should it be determined to dissolve the Corporation, a liquidator or liquidating commission shall be named by the stockholders' meeting. The liquidator or liquidating commission shall represent the Corporation during the liquidation process, paying pending debts, collecting loans, distributing the surplus among shareholders in proportion to the paid-up capital represented by each share, and in general exercising all the functions involved in the liquidation process.

The shareholders' meeting that designates the liquidator or liquidating commission shall place a time limit on the activities of one or the other and establish the basic rules governing the liquidation process. On conclusion of the assignment, or of the time limit fixed by the shareholders, the liquidators shall submit a detailed report of the activities accomplished, and finally shall present an equally detailed report on the liquidation as a whole.

ARTICLE 45
ARBITRATION

Should disagreement arise between the Corporation and its shareholders, the controversy shall be submitted for arbitration to a three-man board.

One of the arbitrators shall be named by the Corporation, another by the interested party, and the third by common agreement between the arbitrators. Should they be unable to reach an agreement, the Corporation or the interested party may request that the Joint Commission, or another agency, designate the third arbitrator.

None of the arbitrators may be of the same nationality as the interested party in the controversy.

Should all attempts at a unanimous agreement fail, decisions shall be taken by majority vote.

The third arbitrator may decide all matters of procedure and competency in instances where the other parties are in disagreement.

CHAPTER VIII: IMMUNITY, EXEMPTIONS, AND PRIVILEGES

ARTICLE 46
SCOPE OF THIS CHAPTER

In order to attain the objectives established in this Agreement, the Contracting Parties concur that the Andean Development Corporation shall enjoy in the national territory of each the immunity, exemptions, and privileges established in this Chapter.

ARTICLE 47
ASSETS IMMUNITY

Corporation property and other assets, wherever they are located, shall enjoy immunity with regard to expropriation, investigation, confiscation, attachment, sequestration, embargo, retention, or any other form of forced seizure that curtails the Corporation's control over these assets by effect of executive or administrative acts on the part of any of the Contracting States.

These properties and assets shall enjoy the same immunity with regard to legal action while no definitive verdict has yet been pronounced against the Corporation.

ARTICLE 48
TRANSFERABILITY AND CONVERTIBILITY

Assets of all kinds pertaining to the Corporation shall enjoy free transferability and convertibility.

ARTICLE 49
INVIOLABILITY OF ARCHIVES

The Corporation archives are inviolable.

ARTICLE 50
EXEMPTION FROM RESTRICTIONS ON ASSETS

In order that the Corporation shall accomplish its objectives and functions, and carry out the operations provided for in this Agreement, the institution's property and other assets shall be exempt from all restrictions, regulations, and measures of control or delay, unless this Agreement specifies otherwise.

ARTICLE 51
PRIVILEGED COMMUNICATIONS AND CORRESPONDENCE

The Contracting States shall grant official Corporation communications the same treatment afforded official communications of the other contracting countries.

Corporation correspondence, including packages and printed matter, that bears its franking seal shall circulate postage free throughout the Contracting States.

ARTICLE 52
TAX EXEMPTIONS

a. The Corporation is exempt from all kinds of taxation and customs duties on income, property, and other assets, as well as on operations and transactions effected in compliance with this Agreement. The Corporation is also exempt from all responsibility with regard to the payment, retention, or collection of any tax, contribution, or duty.

b. The wages and emoluments the Corporation pays to its Directors, alternate Directors, officers, and employees who are not citizens or nationals of the Corporation headquarters' country shall be tax exempt.

c. Obligations or certificates issued by the Corporation, including dividends and interest derived therefrom, shall be tax exempt, whatever the nationality of the holder:

(1) should taxes be used to discriminate against these obligations and certificates for the sole reason of having been issued by the Corporation; or

(2) should the only jurisdictional foundation for these taxes be the place or currency in which the obligations or certificates have been issued, paid, or are payable, or the location of any office or business base maintained by the Corporation.

d. Nor shall taxes of any kind be placed on obligations or certificates guaranteed by the Corporation, including dividends or interest derived therefrom, whatever the nationality of the holder:

(1) should taxes be used to discriminate against these obligations and certificates for the sole reason of having been issued by the Corporation; or

(2) should the only jurisdictional foundation for these taxes be the location of any office or business base maintained by the Corporation.

ARTICLE 53
PERSONAL IMMUNITY AND PRIVILEGES

Corporation Directors, Executive President, Vice-Presidents, executive officers, experts, and technicians shall enjoy the following immunities and privileges:

a. immunity from legal and administrative proceedings related to acts they perform in their official capacity, unless the Corporation expressly revokes the privilege;

b. immunity from immigration restrictions, registration of foreigners, and military service obligations when they are not nationals of the country; and the same facilities regarding money exchange that the country grants to representatives, functionaries, and employees of comparable rank of other member countries; and

c. the same privileges regarding freedom of travel that the Contracting States grant the representatives, functionaries, and employees of comparable rank of other Contracting States.

ARTICLE 54
LEGAL PROCEEDINGS

Legal action against the Corporation may be brought only in a court of competent jurisdiction in a Contracting State where the Corporation has established an office, or where it has named an agent or representative authorized to accept a court summons or notice, or where it has issued or guaranteed securities.

The Contracting States of this Agreement and persons authorized by or representing them may not bring any legal action against the Corporation. However, shareholders may use this right according to the special procedures provided in this Agreement, in Corporation regulations, or in contracts in order to settle controversies that may arise between them and the Corporation.

CHAPTER IX: WITHDRAWAL AND SUSPENSION OF SERIES "A" SHAREHOLDERS

ARTICLE 55
RIGHT OF WITHDRAWAL

Any series "A" shareholder may withdraw from the Corporation, in which case the Corporation shall purchase the shares. Notification of withdrawal shall be submitted in writing to the Board of Directors.

Series "A" shares shall be paid according to the book value they represent, and the Board, according to the Corporation's financial position, shall determine the terms of payment, which shall not be more than five (5) years.

Series "B" shares owned by natural or legal persons of the series "A" shareholding country that has decided to withdraw from the Corporation may be freely transferred in the subregion, provided the proportion assigned to natural or legal persons in point (b) of Article 5 is observed.

In the case of withdrawal by a series "A" shareholder, the following ordinary shareholders' meeting shall adapt the Agreement's pertinent dispositions to the new situation created.

ARTICLE 56
SUSPENSION

Any series "A" shareholder who in the Board's judgment has seriously failed to fulfill certain of his obligations with the Corporation may be suspended by decision of the shareholders' meeting.

The suspended shareholder automatically ceases to be a member of the Corporation fifteen (15) days after the date of suspension, unless the shareholders' meeting determines otherwise.

While the suspension is in effect, the shareholder may not exercise any of the rights conferred by this Agreement, except that of withdrawal.

CHAPTER X: FINAL DISPOSITIONS

ARTICLE 57
ENTRY INTO EFFECT

This Agreement enters into effect when documents of ratification have been deposited with the Ministry of Foreign Affairs of Venezuela by representatives of three (3) signatory countries, including the headquarters country.

If in the term of one year after the last of the three countries has deposited its ratification document the remaining countries have not yet done likewise, the Board of Directors shall call an extraordinary meeting to adapt the Agreement's pertinent dispositions to the number of countries that have presented their ratification documents.

Countries that have deposited their ratification documents before the date this Agreement goes into effect shall be members as of that date. The other countries shall be members as of the date they deposit their documents of ratification.

ARTICLE 58
RESERVATIONS REGARDING THE AGREEMENT

The signature and ratification of this Agreement may not be the object of any reservation.

ARTICLE 59
ADHESION

Once this Agreement is in effect, all those States that undersigned the Bogotá Declaration on August 16, 1966, and were accepted by the Joint Commission, may present their adhesion.

The Agreement shall go into effect for the new member State thirty (30) days after it has deposited its document of adhesion. In this case, the shareholders' meeting shall consider and resolve if any adjustment in the Agreement's pertinent dispositions is required.

ARTICLE 60
REINCORPORATION

The shareholders' meeting shall determine the conditions for reincorporation of a series "A" shareholder that has withdrawn from the Corporation.

TRANSITORY DISPOSITIONS

First. The headquarters country shall call the first shareholders' meeting within sixty (60) days after the date this Agreement goes into effect.

Second. From the time the Agreement goes into effect to the holding of the extraordinary meeting referred to in Article 57, the Andean Development Corporation shall be provisionally administered as determined by the shareholders' meeting in compliance with the general norms established in this Agreement.

Third. Should three (3) countries ratify this Agreement, but not the headquarters country among them, three months as of the date the last document of ratification is deposited, the ratifying countries shall select another headquarters country.

Drawn up in the City of Bogotá, on the seventh day of the month of February of nineteen hundred and sixty-eight, in the Spanish language, in six equally authentic copies.

In certification of which the undersigned Plenipotentiary representatives have subscribed the present Agreement.

Federation of Malaya and Singapore Common Market

Although many proposals made in Southeast Asia during the past ten years have advocated regional economic cooperation, the August 1963 treaty establishing a common market with participation by the Federation of Malaya, Singapore, Sarawak, and Sabah represents the only case in which such initiatives were actually translated into a formal commitment involving a group of neighboring Asian countries. The merger of these territories into the Federation of Malaysia through an agreement with the United Kingdom signed in London in July 1963 was the immediate catalyst of this action. The common market treaty took the form of an annex to the agreement establishing the Federation.

The general framework of the Malaysian common market was elaborated by a mission of the International Bank for Reconstruction and Development (IBRD) that visited the area in early 1963. The mission's terms of reference, jointly agreed upon by the United Kingdom, the Federation of Malaya, and the State of Singapore, were to report on the feasibility of, and problems inherent in, close economic coordination among the prospective parts of the new Federation, with special consideration of the possibility of a common market arrangement. The mission was to recommend concrete steps toward economic coordination that would maximize the advantages for all territories and to recommend administrative arrangements for the coordination and integration of planning, including planning for industrial development. In a report presented to the governments involved, the IBRD mission came to the conclusion that despite important differences among the prospective participants of the Federation of Malaysia in economic structure, trade policies, and development needs, the merger of these territories could contribute substantially — given appropriate policies — to a solution of their development problems. Unification would create a large economy more diverse than any of its component parts, and a common market would offer greater opportunities to local producers of commodities consumed in significant quantities throughout Malaysia. In the field of agriculture it was recognized that the output of a number of products traditionally imported from the outside could be expanded. The greatest potential appeared to be in manufacturing, however, despite the fact that the territories comprising the then future Federation of Malaysia had been outdistanced in industrial development by, among others, Thailand and the Philippines.

The main reason for the area's extreme industrial lag has been the attractiveness of alternative opportunities for investment — in rubber plantations, tin mining, and trade, which is especially encouraged by the low import duties in force in Malaya and Borneo and by the virtual absence of tariffs in Singapore. The potential Malaysian market also has been limited by the protective tariff walls of each territory and the possibility that Singapore, after independence, would also erect such walls. The IBRD mission considered it urgent that a common market be established in the region concurrently with the setting up of the Federation of Malaysia, because it had discovered that each territory of the future federal state was accelerating its own economic development program without considering the longer-run limitations arising from the small size of markets and the scarcity of financial resources.

The negotiation of a common market arrangement in Malaysia was especially difficult on account of the formidable differences in the development levels of the Malayan states, Singapore, and the two Borneo colonial territories and of the key role of the entrepôt trade for the economy of Singapore. It became apparent at an early stage of the negotiations that the traditional approach, limited to the freeing of trade, was especially unsuitable in these circumstances, and that any arrangement politically and economically acceptable to the future members of the Malaysian common market would have to fulfill three conditions. It would have to devise measures aimed at effectively insulating Singapore's entrepôt trade with third countries from commercial exchange within the region; find ways to compensate the less developed partners (the Malayan states and the two Borneo territories) for the loss of revenues resulting from the freeing of trade within the region; and provide for some pooling of resources for the development of the most backward participants (the Borneo territories).

Consequently, it was recognized that (1) a Malaysian common market should cover only the domestic products of the participating countries; (2) a Tariff Advisory Board, an independent consultative body that would command the confidence of governments and of private business circles, should be established to implement a common tariff policy; (3) tariff harmonization for the protection of regionally produced goods should be introduced gradually over a five-year period; (4) in view of the importance of Singapore as a transit place for trade of the rest of Malaysia with the outside world, some agreement should be reached about the allocation of customs revenue to other members of the common market; and (5) some coordination of industrial policies should be enforced.

All of these major IBRD recommendations were incorporated in the agreement annexed to the treaty establishing the Federation of Malaysia. The common market treaty offered the participating countries a number of important mutual concessions. Thus, in view of the paramount importance of the tariff policies to be elaborated by the proposed Tariff Advisory Board to the Federal Government of Malaysia, Singapore was granted (for a five-year period) the right to veto any appointment to the office of the Board's Chairman and to nominate one of his three deputies. The Federal Government of Malaysia was explicitly enjoined from imposing or changing any protective duties with respect to Singapore without the specific advice of the Tariff Advisory Board. Moreover, the Singapore government was granted the right to require a delay, no longer than one year, of the imposition in its territory "of any revenue duty . . . on the grounds that it would significantly prejudice the entrepôt trade." The treaty defined entrepôt trade to cover not only trade in goods and products imported into Singapore from outside Malaysia for re-export to third countries but also primary products imported into Singapore from other parts of Malaysia for subsequent re-export, regardless of any further processing, to the rest of the world.

In exchange for these concessions, Singapore agreed to transfer to the Federal Government of Malaysia (a) customs duties and other charges collected in Singapore on goods to be exported from or imported into Malaysia, except those for consumption in Singapore; (b) income taxes collected in Singapore but attributable to income derived from the Malayan states; and (c) 40 per cent of all other revenues collected in Singapore, with the exception of property taxes. Moreover, the Singapore government committed itself to extending long-term development loans to the Borneo territories.

Despite the large degree of mutual economic dependence between

Singapore and the remaining members of the Federation of Malaysia, the actual implementation of the common market provisions has never begun. The reasons for the failure of the scheme are both economic and political. In May 1965, when the Malaysia Tariff Advisory Board finally submitted to the federal authorities a first list of more than one hundred free trade items to be covered by the single common traiff vis-à-vis the outside world, the Federal Government refused to act on the Board's recommendations unless Singapore increased its share of revenue transfers to the Federation. At the same time, Singapore sought, without success, more autonomy from the Federal authorities in economic and political matters. In August 1965 Singapore left the Federation and reimposed license and quota restrictions on manufactures from Malaya in defense of its own industries. Singapore's authorities claimed that while they dropped all trade restrictions on imports from Malaya after the establishment of the Federation, Malaya and the two Borneo territories continued to impose duties on virtually all products from Singapore by delaying action on the Tariff Advisory Board's recommendations.

Shortly after Singapore left the Federation, a joint committee was established to discuss trade problems. Its recommendation that Malaysia and Singapore carry on trade under conditions prevailing after August 1963 was accepted in principle by the two parties. Trade flows were restored through a formal agreement lifting Singapore's restrictions on products from Malaysia in exchange for provisions allowing some Singapore-produced manufactures duty-free entry into the markets of the former members of the common market. Nevertheless, the common market arrangement providing for harmonization of tariff and industrial investment policies became a dead letter. Thus the only regional cooperation agreement in Southeast Asia joined a long list of never-implemented proposals.

Although the Malaysia-Singapore common market was largely a victim of unsettled political conditions in that part of the world, its failure offers interesting lessons for other groupings. The treaty itself represented an ingenious attempt to face the problem of a serious imbalance arising from the freeing of trade among countries with large disparities in development levels and in production factor endowments. The problem was further complicated by the dependence of the most advanced member, Singapore, on entrepôt trade. The proposed formula called for simultaneous action on four different fronts: trade liberalization, equitable distribution of fiscal revenues, economic assistance to the least developed members, and coordination of industrial development plans. The Malaysia-Singapore experiment failed, but not without providing further support for the hypothesis that, to succeed, any multilateral agreement on regional cooperation must provide an acceptable formula for the distribution of benefits and losses arising from trade liberalization, the location of industrial development projects, and other aspects of the integration program.

Bibliographic References

International Bank for Reconstruction and Development. *Report on the Economic Aspects of Malaysia.* Washington, D.C., July 3, 1963. Mimeographed.

Johnson, Christopher. "Singapore and Malaysia," *The Financial Times* (London), August 10, 1965.

AGREEMENT BETWEEN THE GOVERNMENTS OF THE FEDERATION OF MALAYA AND SINGAPORE ON COMMON MARKET AND FINANCIAL ARRANGEMENTS*

Common Market

1. (1) The Federal Government, in order to facilitate the maximum practicable degree of economic integration of the territories of Malaysia, while taking account of the interests of the entrepot trade of Singapore, Penang and Labuan and those of existing industries in Malaysia, and the need to ensure a balanced development of these territories, shall progressively establish a common market in Malaysia for all goods or products produced, manufactured or assembled in significant quantities in Malaysia, with the exception of goods and products of which the principal terminal markets lie outside Malaysia.

1. (2) Where the same protective duties or revenue duties are applicable throughout Malaysia in the case of any class of goods or products, then no tariff or trade barrier or trade restriction or discrimination shall be applied to such goods or products in regard to their circulation throughout Malaysia.

1. (3) The provisions of the preceding sub-paragraph shall not be construed to prevent the imposition of —

(a) any special production tax on producers in a low-tariff State which would offset the cost inequalities arising from the differential import duties; or

(b) any export duty or export restriction on primary products where the principal terminal markets lie outside Malaysia.

Tariff Advisory Board

2. (1) The Malayan Government shall take steps to establish by law before Malaysia Day [August 31, 1963 — Editor] a Tariff Advisory Board to advise the Federal Government generally on the establishment of the common market

* Signed in London, July 9, 1963. This is the official text, published as Annex J to *Malaysia: Agreement Concluded Between the United Kingdom of Great Britain and Northern Ireland, the Federation of Malaya, North Borneo, Sarawak and Singapore* (Cmnd. 2094; London: H. M. Stationery Office, 1963). [Editor's note.]

as defined in paragraph 1 above, including the establishment and maintenance of a common external tariff for the protection (where required) of goods for which there is to be a common market.

2. (2) Appointments to the Board shall be made by the Federal Government but until five years from Malaysia Day the appointment of the Chairman shall require the concurrence of the Singapore Government; the first Chairman shall be appointed as soon as possible after the conclusion of this Agreement. During the first five years, there shall be three Deputy Chairmen, one of whom shall be nominated by the Singapore Government. In appointing members of the Board regard shall be had to the areas and interests involved.

2. (3) The Board shall sit in public to receive evidence except where the Board deems it necessary to receive evidence *in camera*. Within six months after their receipt the Federal Government shall publish the reports and recommendations of the Board other than those of which publication is not in the public interest.

Protective Duties

3. (1) For the purposes of this Agreement a protective duty shall be defined as a duty which is levied in respect of a class of goods or products which are or are to be produced, manufactured, assembled or prepared and used or consumed in the Federation in significant quantities, or which are used or consumed in the production, manufacture, assembly or preparation in the Federation of goods or products of such a class or which are of a description providing a substitute for or alternative to goods or products of such a class. All other duties shall be defined as revenue duties. A duty shall be regarded as imposed in Singapore, if it is imposed on goods imported into Singapore for use or consumption there and not otherwise.

3. (2) Except in cases where it deems preventive action to be urgently necessary, the Federal Government shall not in Singapore make any class of goods or products subject to a protective duty or vary any protective duty before receiving the advice of the Tariff Advisory Board. In cases where a duty has been imposed or varied without prior reference to the Tariff Advisory Board, the Federal Government shall seek the advice of the Board thereon as soon as practicable thereafter.

3. (3) For a period of 5 years from Malaysia Day the Singapore Government shall have the right to require a delay not exceeding 12 months in the imposition in Singapore of any protective duty on the grounds that the duty would significantly prejudice the entrepot trade. In any enquiry by the Tariff Advisory Board on a proposal to impose such a duty, the Singapore Government shall inform the Board of any item on which it may wish, in the interests of the entrepot trade, to avail itself of this option. In regard to such items, the Tariff Advisory Board shall consider the possibility of anticipatory action in Singapore and shall, if necessary, include in its recommendations proposals to prevent such action. During the period of delay, the Singapore Government shall not grant any licence, concession or inducement to any industry which may be affected by the proposed protective duty without the concurrence of the Federal Government.

3. (4) The Tariff Advisory Board shall be required within six months after Malaysia Day to make its first report as to what protective duties should be imposed. For this purpose it shall consider any proposals made to it by the Federal Government or a State Government.

Revenue Duties

4. (1) In formulating its policy relating to the harmonisation of revenue duties, the Federal Government shall pay due regard to any representations made by the Singapore Government on the economic, financial and social implications of such harmonisation.

4. (2) Revenue duties in force in Singapore on 1st July, 1963, and the corresponding duties in force in the Federation of Malaya shall be harmonised as soon as practicable.

4. (3) Until 31st December, 1968, no revenue duty shall, except at the request or with the consent of the Singapore Government, be imposed in Singapore by the Federal Government in respect of any class of goods or products not chargeable with such a duty on 1st July, 1963. Such consent shall not be withheld except on the grounds that the duty would significantly prejudice the entrepot trade of Singapore.

4. (4) Before 31st December, 1968, the Tariff Advisory Board shall review the revenue duties in force at that time in Singapore and in the remainder of Malaysia and shall make recommendations regarding the amendment of such duties or the imposition of additional duties. As from 1st January, 1969, the Singapore Government shall be entitled to withhold its consent to the imposition in Singapore of any revenue duty in respect of any goods or products referred to in sub-paragraph (3) for any period up to 31st December, 1975, on the grounds that it would significantly prejudice the entrepot trade, and, in the absence of such consent, no such duty shall be imposed provided that the Singapore Government shall pay to the Federal Government annually compensation equal to the loss of revenue suffered by the Federal Government as a result of the withholding of such consent.

4. (5) For the purposes of this agreement, the entrepot trade of Singapore means trade in goods and products imported into Singapore from outside Malaysia and primary products imported into Singapore from other parts of Malaysia, which goods or products, whether further processed or not, are subsequently re-exported from Singapore to destinations outside Malaysia.

Tax Collection

5. Subject to the provisions of the Annex to this Agreement, executive authority in respect of the collection in Singapore of customs duties and excise and income tax shall be delegated to the Singapore Government. The Federal Government may revoke this authority if the Singapore Government fails to comply with any direction properly given to it by the Federal Government for the collection or protection of these taxes or shows itself unwilling or unable to discharge these functions efficiently. This authority may extend to customs duties and other charges collected in Singapore on goods exported from or to be imported into Malaysia outside Singapore.

Division of Revenue

6. (1) All revenues collected in Singapore, with the exceptions specified below, shall be paid into a separate fund in a branch of the Central Bank to be established in Singapore and the fund shall be divided between the two Governments and paid to them at least once in every year, in the proportion of 60 per cent. to the Singapore Government and 40 per cent. to the Federal Government. The exceptions are —

(a) the revenues specified in Part III of the Tenth Schedule to the Federal Constitution, including property tax in lieu of rates (to be paid into the State Consolidated Fund);

(b) customs duties and other charges (including excise not in force at the date of this Agreement and any production tax imposed in respect of goods to which a protective duty is applicable) collected in Singapore on goods to be exported from or imported into Malaysia outside Singapore (to be paid into the Federal Consolidated Fund);

(c) income tax collected in Singapore and attributable to income derived from the States of Malaya (to be paid into the Federal Consolidated Fund).

6. (2) 60 per cent. of income tax collected in the States of Malaya but attributable to income derived from Singapore shall be paid to the Singapore Government.

6. (3) Income tax attributable to income derived from Singapore and collected by an Agent outside Malaysia shall be paid into the separate fund referred to in paragraph 6(1) above.

6. (4) From the beginning of 1964 paragraphs 6(1)(c) and 6(2) shall apply as if references to the States of Malaya included references to the Borneo States.

6. (5) The provisions of Article 109 and Clauses (3), (3A) and (4) of Article 110 of the Federal Constitution shall not apply in relation to Singapore.

Federal Projects in Singapore

7. The Singapore Government shall pay to the Federal Government the cost of capital development of Federal projects in Singapore other than projects for defence and internal security. The two Governments shall agree together on projects to be covered by this paragraph which do not provide predominantly local services.

Financial Review

8. The arrangements specified in paragraphs 6 and 7 above shall remain in operation until 31st December, 1964. The two Governments shall then review these arrangements and shall decide upon any amendments to be made to them in respect of the two year period commencing 1st January, 1965. There shall be a similar review in respect of each subsequent period of two years. In default of agreement between the two Governments, any issue in dispute shall be referred to an independent assessor appointed jointly by the two Governments. In default of agreement between the two Governments on the choice

of an assessor, the Lord President of the Federal Court, after considering the views of both governments, shall appoint an assessor from among persons recommended by the International Bank for Reconstruction and Development as being persons enjoying an international reputation in finance. The recommendations of the assessor shall be binding on both governments. Such reviews shall have regard to all relevant factors.

Finance for Borneo Territories

9. To assist development in the Borneo territories the Singapore Government shall make available to the Federal Government:

(a) a 15-year loan of $100 million, bearing interest at current market rates in the Federation, subject to the proviso that the loan shall be free of interest during the first 5 years after drawing and that if, having regard to the economic growth in Singapore, it is so recommended in the financial review in respect of the period of two years commencing 1st January, 1969 under paragraph 8 above, the loan shall be free of interest for a further period of 5 years; and

(b) a 15-year loan of $50 million bearing interest at current market rates in the Federation.

The above loans shall be drawn in equal annual instalments over a period of 5 years, commencing in 1964.

Disputes as to Interpretation or Application of this Agreement

10. Any dispute between the Federal Government and the Singapore Government as to the interpretation or application of this Agreement may be referred by either Government to the Federal Court for determination by that Court in exercise of the jurisdiction conferred upon it by Article 128 of the Federal Constitution.

PART I
CUSTOMS AND EXCISE

ANNEX TO ANNEX J

Subject to the provisions of Paragraphs 1–4 of this agreement the following powers under the Singapore Customs Ordinance are reserved to the Federal Government —

(1) The power to fix the rate of tax, duty or excise on any class of goods;

(2) The power to fix by order the value of goods for duty or excise purposes;

(3) The power to grant exemptions or refunds in respect of duties or excise other than in particular cases where the duty or excise is less than $2,000 in any one instance;

(4) The power to make regulations both in relation to Customs and Excise.

2. The Federal Government will also have the following powers: —

(1) The power to appoint Federal officers to inspect the Customs and Excise Department, Singapore. Reports would be submitted to the Federal Government direct with a copy to the Singapore Government and the inspecting officers would have the right of access to all documents and records of the Department.

(2) The right of the Federal Minister responsible for Customs to issue directions to the State Government which he considers necessary to ensure the effective collection or protection of Federal customs duties and/or excise.

PART II
INCOME TAX

Powers to Be Exercised by the Federal Government in Relation to Collection

(the references are to the *Singapore Income Tax Ordinance*)

SECTION 3A

The power of the Minister to give the Comptroller-General directions of a general character.

SECTION 13(2)

The power of the Minister to provide that interest on any loan charged on the public revenue of Singapore or the Federation shall be exempt from tax.

SECTION 106(1)

(1) The power to vary or revoke the whole or any part of any schedule to the Ordinance.

(2) The power to exempt any person or class of persons from all or any of the provisions of the Ordinance.

Powers to Be Varied

SECTION 7

The powers of the Malayan Board of Income Tax as at 4th June, 1963, to be retained with the deletion of subsection (3).

SECTION 19(2)

The Comptroller's powers to vary the rate of capital allowances prescribed for machinery and plant should be transferred to the Comptroller-General.

Pioneer Industries Ordinance

Certificates granted by Singapore to be subject to approval of the Federal Minister of Finance.

Industrial Expansion (Relief from Income Tax Ordinance 1959)

SECTION 5

Orders made by Singapore to be subject to approval of the Federal Minister of Finance.

INCOME TAX BILLS

The powers conferred on the Minister or the Comptroller by any Income Tax Bills introduced between the 1st June, 1963, and the date of formal acceptance of the Heads of Terms of Agreement and enacted prior to Malaysia Day.

Between the date of formal acceptance of the Heads of Terms of Agreement and Malaysia Day the Singapore Government should not introduce any new legislation with respect to matters the subject of that Agreement.

Powers to Be Retained

SECTION 4(2)

The Income Tax Department of Singapore shall be subject to detailed inspection by the Comptroller-General in accordance with the existing provisions of Section 4(2) which require the Comptroller and his officers to be subject to the supervision and direction of the Comptroller-General.

Powers to Be Reserved

The right of the Federal Minister responsible for Income Tax to issue directions to the State Governments which he considers necessary to ensure the effective collection or protection of Income Tax shall be recognised.

General Bibliography*

Baerrensen, Donald W., Martin Carnoy, and Joseph Grunwald. *Latin American Trade Patterns*. Washington, D.C.: The Brookings Institution, 1965.

Baerrensen, Donald W. "A Method for Planning Economic Integration for Specific Industries," *Journal of Common Market Studies* (Oxford), Vol. VI, No. 1 (September 1967).

Balassa, Bela. *Economic Development and Integration*. Mexico City: Centro de Estudios Monetarios Latinoamericanos, 1965.

———. *The Theory of Economic Integration*. Homewood, Ill.: Richard D. Irwin, 1961.

Brewster, Havelock, and Clive Y. Thomas. *The Dynamics of West Indian Economic Integration*. University of the West Indies, Institute of Social and Economic Research, Studies in Regional Economic Integration, Vol. 1. Jamaica, 1967.

Brown, A. J. "Economic Separatism versus a Common Market in Developing Countries," *Yorkshire Bulletin of Economic and Social Research,* May and November 1961.

———. "Should African Countries Form Economic Unions?" In E. F. Jackson, ed., *Economic Development in Africa*. Oxford: Basil Blackwell, 1965.

Castillo, Carlos. *Growth and Integration in Central America*. New York: Frederick A. Praeger, 1967.

Cooper, C. A., and B. F. Massell. *Toward a General Theory of Customs Unions for Developing Countries*. (The RAND Corporation, Memorandum P. 2919-1.) Santa Monica, Calif., [1964]. Mimeographed.

Dell, Sidney. *A Latin American Common Market?* New York: Oxford University Press, 1966.

———. *Trade Blocs and Common Markets*. New York: Alfred A. Knopf, 1963.

Demas, William G. *The Economics of Development in Small Countries, with Special Reference to the Caribbean*. Montreal: McGill University Press, 1965.

Diab, Muhammed A. *Inter-Arab Economic Cooperation, 1951–1960*. Beirut: American University, Economic Research Institute, 1963.

Economic Commission for Africa. *Background Paper on the Establishment of the African Common Market*. (E.CN.14/STC/20.) Addis Ababa, October 13, 1963. Mimeographed.

———. *Elements of a Model Convention for Sub-Regional Common Markets in Africa*. (E/CN.14/WPI/1.) Addis Ababa, July 16, 1965. Mimeographed.

* Includes only literature available in English.

————. *Report of the Symposium on Industrial Development in Africa (Cairo, 27 January–9 February 1966)*. (E/CN.14/347.) Addis Ababa, March 16, 1966. Mimeographed.

Economic Commission for Asia and the Far East. *Regional Economic Co-operation in Asia and the Far East (Report of the Ministerial Conference on Asian Economic Co-operation, Manila, Philippines, 3 to 6 December 1963)*. (United Nations Publication, Sales No. 64.II.F.14.) New York, 1964.

————. "Regional Trade Co-operation: An Exploratory Study with Special Reference to Asia and the Far East," *Economic Bulletin for Asia and the Far East* (Bangkok), Vol. XII, No. 1 (June 1961).

————. "The Scope for Regional Economic Co-operation in Asia and the Far East," *Economic Bulletin for Asia and the Far East*, Vol. XII, No. 3 (December 1961).

Economic Commission for Latin America. *The Economic Development of Latin America and Its Principal Problems,* by Raúl Prebisch. New York: United Nations, 1950.

————. *The Latin American Common Market*. New York: United Nations, 1959.

————. *Multilateral Economic Co-operation in Latin America*, Vol. I: *Texts and Documents*. (United Nations Publication, Sales No. 62.II.G.3.) New York, 1962.

————. *Possibilities for Integrated Industrial Development in Central America*. New York: United Nations, 1964.

————. *Towards a Dynamic Development Policy in Latin America*. New York: United Nations, 1963.

Green, R. H., and K. G. V. Krishna. *Economic Co-operation in Africa — Retrospect and Prospect*. Nairobi, London: Oxford University Press, 1967.

Griffin, Keith, and Ricardo Ffrench-Davis. "Customs Unions and Latin American Integration," *Journal of Common Market Studies,* Vol. IV, No. 1 (October 1965).

Haas, Ernst B., and Philippe C. Schmitter. "Economics and Differential Patterns of Political Integration: Projections about Unity in Latin America," *International Organization* (New York), Vol. XVIII, No. 4 (Autumn 1964).

————. *The Politics of Economics in Latin American Regionalism*. Denver, Colo.: University of Denver Press, 1965.

Hansen, Roger D. *Central America: Regional Integration and Economic Development*. Washington, D.C.: National Planning Association, 1967.

Herrera, Felipe. "The Inter-American Development Bank and the Latin American Integration Movement," *Journal of Common Market Studies,* Vol. V, No. 2 (December 1966).

Inter-American Development Bank. *The Inter-American Development Bank and the Economic Integration of Latin America*. Washington, D.C., November 1967. Mimeographed.

Kitamura, Hiroshi. "Economic Theory and Regional Economic Integration in Asia," *Pakistan Development Review* (Karachi), Vol. 2 (1962), No. 4.

Lindeman, John. *Preferential Trading Systems in Latin America*. Washington, D.C.: International Economic Consultants, 1960.

Lipsey, R. G. "The Theory of Customs — A General Survey," *The Economic Journal* (Oxford), September 1960.

Little, I. M. D. "Regional International Companies as an Approach to Economic Integration," *Journal of Common Market Studies,* Vol. V, No. 2 (December 1966).

Mikesell, Raymond F. *Liberalization of Inter-Latin American Trade*. Washington, D.C.: Pan American Union, 1957.

──────. "The Theory of Common Markets as Applied to Regional Arrangements among Developing Countries." In Roy Harrod and D. C. Hague, eds., *International Trade Theory in a Developing World*. London: Macmillan, 1963.

──────. "Towards Regional Trading Groups in Latin America." In Albert O. Hirschman, ed., *Latin American Issues: Essays and Comments*. New York: Twentieth Century Fund, 1961.

Ndegwa, Philip. *The Common Market and Development in East Africa*. Nairobi: East African Publishing House, 1965.

Nye, Joseph S., Jr. *Central American Regional Integration*. Carnegie Endowment for International Peace, *International Conciliation*, No. 562 (March 1967).

──────, ed. *International Regionalism: Readings*. Boston, Mass.: Little, Brown, 1968.

Perloff, Harvey S., and Rómulo Almeida. "Regional Economic Integration in the Development of Latin America," *Economía Latinoamericana* (Washington, D.C.), Vol. 1, No. 2 (November 1963).

Pincus, Joseph. *The Central American Common Market*. Mexico City: U.S. Department of State, Agency for International Development, September 1962.

Plessz, Nicolas G. *The African Common Market: Myths and Realities*. Charlottesville, Va.: University of Virginia, The Thomas Jefferson Center for Studies in Political Economy, June 1962. Multilith.

Segal, Aaron. *The Politics of Caribbean Economic Integration*. University of Puerto Rico, Institute of Caribbean Studies, Special Study No. 6. Río Piedras, Puerto Rico, 1968.

Tinbergen, Jan. "Customs Unions: Influence of Their Size on Their Effect." In Jan Tinbergen, *Selected Papers*. Amsterdam: North-Holland Publishing Company, 1959.

──────. "On the Theory of Economic Integration." In Tinbergen, *Selected Papers*.

Triffin, Robert. "International Monetary Arrangements, Capital Markets and Economic Integration in Latin America," *Journal of Common Market Studies*, Vol. IV, No. 1 (October 1965).

United Nations Conference on Trade and Development. *Payment Arrangements among the Developing Countries for Trade Expansion: Report of the Committee of Experts*. (United Nations Publication, Sales No. 67.II.D.8.) Geneva, 1966.

──────. *Trade Expansion and Economic Co-operation among Developing Countries: Report of the Committee of Experts*. (United Nations Publication, Sales No. 67.II.D.2.) Geneva, 1966.

──────. *Trade Expansion and Economic Integration among Developing Countries: Report by the Secretariat*. (United Nations Publication, Sales No. 67.II.D.20.) New York, 1967.

Urquidi, Víctor L. "The Common Market as a Tool of Economic Development." In Albert O. Hirschman, ed., *Latin American Issues: Essays and Comments*. New York: Twentieth Century Fund, 1961.

──────. *Free Trade and Economic Integration in Latin America*. Berkeley, Calif.: University of California Press, 1962.

Vanek, Jaroslav. "Payments Unions among the Less Developed Countries and Their Economic Integration," *Journal of Common Market Studies*, Vol. V, No. 2 (December 1966).

Wionczek, Miguel S. "Experiences of the Central American Economic Integration as Applied to East Africa," *Industrialization and Productivity* (United Nations, New York), Bulletin 11 (1968).

──────, ed. *Latin American Economic Integration: Experiences and Prospects*. New York: Frederick A. Praeger, 1966.

———. *Latin American Free Trade Association.* Carnegie Endowment for International Peace, *International Conciliation* (New York), No. 551 (January 1965).

———. "Latin American Integration and United States Economic Policies." In Robert W. Gregg, ed., *International Organization in the Western Hemisphere.* Syracuse, N.Y.: Syracuse University Press, 1967.

———. "The Montevideo Treaty and Latin American Integration," *Banca Nazionale del Lavoro Quarterly Review* (Rome), June 1961.

Index